Combats & Kisses

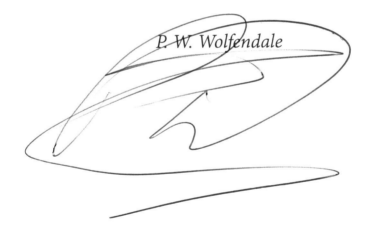

P. W. Wolfendale

Clink Street

London | New York

Published by Clink Street Publishing 2018

Copyright © 2018

First edition.

ISBN: 978-1-912562-05-3 paperback
978-1-912562-06-0 ebook

In Loving Memory of Ellie Bloomfield

Ellie helped to edit the first part of this book for me, enabling me to complete this work without further assistance from her, and for that, I will always be in her debt. Ellie was an extremely caring intelligent woman with a lust for life, taken far too soon at just 27 years old. She is sadly missed

ACKNOWLEDGEMENTS

Paul Simpson
Paul and I go back to our classroom school days. I would like to thank Paul for finding time in his busy schedule to read through a vast proportion of my manuscript. Paul is a highly educated person and is a master with words. I've learned so much from my time working with Paul.

Emily Cromwell
Emily is my daughter and was always there to help me with any part of my book I was unsure about, Emily spent hours reading through my book with a fine tooth comb, her feedback whether positive or negative was vital to the publication of this book.

The Lads of the Military
A big thank you to all who gave me their input with their "pull up a sandbag" stories, 42 years is a long time to remember every event that took place during my service.

ROLL OF HONOUR

Some of the Brave Men I Served with

NAME	RANK	TIME SERVED
Paul (Dusty) Ashman	Bdr	1979-1995
Ken Baily	L/Bdr	1970-1985
Brian (Butch) Barber	Bdr	1967-1976
John (Dinger) Bell	L/Bdr	1972-1981
Keith Booth	Gnr	1976-1982
Don (San) Bowles	Gnr	1974-1977
Denis Bowen	Sgt	1977-2000
Eddie (Jock) Burns	Gnr	1977-1981
Eric Callaghan	Bdr	1974-1984
Phil Card	Gnr	1975-1980
Alan Carvell	Bdr	1972-1981
John (CJ) Cartwright-Jones	L/Bdr	1975-1986
Andy (Weeble) Clayton	L/Bdr	1974-1983
Danny (Scouse) Considine	L/Bdr	1976-1987
Ian (Nipper) Coulson	Gnr	1976-1985
Billy Dalzell	Bdr	1973-1986
Danny Dalzell	Bdr	1971-1983
Dave Dalzell	Bdr	1971-1983
Brian (Betty) Davies	Sgt	1972-1997
Mark Davies	Sgt	1974-1992
Pete (Ragsy) Dodd	WO2	1967-1990
Sammy Douglas	Sgt	1967-1979
Ken (Taff) Dominy	WO2/TSM	1975-1997
Paul (Drabs) Drabarek	L/Bdr	1980-1994
Joe Elward	Sgt	Not Known
Alan Green	Gnr	1973-1976
Dave Hewer	Bdr	1979-1990

Gavin (Hammo) Hamilton	Gnr	1977-1980
Sandy (Paddy) Harkin	Not Known	Not Known
Dennis (Big Den) Heron	L/Bdr	1971-1983
(Gripper) Higginson	Gnr	Not Known
Ricky (Slug) Hill	Gnr	1974-1979
Jon (Jess) James	WO2	1965-1990
Jimmy Jewell	Bdr	1976-1992
Stu Jenkins (RQMS)	W02	1974-1997
Steve Jenkins	Gnr	1975-1978
Ronnie (Jonah) Jones	Bdr	1973-1976 and 1980-1993
Ray Kennedy	Gnr	NOT KNOWN
David (Limpy Lou) Lewis	Gnr	1970-1979
Steve (Stigger) Leech	W01	1979-2003
Kev Long	Gnr	1979-1982
George (Jock) Lynch	Sgt	1974-1992
Douglas Massey	S/Sgt (BQMS)	1963-1985
Colin Mcinnes	Cft	Killed in Londonderry 1975 I.R.A Bomb
William Mills	Major	1977-1994
Cyril (Daddy Mac) Macdonald	Gnr	killed in Londonderry 1975 I.R.A Bomb
David (Nobby) Naylor	Bdr	1973-1980
Dennis Norris	W02 QMS (AC)	1974-1993
Pete (Priggers) Prigmore R.I.P	L/Bdr	1977-1984
Kevin Pardue	S/Sgt	1973-1995
Steve (Sheep) Parry	Gnr	1974-1977
Kev Partridge	Sgt	1979-1992
Charlie Pearce	Gnr	1979-1980
Peter (Riggers) Rigby	W02	1974-1998
Steve Rigby A.P.T.C	Acting Sgt	Medical discharge 1982
Stan Rigden R.I.P	Gnr	1980-1990
Karl Rimicans	Not Known	Not known
Stu Rodger	Gnr	1979-1985

Robbo Robinson	Sgt	1974-1996
Gordon (Sammy Sampson)	WO2	1974-1998
Jon Shaw	Gnr	1967-1975
Mick Shaw	Gnr	1972-1975
Steven Shaw	L/Bdr	1973-1977
Paul (Sherry) Sherrington	L/Bdr	1972-1979
Fred Schule	Gnr	1970-1979
Steve (Schoie) Scohfield R.I.P	Sgt	1974-1993
Michael (Geordie) Stanton	L/Bdr	1974-1979
Simon (Tats) Tattersall	Sgt	1977-1997
John (Thunder) Theobold	Gnr	1973-1977
Bernie Tittle	Sgt	1974-1998
Declan (Tommo) Tomkinson	S/Sgt	1975-1998
Dave Turner	Gnr	1974-1978
Richard (Geordie) Walsh	S/Sgt	1973-1985
Ian (Eddy) Waring	MOQ	1977-2000
Dave Waterman	Sgt	Not Known
Adam (Toyah) AKA Wilcox	Gnr	1981-1987
Paul (Wolfie) Wolfendale	L/Bdr	1974-1984
Bill Young (Chief Clerk)	S/Sgt	1967-1989

AUTHORS NOTE

This is a true story of events about me, a fifteen year old boy who was brought up by his grandparents since being knee high to a grasshopper. My grandparents had fourteen children of their own and yet still found time to take my sister Zoe and I into their family home.

Eight boys and eight girls with me being the youngest member to the family meant a warm and loving environment was had by all. In this book I refer to my grandparents as mother and father, and my aunties and uncles as my sisters and brothers, just like it was back in those days. My surname would always cause confusion among my friends with it being Wolfendale as opposed to Cooper, my grandparents' name; even now I find myself trying to explain how it all came about.

A new and amazing adventure lay ahead for me as I paved the way to make my parents feel proud of what they had done for me and my sister; joining the military and following in my father's footsteps was something he always talked to my mother about, hoping that one day, one of his children would sign on the dotted line. With everybody now left school and doing their own thing, it was left to me to take the Queen's Shilling and make my father's dream come true.

WARNING
Limited swearing is buried in the nature of how British Soldiers speak

CHAPTERS

CHAPTER ONE
A RUDE AWAKING

As I lay asleep on my spring mattress, tossing and turning, trying to avoid the odd spring or two that was protruding through the cotton cloth that embalmed the mattress, I could hear my mother shouting up from the bottom of the stairs, "Paul, get out of bed! It's time to get up for school!" I opened my eyes to see the light of day peeping through a gap in the curtains, at the same time trying to wrap the threadbare sheet and blanket around my body. There was no central heating in our house, so getting out of bed was a challenge within itself. My four brothers that were still living at home had already gone to work on their respective farms, so the room that we all shared was feeling very empty.

I slid my feet out of the bed onto the creaky black wooden floorboards making sure I kept hold of the bed covers, just like I would on any normal day. Normal day, you may ask? It would be one of those get out of bed days that we all have from time to time, one of those days that would change your life; I do believe a crystal ball would have struggled to make sense of what the next ten years would bring.

How could I have possibly known that in less than twelve months I would be standing on a military parade square in front of my parents with some of the most unparalleled mates I could ever meet?

In less than two years I would be fighting on the streets of Northern Ireland and, at the same time falling in love with a young Irish girl that I met on an Army vehicle checkpoint, a girl that I was infatuated with, a girl that I put my life on the line for, and a girl that could never be mine; how could anyone even come close to understanding this segregated relationship?

Stood bolt upright next to my bed in nothing but my Y-fronts, I finally plucked up the courage to throw down the covers that were keeping my body warm; one...two...three "Arrrgh, bloody freezing!" I said to myself. I could feel the cold damp air that was seeping through the rotten window frames on my bare skin; my teeth were starting to chatter their own unmelodious tune.

Briskly, I walked over to the window, still half asleep; the bright end of June's summer sunlight caused me to squint as I drew back the dark coloured curtains. As I wiped the cold condensation from the window panes with my already cold hands, I could see my father and brother working in the farm yard that was no more than about fifty metres from my window, just beyond the garden, the garden that would keep us fed for the next twelve months: potatoes, carrots, peas, onions, beans... You name it, my father grew it.

That's how it was. Sixteen pounds a week were my father's wages for working on the farm. My sister was carrying metal buckets full of milk for the calves; I could see the milk slopping over the edge of the buckets and down into her Wellingtons as they brushed the side of her legs. She was walking with a kind of stiffness in her body, trying to spill as little milk as possible. I turned around and walked away from the window towards the bathroom before the starlings could be scared away by my scrawny body.

The bathroom was diminutive, with a white enamel sink on the right as you walked in, and a bath on the left. The toilet was in striking distance from the sink if I needed a pee and could easily be reached whilst having a wash with the right trajectory and elevation. The taps on the sink were very difficult to turn on and off; it would take about three or four full turns before any water would start to drip out into your hands then, without any indication or warning, it would shoot out like a bullet from a gun. You could hear the pipes rattle with the force of the water, combined with the air that was trapped in the system, if you were lucky enough; there was a slight possibility that you might get some hot water, provided you weren't the last one out of bed or to use the bathroom. On this occasion, I wasn't so lucky.

I threw the cold water from my hands over my face, exclaiming "Shit!" and "Bloody hell!", before grabbing the cold, damp towel that was hung over the edge of the bath to wipe away the water from my face and, at the same time trying to relieve the sharp stabbing pains that I was enduring.

The water was heated by the coal fire that my mother would light when she got up in the morning. It was then stored in the cylinder next to the bathroom, on a good coal fire day, you could hear the water bubbling in the tank, which meant you had to be extra careful when turning on the hot water tap. The water would get that hot that it would scorch the copper off the inside of the tank; it would be brown in colour as it came out of the tap.

I made my way back into the bedroom, trying to find my school clothes that were screwed up on the floor somewhere by the double bed that I shared with my brother. I was just putting on yesterday's socks when I heard my mother shouting up the stairs once more. "Are you out of bed yet?"

"Yes!" I replied. "Be down in two secs, mum!"

"Well, get a move on," my mother said. A few years ago it would have been "if I have to come up those stairs I will tan your backside" but now, all that is just a memory. With yesterday's socks still affectionately covering my feet I continued to get dressed in quick time. First was my flannelette grey trousers, followed by my cotton grey shirt that was already buttoned, my size nine lace up black shoes were next – and, on a lazy can't-be-bothered day, I could force my feet into the shoes without untying the laces; however, this sort of behaviour didn't go down too well with my mother in respect, that we had little or no money to buy a new pair.

I was now feeling ready to take on the world, well at least the small simple world that I lived in. I had a quick tidy up of my bed and bed space before one last look at all my football pictures on my bedroom wall, and then, it was down stairs, or as my mum would say, "Get down them dancers now."

It took less than a minute from getting dressed into my school uniform to reaching the bottom of the creaky wooden stairs. Finally silence could be heard as I stepped off the last step, onto the cold quarry tiled floor that led into the kitchen/dining room. "Morning mum," I would say, making my way into the dining room area. I didn't always get any response from my mum; she was always too busy making sure all of her now grown-up children were up and ready for work, or in my case, school. My mum would get one of my sisters to put on my school tie, but it was always done under duress: "Why can't he do it for himself?" my sister Gwen would ask. Eventually, she would oblige, by almost choking me as she pushed the knot of the tie up against my Adam's apple. There were still five of my eight sisters living at home that meant one sister for each of the five school day's would have the pleasure of choking me. My sisters were all younger than my brothers who, at this point, had already gone to work.

Most of my sisters would not leave for work until after 8am that meant the kitchen area was quite chock-a-block and would become even more occupied when my brothers and my father came home for their breakfast. Porridge made with water was always on the menu; however, eggs and toast were also available on some days. The porridge was always first choice for me, with sugar or syrup to sweeten. The only time I would consider toast or eggs was when you could smell the porridge burning from my bedroom; I would stand at the top of the stairs for a few seconds, enjoying the aroma of the wonderful smell of burnt porridge, before plucking up the courage to venture down into the kitchen. Sometimes mum would forget to turn the heat down on the electric cooker then, with everything else going on around her, she would forget that the porridge was burning. My mum was a very loving person, however you wouldn't want to cross her path when things weren't going well; she had a very strict regime. If the porridge was burnt she always had a way of saying, "Get it down you. It won't do you any harm!" Before you knew it, the bowl of porridge was staring you in the face; you knew then that not eating it wasn't an option, well, at least if you knew what was good for you.

We were brought up to be very independent, but we were also very careful not to cross any boundaries. Once I had eaten my breakfast, I put on my school blazer and headed for the front door. It was a quick, "Bye mum!" However, I don't think she heard me with so much going on. I normally left the house about 0750am, just before the time my sisters would be going to work and, just before my father and brothers would be coming home for their breakfast. I use to have to walk the two and a half miles to school for the first three years at high school. However, when I reached the age of thirteen, I managed to get myself a job at the corner shop. I would earn sixteen shillings a week before decimalisation was introduced in 1971, and then it became 80p. The money I earned allowed me to purchase a bike from my friend; I would pay him ten shillings a week for ten weeks, accumulating to a total cost of £5. The bike ride would take me about twenty minute's tops.

The journey was very scenic from my house, which was about a mile from the outskirts of my nearest town Nantwich. I would pass over the canal bridge that spans over the Shropshire Union Canal. The canal straddles Staffordshire, Cheshire and Shropshire; it also connects with the Llangollen Canal, which is about two to three miles from where I would stop on top of the hump-back bridge. I would pause only for a few seconds to admire the narrowboats that were moored up and, maybe, if I was lucky, see a fish or two being caught by the many fishermen who had decided to make an early start.

The journey continued along Queens Drive, past the house of Paul Simpson, one of my school friends, who was almost part of the family with the fact that my mother thought as much of Paul as she did myself; maybe it was the name she liked. Riding through Nantwich with all its black and white Tudor buildings was next. At the far end of the town, I would cycle over a railway crossing with its old-fashioned gates and signal box. I would always be hoping that the gates would close and a train would come past; how times have changed. Today, everybody seems to rush around at 100 mph, getting frustrated if they so much as have to give way to a pedestrian crossing the road. After the crossing, it was about another half mile to my school. This is where I would take the opportunity to pick up some speed. I had a speedometer on my bike, so getting my speed up to 30mph was a must; with my bum in the air and my legs going up and down like a fiddler's elbow it took only a few seconds to reach max out speed. It would take me no more than a few minutes to complete the final stages before arriving at school.

It was an all-boys' secondary school, with the girls' school actually connected by a corridor. I was always the first pupil to arrive, with the exception of the odd occasion when I was running late. I would see some of the teachers arriving in half decent cars as I made my way over to the bike shed that was just behind the playground. This is where I would wait for my mates to arrive so we could have a game of football.

Within minutes, they all started to arrive by their various modes of transport: bikes, buses, cars, on foot, whatever it took to get them away from their parents for a few hours. Once there were enough of us to start the game, we would place our blazers on the ground to represent the goalposts. I was football mad and could not get enough of the national game, whether it was playing, reading or watching; I was an encyclopaedia of knowledge. We had to play with a tennis ball in the playground for safety reasons. Those were the rules that we had to abide by. The fun and excitement was just the same though; scoring a goal with any kind of ball always gave me a buzz. We would play until the bell rang at 8.55am and then, line up in long files military fashion, before being escorted into the assembly hall for the morning's assembly.

On arrival in the assembly hall, we all took our seats waiting patiently for the Headmaster to address us. I remember looking up at the huge stage; there were many seats strategically placed for all of the teachers, a piano was to the left of the stage for the music teacher to show his skills. It was very noisy in the hall, with the sound of our chairs being scraped on the wooden floor, and the fact that everybody had something to chat about. Personally, all I would be chatting about was whether or not I had made the school footy team for the game later on that week. The teachers arrived. "Quiet everyone," was the command. They made their way onto the stage and took their seats. You could hear a pin drop as we waited for the Headmaster to arrive. Finally, the head arrived. I can still see him now with his National Health glasses and his funereal suit. He would march onto the stage as opposed to walking. His arms would always be swinging like a continental soldier. Once on stage, he would address you, looking over the rim of his glasses as he stood behind his podium. "Good morning," he would say in a quiet but stern voice. "Good morning, Sir," was the reluctant reply from the floor. "Stand up everybody for our first hymn," said the Headmaster. I could see the very old, grey-haired music teacher Mr Kirkham getting all excited; it was his time to show us all how he could knock out a bloody good tune on the ivories. To be honest, I was one of a few that actually enjoyed singing hymns; I spent quite a few years in the local choir, as well as having to go to Sunday school with my brothers and sisters. The assembly would last about thirty minutes, with the Headmaster talking to us about various topics and bringing us up to speed on any developments that would be of interest to us and the school. Little did I know at this moment in time that what he was about to say next would have such a bearing on my future.

"Later on, this afternoon, we will be welcomed by the Army Recruitment Team. They will be giving you all a talk on life in the British Army, they will be showing you a short film on what it's like in the Army and whether you feel it may be the life for you." At first, all I was thinking about was what lesson I would be missing; I never thought for one minute of joining the Army, I mean to say, I was just a fifteen-year-old lad still attached to my mother's apron strings. I wouldn't harm a fly, let alone be able to shoot someone if needed. I did get into a few fights at school but surely that doesn't count? With assembly finished, I made my way to my form class for registration then on to my first lesson of the day.

The narrow corridors felt so claustrophobic with everybody hustling and bustling and occasionally banging into each other, trying to get to their respective classrooms on time. The swing doors were flung open repeatedly, banging and crashing every few seconds. My mother was a very superstitious person and would always say that you shouldn't pass on the stairs. That worked fine at home, however, at school, not a chance. I don't think a day went past when I didn't meet someone else coming up or down the two flights of stairs. I'm afraid that superstition went out of the window on day one.

The first lesson of the day was normally an hour long, followed by a twenty minute break before our next lesson. There was a clock hanging on the wall behind the teacher's desk that everybody could see quite clearly, and, as I didn't have a watch of my own, I would find myself looking up at the clock and staring at it at every opportunity; I was drawn to it like a rabbit to headlights until the final minute ticked by.

"Okay, put your books away" said the teacher in a loud and clear voice. "Tidy up your desk and place your chairs quietly underneath." We made our way quietly and slowly out of the classroom, until out of sight of the teacher. Our pace gradually got quicker and quicker as we raced down the two flights of stairs to the ground floor. Normally, it would be straight onto the playground for a quick game of footy; however, on this occasion, I had some money in my trouser pocket that my brother Allan had given to me for running him an errand. The going rate for going to the shop for my brother was 10p; six bags of crisps and six chocolate bars is what my brother would ask me to go and buy for him. I was fine with that; he could have bought the whole shop of chocolate for all I cared, as long as I got my 10p. I could almost hear the tuck shop calling my name from the bottom of the stairs. The tuck shop was always run by one of the school teachers, on this occasion, it was Mr Green, the woodwork teacher, who would set up a wooden table in a small part of the corridor: Chocolate Fingers, Jammy Dodgers, Marshmallows, Potato Puffs, Ice Buns and all sorts of other amazing goodies. Jammy Dodgers and Potato Puffs were my favourites; they would always be my first choice, unless my funds were running low, then, it would have to be the cheaper option of Chocolate Fingers. The Jammy Dodgers were to die for; I would normally gorge on them first and then fill my jacket pockets with two or three bags of potato puffs to eat discreetly in my next lesson. Depending how much time was left before the bell rang for next lesson; I would go and have a kick around with my mates.

The rest of the morning would be roughly the same, with one double or two single periods before lunch. Lunch break was about a half hour long and, this time, it was straight onto the playground for at least half hour of footy, before trying to prise myself away to eat my lunch. Lunch was served in the dining room that bordered the assembly hall, by the time my mates and I arrived for lunch there was an upside, there was no queue; everybody else had eaten. On the down side, there was not much choice left, but I suppose I wasn't too bothered; after all, I was still full up from the Jammy Dodgers and Potato Puffs. Just before leaving the dining hall, my mates and I could see the Army moving in. They were setting up all their equipment onto the stage for the afternoon recruitment campaign. We looked at them with curiosity running through our minds; without so much as a single blink, I could see them looking back at us. I felt hypnotised. I couldn't seem to look away. It felt as if their eyes were talking to me, saying in a loud voice, "You're mine, my lad."

I headed back to the playground, still feeling transfixed; with only a few minutes to go before the bell would ring, I needed to clear my head of any thought of me joining 'The Professionals'. The bell finally rang to end what seemed to be a much shortened lunch break. You would see the odd teacher hurrying us along as we started to trundle back to our respective classes, still chitchatting away, for our afternoon registration.

"Bradley!"

"Sir"

"Cornes"

"Sir"

"Moss"

"Sir"

"Taylor"

"Sir"

"Wolfendale"

"Sir"

I was always the last name to be called, as registration was always called in alphabetical order. I just wish sometimes they could have maybe called the register in reverse alphabetical order, just so I could hear my name being called out first.

Even if I'd suggested the idea, it would have fallen on deaf ears.

"OK everyone, listen to what I am about to say," said the form teacher. "Shortly, we will be making our way over to the assembly hall in a quiet and orderly fashion. For the benefit of all of you who were not listening in this morning's assembly, and also for all of you who were listening but have forgotten, this afternoon, the Army will be doing a presentation for those of you who have any ambition in life. If you think you have what it takes to become a soldier, then far be it for me to stand in your way."

In the light of the day I was thinking to myself, *"What gives him the right to address us in such a patronising way?"* OK, some of us were not the brightest sparks on the planet, but I personally, would not talk to anyone in an unfriendly manner.

The teachers didn't seem to have time for anyone who couldn't keep up to the same standard as the boy who was destined to be an astronaut, but I'm afraid that's what it was like at a secondary modern school; classrooms full to the rafters with one teacher in charge of about thirty plus students. It wasn't an ideal situation, and it certainly didn't work. After one more final humiliation speech by our form teacher, we made our way to the assembly hall, along with the rest of the school. I think the only people that were excused from the presentation were the ones that were too old to sign up; you've got it, all the teachers. As we entered the hall, we were told to sit anywhere we wanted by the skeleton staff of teachers that could be bothered to attend. The noise level was double what you would have expected it to be.

"Quiet everyone, stop talking!" said a loud voice that came from one of the teachers that was standing at the side of the hall. I think he was just trying to impress the Army personnel who we could all see on the stage standing very stiff and upright in their uniforms and shiny boots, waiting for the signal to start. With the hall now silenced, the teacher handed over the assembly hall to the Army personnel, who were now ready in all respects to start their presentation.

"Welcome everyone. First of all, I would like to tell you a little bit about myself and my recruitment team over on my right hand side. My name is Sergeant Boucher. I was a young lad once, just like all of you sitting out there in front of me today, confused with what I wanted to do with my life. Do I want to be a train driver, or maybe a farm worker? Maybe I'll end up in one of the local factories where some of my family worked.

"All these ideas were going through my mind, until one day, I was walking down Nantwich Road in Crewe, when I stumbled upon the Army Careers Office; the posters in the window were very inspiring. 'Come Join the British Army' was printed on all of the posters. 'See the World', 'Come Have Some Fun.' 'The Army Needs People Like You'. I peered through a small gap in between the posters to see this military man, sitting at a desk, talking on the phone. I am not sure if he saw me or not, peering through the window but, what I do remember is, within seconds, I was sitting in front of him, looking up at this fine specimen of a man. Although he sold the Army to me, it was still my decision to join. I have never looked back once since the day I walked into the Army Careers Office on that day.

"I joined up in 1961, some twelve years ago: *Join the Navy and See the World, Join the Army and Sweep it,* was the motto. Well, if that were the case, I wouldn't be standing here today; if I'd wanted to be a road-sweeper then

I'd have joined the local council. Over on my right are Corporal Dobbs and Lance Corporal Evans, both of whom have recently come back from a tour of Northern Ireland."

Sergeant Boucher continued with his speech, telling us about different regiments and corps' you could join; it sounded impressive, however, it meant little or nothing to me. I was a young lad from a hard-working farming background, the only gun I knew about was a twelve-bore shotgun that my father had locked away in his shed. He would use the gun to help feed us all by going up the farm fields to find a rabbit or two for Sunday lunch. It wasn't long before the Sergeant was asking the Corporal to start the projector rolling. "Lights out and close all side curtains," said the Sergeant. No sooner said than done, was the response from the two or three teachers that were present.

With the hall now in darkness, the Corporal switched on the projector to start the recruitment film. We all waited with bated breath, our eyes fixed on the screen that was hanging from the top of the stage; within seconds you could hear loud military music vibrating from the school speakers that were strategically placed on the stage, then, the screen lit up with the sight of a military band marching across an Army parade square. The film lasted about forty minutes before all of the curtains were reopened and the lights came back on. I suppose, looking back on it now, it was just propaganda, or in Army terms, 'bullshit'. Everything they wanted you to see was included and everything they didn't want you to see was kept within the confines of the Army.

I am not sure how many of us were taken in by the film, but from a personal point of view, I was impressed by what I saw. 'Sucker', you might think, and you know what, you might be right. But there was no doubt in my mind that life in the Army was something I would be seriously considering when I left school.

We were invited onto the stage in an orderly manner to chitchat to the Army personnel and to take home some paraphernalia. I remember, just before I stepped down from the stage, asking the Sergeant what regiment he was with. He took off his beret and pointed to his cap badge and said, "This, lad, is the badge of the Royal Artillery and, if you do decide to sign up, I would like you to bare that in mind when you choose which corps' you would like to join."

"OK," I said nervously. "Thank you again for the presentation; it has been very enjoyable and informative." He shook my hand with a vice like grip that had me saying, "Ouch!" under my breath; however, I wasn't showing *him* that it hurt. Eventually I managed to prise my hand away from his hand with my fingers all stuck together.

There was a final closing speech by Sergeant Boucher and his men before the show was finally over. It was now time for one of the teachers to step up onto the stage in a very unmilitary manner to thank Sergeant Boucher and his men for all of their hard work and endeavour on putting on a great presentation. I was actually feeling very disappointed that it was all over, as the teacher asked us to put our hands together for Sergeant Boucher and his team. They were going back to serve their country and I, well, it was back to my daily routine for me: five days of school with weekends off. Still, I thought to myself with a smirk on my face, I only have about ten months left at school then, maybe God willing, I too can join the Army and become a soldier.

"Listen in, everybody!" was the cry from the stage, "I would like you all to make your way to your form classes for the end of school registration, where your form teacher will be waiting for you. Please leave in an orderly manner starting with the front row first."

After the first few rows of pupils had made their way out of the assembly hall, it was like a stampede: chairs being scraped along the floor once more, people pushing to get through the swing doors; typical school chaos at its best. I made my way the short distance along the corridor to my form classroom, where most of my class had already arrived. "Sit down and be quiet," said our teacher. "Say your name when I call it out."

I knew it would be at least two minutes before he called my name out, so I started to read the leaflets that I had taken from the stage; I was so engrossed in them that the teacher had to call out "Wolfendale!" twice before I answered.

"Sir!" was my reply feeling startled.

"About time," he said. "OK, sit up straight. I shall be letting you out of school ten minutes earlier today; there is not a lot of point in starting something new."

We just looked at each other and smiled like Cheshire cats.

"Class dismissed," said the teacher.

I was out of the school main entrance like a bat out of hell, almost forgetting I now had a bike to ride home on.

It made a nice change for me to be able to ride through the school gates and along the road without having to worry about running one of my school mates over, who would normally be walking in the road. Four or five abreast they would walk, without a care in the world. I could see all the girls in their respective classrooms as I rode past their school. I felt like an escapee from a prisoner of war camp, as I picked up speed and headed home, with not another pupil to be seen. The journey home was as per normal: across the railway crossing, through the town, over the Canal Bridge then out into the countryside. As I cycled past the farm that was on my left, just before my house, I could hear the droning noise that the generator made when it was switched on. It supplied the air pressure for the milking machines; you could normally set your watch by the sound of the generator being switched on. I could also see the grey smoke tunnelling its way out of the chimney of my house and being blown up into the cloudy sky.

I finally turned left into my drive. There were three farm cottages on the drive that were all attached together. I lived at number three, the one at the end of the drive. It had a big open wooden garage even though we couldn't afford a car. There was also my dad's shed, a shed that was always locked up, in respect that it was where my dad and my brothers kept their shotguns. I would always say hello to the two dogs we had, one of them was called Patch and the other called Judy. Patch was always chained up, which at the time seemed quite normal back then, but now as I look back some forty years on, it fills me with unremitting sadness. We had acres of fields in front of our house, so even now find it hard to understand why this beautiful black and white collie dog spent most of its life chained up. Judy was a corgi, who for some unknown reason had the run of the house. She wasn't one of these dogs that would welcome you with a smile; in fact, she had a tendency to bite whenever she felt inclined. I still have a scar on my right arm to prove it. However, dogs will be dogs and bygones will be bygones.

The huge, heavyweight front door was partly open with the weather being warm, so with a slight push of my hand, the door opened to reveal the steep flight of stairs that led to the bedrooms. Without knowing whether anyone was at home, I made my way briskly and loudly up the staircase into my bedroom. Within minutes I was changed into my play clothes, (not that I had a lot of clothes} ready to take on the world. There was no homework in my day, so when school was out, that meant school was out. I placed the Army leaflets that I had acquired underneath my mattress, along with all my football magazines, for safekeeping.

It was most definitely the safest place in our house if you didn't want to lose anything. As I made my way back down the stairs, I noticed that there was some form of human life in the house after all. It was my mum, pottering around the kitchen in her slippers and apron. I think at my age, as a young fifteen year-old lad, you just don't take any notice of your surroundings; the house could be getting ransacked and I probably wouldn't have noticed or cared for that matter; getting on the field in front of the house for a game of footie was all I was interested in. My mum never had much to say, like, "how was your day?" or, "how come you're home early?" As long as she could see some sort of movement from my skinny frame, and as long as I looked like I was still breathing, that was fine.

My mum had more important things to concern herself with, like cooking dinner for all the hungry mouths that would be coming home in the next hour or two. I was tempted to tell my mum about my day and how I was contemplating joining the Army, however, I thought I would ponder the idea a little longer, maybe wait for the right opportunity to tell both of my parents together.

After a quick rummage in the fridge for my daily intake of milk, I was soon in the field, kicking a football around on my own, trying to avoid all the cow pats that were lying randomly on the playing area. Unfortunately, the cows didn't understand that it was a no shitting area. Sometimes, one or two of my mates would cycle up to my house for a game, and then when my brothers came home from work, about six o'clock in the evening, they would have their tea (a northern word for dinner) before joining me and my mates in the field. We would normally finish about eight o'clock, but the problem was, as soon as one of us had called time, I knew then, it was time to make a quick dash across the short distance towards to the fence that divided the field from the drive. I use to high-jump the fence before my menacing over-size brothers could catch me. As soon as I was over the fence, I felt safe. I knew I could make it into the house and into the safe haven of the living room to where my mum and dad were.

My older brothers, for some reason, would attack either me or one of my school mates and inflict a lot of pain on one of us. They would get you into a Boston strangle (a wrestling term) where they would turn you over and sit on your back whilst at the same time, pulling your legs up in to the air. Technically, it was like they were trying to snap your back. Unfortunately, I had failed to inform one of my mates as my brothers attacked him like a lion pouncing on its prey. He had little or no chance of getting out of the hold he was in. He was subjected to a lot of unnecessary pain; screaming to the point where he was actually crying, they finally let him go. To them it was just a bit of harmless fun, but you try telling that to my mate. He still stayed my mate for the next eight months or so that I had left at school, however, he never did come back to my house. He had been scarred for life. If I ever see him now in the street, it is always the topic of conversation. I didn't like to mention the fact, but he always seemed to walk with a kind of concave curve in his back, unless it's just my imagination. Who knows, maybe it's just my eyes playing tricks on me in my old age?

When we were all a lot younger we would have to go to bed at eight o'clock, right after Coronation Street. Judy the dog would always bark as soon as she heard the trumpets of the theme tune to bring Coronation Street to an end. She would round us up like sheep until we were all out of sight and in our bedrooms. Now, with me being the youngest, the boundaries had changed. I would go to bed whenever I felt like it, within reason. Television programmes would end at about eleven and, unless you wanted to watch the test card all night, there was very little to do. It was warmer in my cold bedroom than to stay downstairs watching the embers of the fire slowly die out. I would normally go to bed about ten o'clock, the same time as most of my sisters. Occasionally, I would go into the girls' bedroom, sit on the end of their bed and chat about general things before turning in.

Most of my brothers would spend a couple of hours at the pub that closed at eleven, before making their way home and waking me up as they got into bed. Judy always slept on the end of the bed right by my feet. The only problem with that was if I wanted to turn over in the night or just stretch my legs out, she would start growling as if to say, "This is my space. One false move and I will bite your toes off." This night was one of those nights when she was giving me a hard time; I woke up in the early hours of the morning and was just about to move my legs when I heard her growling. I just froze as the growling got louder. I was too terrified to move. I started shaking my brother. "Allan! Allan! Wake up, I can't move my legs! Judy is growling at me!"

"What's up?" said Allan still half-asleep.

"It's Judy!" I said. "Please get her to move… she's growling at my feet!" But before my brother could move her, she sank her teeth into my big toe. I was almost in tears with pain. My brother managed to kick her off the bed onto the floor. All I heard was a thud, then the sound of her little feet on the wooden floorboards, walking away from my bed. I think she must have been trying to find a warm spot somewhere else to curl up and go sleep.

I had to wait until the morning when it was light to inspect my toe. Oh yes, she had drawn blood. I could see four teeth marks on my toe. I was going to tell my mum what had happened, but thought better of it; it was my problem, so deal with it, is what she would have said. That's how it was with us all. We all learned to take care of ourselves. I had more scars on me than I care to remember. It wasn't long before I was making my way to the Army Careers Office in Crewe without a word to my parents. As far as I was concerned I was only expecting to have a formal introduction into Army life, how wrong could one be; when I was asked to take an IQ test that I was unprepared for.

CHAPTER TWO
ARMY CAREERS OFFICE

It was now mid-July and the school summer holidays were almost upon us. I would be entering my final seven months when I returned to school in September. It was in the summer holidays I decided to venture out to Crewe without telling anybody. "Bye mum" I said "just going out to play." If I was lucky she might respond with, "OK."It was only when it got dark that my mum would start to question my whereabouts. "Where's our Paul? He should be in by now," she would say.

I walked the two miles into Nantwich to catch the bus that would drop me off near the Army Careers Office on Nantwich Road in Crewe. Top deck, front seat, looking out of the window was my favourite position on the double-decker bus; I use to find myself ducking my head at all the branches from the overhanging trees. Every time we went around a corner, it seemed certain we would hit a house or two. I suppose that is why I liked it on the top deck. I think I must have been born with the fear factor running through my veins. The half-hour journey seemed like forever until the bus finally arrived at my stop.

There were no doors at the back of the bus, just an open space where the conductor would stand when he was not collecting fares. I always took the opportunity to jump off the back of the bus just before it had fully come to a stop, in a kind of audacious way. Occasionally, I would fall over my own feet onto the pavement; it got a few laughs from bystanders that were walking past, minding their own business; however, I would just get up, brush myself down and carry on as if nothing had happened. Luckily for me, on this occasion, I managed to stand up on my own two feet. It was probably a good job because when I managed to get my bearings together, I realised that I was standing outside the Army Careers Office with one of the soldiers doing some window-dressing.

I looked over my shoulder towards the road, to hear the roaring sound of my bus driving away; I could hear the grinding of the gears as the bus struggled to pick up momentum. This was it. I felt quite alone even though the streets were full of traffic and pedestrians. It reminded me of standing outside the dental practice, not wanting to go in but, at the same time, knowing that I must. Regrets are something I don't take kindly to, my philosophy is, go for it: better to have tried and failed than not tried at all.' I tightened my lips together and at the same time, trying to control my squeaky bum, took one last breath and made my way through the beautiful, shiny glass door that was covered in decals. The waiting room that welcomed me was very small and triangular in shape, decked out with military posters wherever you looked. There was probably enough room for about four or five people maximum.

As I took a seat, I could see another glass door immediately in front of me. The door was partially open. I could see a military man sitting behind a large heavy wooden desk. It was all coming back to me now, the things Sergeant Boucher was talking to us about just a few weeks ago. The soldier that I saw dressing the window was the first to greet me, as he stepped down from the window ledge. In a stern but gentle voice; dressed in his immaculate Army uniform, he said, "Hello, how can I help you, son?"

"I am interested in joining the Army," I said with a kind of nervousness in my voice. I am sure he must have noticed that I was nervous, but at the same time, he made me feel very comfortable by not saying anything.

"Brilliant. Joining the Army, hey" he said with a smile on his face? "Just give me a minute and I'll be with you."

"Thank you, that's fine," I said, as I watched his every move until he was seated alongside his military comrade.

"OK, would you like to step forward please into my office."

I was smartly out of my seat, thinking, *the Army is no place for losers*. In simple terms, I was trying to make an impression.

"Take a seat," said the soldier. "OK, my name is Sergeant Dave Boucher. You're more than welcome to call me Dave or Sergeant Boucher, if you prefer. Sitting next to me is Corporal Gavin Batty, who is here to assist me in my duties… So you want to join the Army? Then tell us a little about yourself: how you got to hear about us and the reasons why you think the Army would be the life for you."

I replied in a slightly high-pitched voice, as my voice had not fully broken yet. "My name is Paul Wolfendale, I'm fifteen years old, soon to be sixteen. I go to the boys' secondary modern school in Nantwich; that's where I first got the inspiration to join the Army… I was present at your recruitment campaign."

"Ah right; that was about six weeks ago, if mind serves me right," said the Sergeant.

"Yes," I said. "I recognise you both from the fine presentation that you put on for us all."

The Sergeant replied by saying, "It's nice to see that our time at your school hasn't been a total waste of time and effort. You're actually the first boy to have shown any kind of interest, so I would like to thank you once again for coming here today."

Ten minutes of what I would describe as interrogation, to find out whether or not I had what it takes to join the professionals was next. "How do you think you'll cope when faced with hostilities on the streets of Northern Ireland?" they said waiting for my answer.

"I will probably be scared at first, I won't deny that," I said, "but it's something I've thought about and I am pretty sure I will be ready for the task."

"How do you think you'll react when being kicked out of bed at 0530hrs in a morning? Your mum won't be there to wipe your nose," they said pushing me once more for a more than one word answer.

"I come from a large hardworking family," I said "so I am use to fending for myself." After a few more questions the interview was over. They seemed pleased with everything I had told them, making me feel a lot more comfortable with everything.

"OK," said Sergeant Boucher. "Would you have any objection in taking part in an IQ test?"

"Did you say an IQ test?" I said in a shocked voice."

"That's correct, an IQ test" said Sergeant Boucher.

"Err, yes, I don't mind at all, when would you like me to come back?"

"Come back, Come back young man! You don't need to come back, you can do it right away!" he said chuckling to himself.

Ouch, I thought. I wasn't prepared for this. Unfortunately, I could not think of one solitary reason for not doing the test right now. "Yes," I said. "Of course I will," I said in a kind of, *I am ready for anything you can throw at me* type of voice. I was still feeling uncomfortable with the situation but thought, 'what the hell; just go and do the test and see what happens.'

"Corporal Batty, could you escort Paul upstairs and get him started on the test please."

"Yes, Sarge," said the Corporal as he stood up from his seat. "OK Paul, would you like to follow me please, if you could just make your way up those stairs on your right and I will follow you up."

They were just like the stairs from my house: very narrow, very dark and very squeaky. At the top of the stairs a voice from behind me said, "There is a door on the right Paul, which should be unlocked. Just press the handle down on the door then give it a little nudge."

No sooner said than done.

"You should see the light switch on the wall by the door."

The room lit up as I pressed the switch to expose the room to my eyes. It was just like a small store room, with no windows, just a wooden desk and a wooden chair. There was a grey metal locker standing up against the wall that was locked and, to be honest, that is about as descriptive as it gets. The Corporal followed me into the room and made his way over to the grey metal locker. He reached into his pocket and pulled out a bunch of keys, one of which unlocked a small brass padlock. "Just take a seat Paul, and relax," he said as he removed the padlock from the locker.

I could see lots of paper work on the shelves in the locker as the Corporal opened the locker doors. He reached into the locker and pulled out some sort of pamphlet. "Be with you in a second just need to lock the locker up." The Corporal put his keys back into his pocket and then placed the pamphlet on the desk in front of me. "Just keep the pamphlet closed for now until I tell you to open it," explained the Corporal. "You will have thirty minutes to complete as many questions as you can from the time that I tell you to start. If you don't know the answer to a question, don't spend too much time dwelling over it; just move onto the next one or before you know it, you'll find yourself running out of time. Are there any questions that you would like to ask before you start the test?"

"I cannot think of any at the moment," I said as I was staring down at the test sheet.

"OK then, I will leave you to get on with it. You can now open the pamphlet in front of you and start the test when you're ready. Good luck," said the Corporal as he left the room, closing the door behind him. I could hear his boots working on the wooden steps as he made his way down the staircase and back into his office. I was now feeling even more alone without a care in the world. I had one last look around the room (for what earthly reason I just don't know).

I opened the pamphlet without any clue to what I might find or be faced with. It was very self explanatory, it was just a series of puzzle with questions like, what number precedes the following: 1 2 4 7 11… answer 16; 1 + 1 = 2, 2+2 = 4, 4+3 =7, 7+4 =11 so, naturally, 11+ 5… the next numbers would be 16+6, as the numbers that you add go up in a numerical order (1, 2, 3, 4, 5, 6); which was the odd one out of 17, 26, 35, 44, and 54… answer 54, as all the other numbers add up to 8, if you add the two numbers together. I felt myself rattling through the questions very quickly, and was just thinking to myself that I might get through the whole test at this rate, when suddenly I heard the office door open and the sound of someone coming up the stairs. I was pretty sure by the sound the stairs were making that it wasn't the Fairy Godmother coming to help me.

"OK, stop writing," said the Corporal as he opened the door.

I probably had a few more pages left of the test, but felt quite satisfied I had done well enough.

"How did you find the test Paul?" said the Corporal with a smile on his face.

"Yeah, not too bad, thanks. I managed to finish most of the questions."

"Good," said the Corporal. "If you would like to make your way back down the stairs and take a seat in the waiting room, I will follow you down and then mark your test paper."

Once in the waiting room, I could see the Corporal sitting next to Sergeant Boucher, marking my test sheet. He had a kind of stencil that he put over the page, with little square holes in it and, if your answer was correct, it would show up in the respective square hole. If your answer didn't show up, then it was obviously wrong. I waited anxiously, but at the same time, I remember not feeling too worried. I think I did as well as I could within the allotted time. I saw the Corporal having a kind of whispered conversation with Sergeant Boucher before he finally stood up and inviting me forward into their office. "OK Paul, if you would like to step into my office and take a seat please."

I wasn't sure where to look or where to put my arms, I felt myself fidgeting in my seat… *please put me out of my misery,* I was thinking.

"Right Paul, let me first put you out of your misery," said Sergeant Boucher – as if reading my mind "You have passed."

My hand that was covering my mouth slowly slid off the end of my chin to form a clenched fist, my head went back as I looked up to the heavens as if to say, "Thank you, Lord. Thank you." I brought my head down from the heavens and looked at Sergeant Boucher, breathing a sigh of relief. "Thank God for that," I said.

"You actually did very well Paul; your score was far more than you needed. What you will need to do now, because you're still only fifteen years of age, is come back in about six months time, around February time, then we will take things forward to the next stage of you joining the Army. Are there any questions you would like to ask myself or my Corporal before you leave?"

"Just one," I said. "Will I need to do the test again when I come back in February?"

"No, of course not," said Sergeant Boucher. "Your test will be filed away until you return in the New Year. Do you have any more questions?"

"No, that's fine, thank you," I said feeling contented with how it all went.

"OK then Paul; we shall both look forward to seeing you soon."

I stood up and was greeted with two firm handshakes from Sergeant Boucher and Corporal Batty, who wished me all the best.

I felt like a million dollars as I exited the Army Careers Office and stepped back into civilisation. I made my way across the other side of the busy road to the bus stop whilst, at the same time, trying not to get splattered as I dodged the traffic. There were about four other people already at the bus stop, all a lot older than me I hasten to add. I was yearning to tell one of them about my day. I was hoping that someone might start up a conversation with me as I stood and waited for the bus. I looked up to the sky to see the sun shining in between the white fluffy clouds, very representative of the day I was having. *Pathetic fallacy* is what I believe this is called. To be honest, I felt I had more chance of getting a conversation from the sun that seemed to be trying to tell me, "Well done, young man. I am shining my warm beautiful sun rays down just for you."

Finally, I could see the bus in the distance among all the slow moving traffic; the noise of the diesel engine could be heard for miles. It seemed to take ages for the bus to arrive, along with the fact that I could not wait to get home and tell my parents the news. The bus eventually pulled up along the edge of the kerb, with its squeaky brakes working on its massive wheels before coming to a complete stop. I allowed all the other passengers that were waiting with me to embark first before I got on and made my way up the metal stairs to the top deck. I was hoping to sit at the front like I would nor-mally do; with the fact that the bus had just come from the main bus station it was quite full so sitting at the front wasn't going to happen. I decided that the next best seat would be to sit on the right-hand side of the bus so that I could look out of the window at the Army Careers Office, and reflect on what I had just done as the bus drove away. By the time the bus had reached Nantwich main bus station, I had made my way to the front seats on the top deck with most of the passengers already disembarked.

With the bus now parked up, I made my way home. It was about a half hour walk through the busy town out into the countryside, before finally reaching my house mid-afternoon. As I entered the house, everything was as normal as could be, apart from the fact my father was at home along with my mother. My father was now retired but occasionally would help out on the farm when asked. He was sitting in his normal place on the settee watching the 21" colour television we had, with his cap on, smoking a woodbine. It could be difficult enough for me to talk to my father at the best of times, let alone when he was watching his beloved television; disturbing him wasn't an option. I decided it would be best to tell my mum first, then she could tell my dad the good news later. "Mum," I said, "I have something to tell you."

"What is it now?" she said as if she had better things to do than listen to me.

"I am thinking of joining the Army," I said in a firm voice.

Her attention was forthcoming. "Joining the Army" my mum asked?

"Yes," I replied. "I caught the bus into Crewe today and went to the Army Careers Office. I did an Army IQ test and passed it."

I don't think my mum knew what to say; she seemed a little perplexed to say the least by what I had said. "That's wonderful," she said. "Your father will be really pleased and so chuffed with you."

It made me feel so proud to hear those words from my mother, knowing that joining the Army meant so much to her and my father.

My mother went off into the living room to tell my father all about what I had just told her about joining the Army. I don't know how the conversation went as I'd already gone outside onto the field to practise my footy. My parents were one of the main reasons why I decided to join the Army. My father served in the Army between the two world wars. He enlisted on the 28th of December 1923, at the age of 19, into the Kings Shropshire Light Infantry, and had an honourable discharge on the 18th of September 1931. I know from talking to him and my mum that they would have liked for one of their sons to have joined the military. One of my brothers, Robin, did deliberate with the idea of joining the Army, but then decided against it; I guess I was the last chance saloon for one of the eight lads to follow in my father's footsteps.

Later on that evening, I ventured back into the house after several hours of climbing trees in the near-by woods. I don't remember too much of what my father had to say (like I said he was a man of very few words), however, it didn't matter a fig to me because, deep down, I knew that he and my mother were both equally as proud of me as I was to have them as my parents.

September arrived, the month I always looked forward to. It was my sixteenth birthday (on the 14th to be precise) and, instead of the normal toys and games I would receive from my parents, I received clothes. I felt very disappointed and remember thinking *what do I want with clothes*? It was a major shock to the system, but I guess it is all part of growing up in life; dealing with these sorts of changes was something I would have to get use to. One day, you're a boy without a care in the world then, the next day you're a man with responsibilities. I soon got over the shock and started looking forward to Christmas; the colder months and darker nights meant that football was limited to the school playground. I started to learn how to speak German at our local college along with my school buddy Paul Simpson. I use to go one day a week from school and would practise it at home in the evenings whilst lying in my bed under several blankets. I knew that speaking German would be advantageous to me, with the fact that a huge part of the British Army was based in Germany, and I myself, might get posted overseas one day.

Christmas soon arrived, with me knowing that this would probably be the last traditional Christmas that I would be part of. My presents would still be laid out on the settee alongside all of my sisters' presents; I knew I would be getting more clothes again, so it didn't come as such a shock when I opened my presents: Trousers, shirts, pullovers, socks, underwear and, of course, some obligatory hankies were the format for the day. I was always grateful for what I got, but it felt like Santa had deserted me this year. After the festive period had come and gone, it was now time for me to start preparing for 1974. I had about four months left at school before stepping out into the real world. I wasn't too sure what the first few months were going to bring, shocks and surprises of plenty I was expecting, but even I was taken aback when I went to see my local GP. What he asked me do was something I was not fully prepared for, it was that smile on his face that will stay with me forever as he went about his business.

CHAPTER THREE
DROP YOUR TROUSERS YOUNG MAN

As February dawned, the snow was laying nipple deep on the ground. It was about 7.30am on this very cold Friday morning. I had just got dressed ready for school. I took a quick look out of my bedroom window; all the fields that I could see to my right looked liked they had been covered with the biggest white blanket I had ever seen. I looked over to the farm that was immediately in front of me to see if I could see any activity, it was as if time had stood still; all the cows were being kept in the cowsheds until the weather improved. My brother and sister were nowhere to be seen. With the fact that milking was almost over, I guess they were probably having a warm cup of tea somewhere.

It wasn't long before I made my way down the creaky stairs and made myself a brew.

"When are you going back to the Army Careers Office?" asked my mum as she handed me my bowl of un-burnt porridge.

"On Monday morning," I replied in a cheerful voice. "I will tell my form teacher today that I won't be in school because I have a careers interview."

"Oh, OK then," said my mum. "You must make sure that you dress smartly; we don't want them thinking that you can't dress yourself, do we now?"

"No, mum, you're right," I said sarcastically.

"I will sort some clean clothes out for you and put them on your bed," said my mum.

"Thanks mum," I replied.

"Make sure you have a bath on Sunday night. I'll make sure there is a good fire burning in the grate so that the water is piping hot," said my mum.

I gulped down my porridge then finished my cup of tea before saying goodbye. It was a nightmare of a journey in the snow and, by time I had reached the school gates, the bottom of my trousers were soaking wet. I wasn't sure whether we would be allowed to play football in the playground or not, but luckily for me, the teachers were showing some sort of common sense for a change allowing us to play.

Most of the school decided to stay inside at all break times that we had throughout the day. It was only me and a few of my mates that would brave the elements. We had a few snowball fights and a few rolls in the snow; *it's what's known as having fun*, I thought, as I looked towards the school to see the rest of the pupils in their respective classrooms. At the end of the day it was make your way home time once again. The snow was now very slushy and, just when I thought I couldn't get any wetter, I was completely wrong; every time a vehicle drove past me as I cycled home I got an absolute drowning with dirty, slushy, freezing cold water. I arrived home to the sound of my mum saying in a loud voice, "Look at the state of you, our Paul!" Then (in a stern voice), "What have you been up to?"

"Don't blame me mum! It's all those crazy drivers on the road; they don't even slow down when they pass you, 'In fact', I think they speed up on purpose to see if they can get the slush to go over your head."

"Get your shoes now, I will stuff them with old newspapers and put them by the fire to dry," said my mum.

No sooner said than done; my feet were like ice blocks. I went upstairs into my bedroom to find some dry clothes to change into, before making my way back downstairs. I put my bare feet close to the flames on the open fire to thaw them out, almost burning my toes in the process. My mum brought me some clean, warm socks that had been drying out on the cylinder upstairs and gave them to me. "Put these on," she said. "They will keep your feet warm."

As I put them on, the feeling of the warm socks on my cold feet was to die for; I was feeling so much warmer now, so decided that football was definitely off the menu. I went into the living room where my father was watching television in front of another raging fire. "Hi dad," I said in a kind of happy voice. My father just nodded his head downwards to acknowledge that he had heard me then continued watching the television.

It was always nice to have the weekend off, although I didn't have any plans to do anything. All my thoughts were now focused on Monday morning and nothing else. The weekend passed quickly, as is normally the case when you're not at school. Saturday morning was spent playing in the woods and in the nearby council yard across the road at the end of my drive. My sister and her friend came along later in the morning to see what I was up to and just to have a chat. "What are you up too? Ah Paul" said my sister.

"Not a lot. Just playing around, climbing trees and playing in the sand," I replied.

My sister then said, "I've just been telling my friend Amy about all the clothes that mum and dad have bought for you instead of toys and games. I also told her about the dicky bow that they had bought for you."

I was sat thinking, *why did you need to tell her about my dicky bow?* But, before I could say anything, Amy and her super-quick thinking shouted, "Wow, that's good. I have a dick but it's not in a bow yet." I was stunned in to silence and didn't know what to say.

After a while we all made our way back home. My sister and her friend Amy went to the girls' bedroom to do what girls do, and I went into the dining room to listen to the afternoon's football on my transistor radio. I would normally watch the television, however, come four o'clock my father would always be watching the wrestling; all this meant is, that I would not get to find out how my beloved team, Leeds United, were getting on. Saturday night was *Match of the Day* night. The problem I had was staying awake; there would be times when I would be watching the news on my own, waiting for *Match of the Day* to start, then all of a sudden, I would wake up to the tune of *Match of the Day*, signalling that the programme had finished. I would be fuming, basically because that was it; it would never be repeated in respect that we didn't have modern technology like a VCR. I would go to bed all disgruntled and have to settle for reading the football stories in the Sunday paper the next day.

Sunday was pretty much the same as Saturday without the sport; we did use to have to go to Sunday school when we were younger, but all that has stopped now that we were older. Sunday evening was soon upon us. I was sitting in the dining room talking to one of my sisters, when I suddenly heard the water pipes rattling upstairs in the cubbyhole where the cylinder sat. The next thing I heard was my mum saying in a loud voice, "Paul, I am just going to run the bath water for you to have a bath. Don't be too long or the water will be cold."

Not a chance, I thought. The water would get that hot in the bathroom that it took the paint off the walls. "I'll be up right away," I said, in an *anything-you-say-mum* kind of voice.

"I have put your clothes that you will be wearing tomorrow on your bed; try to make sure you don't crease them up," my mum said.

I was just about to go upstairs when I saw my mum making her way downstairs.

"Don't you come up, our Paul, until I reach the bottom," my mum said with her superstitions kicking in again. I waited until my mother was at the bottom of the stairs before being allowed up into the bathroom. It felt more like a sauna than a bathroom; there was steam everywhere. I turned the cold tap on and left it running until I was undressed.

I decided to get an early night after my bath. I spent a little time with the light on practising my German. "Ich heisse Paul Wolfendale," I would say to myself before my eyes wouldn't stay open any longer. I just about managed to switch the light off before my head hit the pillow. The next thing I knew, it was Monday morning and I was eagerly waiting to see what the day had in store for me. I felt excited; it reminded me of the time we would all get up on a Sunday morning once a year in the summer holidays for our annual Sunday school trip to Blackpool. I got dressed in the smart clothes my mum had laid out for me: nicely pressed trousers that would be more suited to a golfer, not quite plus-fours, but similar, my shiny lace up winkle-pickers type shoes and a zip-up blue pullover.

I had more colours in my clothes than a technicoloured yawn. My mum would always take one last look at me before I left home. Even though we were a very poor family, smart and tidy was top of her agenda; there was no excuse for scruffiness where my mum was concerned. "Stand still," my mum would say to me. She would then get out her hankie and spit on the corner of it before wiping the edge of my mouth to get rid of any remaining food that may be present. I still feel the impact of that now as I write this book. The spit had a kind of smell of its own, it was disgusting.

My mum and dad wished me good luck as I started my eagerly awaited voyage. First it was on foot to Nantwich, and then I would catch the bus to Crewe. The Army Careers Office was open as I arrived about 10.30am. There was no hesitation this time; I just marched right into the waiting room. Everything seemed the same as it was some six months ago until I noticed that Sergeant Boucher and Corporal Batty were no longer present; there were two different soldiers sitting at the desk where they would normally be seated. "Hello, how can I help you?" said one of the soldiers.

I replied by saying. "I was here some six months ago. I was interviewed by Sergeant Boucher and Corporal Batty who asked me to take part in an IQ test that I passed. I was told that I was too young to join the Army at this moment in time, so I would need to return when I was sixteen. Come back and see us in February they said."

"Well unfortunately, Sergeant Boucher and Corporal Batty have now returned to their units. My name is Sergeant Danny Cromwell and this is

Corporal David Huxley. We have now taken over their duties for the next two years. Did you say that you passed the IQ test?"

"Yes," I said in a confident voice.

"Bear with me a minute," said Sergeant Cromwell. "I will just need to check the files that should be in here somewhere."

After rummaging in the filing cabinet for a few minutes Sergeant Cromwell turned to me and said, "I am sorry, but there doesn't seem to be any recollection of you being here six months ago."

"Oh," I said, disappointed and confused. "Well, I definitely was here; it's not the sort of thing I would lie about."

"No, I understand," said Sergeant Cromwell. "That is not in dispute. All it means is that you'll have to do the IQ test again."

"I was told I would not have to do the test again," I said feeling annoyed.

"Yes, I know," said Sergeant Cromwell, trying to show some sympathy. "I understand how you feel, without the paperwork from the test you say you did, I'm afraid there's nothing I can do."

I was not happy at all, I'm just glad there wasn't a cat roaming around otherwise it would be feeling ill. All that said; I still had to understand that mistakes happen in all forms of life.

Corporal Huxley escorted me to the so-called store room just like six months ago. After the time had elapsed, I was escorted back into the waiting room and waited for the Sergeant to mark my test sheet once more. "OK, Paul. Would you kindly make your way into my office and take a seat please," said Sergeant Cromwell.

I sat down and waited my result.

"Well done Paul, you have passed the test with flying colours, and once again, I apologise about the mix up with your last test."

"No problem," I said. I was just glad to have passed it for a second time. "What happens now?" I asked.

"OK, what will happen now is that I will need to take all your details down: date of birth, where you were born, address, your religion, etc. All in all, it should take about ten minutes to complete the paper work. Corporal Huxley, could you get me the registration forms from the filing cabinet please?"

"Right away," said the Corporal. The Corporal handed over the forms to his Sergeant, who then started by saying, "Your full name please?"

"Paul William Wolfendale," I said feeling good that I'd got that one correct.

"Date of birth?"

"Fourteenth of the ninth, 1957," I answered

"And who is your next of kin?"

"Charles William Cooper and Adeline Harriet Cooper,"

It seemed to take a lot longer than ten minutes to fill out all of the forms, but finally, the Sergeant said, "OK, I think that's about it. I will just have one more look to make sure I haven't missed anything out." He checked the forms up and down several times before declaring. "Yes, I can't see anything else that needs filling out; all the questions have been answered."

After all the forms had been neatly filled in using block capitals, I felt that the Sergeant knew more about me than I knew about myself. "Right, Paul," said the Sergeant. "Now all the paper work is complete, the next step is to arrange a medical with your GP. I have all the details, so I shall be in touch with him right away; you should receive a letter in the post within the next few days explaining when your appointment is. After that, and, providing the medical goes well without any major issues, we will be in touch with you again by form of a letter for a further interview about the next stage."

"How long will all this normally take?" I said.

"All being well, I will phone your GP later on today to arrange a medical for you. Hopefully it will be no later than the end of this week; once your medical is complete I should get the result back the following week."

"That's great!" I said feeling contented that things were now moving forward. "I look forward to hearing from you soon." I shook the hand of both the Sergeant and the Corporal before saying, "Thanks again. See you soon."

"Bye, Paul, have a safe journey home."

I made my way across the road to catch the bus that would take me back to Nantwich before the enduring two mile walk home. It felt just like the last time except this time, I really felt that this was it; there was no turning back now. I was now that much closer to joining the Army and 'taking the Queen's shilling.' I decided to skip school for the rest of the day although I must say, it was a close decision, I just felt the road home seemed a more attractive proposition than an afternoon of lessons; well it was certainly more scenic.

As I walked home, I could sense I was the only school pupil in the town. *Where were my mates when I needed them?* I felt like a stranger in my home town; people would stare at me as if to say, *what are you doing, my lad, you should be at school?* I took a few short cuts through alleyways and deserted car parks to avoid being compromised by all and sundry; it wasn't until I eventually crossed over the canal bridge, some half a mile away from my house that I felt in my own comfort zone. It was all quiet at my house as I walked up the path to the front door. The only noise I could hear was from Patch, as she paraded up and down the length of her chain. I stopped for a few minutes to give her a hug and a cuddle before stepping through my front door.

Judy was next to welcome me, with a little snarl; she liked to show me her teeth from time to time. *I am the boss around here* was the message I was receiving. Although the house wasn't that big, three-up and three-down, including the kitchen, my mum and dad were nowhere to be found. It wasn't long before I set eyes on my mum. She had been hanging out the washing in the back garden. "Oh, you're home already," my mum said in a surprised voice as she walked into the kitchen. She caught me swigging down a pint of milk from the small white stand up fridge.

"Where's dad?" I asked.

"He's in the garden, digging up potatoes for tea," said my mum. "How did you get on today?"

"Well, everything went well," I said. "They made me do another IQ test that I passed with flying colours, they said the next step will be for them to send me an appointment letter for a medical at our local GP within the next few days and, providing the medical goes well, they will need to see me again soon after to discuss matters further."

"I am so pleased!" said my mother. "I will tell your father when he comes in from the garden."

I could tell from the look on my mum's face that she was chuffed to bits with what I was doing; I also knew that my dad would be sharing the same sentiments. I can never remember my dad saying anything at all about me joining the Army after he was told the news by my mum, but he didn't have to. Occasionally we would sit on the grass bank in the back garden and have a chat with his woodbine in one hand and a cuppa in the other; I'm pretty sure that my dad would sit there all day if he could. As far as my brothers and sisters were concerned, it was, *I'll believe it when I see it.* I remember one of my sisters being a little judgemental, in saying to me, "can't see you sticking it out. You're too much of a mummy's boy."

Somewhere hidden in that statement was an element of truth; it always seemed in my sisters' eyes that they got blamed for everything that went wrong and, that I was always the innocent party. Well, to put the record straight, I remember at least two occasions when my dad took his leather belt off his trousers and thrashed me hard on my backside. I could feel the anger in the belt as it thrashed against my paltry thin trousers as a lay bent over my dad's knee.

I shared a mutual love with my parents. Deep down inside my heart, I loved them more than anyone could ever know. Maybe that's what my sisters saw when they made their judgement call, and, not the fact that I felt so much love towards them; maybe it was a love that could only be felt by my parents.

A few days had past and I was still awaiting the arrival of my well anticipated letter. The post always arrived about 7am, just as I would be getting out of the comfort of my warm bed. Dressed only in my underwear, I heard the postman at the door whilst, at the same time, feeling the coldness of the room air chilling my body. I could hear my mum thanking the postman. I stood motionless for a few seconds, hoping that there was some post for me. Within seconds, my mum had shouted up the stairs. "Paul, there is a letter for you; it looks quite official. I would say by the looks of it, it's probably from the Army."

"Be down in a minute mum; just getting dressed." I said with a shiver in my voice. I felt adrenalin running through my veins as I accelerated my way downstairs missing every other step and jumping the last four.

"What's that noise?" said my mum in a concerned manner. "Paul, are you OK?"

"Yes," I said. "I just missed a couple of steps on the way down."

"Well, be careful you daft bugger, you'll do yourself an injury" said my mum.

"Where's my letter mum?" I asked.

"It's on the table in the dining room in a brown envelope," replied my mum.

"OK, I can see it, thanks" I said." I picked up the letter and carefully opened it, trying not to rip any part of what was inside the envelope.

"Well, what does it say?" shouted my mum from the kitchen.

"Give me a second… I am just about to read it," I said as I unfolded the piece of paper that was in the envelope. "It says that an appointment has been arranged for you at your local GP on Monday the 18th of February at 10.30am."

"That's next Monday," my mum said.

"Yes," I said. "In four days' time, it says that the GP will give me a full examination that should take no more than about twenty minutes… *Please make sure that you take this letter with you and hand it to your GP,*" I quoted.

"Is that it? Nothing else" said my mum.

"No, that's all it says," I said.

My sisters that were getting ready for work were too interested in not being late than bothered about my less concerning medical on Monday morning. That was fine by me, because I also had more interesting things to concern myself with, like getting to school on time and playing footie with my mates.

Monday morning arrived and, after my mum had made sure I was shining like a new penny, I got my bike out from the shed and made my way to Nantwich, not forgetting my appointment letter. The weather was slightly murky with a slight drizzle in the air, so wearing my three-quarter Parka coat with its rabbit fur trimmed around the edge of the hood was a must. It actually did look more like a military coat with all its neatly sewn-in pockets and a pull-cord around the waist. I arrived at the GP clinic and parked my bike up against the wall of the practice, hoping it would still be there when I returned. I made my way into the reception area and walked over to the counter.

"How can I help you?" said the smartly dressed lady in a posh kind of voice. Well, compared to mine, it was posh.

"I have an appointment with my GP," I said as I handed over the appointment letter for her to read.

"OK, if you would like to take a seat please, and wait for your name to be called."

"Thank you," I said politely as I made my way to the waiting room, only to be greeted by all the walking wounded that were hoping for sick notes. There were some magazines available, but of no interest to me: *Women's Own*, *Gardeners' World*, *DIY*, etc. I just bided my time by reading all the notices that they had posted around the waiting room walls, until it was time for my name to be called. No sooner had I finished reading about the impact of drugs, my name was called over the PA system. "Paul Wolfendale to Doctor Crawford please, Paul Wolfendale to Doctor Crawford."

I looked at everybody as I left my seat thinking, *Yeah; go on, it's my turn now. Enjoy your magazines.* Along the short narrow corridor I went, passing several doors that were all closed: Doctor Harris… No, that's not me; Doctor Sinn… No, that's not me either, and then as I looked further down the corridor, I noticed a door on my left that was slightly ajar. I peered around the frame of the door to see this elderly gentleman writing some notes on his desk. I think he must have sensed my presence because, within a split second, he turned and looked up at me from the comfort of his chair. "Mr Wolfendale," he said, with some authority in his voice.

"Yes," I said with trepidation in mine.

"Come in and take a seat," said the doctor. I did exactly what he said then waited for his next command which was, "Shut the door behind you please."

"Sorry," I said apologetically.

"OK, so you're thinking of joining the Army, are you?"

"Yes," I said.

"If you would just like to stand up please and strip down to the waist as I need to examine you." He took out his stethoscope and positioned it all over my body, at the same time telling me to breathe in and out repeatedly. "OK, everything seems fine. Could you now take down your trousers, please?"

Ouch. I felt he was now going to take away what little bit of dignity I had left. I saw him putting on a rubber glove and knew what was coming next.

"Pull your pants down please."

I couldn't believe that I was now standing bollock-naked in front of a man I had never met before. This was the most undignified thing I had ever done in my life. There I was with my trousers down to my ankles and my underpants resting on top of them; standing in front of this strange man with his face only inches away from mine, was making me feel very uncomfortable.

I felt his rubber glove against my undercarriage.

"Cough please," he said as he continued his test to see if there was any sign of a hernia that could put a stop to my Army career right here and now.

As I arched my neck back I made sure I kept my mouth closed, just in case I fired a foreign body out of my mouth. I remember the way he was looking at me, a way that made me feel that he was actually seeing whether I was enjoying the experience.

"OK, that's fine. Just take a seat please while I fill in my report," he said.

A few seconds later, after he had finished his report, he said, "I just need to do a test now to test for colour blindness." He showed me a book with numbers that were hidden in a mass of bubbles on each page, my job was to recognise and call out the number that I could see on each page. I could see that I was struggling on one or two of the numbers; in fact, there was the odd one or two that I couldn't even see at all. I knew then that all was not well. I felt a magnitude of sadness inside me as the doctor explained that I was suffering from a mild case of colour blindness that he would have to put down in his report.

"I shall have the report sent out today so you should get a letter from the Army Careers Office very soon," he said.

"Thank you," I said as I turned towards the door, feeling like I had just been kicked in the undercarriage and not just having it felt.

Back home, I explained to my parents what the doctor had said, but ever the optimist, my mum said, "Oh, don't worry, you'll be fine. You'll see, don't get yourself down."

I just agreed and thought, *yes, my mum is right as usual. There is no point worrying over it; I shall just have to wait a couple of days to see what the result of my medical is.* I could see the chances of me joining the Army receding with every word that was spoken by my mum.

The letter arrived on Thursday morning. I was just having breakfast with my sisters when the post arrived, along with some other mail. The letter seemed a lot larger than I was expecting; it was a large brown envelope that was bursting at the seams. My mum was urging me to open it.

"OK!" I said to my mum. "Just give me a moment." I pulled out a three page letter that was stapled together and started to read it out aloud to whoever was listening.

It read something like this. *'Thank you for attending your medical on Monday 18th of February. Your GP has given us an unbiased report on your health, in respect to joining the Army. I am sure you understand that it is important for all potential soldiers to be medically fit for service, so as to take on any task in the Army that they're given. A full report of your medical can be seen and explained overleaf.'*

"Well, what does it say?" asked my mum.

I found it hard to completely understand the report as I scanned my eyes across the page; everything seemed in order until I reached section at the bottom of the page. It explained that due to my mild condition of colour blindness, I would need to be referred to a military doctor to see the extent of my condition. 'We have enclosed a second-class return ticket for you to visit RAF (Royal Air Force) Cosford on Monday 4th March. Details of the whereabouts and a map of how to get there from the station are enclosed on page three of this document.' I looked inside the envelope to find the return ticket, also a claims form for any other expenditure I might encounter.

"Well," said my mum. "That's good news!"

I suppose it was. At least I was still in there fighting. I would just have to stay positive. If nothing else came out of it, at least I would be getting a day out and a free train ride to an area of England that I've never visited before. It seemed to have been a long journey already, with the fact that I've had to do two IQ tests, endure an undignified medical, and now I had to go to RAF Cosford for more clarification of my status to be a soldier. It would be a week or two before I would find out. Was it going to be good news as I stood apprehensively in front of my parents about to open the letter?

CHAPTER FOUR
OPEN IT UP PAUL, LET'S HOPE IT'S GOOD NEWS

Back at school, some of my friends and I were all getting quite excited that we would be leaving in about four weeks time. Because of our age, we were all entitled to leave at the Easter half term at the age of sixteen. I am not sure if they all had jobs to go to but, what I do know is that none of them apart from me was joining the forces. One or two of my teachers knew that I would be leaving to pursue a career in the forces and made their feelings known to me. It felt good that they were finally taking an interest in me and my ambition to be a soldier.

On Monday 4th March, I was out of bed early, making sure I didn't miss my train to Cosford. My mum was busy doing the washing, so I thought I would make myself some breakfast: boiled eggs with soldiers swilled down with a cup of tea was the theme for the day. I seem to remember the advertisement on the television the night before, 'Go to work on an egg' in a nice tuneful way, so what better way to start off the day; after all, I had a long day ahead of me. I left my dirty plate and egg cup in the sink for mum to wash then made my way outside. "Bye mum! Bye dad!" I said.

"See you later on," they said.

"OK, bye. Should be home later on in the afternoon," I said.

On arrival at the railway station, I made my way through the glass doors into the station. I felt a feeling of entrapment as the doors closed behind me to hide the noise of the traffic outside. The station seemed quite full of people for a Monday morning. I looked across and, in front of me, towards the ticket booths, there was a smart gent standing in front of one of them, donning a dark coloured full-length coat carrying a leather briefcase. "A first class return ticket to London please," said the gentlemen in a posh voice.

"Certainly Sir," said the ticket master.

"Two cheap day return tickets to Blackpool," said two elderly ladies in a language more common to me. Everybody else seemed to have a companion of some sort with them. Not me. I was on my lonesome, thinking to myself, *where the hell do I go?* It was only then that I remembered I already had my tickets tucked away safely in my pocket. I turned to my left and saw a stand that was selling all sorts of goodies and magazines; I had a few bob in my possession, so I thought I would treat myself to some chocolate before making my way past the ticket booths to the small entrance that led to the train platform. The entrance was manned by a ticket master dressed smartly in his British Rail uniform. I handed over my yellow ticket, or was it orange, blue, brown, how the hell do I know… I am colour-blind. He punched a hole in my ticket with his small little hand punch. "Thank you," he said. "Platform three to Wolverhampton should be leaving in about twenty minutes."

"Thank you," I said as I made my way down the wide open stairs onto the platform, at the same time looking for platform three.

I had only been on a train about three or four times in my life; it wasn't the sort of thing that we could afford, so naturally, I was feeling a little nervous. There were whistles blowing all around me, and PA systems echoing, "The next train to arrive at platform three will be the nine twenty to Birmingham, stopping at Stafford, Wolverhampton. Passengers for Cosford change at Wolverhampton."

Shit, I was thinking, *that's my train*. I could hear the wheels of the train working on the track as it slowly pulled alongside the platform that I was standing on. It seemed to go on forever. Carriage after carriage went passed me until, with a final screech of the wheels, the train stopped. Luckily for me, a lot of passengers disembarked at Crewe, leaving plenty of seating space in the second-class carriages. The train had small segregated compartments with closing sliding doors. Each compartment would hold about six to eight passengers. I managed to get myself a window seat so I could watch the world go by as the train picked up speed along the rails; if I remember correctly, there were only two other people of a more mature age in my compartment.

I could hear all of the carriage doors closing; each one seemed to have its own distinctive bang, one after another *bang, bang, bang…* Then there was a loud whistle from the platform to signal the departure of our train. Within minutes, we had picked up speed and were heading out of the station into a more rural setting. There were lots of fields and woodlands to admire. The two gentlemen in my compartment got out their copies of the daily newspaper. I was quite content just looking out of the window, taking in the beautiful countryside. Occasionally, I would be snapped out of my day dreaming by the ruffling of their newspapers every time they turned to a new page; rattling their pages as loud as they could had me thinking they were in competition with each other to see you had the loudest rattle. It wasn't too long before we were pulling into Wolverhampton station and saying goodbye to the countryside. I was just about to ask a railway porter as I stepped off the now stationary train, what platform I needed for Cosford, when I heard over the PA system, "Passengers for Shrewsbury please make your way to platform two."

That's my train, I said to myself, *that's the one that stops at Cosford.* I was getting the hang of this now, feeling quite proud that I hadn't yet got lost.

A short train ride of about twenty minutes into rural Shropshire countryside and we were in Cosford. It was about a half mile walk to the barracks, whereupon I produced my letter of confirmation that I had with me to the person on duty at the Guardroom gate. After my identity had been established, I was given verbal directions of where I needed to be. It was a short walk across the barracks to the medical room. The whole format was much the same as it was with my own GP, except, this time, I knew I wouldn't be subjected to flashing my meat and two veg.

"Could you read the numbers on each of the pages in the book please" said the military medic in a serious voice.

Two, five, nine, one, don't know, four, don't know, seven, was how it went. It only took a few minutes to complete the colour-blindness test. "Your result will be sent to Army records and then you should hear from them within a few days," said the Army medic.

I was thinking *Yes, I know everything always seems to take a few days.* I was getting use to this now as I smiled to myself. "Thank you; am I free to leave now?" I said.

"Yes, that's it. All finished," said the medic, "have a safe journey home."

Well, all I could do now was head back home and wait for the news that could change my life.

After a straightforward journey back, I arrived home late afternoon. My mum and dad were both in the living room watching something on the TV. I think my dad was listening to me as I stood in the middle of the living room with my back to the fire, a fire that was lightly burning. I started by saying, "They will let me know in few days… that's all that they could tell me. I should receive a letter in the post telling me about my result."

"How do you think it went?" asked my mum.

"It's hard to say." I said, "I saw some of the numbers they wanted me to read, but there were also some I couldn't see at all."

My dad just looked towards me without so much as a word and just continued watching whatever he was watching. I suppose it was more appealing than what I had to say. I didn't take any offence to the fact that he continued watching television; that is the way my dad was. He was a great guy.

It was Friday 8th March before I heard from the Army. Unfortunately, the post was late that day that meant I had already gone to school. It was only when I came home that afternoon, after school, that my mum came rushing towards me with the letter I had been waiting for over the last two days.

"Here, Paul. It has arrived. Open it up! Let's hope it's the news we've been waiting for."

This was probably the most tension I have ever felt in my entire life. My stomach was churning. I just took a deep breath and went for it. I knew my mum and dad would be so disappointed, not with me, but with the result if it wasn't the news I yearned for. A small but important letter was now getting the better of me. I pulled out the letter that was neatly folded and started to run my eyes across the sheet of paper, trying to see if I could see my result without reading all the other jargon that was printed on the paper. There it was about four lines down: 'Congratulations'. I am pleased to say the result of your colour-blindness test is of a required standard to join the Army. You have been marked as CB 4 (Colour Blind 4).' I still don't know to this day what the hell it actually meant, but to be honest, I didn't give a fig. I continued reading the next line of the letter, that read. 'This is the minimum requirement to join the Army.' I looked towards my mum with my eyes wide open and a huge smile on my face. Before even reading any more of the letter it was so obvious to my mum that it was positive news.

"Well done," she said. "I will go and tell your dad. He will be so pleased!"

My mum went to find my dad leaving me to continue reading my letter in a more methodical order: my address, my name and 'Dear Paul'.

The main part of the letter read 'We would like to see you one day next week to arrange for you to go to an Army training unit based in Harrogate in the North of England for a two-day assessment: You'll be assessed on your maths, English, spelling, current affairs and one or two other tests. You'll get chance to put any questions forward to our training team, who are there to assist you in all your needs. I put the letter back into its envelope and made my way to the back garden where my mum was telling my dad the news. I explained the rest of the letter to my parents, who seemed to be overwhelmed with joy; even my dad had a smile on his face. It was a euphoric moment for me and my parents. I could finally see some light at the end of the tunnel, even though I still had some more tests to do. *One step at a time*, I thought to myself. It was only now when I thought I'd better get myself down to the barbers and get rid of my precious locks. Have you ever wondered what items were on sale in a barbers shop, me neither.

As I sat in there in the Barbers chair looking at the items on the shelf that were in front of me, I was absolutely shocked to see a certain item that I had only read about in an adult magazine staring me in the face.

CHAPTER FIVE
SHORT BACK AND SIDES

Over the next few days, before I would return to the Army Careers Office in Crewe, I felt that my sisters and brothers were showing me a little more respect. In their eyes, I was no longer 'Mummy's Little Boy'; I was now turning slowly but surely into a man in my adolescent years. All I needed now was for my voice to break, and try to grow a little bum fluff on my chin. Unfortunately, I had to take another unauthorised day off school so I could go to the Army Careers Office. Taking days off was now becoming habitual, but there would be no complaints from me; I had an exemplary attendance record with only two unauthorised days off in the twelve months leading up to me leaving; a few days off here and there went unnoticed.

I returned to the Army Careers Office on Monday 9th March at about 9.30am. It was a miserable wet Monday morning that meant I was absolutely soaking wet as I stepped off the bus, not that the bus was a convertible, it was just from walking from my house to the bus station in Nantwich. I thought I would have dried out by time I got to Crewe, given that the journey would take about half an hour. Not a chance. I looked like I had been dragged through a puddle backwards; I quickly made my way into the Army Careers Office to get out of the now persisting rain.

"Hi Paul," what's the weather like outside?" said Sergeant Cromwell with a huge smile on his face.

"Fine," I said in a sarcastic voice. "There are just a few drops of rain, but otherwise, not too bad."

"Sorry," he said. "Was just having a laugh; couldn't resist saying something. Please take advantage of this one time offer that this amazing caring Sergeant is going to offer you: would you like a cup of tea? You look as if you could do with one to warm you up."

"That would be great, thanks," I said gratefully.

"OK, just take a seat. Corporal Huxley, put the kettle on will you. We have a guest!" shouted the Sergeant.

"Why have a dog and bark yourself, eh, Paul!"

"Good point," I said in a quiet and perplexed voice. I didn't want Corporal Huxley to hear me, or bang goes my cuppa.

"OK, Paul. So glad you have now completed your medical; I have the result here in front of me. There is no major concern apart from you may be slightly restricted to what corps' you join because of your ability to recognise certain colours."

"Yes," I said. "I understand; just glad that I've managed to pass that part of the test."

"Is there any corps' you have in mind that you would like to join?" said the Sergeant.

"Yes," I said. "I was thinking of joining the Royal Artillery. I remember chatting to Sergeant Boucher the last time I was here. I commented on his cap badge and he said that he was a member of the Royal Artillery. He went on to say you won't go far wrong in the Royal Artillery; there are lots of opportunities for you in the Artillery, so I thought, why not. What do you think?"

"Well, I certainly wouldn't disagree with what Sergeant Boucher told you. Yes, the Royal Artillery sounds a great choice. Corporal Huxley is that cup of tea ready yet?" shouted Sergeant Cromwell.

"Just coming now, Sarge," said the Corporal.

Within seconds, there were two Army size mugs of tea sitting on the desk in front of me.

"Thank you, Corp," said the Sergeant. "OK, now we can get down to the business end of this conversation."

I took a sip of my NATO (North Atlantic Treaty Organisation) standard cup of tea (milk and two sugars), before placing the mug back onto the desk just to the side of me; I looked the Sergeant in the face as if to say, *I'm ready for you now. You have my undivided attention.*

"OK, Paul, you probably already know from the letter you received last week that you'll now be sent to an Army training camp for a two-day assessment. The camp is in Harrogate, North Yorkshire like I mentioned, it's the home of the Royal Signals apprentice training. We will send you out a letter with all the details of what is expected from you while you're there, and a list of items you need to take with you," he continued. "This will be the last stage of your recruitment in to joining the Army and, providing everything goes well, we will be seeing you when you get back."

I took another gulp of my tea before asking in a curious voice. "So, even though I've passed my medical and my IQ test twice, I am still not yet guaranteed a place?"

"That's correct," said the Sergeant. "However, I can't see there being any stumbling blocks. Your score on the IQ test was very high; there is nothing they'll throw at you that you won't be able to handle. Anyway, you owe me a cup of tea so you'd better come back," said Sergeant Cromwell with a serious smile on his face.

"OK," I said. "You win. I will see you when I get back and return the favour." I finished my cuppa then headed back home. As the bus drove along the bumpy road I really felt as if I was part of the Army now. I felt as if I was already signed up. After all, I had been drinking their tea. For the first time, I felt that camaraderie that can only be felt by military personnel. *Bring it on*, I thought. I didn't want the bus journey to end. I was in my own little bubble without a care in the world. Unfortunately, I was brought back to earth as the bus pulled into the bus station; at least it had stopped raining now, there was hardly a cloud in the sky.

It was now left to the postman once again to bring me even more mail. I think I must have been the most popular person in my household; I was getting more mail than all of the rest of my family put together. Not that I was complaining. It made me feel very important every time the postman arrived with a letter that was addressed to me.

I was leaving school within the next few weeks, at the beginning of April, Friday the 5th to be more precise. I was hoping that my two-day assessment would be after I had left. I just felt, with school out of the way, I could then concentrate on preparing myself for the big day, the day when I would finally join the Army. Thursday the 12th was when I received my confirmation letter. I was the first to the door on that day, as I caught sight of the postman through the kitchen window coming up our drive, and then I heard Patch barking resolutely. I think by now, the postman had got the measure of the length of the dog's chain, as he walked on the left hand side of the path, just out of reach of her bite. To be honest, I don't think Patch would have bitten him if he was covered in gravy; either way, he was taking no chances. He would have had more chance of getting a bite from Judy if he had decided to venture through the half open door.

"Thank you," I said, as he handed over the post. "Have a nice day."

"You too," said the postman.

I noticed that he was keeping one eye on Patch as he sidled his way past towards his bike that was propped up against the fence. I wasn't too concerned about the letter today, as I pretty well knew what it contained. 'Dear Paul. A reservation has been made for you at the Army barracks in Harrogate, North Yorkshire, on Wednesday 10th April. You'll need to report to the Guardroom no later than 1000hrs on the morning in question, where upon you'll be taking to and, shown your accommodation. You'll be expected to wear smart clothes on arrival and, for the two days that you'll be there, a military member of the training unit will address you at 1100hrs. You'll then be shown the whereabouts of the cookhouse; lunch will be at 1230hrs. In the afternoon, you'll take part in some military exams in the education centre and be shown a short film. The evening will be at your own leisure; you may go out into town, but please remember, that you'll be representing the Army, we will not allow anyone to misbehave.

There will be zero tolerance on misbehaving and you'll be sent straight back home without any hesitation. Reveille (getting out of bed) on day two will be at 0700hrs, breakfast will be served in the main canteen between 0730hrs until 0830hrs. There will be a parade outside the accommodation block at 0900hrs, where you'll be briefed on the day's activities. You shall all be finished about 1500hrs then, one-by-one; you'll be interviewed and told of your acceptance into the British Army. After that, you'll be free to leave the barracks at around about 1600hrs. A guide of what you should bring with you can be seen overleaf; please do not bring any unnecessary items with you that you don't need.'

Well, that was it. I had a month to wait. I was thinking it was about time I got my hair cut; my beautiful, shoulder length straight hair was now under threat from Mr Stubbs, my local barber. My mum agreed with me and said, "Paul, I want you to call at the barbers on the way home from school one day next week. I'm afraid those locks are going to have to come off."

"Yes, I know," I said, mumbling underneath my breath. I called in at the barbers shop the following week on the way home from school, just like requested. I could see the barbers red and white pole revolving round from up the street outside the shop. As I got closer, I had reservations about entering the shop, but realised I had no choice in the matter. I was now at God's mercy.

I stepped inside to find that there were only a few gentlemen waiting. All the hardback kitchen-type chairs were pushed up against the walls. There were four on one wall and about six along the other side. In front were the three swivel adjustable leather chairs. I could see and hear the buzzing of the electric shears, the snipping of the scissors and the quiet chitchat that went on between the barber and the customer. You became the barber's new best friend for the next ten minutes or so that you were in the chair. You would converse with him through the huge mirror in front of you that was fastened to the wall. There were personal touches, like the way he placed the poncho-like cover around you to prevent you from getting covered by your snipped hair… It was always the barber's job to make you feel important.

Within minutes of reading the sports pages of the newspapers that were available for customers to mull over, one of the three barbers that had just finished cutting someone's hair looked over to me and said, "Next please," in a quiet voice.

I made my way over the vinyl floor that had just been swept, and then shuffled my backside into the comfort of the leather seat. The barber then hoisted the seat up to a height that he could safely cut my hair; I was thinking, *a few more pumps of his foot and I would have been saying hello to the ceiling.*

"How would you like your hair cut, Sir?" said the barber in a quiet voice.

"Short back and sides," I said, as I closed my eyes in disbelief to what I've just told him to do to my fine hair.

"Are you sure?" said the barber "there is a lot of hair to cut off."

"Yes," I said. "I am hoping to join the Army soon, so it as all got to go."

"Very well," he said. "I will cut it to your specifications, but you might find that the military will have their own version of a short back and sides."

The barber was chatting away to me, but to be honest, I wasn't paying much attention to what he was saying. All I could think about was my hair that was now falling on the floor in great bundles. I tried to take my mind of what he was doing by seeing what products were for sale. There were lots of items in front of me on the shelf by the huge mirror that housed my face: Brylcream, combs, razors, razor blades and then, out of the corner of my eye, I noticed Durex in packets of three. With the fact that I was being groomed by a man, and everybody else was at a more grown-up age than me, it made me feel very concerned; after all, I had never seen Durex for sale at such close quarters. In fact, that is the closest I had ever been to one. I mean to say I was only sixteen and still learning my trade.

Before I knew, it was all over and the barber's mirror came out. He placed it at the back of my neck.

"Is that OK, Sir?" he said.

"Yes, that's fine. Thank you."

"Would you like some spray on your hair, Sir?" he asked.

"Why not," I said still feeling shocked at what I saw.

I took one last look in the mirror before I got a brushing down.

"25p Sir," said the barber, "I hope everything works out well for you in the future."

I paid the man and said 'thank you' before leaving. It felt cold around the back of my neck and around my ears as I made my way back home on my cycle, but the deed was done. It took a lot of my friends a while to get use to my new hair style; the badgering lasted about a week.

"Woo! Nice hair!" they would say.

"Paul, did you get his name?"

"What name?" I would say.

"The name of the man that attacked your hair, just find out his name and we will sort him out," they said.

Laugh all you want, I thought. *Soon, I shall be meeting new friends from all parts of the country, all with the same type of hair cut as me, short back and sides.*

In the weeks leading up to me leaving school, nothing much more happened: it was just the usual burnt porridge, school, home time and football with my friends. I kept up my good attendance record all the way to Friday 5th April, the day I would be leaving. I made my way to school for the very last time on a fine sunny day. Everything seemed the same. The only thing I felt different was that I was more observant this time around; my eyes were working in synchronisation with my feet, I was taking in more information about my school than ever before. My head was almost turning 180 degrees with every step I took.

There was an element of sadness running through my body, but at the same time, I was ready for saying goodbye to my school days. It wasn't until after lunch, when the Headmaster got all the Easter leavers together outside his office. There were no more than about ten of us that were eligible to leave. We lined up for what should have been a firm handshake and a good luck message for the future from the Headmaster. It was one of those times when I felt that the Headmaster was painting everybody with the same brush; he didn't even have the decency to say any more than 'good luck' with a handshake. He couldn't even look me in the face when he said those futile words. I was leaving for a career in the Army, to serve my country; all he could do was to look down at my worn-out shoes.

The whole leaving parade took no more than one minute to complete, from the first handshake to the last. Just before the Headmaster made his way back to his office, he looked up at us for the first time and said, "I shall be glad to see the back of you all. Goodbye."

I just shook my head from side to side in disbelief at what I had just heard. I didn't even have it in me to return his goodbye. My friends and I made our way out of the school gates for the last time. Leaving school wasn't what I imagined it to be, thanks to our Headmaster. He made me feel like I had no right to be walking on the same earth as him; maybe it is part of the criteria to be a Headmaster: just be the biggest bastard you can be and you should make Headmaster within a few years… that's how he made me feel. Exams of plenty was going to be my next obstacle as I spent two days at the Harrogate assessment centre; waiting nervously outside the Majors office had me wondering, had I done enough to accomplish my dreams?

CHAPTER SIX

HARROGATE ASSESSMENT CENTRE

I made the most of the final five days before going to Harrogate. I went to see a lot of my friends and managed to get some fishing in down the canal with a rod that the farmer's son bought me for my birthday. Tuesday evening was soon upon me, I found myself having a long soak in the bath. My small holdall of a bag was waiting to be acquainted with its final items: towel, soap, toothpaste etc., before it would be zipped up ready for the morrow. A good night's sleep was on the agenda, as I had to be up at five in the morning. I would normally be up early anyway, to be on the safe side, my father said he would give me an early morning wake me up call. There would be no room for any error; I couldn't be late for one of the most important days of my life so far. I snuggled down into my bed with my face pressed up against the wall. Alan Clarke, Peter Lorimer, Eddie Gray, Norman Hunter, Billy Bremner… the whole damn Leeds team were wishing me a good night's sleep as I looked at all my posters on the wall.

I found it more entertaining than counting sheep; that old wives' tale never did work for me. Lights out and my eyes were closed. I was now playing football at Elland Road for the next eight hours until, "Paul! Paul! Come on, it's time to get up. It's 5am," said my father.

It was still dark so there seemed no requirement to wake my brother up, who was lying next to me. Unfortunately, I had to climb over my brother to get out of bed. I may have accidentally kneed him in the back. I'm not sure, either way, by time my feet had hit the wooden floor boards, he was awake.

"What time is it?" he said.

"5 o'clock" I muttered.

My brother was due to get up shortly anyway, so I was doing him a favour, although he probably wouldn't agree with my sentiments. I seemed to be getting preferential treatment. I heard my mum getting up as I was in the bathroom splashing cold water on my face (no fire, no hot water). I needed to leave at about 6 to arrive at the railway station for round about 6.30 to catch the 6.45 train from Crewe. My sister's boyfriend was giving me a lift in his yellow Vauxhall Viva, so there would be no walking to the bus stop for me. There would also be no long bus journey driving around every housing estate in Crewe and Nantwich and, no elements of the weather to deal with. With all the goodbyes out of the way from my family (mum, dad, brothers and sisters), I got into the back of the Vauxhall Viva.

My sister Pauline came along to the station for a ride with her boyfriend, and a bit of moral support. There was a bit of chitchat on the way, but my head was elsewhere. I was away with the fairies. I said goodbye to my sister and her boyfriend as I made my way into the station with my holdall, one final check that I had all of my documentation and then it was onto the platform. A three-hour journey with two stops at Manchester and then Leeds awaited me. The train and connecting trains were all on time, so I arrived in Harrogate at 9.30am or thereabouts. I hailed a taxi for the short journey of about three and a half miles to the barracks with what bit of money I had. This was all my own money, I hasten to add, from my endeavours to find work: paper boy, turkey farm, corner shop, cleaning cars and, of course, not forgetting the errands I ran for my brother. I arrived in good time to be greeted by a soldier who was manning the Guardroom gates. After checking my details, he asked me to report to the window of the Guardroom.

"Name" said a voice, whose face I could hardly see through the tiny open window?

"Paul Wolfendale," I said.

He checked his list to see if my name was on there then said, "OK, if you would just like to wait over there by the corner of the Guardroom."

There were one or two others already standing there looking nervous, scared and full of apprehension. Within about ten minutes or so, a Corporal came over and escorted us all to our accommodation. We were about fifteen strong, although the Corporal said that there would be more arriving within the hour.

With everybody now present, the day was conducted in a very military fashion way, just like the letter had said: at 1100hrs we were taken to the education centre in a kind of orderly shambles for a brief on the itinerary for the day; it was just like walking home from school, four or five abreast, some of us on the road. "I know that you have all passed your IQ test back at your local Army Recruitment Centre" said a Corporal, "however to assess you further and to find out more about your level of intelligence you'll be tested with several exam papers over the next two days, this will allow us to judge which corps' you would be more suited for. At the end of the two day assessment and all being well, you'll be offered a corps' to join, have you any questions, no? OK, then I will see you after lunch, do not be late."

We were taken to the cookhouse that was just across the way from where we were. It was packed with military personnel staring at us with a kind of smile and snigger on their face; they seemed to be thinking, *this will be you soon, get use to being treated in a namby pamby way; enjoy it while you can... it won't last.* We definitely felt like outsiders. It was like a form of segregation: them and us, but what of it, we all need to start somewhere. After lunch it was a short thirty-minute break before heading back to the Education Block. With the first test out of the way I made my way to the drinks machine for a cold refreshment. I didn't care much for smoking, although I had tried the odd one before; a smoke break to me meant a drinks break. There was about twenty minutes between the maths exam finishing and the next exam starting.

I found the English exam paper a little more challenging but still managed to complete it within the hour. The Corporal got us all together for a final debrief then explained, "That's it for today. Your time is now your own. Evening meals will be served at the cookhouse then after that; you'll be allowed to leave the camp if you so choose. Alternatively, you may stay on camp, where you can use the NAAFI (Navy Army Air Force Institutes) facilities. You can get yourself a drink there... At least, those of you that look eighteen will. You may also watch television or just chill out. I will see you all in the morning at the education centre at 0900hrs, not outside your block like your acceptance letter said. Breakfast is at 0730hrs until 0830hrs for those of you who want breakfast. Get away and have a good evening. Don't get too drunk, and don't forget, we do expect a certain amount of decorum from you all. Go on; get out of my sight before I change my mind."

No sooner said than done, I went back to the accommodation block with the rest of the lads and prepared for dinner. As a group, we soon became very fragmented, but as individuals, everybody had made at least one or two friends.

"Anyone coming to tea?" said one of the lads.

"Yes," I said. "I'm starving."

"Me too!" said another voice.

Before I knew it, there was about five of us making our way to the cookhouse; chitchatting away, engaging in a post-mortem over the two exams we had taken.

"A load of shit!" said one of the lads. "Never was any good at maths."

"I found some of the questions difficult," said another lad, although he felt he had done well enough.

I just kept my thoughts to myself, trying not to give too much away by saying, "Yeah, not too bad. I'll just keep my fingers crossed for tomorrow."

The food in the cookhouse was nothing more than amazing from what I was use to; there was a least four choices of meat, roast potatoes, mashed potatoes, chips, four different veggies, sausage burgers, that was just the main course. There were all different kinds of puddings; there was also tea, coffee and orange juice… Just amazing! I can see where the phrase 'You can't go to war on an empty stomach' comes from. With that much food on offer, you would find it difficult to disobey the Queen's Regulations. After tea, it was back to our room. I just lay down on my bed for a while, giving my stomach a well-earned rest. I was smiling like the cat that had just had the cream. My eyes were closing with every second that passed until I fell asleep. I woke up about an hour later to find most of the lads had disappeared, except for one or two. My mind was now focused on going down to the NAAFI for some refreshments and social time. "Anyone fancy a walk to the NAAFI?" I said, still rubbing my face with my hand.

"Yes, why not" said a couple of the lads who were not up to much anyway.

"Great," I said. "Let's get going."

I wasn't one for drinking, despite having seven other brothers that did. It was just nice to chill out with a couple of mates. A couple of glasses of Coke and a bag of salt and vinegar crisps was reward enough for my stomach that was still bloated. My two other colleagues had a pint or two; despite their boyish looks they got served by the busty barmaid. It must have been their charm that did it. They never stopped talking about her and her 'Oh my god… tits!' all night until it was time for us to leave and head back to our room.

One by one, we all turned in for the night; some were a little inebriated and could hardly find their way back to their beds. I just turned over and tried to get some sleep, knowing that I still had a long day ahead of me tomorrow. Eventually the room fell silent amongst the darkness of the night. Occasionally, I would hear a short sharp cough and the odd fart. It was sometimes difficult to distinguish between the two; the only way I could tell whether it was a fart or a cough was if someone was giggling, you knew then to hide under your sheets before the smell could drift up your nose. The smell always seemed to hang over you like a cloud so I would normally leave it about five minutes before I gave it the all clear. There was that much gas circulating around the room I was frightened that we would all become air-borne; tossing and turning throughout the night made me feel grateful when the first glimpse of light appeared.

At last I could hear the sounds of military vehicles outside the block. I turned over to look at my watch that was on my bedside cabinet (the watch that my parents had bought for me a couple of days ago – just a cheap one, but it did the job). I stared at my watch, eyes wide open. 0645hrs was the time; I decided it was time to get out of bed and make my way to the bath-room. By the time I had made my way back to my bed space, everybody else was dragging themselves out of their pits (military term for beds) with a kind of can't be bothered attitude.

I was now dressed and waiting for a couple of my mates I had become acquainted with to get dressed.

"Breakfast," I said to my mates in a loud voice.

"Yes," they said. "Ready when you are."

On the way to the cookhouse, I was wondering whether breakfast would be as amazing as tea was last night. I could smell the food as soon as we walked through the doors: there were trays of sausage, bacon, mushrooms, beans, tomatoes, fried bread, scrambled eggs and fried eggs to order. There were at least four types of cereal: orange juice, tea, and coffee; you could even make your own toast. Well, I didn't over-face myself, but I certainly made the most of the Army's hospitality.

With breakfast finished, my mates and I made our way back to our room. There were still some people just getting up; they obviously weren't interested in breakfast. Looking at the state of some of them, I think the sight of a greasy egg would have pushed them over the edge. 0845hrs and we all started making our way over to the Education Block for our final exams. I think everybody made it on time. What I am saying, is that I could see no spare seats in the exam room. General knowledge was our first exam, followed by a spelling exam; the general knowledge exam was more to do with the world at present, and one or two military related questions. After lunch, we were shown a military film whilst our exam papers were being marked. Once the film was over, the Corporal said, "OK, listen in carefully. I want you all to go and get your bags from your room and report back here to the Education Block by 1500hrs. You'll then find out whether you have been accepted into the British Army. See you later."

We were all feeling a little excited, but at the same time, apprehension was kicking in; we were all unsure whether we had made it or not. The mood had definitely changed amongst the group from yesterday. You could sense that some of us were feeling scared of the outcome. 1500hrs and we were all waiting in the education rest room area to be called forward. One by one each individual that was called forward was taking no more than about five minutes to be given their results.

"Paul Wolfendale. You're next," said the Corporal, in a kind of *get a move on* voice. "Just go through the door in front of you and take a seat."

I made my way into the small office and sat down on the seat in front of the desk.

"Hello, Paul," said this smartly dressed military man, in a soft voice. "My name is Major Eladneflow. I have all your exams results and medical details here in front of me." He stared me in the eyes, paused, and then continued by saying, "I am delighted to tell you that you have been accepted into the British Army. Well done! I can offer you several corps', however, because of your colour blindness there will be a limitation on some units you'll not be suited for."

Bring it on, I said to myself.

"Is there any corps' that you have given any thought to joining?"

"Yes," I said. "I was thinking of joining the Royal Artillery. I don't know too much about the Artillery. Well, in fact, I don't know too much about the Army, if I'm honest; however, my Recruitment Sergeant in Crewe is part of the Royal Artillery. He told me that the Royal Artillery was a great corps' to join."

"How right he is," said the Major in a fine voice. "Well, if that's the corps' you would like to join, I am pleased to say we can more than accommodate you. 'Congratulations', young man. I wish you a long and prosperous future in the British Army."

We both stood up and gave each other a firm hand shake; I didn't want this moment to end. Unfortunately, there was still another six or seven candidates to be seen. I walked out of his office, feeling swollen with pride.

"How did you get on, Paul?" said some of my mates.

"I'm in" I said", "Joining the Royal Artillery, Can't wait!"

"Well done, mate. We all got in as well," they said.

"Great news" I said.

Unfortunately, there were about three or four that didn't make it. It was difficult to know if they were upset by the news or not. I saw them leaving the building looking very disgruntled, but in the same breath, they seemed to be laughing at the fact they had not got in.

We said our goodbyes to the Corporal and the rest of the military staff, who wished us all the best as we made our way out of the barracks to civilisation. A military bus drove us the three and a half miles to the train station. It was an emotional feeling, saying goodbye to my friends; friends that I would never set eyes on again. My train was leaving at 1645hrs so I only had about twenty minutes to wait. I just took a seat on one of the wooden benches on the platform and watched passengers go to and fro. I arrived back in Crewe at around 1930hrs; I had to catch a taxi back home. With the fact that none of my family had a phone, keeping in touch was always a problem. One of my brothers did have a phone, but didn't have a car. All he had was a scooter, and I certainly didn't fancy a lift on that.

I arrived home just before eight, when it was still light outside. I paid the taxi fare with what money I had left and made my way up the drive to my front door; it was quiet outside, but as soon as I opened the front door, I could hear my sisters' and brothers' voices echoing around the house. I walked into the living room to find my mum and dad sitting on separate settees watching television. They turned their heads towards me.

"It's our Paul!" said my mum. "Turn the television down."

"I made it." I said, "I am joining the Royal Artillery."

My mum gave me a warm hug. I could feel my dad's whiskers on my choir boy face as we embraced. It was a heart-warming moment for me, knowing that what I was doing meant so much to them. I think this is the most emotion I have ever seen from my parents. I sat down next to my mum and spent at least an hour talking to her and my dad about the Army and my time at Harrogate. It was now a case of waiting for my signing on date to arrive then say my final goodbyes to all of my family and friends.

CHAPTER SEVEN
THE QUEEN'S SHILLING

Ten days later, on Monday the 22nd April, I was making my way back to the Army Careers Office in Crewe, having received my confirmation letter. This was it. I was now ready to take the Queen's Shilling. On arrival, Sergeant Cromwell and Corporal Huxley shook my hand and said, "Well done, Paul. Just take a seat. We will be with you in a short minute."

There were four other boys all ready and waiting, who had arrived a few minutes earlier. I took a seat next to one of them before saying. "What happens now?"

"Not sure," said the person next to me. "I think we will be called forward one at a time into the office. There, we will be asked to sign some sort of paperwork and then we will be given our joining dates. I think one of the downstairs store rooms has been turned in to an office; I don't remember it from the last time I was here."

Just then, and to our surprise, we were all called forward at the same time by the Sergeant in a very polite and serious voice. "OK, if you would like to follow me please." There wasn't a lot of room in the office; it felt like a game of musical chairs where someone was destined not to get a seat. Luckily, there were enough seats for us all.

The Sergeant introduced us to this high ranking officer who seemed to be sizing us up for his dinner. His piercing eyes were scrutinizing our bodily worth as they slowly moved from left to right. He called us forward individually to congratulate us with a firm handshake at the same time informing us all that his name was Major Watkins. "Take a seat, Paul," he said. "I am now going to read your enlistment papers to you, then, you'll be invited to read the Oath of Allegiance. Once I have read them, you'll be free to ask me any questions you may have. I will then ask you to sign on the dotted line, so to speak. Since before 1876, anyone joining the Army was given the Queen's Shilling; nowadays, you'll be given the equivalent of a day's pay and also any expenses you may have incurred on the way here today."

The enlistment papers were read out to me and, to be honest, I probably didn't understand a word of the military jargon. I just wanted to get it signed; I could have been signing my death sentence for all I knew.

"OK, Paul. I would now like you to read the Oath of Allegiance. Do you have any questions before we continue?" said the Major.

"No, I think that's all fine, thank you," I said.

"OK, if you would like to read the Oath please."

I Paul Wolfendale, do swear that I will be faithful and bear true Allegiance to Her Majesty Queen Elizabeth, her heirs and successors, according to law. So help me God.

"I would now like you to sign at the bottom of the paper," said the Major. "And then you can sign for your pay."

I signed both papers and was handed a small, light brown bible that was no more three inches by two inches. The Major then said, "I hope this book will serve you some comfort throughout your prosperous Army career."

On the outside of the small brown bible read: 'The Soldiers' Testament with the Psalms in Metre', and in the front cover was a label that read, 'This Book was used in the Attestation Ceremony of Paul William Wolfendale, on enlistment into the Army at Crewe on 22 April 1974. It is presented on behalf of Her Majesty the Queen, for personal use, as a source of spiritual and moral guidance during Army Service.' I was handed £1.57, to my knowledge, and my return bus fare. That was it; I was now officially a soldier in the British Army. Once everybody had signed their enlistment papers, we went back into the waiting room. Sergeant Cromwell came over to us and said, "Right, I will now give you your starting dates: Paul Wolfendale, you'll be joining the J.L.R.R.A (Junior Leaders Regiment Royal Artillery), based in Nuneaton at Bramcote. You'll report to Gamecock Barracks on Tuesday the 7th May; details will be sent to you in the next few days, including rail tickets and a list of what you'll need to bring with you. If you have any queries between now and your starting date, Paul, then please don't hesitate to come along and see me. I will be more than willing to answer any question you may have."

With all the ceremonies now over, we made our way across the road to the Earl of Crewe pub for a lunch time celebratory drink. I thought, *how preposterous,* building a pub across the road from the Army Careers Office. What were they thinking, were they insinuating that all soldiers like the odd pint or two, come on, pull the other one. I felt like a man now, drinking with mates. This was an unusual situation for me to be in; this was the first time in my life that I had sampled a pint of beer. A pint of lager is what I drank as I chatted to my Army mates. We were all feeling very excited and proud. We stayed for about an hour in the quiet surrounds of the lounge area of the pub. We all left about the same time and staggered our way back to our respective homes. *One pint, and I am anybody's,* I was thinking to myself. I felt fine but slightly merry. Fifteen days and counting; I had lots to sort out, people to see, I needed to be ready in all respects.

My mum bought me numerous things that I had never possessed before: my own toothbrush, not one I shared with my brothers: a dry razor, towels, soap, my own personal soap dish, shampoo, deodorant, pens, paper, stamps, Kiwi polish and Brasso. It was quite refreshing being able to have two weeks of recreation before finally starting my basic training. Saturday the 27th April saw my beloved team, Leeds United, beat Queens Park Rangers 1-0 and become champions. Abba was winning the Eurovision song contest down in Brighton, and I won a few quid on the Grand National – I had a 50p each way wager on Red Rum. May arrived and my brothers and I were swapping the goalposts for a cricket bat and wickets. During the next few months, it would be cricket for us all. We had a homemade cricket bat that weighed as much as I could lift. It was made from a piece of wood that measured about four inches wide and about three inches thick. My brother whittled the handle down with his pen knife. You could just about get both hands around it. I remember you would have to pick your bat up about five seconds before the ball was bowled; if you didn't, the ball would be passed you before you could say 'Yorkshire'. No pads, no gloves; the good old corky ball would leave its indentations on your body for weeks. We took no prisoners. We just bowled it as fast as we could. It reminded me of the Body Line method between Australia and England in 1932–1933 series, where instead of bowling at the bat the bowler was ordered to bowl at the body. This would be the last time for a good while that I would have the opportunity to enjoy the company of my brothers in a sporting way, something that I know I would miss until I returned home in some six weeks' time. Making new friends was something I was looking forward too. All sorts of thoughts were going through my mind, *will they like me, will I like them, and will I find someone that share the same interests, maybe even someone that doesn't drink alcohol.* It wasn't long before all the questions would be answered as I met my first new friend on the train, a friend that is still my friend today; standing in the area that separates the two carriages having a cigarette, made my decision too stretch my legs for a second, one of the best decisions I have ever made.

CHAPTER EIGHT
"BYE SON" SAID MY DAD

It was Monday 6th May and I had just got out of bed. It was that quiet I could hear the mice racing around underneath the floorboards searching for food. I knew this was the penultimate day; tomorrow I would be saying goodbye to all of my family and all my surroundings; thinking of how best to make use of my last 24 hours before I handed myself over to the Army was at the forefront of my mind.

The first thing I did was make sure I had all my belongings packed safely in my brown, shoddy suitcase. I checked all my documentation was in place and then, it was just a case of chilling out. I just wanted tomorrow to arrive as soon as possible, even though I was very apprehensive at what lay ahead. I sensed a deathly silence from my parents that I had never felt before; my mum in particular was very quiet all day. It wasn't until my brothers and sisters came home from work that everything seemed to get back to normal. There was some general chitchat about me leaving home, but all in all, it was still Monday night dominoes for my brothers and for my sisters, they did whatever sisters do on a Monday night.

"I'm off to bed now," I said to my parents.

"OK," they said. "See you in the morning – nice, bright and early."

It was only ten o'clock, but as long as it was dark, I could normally get to sleep. I was expecting my brothers home about midnight from the pub and they didn't disappoint.

"Hey Paul, We won 4-1… Top of the league!" said Allan.

I must admit that I did take an interest my brothers' dominoes, but I needed to sleep.

My brother must have kicked me ten times or more as he climbed over me. At least I was spared the humiliation of Judy biting my toes; she was left downstairs in the kitchen.

Tuesday 7th of May brought my last few hours at home. My sister's boyfriend was picking me up at 9.30am to catch the 10 o'clock train from Crewe to Nuneaton. My bag was by my side in the living room. My mum was fussing around me and my dad was just being his normal self, sitting on the settee watching television. I had already said my goodbyes to my sisters and brothers, who were now at work. Although wearing the watch bought by my parents, I still felt myself checking the clock on the mantelpiece at regular intervals: 9.05, 9.15, and 9.25; it was then I heard a car pull up the drive.

"That will be him now," said my mum.

I was really feeling uneasy now. My mum and dad both stood up, not knowing what to do next. This was a situation that none of us had experienced before. I took the first move by giving my mum a warm embrace, followed by a hand shake from my dad. I made my way to the front door with my suitcase in hand, followed closely behind by my mum and dad. There it was: the yellow Vauxhall Viva to take me away from my family.

My sister's boyfriend Phil helped me with my case in to the boot of his car before one last hug from both of my parents. I could tell it was very emotional for my parents, but as you already know, they were very good at hiding their feelings. I am pretty much the same; I show very little emotion. I always seem to bottle things up. I do wish sometimes I could show my real feelings so that people could feel the real me; I am not cold… I just keep my feelings in the confinement of my heart.

"Keep in touch, love," said my mum, passionately. "We will all be thinking about you."

"Will do, mum. I will write to you as soon I'm settled in."

"Bye, son," said my dad.

"Bye, dad," I said "take care of yourself. I got into the front of the Viva and settled down for the short, thirty-minute journey. This was it, with the engine now started the car started to move slowly away from my home. My parents were now becoming a distant image as I waved at them through the side window. I turned my head around so as to look out of the back window for one last time.

"Bye mum. Bye dad." I said under my breath as we turned right out of the drive onto the main road. At this moment in time, I was feeling lost in my own surroundings; nothing seemed to be making any sense.

It was such a strange feeling that I had never felt before. We passed the Army Careers Office and the Earl of Crewe pub on my right. We were only about half a mile away from the railway station now; I could see Rail House, the tall building in the distance next to the British Rail station. Every time

I looked out of the window, I found myself reminiscing. Even the weather wasn't spared my thoughts. We arrived at the station with my mind still in overdrive. I needed to get to grips with myself and start thinking about the future, not the past.

I finally snapped out of my daydreaming and removed my suitcase from the boot of the car. My sister's boyfriend wished me good luck: "You'll be fine," he said in a typical man voice as he shook my hand.

"Thanks. See you when I get back." I said. I didn't look back once to see him drive away. I just made my way into the station then onto the platform for my journey into the unknown. As I sat on one of the cold wooden benches, I looked up and stared into oblivion. I could almost hear my mum saying in a quiet but slow voice, "You'll be OK. Don't need to worry. You might feel lost from time to time, but I know you'll find a way through it. We will all be thinking about you. You may be out of sight, but you'll be always in our thoughts." I now felt inspired, ready to venture into unknown territory. *The train arriving at platform four is the 10.05 to London Euston, stopping at Stafford, Nuneaton and London Euston,* was the sound I heard from the echo of the PA system. I stepped forward to the edge of the platform and took a look down the track. I could see the train making its way across several points, before it finally pulled up alongside the platform with its screeching brakes. I noticed that there were some other boys all about the same age as me already seated on the train; it made me feel as if I wasn't alone any more. *Were they going to Bramcote* I asked myself? *Maybe, Maybe not,* I thought.

I made my way onto the train, at the same time, not letting my suitcase out of my sight; I caught sight of some other boys lugging their suitcases onto the train with their short back and sides. Once on the train I could feel we were all eyeing each other up like it was some sort of competition for the girls we would eventually hope to meet. Occasionally, I would look at someone thinking that if he can make it, then so can I. It felt quite intimidating for the first few seconds but I was thinking, *what of it, this is the life I had chosen and my aim is to fulfil my dreams.*

The train was now picking up pace on its way out of Crewe; passing the football ground along with several dilapidated buildings and then, on too pastures new. Half way through the journey, I decided to stretch my legs; this was going to be one of the best decisions in my life so far. I made my way to the area that joins the carriages, where the toilets are. I started talking to a boy who was having a fag, with the window of the door partially down.

"Are you off to Nuneaton?" I said.

"Yes," he said, in an accent I wasn't familiar with.

"Me too," I replied. "I got on at Crewe. Where have you come from?"

"North Wales," was his answer, taking another drag from his fag. "My name is Steve."

"Mine's Paul," I said. "However, some of my mates call me Wolfie or Woofer."

"My mates call me sheep, but you can call me Steve," was his quick reply. I was later to find out that I should have called him Steve 'I-like-collecting-hangovers' Parry.

"I will bear that in mind," I said.

Steve found it amusing, by continued saying, "I use to be a wolf but I'm all right nowwwwwww."

We seemed to get on really well, taking the mickey out of each other for the rest of the journey. Now that the ice was broken, I felt that I had made my first friend; I was now feeling more self-assured about myself.

It wasn't long before the train was pulling into Nuneaton station. I could see all the short-back-and-sides getting out of their seats with their cases making their way to the exit doors. As I looked out of the window, I could see two soldiers standing on the platform; they were looking very smart but also very scary.

"Anyone for Bramcote, the Junior Leaders Regiment Royal Artillery?" said one of the soldiers in a loud voice. We all looked over to where the soldiers were standing before about thirty or more of us could be heard saying.

"Yes."

"OK, make your way over here please and stand by the wall," the soldier grinned. "Welcome to Bramcote home of the Junior Leaders Regiment Royal Artillery. My name is Bombardier White and this is Bombardier Walsh. Please address us as 'Bombardier' and we will get on just fine. If you do not address us as Bombardier, you will have us to answer too, do you under-stand?" He sounded like a right Nasty Pasty.

We all shouted in a military kind of voice, "Yes, Bombardier!"

The Bombardier shouted back, "Very well, then. Make your way out of the station, where there is a green military bus waiting to take you to your bar-racks. I would like you to give your name to Bombardier Walsh before get-ting on the bus. It's about a ten minute bus ride so don't get too comfortable."

Comfortable, I thought. The seats were that hard I felt certain things bang-ing together like someone was playing a game conkers.

I am not certain where my mate Steve was sitting, but I'm sure he was on the bus somewhere. Within minutes the bus was turning into the barrack gates, my eyes seemed to be glued to the posh building on my right. You could smell the sweetness of the freshly mowed lawns and see the shadows of the huge trees that stretched across from one end of the grass to the other. I could almost feel the cool breeze from the shadow areas as I sat sweltering on the bus.

It was nothing like the war time movies I had seen on television; it turned out that the building I was hypnotised by was RHQ (Regimental Head Quarters). Say no more. The building on my left was the Guardroom, again, a beautiful structured building. I could see that we were expected by the presence of the military personnel standing tall on top of the steps. The two Bombardiers stood up from their seats at the front of the bus; they turned and faced us. In school, the teacher would say, "Quiet, please," but we knew as soon as their eyes met ours, it would be a military command. The bus fell silent within seconds. A loud voice could be heard ringing in my ears, "Right, you lot! I want you to make your way off the bus in an orderly fashion. Make sure you take all your belongings with you. Once off the bus, I want you to fall-in into three ranks. For those of you that don't know what the difference is between a wank and a rank, just stand shoulder to shoulder with the man on your right." I was expecting a certain amount of swearing, but maybe not so soon.

By some sort of miracle, we all seemed to fall into line like sheep; my mate Steve must have felt right at home. The Bombardiers handed over the nominal roll to one of the soldiers who were standing on the steps of the Guardroom. I could barely hear what they were saying; it was something like, 'All present, Sir,' and 'Thank you, Bombardier.' I was now thinking, *this must be someone important.* Even the teachers in my school didn't get that sort of respect.

A rather posh voice addressed us with. "Welcome to the Junior Leaders Regiment," in a slow but decisive manner. "My name is Lieutenant Harris."

I was right: he was important.

"I hope and trust you all had a pleasant journey here today. For those of you who make the grade, this will be your home for the next twelve months. I would like to start by saying that you are the first intake of sixteen-year-old recruits ever to serve at these barracks; there will be about 1,200 of you over the next twelve months. I would, first of all, like to give you a little history lesson of the now called 'Gamecock Barracks'. From about 1939, the start of World War Two, the barracks was the home of the RAF. The barracks were then called 'Bramcote Barracks'. Then, in 1947, the Barracks were taken over by the Royal Navy flight units, and they were then named after the ship, HMS Gamecock. In 1959, the barracks were then taken over by the Junior Leaders Regiment Royal Artillery. The Regiment was tasked with producing future NCOs (None Commissioned Officers) and warrant officers for the Artillery: The training included skill-at-arms, drill, field craft, first aid, NBC,(Nuclear Biological Chemical Warfare) character building, map reading, education, physical training, gunnery and signals. The regiment was divided into four batteries: 2 Baker Battery, 33 Campbell Battery, 39 Roberts Battery and 40 Wardrop Battery. Each battery consisted of four troops. Each battery and troop carried the name of a famous gunner of the past."

Camaraderie was built up through the system of troops and batteries, and there was a great deal of healthy competition in all areas, especially sport. Lieutenant Harris continued with his speech by saying, "I know it has been a long process for you all just to get this far, so I would like to congratulate you on your effort and commitment. This is now where it all begins; you'll be delegated to one of the four batteries that we have in the barracks. There, you'll meet your highly trained staff; they will ensure that you're trained to the highest standard that is expected from a soldier in the British Army. You'll be worked hard throughout your time here at Gamecock Barracks; all we expect in return is for each and every one of you to give it your best. I know this is a big step for a lot of you, but the rewards are immense. In six weeks' time, I will hope to see you all again on the parade square, parading in front of your family and friends and, believe me when I say, it will be one of the proudest moments of your life. Thank you for your time, I will now like to wish you all the best of British and hope your stay at Gamecock Barracks is an enjoyable one. When I call out your name just answer 'Sir', and I will tell you which battery and troop you'll be joining."

CHAPTER NINE

WINGATE TROOP

The names were read out clearly and precisely in a loud voice; we were all feeling anxious and, at the same time, excited. Everybody seemed to be sizing each other up and a down with a kind of trepidation, wondering who they were going to be sharing a room with for the next 12 months. Rigby, 33 Campbell Battery Wingate Troop; Fielding, 2 Baker Battery Porter Troop, and on and on it went… Parry, 33 Campbell Battery Wingate Troop. "Sir," was the reply in a voice that seemed familiar to me. I looked over to see who it was; it was Steve, the guy I had met earlier on the train.

Before long, my name was called out: "Wolfendale." Now all eyes were on me. I could feel the nerves travelling through my body until my legs were feeling like jelly.

"Sir," I said in my squeaky voice feeling embarrassed. *Why me* I thought, *why do I have to be the one with the squeaky voice?* Before I had time to think any more about my voice, came, "33, Campbell Battery Wingate Troop."

Wow, my head was banging with excitement. "Yes, yes!" I was saying under my breath. I made my way over to where Steve and all the other Wingate lads were standing, as the roll-call continued, until everybody had been accounted for.

"OK lads. Listen in," said a loud, clear and slow voice. "You're now going to be given your Troop Sergeant and Troop Bombardier. They will be your mum and dad for the next twelve months." I am sure we were all thinking, *which one is the feminine one?* We were to find out later that it was wise to keep those kinds of thoughts under lock and key.

"Wingate Troop: Sergeant Preece and Bombardier Bartlett."

All I could hear was the sound of the metal on the bottom of their ammunition boots as they both made their way towards us. The Sergeant was holding some sort of walking stick; I was later to find out it was a pace stick used for drill on the parade square. His boots were bulled up like mirrors, again, words I had never heard of. Everybody in the Army speaks a different language. It took me a while to pick up the lingo. Bullshit, Nosh, Eating Irons, Right Wheel, NAAFI, RSM, BSM, rissoles, casseroles, arseholes, Officers' Mess, Sergeants' Mess, You're a mess. *Calm down,* I said to myself.

Sergeant Preece and Bombardier Bartlett stood shoulder to shoulder, facing us about a metre from the front row. You could smell the cherry blossom on their boots, and the starch on their crisply ironed uniform.

"Right, listen in you lot, my name is Sergeant Preece and on my left is Bombardier Bartlett." They addressed us for about five minutes with a few 'do's and 'don'ts, before finally saying. "We are now going to show you your accommodation; this is where you'll be sleeping for the next six weeks. It's called Recruits Block. You'll then be moved just across the way into Wingate Block for the rest of your time here with us. Turn to your right," said Sergeant Preece in a friendly voice.

We all turned in a kind of leisurely way, falling over our suitcases at the same time. I was thinking, *penny for your thoughts, Sergeant.* He must have been thinking, *what a shower we have here.*

"OK, follow me and Bombardier Bartlett."

It seemed like a half mile walk, swapping our suitcases from our left arm to our right arm without trying to lose pace with the rest of the crowd.

"Keep up with the man in front of you!" was all I could hear. I had never been so close to a man's arse in my life.

We finally arrived outside the Recruits Block, where we were would be housed for the next six weeks before being moved to our troop accommodation, then finally our passing out parade.

"OK, stop," was the call. "Turn to your left."

We were now facing the building. We were standing on a road that had no potholes and not so much as a cigarette butt anywhere, there were soldiers being marched around, *Left Right Left Right Left Right Left;* or words to that effect as the sun was shining down on our now worn out bodies; we were now the new NIGs (New Intake Gunners.) You could feel the laughter of the more senior recruits as they glared over towards us, whilst they marched past with their arms swinging up to the horizontal and then back as far as they would go.

The block that we would be occupying was the shape of a letter H, if you were to look at it from the sky above. Everything was regimental; big swinging doors with three windows on the right and three windows on the left; a two tiered, all-bricked building was how it was. There was about a metre in width of freshly cut grass from the building to the footpath that we weren't allowed to set foot on without permission. We were now split down in to smaller groups of about 20 to 25. I was now in Bombardier Bartlett's section, along with my mate Steve-the-sheep Parry. Sergeant Preece was still in overall charge because of his seniority. We made our way into the block and up the wide staircase that was in front of us. The floor was made from a hard lino-like covering, in Army green, or maybe brown (my colour blindness kicking in again). The room or, should I say, dormitory we were staying in was full of metal bunk beds. One by one we were given our bed space.

"Wolfendale, top bunk," said the Bombardier.

"Gandy, Bottom bunk!" and so on until all the beds were full.

The lockers were grey metal, about a metre in width and two metres in height. On opening your locker, on the left side were several shelves and a personal lock up part for your valuables.

We were standing around like lost sheep.

"Put your suitcase and any other items you have onto your bed, then, make your way outside in an orderly fashion."

It was just a spring metal grey base deficient of a mattress; getting rid of my luggage even though it was only for a short while was pure bliss.

Back outside on the road and lined up in three ranks, we stood awaiting our next instructions.

"Listen in, lads. We are now going to take you to the BQMS stores." (Battery Quarter Masters Sergeant)

That one went straight over my head. *No problem,* I thought. *Just follow the rest of the lads.* I'm sure I wasn't the only one that had not heard of the BQMS stores. A short walk was all that was needed before we arrived at the stores. I couldn't see anything interesting like: chocolate bars, ice cream, milkshakes, etc. We had to line up in single file and then make our way into the building; it looked like my worst nightmare.

It was where we were getting kitted out with all our Green Army uniforms. It was very much like a well oiled production line until I peered down the line; organised chaos was what I was looking at.

"What is your shoe size?" said the BQ (Battery Quartermaster).

"Size 9," I said, as he handed me over two pair of boots: Socks (four pairs), insoles (two), No. 2 dress shoes (one pair) and plimsolls (one pair). When you reached the end of the line you were fully assembled, or should I say, you had all the parts you needed to become a soldier. You then had to take your kit away and figure it out for yourself. Everything had to be signed for on an 1157 Form. Some items were recognisable: trousers, shirts, coveralls, kit bag, combats, etc. But then others, I literally had no idea about: cap-comforter, gaiters, button stick, housewife and lanyard; however, these were items that we would get more familiar with throughout the next few weeks.

After several trips and with our arms aching, it would be expected that we would be dropping the odd item or two onto the tarmac road, it was time to sign for our bedding: two cotton sheets, two grey blankets, two pillows with pillow cases and a mattress cover.

We all assembled back in the block; sat on our beds we were given a lecture on how to make your bed Army style. Hospital corners were a must. We put the mattress into the mattress cover with lots of laughter; the mattresses were being thrown over our shoulders fireman's lift style. At least we were becoming closer as a group now, or in other words, we were all looking like idiots. Eventually, we had our mattress assembled and on the bed springs. The sheets and the blankets were next: bottom sheet to lie on, then the next sheet and then two blankets. The last bit I liked, being artistic as I am; neatly folding the corners of the blanket into the hospital corners we were told about gave it that finishing touch. Pillows and pillow cases were next; there we had it, like something from Blue Peter. The dormitory was looking a little more like it should, although we now had the task of sorting out all our military equipment.

The time was now getting on and Bombardier Bartlett decided that it would be better to have a break and continue with sorting out our Army gear after lunch. We were still being ushered around, in other words, we were not ready to be trusted on our own. I don't think we needed a map to find the cookhouse as we assembled outside, We could see people coming back from lunch, swinging their right arms; their left arms were folded around their back with their knife, fork and spoon in their plastic green cup. We were still in our civilian clothes and standing out like sore thumbs as we made our way into the cookhouse; it was to be the best time of the day over the next twelve months. Three squares a day is what the Army is about: a soldier marches on his stomach, or so it is said.

We were allowed to navigate our way back from lunch on our own, at the same time, still remembering that we were soldiers in civvie clothes. Army discipline still applied. When we arrived back at the block, we had a half hour break before Bombardier Bartlett came back from his lunch break. We decided to lie on our pits for a short while and, at the same time getting to know one another.

All of a sudden, we could hear the noise of the outside doors swinging open, and, then the sound of Bombardier Bartlett's boots as he marched up the stairs. We thought it would be better if we showed some respect by getting up from our pits.

After entering the room, Bombardier Bartlett told us to assemble outside in three ranks, a term we were now getting use to. Now, and for some reason unknown to me, I took my eating irons (knife, fork and spoon) and cup with me. No one seemed to notice, not even me, until we were told that we were going down to the Regimental Barbers to get a military hair cut. My hair was already short, but apparently not short enough. We walked into the barbers shop and tried to find a seat. Seating thirty people at the same time is quite a feat within itself, considering there were only about ten seats in all. This is where I felt like a complete idiot for the first time since arriving this morning; waiting to get my hair cut, holding my eating irons and cup was just laughable. One smart Alec said, "Have you brought your cup to put your hair in?" I was lost for words. I didn't know this guy and just didn't know how to reply to that remark. He was right though, why the hell did I take them with me?

This would be the start of lots of embarrassing moments for me and other recruits. I thought, *just grow a pair and get on with it… it's the British Army not the Salvation Army.* Short back and sides was the norm, plus a bit. We made our way back to the block in droves until we were all accounted for, this is where I got my first chance to get rid of my eating irons and cup and put them back into my locker. Better times lay ahead as we stood by our mirrors feeling high and mighty with what we were seeing. It was one of those "leave me along with my thoughts" moments.

CHAPTER TEN
THE BADGE OF THE ROYAL ARTILLERY

It was now mid-afternoon, time to get out of our civvies and into our Army green uniforms. To start with, we were told to get in to our lightweight trousers. It felt slightly uncomfortable, stripping off in front of strange men. I had met Steve on the train about three hours ago, now here I was undressing in front of him, showing him my underwear. You could almost feel your mates staring towards your lunch box area. Even now, I don't like to think about what they were looking at. They were really nice well-fitting trousers with deep side pockets on each side. Next came our cotton shirts, these were uncomfortable: thick material with long sleeves and buttons up the front. I really felt like, *this is it... I'm a soldier now.* Socks that were thicker than a politician were next, followed by my DMS (Direct Moulded Soul) size 9 boots.

Once dressed, our civvie clothes were put away and never to be seen again, well at least for the next six weeks. I took one last look at them, including my football boots that I was hoping to get some use out of before closing the suitcase shut. It was so strange wearing Army boots; it felt I was going in to a gang fight. If you saw someone walking around your neighbourhood in boots like the ones I was wearing, you would stay well clear. 'Bovver Boots' was the nickname they were given. We continued in to the afternoon putting away all our equipment into our lockers in an orderly manner, still under the supervision of Bombardier Bartlett.

We were allowed a five-minute smoke break, for those who would like a quick puff. I was a non-smoker at this time; however, it didn't take me long to try a fag or two. Anyone caught putting a cigarette butt out on the road would be in serious trouble. Not just trouble, but serious trouble. In your pockets they went or into the first bin you could find. This was the first time I felt the Army discipline kicking in: you eat when I say, you speak when I say and you shit when I say. It was all coming back to me now from some of the Army films that I've watched in my time.

It was getting close to tea-time now, but before then, we were taught how to shape our berets. 6 and ¾ was my size. We all went into the washrooms and soaked them in a sink of warm water before squeezing the life out of them. You would repeat it several times and then, place it on your head. Once on your head, you would need to groom it by pulling it down to the right; this would result in a flap forming. Again, you would repeat the process until you or your Bombardier was happy with it. Putting it on whilst wet means that it shapes itself to your head. We were now almost assembled. One last thing was the cap badge; this was the proudest part of the uniform. There was a little slit in the front of the beret where you would slide a clip into that would be attached to the badge.

"OK," said Bombardier Bartlett. "I now want you to open your lockers and stand in front of the mirror that is attached to the inside of the left hand door. You now need to make sure that your cap badge is in line and, above your left eye. Do you understand?"

"Yes, Bombardier!" we all shouted.

I felt so proud when I looked in the mirror and saw the badge of the Royal Artillery over my left eye. I thought; *if only my family and friends could see me now.* You could have heard a pin drop as everybody stood in front of their mirrors with the same emotion that I was feeling. During those few seconds of silence that we were all enduring, it felt that we were no longer boys. We had finally turned into men.

"Turn to your front," a loud voice ordered.

I felt I had just been woken up from an amazing dream. It was Bombardier Bartlett standing in the middle of the room.

"Just relax and stay where you are."

Bombardier Bartlett presented himself to us all one-by-one and showed us how to wear our beret Army style, at the same time issuing us with our name tags. It was about three inches long by an inch wide, with your name in block capitals. It would be pinned to our shirts like you would fasten a safety pin.

We were all now starting to look more and more like soldiers even though it was only our first day. It was now time for us to find out a little more about each other and where we all came from: some had travelled from as far as Scotland, Wales, Newcastle, Plymouth and Devon, there was also one of the lads who lived only about five miles away in Hinckley. I had never ventured far from where I lived before, apart from the annual Sunday school trip to Blackpool, so to meet so many people from all of these places broadened my horizon of the UK.

It wasn't long before I understood words like: Jock, Taff, Brummie, Geordie, Sheep, Paddy, and 'I am a cider drinker'. Bombardier Bartlett left us alone for about half an hour while he went to do what a Bombardier does in half an hour. We were left to sort out our lockers with all our belongings: It was organised chaos once more: hanging our lightweight trousers and shirts onto coat hangers, folding up our red PT vests, dark blue shorts, woolly-pulley jumpers, Army underwear, white long johns, green shorter pants, socks, string vests, 56 pack webbing, mess tins, cap comforter, plimsolls, dress shoes, second pair of DMS boots, dress shirts, dress ties, dress hat, barrack room trousers, button stick, etc. Most of us were now nervously enjoying a laugh; starting to feel like we were part of a team and working together was how it was starting to feel.

It didn't take long for us all to inherit a nickname, mine being Wolfie; the name kind of grew on me after a while, anyway it was better than my nickname I had at secondary school, 'Kodak', the reason behind the name was because I use to squint like an instamatic camera.

It was now about 1700hrs and we were just sitting on our beds, we heard Bombardier Bartlett and his ammo boots thundering up the stairs. The doors swung open and closed just as quickly. Bang! Bang! And then they came to a gentle halt.

"Right, you lads, get your KFS and your green plastic mugs and line up outside."

Even something as simple as that was causing confusion within the ranks. Some forgot their berets, some couldn't even find their fork or knife, and mugs were being dropped down the stairs. We eventually formed up outside the block in three ranks with all our eating irons tucked into our mugs and held in our left hand; with our left hand now pressed up against our back we were ready in all respects.

"Turn to your right in threes," said Bombardier Bartlett.

It was a bit like Dad's Army. What should have been done in a split second took us about five seconds to be all facing the correct way, "By the front, quick march." Left, right, left, right, left, right, left…

What the hell? I thought. We only had one arm to contend with and that was proving difficult. We were all kicking each other's heels on the occasions we got out of step.

We finally arrived at the cookhouse. "SQUAAAAD HAAALT," Shouted Bombardier Bartlett.

It was like a machine gun going off: bang! Bang! Bang! We all stopped at millisecond intervals.

"LEEEEEFFT… TUUURRN-A…"

Bang! Bang! Bang! The machine gun sound could be heard again.

"OK, stand easy."

I had no idea what that meant until a few weeks into our training.

"You're now going to be fed for the second time today, you lucky bastards," said Bombardier Bartlett. "When I say go, I want you to get your arses into the cookhouse pronto. Do you understand?"

"Yes, Bombardier!" we all shouted.

"Go! Go! Go!" said the Bombardier.

We shot into the cookhouse quicker than a rat up a drain pipe. I was wondering, *what has happened to the nice Bombardier we were talking too earlier in the afternoon?* I wanted him back; I didn't like this new one that was now swearing and shouting.

The nosh again was like a banquet to me, with so many choices. You could feel the eyes of the chefs staring at you, as you helped yourself to the food. If you decided to put a second portion of food on your plate, you could be sure you would get a whack with a metal ladle from the chef on your fingers. Bombardier Bartlett would watch our every move; he would watch every mouthful of food that entered our mouths. He was tapping his pace stick on the wooden floor and, occasionally, he would crack a joke or make a remark that we were expected to laugh at. Although other soldiers were looking in our direction, we felt a little more like one of them now that we were in our uniforms.

Twenty minutes was about the time we were given to wolf and wash down our nosh with a mug of tea.

"Outside, now!" said the Bombardier, as the tapping of his pace stick became louder. Chairs were being scratched and banged as we made our way outside to line up in three ranks in front of the cookhouse. Once outside, we lined up as usual in no particular order and marched back to our block. 'Quick march', 'squad halt', 'right turn', 'stand easy' and 'fall out' were becoming familiar orders now; even after only one day, we were getting to grips with the Army lingo. Back in our room, we put our eating irons back into our locker along with the green mug. This was to become the norm as the weeks went by; anything that was left out of your locker would be thrown out of the window by Bombardier Bartlett. He didn't give two monkeys if it got broke or damaged – not his problem. You would have to go to the BQMS stores and sign for replacements that you had to pay for. The cost would be deducted out of your wages at the end of term.

All this discipline would teach us to lock all our items away. Tea leafing was a common affair in the Army, as we were all to find out through the coming months. We were all told to bring a lock for our lockers and also a lock for the personal small drawer inside the locker. If you didn't have a lock or had forgotten to bring one, you could purchase one from the NAAFI shop that was on the barracks.

Bombardier Bartlett spent a couple of hours with us that evening, bringing us closer together and getting to know more about us including our names. We sat at the end of our beds while he explained a few Army regulations to us, at the same time, allowing us to ask any questions we may have. Lights out would be at 2200hrs and reveille would be at 0530hrs. We all looked at each other with open mouths when he said those words; we were all thinking, *what? Five thirty in the morning. Not a chance!* But, as we discovered throughout our training, not a chance of us 'not' getting up was what we meant.

At about 2130hrs Bombardier Bartlett told us to get ready for bed, and that he would be back at about 2200hrs to turn the lights out and tuck us in. It was nice to hear those words. Bed! After such a long day, it was no sooner said than done, we were all undressed within seconds: Some of the lads had decided to wear shorts, a few were in their undies, and quite a lot of us in pyjamas. I had never worn pyjamas in my life, except the time when I was in hospital after getting run over by a motorbike when I was fifteen years of age. They were red nylon pyjamas, and although not to my taste, at least it covered my bits. With impeccable timing Bombardier Bartlett arrived back at 2200hrs.

"OK, get yourselves into bed," he said.

I was on the top bunk, so it was a small hop and a quick swing of my legs before I was planted on my mattress. It was so unreal: clean crisp sheets, two soft pillows and my own bed – something I had not experienced before. No dog at the end of my bed about to bite my feet if I dared to move. I felt the iron frame of the bed move as the person underneath me; Sam Gandy was climbing into his bed. There were about twenty of us in the room, with the same amount in another room.

"Get yourself a good night's sleep; I will see you in the morning at 0600hrs. Make sure you're all dressed ready for breakfast: lightweight trousers, short sleeved shirt and DMS boots. Any questions?" said the Bombardier.

"No, Bombardier," we all said in unison and with a kind of loudness to our voices.

"Goodnight," said Bombardier Bartlett as he turned the lights out and walked out of the room.

There was no way we were going get to sleep straight away. Although I wanted to sleep my head was saying, stay awake, and listen to what is being said.

"Woofer," said a voice in the dark.

"What?" I replied.

"Where are you from?"

"Nantwich in Cheshire," I said in my embarrassing squeaky voice.

This sort of chatter went on all through the night. Names I seem to remember are: Riggers, Jock, Sam, Bulldog, Muckers and Parry. There was the occasional giggle of laughter around the room until it gradually got quieter, and then finally, there was silence as we all fell asleep. Just before I fell in to a coma, my last thoughts were of my now distant family. I could almost hear my sisters and brothers passing through my bedroom to get to the toilet and my mum saying, "Paul, get to sleep, school in the morning!" *Where am I? What am I doing here?* I kept telling myself to go to sleep and maybe all will be well.

During the night, I could hear the occasional snoring, people tossing and turning or even the odd one or two getting up to go the loo. I had no way of knowing what time it was. I had left my watch in my locker; it was just a case of waiting until we got woken up. There was going to be so much going on over the coming weeks; bed blocks, bulling boots and locker lay outs were just some of the skills we needed to learn.

CHAPTER ELEVEN
BASIC TRAINING BEGINS TERM ONE

Pitch black dark, I could hear the sound of ammo boots again, echoing around the building. I could hear doors swinging open with some force and voices at full volume, shouting, "Get out of bed!"

The sound of the boots was now getting closer to our room. I, like many of my companions, were hoping they may forget to come into our room, as we hid under the sheets of our beds; Too late. "Bang!" went the doors and on came the lights.

"Get out of bed! Hands off cocks and onto socks!" said the guard with a well rehearsed speech.

My hand was not on anyone's cock, at least I hope not. We had to get our feet onto the wooden floor before the two guardsmen would leave. A few beds got rattled for some of the slow ones. I just sprung out of the top bunk onto the floor, nearly breaking my legs that had not yet woken up in unison with my body. No sooner had the overnight guard disappeared to wake up their next victims, we made our way into the washroom; everybody was a lot quieter now as you could imagine, rubbing our eyes and dragging our feet as we looked down at the floor and, occasionally bumping into each other. With my wash-bag full of all sorts of wonderful things that my mum had packed for me, I made my way to the nearest sink. There were about ten enamel sinks with several showers and a couple of baths.

It looked like a steam-train had just driven straight through the washroom, with the fact that all the sinks were being used at the same time. I unzipped my wash bag and sieved through the bag to find my toothpaste and brush, followed by my razor. Shaving was a thing I had never indulged in before; not only was my voice squeaky, but my face was that of a well-groomed choir boy. There was a little bit of bum-fluff around the upper lip area, but still it had to go. I took out my small can of shaving cream from my wash-bag with not a clue what to do with it. I just followed the lead of all my Army mates:

lid off, a little squirt into the palm of my hand, followed by a rubbing session until it had turned into foam.

I put it onto my face like a professional, feeling proud of myself. I now took the plunge and started to shave my top lip with gentle precision before tackling the rest of my face. A dab of cold water and it was all over, easier than I thought. As I glanced first to my right and then to my left, I could see dribbles of blood in some of the sinks, mainly from some of the lads that had shaved the tops of their zits. I was lucky in that department that my face was so angelic in comparison to some of the other lads; I think some of them must have been shaving before they were out of nappies.

Next, back to the room, where I endeavoured to get into my Army uniform along with the rest of the lads. We all spent a good while checking each other over, making sure there was nothing out of place. A quick look into my mirror to add the final touch to my beret, *yes*, I thought, *looking good*. Making our beds was next, hospital corners etc, then a quick tidy up of our bed space. It was still only about 0600hrs, according to some of the lads who had a watch. Daylight had already broken. As we were standing around chatting, we could hear Bombardier Bartlett arriving. He told us that we could make our own way down to the cookhouse for breakfast that started at 0630hrs: "I will see you back here standing by your beds at 0730hrs," he said in a loud and clear voice. "Make sure you march down with your eating irons and mug in your left hand neatly behind your back whilst, at the same time, swinging your right arm to the horizontal and as far back as it will travel. You'll return in the same way; anyone caught not marching in the correct manner will have me to answer too, do you all understand?"

"Yes, Bombardier!" we all shouted that seemed incorrect for this time in the morning.

"OK, see you all back here at 0730hrs."

Breakfast was a fine affair: sausage, bacon, scrambled egg, fried egg, poached egg, mushrooms, fried bread, beans, tomatoes, cereal, tea, coffee, orange juice. *Get stuck in*, I thought, like all the rest of the lads.

Back in the block, we went to the washrooms to clean our eating irons and mug before returning them to their rightful place in their locker.

Bombardier Bartlett returned with supreme punctuality once more at exactly 0730hrs.

"Stand by your beds," he said. (This was a term we now getting more familiar with.) He walked from one bed to the next, eyeing us up like a hawk, ready to pounce on any minor error he could find. He would stand upright, about a metre away from your face, then move one step to the left and one step forward to investigate your locker. At the same time, he made sure you were still facing forward and standing in the attention position. What he was looking for was beyond me: he just checked everyone's dress, locker, bed space and bed. It was quite apparent that basic training had now started for real. Once finished, Bombardier Bartlett told us to relax and in a few short minutes the rest of Wingate Troop would be joining us to go through the itinerary for the next six weeks or so, leading up to our passing out parade.

My mind was whirling with all manner of thoughts and uncertainty at this moment in time. I just didn't know how I should be feeling: nervous, excited, proud… It felt like being thrown into the deep end of a swimming pool. Sink or swim – my choice. Sinking was not an option. It wasn't long before all the rest of Wingate arrived in our room. They all sat on our well-groomed beds.

"OK, settle down," said Bombardier Bartlett. "Shortly, Sergeant Preece the Troop Sergeant will be joining us. When he comes in, I would like you all to stand up on my command."

After a brief pep talk, Sergeant Preece arrived.

"Stand by your beds!" said the Bombardier in a loud voice.

Sergeant Preece's boots seemed twice as loud as Bombardier Bartlett's. His pace stick seemed twice a long and his voice was deeper. Respect sprang to mind as I looked him up and down. Bombardier Bartlett looked at Sergeant Preece and said, "All present and correct Sarge."

"Thank you, Bombardier, have them relax," said Sergeant Preece.

"OK, lads, relax and listen in. Sergeant Preece will now address you."

We all listened in with our ears pinned back.

"Today is your first full day of your Army career. This is when you become men. You'll be worked hard from dawn to dusk. You're now part of the British Army. You have signed an allegiance and taken the Queen's Shilling. You're now under military law. Bombardier Bartlett and I, along with some junior NCOs, will be responsible for your well being and your military training for the next twelve months. You will address me as Sergeant Preece, you will address Bombardier Bartlett as Bombardier and not Bomb. The only time you address him as Bomb is, if you see him with a fuse up his arse."

We all chuckled at that remark only to be told loudly to 'shut up'. We weren't even allowed to laugh at what we thought was a funny remark.

"We also have L/Bombardiers Lewis and Hogg; you will also address them as Bombardier. Later on today, you'll be introduced to your TC (Troop Commander), Lieutenant Waddington. You will address him as Sir or God. Please remember that when you're out and about and you pass an officer, you will salute them with your right arm, like so." Bombardier Bartlett gave us a demonstration.

"Remember, you're saluting the Queen's commission. The rest you'll figure out for your selves. There are plenty of spare places in the Glass House (Military Prison), so make sure you get it right."

At this point, I could feel the expressions on all our faces; being threatened with Military Prison on our first day was something that we didn't need to hear.

"If you do not understand anything, or are not sure about something, then we will expect you to ask. We are working as a team and our aim is to be the best. I want to see Wingate Troop winning everything. Pull you weight, work hard, and life will be pleasant. Any one individual that fouls up means you'll all suffer the consequences.

Today you'll be shown around the block and the camp. This will take a couple of hours then, the Bombardiers will show you how to wear your uniform with pride: they will show you how to bull your boots and iron your kit, clean your brasses, brush your beret, and how to make a military bed block. I expect you to be looking like military soldiers tomorrow morning on parade."

Wow, I thought, *can't wait.*

"The regimental photographer will be with us this afternoon to take your mug shots for your ID cards and then, you'll also be given your military number."

"Wolfendale!" shouted Bombardier Bartlett. "Where's your name tag?"

"In my locker, Bombardier," I said nervously.

"Get it on now! And that goes for anybody else who have not got theirs on."

There was a mad rush as about half of the troop had also forgotten their name tag.

Outside in three ranks was the command from Bombardier Bartlett. One last check of my clothing: locker locked up and bed space tidy before leaving the room was imperative. Everybody made their way down the stairs like there was no tomorrow; with the senior ranks close up behind, we were ready for our first full day. Once assembled in our ranks, we stood there waiting for our next command.

"What the hell do we have here?! You look like a rollercoaster gone wrong!"

We had no idea what he was on about until he explained. Our height varied from about 6ft 5in to 5ft nothing. There were tall and small people dotted around the ranks in any sort order; to us it meant nothing, to the Army it meant everything.

We were sorted out into a more fashionable order: tall ones at the end, small ones in the middle. Sergeant Preece now took over the commands: "SQUAAAAD! SQUAAAD! SHUN! Turn to your right in threes… Righttttt! TURN!"

We were now getting the hang of military jargon, basically, we were all facing the same way following the 'right', 'quick march', 'left', 'right', 'left', 'right', 'left', 'right', 'left' commands. It sounded more like 'oft', 'ight', 'oft', 'ight', 'oft', 'ight', 'oft'. Did it matter? Not in the least. We were looking good: arms swinging in unison and our chin up; *left right left right left right left….*

We were taken to the parade square, which was about 100 metres from our block, before we were told to halt.

"SQUUAAAD HALT!" was the command.

Not quite as good as when we moved off from the block, but we got there. A few of us managed to clip the heels of the guy in front as he stopped; however, this was not an uncommon thing.

"RIGHT TURN!" continued the instructions.

Wow, we were all facing the correct way again.

"Stand at ease. Stand easy," said Sergeant Preece. "OK, gather round. This is the parade square where you'll be every day from 0830hrs until 1000hrs Bombardier Bartlett and I will be teaching you how to march with precision. This is where you'll practice all your military drill from now until your passing out parade in six weeks time. There is not one inch of this square that you won't march on. The parade square is out of bounds at all times unless you're being taught drill. Do not use the square as cut-through. Do you understand?"

"Yes, Sergeant!" we all shouted.

"Over to your left is the Education Block, and just to the right is where you'll be beasted every day of the week by highly trained PTIs (Physical Training Instructors)."

We continued the 50p tour: first was the Guardroom and then, opposite, was RHQ. This is where the CO (Commanding Officer) and all the hierarchy had their offices. The medical centre was also close by just at the end of

RHQ; little did I know that one day, I would end up being bedded down there while my mates went on annual leave.

We were then shown the beautiful, very modern and diamond-shaped Church of St. Nicholas that we had to attend once a month for Sunday morning church service. Beyond that was the assault course that became a big part of our Army training.

We were then taken to these big aeroplane hangars that were used by the RAF and the Royal Navy flight units. This is where we would do our personal weapon training and also, practise drill, in the event that the weather was so unkind to not allow us to practise on the parade square. Further away from the barracks, but still within the perimeter, was a huge area called the windbreak. It was a massive clump of trees that formed a wood. The circuit must have been at least a mile round; this is where we would do a lot of our cross-country running:

Also on the camp were the Post Office, the barbers shop that we had already had the pleasure of visiting, the Officers' Mess, Sergeants' Mess, and a squash court that was situated behind our block. After that were football and cricket pitches, and then the tour was just about complete. The camp gave you a feel of a small town, just like the one I was from in Nantwich. The only difference was, in Nantwich there were a number of pubs that lined the streets. The Odd Fellows Arms to name one, where all my brothers would frequent.

"Right, listen in," said Sergeant Preece. "Form up in three ranks," he ordered, in a kind of quiet voice. "Bombardier Bartlett will now march you back to Recruits Block. Once there, you'll be allowed a twenty minute NAAFI break. Bombardier Bartlett will explain what you'll be doing after that, any questions?"

"No, Sergeant," we all shouted.

"Very well, take them away, Bombardier."

After being brought up to attention, it was a case of, "Right turn, by the right, quick, march."

It took no longer than about two minutes to reach Recruits Block.

"SQUUUAAAAD HALT!" said the Bombardier. 'Right turn', 'stand at ease', 'stand easy' were the next commands that we were all getting use to now.

"OK, Anyone wanting to go to the NAAFI to get a drink or something to eat, do so now, but only when I say. Or, you can just go back into the block.

Either way, I want you all back in your rooms standing by your beds by 1030hrs. Do not be late. OK, fall out."

I decided to go down to the NAAFI with one or two of the other lads that I was getting familiar with: Pete Rigby (Riggers) Steve Parry (Sheep), Sam Gandy, George Lynch, (Jock) Dennis Norris, Andy Clayton, Mark Davies and a lot more I would become friends with as the weeks went by. We all had to march down with our arms swinging as far back as they would go and as far forward to the horizontal as possible. It was nice to be able to chat and feel more relaxed when we entered the NAAFI shop. I suppose you could describe it as a very small supermarket. In one area there were all the essentials: like polish, Brasso, yellow dusters, soap, toothpaste etc., and then, over the other side, all the luxury items: sweets, chocolate, biscuits, drinks, crisps – not too many savoury items. There was a section where you could buy fresh made up bread rolls (ham, chicken, egg and salad). I decided to buy a couple of egg rolls and a fizzy drink.

All the food had to be eaten on the premises. We had about ten minutes to wolf it all down before making our way back to the Recruits Block. On the way back, we passed an officer. This was it… our first chance to practise our perfected salute. First to salute was Riggers, then Sam followed immediately by Steve. I thought, *Oh my God!* My turn was next. I looked right towards the officer and went for it. It was a proud moment when the officer returned the compliment with a smirk on his face. We all continued marching until we got back into the block. We were all feeling as if we had just conquered Everest. As we made our way back into our room, we were all going *up one two, down one two.* The arm would go up the longest way and down the shortest way.

Within minutes of arriving back, "Stand by your beds," was commanded. It was our Bombardier, back from his NAAFI break, along with two L/Bombardiers. "From now up until lunch time, myself and the two L/Bombardiers will be teaching you the basic skills of how to bull your boots to a standard that you can use them to shave in: they will teach you how to iron your clothes to a standard that you could cut yourself on the creases of your lightweight trousers; they will show you your locker layout: they will show how to make a bed block, clean brasses, room jobs, and all other aspects of being a soldier in the British Army." Bombardier Bartlett then put us in groups of about eight men, and then, we were assigned to one of the three Bombardiers. Out of the lads I was now becoming good friends with,

George and Dennis were in my group, along with some more unfamiliar faces: Fitzgerald, Whiteman, Machin and Slowther. The Bombardier that was assigned to us was Bombardier Bartlett.

We gathered around my bed space before relaxing by sitting on any part of the bed that was vacant.

"I need a pair of boots to start with," said the Bombardier. No sooner said than done.

"You can practise with mine," I said as I got my spare pair of boots out of my locker.

Bombardier Bartlett took the lid off a small tin of black boot polish. I could smell the cherry blossom from where I was sitting.

"Whiteman! Go and get me some water," said Bombardier Bartlett as he handed over the lid off the polish tin to Junior Gunner Whiteman. That was our title from now on, Junior Gunner. "Take the lid, fill it up with water, and mind you don't spill a drop on the floor," said Bombardier Bartlett.

"Yes, Bombardier," said Junior Gunner Whiteman, with a smile on his face.

Trying to walk in a straight line and holding a boot polish lid full of water is a task within itself; however, that was something we had to get use to.

Junior Gunner Whiteman returned with his hand as steady as a rock.

"Careful… careful…" we all said as he approached with his eyes glued to the lid. A little wobble here and a little wobble there. "Steady… steady…" Whiteman slowly lowered the lid onto the bed beside the Bombardier. A big sigh of relief came over his face as the lid finally came to rest. His job was done. He then walked slowly backwards, still keeping his eyes on the lid until he sat himself back on the bed.

Yellow duster in one hand, folded around the finger was the start of the demonstration. Then, the finger that was covered with the yellow duster slid across the polish so that you would have a dab of polish on the duster. You would then dip the same finger with the polish on into the lid full of water, being careful not to soak the duster. Next was the delicate bit: you would do small circles, normally clockwise on the top of the toe cap of your boot, making small circles that would be called 'bulling rings'. When you felt that the duster was not running smoothly across the toe cap, it would be time to apply more polish or water onto the duster. Some of us were really a natural at this sort of thing and others found it more difficult. I still don't know to this day why some could do it better than others – you either had the gift or you didn't.

My mate Steve Parry was an absolute master at the art of bulling boots; he could bull them up like mirrors. Myself, I would say I worked bloody hard with the help of Steve to achieve his standard; however, there was no way on this planet that I was ever going to reach his high standards. Mediocre, I would say at best. I would say I was better than some, but not as good as others.

The demonstration lasted about twenty minutes then, it was down to us to work out better ways of getting our boots to look like mirrors. We were told that toes and heels were what are expected on our everyday boots. For our best boots, they would need to be bulled all over, including the soles. There is a part on the bottom of the boot that does not touch the floor when marching. It rises up from the ground by the heel.

Next on the agenda, was being shown how to iron our clothes ready for our morning parade. All the polish and dusters etc. were now put away out of site. Bombardier Bartlett then produced an iron from a bag that he had. I thought he was taking the Michael when he said, "First, you have to plug the iron into the plug socket that is in the wall and switch it on. The iron will then become very hot. Please do not touch the silver shiny side or you will get burnt. Follow me."

We all followed like sheep over to the far end of the room, where there was a square sort of dining table. A sheet or blanket could be used to cover the table ready for ironing. It was a basic iron, not one of those that squirt water at the press of a button.

"Slowther, take your trousers off," said the Bombardier. "We need a pair of trousers to practise with."

We all looked at Junior Gunner Slowther with open eyes, at the same time thinking; *Thank God he didn't ask me.* His face was a picture. You could see he didn't know what to make of the situation. *Was the Bombardier being serious? Should I do what he has commanded? Will I be in trouble if I refuse?* He was just about to undo his belt that was holding his trousers up when the difficult decision was made for him: "Slowther, that's enough," said the Bombardier with a smirk on his face. Bombardier Bartlett produced a pair of lightweight trousers from his bag of tricks. There were all sorts in there: cotton shirt, woolly-pulley and loads of other things.

The creases in Bombardier Bartlett's trousers were so sharp. "This is how I want your trousers looking tomorrow morning. Notice there are no tram lines."

He demonstrated how to iron them with precision and then, showed us how to iron our shirt and jumper. It seemed easy enough. We would have to wait and see on tomorrow morning's parade. We only had the one iron to start with among about twenty of us; however, because we had so much to do, we would do other things with our kit until the iron became free.

"OK, go and have a smoke break for ten minutes," said Bombardier Bartlett. "For those of you that don't smoke, get yourselves outside at the back of the block and get some fresh air; in other words, get out of my sight."

It felt good, chatting away having a laugh with my now mates, tucked up by the wall and out of sight from people like the RSM (Regimental Sergeant Major). With the allotted ten minutes now up, Bombardier Bartlett yelled out in his sharp voice, "Right, you lot! Get yourselves back inside now."

There was one or two of the lads burning their fingers on their cigarettes as they tried hurriedly to put them out before putting the butts in the bin at the front.

We made our way back up to our room, where it was now time to be shown how to do a locker layout. We had metal coat hangers. Anything that had to be hung up was hung up with the sleeve pointing forward at a 45 degree angle. There were about six or seven items that had to be hung. All you should have been able to see was the sleeve of the garment that needed to be spaced out with the same space between each one: the shelves were used for items like pullovers, vests, shorts and towels, all neatly folded into small squares. Your socks would be folded into small balls and placed at the side of those items.

On the top shelf was your PT kit along with your No. 2 dress hat that would be placed on top of your vests. To the side of them were your mess tins; these would be used instead of plates when you went on exercise. Your boots would be at the bottom of your locker, along with things like: webbing, poncho, and No. 2 dress shoes. Some regiments may set their lockers out differently, but that was our basic layout. I think it was going to be a case of trial and error over the next few days and weeks before we would get it completely correct.

It took us some time to work out where everything went; our lockers were now laid out in a way so that we could actually find things if we needed them. We just had about enough time to be shown how to make a bed block before lunch. This was to prove more arduous than I would have thought: you would have to fold your two sheets (that would be about twenty inches in width and about fifteen inches depth) and a couple of blankets; the height of the bed block would be about six to eight inches. Once folded, you would then fold the blankets in the same fashion. The sheets would be in the middle of the blankets so; it was blanket, sheet, sheet, and then blanket. If you are still with me so far, then, you would fold another blanket around the sheets and blankets to bind them all together; the blanket would then be tucked in like the flap of an envelope. You would then have to turn it over as if you were tossing a pancake so that the flap would then be at the bottom out of sight, at the same time trying to keep it all together without it falling apart.

Squaring the bed block was the next task. If you got your mess tins out of your locker, you could slide one along the top and one up the edge of the bed block. They would meet at the corners, producing sharp neat corners. Making bed blocks to a precise size so that they were all the same was practically impossible. Some looked like they had just been slept in and some were as flat as a pancake.

Time was getting on now; we had about five minutes to make our own bed blocks. "Get your eating irons and mug together! Get yourself down to the cookhouse, I will see you all back at 1345hrs do not be late – we have a lot to get through!" said the Bombardier, a lot being the operative word.

A lot of bulling boots was the priority over the next few days and weeks. Some were poor, some were average and then there was a pair that had professionalism written all over them. Whose boots were they, was the question as Bombardier Bartlett held them up in front of the troop?

CHAPTER TWELVE
CHAIN OF COMMAND

We were now given a little more freedom. We all made our way down the stairs at a gallop and then, once outside, it was arms at the horizontal once again as we marched our way to the cookhouse. Once in the cookhouse, we were asked by one of the several chefs who were working behind the buffet counter, "What would you like?" in a deep voice, a voice that put my squeaky voice to shame. I was still embarrassed about my voice and I was thinking, *when I open my mouth and tell him what choice I would like; he would probably question my gender.* After all, I did sound very feminine. All I needed now was a skirt and high heels and I would have had the full package. I was determined to do something about it. I looked him in the face and said, "Pork, please," in the deepest voice I could master.

It sounded so unreal to my ears; however, the chef never batted an eyelid. To him, it sounded normal. I thought, *my God, I have finally managed to break my own voice!* Even my mates, never really noticed the change in my voice. So that was it, my voice had finally broken. Now and then I would still come out with a little squeak, but generally, I had mastered my demon; the squeaky voice syndrome.

After lunch, we made our way back to the block via the NAAFI. I thought it would be a good chance to buy some polish and a duster in readiness for the evening. 1345hrs soon arrived when we heard Bombardier Bartlett cry: "Outside in three ranks now!"

We all closed our lockers in quick time. Bang! Bang! Bang! You could hear all the locks being locked securely; a little rattle of the lock to make sure it was not going to come loose and then a mad dash through the swinging doors was how it was. If you were unlucky, you might just get a bash in the face from the door as it swung back cracking you one on your temple.

Halfway down the stairs, you would always merge into other half of the troop from their respective room; they were also making a mad dash to get on parade. Forty plus NIGs trying to get on parade in quick time was a sight not to be missed. No one wanted to be the last one on parade, but unfortunately, someone had to be. *Just make sure it's not you.* I could guarantee if you were the last man, it would be etched on the mind of Bombardier Bartlett the next time we got on parade. In other words, you got one chance. *Just make sure it's not you again next time.* If it was, you could rest assure that you would be running around the block two or three times.

"Get fell in now!" was the order as we were tripping over each other, all that said, still in an orderly fashion. We all now knew our position in the ranks so, if someone was a few seconds behind you getting on parade, it would make it difficult to know where to stand. You would be standing next to a space. You would always be looking for the person you stand next to in order to help you get your correct position. I would stand next to Mark Davies (not because I fancied him) because he was roughly the same height as me, and that's how it was for a while.

"OK, stop fidgeting, and listen in!" said the Bombardier. "That means you too, Parry!"

Just then, Sergeant Preece arrived for his speech. This is how it always went. It was known as the Chain of Command. Next to arrive was the BSM (Battery Sergeant Major), who had a few more words to say. One thing I did notice was the higher the rank, the more distinguished the person looked. The Sergeant Major was wearing a khaki-coloured peak cap , a white coloured shirt, smart khaki trousers (complete with a stable belt), bulled boots, a pace stick and he had a large crown strapped to his right wrist, the size of a very large watch. *Very smart,* I thought. *He looks important.* We were now waiting for the arrival of our TC. These are the people we apparently have to salute. They have pips and crowns on their shoulders, this is one of several ways we would recognise them from all the other ranks; the way they walk plus, the way they speak were also noticeable features.

With the fact that the TC warranted more respect than the Sergeant Major (in respect that he was an officer), I still felt that the Sergeant Major was the governor, especially when it came to Army discipline. Sergeant Preece brought us all up to attention whilst we were awaiting the arrival of the TC: "Listen in! Squad! SHUN!" rattled out of his mouth. I could see the TC strolling towards us out of the Battery Block that was next to our Recruits Block, with a kind of swagger. He was a lot smarter than us; he was dressed very much like the Sergeant Major: a khaki peak cap, a white thick cotton shirt (neatly ironed), two pips on both shoulders, heavyweight khaki trousers and shiny brown shoes that were tipped with metal studs, toes and heels. His stable belt was full of the colours of the rainbow: red, blue and yellow stripes all around the belt – they're the colours I seem to remember – which was fastened with buckles and leather straps. He was a lot younger than I thought he would be; mid twenties I would say.

The TC introduced himself, with Bombardier Bartlett, Sergeant Preece, and the Sergeant Major all standing in close attendance. Again, the chain of command sprang to mind; however, we still had to listen to everything he had to say without falling asleep. I suppose he was trying to put forward some of his own thoughts, I can't remember taking anything on board I didn't already know. I suppose he was just following orders like we all do in the British Army. I can still remember the last few meaningful words he said: "Work as a team, work hard and you will get your just rewards. You're representing Wingate Troop 33 Campbell Battery. Let's show the rest of the regiment that we are the best. Good luck, lads."

We were brought up to attention by the Sergeant Major who then turned to his left and saluted the TC.

"Carry on, Sergeant Major," said the TC as he returned the salute. The TC then turned away and headed back into the Battery Block and into the cosy confines of his office.

"Stand at ease. Stand easy," said the Sergeant Major as he handed command back to Sergeant Preece. "When I give you the command to fall out, I want you all to make your way into the lecture room that is located on the ground floor just to the left as you walk in. You're going to have your photograph taken by the regimental photographer for you ID cards. You'll also be given your Army Number at the same time. This number is your identity from now until you leave the Army. Are there any questions?"

"No, Sergeant!" we shouted.

"Very well, listen in: Attention, turn to your right, march three paces forward."

Apparently, that is how you fall out. We would get to know all about these type of instructions when we started learning our basic drill moves.

Once inside the lecture room, we would be called over one by one. Each picture would only take about a minute to complete. It was just like a photo booth, I suppose: don't smile, beret off, look into the camera and, before you knew it, it was all over. The only problem I had was that as soon as I sat down for the photo, I could hear and see people like Riggers and Parry (among others) saying things like, "Wolfendale take your gas mask off!" or "Don't break the camera!" They were making face gestures behind the photographer's back. How could you not laugh? I was now getting grief from Bombardier Bartlett: "Wolfendale, stop smiling. Keep still before I give you something to smile about!" as he pointed his pace stick towards me. If I was that way inclined, yes, I do believe it would have made me smile.

I was given my Army Number that I was never to forget: 24311682 Junior Gunner Wolfendale. That was it, I was just a number, an Army statistic, or at least that's what it seemed like.

We all returned to our respective rooms, which in our case was the dormitory. Bombardier Bartlett lined us up in the corridor just outside our room. He showed us our schedule for the next six weeks that was pinned up on the notice board, subject to change at any given notice. Tomorrow would be Wednesday the 9th May; this would be our first full day of military training. Over the last 36 hours or so, we had been taught the basic essentials before the real fun began; make or break time is a term I would use. Reading the notice board it said. Reveille would be at 0530hrs, breakfast would be at 0630hrs and we needed to be back by 0715hrs. All room jobs needed to be completed by 0745hrs. "Room jobs?" we all said, looking to each other. Just to the right of the schedule was another notice; it was a list of all the room jobs that we would undertake. Next to each room job was the name of the person or persons that were to undertake that task. Our attention was taken away from the original schedule, as we were all trying to find out what room job we had been allocated.

It was like feeding time for a very hungry litter of pups. We were all trying to get our heads into the very small space to see the notice. I managed to get a quick look to see which job I had been sentenced to: showers and washrooms, along with Muckers (Chris Muckersie), Clive Davies and Slug (Ricky Hill). That would do for me. I wasn't really concerned about what the rest of Wingate Troop duties were.

At 0800hrs, we would be stood by our beds for a preliminary check of our lockers and bed blocks, followed by parade outside the Recruits' Block at 0830hrs. Drill on the parade square was going to be a regular thing in the morning, straight after first parade. At around 1000hrs, we would have our well earned NAAFI break that would last for about twenty to thirty minutes. This would also give us a chance to see if we have received any post from our love ones which, in some cases, our girlfriends: sounding (learning how to blow a bugle) was a 1030hrs (for half an hour), followed by PT at 1115hrs in the gym. At 1200hrs, we would then be free for about fifteen minutes to get showered and changed before making our way to lunch.

The afternoon would start at around 1345hrs. Wednesday would be sports afternoon, and then it would vary from day to day: more square-bashing, education and first aid, assault course, lectures, field craft, cross country, skill at arms, NBC training… In other words, we were going to get gassed. There were some days that had small slots marked on the schedule that said 'TCs disposal'. That meant the TC would choose what he thought we needed more work on. Evening meal would be at 1730hrs and then back to the Recruits' Block for an evening of fun: bulling boots, cleaning brasses, ironing clothes, dusting, polishing and scrubbing. The list was endless. We would not be let out of the barracks for the first six weeks until after our passing out parade; in Army terms, it means confined to barracks. Just as I was processing the last few lines of the schedule I heard.

"Get back to your rooms! You have got a couple of hours before tea, so make the most of it" said Bombardier Bartlett. "This will give you plenty of time to practise bulling your boots. I will be back at 1700hrs to inspect them and see how you're managing. Remember, work as a team; if any one of you is struggling, get someone to help you. See you in about two hours, oh and one last thing: anyone needing to go to the NAAFI to get some polish, dusters and anything else etc., that's fine, but get a move on. I don't want you to be hanging around there. Buy what you need and get straight back."

No sooner had he gone, there were cries of, "Who's coming to the NAAFI? I need some polish and a duster!"

Lucky for me and one or two others, we were already organised, so we went straight to the washrooms with our lid off the cherry blossom polish tin to fill it with cold water; of course, making sure we didn't spill any on the way back to our pits. I remember gently placing the lid onto my top bunk along with my polish, and then carefully climbing up onto my bed, trying not to spill a drop; it was like trying to drive a toaster through a car wash. I started to bull my boots just like I had been taught: duster over hand, point your finger out, slide it across the polish and then a little dab of water; small circles in a clockwise direction all over the toe cap, and hey presto. It was more difficult than Bombardier Bartlett made it look.

"Wolfie!" shouted one of my mates. "Can you see your face in them yet?"

"What the fuck do you think?" I said. "Can't see much difference to when

90

I started bulling them about twenty minutes ago." I was thinking, *it's going to take me until the passing out parade to get them shiny.*

Just then, all the ones that went to the NAAFI were returning with their products. They couldn't wait to have a laugh at my expense and all the other lads at our feeble effort so far. To be honest, I think they were just as worried that they were going to have the same problem. The bottom line was, we were already twenty minutes ahead of them and we only had two hours or thereabouts to produce a shine. We all knuckled down to our task in hand, at the same time, messing around and having a laugh. I believe if we didn't we'd go crazy.

My wrist was feeling a bit stiff so every few minutes or so, I would have to stretch and move it a little as I felt some sort of cramp within the wrist itself. Occasionally I would get down from my bunk, then have a walk around the room, taking in my own inspection. I was trying to get some advice from Steve on how to get my boots looking like his, but to no avail.

"How the hell have you got your boots to look like mirrors?" I said.

His explanation was simple, yet hard to understand. I tried out several different methods that he told me to try but without the same success. Sometimes I would try a thicker layer of polish, sometimes more water on my duster: smaller circles, larger circles, washing my duster to make it softer; it was no good. I had to accept that I was never going to get my boots to be as shiny as Steve's.

I bulled my boots to what I thought was an acceptable standard. I was judging that by everybody else's boots. They were better than some, the same as others, and quite a long way behind Parry's. We all kept bulling our boots until Bombardier Bartlett arrived and our wrists were dropping off. It was quite a relaxed room when he walked in; he could see that we were all hard at work, occupied in bulling our boots. With that in mind, he just said in a calm voice, "Carry on with what you're doing. I will come around and have a look to see how you have fared."

To be honest, I got the impression that he was happy with everyone's effort, mine included.

"Nearly as good as mine, Wolfendale," he said with a tinge of irony. "Still can't see my beautiful face in them – more work needed."

I felt like saying, *you'll never see your beautiful face in my boots… you need a beautiful face before that could happen.* Best keep those remarks under my beret.

"OK, listen in. Well done on your efforts this afternoon. Still lots more bull needed."

We could all see that he had a pair of boots in his hand; the question that needed to be asked, whose boots were they?

"This is how I expect your boots to be looking in the next few weeks. Parry, come and get your boots back."

To be honest, I wasn't surprised that they were his. I'm not sure if Steve felt embarrassed; knowing Sheep, though, probably not.

We were now free to go to tea at our leisure; however, we would need to be back in the block by 1900hrs. It felt good marching to tea in half shiny boots for the first time.

"Don't come near my boots!" we were all saying to each other. Some of them would do it on purpose.

"Get away!"

"Piss off!"

"Fuck off, Riggers! Don't stand on my boots!"

I think we had almost forgotten that we were supposed to be marching to tea; we looked a right shambles. We were hopping, running; pushing each other away; we'd have been in serious trouble if we had been spotted by any of the senior ranks that were roaming the camp. Luckily for us, we made it there and back without too many scratches on our boots and without being spotted.

Back in the block, we just relaxed a little, awaiting the arrival of our infamous Bombardier. Some of the lads were taking a welcome shower and were caught off guard when he arrived.

"Get your scrawny bodies out of the showers and back into your room now!" yelled Bombardier Bartlett.

The lads came running in with Army green towels covering their waists looking like drowned rats. The whole episode reminded me of a Jekyll and Hyde scenario. Before tea, Bombardier Bartlett was chilled and relaxed; now, well let's just say, he was like a raging bull.

"I said 1900hrs – back in your room!" he shouted, with his voice getting louder and his nostrils getting wider. "When I say 1900hrs, I mean 1900hrs, and not a second later! What were you doing in the showers? Don't answer that one. It is now 1904hrs. That means you're four minutes late. The Army functions on punctuality; remember that. You know what? Because you like the showers so much, you can get yourselves back in there after I've finished with you. I want the showers and the washrooms immaculate when I come back tonight at 2200hrs."

I think he must have been upset by something or someone; the fact that he had to come back and tuck us up in bed at 2200hrs probably didn't help. *Not our fault* I'm thinking. I'm quite sure we were capable of tucking ourselves up in bed. Well, I don't know about my Scottish mates.

"Room jobs, take a look at the notice board to see what room jobs you have been allocated. Those of you who should have been on washrooms and showers are excused, courtesy of Bousefield, Quinn, Russell, and Vann. Those mentioned will also have to do their own nominated room jobs, so unless your room job was washrooms, you'll have two room jobs to do to night wont you?"

Yes, I said to myself. *No room job for me tonight.* I could also see Muckers and Slug Hill smiling, out of the corner of my eye.

The Bombardier showed us all where all the equipment was for the relevant jobs: bumpers, floor polish, bass brooms, old blankets, scouring powder, toilet brushes, etc.

"I shall be back at 2200hrs." said Bombardier Bartlett.

We were all thinking *I hope he's on a promise tonight;* otherwise, we could be the ones that would feel the brunt of him not getting his leg over when he returns back from his Army quarter that is situated on the barracks. With no room job to do, it gave me more time to get my kit ironed before getting stuck into bulling my boots. It was nice to have the extra time to myself; however, I felt it only right to give the lads a hand with some of their tasks. It was all hands to the pump: we had less than three hours to do our kit, room jobs, have a shower and get ourselves ready for lights out. We made sure we were all done and standing by our beds at 2150hrs. We were dressed in shorts, PJs and long johns (for the weirdo's amongst us). Basically, we were all ready for bed.

It was now dark outside; looking out of the window you could see the regimental guard marching around in two's in their combat suits. We closed the curtains just in time to welcome the arrival of Bombardier Bartlett.

"Stand by your beds," was heard as he came through the door. He had a quick look around the accommodation before he came up to each and every one of us individually; "Hands out in front of you!" He inspected our fingernails, toenails, and then walked around the back of us and checked behind our ears; I don't think anyone was expecting this; however the inspection went well as far as I can remember.

"Get yourselves a good night's sleep," said the Bombardier, as he turned and switched the lights off without so much as another word.

It was certainly a lot quieter than last night; we were all a little tired and not feeling much like chatting. I could hear the odd whisper along with the odd chuckle or two, before I was in my own little world. *Please don't wake me up; let this moment last forever,* I thought to myself. The following morning was to be a locker inspection; although every one of us was expecting to be picked up for something like dust on the top of your locker, or your KFS not been cleaned, it was a complete shock when Bombardier Bartlett inspected my personal locker and found a magazine, a magazine that had him asking, "what the hell do you get up to in your spare time?"

CHAPTER THIRTEEN
STAND BY YOUR BEDS

The following morning all my thoughts and all my dreaming were brought to an abrupt end. I must have woken up several times before I heard the regimental guard once again, slamming the swinging doors as hard as they could. I think the majority of us knew what to expect before they entered our room. My mind was already out of bed; it was just a case of getting my body to follow as the lights went on.

"Out of bed!" they shouted.

I was now waiting for the next order: hands off cocks onto socks, just like the night before. Sure enough, before my feet hit the floor, the predictability rang in my ears.

I grabbed my wash bag and made my way to the washrooms before it got too overcrowded. We were all rushing around, sorting ourselves out and getting ready for breakfast. I think we all knew that time was of the essence and we weren't going to be dragged down by time-wasters who couldn't be bothered to pull their weight. As far as I can remember, some of the lads didn't even make it to breakfast. Cereal and full English was the agenda for the day, and then back to the room for our room jobs. It was a case of, all hands to the pumps. as we got stuck in to our room jobs: with this being our first inspection of the block, our bed blocks, lockers and uniform meant we needed to put on a good impression. We just about managed to finish all of our room jobs by 0745hrs and were awaiting Bombardier Bartlett's presence. We were darting around like headless chickens checking each other's dress, and I don't mean in the feminine sense. We would also be inspecting each other's locker layout for uniformity. Bombardier Bartlett arrived with precise punctuality and just stood there in an upright position with his pace stick down by his side. "Stand by your beds!" he shouted at the same time giving us a few seconds to get ourselves organised; we had to stand to attention at the side of our beds looking at the person opposite and trying not to smirk or even smile.

One by one, Bombardier Bartlett inspected our lockers and bed blocks: "Not bad Parry. Did you iron your No. 2 dress shirt?"

"Yes, Bombardier," said Steve.

"Well, next time, try turning the iron on."

I was trying not to laugh at the remark as I clenched my lips together. I could see Dennis, who was standing opposite me by his bed, donning a huge beaming smile. It was easier said than done not to laugh. Once one person laughs, it becomes infectious. How we managed to keep straight faces is beyond me, but we did. Out of the corner of my eye, I could feel Steve's eyes glancing over towards me. I could tell what he was thinking, *soon be your turn, Wolfendale*, and he was right. I don't think anyone got away scot-free.

"Lynch, need to sort out your webbing!"

"Riggers, your tooth brush looks like you have been cleaning the toilet bowl with it!"

"Muckersie, call that a bed block, well do you? It looks like you have fucking slept in it."

Bombardier Bartlett finally made his way over to my bed space; talk about squeaky bum time... I was bricking it. I felt like my arse was falling out of my trousers. Each second he was searching through my locker felt like an hour. Just when I thought I was home and dry I heard the inevitable cry from Bombardier Bartlett, "Wolfendale."

"Yes, Bombardier," I said.

"Turn round and face your locker."

A swift swivel around and I was now facing my locker with Bombardier Bartlett breathing down my ear.

"Take a look in there," he said, as he pointed to my personnel belongings, "What the fuck his that?"

I had hidden a copy of an adult magazine behind my wash bag.

"I don't remember seeing this on your 1157," said the Bombardier. "If it has not been Army issued, then it goes away in your suitcase until the end of term. So we now know who the biggest wanker is, don't we, Wolfendale?"

"Yes Bombardier!" I said in a very thunderous voice.

"You haven't gone deaf then yet?" said Bombardier Bartlett.

"What was that you said, Bombardier?"

"Don't you be insolent with me, Wolfendale, otherwise it will take a good surgeon to remove my pace stick from where the sun doesn't shine." *Not that bloody pace stick again* I was thinking. "Close your lockers and don't forget to lock them. Make your way outside the Recruits' Block in three ranks. Goooooo! Get outside, now!"

We charged down the stairs and lined up for first parade in double quick time and then, waited with bated breath for Bombardier Bartlett to arrive. It took us no more than about thirty seconds to form up in three ranks, just in time to be greeted by the words, "Stand still and don't move a muscle!"

We didn't dare. We were brought up to attention and then the front rank had to take one step forward, and the back rank took one step back. This would leave a space in between the ranks big enough for the Bombardier to walk up and down the ranks and inspect his men – yes, his men.

One by one, he inspected our dress: beret, shirt, lightweight trouser and belt, your boots needed to be shiny, with no sign of any dirt in the welts of your boots. He would check that we were properly shaven, with no sign of bum fluff anywhere on our faces. The next step was to walk around the back of the ranks and check for anything that might be out of place; every button would need to be fastened, including your side and back pockets, then one final look to see if your cap badge was over your left eye, etc. Bombardier Bartlett made his way back to the front of the squad and brought us up to attention before getting us back into close order; in other words, he got us to close ranks again.

"Well done today, on your first inspection. This is just a taste of what you can expect over the next few weeks; there is a lot more work to be done on your lockers and rooms before I am satisfied, as far as your dress is concerned, good turnout."

'Praise before criticism' springs to mind, It was nice to get praised, however, I think it's the Bombardier's way of saying; *you're going to get a lot more of what went on this morning.*

"We shall be making our way onto the parade square shortly, for your first session of square bashing (drill). We shall be met by Sergeant Preece and the other half of Wingate Troop. Sergeant Preece and I will be educating you in the art of military marching. We will be teaching you to change direction as a troop: right wheels, left wheels, quick march, slow march, saluting whilst marching, change step on the march and lots more. All will be explained once on the square. Attention! Right turn! Quick march! Left! Right! Left! Right! Left! Right! Left!"

Before we knew it, we were on the parade square. The parade square seemed so spacious now that we were on it; it looked a lot smaller when we were marching past it on our way to the cookhouse. The weather was overcast with a slight breeze in the air. That was a God-send. It provided us with some air conditioning to keep us cool. While we waited for the other half of Wingate Troop to arrive, we were allowed to rest a little whilst still formed in three ranks. We were all just chitchatting away and giving each other banter.

"Bulldog!" someone said. "I bet you feel at home here. All this open space for you to run around in!"

"Here, boy, come on then!" said someone else.

Some of the lads were patting their thighs, at the same time as looking at Bulldog.

"Good boy, Bulldog."

You could tell we were getting more familiar with each other, with the fact we were taking the mickey out of certain individuals, and at the same time, trying not to overstep the mark. There would always be someone who would take offence. Broad shoulders were the theme for the day; if you can't take it, then maybe you shouldn't dish it out.

"Left… Right… Left… Right… Left… Right… Left!" could be heard over to our right. I think we all recognised that voice as it echoed across the parade square. "Left! Right! Left! Right! Left! Right! Left!" It was the familiar voice of our Troop Sergeant, Sergeant Preece. We were all slightly curious as you naturally would be; although they were part of Wingate, they were still our competitors when it came to drill or any other competitive event. Bombardier Bartlett got us to come to attention; facing forward without so much as a glance to the right Sergeant Preece marched his section onto the square and alongside our section. With a quick shuffle of our feet as we stood still, we became joined at the hip. Sergeant Preece gave us a pep talk and explained what we were going to be doing within the next hour and a half. We were now split up into our original sections once more. A-section was Sergeant Preece's mob, and B-Section was the elite section. *Bring it on,* I thought, in my competitive nature. I could tell Bombardier Bartlett was very competitive by the way he addressed us. Second place did not have any place in his vocabulary.

After parting company with A-Section, we were again split up into pairs. I was paired with Dennis. He became my bosom buddy (so to speak). *Hurray,* I thought. We had to march towards each other, and then shout out orders; it sounded like World War Three was about to start. To be honest it felt embarrassing, however, we just had to get on with it. We would have to shout at the top of our voices: "Right Turn, one, two three—one, two three—one, two three—one! By the front—quick march! Left! Right! Left! Right! Left! Right! Left!"

Your buddy would then have to tell you to halt in a kind of regimental way if he could. It is difficult to tell one person to halt by command, so we both agreed to say our name.

"Wolfendale—Halt!"

"Miss... one two!" I would say. ('Miss' means misses a step, not like being back at school: Yes, Miss; please Miss; I know the answer, Miss.)

Eventually, after losing a percentage of our hearing, we would be formed back up in three ranks; we would practise the skills we had taught ourselves, but this time as a squad. *Move to the right in threes* would be the command. *One, two three—one!* We were looking good. *By the front—quick—march!*

Our arms were now swinging in unison with our legs for the first time. You could feel the collective determination of the troop as we marched around the parade square.

"Open your legs up!" was the cry from Bombardier Bartlett, as the pace increased.

"Clayton! Open your legs wider! They're not going to fall out, there in a sack! Left! Right! Left! Right! Left! Right! Left!"

After a full circuit of the parade square, we were now back where we started.

"Squad halt! Right! Turn! Stand at ease. Stand easy. Listen in," said Bombardier Bartlett. "You now have a twenty-minute break; after that, you'll make your way onto the grass area that is situated behind the parade square. There, you'll be met by the Trumpet Sergeant Major for your sounding lesson. Do not be late!"

We were brought up to attention and then told to fall out: "One, two three—one, two three—one, two three!" we all shouted.

A quick toilet break was needed first and foremost. I decided to give the NAAFI a rain check this time around and make my way back to the block. There were only a handful of us who went back; the rest went to the NAAFI for some light refreshments. It felt strange in the block not having to fight for the toilet for a change. I lay on my bed for a quick catnap, being watchful not to get caught by any senior ranks that might be patrolling around. Egyptian PT was the Army term for it. To be honest, it didn't seem worth it. No sooner had I lay on my bed, it was time to go to sounding.

Sounding was to be an every-other-day routine, initially with an original view to providing the RA (Royal Artillery) with buglers. The training was conducted by members of the RA band who were posted to the JLRRA as permanent staff to manage the junior's band and, presumably, with a brief to look out for talent too. You had to show promise and musical ability to join the band that was done on a voluntary basis. The bandmaster also held auditions to give unknown trumpeters and drummers the opportunity to step forward. There were times when if you were musically minded, you would be selected for the band, but if they were getting a little low on numbers, you only had to look like you were musically minded and you were in. This would not go down too well with your Troop Sergeant. He expected you to fuck up big time, and, there was no way he wanted to lose one of his men to the RA band.

Just before we went to sounding, whilst on parade outside the Recruits' Block, we got one last minute lecture from our Bombardier in no uncertain terms: "If any of you get chosen for the RA band, you will have me to answer too. When you're asked to blow the bugle, I want you to act as if it is your girlfriend: stick your tongue in the hole and blow around the mouth piece making sure you don't make a fucking sound. That will do the trick. Those of you who do not have a girlfriend, I suggest you get one quick. Fall out, and get yourselves over to sounding now."

I had never blown anything in my life. I wasn't that way inclined; however, I had little choice in performing my first blow job.

We were all standing in a semi-circle with our bugles that we had been presented with at the ready. To be honest, some of us couldn't blow for laughing. I think we were all thinking of what Bombardier Bartlett had told us minutes ago. There was no way I could get a note out of the bugle, I think I might have got the odd beep, but that was as good as it got. I was blowing for England without too much success. My cheeks were bursting; it was like trying to blow one of those long shape balloons up. It was definitely not for me. At the same time, I did hear some notes that sounded like they weren't out of place. The whole lesson took about forty minutes before we could rest our cheeks and be dismissed. Bombardier Bartlett came along for the last five minutes to make sure we were not going to be plucked away from his troop and into the hands of the RA band.

"OK. Form up!" said the Bombardier. We were marched back to the block that was about a minute away and told to get into our PT kit and form up outside. Although I was brought up climbing trees jumping ditches and basically being able to fend for myself, the gym should've been a walk in the park. I didn't take in to account that climbing ropes could be painful; actually, climbing up to the top wasn't too much of a problem, it was the descending that left its mark on my hands.

CHAPTER FOURTEEN
LETTERS FROM OUR LOVED ONES

RAPTC (The Royal Army Physical Training Corps') is responsible for physical fitness and physical education. Its members are all PTIs (physical training instructors). The RAPTC was formed in 1860 as the Army Gymnastic Staff. It was renamed the Army Physical Training Staff in 1918 and was given its present corps' status by Army Order 165 in 1940. Based at the ASPT (Army School of Physical Training) in Aldershot, its instructors are based in every battalion and regiment in the Army. It is not possible to join the RAPTC directly from civilian life. Prospective PTIs must first join another regiment or corps' and then qualify as Regimental PTIs after a nine week course at the ASPT. They then return to their unit and only after further experience can they attend selection for the RAPTC. If they pass the selection course, they follow a thirty-week intensive training course before qualifying as an APTCI and transferring to the RAPTC.

It was a quick five minute turn around: blue almost knee-length shorts, a red short-sleeved vest (neatly tucked into your shorts), laced up plimsolls (smartly polished) and Army green socks was the dress.

"Outside!" was the cry.

We all lined up as normal, ready for our first PT session, which was to become a daily experience for the first six weeks. I don't know why, but as soon as you get into your PT kit, you seemed to have this natural urge to jump up and down on the spot. We couldn't stop fidgeting. I think we must have felt as if we had been set free from our normal Army routine.

"Right turn double march!" was the order, given at a speed we were expected to move our arses at.

It was OK for the Bombardier in respect that, every time we got away from him, he would give the instruction to mark time. That order means double on the spot until he catches up, and then, the order to double march is given again. What would normally be a two-minute walk, would now take us twice that time, even with the fact that we were running. Sometimes we would mark time for about thirty seconds at any one time. We eventually arrived at the gym.

"Fall out," was the command. "Get yourselves inside, now! Double!"

Once inside, we were lined up in the corridor area. The smell of sweat permeated the warm air of the gym. You could smell the brine from the swimming pool. Everything seemed to echo. The huge size of the gym made me feel I had dwarfism. I remember the brown double doors swinging open as this huge figure of a man came towards us; Bombardier Wes Goodman, a West Indian man. He was as black as two o'clock in the morning. He looked liked a black version of Desperate Dan, someone I had read about in one of many of my childhood Comics. He wore a white PT vest with red trims and white shorts. He was a right 'meathead' (although, that sort of comment you kept to yourself). His neck was bigger than my thigh and the muscles in his arms were something like a man made mountain. His accent was the thing I remember most.

"Get your white arses in the gym, now!"

"Does that include me?" said Junior Gunner Whiteman, who was hiding in the background. Dave Whiteman was just as black. He was from Malawi and such a favourite with the rest of us.

"Yes, it does," said Bombardier Goodman in a sarcastic voice. "What is your name?"

"Junior Gunner Whiteman, Bombardier."

"Then maybe you would you like your own personal invitation, Junior Gunner Whiteman. What kind of name is that for a black man? Get your black arse in the gym now."

There was more to follow as Mr Universe walked in. Wow. I could feel each and every one of us glued to his physique. Was I turning gay? Oh my God. Why am I looking at this man in this way? I am just so glad he didn't say touch your toes. I would have been out of there quicker than a ferret up your trouser leg. These men warranted respect and respect they got. After entering the gym, there were a few 'do's and 'don'ts, before we were running around the perimeter of the hall: past the ropes, climbing frames, gymnastic equipment, mats and medicine balls. To be honest, we didn't have time to take in the view; we just had to keep running until told otherwise.

Everything was done at a frenetic pace, a pace I was unfamiliar with.

"Form up in a straight line!" yelled the PTI. Before the last man was even in line, it was, "Sprint to the end of the gym, touch the wall and sprint back.

I want to see the last man back!" Then we had to sprint backwards, touch the wall, bunny hops, and touch the wall again, a few stretches and running around the gym. Apparently this was just the warm up; we were painfully knackered. We eventually got some respite from running around the gym, only to be told to line up by four ropes that were hanging from a frame. This seemed a blessing in disguise; it gave us a little breathing time, however, we still had to run on the spot while we waited for our turn to climb the rope. I had never climbed ropes before, just the odd Tarzan across small brooks: arms, legs, arms, legs, arms, legs… all the way to the top. The hardest part was wrapping your legs around the rope to act as an anchor; if you got that right, you could straighten your legs whilst, at the same time, pushing your body up the rope. Unfortunately, I had no co-ordination. I was using my arms for the majority of the climb which was a major handicap. Once at the top, you had to feed the rope through your hands on the way down. Not a chance. I still have the blisters on my hands now. You could almost see the smoke venting from my hands as I reached the bottom of the rope:

Press ups, sit ups and step ups followed and then, to finish off, more running around the gym.

"Outside!" said the PTI.

As much as we tried to run, our legs were not having it; they were like jelly: Hands on hips, breathing heavy and heads rolling around, was the way we all exited the gym. Bombardier Bartlett was there to meet us: "Line up in three ranks!" He was showing no mercy. "Right turn Quick march!"

Back at the block, it was shower time and then back into short sleeve dress: lightweight trousers, shirt, boots, beret, and then off to lunch. The afternoon was a quieter affair: an hour of drill, followed by education in the Education Block. Education was a lot to do with map-reading, world affairs, how to use a Silva compass, etc. and, in some cases, how to use a knife and fork. Week one was pretty much the same daily routine: sounding, PT, drill and room jobs. We were being put through our paces and being built into shape.

After the first couple of days, we were told about mail we might receive from our loved ones and girl friends. We would stand by our beds just after our 1000hrs NAAFI break and wait for the Bombardier to arrive. It was an exciting time for all as this was the only communication we had with the outside world. We all waited for our names to be called out.

Rigby: one letter.

Gandy: one letter.

Norris: one letter.

"Norris!" said the Bombardier.

"Yes, Bombardier?" said Dennis, as the Bombardier put his nose on the envelope.

"This letter stinks of perfume, you puff!" as he handed the letter to Dennis.

"Lynch!"

"Yes Bombardier," said George. I could see George smiling out of the corner of my eye.

"No mail for you today."

What a choker. I could see Jock shake his head in disbelief. I am sure he was thinking, *you bastard*. I am so glad he didn't say it. I don't remember getting any post for a few days, but when I did, it felt so emotional. I would open the letter and have a quick read before we were summoned to get outside for whatever they had in store for us that day. I would normally wait until I had a quiet moment to myself before reading the letter again. I would lie on my bed, facing my pillow, and savour every word that had been written:

Dear Paul.

Hope this letter finds you in good health. We are all missing you so much! At the same time, we are proud of what you're doing, everybody here is fine. How is the food? Have you made any friends? Lots of people are asking about you. Mrs Billington up the road and Mr Bullen – they all want to know how you're doing. Weather is fine. Coal man has just delivered a tonne of coal – should last us a few months if the weather keeps! Must go now, got to get the tea on for your father and the rest of your brothers and sisters; Dad's just digging up potatoes from the garden.

Take care!

Love mum xxx

This was one of those moments when we all wished we were at home with our family and friends. The letters we received were such a comfort to us all: no swearing, no shouting. You could feel the love in the art of the writing. Five minutes on my bed with my letter was all I needed to recharge my batteries. My family were out of sight, but never out of mind. I was now ready to take on the world again. Bring it on, Bombardier Bartlett!

Friday was pay day. Around lunch time, we were ordered in front of the TC. We would be lined up in the corridor outside his office feeling excited like children in a sweet shop.

"Form up in alphabetical order!" was the cry from the Bombardier. None of us knew what to expect or the amount we would be getting. I can't remember anyone saying, bring a wheelbarrow with you, and with that in mind, it gave us some idea that the amount we received was going to be minuscule. The Bombardier stood smartly outside the TCs office. The door was wide open so that the Bombardier could keep an eagle eye on us as we waited for our turn. He could also keep one eye on the person getting his pay, making sure that he did the correct drill and say the correct wording.

I was one of the last in line as per usual (W was still at the back end of the alphabet) to be ushered in.

"Attention!" was the order.

Everything was done in quick time: *Left, Right, Left, Right, Left, Right, Left, Mark time, Halt, Right turn, salute your TC and stand still.* Wow. I was still in the state of shock to even listen to what the TC had to say. The room was more like a small bedroom: about three metres square with a window looking over towards the parade square (a sea view room springs to mine). He was sat behind a solid wooden table, decked out with paperwork and a phone. With his hands firmly on the table he looked up and stared me in the eyes as if to hypnotise me. There was about a three second pause, and then: "Number rank and name?"

"24311682 Junior Gunner Wolfendale Sir," I said nervously.

"Check your pay and pay book is correct."

"Pay and pay book correct, Sir!" I said as I signed against my name in the pay book. To be honest, I cannot imagine anyone saying, "Pay incorrect, Sir!" If I remember correctly, the pay was 50p a week. All other monies owed would be given to you at the end of half-term in the form of a cheque. I believe that 50p is all they would trust us with. In 1974, you could buy a lot of Smarties for 50p. I then had to come to attention, salute, about turn and march out: when you think that a postage stamp was 6p, a pint of beer was 20p, chocolate was from 5p a bar, it gives you some idea of the value of 50p. You literally had nothing to spend your money on. We weren't allowed out of camp and we had three squares a day; it was just enough money for a few extras. Over the coming days we were all turning into right little house wives, I felt that could certainly look after myself far more now than when I was living at home. So how come a simple task, like switching on the troop washing machine, had Riggers regretting he ever went near the dam thing?

CHAPTER FIFTEEN
RIGGERS GETS A SHOCK

Friday afternoon was spent defacing our kit. Yes, you heard me correctly.

"Get your spare pair of DMS boots out of your locker," said Bombardier Bartlett. L/Bombardier Lewis and L/ Bombardier Hogg will be along shortly to show you how your best boots should look. Get your bulling rags and polish at the ready. You'll also require your fork or spoon from your KFS."

We were all a little bamboozled by that remark; surely, they were not going to make us eat our boots? Before long, the two L/Bombardiers arrived; they were a little more casual and laid-back than Sergeant Preece and Bombardier Bartlett. We were split into three groups. I was with L/Bombardier Lewis, along with Steve Parry and one or two others. We all sat on two beds that were opposite each other with our boots, polish, fork or spoon. It was only now that it was explained what the fork and spoon would be used for.

"Has anybody got a lighter on them?" said L/Bombardier Lewis.

About three of us had one.

"OK," said the L/Bombardier. "Now, get your spoon or fork and put the non-eating end over the naked flame of your lighter. Keep it there until it becomes very hot; about a couple of minutes should do it."

This is fun, I thought. We could get burnt or, better still, I could burn Steve; accidentally of course.

"Now, put your left hand in your boot and take your hot utensil holding it by the end that isn't hot. Put the hot end on the upper part of your boot and smoothly run the utensil over the upper part."

We were now defacing our boots. What we were actually doing was burning all the rough areas of the boot. Once smooth, it would be easier to bull to a mirror shine. I could feel the heat seeping through the leather and onto my hand. It was fucking hot. I had to keep swapping my hands around every minute or so to prevent my hand being scarred. The smell was very potent from all corners of the room. It was a good job we didn't have smoke alarms in the room: sixteen-year-old lads with cigarette lighters was a recipe for disaster.

We eventually burnt all the upper parts of the boot and all around where the lace holes were. Over the coming weeks, we were using candles as well as our lighters on our best boots; it was a cheaper and easier option.

After tea, we were left alone again, although we did have lots to do on our kit and room jobs. Around 2000hrs, there was a cry of, "Burger van outside!" Apparently, this was a regular thing on a Friday night and sometimes in the week. It was a mass brawl:

"Get us one!"

"Fizzy pop for me!" said someone else.

"I'll have a hot dog!" I don't think anyone listened to the demands of the lazy twats that couldn't be arsed to get off their beds; we all just legged it downstairs to the van, I had a most wonderful burger and all washed down with a can of fizzy pop. I liked the Army food, but this was something else. This become a regular event on a Friday night; the only drawback was that, somewhere within the ranks, some smart Alec, decided it would be a good idea to say crumbs or drops. What that meant was, when you returned into the block, the first one to shout 'crumbs' got the last bite of your burger, and the first one to say 'drops' would get the last dregs from your can of pop. It caused so many arguments. As soon as the door opened, all you could hear was 'crumbs' from about six people. I would normally give it to the one who had the biggest muscles; it would save me from a pillow in the head when we went sleep at night.

Saturday morning was just like a week day for us NIGs: breakfast, room jobs, stand by our beds, and then parade outside. There would be a thorough inspection of our uniforms and then it was onto the parade square for a couple of hours of drill. After NAAFI break, we were told to get into our PT kit; we would be doing some cross country running around the wind break. All this was at the far end of the camp. Most of all sports would be played here: football, cricket and rugby. Also, the assault course was nearby. Being a sporty kind of person, this was to be my comfort zone. I loved playing any kind of sport; however, cross-country was not the sort of thing I would choose to do on a Saturday morning. The TC decided to pay us a visit. Looking at the way he was dressed, there was no way he was participating: shiny shoes, trousers, shirt, peak cap, pace stick, etc.

"OK. Line up!" said the TC in a posh voice. He was definitely no Bombardier Bartlett. "Are you ready? One circuit of the wind break… GO!"

I was quite a good runner and would expect to be near the front or thereabouts, however, we had some right fit guys amongst us. Steve Parry and George Lynch to name just two, and also Lester Fitzgerald; these guys could make my running look like I was towing a caravan. On the turn into the home straight, I was within the top ten, but quite a distance behind Steve, George and Fitzy.

Saturday afternoon meant we were at our own disposal; we still had to respect that we were soldiers of the British Army and, if we stepped out of line, we would be for the high jump. It gave us time to do our laundry. There was a washing machine in the Recruits' Block however, the chance of it being available was next to none; washing everything by hand was a far better option. I can remember lying my lightweights on the floor of the washrooms and scrubbing them with a bass broom: a little soap powder on the trousers, followed by some hot water and then a little elbow grease, scrubbing as hard as you could. Once clean, you would then wash all the soap out in the sink or shower and then, take them into the drying room to dry.

Later on in the day, you would come back, hoping to find your kit still there. This is the part where you would lose some of your items if you were not careful. If someone had indiscriminately messed up while washing their pullover, and it had the look that it belongs to a six-year-old (short body, shrunken arms, etc.), they would quite easily take the best looking jumper they could find. This sort of thing was not uncommon. The problem you had was that if you needed to exchange an item at the BQMS stores, you would be billed for the item if they thought it was neglect. There was another system in place whereby you could get about five items of clothing cleaned each week at the local laundry; you would wrap the items up in your green Army towel, tied with a bit of string, and a blue label with your name and items written on it. They would be collected on a Monday and then returned the following Monday. There would be a small charge for this service that would come out of your wages at the end of term.

With it being Saturday and purely by chance I was walking in from outside the block, I noticed that the washing machine was free. I rushed upstairs to get my washing whilst, at the same time, shouting: "Riggers! Quick! Get your arse into gear – the washing machine is free. We can share it together!"

"OK, Wolfie, mate!" said Riggers. "Go down and make sure no one else gets it. I'll be with you shortly – I'll bring some washing powder."

"OK," I said, as I legged in downstairs. *Still empty*, I said to myself as I put my washing on the table that sat beside the washing machine. Within seconds, Pete (Riggers) arrived with his sack full of clothes: lightweight trousers, shirts, socks, underwear, etc. Remembering that we were all use to our mums washing our clothes, it proved to be an experience within itself. After putting our clothes in the machine, it was time to switch it on.

"Riggers switch it on," I said.

"OK," said Pete.

As soon as Pete pressed the button, he got one massive shock that ran through his body.

"Arrrghh Fucking hell!" was the cry from Pete. The washing machine was alive and kicking, it was no wonder there wasn't anyone using it; the bloody washing machine was a death trap!

We decided to unplug it from the wall and put a notice on the machine saying out of use. We took all our clothes to the washrooms and decided it would be safer to wash them by hand before taking them to the drying room. On returning to our room, there were a few people on their beds. "Muckers," I shouted. "Did you know the washing machine is a death trap?"

Muckers couldn't stop laughing when I told him about Riggers and the electric shock he got.

"Yes I did know, you daft bastards," said Muckers. "That's why there is no one down there. Clayton got a shock from it before!"

"Nice of someone to tell us!" said Pete. "I think we were the only people that didn't know about it."

The rest of Saturday and Sunday was much of the same. I wasn't one for socialising down at the NAAFI. Not my scene. Bulling boots, ironing… It gave us chance to reshape our locker layouts. I remember Saturday night being a little rowdier. I think it was just the excitement of knowing we could have a bit of a lie-in on the Sunday morning. This was to be a rarity in the coming weeks. There would be pillow fighting in the dark. You could hear someone creeping around in the dark, and then: "Arrrghh! Bastard!" as someone was smacked around his face with a full-on swing of a pillow. To be honest, It was funny as hell (when it wasn't you), however, if it was you, revenge would be sweet. You just crept over to the direction where you thought the perpetrator came from and let fly with your pillow. Another, "Arrrghh bastard," again could be heard. You would occasionally hear the perpetrator stub his toe on the metal frame work of someone's bed, as he would hurriedly try to discreetly get back into his bed. That bit was even funnier: "Arrrghh! Fucking hell! My fucking toe! Ouch!" You were pretty sure then who the culprit was.

If he was bigger than you, you just let it go. If he was smaller, then you would give him the pillow treatment of his life, Bang! Bang! Bang take that you moron! I remember once, someone was standing by the light switch; just then as the cry of bastard was heard, the light was switched on.

"Muckers, you twat, you've been compromised," said a voice. Muckers jumped hurriedly back into bed and still had the bravado to deny it.

A good hour of having your face splattered was enough for anyone. We were getting tired now. Finally, we were down to the last little murmur before we all fell asleep.

Sunday was a rest day: writing letters, going down to the NAAFI, playing squash and chilling out. No church parade this Sunday meant we spent most of our precious time getting ready for Monday. After breakfast, I decided to write a letter to my parents before everybody was fully awake. Some of the lads had skipped breakfast and were still asleep; some were doing their washing. I got out my writing set that was in a zip-up case, it was what my mother and father had bought me as a present before I left home: writing paper, envelopes, stamps and pens. I lay on my bed and started to write my thoughts.

Dear Mum and Dad,

Thank you for your kind letter. It was received with pure excitement. I am missing you all so much, especially after last night's pillow fight. My nose is broken and I've have a split lip.

That is my sense of humour

Only joking, we did have a pillow fight, but all in good fun. I am settling into Army life even after the first week; today is a rest day so I thought it would give me time to write to you. We do not get much time to our selves, so I will be writing when I can. We only get 50p a week of our wages at the moment and the rest is put into savings . We then get a cheque at the end of our first half term – in just less than six weeks' time! Some of the lads say they will be getting a parcel full of goodies and I was wondering if it would be possible for you to send me one – 50p doesn't go a long way! I hope the weather is nice where you are; it is raining now, where I am. I will close for now.

Write again soon.

Love and miss you so much.

Paul xxxxx.

After writing a letter to my parents, I said to Dennis, who was lying on his bed, "Fancy a walk to the NAAFI? I need to post a letter and I would like a look around."

"Yeah why not," said Dennis. "Got nothing better to do at the moment, just give me a second." The rain had stopped now, which was a good thing as, unfortunately, umbrellas were not part of your 1157. We had a great chat as we were walking along, about our home life and where we lived: our interests, life style, hobbies, etc. I was getting to like Dennis, and over the next few months he was to become one of my best mates. We could see the squash courts behind our billet and thought it would be a good idea to give it a go, even though I had never played it before. I asked Dennis whether he had played squash, and to my surprise he said yes. Well, that was it. He could teach me how to play. We called in at the gym on our way back from the NAAFI and asked about using the facility.

"You need to book a slot," said the PTI. "What time were you thinking of playing?"

"Later on today would be fine, if there are any free slots," I said.

"What about seven to eight tonight" said the PTI?

"What do you reckon, Dennis?" I said.

"Yeah fine by me," said Dennis.

"OK," I said. "We would like to book it."

The PTI put our name on the sheet and that was that. It was booked.

It was back to the block for some more Egyptian PT however, it was never going to be that easy when there is so much noise going on. Everybody seemed to find something to do: bulling boots, ironing, washing, locker lay out, writing letters, or just general Army chitchat. I went to lunch with Dennis, Riggers, and Steve Parry; they were becoming my close friends now, as well as George Lynch, Sam Gandy and Muckers. We all had our little groups; however, we were still friends with most of the other lads. There was a lot more familiarity now between the ranks. Some were even asking what time would the 'Bomb' be back, instead of Bombardier. That was something you really didn't want to get into the habit of saying if you valued your life. After tea, Dennis and I got into our PT kit and made our way to the squash court. I think there were about three courts inside the building. Although I had never played it before, it didn't take me long to work out the rules, with a little help from Dennis. It was great for our fitness levels. I was quite taken aback of how many miles I must have run in the hour we were there.

A short walk back to the block and then we got on with our room jobs. We had gone all day without seeing Sergeant Preece and Bombardier Bartlett but that was soon to change. At about 2000hrs, Bombardier Bartlett arrived to inspect the block and to see how we were progressing with everything that was expected from us. After all, he was here to blow our noses; we were only sixteen and irresponsible, or so we kept getting reminded.

Bombardier Bartlett would return later in the evening at 1000hrs for his usual inspection of our hygiene. It was fingernails, toenails and just a general look behind the ears time once again. To be honest, I didn't envy his job. I don't know whether he got a kick out of what we would call, messing us around, but looking at the state of some of the toenails; you couldn't have paid me to inspect them.

"OK. Get your filthy bodies into your filthy beds. Tomorrow is sheet exchange. I will nominate two of you to get all of the sheets and pillow cases together and then, get them down to the BQMS stores in the morning. I still expect your blankets to be folded correctly; you can still make a bed block with blankets only."

Before we could blink, the lights went out and the swinging doors finally came to rest.

"Riggers," someone said in a quiet voice.

"Shut up and go to sleep!" said someone else.

"I've got a hard-on!" said someone else.

That started everybody chuckling.

"You'd better not make a mess on those sheets! If I get nominated to do the sheet exchange tomorrow, you can exchange your own fucking sheets," said Riggers.

"Get to sleep, will you!"

It was just guesswork, as to who was saying what. Eventually we all fell asleep. I had a great night's sleep and didn't wake up until the guard flung the doors open at 0530hrs and turned on the lights.

No sooner did your feet touch the floor, you would strip your bed. You would get your two pillow cases and two sheets and put them into a trolley that was outside the room. If you had any damaged pillows or blankets, you could exchange them at the same time, as long as you had not been negligent. If that was the case, you would be made to pay for those items. The fee would be stopped out of your wages, another way of making our pay check smaller. There was a rumour doing its rounds that the assault course was now awaiting us, *no problem* I thought, *fit as a butcher's dog me.* Why didn't I guess that I would be the one to be chosen to climb over the twelve foot wall singlehandedly after everyone else had been aided? Was it because of my paranoia with everything I do is always in alphabetical order, or some other bazaar reason? I was soon to find out as we were made our way down to the mandatory assault course.

CHAPTER SIXTEEN
CHURCH PARADE

Monday morning was a normal routine day: drill, sounding and PT. The only difference now was that our mail would be available for us be picked up by ourselves from the Battery Office. This is where the Battery Clerk, Sergeant Major and BC (Battery Commander) offices would be.

As you walked in, there was a whiteboard situated on the wall in the corridor. If you had a letter, your name would be displayed on the board in highlighter. If you had two letters, it would say x2 next to it. A parcel would be displayed in the same way, except it would say parcel. In the afternoon, we were marched down to the assault course, dressed in our combat trousers and red PT vest. This was the first time we had worn combat trousers. I found them very uncomfortable; cotton lining sewn into the trousers was suppose to make you feel exceptionally grateful, never worked for me, I just found them so tight against my legs. They were a lot heavier than regular Army trousers – not the sort of trousers you would want to wear on a regular basis.

Again, this was like a test of our fitness and agility, just like the cross country. We had a full house with us: TC, Sergeant Preece, Bombardier Bartlett and the two L/Bombardiers; they were there to put us through our paces. The TC was mainly there to watch his troop perform. As for the rest of the senior ranks, they were there to beast us and to teach us how to negotiate each obstacle. On arrival, I could see all of these unwelcome obstacles. The look on our faces was saying 'welcome to hell'. The first obstacle was the twelve foot wall without a brick out of place. Looking at it, I would say there was no way we could get over it without sustaining injury. How wrong could one be?

We were given a demonstration of how to get up and over the wall as a team: two men would stand at the base of the wall, with their backs pressed up against it. Then, two other men would run forward to the wall at pace; each one would then step into the hands of one of the men with his right or left foot; they would then be catapulted up at the same time grabbing the top of the wall. With all the strength you could muster you would pull yourself up onto the top of the wall, and then, you would turn your body around so that you were hanging over on your stomach, facing the rest of the team. Your job now was to pull the rest of the men over the wall after they had been catapulted up the same way.

All seemed easy and, to be honest, it wasn't that difficult. However, the question that needed to be asked was, when everybody had been catapulted up the wall, what would happen to the men standing at the base? I was soon to find out. I was brought up in the countryside, learning how to look after myself: climbing trees, jumping ditches, walking on roof tops, working on the farm... It was all kids' stuff to me; little did I know that these sorts of skills one day would stand me in good stead for this sort of thing. I could see that the senior ranks had their eyes on me.

"Wolfendale!" was the cry from Sergeant Preece. "Get your body over here; you're going to be the last one over the wall."

What the fuck! I thought. *Why me?*

It started with me being one of the men at the base; it was hard enough throwing everybody over the wall let alone getting over it on my lonesome. After catapulting Muckers, the other man that was standing at the base of the wall to the top, it was down to me to make my own way over.

I had to take a long run at the wall and try to climb the wall with some force then, stretch my arms out above my head. The two men on the top of the wall would grab my arms and try to pull me up and over the wall. I still had to climb with my feet at the same time as I was being pulled up to the top. The belt of my trousers was next to be grabbed; this was the point when I felt my squeaky voice come back; I think it is called a wedgie.

It was hard work, even by my standards. There were occasions when I would have to take two or three goes to get over the wall; however, most of the time, it was first time. It was now down to me and the two men on top of the wall to catch up with the rest of the lads. There were a couple of ditches to jump – one full of water: a four foot wall, monkey bars, a balance bar and the scramble net to finish. There were some other obstacles like pipes to go through, but the ones that I mentioned before made up the majority of the assault course. We were taught how to negotiate all the obstacles in the two hours we were there. For the first time, I felt that I had earned the right to be part of Wingate Troop. It felt that more people wanted to be my friend. I could look the senior ranks in the eye knowing, that I had earned their admiration, at least for a short while, as it could soon change.

Friday was much the same as week one. We now had our ID cards with our name, number and blood group printed next to our photos. All ID cards were to be placed in the top left hand pocket of your shirt; they were about 3" by 2" in size. We were also introduced to how to use starch on our uniforms without using too much (causing white-looking lines on your kit). You could get really sharp creases on your shirt sleeves and the front of your trousers; it would make your trousers look like they were standing to attention. We were introduced to an alternative use of aftershave: if you put a drop or two in the water that you use for bulling your boots, the result would be a deeper shine on your toe caps and, not just to make them smell better. Friday night was burger night. As usual, 'crumbs' and 'drops' could be heard in the barrack room.

Saturday morning was an early start in readiness for BSM's parade. We would fall in on the parade square and await his arrival. This parade had a little more of a twist to it than the normal parade, in respect that the BSM was on the lookout for some bodies to do fatigues over the weekend: working in the cookhouse, Sergeants' Mess, Officers' Mess, and any type of work that was required over the coming days. Basically, you were volunteering yourself by turning up on the BSM's parade.

I remember the BSM walking the ranks, getting closer to me. He had already detailed about three bodies for petty offences: fluff on your beret, a hair on your face that your razor didn't pick up, collar of your shirt not lying flat… I was feeling a little concerned as I was now face to face with him. *Do not smirk, stand still and up right, do not show him that you have no respect for his parade.* It felt he was taking an eternity to inspect me; he must have walked around me about three times before he decided he could find nothing at all wrong with my dress. I was so relieved when he went on to his next victim. At last, my bum had stopped twitching. Three ended up to be the final score that would have to do fatigues over the weekend.

We had a good ninety minutes of drill watched by the BSM, before being marched back to the block. It was about 1015hrs and we were told to get into our PT kit.

"You have a half hour break now," said Bombardier Bartlett. "I will see you outside with your football boots or trainers at 1045hrs."

Wow, I thought. *I am getting paid for playing football.* Apparently, we get paid twenty three hours and fifty nine minutes of the day; in other words, we have one minute of the day to ourselves. There was mixed feelings in the block, some of us couldn't wait to get on the field, but there were others (the ones that could blow the bugle) that looked uninterested.

"Outside, now!" was the cry from the Bombardier.

I must have been one of the first out, followed by the bugle blowers. A five minute jog to the footy pitch and then we were split into two teams. Not many people knew my passion for football, and sport in general, but they were about to find out.

I was a completely different person on a football pitch; I took no prisoners. There wasn't a blade of grass that I didn't cover. I would run twenty metres in quick time just to get the ball. Anyone caught ball watching for a split second would feel the full force of my tackle. I got a lot of praise from some of the lads as we came off the pitch and again, making a lot more new friends.

After returning back to the block, it was showers and then lunch. We would be free for the afternoon except those who got singled out on the BSM's parade for their kit not being up to standard. They would be down the cookhouse for 1400hrs, washing pots and pans, peeling potatoes and cleaning floors. They must have been feeling really down in the dumps. I felt sorry for them, but, at the same time, glad it wasn't me. I 'm pretty sure that one day my time would come.

Lying on my bed, for an hour or two in the afternoon was on my list of things to do before I die. Then, after tea, I got booked in for a game of squash with Dennis. I spent a couple of hours doing my kit, including my best boots when I noticed I had a button that had almost detached itself from the side pocket of my combat trousers; it must have happened when we were on the assault course.

"Anybody used their housewife yet?" I said. I heard a few moans and groans from some of the lads.

"What the hell is a housewife?" said someone else.

"This little green pouch," I said, as I got mine out of my locker. "I have a button that needs some attention so I think I will try it out."

I opened it up to find some sewing needles and green cotton, as well as some things I wasn't too familiar with. I had seen my mum and sisters sew various items from time to time, so was not too unfamiliar with the art of sewing a button on. I got out a needle that I thought was the size that I needed and then managed to thread the cotton through the eye with some precision. I tied a single knot at the end of the cotton and then, let the sewing begin. It all went better than I could have ever imagined; before long, the button was secured in to place. The only drawback was, I had more pricks in my finger than a second-hand dart board. A trip to the washrooms for a cool shower and then it was bed for me once more.

Sunday would normally be at the TCs disposal however, this Sunday was Church Parade. It would be about every four weeks, unless there was some special occasion like Easter Parades, Armed Forces and St George's Day, VE (Victory in Europe) day, D Day or Remembrance Day (Poppy Day). In these cases, we might be expected to attend more often than one week in four. The service was at 1100hrs. We were paraded down to the Church of St Nicholas: dressed in our lightweight trousers, shirt sleeve order and, nice shiny bulled boots. I wasn't too unfamiliar with the church as my parents made sure we went to Sunday school every Sunday morning at the local chapel. I then joined the choir at the C of E (Church of England) church about two miles up the road from where I lived.

The church was full to the rafters with senior and junior ranks: officers, junior leaders, and of course, NIGs. We all sat together as a battery in a small section of about two to three rows. We were made to take our berets off, as normal practice, and place them underneath the epaulet on our left shoulder of our shirts. We were treated to a local duet half way through the ceremony. A young, good looking female and a young, not so good looking man took to the stage and sang the 1974 Christmas hit 'Streets of London' by Ralph McTell. It was the highlight of the service. I felt mesmerised by their beautiful harmonising. Inside the church, I felt like I had been taken to a place I didn't want to leave. I felt that much closer to my home. I was daydreaming. I could almost feel all my family and friends, as if they were sitting next to me.

Outside the church, it was like another world. It felt like being imprisoned and much further away from civilisation. I thank God for those brief moments I endured in the confines of the church that stay with me forever.

At about 1200hrs, we were marched back to the block. It was lunch time, and then the afternoon was our own. Later on that evening, I took a stroll down to the NAAFI. I just needed to get out of the barrack room for a while. Steve Parry, Pete Rigby and Sam Gandy decided to join me. You could watch whatever was on TV (an episode of Hawaii Five-O was showing); you could have a game of pool if you were willing to wait. There was also a jukebox playing in the corner; 'Sugar Baby Love' by the Rubettes, 'Seasons in the Sun' by Terry Jacks, 'Billy, Don't Be a Hero' by Paper Lace and 'Devil Gate Drive' by Suzi Quatro were just some of the seven inch records in the jukebox.

It was nice just to chill out for a while with my mates. I remember Parry asking me, "Wolfie?"

"What?" I said.

"Who sang 'My Ding-a-Ling'?"

"Chuck Berry," I said, feeling intelligent. No sooner had I given him my answer, my beret was being flung across the NAAFI floor.

"What the fuck was all that about?" I said.

"You said 'Chuck Berry', so I did!" said Parry, with a kind of *I'm just doing what I am told* sort of face. A bit of a tussle broke out between us as I tried to grab his beret; it was all in good fun though however, we still had to make sure we didn't divert any attention to ourselves; the last thing we both needed was to be reported to our Troop Sergeant. This was the start of lots of pranks we would endure over the coming weeks. We all made our way back to the Recruits' Block for around 2100hrs and then got our kit ready for the morning parade. At around 2200hrs, the ROS (Regimental Orderly Sergeant) was doing his rounds.

"Right, you lot. Get your disgusting bodies into your pits. The lights will be going out in about ten minutes' time when I return."

We didn't need any second warning. We made sure we were soundly tucked up in bed before he arrived back to switch off the lights. Silence was golden all through the night; even when I occasionally woke up to turn over there wasn't a sound to be heard. If Steve and Dennis had known what lay ahead for them the next day, I'm pretty sure they would have been tossing and turning throughout the night; I believe staying in bed would have been a better option.

CHAPTER SEVENTEEN

NIGHTMARE AT THE GYM

Monday morning arrived. That meant we were now two weeks into our training. Drill and PT was getting harder. Sounding was becoming a bit of respite – just standing around for half an hour, trying to blow a bloody bugle. On the parade square: we were learning how to salute on the march, right wheels, left wheels, cartwheels, slow marching, advancing in review order, and even changing step on the march.

It wasn't long before changing step became 'change sex'. Instead of us doing a quick Ali shuffle on the command 'Change sex!' we would put our right hand on our hip and put our left hand in front of us with a kind of limp wrist action. We would all say at the same time, "Up, two – three – four – five, down, swing!" in the campest voice we could muster, and then carry on marching. This was just a joke thing that the Bombardier got us to do every now and then.

One of the PT sessions that week showed us why we shouldn't slack whilst under the command of the PTIs. The PTIs could be a nasty group of sadists if upset. They would enjoy nothing more than to see us all in pain and were particularly good at making even the fittest soldier wilt in the gym, especially during the dreaded gym assault course, where you had to work on one piece of equipment at a time; with the PTI bellowing in your ear to work harder, and ordering us to change equipment at the blow of a whistle, you made sure you didn't slack. We were all working our Army socks off, or so I thought, when one of the PTIs noticed that two of the lads weren't working to their expectations. The lads concerned were both my mates, Dennis and Steve. I am sure they both thought *Why me? Why not Wolfendale and Lynch? We are working just as hard as them.* They both looked at the PTI in horror and disbelief. There was no answering back.

"Get your arses onto the wall bars, now!" could be heard all around the gym. They were made to hang off the wall bars by their arms for the remaining ten minutes whilst the rest of us continued getting beasted. None of us dared to even so much as peek towards them or we would have been given the bar treatment as well.

Over lunch, I asked Dennis what happened after we all went for a shower.

"We got fucking beasted, that's what fucking happened." Dennis wasn't one for swearing so I knew then he was engulfed with rage; everybody has his breaking point and Dennis was close to his. He continued saying, "I thought that was the end of it when the session had finished. Instead of letting us go, and have a shower, we had our own individual PT session under the direct instruction of four PTIs. It was the longest fifteen minutes of my life where we literally, crawled out of the gym. We then had to get showered and changed and join the troop immediately for drill parade. My arms and legs were like jelly; Steve and I were marching like we were on day one of our training."

I could see that Dennis was still in a state of shock by the expression on his face. There was no way he could even raise a smile, let alone anything else. He must have been thinking, *what the hell have I volunteered for?* I do believe that at this point, if he had been given the option to stay or leave the Army, he would have chosen the latter of the two.

Also in week three, we were given our red Wingate tracksuits. This was a non-optional requirement. The cost would be taken out of our wages at the end of our half term. There was more education and, of course, our mail. Education was more to do with enhancing our knowledge of the British Army and their ranks, from Lance Bombardier to RSM, from 2nd Lieutenant to General. I suppose it was advantageous to us all; I now possessed a full knowledge of who I should and who I shouldn't salute – no more saluting the RSM for me!

As far as the mail was concerned, I was hoping for the big one. Yes: a parcel for Wolfendale. Sure enough, on Thursday after drill parade, I walked into the Battery Offices to see my name on the white board: Wolfendale parcel x 1, Wolfendale letter x 1. It felt like Christmas come early. I walked over to the small hatch of a window.

"Yes? How can I help you?" said the Battery Clerk (the rank of a full Bombardier).

"I have just seen my name on the white board," I said, with a huge smile on my face. "It says I have a letter and a parcel."

"What's your name?"

"Junior Gunner Wolfendale, Sir."

"Do I look like an officer?" he said in an angry voice.

"No, Bombardier," I said in a sulky voice.

"Then don't call me Sir. I work for a living. You can call me 'Bombardier' or 'Battery Clerk'. Do you understand?"

Is there no one I don't get a bollocking off? I thought. *All I want is my mail. Maybe no one has sent him a letter and that's why he's spitting his dummy out.*

He reluctantly handed over my parcel and letter that I had to sign for.

"Thank you, Bombardier!" I said out loudly. *Fuck off, Bombardier,* was what I was really thinking. It's amazing how good news travels fast; no sooner had I returned to the barrack room than everybody who was in the room seemed to know that there was a parcel about to enter the room.

"Wolfie!" was the cry from the room. "How're you doing mate?"

For the next few minutes, everybody was my best mate; even the senior ranks were getting in on the act.

"Wolfendale!" shouted Bombardier Bartlett. "Come with me." He escorted me to my bed at pace whilst, at the same time, telling everybody else to stay by theirs. I was ordered to open my parcel; it was full of all sorts of goodies. With it being Thursday, everybody was broke until Friday's pay day, so a chocolate biscuit or two would be like a king's ransom: In the parcel were two packets of chocolate digestives, two packets of chocolate bourbons, Smarties, Opal Fruits, Fruit Pastels, Mars bars and Picnics.

Bombardier Bartlett was first to sample my chocolate biscuits. I was his best buddy for all of two minutes. No sooner had he left the room, everybody else converged into my bed space. To be honest, I didn't mind one bit; it was a nice feeling to feel popular for a short while. I shared out my goodies with the rest of the lads before locking the remainder away in my locker for a later day. There was going to be quite a shock for the TC when, to his delight, he was to be told that he had a recruit in his troop that was as quick as anyone over the assault course, and could fly across the scramble at the speed of lighting. Now who could possibly be that brainless to even remotely think about running along the top of the net and then jump off the end without a parachute. Who could that possibly be? It was going to be like a little murder mystery among the troop until, one sunny afternoon on the assault course, all would be revealed.

CHAPTER EIGHTEEN
PARCEL FOR PARRY

On Friday afternoon, at about 1500hrs, we were marched down to see the tailor, to be measured up for our best uniforms (more noted as No. 2 dress uniform). This was the first time for a long time that I felt we were now getting closer to our passing out parade that was only three weeks away. I must admit I knew naff-all about getting measured up for a suit, I mean to say, I had never owned one before, well, at least one that would fit. It felt very personal; especially when we were all asked, what side do you dress on? Did the tailor not understand that we were just sixteen year old boys without any knowledge of what that comment meant. Bombardier Bartlett could see that we were confused by that remark and so decided to take matters into his own hand: "Get lined up in two ranks facing each other," he said "about a metre apart."

I was standing facing Riggers, staring him in the face and trying not to laugh. We were all thinking, *what the hell is all this about?* Bombardier Bartlett continued saying. "Now, I want you to bend your head forward and imagine that the person in front of you is in competition with you for the girls in your life. Take a good look at the swelling in his trousers and then tell the person in front of you which side it's hanging, in other words, 'the angle of the dangle', for those of you that can't see any sort of bulge then take a step forward and feel for yourself."

On your bike, was the thought of everyone; I had never put my hands anywhere near a penis before, apart from my own on the odd occasion, I unquestionably wasn't going to start with Riggers, even though I couldn't see his bulge. I just took a guess and told Riggers he was hanging to the left.

"Now get yourself back into single file again facing the tailor!"

As I stood in front of the tailor (you just knew what he was going to ask you), I already had a smirk on my face as I awaited the question.

"Which side to you dress on?" said the tailor.

"Right side," I said looking down at my invisible bulge.

He then got his tape measure out, which, I must admit, got me a little worried at first. I thought, *what the hell is he going to measure?*

"Inside leg 40 inches, waist: 32 inches; chest: 38 inches" said the tailor.

It was a relief when I saw him put the tape measure away without me having to expose myself.

"Thank you," said the tailor. "I have all the measurements I need. Next man, please." And so it went on until we had all been measured up for our uniforms.

We arrived back at the block about 1600hrs, giving us an hour's rest bite before tea, or so we thought. Bombardier Bartlett came into the room just as we were about to relax and said, "Get your No. 2 dress hats out!"

The hat was dark blue on top and red around the sides; it had a shiny peak attached at the front and was complete with a chin strap that was fastened around the front of the hat, just above the peak by two shiny buttons. The strap was adjustable and had to be adjusted so it would lay tight against your hat. Inside the hat, it had a kind of sweat band that was sewn into the hat itself. They could be quite uncomfortable to wear, especially when you had to stand for up to an unlimited amount of time on a military parade square.

"I am going to give you a demonstration on how to clean your hats," said Bombardier Bartlett. With our hats in hand, Bombardier Bartlett took us to the washrooms with our clothes brush in hand.

The process of cleaning your hat was called spinning. You would get your clothes brush and sprinkle water onto the soft bristles then, put the brush on the top of the hat and turn it in a kind of spinning motion, hence the word spinning. You would do this several times until you got your hat shining like the rain drops in a rainbow. Your hat was then placed on the top shelf of your locker just like a trophy that you had won. I remember stepping back about a metre from my locker and admiring my hat, thinking, *it won't be long now before my passing out parade.* I would be wearing it with smugness in front of my proud parents.

After tea, I got into my Wingate tracksuit for the first time. Considering I had never owned a tracksuit before, it made me feel like a professional sportsman. You can imagine how it must have felt to get out of your Army uniform and DMS boots. I suppose it was like coming home from work after a hard day's slog and kicking your shoes off, and relaxing with a cool glass of wine. Unfortunately, we weren't allowed any alcohol. Later on that evening it was the Friday burger van and fizzy pop again. Yes, you've guessed it: 'crumbs' and 'drops' could be heard around the room as usual; a trip to the NAAFI just to get that weekly feel of civilisation brought the evening to an end. I don't think I could have got through the week without my weekly ration.

Saturday morning was the weekly BSM's parade and, just like last week, the BSM was on the prowl for some bodies to do fatigues. Three new bodies were chosen. I thanked God again it wasn't me, although I felt my turn was just around the corner. After two hours of square bashing on the parade square, we were marched back to the Battery Block.

"I want to see you outside the Battery Block in combat trousers and red PT vest in thirty minutes' time," said Bombardier Bartlett in a stern voice. "Don't anyone be late. We will be going down to assault course. Fall out."

I wasn't too bothered about the NAAFI so I went straight to the Battery Office to see if I had any mail. *No mail for me today*, I thought as I scanned down the list; however, I did notice that there was a parcel for Steve, my mate Parry. I rushed out of the Battery Office and across the road into the Battery Block.

There was no way that Parry was getting away without anyone knowing he had a parcel full of goodies. "Parry's got a parcel!" I shouted from the top of my voice: Biscuits, chocolate sweets… we were all thinking, and we weren't wrong. Within minutes, Parry was seen by our lookout, Mr Gandy, from the Recruits' Block window. "He's just coming into the block now," said Sam. We could hear the swinging doors crashing back and forth as he entered the block; we could hear him coming up the stairs. "Parry!" we all shouted.

"Fuck off!" said Steve in a loud and serious voice, knowing that we already knew of his windfall. We all surrounded his bed space, willing him to open his gift. You could smell the sweetness of the contents seeping through the brown paper that it was wrapped in.

We were all drooling as he opened his parcel. *Bingo,* just like we thought: full of confectionary. We just had time for a quick taste of his goodies before we had to parade outside.

A quick three minute run to the assault course was just the tonic we needed to get us warmed up for what lay ahead. We had all been semi-trained in the art of how to handle all the obstacles on the assault course, so it was a case of putting our entire specialist training into action.

"Wolfendale… Muckersie! Against the wall!" was the cry from Bombardier Bartlett. *How did I know that was coming?* "The rest of you, line up. Lynch and Hatton, I want you two to be first up the wall and then when you reach the top of the wall, turn yourself around so that you're facing to the front. I then want you both to help the rest of the troop over the wall. Wolfendale, you're going to be the last one over. All understand?"

"Yes, Bombardier!" we shouted with a kind of *do we have a choice* look written all over our faces.

"Get ready!" There was a pause of silence of about five seconds before we heard, "Gooooooooooo!"

It felt like a stampede coming towards me; no sooner was I catapulting Riggers up and over the wall, I could hear Parry thundering towards me, Parry shoved his size-ten boot into the palm of my hands without any mercy. "Up you go, Sheep!" I said.

"Next!" said the Bombardier.

It was really frantic with no time to draw breath. After they had all been thrown over, there was only me and Muckers left.

"Come on then, Muckers. Your turn next," I said as I threw the huge figure of Muckers over the wall, with his size-eleven boots planted well into my stomach; I didn't even have time to say, *you bar-steward, Muckers,* before it was my turn to climb the wall. I was feeling well battered and bruised, but this was no place for losers, it sounded like a battlefield the other side of the wall. All I could hear was "Get up off the ground, Hill! Catch up with the man in front of you, Gandy. Norris, get your little scrawny body over the monkey bars, now! Don't you dare fall off," It was literally every man for himself; even though we were working as a team. At this moment in time, I wasn't too sure if I wanted to get over the wall and onto the other side. It seemed a lot calmer on my side.

With Muckers now on his way, it was my turn. For some reason, it just didn't seem normal; I mean to say, what idiot would run full pelt towards a twelve-foot brick wall? Oh well, orders are orders and follow them you must. I ran full pelt before planting my right foot firmly onto the brick wall. I managed to get enough momentum to propel my body up the wall with my stretched out hands. I was grabbed by Lynch and Hatton; they pulled me up with force and aggression that was written all over their faces. My legs were still climbing the wall to the point where my legs were now overtaking my body; folded in two is how I would describe it, either way, it was fucking painful. My legs were now over the wall, but my body was facing the ground.

"Don't let go of my arms!" I said in a loud voice. "Pull me up." I felt like I was a millisecond from being planted into the ground, head first.

With a bit of a tussle, I managed to get my body above my legs and get a firm grip with my hands on the top of the wall. It was now a case of catch up time with the rest of the troop. By time I got to the scramble net which was the last obstacle, I had caught up with the majority of the men. The scramble net was about the same height as the wall. You would climb up the net, just like you would climb a rope ladder; little tiny steps were the way to do it. Once on the top of the net the conventional way of getting over would be to do an Eskimo roll. It was about fifteen feet from one end to the other, so a few rolls and you were ready to climb down a single rope that was attached to the metal framework.

I had other ideas. Very unorthodox, I agree; however, I did it the Wolfendale way. Once on the top of the net, I just ran like a bat out of hell across the net, trying not to worry about one of my feet falling through the gaps in the netting. My wedding tackle was now on the line, it meant that slipping through the net wasn't an option. I thought; *I will cross that bridge when I have to.* It took me no more than three seconds flat to reach the other end, and then I just leaped off the top of the framework without any thought for my knees. I bent my legs and did a forward roll and then, hey presto. There were a lot of shocked faces within the ranks. I am pretty sure that they were all thinking, *I hope we aren't going to be expected to do that.*

"Wolfie, you're a fucking nutter!" was all I could hear from some of the lads, or words to that affect. It wasn't long before the word got back to the TC about my physical attack of the assault course.

We spent about an hour perfecting certain skills on the assault course before we made our way back to the Recruits' Block for showers and lunch. The weather wasn't so kind in the afternoon – showers… sometimes a little thundery – but it didn't really matter as we weren't allowed out of the barracks anyway. You would think that we would get bored, being stuck in our rooms and the close surrounding areas. Not a chance. We had so much to do, the tasks we were given would never go away.

It was nice to be able to spend more time at the cookhouse on Saturday evening, in the respect that you had nothing to rush back for. We managed to converse between each bite of food, and even have a second cup of coffee if you got caught up in an intelligent conversation for a change (one without any swear words). Swearing was not my thing, but it was the only language that a lot of my mates understood. I couldn't imagine Bombardier Bartlett saying "could you please get on parade for me Paul?"

in a soft and gentle voice, "please don't rush, we don't want you hurting yourself now do we?"

After a good night's sleep, it was down to the cookhouse at 0800hrs for my full English, washed down with a mug of tea. Again, it was nice not having to wolf it down. Some of my mates arrived in dribs and drabs and joined me at the table. The weather was a lot more presentable: sunny skies and white fluffy clouds could be seen from every part of the barracks. I had not got anything planned for the day, like a nice trip to the coast, so I made the most of the sun by sitting on the grass behind the block in my PT vest and shorts. I took my polish and got stuck into bulling my best boots. With us only being sixteen years of age it would be reasonable to think that none of us were married, in fact there were only a few that had a girlfriend back home. Why is it then when Junior Gunner Owen got confused with what the BC was asking him he said "I'm not married Sir?"

CHAPTER NINETEEN
OWEN NEEDS A HOUSEWIFE

Bombardier Bartlett arrived later on in the afternoon to inform us that there would be a BCs parade tomorrow morning at 0800hrs, everything needed to be on the ball. "God help anyone whose kit and locker layout is not up to standard. I will be back tonight at 1900hrs and I want to see you all dressed in your coveralls, standing by your beds. Make sure you inform the rest of the troop that is not here at the moment. I don't want anyone to be late, understood?"

Bang went our rest time; it was only an hour to go before tea; Sunday basically was now well and truly over.

After tea, we all arrived back at the block to get into our coveralls. This is the first time I had worn my coveralls. I didn't like them one bit. I don't know whether it was the fact that I knew it meant lots of hard graft or, the fact that they were so uncomfortable. They felt quite tight above the waist, with the fact that they were fastened with small silver press studs, and below the waist, they felt very baggy especially around the crotch area. I also think that it must have been a standard universal length in the leg department; my coveralls were about two inches too long. They kept getting stuck underneath my plimsolls, almost legging me up.

Going to the toilet was also a challenge within itself; I was completely stripped down to nothing, just to go for a tom tit. My coveralls were folded up around my ankles. I was so use to just dropping my trousers and not doing a complete strip.

At 1900hrs, we were all ready and waiting for Bombardier Bartlett to arrive. It wasn't long before he slung open the swing doors and addressed us: "Tomorrow will be the most important room inspection so far since your time here," he said in a serious voice. "Tonight, I want the whole of the block bulled-up immaculate and, ready for the BCs inspection tomorrow morning. I shall be popping in from time to time to see the progress you're making, I want this place looking fit for a king; don't let me down." Bombardier Bartlett then left us to our own devices, basically to get on with our respective room jobs.

Everyone would have to help each other; if your room job was finished, you would be expected to help out with someone else's room job. There was no room for slackers. Some of the lads were becoming quite anti with the pressure they were under. I think this was the first time I actually noticed any major aggression from one person to the next. The washrooms were just about out of bounds: "Don't anyone go into the washrooms!" was the cry. How the hell were we supposed to have a wash before we went to bed or in the morning? It was like there was an all night guard on the washrooms. We finally came to a compromise where we were allowed two sinks, one shower and one toilet until after the parade.

The dormitory floor was also out of bounds; it had been polished with a yellow coloured substance that looked like it belonged in a new born baby's nappy. The stench was just as bad. You would scoop a handful of the polish out of a large tin with your fingers and throw it onto the floor at about one metre intervals around the room, trying to make sure it didn't get onto your bed or anywhere else; getting down on your knees and rubbing it into the floor meant the jobs a gooden. Once rubbed in, you would leave it for a few minutes before getting out the huge bumpers – they were just like the brushes you would use to sweep the floor except they had a big metal foot on the end of the handle. On the bottom of the metal foot was a soft wool-like material that would be used to polish the floor. You would swing the bumper backwards and forwards with some effort almost tearing your arms out of their sockets. Occasionally, we would use a torn blanket underneath the bumper to give an extra shine to the floor; tiptoeing around the edge of the floor, trying not to erase the shine that was now beaming from the floor was a skill within its self."Keep to the left!" was shouted from the bumper brigade.

"Don't use those sinks!" said the washrooms party.

"Don't step on the stairs!" said the staircase performers.

The only safe place was on your pit; even then you would get a bollocking for not working. Basically it was a night to forget.

At 2200hrs, Bombardier Bartlett came around for the last time. We stood by our beds, dripping with sweat as he inspected the block. To be honest, and to our surprise, he was relatively pleased with the effort, just a few minor details needed attention, nothing that couldn't be sorted out in the morning. It took everybody a good hour to have a shower with the fact that they were all closed off, apart from the one we could use. We were allowed to have the lights on for an extra hour to give us time to wind down; 'Silence is golden' was the theme of the night. Not a sound could be heard from any corner of the room as the guards came to make sure the lights were being turned off. I was that knackered that my mind couldn't even sum up enough effort to have a dream.

Monday 27th May. Just less than three weeks to go before our passing out parade. We were woken up in the usual way: swinging doors crashing back and forth to get your attention and to open your eyes, then, almost at the same time, the guard would turn the lights on, which would have the adverse effect and make you close them again; if you didn't, you would be blinded. Then, with the loudest voice possible the habitual: "Hands off cocks onto socks!" was perforating our eardrums. Your eyes would be open again and your bed would get rattled: "Wakey Wakey, you lazy bastards, out of bed now." Some of us just sat on the end of our beds for a few seconds while, at the same time, rubbing our eyes which felt like they had sand in them. Next was a quick trip to the partly closed washrooms for my three 'S's: shit, shower and shave, then back to my bed space to get dressed before making my way down to the cookhouse for breakfast. I could hear the birds singing in the trees. I thought, *what are they so they happy about?* At this moment in time I was wishing I was one of them. Singing in the trees seemed like a good idea. Maybe I could have flown over the person that woke us up and shit on his head.

I arrived back at the block at about 0715hrs to all the chaos that was going on. We had about 30 minutes left to finish of all the room jobs and be standing by our beds before Bombardier Bartlett arrived: bumpers away, bed blocks made and a final dust around meant we were ready for action.

"Stand by your beds!" Was the cry, as Bombardier Bartlett walked into the room. The chain of command was now here for us all to see. If the inspection wasn't up to standard, then we would all get it in the neck. First would be the BSM, then Sergeant Preece, followed by Bombardier Bartlett, and then the buck would stop at us NIGs; getting it right was imperative.

"OK. Listen in," said Bombardier Bartlett. "When the BC arrives, I will bring you all up to attention. The BC will then get me to stand you at ease. He will then make his way around each one of you in turn. When he approaches you, I want you to come to attention and salute the Battery Commander in the correct manner. At the same time, I want you to shout out your number rank and name."

Within minutes, the BC arrived, along with the TC. He was a lot stockier than the Troop Commander, and shorter. His uniform was the same, apart from he donned a crown on his epaulets (for the rank of a Major), whereas the TC donned two pips (the rank of a full Lieutenant).

"Room, shunnnn!" was the cry from Bombardier Bartlett. We all came up to attention. Bombardier Bartlett saluted the BC who, in turn, told Bombardier Bartlett to stand the men at ease.

"Stand at ease!" said the Bombardier. We all stood by our beds, staring at the person opposite, making sure we didn't make a sound; staring at your roommate and not smirking was quite a difficult task.

The BC approached the first recruit that just happened to be Steve Parry. I could see the BC out of the corner of my eye inspecting Steve's locker, which was next to mine. I could hear him saying things like, "What made you join the Royal Artillery then, Junior Gunner Parry?" As simple as the question may seem, I thought, *I hope he doesn't ask me that sort of question.* I hadn't got a clue about why I joined the Royal Artillery; it was just one of my preferred options. I am pretty sure that's not the answer he would be looking for. "Thank you, Junior Gunner Parry," said the BC. I knew then that, that was the signal for me to come to attention. Within a split second I was standing to attention – right leg to the horizontal, slammed down onto the wooden floor. I could feel the shock waves shooting up my leg. I tried not to show the pain I was enduring as I saluted the BC; at the same time, saying, "24311682, Junior Gunner Wolfendale, Sir!"

The BC and the TC looked like they were joined at the hip as they both walked around the back of me to inspect my locker. I wasn't allowed to turn around unless asked to by either one of them, I just had to stand firm again staring at my roommate. The BC seemed satisfied with what he had seen so far as he walked around to the front to face me. He was that close to my face that I could smell his aftershave.

"How are you finding your time at Bramcote so far?" he asked.

I was thinking, *do I tell him the truth or do I tell him a fib?* I chose the latter; after all, that is what he wanted to hear.

"Really enjoyable, Sir," was the answer I gave, with a huge smile on my face.

"Excellent," said the BC.

I could feel the eyes of the TC and Bombardier Bartlett staring at me as I gave my answer. Their stare said it all; I didn't dare say anything derogatory unless I wanted to see the inside of the cookhouse over the following weekend.

Junior Gunner Owen was next in line.

"Name," said the BC.

"Junior Gunner Owen, Sir."

Owen had a very supple voice and was a little on the chubby side – just about the shortest in the battery, I would say. He was the sort of guy that wouldn't say boo to a goose. On inspection, Junior Gunner Owen didn't notice (and neither did any of his mates) that he was deficient one of his shirt buttons, just around the belly button region. It may have just popped off when he was standing to attention, we may never know however, the eagled-eyed BC was not to be fooled; after all, he wasn't the BC for nothing.

Anyway, it was spotted: "Junior Gunner, Owen, you have a button missing," *Oh my God. What would happen to him? We were thinking.* The Guardroom was the least we would expect for this offence.

We stood awaiting the outcome. After a few seconds, the BC said, "Do you not have a house wife?" (Referring to his little pouch that housed his needles and thread)

Very nervously, Owen said, "I… I'm… I am not married, Sir, I haven't even got a girlfriend."

There was no way that the rest of the troop (including myself) could keep a straight face. All you could hear was a kind of grunting noise from our mouths as we tried not to laugh. Tight lips were the order of the day. We were literally shaking as we stood by your beds.

"Keep quiet!" said Bombardier Bartlett, who was also finding it difficult not to laugh and keep a straight face.

The BC was not impressed by Owen' amusing, but honest reply, he just shook his head and continued inspecting the rest of the troop. Bombardier Bartlett made a note on the note pad he was carrying, along with all the rest of the notes he had compiled. After the last person had been inspected, we were brought up to attention again for the departure of the BC; a few minutes spent walking around the accommodation and inspecting all our hard work meant the inspection was now over. It wasn't long before he left the block and headed back to his office, just across the road. *Try not to get run over,* we were all thinking. An Army Land Rover could make quite a mess of you if it accidentally hit you. We could see the BC chatting to Sergeant Preece and Bombardier Bartlett before the obligatory saluting took place.

"Outside, now!" was the cry from Bombardier Bartlett, in a loud and stern voice.

We hardly had enough time to lock up our lockers before we were bullied into getting our arses down the stairs and line up outside in three ranks.

Everything felt so frantic. For the first time for a while, I felt so disorganised. It felt like I was back in week one of basic training.

Bombardier Bartlett, along with Sergeant Preece, were standing in front of us with their pace sticks at the ready; when I say ready, I mean ready to crack them around our heads. Sergeant Preece took the reins and addressed us: "Listen in," he said, in his deep voice. "The BC was impressed with your efforts; only three weeks into your basic training and the standard you have achieved is to be commended… But remember, these are the words from the BC and not mine or Bombardier Bartlett's."

I could feel a slight sigh of relief around the ranks, but knew we mustn't get confused with complacency; after all, Sergeant Preece as made it crystal clear, not clear, but crystal clear that these are the words from the BC and not himself or Bombardier Bartlett.

"Rigby,"

"Yes, Sergeant," said Riggers.

"Dust on the top of your locker – not acceptable," said Sergeant Preece. "Clayton!"

"Yes Sergeant,"

"Your mug is fucking disgusting. Try washing it once in a while. Owen, you idiot, we know you're not married. I am sure the BC can work that one out for himself. Wolfendale, more work needed on your best boots. Parry, you need to plug in the iron the next time you iron your lightweights. Muckersie, get yourself down to see George after this parade for a neck shave. Norris, you need to get yourself down to the BQMS stores and get a chest that will fit your shirt or, better still, get a shirt that will fit your chest."

It could have been a lot worse. There was no way we were going to get away scot free; it was like a warning to what was to come. Drill parade was next: *Left! Right! Left! Right! Left! Right! Left!* Was the cry from both Bombardier Bartlett and Sergeant Preece, who seemed to be getting more involved with our drill sessions now that our passing out parade was looming ever nearer; drill was becoming a lot more tolerable now. I suppose you could relate it to as learning to drive: difficult at first but then, when you get the concept of the basics skills required, it becomes second nature and more enjoyable. Just when we were all getting use to wearing what felt like uncomfortable Army uniforms, we were hit with; you are now going to feel even more uncomfortable. We spent hours assembling all theses bits and pieces together that seemed at the time unwarranted. I was wrong, I mean, where else would I put my magazine and two hundred fags?

CHAPTER TWENTY
ISSUE OF WEBBING

Sounding was now a thing of the past; anyone who got chosen to be part of the band (not me) would have designated times throughout the week to practise with the Trumpet Sergeant Major. There was about two or three of the troop that disobeyed Bombardier Bartlett's orders, basically those few managed to get a tune out of the bugle during the half hour that we to doing sounding. Straight after NAAFI break, we were put to good use by the senior ranks: extra drill, lectures, room jobs, haircuts, etc., and on this occasion, we were taught how to assemble our webbing. It was like trying to assemble a jigsaw puzzle that had pieces missing. We sat on our beds and laid out all of the pieces, awaiting instructions on how to connect it all together.

First was the belt: you would attach the two brass buckles, one was called the female end and one called the male end, and then, you would slide two brass slides through the ends of the belt and then slide the buckles through the ends, making sure the female buckle was on the left side and the male on the right side of the belt (very sexual). You would then fold the belt around the buckles and then clip the hook (attached to the end of the belt) into one of the small holes that were located on the belt. Your waist size would be the telling factor as to which slit you would decide to clip the hook into. Once the hook was in place, you would then slide the brass slides forward as close to the buckles as you could, thus pressing against the folded part holding the belt in place. We all stood there looking at each other as we fastened our belts; male buckle goes into female buckle. I was trying not to make any innuendoes... I mean to say, belts, webbing and straps... all we needed now was for something to be called a whip and we would be talking about a completely different subject.

One or two of us had to re-size our belt to get it to be a perfect fit. We then took them off and attached the yoke. This is the main body that went over your shoulders like braces for your trousers. It was attached to the back of your belt by two straps and also attached to the front of your belt by two adjustable straps; you could tighten the straps to suit your frame. There were also small side straps: one on the left side and one on the right side. These were also adjustable straps and could be attached, by hooks, to a clip that was on the pouches that we were yet to fit to our belts. You must remember that we could march tens of miles with our webbing and it needed to be as comfortable as we could possibly make it. There were several loops and hooks on the yoke for attaching things like picks and shovels.

Next were the two front ammunition pouches; they had two prongs at the top of the pouch and two prongs at the bottom; the prongs were on the back of the pouch and you would connect the prongs into small slits that were on the inside of the belt. There were lots of these slits in case you were required to have more than two pouches on your belt at one time. My fingers were working overtime trying to get the prongs into the slits. It was bloody hard work. The ammunition pouches were about the size of a house brick and opened up at the top with a small flap that could be easily closed and fastened with a small strap that went through a metal clip to secure it into place.

On the right of your belt was a pouch for your water bottle and mug. It was attached in the same way as the ammunition pouches. The black, hard plastic bottle reminded me of a rotund person. The mug would sit on top of the water bottle, nice and snug, with two folding metal handles for storage purposes. The handles would be used for holding the mug when needed. Around the back of the yoke, you would attach two kidney pouches, about the size of a mess tin. These could be used for your washing kit, mess tins, NBC kit, etc. You could even fit about 200 cigarettes in each pouch, for those of us that smoked.

Above the kidney pouches was your backpack, which was about the size of a rucksack. It, too, had adjusting straps. Your sleeping bag would be fastened on top of your backpack by two straps. Once the sleeping bag was in place, you would then connect the backpack to your webbing. There were two straps that would go over your shoulders and clip onto your yoke at the front. The straps could be pulled tight so that the backpack would fit snug to your back. The backpack would be used for your clothes, spare boots any extras and of course, a copy of an adult magazine was a must for the most discerning soldier.

Attached to the bottom of your kidney pouches was your poncho roll. It ran the length of your butt and was about the thickness of your arm when rolled up. It was designed for carrying your poncho, but like all the other parts of your webbing (including pouches), it's not what it's designed to do – it's what it can do. You would adapt to suit your needs unless ordered otherwise.

Once assembled, Bombardier Bartlett would come around and adjust our webbing so that we understood exactly how it should feel. It wasn't the most comfortable garment I had ever worn; however, it was something I would have to endure; I was in the Army, not the Girl Guides.

"OK. Put your webbing away and get yourselves ready for PT," said the Bombardier, with a merciless smile on his face. Within minutes we were down the gym getting beasted again: circuit training and a game of murder ball to finish the session. A war of attrition sprang to mind: all-out war was the rules of the game. First team to get the medicine ball from one end of the gym to the other and place it on the rubber mat would win; a few more bruises aches and pains to add to the ones I already had was becoming a way of life now.

After lunch, It was a pleasant relief to lie on my bed for a short while nursing my aches and pains, before the afternoon's activity. Around 1345hrs, and just before I was about to go into a coma, the battle cry from Bombardier Bartlett could be heard echoing up the stairs and into my ears: "Outside, now! With your webbing on! Come on, hurry up! Get a move on!" It was unconditional chaos trying to squeeze through the double swinging doors and down the stairs without your webbing on, but now, it was twice as difficult. We were all about a foot wider. At one point, I think I was wearing someone else's webbing, with the fact that my webbing was interlocked with theirs.

There wasn't much space between the ranks as we stood to attention on this sunny Monday afternoon. The webbing was certainly causing an issue: there seemed to be no space for my arms to rest down by my side, and my shirt felt all scrunched up and uncomfortable. It was just something we all had to get use to. We were now all still feeling a little in the dark about what the afternoon had in store for us; it was only revealed when Sergeant Preece spoke up and said, "This afternoon, you'll be issued with your personal weapon." (*Wow,* I thought.) Sergeant Preece continued: "You will be taken down to the armoury, where you'll be allocated your SLR (Self Loading Rifle) – the main weapon of a British Soldier. We will then make our way over to hangar one, where you'll be shown how to take your weapon apart and how to assemble it again." I didn't realise that we could be in severe danger of being shot-at from Sergeant Preece's married quarter. But it was soon made clear when we were told the range of the SLR rifle.

CHAPTER TWENTY-ONE
SLR RIFLE

As we made our way down to the Guardroom where the armoury was, the instructions were: "Right turn! Quick march! Left! Right! Left! Right! Left! Right! Left! " Once outside, we were told to fall out and line up in single file. One by one, we signed for our SLR: complete with a sling, two magazines and an SLR cleaning kit. These weren't your everyday sleazy magazines that we are talking about; these were like metal objects that you load your bullets into, and then attach the magazine to your rifle. On this occasion, the magazines were put into our ammunition pouches which were then fastened up, your SLR cleaning kit would be put into one of your other pouches. Next, we were shown how to attach the sling to our rifles by threading it through a clip at one end of the rifle and another clip about half way along the rifle, just before the barrel. You would then fold the sling-strap over and connect it to the sling at a position that would suit the length you required. The rifle was now ready to be carried over your right shoulder by the strap, with the barrel pointing upwards.

I was quite surprised how easy this part of assembling the strap was; even I managed to connect the strap without any issues. We made our way down to hangar one, only being able to swing our left arm. The SLR rifle was pressed up firmly against the side of our body, making sure it didn't rattle around. We finally arrived outside this massive hangar. Its huge steel doors that were already open were the first thing that struck me. The hangar itself was about the size of a couple of a football pitches and just as tall – remember, these hangars were used to house aeroplanes. I remember it being very echoing, cold and eerie. There were quite a few large type guns on wheels that I had only seen before on television while watching the Queen's birthday celebrations; apparently they were small artillery field guns, 25 pounders to be more precise. There was also a large artificial ski slope for those who wanted to take up skiing throughout the coming months.

"Fall out," was the command from Sergeant Preece. "Make your way into the hangar and line up facing towards the far wall."

We didn't have to acknowledge the order like we normally would from Sergeant Preece, like a naughty school kid who had done something wrong – we were now in possession of a British Army Rifle that could kill (no sarcasm intended). I think that alone deserved respect. We just followed his command and made our way into the hangar as ordered.

We were given a small talk on the weapon and its safety features before we were allowed to dismantle it. Holding the rifle in his hands and facing us, Sergeant Preece started to explain, "These rifles have been part of the British Army since around 1954. It uses 7.62 x 51mm NATO standard ammunition."

This didn't mean a lot to me at this moment in time, however, I listened and learned.

"It is gas operated and has a tilting breech block. It is a semi-automatic rifle and has a detachable magazine that can hold up to twenty rounds of ammunition at any one time. Its effective firing range is up to 875 metres; the distance from my married quarter to the Recruits' Block is about 350 metres. Take note: you have been warned…" said Sergeant Preece with a brutal smile on his face. "Wolfendale,"

"Yes," I said.

"This is the dangerous end," said Sergeant Preece sarcastically and pointing to the end of the barrel.

You don't say, I thought.

"This is the end that you point at your chosen enemy; however, the other end can also be just as dangerous." He was pointing to the butt. "It can make a mess of someone's face if used in the correct manner."

I could see everybody looking at each other, thinking: *I hope you have good dentist cover.*

"Take you webbing off and remove your poncho from your poncho roll. At the same time, open it up and lay it on the concrete floor in front of you."

Although this wasn't rocket science, it still took us a few minutes to complete this simple task; let's just say some of us were a little slow. We were now told to stand up with our rifle held across the front of our body, with the barrel facing the floor. One by one, Sergeant Preece and Bombardier Bartlett came around us all and showed us how to cock the weapon so they could check that there were no rounds in the chamber of the rifle. This was one of the most important safety features of the rifle that we would be expected to carry out. You would first check that your safety catch was applied and then, you would point the barrel of the rifle up at a 45 degree angle with the butt of the rifle against your body for support. On command, you would pull back a small metal handle called the cocking handle; it would then lock itself into place. It would take a lot of strength to pull it back as it was under spring pressure. Your IC (In Charge) would then check into the chamber and shout: "Clear ease springs!" You would then take off the safety catch and point the weapon down the range or, in this case, towards the wall in front of you. You would then fire the weapon and reapply the safety catch.

We were now told to lay our weapon onto our poncho, making sure not to drop it or, and believe me when I say what I'm saying, you would be dropped from the same height. We were then talked through the parts of the weapon as we dismantled it step by step. First, we had to break the barrel from the butt by flicking a catch. This would open the rifle up, which was now being held by a hinge. We would then remove the contents of the rifle: breech block slide, breech block housing, breech block, gas plug, return rod and spring. This was as far as we needed to strip the weapon down at this moment in time; firing pin and other components would come later on.

Understanding how the weapon worked was making a lot more sense now, especially since firing one pretend round of ammunition. The gas produced by the explosion would be trapped, and the force of the gas would push the return rod and spring back against the breech block. The breech block would then shoot back on a rail towards the butt. On its return, it would take another round from the magazine and into the chamber of the barrel, ready to be fired – hence semi-automatic. One round would fire and then another would replace it. There was also a part of the rifle that was called the gas regulator, which was located near where the barrel began. If your weapon was not performing like it should, and you were getting a blockage (sometimes a round would not be taking forward with the force it should, and then would become stuck in the chamber area), you would then need to adjust the gas regulator by turning the small wheel that was numbered from one to nine. It would make the hole smaller, which meant more gas would be trapped (the smaller the hole, then the more gas is trapped), which would result in the return rod being forced back with a lot more force. This would normally fix the problem; however, it didn't do much for your shoulder.

Other training we did that afternoon was to learn the contents of our SLR cleaning kit, how to load our magazine with 20 rounds, and to take rounds out of the magazine using our berets as a means to keep all our rounds together and not lose them.

In the first few stages of firing the weapon, the IC would carry out this task; later on, you were expected to do it yourself. It would be a while before we would fire the weapon, but I could see by the practical demonstration we just had, why we would not be allowed onto the firing ranges until we were fully trained. We spent most of the afternoon in the hangar, which I found really enjoyable before we were told to assemble our weapons and make our way back to the armoury. It was now the end of our working day; tea, followed by a quick stop at the NAAFI, and then back to the block for room jobs and a bit of prating around. Just before lights outs, Sam came over to my bed for a wee chat as he would say in his native tongue. "Bit worried about tomorrow, Paul."

"What's the problem, Sam?" I said feeling concerned.

"Swimming tomorrow and I'm feeling a little apprehensive about it," said Sam. "Never been a strong swimmer, in a nutshell I can't swim."

"You will be fine, mate," I said, at the same time thinking, *he's going to fuckin drown* "no one is going to drown Sam, they have qualified instructors to help you, I'm not the strongest swimmer in the world myself."

"Just hope I don't make a fool of myself," said Sam, still feeling nervous.

"Well, put it this way, Sam." "Just stay close to me, buddy, and I promise not to let you sink. Let's get some shut eye, Sam, and stop worrying, you daft bugger."

CHAPTER TWENTY-TWO
SINK OR SWIM

We were woken up on Tuesday morning to the sound of torrential rain hammering against the windows. This was the first time since arriving at Bramcote some three weeks ago that we were subjected to such elements. Typical Army: they always have a contingency plan in place in case of bad weather. It was our three-quarter length grey rain coats ('flasher Macs') that we were told to wear for the first time; although, in the case of some of the smaller lads, they looked like full length coats. We assembled quickly outside the block and were double-marched to one of the three hangars for our morning session of drill. Oh yes, there was no escaping drill, especially with our passing out parade only 17 days away.

Remarkably, by time we had finished drill the rain had stopped; there were just a few puddles lying in our way as we marched back to the block at around 1000hrs. I remember there was definitely a bigger effort to stamp your authority on the tarmac road, hoping to splash the fuck out of the person that was in close proximity to you in the ranks. The more you splashed, then the more they splashed you back. We had about six inches at the bottom of our trouser legs that were absolutely soaking wet by time we reached the block. Again, some of the shorter guys looked like they had just walked through a car wash.

I received a letter that day, or so it said on the notice board in the Battery Office. After receiving it from the Battery Clerk I made my way across the road and into the block. I put the letter under my pillow to read later at my leisure as I needed to get ready for PT; our first introduction to the swimming pool awaited our arrival. I got my blue Army issued trunks, which had white piping down the side of them and neatly folded them into my green cotton Army towel. I wasn't in any way looking forward to swimming. I could swim; however I would have rather left the swimming to the fish.

"Outside in three ranks, with your swimming kit!" said Bombardier Bartlett. "If I see so much as anyone stamping their foot in the puddles, then I will stamp my foot on their head. Understand?"

"Yes, Bombardier!" shouted my mate Sheep, expecting everybody to join in. We had minutes to get changed into our trunks before we would get a verbal bashing from the PT instructors, and to get ourselves lined up at the end of the swimming pool. I don't think there was anyone who said they couldn't swim when asked, although people like my mate Sam was 'let's say' a little bit on the shy side when it came to water. We were all told to jump in to the deep end and tread water for a short time before swimming to the other end. Some of the smart ones dived in, like Riggers, Parry and George. I jumped in almost on top of Sam, causing him to give me the daggers look. We were told to get out of the water once we had reached the other end and line up by the three-tier diving board.

"Right, one at a time, I want you to make your way up to the top diving board and jump off. I don't want anyone jumping off until I give you the word. I need to make sure it's safe before you jump in."

We were lined up like lemmings waiting to jump to their death; from the top diving board and looking down the line the queue was stretched all the way to the bottom of the metal staircase.

I could see this wasn't going to be the most enterprising thing I had ever done; however, I was thinking, *I can handle this… don't look down… just go for it.* On the other hand, Sam was as quiet as I had ever seen him. I could see the colour draining from his face with each step closer to the diving board. One or two of the so called professional gang, including my mate Riggers and George, took to diving like a duck to water. Now considering Sam was by far one of the weakest swimmers in the troop, he took it on himself to dive. Why? I have no idea. Maybe he just had one of those inexcusable moments we sometimes get from time to time. We all watched in disbelief as Sam edged forward to the end of the diving board and pointed his hands out in front of him, as if trying to say a final prayer. Within seconds, Sam sprung himself forward in to a beautiful swan dive; he was gliding so serenely towards the eagerly awaiting water until he decided to abort the dive. *Smack.* That was the sound we all heard as Sam belly-flopped. Sam was completely stunned, almost to the point of being unconscious.

We could all feel the pain and humiliation he was suffering. He was fished out of the water by the ever alert PT instructors, spluttering and coughing. The PTIs dragged him along the edge of the pool to a recovery area more suited to Sam's unfortunate crash-landing injuries. That was it for Sam. His swimming days were over until next time. It took Sam a few days to get over his escapade – not just physically, but mentally. We all continued with the lesson until we were told to get out of the pool and get changed in quick time. By the time we arrived back at the block Sam was already lying on his bed taking in a bit of Egyptian PT.

After lunch, there was no let-up: it was combat trousers and red PT vest for the assault course that seemed to be a more regular thing now. On arrival, there was already a troop on the course who was just about to leave. I could see our TC talking to a Sergeant from the other troop (2 Baker Battery). We all waited, wondering what they were chatting about. It wasn't long before we were told the news we eagerly awaited.

"Wolfendale, over here!" said the TC; I made my way over to where he was standing wondering, *what have I done now*?

"Sir," I said.

"I have a challenge for you," said the TC. "Sergeant Danson, from 2 Baker Battery, believes he has got a five-star recruit that can outpace any one on the assault course scramble net. I told him that I've got a recruit, Junior Gunner Wolfendale, who will give his lad a run for his money for certain."

Everyone from both troops were getting excited at the fact there was going to be a duel. Those not involved went over to the scramble net at the end of the course whilst the other lad and me, were brought forward and told that it was a race to get over the scramble net. The first one to touch down on the other side would be the victor. I was not looking forward to this at all, but felt I had no choice in the matter.

Lots of cheering and shouting from my mates meant that I didn't dare lose. We lined up about ten metres away from the scramble net, like a sprinter in his blocks. "Go!" was the cry as we both hit the net about the same time with my unorthodox method and his more strategic method; I was just a fraction behind as we both reached the top. Unfortunately, with the fact that he reached the top first, he did his 'Eskimo roll' across to the other side of the net, thus causing the scramble net to move and shake. It meant when I did my signature tune, which was to run as fast as I could across the top of the net, my foot went through one of the holes. There was no way back, and I had lost. I accepted defeat gracefully, but not the TC. He was a winner, and felt we should have a rematch. We would now run separately. The TC made the decision that it would be a good idea to time us both – a much fairer way to decide which troop would be the champion. It was decided that the first to go would be the other recruit from 2 Baker Battery and then, the idea was when he was clear of the scramble net, I would have my turn.

The TC took off his watch from his wrist, which had a stop watch feature on it. "On your marks, get set, go!" as he clicked the button on his watch. Twenty seconds dead, was his time as his feet hit the ground. "Right, Wolfendale. Line up," said the TC. "Are you ready?"

"Yes, Sir," I replied. (I was hardly going to say no)

"On your marks, get set, go!"

I was away before he could click his button on his watch. There was no stopping me now: I literally flew over the top this time in my unorthodox way and then jumped straight off the end of the scramble net to a rapturous applause from my Wingate mates; "12 seconds dead," said the TC now smiling. It felt like winning the Olympics, I could see all of Wingate Troop cheering in delight that I had won – not just for me or the TC, but for the troop. I felt I had made my mark with the TC, however, his view of me didn't change one bit. He always saw me as a bit of a funny guy, a clown to be more precise. I was never going to win him over; I believe if he had to choose someone he would like to go to war with, I would not be on top of his list.

We continued our training on the assault course for the next hour, before the TC called a truce. Back in the block, it was shower time. There was still a good hour to pass before tea, so I decided to lie on my bed and read the letter that I had received earlier in the day. I reached under my pillow, where it was waiting to be opened. As usual, I laid face down, trying to disengage my thoughts from everything else that was going on around me.

Dear Paul,

I hope this letter finds you well. It was nice to hear from you and to hear that you have made lots of friends. We are all getting excited about your passing out parade. Your father and I will be coming, as well as two of your sisters, Mary and Zoe – they will be coming down on the Friday evening and will be staying over in the barracks. Your father and I will be coming down on the Saturday morning with Phil in his Vauxhall Viva. The weather here is mixed at the moment; some days it rains and then other days it is beautiful sunshine. I have just put in my grocery order with John at the Mace shop. I have ordered some extra packets of biscuits for you. When they arrive on Friday, I will send them out to you.

Miss you loads,

Love,

Mum and Dad xxxxx

I could read my letters all day and all night long, on some occasions, I would get them out of my locker and read them again, just to cheer me up, if nothing else. Spinning my No. 2 Dress hat was also something I needed to do again before tea. It was starting to look nice and shiny on top and I could see my face in my peak as I held it in front of me. I had a more extended evening meal with the fact that there was a lot that had gone on lately – everybody seemed to have a tale or two to tell; 'pull up a sand bag' sprang to mind. Wednesday was just another day with basically the same routine: drill, sport and PT. The day went past unnoticed. Joining the Army is something I always wanted to do, but what came next in our training was a complete shock to us all. Milling! *what the fuck is milling*? We were all thinking as Bombardier Bartlett was about to explain about how we were about to get our heads smashed in.

CHAPTER TWENTY-THREE

MILLING

Thursday was a wakeup call. After drill, we were told that there would be a twist to our PT session today. *Interesting*, we were all thinking as we lined up outside in our red PT vests and blue shorts. "Milling," was the word we all heard from the mouth of Bombardier Bartlett as he smiled at us in a kind of ruthless way. I'm not too sure how many of us were familiar with that word; I certainly wasn't as I was waiting for clarification of what it meant. You could see that Bombardier Bartlett couldn't wait to explain to us what 'Milling' was all about. He started by saying: "The definition of the word 'Milling' means beating or thrashing, according to the dictionary. It is used in the military as part of basic training. It involves a boxing ring and two recruits beating the hell out of each other. The objective behind it is to develop and instil aggression into new recruits, just like yourselves; breaking down your conventional way of thinking before building you back up again to become soldiers."

We are going to get beaten up, I thought. We all just looked at each other with deep trepidation: knees knocking and legs shaking. *I want to go home,* I could hear in my head. None of this was explained to me at the Army Careers Office back in Crewe.

"Attennnnnntion, turn to the right in threes, Right Turn!"(I was tempted to turn to the left and leg it) this was it: we were off… *'Lambs to the slaughter'* was going through my mind. Within minutes we arrived at the gym and made our way into the sports hall as normal; a full size boxing ring greeted us as we walked through the swinging doors. I could almost smell death around the hall and the boxing ring.

"Line up in one straight line in front of the ring!" was the command:

Three PTIs, Bombardier Bartlett, Sergeant Preece, some junior ranks and the TC were all present; there was no way they were going to miss out on the most eagerly awaited event to date.

"Listen in," said one of the PT instructors. "I am now going to size you off to what I think would be an equal match." He stood there with his eyes scanning up and down the ranks until he could spot an equal match. Pointing towards me he said, "You lad, red corner!" Then, pointing towards Junior Gunner Quinn, "You lad, blue corner!"

I now knew who my opponent was. I looked across to Dave Quinn and he reciprocated with the same slight grin that I was presenting on my face. He was a room-mate; beating up my room-mate up wasn't the sort of thing I would normally do, even though I had a reputation for playground fighting at school.

It felt quite tense, waiting for everyone's name to be called out. I took more of an interest in my close mates and who they would be paired with. The PT instructor pointed towards Steve ' The Sheep' Parry and then paired him up with another one of my close buddies, George 'Jock' Lynch: Dennis Norris was paired with Tricky 'Dickey' Davies; Whiteman with Muckersie; Hatton with Slowther; Gandy with Walker; Rigby with Mark 'Yogi' Brame, and so on. We were all lined up in our respective corners, chatting nervously away, trying not to show any signs of our emotions. The first three in line were given their headgear and boxing gloves, me, well I was now looking around for an escape route; with absolutely nowhere to hide it was a case of, you just had to stand there and await your fate.

We all stared, opened-mouthed, as Junior Gunner Stuart Hatton took to the ring for his mad minute against Junior Gunner Paul Slowther. Within the first few seconds, Paul Slowther was on the floor with a haymaker of a punch from Stuart Hatton. If I wasn't nervous enough already, I certainly was now. They got Paul Slowther to his feet and escorted him out of the ring with his eyes still perplexed by the experience. Next to enter the ring were Junior Gunner Dave Whiteman and Junior Gunner Chris Muckersie. This was a bit of a mismatch, in respect that Dave Whiteman could box and Chris Muckersie would rely on his massive physique and the power of his fists. Dave Whiteman was dancing around the boxing ring like a professional, picking Chris off at will. Chris was doing his best to follow in the same footsteps as Dave, but to no avail. *If I could only catch him,* Chris was thinking, *I could lay one of my haymakers on his chin.* Unfortunately, it never happened. Dave was too quick and much too smart to get caught. A great contest though. I was just glad I wasn't fighting either of them.

After a couple more mediocre fights, it was time for Sam Gandy and Steve Walker to enter the ring. As I was watching them both climb in to the ring, I was passed my headgear and gloves from one of the previous boxers who had just fought. I could practically smell the fear in the headgear and feel the aggression in the red boxing gloves. I was now only about three minutes away from my fight as I attempted to engage with my headgear. I wasn't too unfamiliar with boxing gloves as I had a pair when I was about fourteen years old, along with a punch bag. I felt excited back then, but this was different; the punch bag didn't punch back. Steve Walker was slightly taller than Sam and it didn't take long before there was claret running down Sam's nose and onto the white canvas. To be fair, it was a great punch – right on the button. Sam was quite relieved to hear the PT instructor call time before any more damage could be inflicted on his now slightly chewed up face.

It was a stupid question I know, however, as Sam walked past me, I said, "How you feeling, buddy?" Sam stared at me with the contempt that the question deserved and just shook his head. I could see he was hacked off that he had just been subjected to a small beating and was infuriated by my stupid question.

My two buddies, Steve Parry and George Lynch, were up next – two sturdy figures. This was definitely a more equal match, as far as size went. Both were throwing punches for fun. George had got some experience behind him, which took its toll on Steve. The end of the fight saw George as the victor on points (if it were a real contest). One more fight passed before I was entering the ring. I was now experiencing what all before me had experienced, and understood how Sam must have been feeling. *What the hell*, I thought. I stared Dave in the eyes and went for it. It was so awkward, trying to knock the stuffing out of a fellow mate. To be fair, it was an even contest. Dave was mainly defensive and not offering much in the way of aggression and, at the same time, I felt reluctant to smash his brains in. I would have needed a bloody good reason to land a few unwelcome punches on his face; I just couldn't think of one in the short time we were in the ring.

I didn't have much time to get myself composed after stepping down from the boxing ring, before my mate Pete Rigby was up. "Riggers Riggers!" was the cry from his two mates. To be honest, Riggers was quite a popular man. There must have been at least three of us shouting for him. Riggers' opponent was a hefty fellow that made it seem like another mismatch. How wrong could one be: Pete got stuck in with some vicious punches introducing more claret to the now not so white canvas, I suppose this was just typical Pete carrying out an order. It was clear to see that Pete got the better of his opponent with aggression as opposed to skill. The last fight of the day saw Dennis Norris against Tricky 'Dicky' Davies. Dennis was quite a wiry person, especially with the fact that his opponent was quite solid. Dennis wasn't averse to fighting, but then again, fighting in the boxing ring is a lot different from street fighting. Every time Dennis felt so much as a boxing glove pass close to his face, the boot went in. The fight had to be stopped several times in respect that sticking the boot in wasn't what the session was about. A big cheer went up for his efforts; I believe Dennis made a few more friends in the short time he was in the ring.

I suppose we were all glad it was over as we were told to make our way outside. We were doubled back to the block for showers and then back into our short-sleeve dress. As we made our way to lunch, the topic of conversation was naturally all about the fighting. There was a sense of 'don't mess with me' from us all as we entered the cookhouse, with our scarred and reddened faces. I remember thinking; *I don't feel like a NIG anymore.* I believe getting in to the boxing ring was the best thing that could have happened to me. The phrase 'grow a pair' made more sense to me now. This was the day when the entire Wingate Troop grew a pair.

Friday, Saturday and Sunday saw much of the same things for most of us: Drill, PT, room jobs, education, bulling boots, etc. On the more relaxing side of things, there were letters, parcels, Friday night burgers, games of squash, NAAFI and, of course, a little Egyptian PT. It was now getting close to the time when we would be trying on our No.2 dress; standing in front of the mirror looking proud was a moment to savour.

CHAPTER TWENTY-FOUR
NO.2 DRESS UNIFORM

It was now Monday 3rd[d] June: week five of our training. We were now only twelve days away from our passing out parade. It was around 0715hrs with clouds looming overhead. I had just returned from breakfast. Dressed ready for the day ahead, I decided to take a look at the notice board to see what was on the agenda for the week. The main things that caught my attention as I was checking over the schedule, was Monday afternoon No. 2 dress inspection; Tuesday afternoon we would be introduced to our first session of first aid, and on Wednesday, we would be taking our first adventure out of the barracks to do our canoeing test. This meant nothing to me, apart from I knew that I would be getting wet. The rest of the week was pretty much the same: Drill, PT, sport and our second session of personal weapon training in hangar one. Locker inspections were taking a back seat now, although there was no let up in discipline and personal hygiene. In fact, the standard of our dress was now not to be questioned; we were expected to be almost flawless in our turnout. Attention to detail was at a premium: fluff on your beret, tram lines on your uniform, boots with a scuff mark on them, buttons not fastened securely, shirt collar not ironed flat, bum fluff, nasal hair or in need of a neck shave would all constitute in a firm rollicking and additional duties.

Outside the block, we would parade for our daily inspection. Bombardier Bartlett would march up and down the ranks looking for any sign of slackness from each and every one of us, hoping to find fault. However, at the same time, hoping not to. You could see by his reaction that there was a certain amount of contentment in his face. Fewer people were now getting picked up for their dress. Morning inspections would previously have taken up to half an hour, but nowadays; ten minutes would all it would take.

"Good turnout," said Bombardier Bartlett with a warm and welcome smile, which was not to be confused with complacency. "Attention! Right Turn! Quick march! Left! Right! Left! Right! Left! Right! Left! "

We were starting to look like a troop ready for a military parade.

Marching on the parade square was becoming more enjoyable instead of a chore. We would swagger around with an element of grace. There were more smoke breaks and less shouting – just stern orders that we all appreciated. At 1000hrs, it was time for NAAFI break, with no more sounding we had an extra forty minutes unless one of the senior ranks had something more interesting for us to do. Forty minutes was time enough to go to the Battery Office to see if we had any mail from our families and friends; time also to do some extra work on our uniforms. There was no mail for me that day so I just took satisfaction in watching my mates opening and reading their mail.

"Who's your letter from, Steve?" I said.

"My mum and dad," Steve said in his quiet voice. "Normal stuff: look forward to seeing you soon at the passing out parade… everyone's fine… the sheep are all looking forward to seeing you again."

"The sheep," I said. "What bloody sheep?"

"Yes. Didn't I tell you? I've a field full of them. When I go home in one week's time, I shall have my pick of about 55 sheep – spoiled for choice." This was part of the reason why I got on so well with Steve: his sense of humour and quick wit always amused me. It was now time to get into our PT kit for the daily physical bashing. *Only an hour to go before lunch*, I thought. Then it was off to the tailors for our No. 2 dress uniforms. During lunch break, I had a more serious chat with Riggers whilst sitting on his well-made bed. "Not long to go now, Pete, before we pass out."

"Can't wait," said Pete in a saddened voice. "Missing my family so much, like all the rest of us. It has been a lot tougher than I thought it would be, but well worth it. I've already met some great new friends like you and Steve Parry." I felt quite taken aback by Pete's remark.

"I know what you mean, Pete," I said, "I feel exactly the same way. It's going to be so exciting next week though. Have you got many members of your family coming?"

"My mum and dad will be attending on the Friday. Also, my eldest sister and her husband will be staying over on the Thursday night in a caravan on the windbreak," answered Pete.

"I am expecting my mum and dad," I said. "Also, two of my sisters will be coming down on the Thursday night and staying over in the accommodation that has been arranged for family and friends." *Roll on next week*, I thought.

"Outside now!" was the cry from Bombardier Bartlett. "Get a move on, Norris, or I will set Muckersie on you, understand?" I was only just in front of Dennis, so as long as I kept Dennis behind me I was safe from the clutches of Chris Muckersie. We were marched down to the tailor to collect our No. 2 dress uniforms and then marched back to the block to try them on. Stood by our beds, we took the clear film-like cover off the uniform; under the instruction of Bombardier Bartlett we started to put in on. First we coupled our Army-issued braces to the buttons at the back of our trousers, we then got in to our trousers which were so much different to our lightweight trousers; they were heavy and as stiff as cardboard, but at the same time, not uncomfortable. We then put our thick green Army socks on. This was the first time that we were given the opportunity to try on our best boots, which were twice as shiny as my normal working boots and very tight around your feet. This gave us an opportunity to work our boots-in, so they wouldn't be uncomfortable on the day of our parade. A lot of the shiny polish would crack from the upper parts of your boots as your feet were pushed tightly in to the boot. I felt like crying as I looked down and saw more polish on the floor than on my boots; lots more tiring bulling nights lay ahead.

Standing there, feeling proud, we were told to get our No. 2 dress shirts out of our lockers and try them on for the first time. It felt just like a brand new shirt that you would buy from your local retailers. With the buttons fastened, it was then time to throw the ends of our braces over our shoulders and connect them to the front of our trousers – the same way they were connected at the back. Once connected, the Bombardier would come along and adjust our braces so the length of our trousers was just touching the upper part of our boots. I had never worn braces before. I always thought they were for elderly people (like my dad) so, when I felt my trousers being pressed up against my crotch, it felt very personal and uncomfortable. Next was the tie. The tie was no more than about an inch and a half wide, made of cotton. There was one or two that had no idea how to put a tie on. Looking across to my right, I could see some of the ties looking like a hangman's noose. A few minor adjustments to our ties had us looking very stylish. All we were missing now were our jackets.

Before we put our jackets on, we had to attach our bombs and lanyard. On the collar of the jacket, you would fasten two shiny metal objects (the shape of royal artillery bombs), just like where a lady would wear her brooch. A small brass plate and clip would be placed underneath the collar to hold the bomb in place. The bomb would have to be set an angle parallel to the collar and sit firmly in place. The white lanyard would be worn on the left shoulder of the jacket. The lanyard would be looped through your epaulette and pulled tight with a white thin string-like cord. We had now earned the right to put on our No. 2 dress jacket. With an air of pride, we put on our jackets. Four shiny buttons down the front of the jacket needed to be fastened and then a cloth belt, the same colour as the uniform would be wrapped around the waist line to complete the now well-assembled jacket.

Bombardier Bartlett made his way around each and every one of us, just to make sure that our uniforms were hanging and fitting right. Occasionally, he would have to get you adjust your braces to check on the height of your trousers from your boots. Some of them looked liked they had been in an argument with your socks. Finally, we put on our hats; there was not much to check-on with the hats, apart from that we needed to be reminded that the peak goes at the front and not the back.

"OK. Put your uniforms away," said Bombardier Bartlett. "You can spend the rest of the afternoon bulling your best boots and cleaning your brass plates for your bombs. Also, there are two brass clips on the jacket that holds your belt in place; they also need cleaning. I will be back to inspect at 1900hrs."

Brushing all the cracked flaky polish off my best boots was the first thing I did. It felt like starting again from scratch; lots of polish and water coupled with some Old Spice soon had them looking like new again. They were actually looking better second time around. You tended to get a thicker layer of polish and a more mirror-like shine. Next were my back plates for my bombs. Brasso and a clean yellow duster did the trick – being careful not to get the Brasso on any of my uniform or bedding. The clips on your jacket would require you to use your button stick; sliding the stick behind the clip would protect you from getting any Brasso on your jacket. We also spent some time bulling the peak of our No. 2 dress hat and then spinning it. Time was now getting on and it was almost time for tea. Even though it had been a somewhat less energetic afternoon, I was still starving. A good hefty meal was the order of the day – mains and pudding. I could hear Parry in my ear saying, "Fat bastard, Wolfie." It was his favourite saying.

Back in the block, it was a case of getting ready for Bombardier Bartlett's inspection: No. 2 dress hat, best boots, bombs and back plates were laid out on the top of our beds, with our uniforms hanging in our lockers. 'Bullshit' is a common word used by the military and there was certainly lots of that going on when Bombardier Bartlett entered the room. We were all sat on our beds, looking busy, engrossed in bulling our boots and cleaning our brasses.

We pretended not to notice he was present. He was standing and looking at us with a kind of confusion. He would have expected us all to stand up to attention by our beds. Out of the corner of my eye, I could see that he felt that he was being intrusive… *how dare you interrupt our passion for bulling boots and cleaning our brasses!* Deep down inside, we were feeling quite smug with ourselves. For the first time in almost five weeks, we defied the urge to stand up; we were expecting a rollicking, but no. To our amazement, we heard: "Carry on what you're doing, lads!"

Bombardier Bartlett walked around us individually and spent a few minutes with each and every one of us. It wasn't so much as to inspect and give us a rollicking; it was more to educate us in the art of getting us to look our best. Next week would be our passing out parade. The inspection didn't take more than about an hour before Bombardier Bartlett departed out of the doors and back to his married quarter. We carried on for a short while, trying to get an extra shine on our boots before putting them carefully away on the top shelf of our lockers. It felt like we were handling a time-bomb as we put one boot at a time in to its designated place, making sure not to undo all our hard work.

You could feel the excitement within the ranks as we were mucking around in the washrooms, throwing water at each other and of course, also the flicking of towels was now a new thing. Some of the lads had got it to a fine art; you could hear the crack of the green half-soaked towel just before it hit your arse: "Arrggh! Fuck off, bastard! Ouch! Piss off!" was the cry from the washroom. I must have got a few whacks myself before making my way back to my bed. It was funny though; seeing people dancing around as if they were walking on a bed of nails was a show not to be missed.

After a few silly good nights – "Night, George", "Night, Dennis", "Night, Sam", "Night, Riggers", "Night, Sheep", "Baaaaa", "fuck off, Wolfendale!" – We finally closed our eyes and tried to dream of our loved ones. However, by Tuesday morning, all our childishness had disappeared. It was now time to get serious once more with what we were going to be taught next; but why was it that George thought it would be a good idea to ask Riggers if it was all right to brake his leg?

CHAPTER TWENTY-FIVE
FIRST AID

Tuesday morning brought drill and PT. We didn't get much of a break between drill and PT as the drill was more intense today; perfecting some of the more challenging moves was proving more difficult than we all expected. Bombardier Bartlett was searching for perfection and was in no mood to let us off the parade square until it was achieved. I took the opportunity to see if I had received my parcel that I was expecting from my family. Bingo. It had arrived with a letter attached to it; I suppose it saved on postage. I managed to smuggle the parcel into my locker this time without anyone knowing about it, given the fact that most of the troop were at lunch. Keeping my goodies for the trip out on Wednesday seemed like a good idea, I thought – just like when I went on a school trip and my parents would fill up my lunch bag up with all sorts of treats.

1400hrs arrived and it was time for our 'First Aid' lesson in the block's lecture room. We made our way there in an orderly fashion: two trained medics, Bombardier Bartlett, Sergeant Preece and the TC made a five man team that were going to teach us our basic 'First Aid' which would be so essential to us through our Army career.

"Take a seat and keep quiet," said Sergeant Preece, at the same time tapping his pace stick on the wooden floor. It felt like he was not interested in teaching us to cope with someone who may have a runny nose; he just wanted to get us on the parade square and drill us till we dropped.

"OK," said one of the medics. "Today, Corporal Harris and I will be teaching you the basics of 'First Aid'. When you and your buddies find yourself in places like Northern Ireland, I would hope that what you learn today and in the future might save your mates' life. *What is 'First Aid'?* You may ask yourself. 'First Aid' is the first care given to casualties before treatment by medical personnel can be made available. The objective of 'First Aid' is to stop bleeding, overcome shock, relieve pain and prevent infection. It is prioritising casualties in the event of multiple injuries: breathing, bleeding, breaks and burns are the order you would treat a casualty."

It was really interesting stuff that we were learning. I could tell from the attention we were showing that everybody was thoroughly hypnotised by what was being said. They began going on about things that you could use for a splint from your military equipment whilst on exercise or, in war type situations: they included things like your rifle, bayonet, entrenching tool, tent poles, stakes and your webbing belt for strapping. We were told to always use the casualty's field dressing and not our own – something that I would not have thought of. Knowing me, I would have used my own and then been left with the hope that if I got injured, the person who was with me may still have theirs. There was also 'First Aid' on hygiene, especially things like athlete's foot.

"Keep your feet clean," said the Corporal, "and remember, prevention is better than cure." We just all looked over to who we thought had the smelliest feet, giving them the eyes, no names mentioned. "Use Army foot powder on a daily basis and make sure you change your socks every day," the Corporal continued. There was the occasional joke, like asking what would be the treatment for a stoved-in chest? The answer was, take the stove out and treat for heartburn. The session lasted about two hours with a smoke break in between; some of the lads were asking for volunteers to burn with their cigarette lighters so that they could put their first aid skills in to practise. I think the going rate was a packet of biscuits. Not surprising no one volunteered.

Back at the block, the banter continued: "Riggers, can I break your leg?" said Jock Lynch.

"Yes, of course," said Riggers sarcastically and shaking his head. "Go and break your own fucking leg. Or, better still, break both of them!"

"Spoil sport," groaned Jock. "I thought you were my mate."

"Yes, I am," said Riggers. "But on this occasion, it's no mate." After tea, there was even more banter. I remember Parry trying to break my arm. Dennis was being sat on by Muckers; I think he was trying to stop him breathing so he could practise CPR (Cardiopulmonary Resuscitation) on Dennis's skeleton-like body. Breathing, bleeding, breaks and burns. The only one out of the four we hadn't practised was bleeding. I had this horrible thought that, whilst asleep, someone would be circumcised. I was taking no chances; I slept with my wedding tackle well between my legs all night, occasionally having to check to make sure everything was still in order. It was a nice chilled session learning all about 'First Aid' in comparison to what lay ahead; not sure whether or not hanging upside in murky water from your canoe can be classed as being insane, well, someone somewhere thought it would be a good idea.

CHAPTER TWENTY-SIX
CANOEING

Wednesday morning arrived and it was time for our first visit to the outside world since we arrived some five weeks ago. The weather was fine and sunny (thank God); not a cloud in the sky. We were dressed in our compulsory 'you will buy a' red track suit. Underneath our track suit top we wore our red PT vest and then our shiny black plimsolls to complete our dress. We had to bring along our trunks wrapped up in our green Army towel that we carried under our arms. It was such a great feeling not having to get dressed into our Army uniforms. It felt like we were going to have a lazy day at worst (chance would be a fine thing).

"Outside!" was the cry from Bombardier Bartlett. "Get outside in three ranks!" I do believe we were all thrilled by the fact we would be leaving the barracks, even though it would only be for the day. I managed to smuggle some of my goodies that I had received from my parents the day before tucked into my towel: Jammy Dodgers and Chocolate Fingers were going to be the theme of the day. I could see Sam Gandy looking over to my towel with a kind of look that said, *what the fuck have you got in there?* Once outside, we were doubled down to the Guardroom to be greeted by the big green Army bus that welcomed us at Nuneaton Railway Station. The lack of a conventional suspension fitted to the bus was no more an issue. We were now institutionalised in the art of pain. Pain is just a word. No gain without pain was the stuff we got told every time we had a PT session. There was so much activity going on as we stood there, taking in every movement that was flashing in front of our eyes. The guards were cleaning the outside of the Guardroom; officers of all ranks were entering RHQ; the occasional three quarter tonne Land Rover would enter or leave the camp and civilian workers were signing in for work at the window of the Guardroom. It was a bit like Piccadilly Circus at peak time.

As we boarded the bus, a four tonne vehicle full of canoes joined our party. It looked like a big square tent on wheels, with the flaps of the canvas open at the rear of the vehicle. These vehicles were louder than the diesel bus I use to ride on back home. Bombardier Bartlett decided that he would ride in the front of the four tonner, leaving Sergeant Preece, along with the TC and a couple of instructors, to take the bus along with all us NIGs.

"Start up and let's go!" said Sergeant Preece to the civilian driver. As we drove forward, I could see the gates being opened by the new guard who had just come on duty. Such a strange feeling came across me as we drove through the gates into civilisation. My mind was pondering thoughts of *I'm going home*. For a few seconds, I was away with the fairies until I heard Parry say in his Welsh accent, "Wolfendale! What's that you've got in your towel?"

"Nothing but my trunks," I said, feeling compromised

"Don't lie, Wolfie," said Parry. "Sam's already told me. He said he saw you put some Jammy Dodgers and Chocolate Fingers in your towel." There was no way I was getting away with keeping my luxury items to myself.

"Don't tell anyone else," I said quietly, I will share some of my chocolate with you and Sam once we get going. To be honest, I would have shared them anyway. Riggers, Dennis, George, Sam, Steve and myself had scoffed them all before we got anywhere near Leek. We turned left out of the gates, past all the married quarters that were partly hidden by the trees and a metal fence. It took us about forty five minutes to get to Leek. Rudyard Lake was our destination – just on the outskirts of the small Staffordshire town. As the bus pulled up, metres from the lake, we were told in no uncertain manner, "Off the bus, you lot, and wait by the lake until everybody is off!"

Just then, the four tonner arrived, we could all see the smirk on Bombardier Bartlett's face in the reflection of the window as the sun beat down on the windscreen. "Wingate Troop, get over here now!" said Bombardier Bartlett, pointing to the back of the four tonne vehicle. The tail gate was dropped down by the driver to allow us to get the canoes off the back; I counted about twenty canoes as they were laid out on the grass at the edge of the lake. Next came all the life jackets and whores, sorry I meant oars, along with spray decks. "Get yourselves a life jacket," said Bombardier Bartlett. We were all fighting over the best ones because some of them looked liked they had become dismantled and reassembled again with some of the essential parts missing. Bombardier Bartlett continued saying, "Now get out of your track suits and remove your red PT vest. For those of you, who maybe colour blind, ignore the word red."

Yeah, good joke, I thought. *I least I haven't got a screwed up face.*

"Now, replace it with your life jacket. Do you understand?"

"Yes, Bombardier," we all said. It felt like week one all over again. I thought all of that was behind us. I think it was just a wakeup call for us not to get too complacent. It took all of ten minutes before we were lectured on all the safety aspects.

We had already completed our swimming test a few weeks ago, so the permanent staff knew that we could all swim. They had a list in front of them of the ones that had passed. I had never been in a canoe before and the thought of getting into one didn't fill me with joy. The water was calm apart from a few ripples around the open spaces. George and I stepped forward to the edge of the water to test the temperature; George bent over and couldn't resist throwing a double handful of murky, dirty water over Steve and I, who also wanted to check out the temperature. "Bastard!" we both said at the same time. It was freezing. Steve and I were all ready thinking about revenge as we made our way back up the small bank to join our mates.

It wasn't long before we were called forward and told what was going to happen. Our names were read from the list that was carried by the instructor in the order he had them. The first six names were called out: "Slowther, Davies, Rowlands, Norris, Rigby and Gandy!" Making their way forward, I could see that Sam 'I don't like the water' Gandy, was tiptoeing his way forward to the lake well behind the other five.

"Gandy, get a move on!" was the cry from Bombardier Bartlett with an ominous smile on his face. They made their way into the uninviting cold, chilled water. "Stop there!" they were told. At this point the water level was just above their ankles. I could see Sam peering across to Riggers and Norris thinking, *that's it for me – any further and I am off.*

"OK. Now follow me," said the instructor as he turned and made his way in to the deeper parts of the lake. Waist deep and getting deeper, Sam and co continued their journey into the unknown. All six were standing with their feet firmly on the rocky sandy bottom of the lake, awaiting their next command that wasn't far away.

"Now, push off with your feet, like so!" One of the two instructors that were in the water demonstrated what they needed to do. They were now all floating on top of the water like dead flies. One of the instructors told them all to swim forward until their feet were no longer touching the bottom, until they were treading water. They were now bobbing up and down like corks in the water. I could see Sam was still petrified; however, the thought of wearing a life jacket eased the tension from his mind. A couple of minutes treading water and swimming around was all that was needed for the instructors to satisfy themselves that drowning wasn't going to happen; they were all ready for the next stage that was to get them use to the cold temperature.

"OK. Now make your way out of the lake and back onto the grass bank," said one of the instructors. Once on the bank, they were all told to get themselves a canoe of their choice. The twenty-plus canoes lay waiting for them to choose. Getting into the canoes was proving to be more difficult than I was anticipating. We were all looking on with smiles, grins, with laughter written all over our faces. Riggers looked like a professional, Norris looked undeterred and Sam looked like he was about pass out – his face was as white as fallen snow. With spry decks fastened and paddles at the ready, they were now only seconds away from the unknown.

"Right, you lot," said the instructor, looking towards us. "Get yourselves over here and give them a gentle push forward to get them floating." I took no time in running over to Sam, mainly to console him, or at least that was my first thought. I put my two hands on the back of his canoe and started pushing with all my might at first, and then more gently as the canoe started to glide along the still water.

"That's enough!" hissed Sam through his clenched teeth and, in a quiet and nervous voice. A few chosen phrases like 'shit', 'fuck', 'get me out' and 'I don't feel safe' could be heard under his breath. He was finding it difficult to get a nice balance. With his paddle at the horizontal and holding it out in front of him, Sam tried his best to not be the first to hit the cold water. He was waving the paddle from side to side like an acrobat on a tight rope.

Riggers and company took to canoeing like a duck to water with the fact that the fear factor that Sam was feeling wasn't their problem. Once they had made their way about twenty metres or so into the lake, the two instructors got the lads lined up in a kind of semi circle; "Listen in," was the cry from the instructor, "we are now going to demonstrate how to do an Eskimo roll. An Eskimo roll is the best and safest technique to recover yourself if you ever happen to capsize, it is fast and you don't have to hop out of your canoe into cold water and figure out how to empty it and get back in. There are ten different ways to perform an Eskimo roll and I and my fellow instructor will be teaching you one of them."

The instructor continued explaining the complicated but somewhat easy to understand method and then gave a demonstration; within the blink of an eye he was under the water and upright again. *Impressed* was the first thought that came to my mind as the last drops of water dripped down his face and onto the canoe. "Now it's your turn," said the instructor with a serious look on his face; I have no idea what must have been going on in the minds of the six lads as they just sat there in their canoes, awaiting their fate, I just know that I was glad I wasn't first up; Parry was having his little joke again saying things like, "Wolfie, can I have first call on your biscuits that you have left in your locker back at camp just in case you drown?"

"OK," I said, "as long as I can have first call on your best boots when you drown you moron." The banter went on for some time and caused me to lose track of what was going on in the water; we looked over the lake to see Riggers just about to perform his Eskimo roll. The instructor's last word to Riggers just before going under was, if you get into any difficulty whilst under the water then there is a toggle at the front of the spray deck, just pull it hard and it will pull the spray deck off, allowing you to slip out of the canoe – and with a bit of luck, resurface (we all glanced at each other "bit of luck"?) The instructor continued, saying, "Are you ready?"

"Yes," said Pete with a look that said, *bring it on.*

"On the count of three," shouted the instructor, one—two—three, with a little wobble at first from side to side, and then splash!!!! In he went, within a few seconds he was back on top of the water, coughing and the odd splutter or two with a few chosen words thrown in for good measure. "Well done Pete; nice one Riggers you mad bastard," could be heard from the grass bank. Dennis was the next to be called forward to execute his party trick. The thing I liked about Dennis, albeit looking scared, that he was willing to give anything ago, nothing seemed to faze him at all. "Come on, Dennis, mate," I yelled from the cheap seats. I was trying my best to encourage him, but before I got chance to offer more words of encouragement he had disappeared. All I could see now was the bottom of his canoe. I think I must have counted to at least fifteen seconds before he managed to get himself upright. "Well done, Dennis," I shouted as he was trying to get his breath back. He was now looking a proud man as he made his way over to where Riggers was. Slowther, Davies and Rowlands were all next to perform without too much difficulty, leaving Sam to go last.

Sam was called forward by the instructors: "Go, Sam, go," we all shouted; everybody knew that Sam had a total fear of water so; all though we were goading him, we were also trying to show some welcome sympathy. Sam never once took his eyes off the instructor; peripheral vision was now a thing of the past. "OK Sam take your time, said the instructor, "if you feel at any time you're in trouble then I want you to tap the top of the canoe with both hands and I will have you out in next to no time." The instructor continued by saying, "Remember the toggle at the end of the spray deck, just pull it down hard and you'll be released. Get ready Sam, I will count you down."

"Ready" said Sam, barely moving his lips.

"One—two—three—now," said the instructor; Sam looked all set for his Eskimo roll with a little wobble left, and a bigger wobble right, but just at the last minute and, at an angle of about 45 degrees Sam manoeuvred himself upright again.

"I canna do it," said Sam in his native tongue, "I canna do it, I canna do it," with his voice now getting louder. The instructor went through the procedures again just like before, giving Sam more encouragement this time.

"OK, Sam, I am now going to manoeuvre my canoe right next to yours so I will be right there for you if you get into trouble." The instructor demonstrated to Sam how quick he could get him out of the water if necessary that seemed to help Sam with his confidence.

I could feel the aggression in Sam's voice as he turned to the instructor, "Ready," said Sam, "let's go for it, before I change my fucking mind." Sam didn't even wait for the mandatory one two three; within a second Sam was under the water fighting for his life, it looked like he was having his own underwater battle as the canoe was being tossed from side-to-side. I asked Parry who was standing next to me, "Who's he fighting with?" There was only him under the water, unless he was being attacked by a creature from the deep. Sam managed to complete the task; however with a little help; as long as he could find the toggle that he was fighting with Sam was happy. Sam had made it; he emerged to a rapturous applause from all of his mates. "Well done, Sam!" You could see the camaraderie between the ranks once again as Sam was escorted out of the water for a well-earned break.

Sam wasn't the only one before lunch that didn't make the full roll unaided as there was about three or four more that needed help; to my amazement I managed to complete the roll along with my mates George and Steve. Although we still had an afternoon of enjoyment ahead of us, we still had lunch to look forward too; what we weren't expecting was to be graced by two beautiful good looking ladies taking an interest in our activities.

CHAPTER TWENTY-SEVEN
WHO'S THAT ACROSS THE ROAD

It was now lunch time and I was starving, I could have eaten a scabby horse and then gone back for the saddle; in the distance we could hear the distinctive noise that you only get from an Army Land Rover as its wheels raced along the road. Within seconds we could all see the three quarter tonne Land Rover that was delivering our lunch; we could almost taste the food from where we were standing as the vehicle approached. A six-foot wooden table was soon assembled by the driver and the co-driver; two large metal containers with battened-down lids about the size of Christmas hampers, were lifted out of the back of the Land Rover and onto the table. At this moment in time, we had no idea what was hiding under the battened-down lids. Maybe they were Christmas hampers? "OK, line up in single-file by the table," yelled Bombardier Bartlett; with no eating irons present we were all thinking it would be something like sandwiches. How wrong could we be? It was Army fish and chips wrapped up in white paper.

The smell that only comes from traditional British fish and chips was now wafting up my nose. I could feel my taste buds salivating with excitement as I was handed my portion; I sat on the grass bank with my buddies in my now warm and cosy tracksuit. It was like a picnic. We could barely contain ourselves; a tea urn and plastic cups were being brought out of the Land Rover, along with a container of sugar and plastic spoons. I laid my now wrapped-up fish and chips on the grass so I could go and get a cup of tea. "Wolfie," said George, "two sugars for me."

"Lazy toad," I said, "just watch out Parry doesn't nick my food and I will get you one."

"Cheers Wolfie." Within seconds I was back wolfing my food down my neck, swilled down with a nice cup of Rosie Lee. With time running away we just about had enough time for a short smoke break and ten minutes of relaxation before we were called forward to be told about the afternoon activities. It was actually quite enjoyable. We were all in the lake at the same time, having fun at our leisure. One of the tasks we had to do was to join all our canoes together side-by-side. We would hold onto the other person's canoe on our left and on our right; the idea behind it was to make a pontoon like bridge so as to walk across with the balance of an acrobat, or in some cases, crawl across to the other side.

Once lined up and one by one, we all had a go; there was about twenty canoes spread across the water. The lake itself would have taken about four hundred canoes to reach the other side. The person at the end of the line that was furthest into the lake would then step very gingerly out of his canoe that was being held by the person on his right. It would then be your choice either to stand upright and walk/run across or kneel down and crawl like a cat creeping up on its prey. Once completed, you would get onto the grass bank before your canoe would be brought to you by one of the instructors and then join the line again.

It was proving to be great fun with one or two falling in. Some of them were trembling like jelly fish. You could feel the weight push down on the front of your canoe as the next individual stepped onto yours. There were times when I thought I was going to capsize, that had me holding on tightly to Parry's canoe for dear life. Mr Parry and myself had already had our go with Steve taking the easy option and myself the easier-said-than-done method; ten seconds flat and I was on the bank wondering how many canoes I managed to damage in the process. As I looked towards the rest of the troop I could hear a few choice words being thrown in my direction as the lads were trying to stabilise their canoes. I looked down the line to see who was next and noticed it was our mate George. I said to Parry, "When George steps off my canoe push your canoe away from mine to form a gap."

"You can't do that," said Steve thinking I had gone mad.

"Go on Steve, it will be a laugh, "I said trying to get him to change his mind.

Steve chuckled at the thought of getting revenge on Mr Lynch and agreed it would be a good idea. "If he falls in, you can take the blame, Wolfendale," said Steve. Typical Steve – never his fault: "Wolfendale told me too," he would say. George started to scamper across the canoes with a look of; I *am doing this for bonnie Scotland. There is no way I am falling in. It is just not going to happen.* WRONG! As planned, George stepped onto my canoe. "Alright George," I said, thinking about my master plan.

"Well, aye," said George, feeling confident. I looked over to Steve exactly at the same time that George was lifting his left leg to step onto Steve's canoe.

"Push now," I whispered to Steve. The canoes parted like the Red Sea. Splash, head first went George into the murky lake. Steve and I stared at each other with a kind of guilty look that lasted for all of three seconds, just in time to see the look on George's face as he surfaced.

"Bastard," said George, shaking the water off his face.

"What?" said Steve; feeling self-satisfied with the outcome.

"Fucking twat, Wolfendale," said George. Steve and I just burst out with laughter as well as the other lads. I am sure it wouldn't be long before George would get his chance to turn the tables on Steve and myself again. A great and amusing afternoon was had by all as we were instructed to get out of the water and get back into our track suits preparing for our return journey to the barracks. Just then, I noticed a small gathering of uninvited civilians.

"Who's that over there across the road?" I said to Dennis whilst gathering my belongings together.

"I have no idea," said Dennis in an uninterested way.

"Two smartly dressed girls in their twenties at a guess," I said to Dennis, "and one lady a little older. They're staring over at us," I babbled on. Just then I saw Riggers taking an interest in the girls.

"Bloody hell!" he said, "It's my twin sisters and my mum, what the hell are they doing here?"

"Hi Peter," shouted his mum in a delightful charming voice with her arm waving frantically. Pete, or was it now Peter, didn't know what to do or say. He made his way over to where the TC was standing just by the bus. There was a short conversation that went on between Pete and the TC before Pete came back and said he had permission to go and talk to his family. "Five minutes," was the cry from the TC as he turned and looked at Pete. On return, we were all curious with lots of questions. "My twin sisters think I am talking posh," said Pete, "and my mum agrees. I'm not posh."

"Now come on Peter," said Sam in his native tongue, "compared to me and George, you have definitely got a swagger to your voice."

"Yar for sure and let me run this by you isn't normal where we come from," I said. "You are, Pete, you are posh, just take my word for it, on this occasion I have to agree with your family Peter." Pete seemed a little bemused by all our remarks.

"OK, listen in," I said to everybody in my Bombardier Bartlett type voice. "It is now official. Peter Rigby is posh. His voice has been verified my three independent parties: his twin sisters; his mother; and now all of his close friends, from now on he will be known as Posh Riggers." Pete just smiled as only Pete can as we made our way onto the bus.

About halfway down the bus and a window seat is where I parked my bum, with my mate George Lynch taking a seat next to mine. Parry and Riggers were behind us with Dennis and Sam at the front of the bus. There was lots of chitchat going on, mainly about the day we'd had, and also about the fact that we couldn't wait to get back to camp; if nothing else at least to thaw out. On the way back, one of the instructors piped up: "OK lads, listen in. Can anyone here hold a tune?" We all looked at each other with a collective frown and were thinking, a tune? The only tune I can remember were the ones I use to suck when I had a sore throat. The instructor continued: "I'm going to teach you all a typical Army song; this sort of thing goes back to as long as anyone can remember: It is there to boost morale when in conflict, cheer you up when feeling down, and improve camaraderie, nothing better than a good sing-song to keep your spirits up. I am going to teach you a little number from Des O'Connor." We all just shook our heads as we looked at each other. "Only joking," said the instructor, "and if anyone knows of any Des O'Connor songs they can get off the bus right now." I looked over my shoulder to Parry in a kind of relieved way, who to be honest, looked disappointed. That was the first time I had my doubts about Steve; *Des O'Connor fan*, I was thinking.

The instructor once again addressed us, then started to educate us in the art of singing; within minutes we had the words stuck into our minds and ready to give it a whirl.

She wore... She wore... She wore a yellow ribbon... She wore a yellow ribbon in the merry month of May-ay-ay...and if... you ask...her why the hell she wore it... She wore it for a Junior Leader far, far away...Far away, not far enough... far away, too far to stuff... She wore it for a Junior Leader far, far away.

Upon...her tits...she wore a yellow brassiere... She wore a yellow brassiere in the merry month of May-ay-ay...and if... you ask... her why the hell she wore it... She wore in for a Junior Leader far, far away... far away, not far enough ... far away, too far to stuff... She wore it for a Junior Leader far, far away.

Upon… her hips…she wore her yellow knickers… She wore her yellow knick-ers in the merry month of May-ay-ay…and if…you ask…her why the hell she wore them… She wore them for a Junior Leader far, far away… far away, not far enough… far away, too far to stuff… She wore them for a Junior Leader far, far away.

As we drove through the local towns and villages, we were certainly attract-ing the attention of all the locals doing their shopping: arms swinging, heads banging, foot tapping, we must have looked like we had escaped from a local lunatic asylum. God knows what they must have been thinking. It wasn't long before we could see the barracks in the distance; time travels so fast when you're having fun. "Keep your noise down now, lads," said the instruc-tor as we continued to yell out the tune, "We don't want the RSM thinking we have had a fun time now do we? That's not in the RSM's itinerary."

Within seconds, we all shut up and looked miserable as we entered the camp gates. "Back home," I said to George, as the sun continued to shine; past the church and then the cookhouse before the bus came to a halt out-side the Recruits' Block. With everybody now feeling jubilant with the day's activities it was time for a five minute walk to tea, a walk that found me spilling the beans to Dennis about my lack of interest in getting drunk. "So one week to go Paul before we can get down to our local for a pint of two," said Dennis.

"I'm not much of a drinker," I said to Dennis.

"Really, Paul," said Dennis, "you've never been drunk before?"

"Nar, not my thing," I said. "Prefer a glass of milk."

"Well," said Dennis, "wait till I tell the lads, pretty sure they will be inter-ested in putting that right."

"Don't you bloody dare, Dennis," I said feeling worried. I just knew deep down inside that there was no way I was going to be leaving Bramcote in ten months time without getting drunk. How right I was. In the mean time I still had to complete basic training so getting drunk was the last thing on my mind.

There was a refreshing change to Thursday morning's activities, as it was D-Day, the 6th of June. We were marched down to the beautiful church of St. Nicholas for the annual parade service to commemorate the landings on the Normandy beaches of World War Two. This was the first time that the majority of us had ever taken part in such a service. The service lasted about an hour with no one excused apart from the ones that were on essential duties. The padre took centre stage and gave us a trip down memory lane. I believe he was the rank of a Major, in a soft gentle but very clear voice he started his speech: 6th June 1944 entered history under the now legendary name of the allied landings on the beaches of Normandy. It was the most dramatic part of Operation Overlord that marked the beginning of the liberation of German-occupied Western Europe. Four years after the crushing defeat of France, Belgium and the Netherlands in the spring of 1940, the Anglo-American Allies launched Operation Overlord. The aim was to gain a foothold in Western Europe in order to defeat Nazi Germany, along with the Soviet Army on the Eastern front.

You could have heard a pin drop as he continued his chilling speech; it certainly made us understand the story of events that took place on that day and, over the upcoming months before VE Day, May 8th 1945. After a few hymns, the service was over. I felt like I wanted to stay. It felt like I was leaving my comrades behind, like when you have to say your goodbyes to a loved one at a funeral. You don't want to leave them; at the same time, there is little you can do bring them back. It didn't take long for me to be brought back to reality with Bombardier Bartlett shouting out his orders, "Left right left right left right left!" Given the fact that many troops were being marched back at the same time, it was difficult to respond to the commands. We were at times turning left at the same time trying to turn right, whoever could scream the loudest would end up with the most troops following them. I think Bombardier Bartlett had about three troops following in close order from other batteries.

Being versatile is imperative to being a soldier, however I never thought for a minute that I could find another use for my beret apart from wearing it on my head; well it was soon to be explained to us all how our Army 1157 can be used for certain tasks we would never even think about.

CHAPTER TWENTY-EIGHT
INTRODUCTION TO LIVE ROUNDS

Lunch brought an end to the morning activities before we were marched down to the Guardroom to get our personal weapon, the SLR rifle. We made our way to hangar one under the guidance of Bombardier Bartlett and Sergeant Preece, just in time to get out of the rain that was now approaching.

"Listen in," said Sergeant Preece, in his deep voice, "last week you were shown how to disable and assemble your weapon. Today you're going be tested on how quick you can load and unload your magazine of twenty rounds of 7.62 ammunition, just like you were taught the last time we were here. You'll be getting a demonstration on how to use your weapon in a safe manner: learn how to fire it, how to take aim at your chosen enemy, different firing positions, prone, standing up and kneeling positions." Wow I was thinking. We were all called forward one by one to receive a small cardboard box that was no bigger than about two to three inches square."Fall back-in and get yourselves into a semi-circle, do not, open the box until I tell you to," said Sergeant Preece; Bombardier Bartlett was keeping his beady eyes wide open for those of us who may be slightly hard of hearing. "Rigby!" shouted the Bombardier, "are you deaf?"

"No Bombardier," said Riggers.

"Then get your grubby hands away from the box and do as you're told. Put your berets on the floor in front of you and empty the box of ammunition into your beret," said Sergeant Preece, "there should be forty rounds in each box, enough to fill two magazines for those of you who find it difficult to count that far." We emptied the rounds into our berets and on the word "Go" we started to load the rounds into the magazines; there were rounds flying everywhere, which accounted for why at the end of loading our magazines some of us ended up with more rounds than we should, and others with less; I remember at least two rounds came catapulting over into my neighbourhood.

It should take about thirty seconds or so to fill your magazine on a good day, I believe it took us about a minute with a few sore fingers thrown in for good measure. "On the word 'go', I want you to unload them," said Sergeant Preece. "Make sure they stay in your beret." To unload your magazine was a lot quicker, you would take the first round out from the top of the magazine and then press the pointed end of the bullet against the other bullets that were neatly stacked in your magazine; as the magazine was spring-loaded as soon as you pressed down on the first bullet the spring would catapult the next round or rounds out. "Go" was the cry from Sergeant Preece. It was frantic, as again the rounds were finding their way into other people's berets. If you got a run on you could almost fire all twenty rounds out of your magazine in one effort in a matter of seconds; great fun was had by us all, I could even see Bombardier Bartlett grinning furtively under his breath. After a couple of goes, we were all asked to replace the rounds back into their now half-ripped boxes, which were then collected and put safely away before the next stage of our training.

There was no way at this stage into our training that they were going to allow us to have live rounds anywhere near our rifles. We were all told to stand up and put our berets back on by Sergeant Preece. He continued by telling us to hold our rifles in front of us, pointing at a 45 degree angle. We all cocked our weapons so he could walk down the rank and check we had no live rounds in the chamber of our rifle. He would walk around the back of you and tap you on the shoulder, at the same time, saying, "Clear ease springs." On that note: we had to ease the working parts forward, put the rifle in the aim position, take the safety catch off with our thumbs and ease gentle pressure on the trigger with our index fingers, until there was a click. The weapon would be now classified as safe; lowering your weapon from the aim position and placing it out in front of you on the floor, or holding your rifle down by your size with the butt of the rifle on the floor, would confirm to your instructor that your rifle was now safe.

We were now feeling comfortable with the weapon handling including, all the do's and dont's. It was now time to put all of our skills into action. We were told to get out our magazines from our webbing pouches and hold them in our left hands. Our rifles would have to be supported by putting the butt of the rifle into our right hip regions, pointing upwards and held by our right hand. The cry came, in a loud and stern voice: "With an empty magazine… LOAD"

The clicking of the magazines engaging themselves with the slot at the bottom of the rifle echoed around the hangar, drowning out the noise of the rain that was now pelting down on the hangar roof.

"Kneeling position… Down!" said Sergeant Preece. "Five rounds at your target in front, in your own time, carry on," Sergeant Preece continued to say. We took aim; I closed my left eye and squinted through my right and fired five make believe rounds. *Bang! Bang! Bang! Bang! Bang!* We said.

"Stand up when you have fired your five rounds with your rifle facing down towards the wall in front of you," said Sergeant Preece. He continued by saying, "On my command, I want you to unload your weapon and make it safe. Do you understand?"

"Yes, Sergeant!" we all cried.

"Very well, then… Unload!" I can still hear those words now ringing in my ears: Safety catch magazine off, cock the weapon three or four times, let the working parts go forward, point the weapon down the range, aim and fire, safety catch back on and stand easy. The next command would be, "For inspection, port arms!" This is where we would cock the weapon so the firing range officer would come round and check your weapon for live rounds. At the point of him checking your weapon, you would have to say in a sharp stern voice, "I have no live rounds or empty cartridge cases in my possession, Sir!" The firing range officer would then say, "Clear ease springs!" Again, you would point your weapon down the range, aim and then fire, always remembering to reapply the safety catch.

The afternoon session went on for about two hours; just enough time for the rain to ease off: we covered blockages, misfires, and even took the firing pin out of the rifle. We learned more about the foresight and rear sight and, how to adjust them; apart from taking a trip down to Kingsbury ranges that was a few miles down the road, we were ready in all respects to fire our SLR.

Later on in the block, it was lots of bulling boots; you could never get enough bull on your boots. After the first five weeks, that seemed to fly past, my boots were looking like a mountain range with attitude; at least three or four tins of cherry blossom had been used, at the same time, about one tin of polish had cracked and flaked off.

Friday and Saturday passed without too much happening, before Sunday 9th June arrived: a day of relaxation. This was our last chance to impress; I must have spent at least half of the day sorting out my kit… After all, we were now only days away from our big event. I took a walk down to the Post Office with Dennis, to post a birthday card for my father that I had bought earlier in the week. 11th June is his birthday. I said to Dennis, "It should get there for Tuesday, shouldn't it?"

"First class?" replied Dennis.

"Yes," I said. "I've stuck a three and a half pence first class stamp on the envelope."

"Should be there by tomorrow," Dennis replied. "How old is your father?"

"70," I said. This is when I explained to Dennis that I was brought up by my grandparents from the age of about one year old. I continued to say that they became my parents and I always addressed them as mum and dad. Dennis found the story very interesting as he explained more about his life. I found Dennis to be a very understanding person who would always have time for you in times of need; talking to Dennis about my family was very heart-warming. Life was feeling grand and it felt like there was nothing going to change my mood; why was it then that Bombardier Bartlett thought that having two girls in the block meant only one thing in his mind?

CHAPTER TWENTY-NINE
SISTERS IN THE BLOCK

Monday morning meant four more working days before our passing out parade. The week wasn't going to become any easier; however, the excitement within the ranks was there for us all to see. There seemed to be a sense of fulfilment to every task that was undertaken – even the ones that were on toilet fatigues were finding a tune or two to sing: "She wore, she wore, she wore a yellow ribbon," could be heard from the showers. Everybody seemed to be doing everything at double pace, as if it would bring Friday that much closer. The unavoidable Monday morning barrack room inspection took place at about 0800hrs. With the attention more focused on the week ahead, Bombardier Bartlett hurried through it; before we knew it he was up one side of the room and down the other and then telling us to get outside in three ranks.

"Listen in," said the Bombardier. "Today starts the final week of your basic recruits training; the emphasis will be on getting you ready for your Farren (name of a past serving officer) parade on Friday morning. There will be several inspections throughout the week, including a full dress rehearsal on Thursday. There may be several changes to the programme so make sure that you all listen to what is being said." His eyes stared towards Steve. "Make sure you check the notice board every day."

Monday and Tuesday went by without too many changes; however, on Wednesday, we did a full rehearsal in our short sleeve dress, complete with the Junior Leaders Band. Luckily, the weather was on the cheerful side for a refreshing change. This would be the first time that we had marched to the band. The band was positioned at the far end of the parade square, dressed in their normal Army uniforms; with the fact that the band was present, there was a lot of stop/start to our drill until it was all falling into place. It was quite amazing how having the band beating out the rhythm with their drums made it so much easier to keep in step: *Bom-bom-bom-bom-bom-er-dy-bom-dy-bom-dy-bom-dy-bom-dy-bom-bom-bom* went the rhythm. We felt so proud; we were bursting at the seams and couldn't wait for Friday.

The parade included about ten to fifteen minutes of quick marching: slow marching, right wheels, left wheels, right turns, left turns, advancing in review order, saluting to the right, but the most enduring part was standing in front of the dais where the General, or someone of similar rank, would stand; you could be stood there for at least half an hour or more without moving a muscle... The General would then inspect the troops. Many a soldier had taken a fall in the past and we would be no different. It starts off with a little swaying, in a kind of forward motion, and then swaying from side to side until: splat! You would hit the deck.

To help us along with the marching and to get some rhythm into our routine, Bombardier Bartlett taught us a type of rhyme to sing, and it worked: Left, right, left, right, boots are heavy and trousers tight, balls are swinging from left to right, left, right, left, right... It brought so much more sharpness to our drill as we shouted it out to the rhythm of our arms and legs that were now swinging in unison.

Wednesday afternoon meant we were moving from the Recruits' Block and into Wingate Block, just up the road. We had to move all our kit and bedding over, being careful not to scratch the bull off our boots. I made sure mine were covered up with a yellow duster as most of the lads did. It took about an hour to get everything sorted. Most of us were given single beds now, instead of bunk beds, in respect that some of the lads had left. I think they must have found that the Army was not for them. Luckily for me, I got a single bed: top floor, about three beds down on the right next to Riggers. Dennis was opposite me; Sheep and Sam were down the far end, and George by the door as you came in.

Later on that afternoon, we were told we would be having pay parade two days early because of our passing out parade on Friday; it was to be held in the TCs new office, he had moved in unnoticed earlier in the day. We knew this parade would include a cheque of X-amount, but we didn't know how much; it was based on when your birthday was, deductions for loss of kit and anything else that the Army could squeeze out of you. It felt like a king's ransom when I looked at my cheque: £85.47 new pence. I had never had so much money in my life. I found it difficult to drag my eyes away from what I was reading; Lloyds Bank, pay Paul Wolfendale the sum of Eighty Five Pounds 47p only. "How much did you get?" could be heard from certain individuals as they exited the TCs office and into the narrow corridor. I tucked the cheque neatly away into my now open wallet and made my way back to my bed space. I was greeted by the sight of my mates that were smiling for Britain and waving their cheques around above their heads.

Wednesday night was mostly spent chatting to one another about the ever closer well-earned break, sitting on our neatly made beds with best boots at the ready along with our lanyards, brasses and No. 2 dress hats, basically final preparation. There was always something that needed attention. Lights out was at about 2200hrs and then we all, one by one, fell asleep. I tried my dammed hardest to get to sleep, but with the thought of seeing my two sisters tomorrow for the first time in six weeks, meant my mind was too active. I was tossing and turning all night, getting up to go to the toilet and occasionally peering out of the barrack room window for the first sign of light, of the now new dawning day; I felt I could almost hear my mum once again saying, "Come on, Mary! Are you ready yet? Zoe, the train will be leaving soon… You don't want to miss it. Paul will be looking forward to seeing you. Make sure you have your train tickets and your overnight bag."

I returned to my bed and quietly wrapped the warm sheets around my body to the sound of Parry groaning. I think he must have been in a deep sheep… Sorry! I meant sleep… dreaming about something or nothing. Lots of other sounds could be heard around the room that are better off left in the barrack room.

At last, the Thursday morning guard could be heard above the chirping of the birds that were making as much noise as they could; "Out of bed, you lazy! Shower!" was the cry from the smartly dressed guard. Most of us were already up and sitting on the end of our beds, rubbing the last remaining tiredness out of our eyes before they entered the room. The ones that were still in their bed got a swift reminder of what happens when your feet don't touch the floor immediately they walked into the room, their beds were shaken up and down at the foot end like there was no tomorrow .Within seconds, everybody was out of bed and making their way to the washrooms. Back in the room, I was dressed and ready for breakfast before half of the lads had even returned from the washrooms. "Riggers," I said. "Are you coming for breakfast?"

"On my way now," said Pete.

We were joined by George and Dennis as we entered the cookhouse. Another good fry up, followed by a bowl of cornflakes, washed down with a nice sweet cup of tea was the order of the day.

At 0800hrs Bombardier Bartlett arrived at the block from his cosy married quarter: "Listen in, you lot, and that includes you, Parry. For the next hour, I want you to do any final preparations you may need to do to your No. 2 dress, including your boots and brasses. I want you standing by your beds, fully dressed at 1000hrs. You can wear your everyday boots for the full dress rehearsal today; your best boots will be worn tomorrow."

Once dressed, we spent the last ten minutes checking each other's attire before Bombardier Bartlett arrived; we were actually itching to go; kicking our heels we were just standing around waiting for the order to arrive.

"Outside, now!" shouted Bombardier Bartlett.

"Come on, lads," said the well spoken George, as he looked over his shoulder towards us all. We were walking with a kind of stiffness that you would only get from wearing our No. 2 dress; there wasn't a lot of give in the tailored uniform, which made marching more difficult.

It was, again, a stop/start parade, with everything needing to be as near to perfect as it could be. As soon as the band struck up that familiar tune that we had heard earlier in the week, we knew it was the signal to come up to attention.

"'Left... Right... Left... Right... Left... Right... Left!" could be heard as we made our way onto the parade square. There must have been around ten or more troops that were having their recruits' passing out parade. Officers and senior ranks were there in abundance, RSM and the CO included. The officers were wearing their Sam Browns and swords that they would use to salute with; their role was going to be just as important as everybody else's. Everybody needed to get it right for it to be a successful event.

The whole morning was taken up with the rehearsal and, by lunch time, we were all ready for a well-earned break; basically, if we weren't ready now, then we would never be ready.

We went back to block to get changed into our lightweights again and then it was off to lunch. It was only hours away now before I would see my two sisters Mary and Zoe. I got talking to Sam: "Well, Sam, I said, my sisters should be on the train now from Crewe; can't wait!"

"You will have to introduce me," said Sam.

"I will," I said. "I will find out whether they will be allowed in the block when they arrive."

Sam wasn't sure if any of his family would be coming to the parade; unfortunately, Sam mentioned that his mum had passed away when he was twelve years of age. I felt the grief that Sam must have been feeling as I looked into his saddened eyes. "Sorry to hear about your mum, Sam," I said with a kind of disbelief in my voice.

"No worries, Wolfie," Sam said, as if to say, *don't let my concerns spoil your day*. "I am here now and won't let anything get in my way. My father might make it for tomorrow; if he doesn't, then so be it."

It was hard to believe Sam's cavalier attitude; I would be absolutely devastated if I had none of my family attending one of the most important days of my life. Steve Parry was expecting his dad and step-mum, along with two of his sisters; Pete Rigby's family, who we had all had a sneak preview of earlier in the week, would also be attending. Pete's twin sisters would be staying over and his parents would be arriving on the Friday, just like my family. Unfortunately, there was more heartbreaking news when I spoke to George: he said that he wouldn't be travelling back up north to Scotland… he would be staying at one of the lads' houses (Stuart Hatton – one of George's friends). Apparently, there were lots of family feuds going on in his life and he felt it would be better if he made other arrangements. I admired George's strong sense of self-reliance; he joined the Army to get away from his family. I joined to make my parents proud of me. I was certainly not a mummy's boy, but on the other hand, I felt that George had a more street wise upbringing than me. Last but not least, Dennis's father, mother, sister and younger brother were all coming down from Chorley near Preston on the morning of the parade. Dennis came over to me, just before tea, to say that he had been summoned to the Guardroom straight away: "Wolfie?" he said in a worried voice.

"What's up, mate?" I said.

"I've been told I've got to go down to the Guardroom… can't think what for," said Dennis.

"Hope everything is OK," I said.

"Will find out soon," said a worried looking Dennis, at the same time, turning and making his way to the Guardroom.

"Maybe someone has reported you for kicking fuck out of Tricky Dicky Davies in the boxing ring" I said jokingly.

It was about twenty minutes before Dennis returned to the block.

"Dennis!" I shouted. "Come over here, mate, and tell me what they wanted you for!"

With his lips clinched together and staring at me in a way that I have never seen him stare before, I felt the worse.

"My mother, bless her. She has only sent me a telegram to say that she, along with my father, brother and sister will be attending tomorrow, and wishes me good luck with the parade. 'Miss you. Love you loads; can't wait to see you tomorrow'. I was bricking it, Paul. I really was," said Dennis.

I gave Dennis a man hug and said, "Thank God that's all it was, buddy. Come on, let's get down to tea."

After tea we awaited our family and friends; it wasn't long before our family members were escorted over to Wingate Block. We were all waiting outside on this fine sunny evening. It seemed so strange, seeing all these civilians in their colourful clothes, making their way over to where we were. For the past six weeks all we had seen was Army green uniforms. Within seconds, I could see Mary and Zoe among the rest of the crowd. "Over here!" I shouted, at the same time, waving my hands in the air like a cheer leader. I suppose from where they were; all they could see was a mass of Army green uniforms. Eventually, our eyes met at a distance of about twenty metres. It was a fantastic feeling, giving my sisters hugs and kisses.

"What's happened to your voice?" said Zoe.

"My voice finally broke," I said. "It broke in the first week I was here." We had so much to talk about that it was difficult to know where to start. Mary looked a little bemused by my appearance; the last time she saw me, I was her younger brother. Now she was staring at a soldier in a uniform. I think she was finding it hard to believe that I was still her little brother with a deeper voice.

"How was your journey?" I said.

"OK," said Zoe. "Apart from we forgot to get off at Nuneaton."

"What?" I said, feeling confused by my sister's remark. "How can you miss it?"

Zoe continued by saying, "It's the first time Mary and I have ever been on a train so it wasn't until we asked the conductor when will be arriving in Nuneaton that he explained we had missed our stop. We were then only minutes away from Rugby."

"So then what happened?" I said, shaking my head in disbelief.

"We got off at Rugby and caught the next train back to Nuneaton."

"How did you get from the station?" I asked.

"There was some sort of Army transport – I think it was a white mini bus that picked us up; two men in Army uniforms were shouting, 'Anyone for Bramcote, Gamecock Barracks, Junior Leaders Regiment?' I said, 'Yes, over here', so that is how we got here, otherwise we would still be at the station."

"I believe you would," I said sarcastically.

It wasn't long before I invited them into the block and into my room; the looks on the lads' faces were a picture. There was silence for a minute. Most of the lads couldn't even put a sentence together without swearing, so keeping silent seemed the thing to do. "Hi, I'm George."

"Hi, I'm Steve."

Then there was Riggers, Muckers, Dennis, Sam, Ricky the slug, Uncle Tom Cobbley and all. I was everyone's friend for as long as my sisters were by my side. It wasn't long before Bombardier Bartlett arrived in the barrack room to introduce himself to our family members; I saw his eyes almost pop out of his head as he looked at my sisters – the only problem was he didn't believe that the two good looking ladies that were standing by my side were my sisters.

"Wolfendale," he yelled. "Get outside now."

"Yes, Bombardier," I said, making my way outside.

"What are you doing with those two girls in the block?"

"They're my sisters, Bombardier," I said, still wondering what the problem was.

"Don't you fucking lie to me, Wolfendale; if you think I am going to believe you then you have another thing coming. They're good looking. What the hell do you take me for?"

"They are, Bombardier," I said still trying to convince him, "their names are Mary and Zoe."

"If I find out they're not, you will be in serious trouble; do you understand?" said Bombardier Bartlett now spiting fire. "You've got ten minutes and then I want them out of the block."

I returned to explain to my two sisters, that Bombardier Bartlett thought that I had an alternative motive; having two young and beautiful girls in the block only meant one thing as far as he was concerned. My two sisters found it quite amusing, but at the same time, felt slightly disturbed at the thought of why he thought they were there. After a little more chitchat, my sisters made their way back to their accommodation along with the rest of everyone's family and friends. We were now alone again, divorced from the thirty minutes of warmth that you only get from your family circle. A couple of hours before lights out brought the best out of everyone; there wasn't one shred of industrial language being touted around the room. It made a welcome and refreshing change. Everybody was in a merrymaking mood without the alcohol. It wasn't long before we all turned in to try and get some sleep.

Missing our slot on the parade square for one of the most important days of our lives would be unheard of. However, if you could name one person that could cause such chaos, you wouldn't go too far wrong in assuming it might me or one of my close mates 'Wrong'. In fact, I think you would be totally astonished when you found out the name of the person responsible for the near miss. I offer you that as a thought.

CHAPTER THIRTY
PASSING OUT PARADE

To my delight Friday morning finally arrived, we were all smartly out of bed for the first time for ages. There was so much excitement bouncing off the walls that we could hardly contain our feelings; in a few hours time, I would be seeing my parents for the first time in six weeks. I made my way to the washrooms for the final time, complete with wash bag and towel wrapped around my waist; teeth cleaned and then one last shave to remove the small amount of bum fluff from around my face before returning to the room.

We could wear, within reason, whatever we wanted to, to go down to breakfast as long as it was Army orientated; I decided to wear my red track-suit with plimsolls, the same as some of my other mates. Even the chef at the cookhouse had a few humble words to say: "Well done, chappies. Big day, today; hope it all goes well."

"Thanks," we said, in a kind of 'Wow, where did that come from' voice, he was human after all. I could see Riggers looking at me with a shocked look on his face.

"Yes Paul, correct, he is human, after all."

"Bet it doesn't last," said Steve. "Wait till we get back next week and he will be hitting us with his serving ladle yet again. We all laughed and got on to eating our breakfast.

Back in the block, Bombardier Bartlett had arrived before we had returned from breakfast. "Come on, you lot," he said in a cheerful but firm voice. "The weather is being kind to you today." Bombardier Bartlett just wanted to make sure everything was going to plan before he departed to get dressed into his No. 2 dress. It was around 0900hrs when Bombardier Bartlett left; his last minute instructions were: "Get yourselves ready, lads, for your big day. I will be back in about thirty minutes. That should give me enough time to inspect each and every one of you." He turned and left us to our own devices. This was it: the start of what was going to be a wonderful event. It didn't take us to long to get into our tight but well tailored uniforms; sitting down on the edge of the bed trying to put on my best boots was proving to be a task within itself, trying carefully not to crack the well bulled polish off.

Ready and stood up by my bed, along with the rest of the lads, we decided to start walking around very tentatively, occasionally peering down at our boots; God help anyone who got within a metre of each other's boots… they were our pride and joy. It felt like being at home again; instead of my sister making sure my tie was sitting correctly, it was my Army mates.

"Over here, Wolfie," was the cry from Steve. "Can I trust you to straighten my tie without choking me?"

"The best tie on parade," I said with a huge smile on my face. We were all helping each other out until nothing more could be done. Bombardier Bartlett arrived back with boots to die for – his ammunition boots were the result of many years of bulling.

"Stand by your beds," he said in a stern voice. He made his way around each and every one of us, checking for any frailties that he could find in our dress, before giving us the order to form up outside. "I dare anyone of you not to feel proud" shouted Bombardier Bartlett as we exited the room.

On this glorious sun-kissed day we made our way, tip-toeing, down the flight of stairs and onto the road outside the block; facing towards the parade square that was no more than fifty metres away and lined up getting our final instructions from the Bombardier, meant we were now only seconds away from our passing out parade. Bombardier Bartlett was milling around the ranks when, to his surprise, the Junior Leaders Regimental Royal Artillery Band struck the first notes of the tune that we would be marching to; Bombardier Bartlett who was now caught off guard, sprung from the middle of the ranks in lightning quick time, at the same time, bringing us up to attention, "Hurry up, get into step quickly" shouted Bombardier Bartlett feeling troubled that we might miss our slot. "Left Right Left Right Left Right Left" Sang Bombardier Bartlett as we were now only metres away from the square. Just before stepping on to the parade square we thankfully managed to get ourselves into step with the military band giving it their all.

"Left… Right… Left… Right… Left… Right… Left!" said the Bombardier to his relief. The marching was so crisp, we may have been caught off guard by the promptness of the band, but we were all moving in unison like a well-oiled engine.

"Right wheel!" was the command as we turned and made our way onto the parade square. Out of the corner of my right eye, I could see all our families and friends sitting down on the temporary wooden stands that had been erected; there were troops emerging from all corners of the parade square… about ten troops in all. We marched around the outside of parade square, completing one full circuit before coming to our designated spot in front of the dais and all our families. We were ordered to advance in review order; it meant we had to march fourteen paces closer to the now cheering crowd. We were standing as straight as a die with the sun beating down on us, trying not to move a muscle; every movement would have been clocked by the beady-eyed hierarchy that were all standing around the dais. I was trying to pick out my parents in the crowd that were now sitting quietly and waiting for the next part of the parade to commence. Not at chance… needle in a hay stack was the term that springs to mind. I knew they were there somewhere and that's all that mattered to me.

Within seconds, we were told to stand easy. I could see the parade being handed over to the General by the CO.

"Wingate Troop! Attention!" was the cry from Bombardier Bartlett, as the: General, CO, TC, RSM and the BSM made their way over to us. Occasionally, the General, a man to be respected, would suddenly stop at random causing the rest of the party to put on the brakes and almost crashing into each other.

"What's your name, soldier?" he asked.

"Junior Gunner Wolfendale, Sir."

"And where are you from?" The questioning continued.

"Nantwich, in Cheshire, Sir," I said.

"Are your family here today to see you pass out?"

"Yes, Sir," I replied.

"Well, they should be proud of you, Junior Gunner Wolfendale; 'congratulations' on completing your first stage of basic training."

"Thank you, Sir," I said feeling swollen with pride, whilst at the same time trying not to show any signs of emotion. The General continued his inspection from one troop to another which lasted about half an hour. We were allowed to stand easy once the General had passed us by, and then wait for the inspection to be over. I could see the General making his way back onto the dais that meant we were only moments away from passing out.

"Parade, shun!" was the cry from the RSM. The parade was then handed back to the TCs and then the Troop Sergeants and Bombardiers; the Junior

Leaders Royal Artillery Band struck up once more and we were off: Quick marching, slow marching, right wheels, left wheels and, best of all, saluting as we past the dais.

"Salute to your right! Salute!" was the cry.

Our heads cracked to the right in quick time and, at the same time, our right hands were thrown up to our peak hats. The salute lasted about ten seconds or so before the order, "Eyes front!" could be heard. I could hear myself saying, "Miss over," as my head snapped back to face forwards. We continued what I would call a lap of honour until we were given the command to right wheel. We all knew what that meant; we were marching off the parade square.

"Squad… Halt! Right turn!" said Bombardier Bartlett. We were now facing our well groomed Bombardier. "Stand easy," was his last command I remember, apart from, "Well done lads; enjoy your long awaited long weekend. I shall see you back in the block at 1800hrs on Tuesday 11th. Don't be late, get out of my sight now before I decide to cancel your leave."

There was no fall-out command. We hurriedly made our way over to the parade square whereupon we could see all our friends and family, exiting the makeshift stand. My mates were becoming a thing of the past now, as I searched for my parents and sisters, among the hundreds of people who seemed to be looking for their lost children. Just then, I got a glimpse of an elderly gentleman wearing a flat cap. I knew then that it was the unmistakeable cap of my father. My mother was close by his side, followed closely by Mary and Zoe. My father was wearing his dark brown suit and matching waistcoat; my mother was wearing her beautiful flowery skirt and blouse, not forgetting her traditional blue buttoned cardigan that was left undone on this fine sunny Friday lunch time. I was no more than about five metres away from my family before I heard my sister Zoe shout over to my parents, "There he is, Mum!" My mum and dad looked over in my direction at the same time getting ever closer. I gave my father a warm embrace; I could feel once again his whiskers on his well shaven face as I hugged him tightly. A man of few words was my father: a short look of admiration into my eyes was enough for me to understand he loved me and was proud of my achievements.

Next was a nice gentle hug with my mother. "What's happened to your voice?" she said. I explained that it had finally broken within the first week of training.

"Did you see me?" I asked.

"Yes," said Zoe. "You were on the left of the parade square, centre row, last man."

"That's right," I said. We continued chatting all the way to the cookhouse where we received our lunch; I could see my mates close by, but all their attention was now fully on their family members. Occasionally we would have a momentary look and give a brief smile, but that was about it. I said to my parents that I was now going to get changed and I would meet them outside the block in about twenty minutes.

"OK," said my mum. "Phil is waiting in the car for us in the car park."

It took me no longer than ten minutes to get changed and to say my farewells to my close buddies Steve, Pete, Sam, Dennis, George, Ricky the Slug Hill and a few others of the lads that were hanging around the block. There were a few firm handshakes and then I was away. Saying goodbye too Bramcote was going to be easy, however coming back was something I wasn't looking forward to.

CHAPTER THIRTY-ONE
BACK HOME WITH MY FAMILY

It was about a ninety-minute journey home in Phil's Vauxhall Viva. It was so nice to see signs that said 'Nantwich five miles' as we left the motorway at Junction 16. With time getting on, we decided to stop off in my beautiful town of Nantwich to deposit my cheque before the banks were closed for the weekend. I was very unfamiliar with banks and cheques, but found the cashier very helpful: "How can I help you?" the very smartly dressed lady said.

"I would like to open an account and deposit my cheque into it, please," I said proudly as I handed her the cheque.

The lady took my cheque and said, "No problem, Sir."

Sir, I thought. *I am not an officer… I am a junior leader in the Royal Artillery*! It did feel good though.

"Would you like a withdrawal on the cheque, Sir?"

There's that word again: Sir.

"Yes, please. £60, if that's OK."

I saw her reaping all these ten pounds notes from her till. *They will soon be mine,* I thought. She handed me the money: "Ten, twenty, thirty, forty, fifty, sixty pounds, Sir."

Within a matter of moments, I had sixty pounds sterling safely tucked away in my wallet. Oh my God; the most money I can ever remember having at one time was no more than a few quid.

"Would you like me to order you a cheque book, Sir?" the cashier said, still smiling through her teeth.

"Yes, please," I said that would be lovely. I filled in a few forms with all of my personal details, and that was it. I was now a prime target for the odd mugger or two that may be roaming the streets. I felt a million dollars as we made our way out of the busy town streets and out into the rural surroundings to where I lived. Nothing much had changed in the six weeks I'd been away; Patch was still on her chain and Judy was still showing her unpredictable side. All I wanted to do was feel the comforts that I had been missing for what seemed like an eternity.

My Leeds United posters were shouting my name from the bedroom so that was my first port of call. Lorimer, Bremner, Clarke, Gray… yes, they were all there. Everything was the same as I had left it. Back downstairs, my mum made a pot of tea in the tin-like pot; no tea bags – just a sieve on top of the cup was the difference between enjoying your cuppa, or to choke on the tea leaves. I hadn't any plans in place for the four days I was home, except I wanted to see my best mate Dec, nicknamed 'Tommo'. Dec lived about a mile from me, on the edge of the more residential areas of Nantwich; 140 Queens drive to be more precise, just over the canal bridge. Declan lived with his parents, along with his two brothers and two sisters, Margaret, Christine, Mark and Paul being the eldest. I believe I had the occasional kiss or two from his sister Margaret; however, that's as far as it went. I was more interested in my sport. I left it until Saturday morning before making my way to Dec's house. It was on the way to Nantwich so I killed two birds with one stone in respect that I was going to do some well deserve shopping. It was about 9.30am when I arrived at Dec's house. I knocked on the door to be greeted by no other than Margaret.

"Hi, Paul," said Margaret, in a sort of 'shocked to see you' voice. "Come in, Paul; so nice to see you."

"Thank you," I said.

Margaret made me very welcome while she went up stairs to get Declan, "Dec! Paul Wolfie is here!" screamed Margaret at the top of her voice. "Get downstairs, now!"

Margaret made her way into the living room where I was sitting comfortably in an arm chair fit for a king. "Want a brew, Paul?" she asked.

"No thanks, Margaret," I said, even though I was always told it was bad manners to refuse. "I need to get a move on; I am off into town to do some shopping."

"OK," she said. "Declan, are you coming or not? Paul's waiting!" she shouted up the stairs again.

I could hear Dec mumbling from the top of the stairs, "Yes, I'm on my way," in a quieter and more tolerable voice.

"I have just given Declan another shout, Paul."

"You don't say," I muttered to myself.

"He said he is on his way."

"No problem," I said. I heard Dec trampling down the carpeted stairs.

"Hi, mate, how are you?" said Dec with a huge smile on his face. We gave each other a gentle hug and a pat on the back.

"I'm fine, Dec," I said, "Just so glad to see you again, I'm going into town to buy some new clothes; would you like to join me?" It was an overwhelming 'yes'.

"Just gave us a couple of minutes, Paul, and I will be with you." We made our way to Nantwich, chitchatting away. Even the murky weather couldn't dampen our spirits. "So tell me: what's it like in the Army, Paul?"

I told Dec about all my mates: Sam and his fear of water, Pete Rigby's posh voice, how I met Steve on the train, Dennis (my squash partner) and not forgetting George taking a plunge in the lake. Dec was mesmerised by all my 'pull up a sand bag' stories. "Ever thought of joining, Dec?" I said.

"Never gave it much thought, Paul," said Dec. "Wouldn't mind after what you have told me. I'm not sure what I am going to do when I leave school next year."

Once in town, we made our way into the clothes shop on Pillory Street; it was so nice being able to buy basically anything I wanted: fashionable flared trousers, top of the range shirts with shirt collars bigger than donkey's ears, a couple of tank tops and new shoes.

"Would that be all?" said the assistant with a huge smile on her face. The smile became even bigger when she totalled the items up that came to a whopping £33. I think even Dec was taken by surprise, especially when I opened my wallet to pay for the goods. Dec wasn't the sort of person who would comment on the size of my wallet; he was too much of a gentleman to comment, however, he must have been thinking not only was I having a great time, but also earning plenty of money as well.

On the way back from Nantwich, we spent some time reminiscing. We became mates about six to seven years ago. Some of my brothers knew Dec's dad. Dec and I worked on the same farm for a while before Dec moved on to a chicken farm just up the road; we would play in the fields and woods that surrounded my house. We even had the occasional fight from time to time. Although Dec wasn't into his sport like me, he did have a small interest in Tottenham Hotspurs. His boss was a Stoke City fan, so occasionally he would take Dec and I to the Victoria Ground to watch the match. We spent most of our school holiday time together and, to be honest, I was now missing his company and the good times we had. For Dec to follow in my footsteps would be a dream come true; he hadn't ruled out joining the Army – he had just got no idea about his future.

On Saturday evening I decided to treat my parents to fish and chips, which was a rarity in our house: "Cod and three, Cod and four, Cod and six, all with crispy bits please," was my order. It was nice to be able to give something back to my parents now that I was earning. Sunday brought the traditional roast dinner except, this time, my father didn't need to go and gun down a rabbit. I made sure that my mum received some keep money so that she could buy a large joint of beef. Army food was amazing, but you can't beat your mum's Sunday roast.

With so much going on in such a short time, I got to see Dec once more on the Monday before I went back; just enough time to say my goodbyes: "See you in about six weeks," I said to Dec with a saddened face.

"OK. Take care of yourself, Paul."

It was difficult to believe that tomorrow I would be returning to Gamecock Barracks. To be honest, I wasn't looking forward to it. Why should I? I was having the time of my life at home, but all good things must come to an end, or so the saying goes. I was just thinking that the next time I came home; it would be for three weeks and not a paltry four days.

Tuesday morning arrived and, after saying all of my goodbyes to everyone, I made my way to Crewe to catch the 4 o'clock train to London Euston, stopping at Stafford, Nuneaton, Rugby and finally London Euston. It was just like six weeks ago except, this time; I was feeling more self assured. There was no Army bus waiting for us on this occasion, so I shared a taxi with some other recruits that were arriving back. Although arriving back didn't have me doing cartwheels, it was so nice to catch up with my new mates once more. I was also missing the TCs sarcasm; however it didn't take long for the TC to express how he saw me as we were told to choose our hobby. "It has got nothing to do with horses Wolfendale" he said laughing.

CHAPTER THIRTY-TWO
CHOOSING YOUR HOBBY

It was as if time had stood still, as I arrived back for what would be the next six weeks of basic training before seeing my family and friends again; friends, I was thinking, what's wrong with me? I have now got a complete new set of friends that I can't wait to see again. It took no more than a matter of seconds before I was presented with their smiling faces once again; walking into the block and hearing those familiar words."Wolfie," made me feel at home once more.

"Riggers," I said excitedly. "How's it going?"

"Fine," said Pete, still unpacking his belongings. "It was great spending time with my family."

"Me too," I said, "Got some new clothes, spent some time with my best mate Dec, actually, he said he's thinking of joining but he's not sure; some Saturday night pub time and then the rest of the time was spent visiting family relations."

"I wasn't looking forward to coming back" said Pete, but now I'm here it feels like this is where I belong, this is where my new friends are."

"That's exactly what I was thinking Pete" I said, apart from Dec, I don't think I will be missing many other friends, I feel this is the life for me now, upwards and onwards I say."

Steve, Dennis, George and Sam all arrived back in dribs and drabs throughout the early hours of the evening, remembering that Sam had a mighty long way to travel back from bonny Scotland. Before lights out there was only one absentee, Junior Gunner Martin Owen, we were all thinking *he's going to be in big trouble when he returns*. Just then he stepped through the door to be greeted my Bombardier Bartlett.

"Owen, get over here now!"

We all feared the worse for Martin; jail, a fine, an extra duty, maybe extra swimming lessons however, we were all wrong.

After a short ticking off from Bombardier Bartlett, it was all clear that there wasn't going to be any form of execution, his train was late getting into Nuneaton station and then he had to wait for a taxi; whether or not we believed his story didn't matter, the main thing was, that Bombardier Bartlett believed him.

I wasn't looking forward to the regimental guard and the unavoidable 0600hrs wakeup call, but no sooner was I thinking about it, it happened. The doors swung open and then came the inevitable cry of, "Wakey Wakey, out of your beds now!" *Six more weeks of this,* I was thinking… *Gordon Bennet, just give us a break, won't you?* There was no way that was going to happen; out of bed I fled and into normal Army routine.

The first day back brought our first session of pokey drill. To me it was just another form of physical training with SLR rifles; pokey drill has been around longer than the Army, it can be used as a form of punishment or just as physical endurance, on this occasion it was for the more physical side.

We lined up on the parade square and were shown various exercises; holding the rifle out in front of you with your arm fully extended for about five seconds, we then had to swing the rifle slowly and in a controlled fashion, first of all to the left and then to the right keeping your arm extended at all times. It was bloody painful to say the least. Occasionally we would relax our arms by resting the rifle butt down on the ground before trying out some new tricks; swinging your rifle around 360 degrees, all in slow motion, holding the rifle above your head and then doing squat ups with it above your head. This would be followed by your rifle down by the side of your leg and then you would have to lift the rifle up to the horizontal then, hold it out with an extended arm.

After about half an hour of pokey drill and with our arms almost to the point of dropping off, it was down to hangar one, for some more SLR training with Sergeant Preece and Bombardier Bartlett. Wednesday was now also pay day as opposed to Friday's; for some unknown reason a certain person with a little more seniority than me, decided that just because we got paid on the Wednesday before our passing out parade, he would mess around with Army routine and continue the pattern. Still… if it means getting paid earlier, who were we to complain?

"Alphabetical order," was the cry from Bombardier Bartlett.

"Get to the back, Wolfendale!" said my mate Parry with a kind of serious smile on his face, it really was annoying for two reasons, (A) that I would be last again to get my wages and (B) that Parry was right once again. £1.50p was the amount we were now trusted with, *wow* I was thinking. To be honest, it didn't make too much difference, in respect that most of us still had money in our Lloyds account; well I certainly did anyway. We were also given our Post Office savings book; it was our choice if we wanted to put money into the account or draw it out. The account had already had a few pounds in it; it was like an incentive for us to save, a learning curve in how to manage your well-earned money.

I hadn't got a problem with saving money, but I found spending it was more fun. Wednesday night brought pain and laughter around the room; I'm not too sure how it came about, but some of the lads, myself included, decided it would be a good idea to wrap someone up in a blanket and use him to bumper the floor with. About four people at a time would slide the blanket at a ferocious speed; *Crash, bang, wallop* was the pitiful sound that could be heard as the blanket collided with the metal frames of the bed. "Ouch, bastard, fucking stop now!"Could be heard with a pathetic voice, *not a chance*, deaf ears springs to mind. The more you moaned, the more you were subjected to the ever-growing pain that was running through your body, it was hilarious at times, we'd never had so much fun, we were like excited kids at a party and on the plus side; the floor was shining like a new penny.

Thursday was the day we had to choose which hobby we wanted to do, now that we had more time on our hands. We had to choose a compulsory hobby that we had to attend twice a week, initially it was on a Tuesday and a Thursday and then it would be toned downed to once a week on a Wednesday. Bombardier Bartlett came into the barrack room and read us the riot act; a slight cough to clear his throat and then, "Listen in and pay attention. I've attached a list to the notice board, it is a list of an assortment of hobbies that you can choose to do. You'll need to pick one of the hobbies as your first choice and, select a second choice just in case we can't offer you your first; we will do our best to give you your first choice where possible."

"Owen," shouted Bombardier Bartlett.

"Yes Bombardier?" could be heard in a quiet a nervous voice.

"Before you ask, knitting is not one of the choices, you puff."

"Bombardier," said Martin in *an I-know-you-are-taking-the-piss-but-I-don't-give-a-fuck* kind of voice; Bombardier Bartlett continued, "Have a look at the endless list and let me know in the morning what you have chosen."

After Bombardier Bartlett had left we stampeded our way to the notice board, like the Bombardier said, the list was endless. There was so much to choose from.

"George," was the cry from Muckers, "What do you think you'll choose?"

"Not sure," said George with a so called 'thinking look' to his face."I am looking to see if they have tossing the caber as one of the choices, but, erm, I can't seem to find it anywhere on the list."

"Tossing the what?" said Muckers with a confused look on his face.

"Never mind Muckers," said George. "It's not the kind of tossing that you're use to, anyway, what are you thinking of doing?"

"Is there anything like cage fighting on there?" asked Muckers, flexing his huge and now semi naked body.

"No" said George, "Hold on… There's something here for you mate; Barbie doll dressing, you'll be OK with that won't you?"

The banter continued throughout the night until the next morning when we were on parade. "In open order march," was the command from Bombardier Bartlett; he made his way around the ranks and one by one asked us our choice of hobby "Rigby."

"Model making Bombardier," said Pete.

Apparently, the reason Pete was so keen on model making is, that himself and his brother use to make Airfix models as a pastime; some groans could be heard within the ranks. *Model making…* we were all thinking, *whatever floats your boat Pete.*

"Gandy"

"Clay and fashion Bombardier," said Sam. I have totally no idea what that was, I'm just thinking *maybe Barbie doll dressing was on the list like George said.*

"Parry"

"Band, Bombardier," said Steve.

"Fucking Band, Parry?!" said Bombardier Bartlett, shaking his head.

"Wolfendale"

"Water polo Bombardier" I said.

"It's got nothing to do with horses Wolfendale, you have to swim," said Bombardier Bartlett. It seemed to get a laugh from most of the lads however I'm thinking, *let him have his little joke.*

"Norris."

"Table tennis"

"Good choice, Dennis," I said.

"Wolfendale"

"Yes Bombardier"

"Shut your mouth while I am talking, Lynch, Olympic Skiing." *Olympic Skiing!!!* We all just looked at George in disbelief not believing what we had heard.

"Sorry, I meant skiing."

"Slip of the tongue," said Bombardier Bartlett; twice now George has been the subject of Bombardier Bartlett's jokes. Once we had all been told what we would be doing in the spare time that we were supposed to have, Bombardier Bartlett continued saying that the list of our chosen hobbies would be published on the notice board later that day.

"You will be expected to turn up for each and every session, when you get there you'll give your name to whoever is in charge, anyone that doesn't will be classed as absent, god help anyone who doesn't turn up. Basically, it is like missing any form of military parade; you just don't do it and expect to get away with it." The list was duly put up on the notice board that evening and to everyone's amazement, we were all allocated our first choices, starting on Tuesday. There were to be a few changes in our schedule, one that would see us being let out into town on Saturday. I don't remember reading anywhere about us being allowed to get drunk; so why would two of the lads take in upon themselves to get plastered?

CHAPTER THIRTY-THREE
CHANGING PARADES

Friday brought exciting news. It was mid afternoon and we were all in the barrack room chitchatting away. Bombardier Bartlett and Sergeant Preece entered the room with the cry, "Get downstairs and into the lecture room now." No sooner said than done.

"Sounds serious," I said to anyone who was listening.

"Sounds like a bollocking," said Dennis.

"I bet it's all down to you Wolfendale," said Steve.

"On yer bike," I said.

We all made our way into the lecture room where the other half of Wingate Troop were already assembled; you could see by the way everybody was talking that we had no idea what we were going to be told in the next few minutes. Sergeant Preece and Bombardier Bartlett made their way around to the front of the lecture room with their pace stick in hand. Tap, tap, was the sound of the pace stick hitting the wooden floor. Sergeant Preece was the first to address us.

"Now you have completed your first six weeks of recruits' training, you'll be given a little more latitude and when I say little, I mean little. On Saturday, after all duties, you'll be allowed to leave the barracks in smart, civilian clothes, you'll need to book out at the Guardroom and then book back in on your return." The lecture continued.

"The guard will have the right to stop you leaving the camp if they feel you're improperly dressed. On return and no later than 2300hrs, that's 11pm to you Norris, you'll be expected to book in again if you know what's good for you. With the increase in your wages now at £1.50, you'll be able to buy lots of Dolly Mixtures," he said, looking at Parry. In other words, you're not old enough to enter any public houses.

"If there is so much as a whiff of alcohol on your breath when you return, you'll be for the high jump."

I am pretty sure that Sergeant Preece and Bombardier Bartlett had already expected the odd one or two would completely ignore their orders; we were Junior Leaders, soldiers in the British Army, and why have rules if we can't break them? I wasn't sure that being let out meant anything at all to me, after all I didn't drink and wasn't keen on Dolly Mixtures. The thought of going into the town of Nuneaton was appealing with the fact I still had about £25 left in my Lloyds account; added to the £1.50p I was now receiving each and every week would give me a total of £34, divide that by six, the number of weeks before I received another cheque, would give me a total of about £5.67 per week. Maybe I could do a bit of window shopping just to get myself away from my daily routine; it was always nice to see that there was life outside the barracks.

After Saturday morning's parade and activities, we made our way to lunch and then back to the barrack room; civilian clothes could be seen all over the room. I've never seen so many colours in the block; my brown leather elasticated bomber jacket and drain pipe type trouser along with my black shoes was my dress for the day. Everybody looked like they were getting ready for their first ever date. After checking their faces in their little square mirror and splashing on some Old Spice aftershave, they were ready to take on the streets of Nuneaton. We all left in dribs and drabs apart from a selected few who had very little interest in life. I wasn't actually performing cartwheels.

"Come on Dennis, are you ready?" I said.

"On my way now," said Dennis, still trying to tie his shoe laces into beautiful double bows. On the way to the Guardroom we met up with Steve and George in their smart attire. Riggers and Sam were nowhere to be found; they were probably already in one of the many boozers that lit up the town. Once at the Guardroom, and as instructed, we signed out. This was the first time that I had ventured any further than the steps that lead up to the open door of the Guardroom. "Name," said the Bombardier at the desk, to be honest it looked more like a counter that you would get at your local chippy without the smell of those beautiful fish and chips.

"Junior Gunner Wolfendale, Bombardier," I said slightly nervously.

"Write your number, rank and name into the book," he said. As I was writing my name, I noticed that Pete and Sam, as I thought, had already booked out about forty minutes earlier. You had to write the time against your name; I looked over my shoulder to see Dennis hiding behind me, not being able to get any closer if he tried.

"Next!" said the Bombardier in a loud and stern voice. Dennis got himself out of my jumper and signed out next to my name.

We asked the Bombardier if he could phone for a taxi, unfortunately the answer was written in his face, we just turned around and awkwardly walked out without once looking back. Outside the gates we got chatting to some more soldiers, to be frank NIGs, they informed us that the local taxi company had been informed about us going into town.

"There should be a taxi on its way," they said, "You can share one with us if you like? Save on the fare." We weren't going to say no, anything to save us a bob or two; within minutes as promised, the taxi arrived.

"Where to?" asked the bearded taxi driver as we piled in.

"Nuneaton town centre," said one of the other lads that were sitting in the front. Without so much as a word from the taxi driver, we were off like a bullet out of a gun. Time is money for these fellows. It was no more than a five-to ten-minute journey before we arrived at the town centre, "£1.20," said the taxi driver, turning his meter off; *30p each seems good value,* I was thinking. Dennis and I made our way to where the shops were, looking for anything eye-catching. It didn't take too long before I found myself in an electrical shop.

"Come on Dennis," I said, rushing into the shop; I had spotted two items of interest that I felt would be of use, a small transistor radio and a steam iron, both essential commodities.

"Ay Dennis," I said with a smile on my face, "it will be great to be able to listen to some sport on a Saturday afternoon, maybe some music from time to time."

The radio cost as much as the taxi fare complete with two batteries, the iron was a little more expensive at around £4.79; I just about had enough money on my person to pay for the iron, however it would have left me a bit skint until next pay day.

"Let's go halves on the iron," said Dennis, "that way we can both use it."

"OK," I said, "I'm all for that."

Just as we were paying I said to the shop assistant, "You know how the transistor radio comes with batteries?"

"Yes?" said the shop assistant, looking confused.

"Well does the steam iron come complete with steam?" I said humorously.

I don't think he found my sense of humor to his liking as I handed over the money; *if looks could kill* sprang to mind.

Dennis and I spent no more than a couple of hours in Nuneaton before heading back to Bramcote by public transport; on arrival we signed in as ordered and took the short walk back past the cookhouse. It was now close to tea time, you could smell the delicious food wafting out of the doors as people were making their way in and out of the dining room.

Once in the block Dennis and I grabbed our eating irons and made our way down to the cookhouse for our evening meal, it seemed just as quiet in the cookhouse as it was when we arrived back at the block after tea. The camp seemed a little deserted to say the least; having the barrack room half empty seemed a treat, you could actually have a conversation without shouting and spend a little more time on the toilet knowing that there is no one waiting to use it on the other side of the door. By 2200hrs everybody was back in the room; well, at least that's what we thought. It was about 2230hrs when Sam and Riggers came back with a tale to tell. "You'll never believe what happened," said Sam.

"Go on, what?" we all said, waiting anxiously for the evening's gossip column.

"Well," said Sam, "we were just booking in when behind us walked Barry Culf and Malcolm Rowlands looking worse for wear."

"Name?" said the Guard Commander with a stiff upper lip.

"Junior Gunner Rowlands, Bombardier."

"Sign in," said the Guard Commander at the same time looking for any sign of Malcolm being inebriated. Malcolm signed against his name as ordered and then stepped back from the desk.

"Next," said the Guard Commander looking towards Barry, "name?"

After a pause of silence and with a kind of slur to his voice;

"The same as him," Barry said, looking towards Malcolm.

We were all laughing with bewilderment; Muckers almost fell off his bed as he tried to contain his laughter.

"Then what?" shouted the lads. Sam continued to tell us…

"Don't be a smart arse, Sonny," said the Guard Commander.

"And then what?" We said

"Well…" said Sam. "The Guard Commander just looked to Pete and me and said 'What are you looking at? Get out of my face before I put my foot where the sun doesn't shine!'

"The last time we saw them they were still both in the Guardroom," said Sam. *Bloody hell,* I was thinking. Minutes later, the sound of Malcolm and Barry could be heard falling up the stairs. As they entered the room we were all intrigued to find out what had gone on.

"What happened, Barry?" shouted Muckers.

"I got— er— I got— I got fucking charged, that's what."

Wow was the feeling from around the room. For the first time since standing on the station platform some six weeks ago did I feel a sense of nervousness running through my body; I just wanted to hide under the sheets of my bed and pretend this wasn't happening; *who was going to be next, to be brought before the BC?*

We all got our heads down for a good night's sleep, expecting the worst in the morning from Bombardier Bartlett.

Sunday morning meant we could lie in bed for as long as we wanted within reason, it was about 1000hrs when we heard Bombardier Bartlett entering the block for his daily Sunday routine inspection and what should be a civil conversation, after all it is Sunday, a day of rest. The phrase *news travels fast* sprang to mind as he threw open the heavy swinging doors.

"Stand by your beds," was the humiliating sound we all heard; with only a handful of us in the room, he continued in the loudest tone he could master.

"You're let out for one day, one day I say, and what do you do, get fucking pissed, where's Culf?" He raged, "I want to see him now!" I was almost frightened to breathe, let alone tell him where Culf was.

"I think he's gone to breakfast," said Dennis nervously.

"Were you pissed up last night, Norris?" said the Bombardier.

"No Bombardier, I was back in barracks by 1700hrs with Wolfendale, Bombardier."

"What about you, Lynch?" as he continued his investigation.

"Not a drop passed my lips, Bombardier."

"Don't lie to me Lynch; what do you take me for, a fucking idiot?" I am now thinking *don't say any more George, your reply should be yes Bombardier, no Bombardier, three bags full Bombardier, just don't push it George*. Bombardier Bartlett continued his rant, saying,

"I want to see everybody standing by their beds at 1400hrs sharp, do you all understand?"

"Yes Bombardier," we all shouted at the top of our voices.

Throughout the next two hours, everybody returned in dribs and drabs to be told the news, I am thinking *Sunday, day of rest, well that's gone for a burton*, there wasn't a soul lying on his bed which would be the norm for a Sunday afternoon. We were all concerned that the Bombardier might pop back unexpectedly and catch us off guard. I decided to try the new steam iron out.

"Dennis," I said, shouting across the room. "Do you fancy trying out our new toy?"

"Why not?" said Dennis. "I'll go and get my lightweights from my locker."

To cut to the chase, we ended up with more water on our lightweights than in the iron; it didn't seem possible, we put about half a pint of water into the iron but ended up with what seemed like a pint of water on our trousers.

"Wolfie," was the shout from Riggers as he made his way over to where we were ironing.

"Is there any chance of using the iron? You know, mates rates and all."

"Not a chance," could be heard from Dennis and me as we spoke in unison.

"Ah come on," said Riggers "screw the bobbin."

"Mates or no mates; business is business," we said. After a few more minutes of negotiating we called a truce. Riggers decided to contribute towards the iron; it was now a three-way split, and then a six-way split with George, Sam and Steve contributing their share.

It was now time for lunch. It felt like your final meal on death row, there was no way I was going to enjoy my lunch; the feeling at lunch was that of, *I've found a penny but lost a pound.*

We made our way back to the block, which was at slow time; dragging our DMS boots on the litter free pavements. We were all standing by our beds, apart from lookout Sam.

"The Bombardier is a near," said Sam, looking out of the window. We all stood still, but at the same time, sniggering at each other through clenched teeth, we were counting the steps as Bombardier Bartlett stamped his authority on each step, seven, eight, nine, and then ten. We knew then the doors were about to swing open. Everything seemed to happen in a flash and, before we knew it, Bombardier Bartlett was standing firmly to attention with his pace stick at the vertical, pressed up against his leg.

We could smell the anger in his voice and saw the devilment in his eyes; walking up and down the room at a slow pace tapping his pace stick on the floor, he finally turned one hundred and eighty degrees, well at least his head did.

"Listen in," Bombardier Bartlett said in a voice that is only heard from a Bombardier that's pissed.

"I do not take kindly having to come in on a Sunday afternoon to babysit you lot, if one of you fucks up, then you will all suffer the consequences, you should all know that by now, Culf!"

"Yes Bombardier," said Barry nervously.

"Stand in the middle of the room now," said Bombardier Bartlett, who explained what we already knew, whilst at the same time, humiliating him in front of the troop.

"You, Culf, are going to be responsible for this Sunday afternoon nightmare you're about to endure."

This doesn't sound good, I was thinking as I looked over to Parry. It wasn't long before we knew what our punishment was – Changing Parades. It meant naff all to me, not being from a military background, but I could tell by the looks on some of the faces of the so called military lads that it wasn't going to be enjoyable. Bombardier Bartlett explained it to us in no uncertain circumstances:

"You will be expected to get changed into different sets of Army dress at the double and then parade outside." It sounded fun at the time; far from it, it was the worst thing that I had ever endured since joining the Army, the first time I really felt manipulated.

"PT kit now," was the order.

We had less time than it would take you to say *Sergeant Major* to get our kit on and get ourselves in three ranks: blue shorts, red PT vest, green army socks, pumps and then a quick dash down the stairs missing every other step, occasionally jumping three at a time before we were on parade outside.

We could hear the other half of the Wingate Troop being put through their paces by Sergeant Preece as we passed their barrack room. It was utter chaos outside, it felt like World War Three was about to break out: there were some that hadn't tied their laces, some who had only one sock on, vest inside out, shorts wrong way round.

"Fucking shower, get yourselves upstairs now and into your combat suits," shouted Bombardier Bartlett. On the way up, we were trampling all over the other half of Wingate once more as they were trying to make their way down the stairs, a mad dash to my bed space and then I just flung my PT kit into my locker as I searched for my combat kit, complete with combat hat. I was never that quick at getting dressed so this was proving to be a challenge and a half; I could see most of the lads sprinting out of the room not wanting to be last. In a strange sort of way we were all working as individuals and not as a team; it was everyman for himself at the same time if we failed as individuals, we also failed as a troop.

Lined up in three ranks brought more chaos and laughter, god knows why we were laughing, I think we were actually laughing at each individual that was getting a bollocking. No-one was safe from the infuriated Bombardier Bartlett: gators hanging off, berets looking like cow pats, shirt buttons not fastened.

"No. 2 dress uniform now," shouted the Bombardier. An hour of torture and embarrassment brought the session to an end. We were absolutely shattered both physically and mentally,but just when we thought it was all over, Bombardier Bartlett hit us again.

"I will be back within the hour to inspect your lockers."

Our lockers looked like your worst nightmare. Chitchat was now at a minimum, most of us had no energy left to talk; our eyes were mainly focused on Barry Culf as we continued to sort our lockers out. All the fun elements of being with your mates seemed to have been drained from our bodies, we would normally be able to laugh this sort of thing off; it felt like we were at a funeral.

The locker and room inspection took place as intended with Bombardier Bartlett's voice now only registering three on the Richter scale.

"Take this as a warning," said Bombardier Bartlett, "you mess up again and you can expect much of the same." We were finally on our own again with the fact that Bombardier Bartlett was now making his way out of the block.

"Bloody hell" I said to Steve, "that was fucking hard."

"OK for you," said Steve, "I only had one boot on, the other one fell off halfway down the stairs." I had to laugh at Steve's remark, watching him on parade with only one boot was a sight not to be missed.

"Are you OK Dennis?" I asked.

"You mean apart from nearly getting strangled with my own braces? I managed to get the left one over my right shoulder; I had a job to fucking breathe."

It was nice to feel the sense of humor now creeping back into the barrack room, we were now starting to feel more like it was before the changing parade; a shock to the system is how we saw it, but one we probably needed, it certainly made me realise who was calling the tune. Discipline is what makes you what you are, without discipline there is no structure and without structure you have no Army.

Week two brought manic Monday with the normal drill, PT, sports and of course no getting away without some sort of inspection. Tuesday was hobbies night, which all kicked off about 1900hrs.

"See you later," I said to some of my mates as I made my way to the swimming pool, dressed in my red Wingate tracksuit with towel and trunks in hand.

"See you later Wolfie," said Pete.

"Don't forget your arm bands," said the ever-amusing Sheep.

"Why don't you go and blow your trumpet," I said, "and I don't mean in the literal sense," as he made his way to band.

"Enjoy your model making Pete," I said, at the same time still wondering, *what sort of hobby model making* was.

It wasn't long before we all returned with stories to tell. Steve was already sitting on his bed bulling his boots when I arrived back looking worse for wear.

"Bloody hell wolf man, looks like you really did need arm bands," said George.

"First and last time," I said, still feeling the shock of almost drowning.

"For some reason – and I don't know why – I thought that water polo would be fun; throwing a ball around in the water and scoring goals seemed right up my street, it wasn't until I got into the water that I realised I wasn't allowed to stand on the bottom, I had to tread water for the entire game, the only person that was allowed to stand on the bottom is the goal keeper, I never touched the ball once apart from when it hit me on the head. I'm going to see the TC tomorrow about a change; I am categorically not doing that again."

Pete, Steve and Sam who was also back from his hobby, were in fits of laughter. Pete had the easiest night learning more about Airfix models and Steve didn't even get to blow his trumpet; apparently he was put into the drum section. *Drum section,* I was thinking, *he couldn't even beat his meat let alone a drum*, actually I take that back, last night I am sure I heard some abnormal noises coming from his direction at lights out.

On Wednesday I was delighted to receive some mail, it was my cheque book. I had never owned one before but it felt good to see my name on every cheque, P.W Wolfendale. I felt rich, I felt important, my own cheque book, wow.

I made my way back into the block to see whether or not the TC was in his office; I noticed that his door was ajar so nervously knocked three times on the door.

"Enter," said the TC in a nonchalant voice, I marched in, came to attention and saluted the Queen's commission.

"What can I can I help you with, Junior Gunner Wolfendale?" said the TC with a grin on his face. When I explained the situation to him about my water polo experience and the fact that I almost drowned, he almost fell of his seat with laughter.

"If you'd had listened to what Bombardier Bartlett said, you would have realised there were no horses involved," said the TC. "What are you actually asking me?"

"I would like to change my hobby Sir; would it be possible to do the Saddle Club Sir?" I said

"Ah, back to horses again are we Wolfendale?" was his quick-witted reply. "You see, I could see in your eyes that you would be more suited to horses, you'll have to go to water polo on Tuesday and then I will see what I can do."

"Thank you, Sir," I said, feeling relieved. I saluted and then marched out with a sigh of relief written all over my face.

The rest of the week went by without any fuss; more weapon handling was the main focus of the week ready for our first visit to Kingsbury Ranges on Monday morning. Sunday night we were told by Bombardier Bartlett to be ready standing by our beds the next morning at 0730hrs in all respects, combats and stripped down webbing: two pouches, water bottle attached to our belt, the yoke and kidney pouches that would hold our mess tins and KFS.

We spent most of the night in the washrooms, admiring ourselves in the mirrors, just like a woman does on a night out; we needed to make sure that our webbing was correctly assembled and not like it had been pieced together in the dark. I got Dennis to check mine over, looking back now though I'm not too sure why.

CHAPTER THIRTY-FOUR (PART ONE)
KINGSBURY RANGES
MR PERFECT TEN

Monday morning meant we were now already in week three, time was passing us by unnoticed; I was thinking three more weeks and then term one would be complete. It felt strange falling out of the warmth of my bed and getting straight into combats.

At the cookhouse we were attracting attention from all and sundry, we stood out like a beacon on a cold and foggy morning, everybody else we could see was in lightweights and short sleeve shirts.

Back in the block just before 0730hrs, we put our webbing on and just mingled around until we got the call from Bombardier Bartlett to get outside in three ranks. Bombardier Bartlett walked the ranks and inspected his lean, mean fighting machine (Wingate Troop), a tug here and a tug there of our disheveled webbing just to make sure it was correctly fitted. "Norris," said Bombardier Bartlett.

"Yes Bombardier," said Norris.

"You're like a bag of spuds tied up in the middle," said Bombardier Bartlett as he grabbed Dennis's webbing belt and gave it one almighty tug that almost put Dennis on his arse.

"OK, listen in," said Bombardier Bartlett.

"Attention, right turn, quick march, left right left right left right left!"

Within minutes we were outside the Armory lined up in single file waiting to be issued our SLR. Once in the Armory, the Armourer would ask you for your rifle number.

"Number?" he would say in a kind of hurried type of voice.

"24311682," I said.

"Oh right," he said, "we have a smart arse do we, rifle number you clown."

"Oh, sorry," I said.

"It's number 73." I was so use to giving my Army number it was the first thing that came to mind: two magazines, cleaning kit and a rifle sling were placed on the counter.

"Sign on the line," said the Armourer with, *why do I have to put up with all this crap* written all over his face? Before I could even sign on the dotted line he was shouting verbal's at the next person. Once outside we were told to fix the rifle sling to our rifles and put our magazines into our pouches before lining up in three ranks.

We were stood waiting for the infamous green bus to arrive when all of a sudden we were hit with a so-called convoy of a four tonner and two long wheel base Land Rovers, one bearing a red flag.

"Clayton, Davies, you can travel in the front Land Rover," said the Bombardier, "The one that is housing the ammunition; the rest of you, get yourselves onto the back of the four tonner." This was the first time we had been on a four tonner apart from one or two of the lads that were in the cadets; the super heavy tailgate crashed down on its hinges that had foot holes in it to allow us to climb up about three feet and into the truck.

Four wooden green benches attached to the inside of the truck and then a green tent-like canvas over the frame was how I would describe it; a tent on wheels. The seats were solid and cold even though it was a warm sunny day. This was it; it really did feel like going into battle, we all sat there with our rifles between our legs with a vice like grip looking out of the back of the vehicle.

The noise of the vehicle starting up vibrated through my poor excuse of a body, *crunch* was the sound of first gear being selected as we all now looked at each other thinking, *are we going to make it?* We were in for a very bumpy ride without a doubt. The green Army bus now seemed like a Bentley compared to this, second, third, and I think I heard the occasional fourth gear as we made our way to just south of Tamworth near the M42; the journey would take about forty minutes normally, that was providing the MT (Motor Transport) driver could avoid doing too much gear changing.

One or two of the lads managed to get a few minutes sleep in the truck until they felt the unwelcome sharpness of the brakes working on the wheels; the ones that were sitting at the rear of the four tonner would now be at the front, sprawled all over the floor, and if it wasn't for the tailgate, the ones at the front would be lying in the road. There were always a few choice words and some banging with the fist on the back of the cab like, "Slow down you mad bastard." These vehicles weren't built for comfort, they were built for transportation. You could always tell when you were close to your drop off point; the bumpy pot holed dirt track would always be a giveaway. I am pretty sure the sadistic driver was seeing how many pot holes he could hit before arriving at the guarded red and white pole barrier. A few choice words could be heard from the back of the truck before the pole was lifted to allow us into the Ranges.

"OK, get out of the vehicle," was the order from the driver as the he dropped the tail gate. We piled out like cattle out of a cattle truck, the drop didn't look far until I saw Sam falling over on to his back side with his weapon almost coming to rest up his nose, I tried my best to keep my balance and not to follow in Sam's footsteps; as my numb legs made contact with the hardened ground I felt a sharp pain rattle up my body.

This was it, Kingsbury Ranges, or at least that's what the huge sign said as we were marched a couple of hundred metres towards the firing range. We were split into three details (small groups); I was in detail one along with Steve, Dennis and George. Sam and Riggers were in detail two.

"Listen in," said Sergeant Preece, "detail one will be down in the shadows of the butts, detail two, you will be first up to fire and detail three, you'll be stripping down your weapon, let's see what you can remember."

Detail two and three were called upon to unload the ammunition while detail one was led down to the butts with a Junior NCO to be told of their task. I had some idea of what the butts were, but it became a lot clearer when I arrived there. It reminded me of a bus shelter that was about a hundred metres long. About two metres in front of us was a mechanically operated rusty looking frame that the targets would be placed into. There was a small shed like building that would house all the materials that we would need: targets, pointers, glue and stickers were the main equipment that we would be required to use; on the brick wall behind us was a black World War Two type phone, you would pick up the receiver from the cradle and then whiz the handle round to make a connection with the firing consol some three hundred metres behind us. Junior NCO L/Bombardier Lewis bellowed out loudly and gave us a target number.

"Wolfendale target three, Norris target four, Lynch target five, Parry target six, Clayton target seven and so on until all targets were manned. L/Bombardier Lewis continued… "Follow me this way lads." We were taken to the shed where we were given a figure eleven target that needed to be placed into the frame work that was opposite your designated station; I had no idea how to erect it into the stand so I just followed the crowd. I noticed that Dennis who was next to me on target four, seem to have more of an idea of what to do so I just copied him. If Dennis was willing to take a chance it was wrong, then so was I.

There was a long wooden stick like a piece of four by two wood, to those of us that had no idea what that meant, it resembled a lollipop stick. It would be put into a small slot and then screwed tight into place. Once all of the targets were securely fastened, L/Bombardier Lewis got us to hoist the targets up above the height of the shelter with a kind of cranking handle; the targets were now in full view of the detail who were at this time, lining up on the range to fire their SLR.

We were all told to stand back away from the targets and sit down on the benches that were positioned under the shelter; I was just chatting away to Dennis when we heard the World War Two phone ringing, we could see L/Bombardier Lewis pick it up.

"Yes Sarge, OK Sarge, will do Sarge," was all we could make out.

"OK listen in," said L/Bombardier Lewis, "five rounds of ammunition will be fired by each man. At this point I will give you the order to bring your targets down, no one is to move anywhere near the targets until I give you the nod." We all waited with great anticipation, not knowing what to expect next.

"What the hell are we doing down here, Dennis?" I said with a worried look on my face, "What if there is a ricochet?" I was genuinely nervous despite the fact I was pretty sure we were not going to die. Dennis tried to reassure me by saying, "Well at least it will be quick, especially if it hits you in the head."

"Cheers Dennis," I said, "Great help you've been."

It wasn't quite like being on death row waiting for the first round to be fired, but it was certainly squeaky bum time; sat there looking up at my target brought the first crack of a bullet hitting the target, the sound reminded me of someone snapping a thick branch in two, crack, crack, crack, as small bits of wood occasionally came flying into the butts. It took less than a minute for everybody to fire their five rounds until no more firing could be heard.

We all sat there with our eyes rolling around in their sockets wondering if we were going to hear one last round hit its target, just then the sound of the phone rang to bring us out of our daze.

"OK," said L/Bombardier Lewis. "I want you to pick up your pointer, the long stick with an arrow on the end of it, point it to where each round had hit the target, there should be five holes in each target, wait for my order."

We all pointed one at a time when ordered to do so, target one, target two, target three, and so on until all targets had been complete. We were then told to lower the targets and then paste them up; we would get a small paint brush, dip it in a pot of colourless glue, and then paste the target where the bullet holes were; last but not least we would cover the holes up with a white circular sticker about the size of a 10p.

"Now raise your targets again," said L/Bombardier Lewis..."and wait for the next wave of rounds to hit your target." After about an hour of being shot at, it was our turn to leave the butts and make our way up to the firing range complete with webbing.

"Don't shoot, don't shoot!" was the cry from myself and Steve as we put our hands up in the air with our rifle slung over our shoulder, it didn't take long for everybody else to follow suit. We were looking like escapees handing ourselves over to the enemy. As we arrived back to the safe end of the range we didn't think our joke would go down too well with Sergeant Preece and Bombardier Bartlett; lowering our hands and trying to look like professional soldiers seemed the sensible thing to do unless we fancied some extra duties back in the barracks.

"Detail two, get your webbing and make your way down to the butts with L/Bombardier Lewis," said Sergeant Preece. "Make sure you take all your rubbish with you." I could see Riggers picking up Sam.

"What are you doing?" said Sam, wondering if Riggers had lost his marbles.

"Picking up all the rubbish," said Riggers. Sam gave a slight grin at the same time shaking his head and replying with, "I'll set George on to you if you don't behave, all Scots keep together, three cheers for William Wallace."

"Detail three, you'll be firing next, detail one, you'll be cleaning your weapons," said Sergeant Preece; it seemed straightforward until Junior Gunner Owen decided to make his way over to the firing range.

"Owen," was the shout from Sergeant Preece. "What detail are you in?"

"Detail one Sergeant," he replied.

"Then get your poor excuse of a body over to the rest of your detail over on the grass area. You're on cleaning weapons, you good for nothing piece of tripe."

With everybody now at their respective place, we started to strip our weapons down like we had been shown back in hangar one. The only thing difference now was that there was a roll of white cotton flannelette being passed around. We had to tear a piece off that measured about two inches by four, hence the saying four by two flannelette.

You would fold the flannelette like the way you would roll a cigarette and then put it into a loop in your pull through. The pull through had a metal end that would be fed into the barrel of your rifle until it came out at the other end, you would then pull it through with some force which would hopefully clean the barrel.

It was now 1230hrs and we were getting ready for lunch. One of the Land Rovers that had gone back to camp to pick up lunch could be seen entering the range; detail two could be seen making their way up from the butts; a phone call that lunch was on its way had them all racing towards us in an uncontrollable fashion.

Fish and chips, I was thinking, just like at Leek, can't wait; with the Land Rover pulled up we were told to line up with our mess tins at the ready along with our KFS. I was standing next to George in the queue.

"Why do we need our mess tins for fish and chips?" I said.

"Who said anything about fish and chips?" was George's reply. "You're in the Army now; it's not going to be fish and chips all the time Wolfie."

"What do you think it will be then?" I asked curiously.

"Not sure," replied George. "At a guess, Army stew," *Army stew,* I was thinking, *what the heck is Army stew?*

Two large green containers at the back of the Land Rover were carried out by two soldiers with muscles that looked more suited to the PTIs back in the gym. The lids came off with some force and then there it was… we could all smell the so-called Army stew. It actually smelt like stew, except when it was ladled out into my mess tin, it looked liked something I had stood in on the odd occasion. Lumps of meat and lumps of fat made up the main ingredients; a few potatoes and gravy and that was that. There was some white bread available to mop up your gravy along with a large, silver tea urn full of NATO standard tea.

I sat down with Steve, Dennis and George and looked across to the Land Rover to see Riggers and Sam making their way over to where we were sitting; inspecting what was in their mess tin.

"Over here Riggers," I shouted with a slice of white bread being pushed into my mouth.

"Not sure what to do with this," said Riggers.

"Choke on it," said George.

"Can you keep an eye on my food?" said Sam, as he went to get himself a cuppa, *keep an eye on his food* we were all thinking, *you couldn't give it away.*

After about half an hour of chewing and spitting the unwanted remains of the bits of fat and gristle out of our mouths, we were replenished and ready for action; a quick wash of our eating irons and mess tins in the container of hot soapy water before we were summoned to the firing range. The butt party made their way down to the butts waving sarcastically, at the same time shouting, "Good luck lads, break a leg."

We were all given a number and told to line up on the range against that number facing our target. We made our way down the range to within one hundred metres of the butts.

"Rest your rifles on the ground at the side of you," said Sergeant Preece, "place your beret next to your rifle and get your two magazines out of your ammo pouches."

Sergeant Preece came to us one by one and gave us fifteen rounds of ammunition that we placed into our berets.

"I want you to put ten! I say again ten! Rounds of ammunition into one of your magazines and five rounds in the other," he said. I'm sure the way he was addressing us made me think that he thought we couldn't count.

"Put the magazine of ten rounds back into your ammunition pouch and keep the one with five rounds at the ready," he said, as we were now all set for action.

"With a magazine of five rounds, load," said Sergeant Preece firmly, "check your magazine and then attach it to the rifle." You could hear all the clicking as each magazine was firmly engaged into its slot at the bottom of the rifle.

"With your rifle pointing down the range, take your ear defenders out of your pocket and insert them into those weird flappy things on the side of your head." Green, small, rubber plugs about the size of your fingernail were neatly pushed into place; everything now seemed muffled apart from the unmistakable tone of Sergeant Preece's voice.

This is it, we were all thinking, I looked across to my left to see Steve and Dennis looking more like action men.

"Listen in," said Sergeant Preece. "You will be firing five rounds initially at my command; this is to zero your weapon, prone position down!" We all collapsed onto our front lying horizontal towards the butts. It felt quite uncomfortable at first with the fact that your webbing was fastened around your waist; a quick shuffle of my webbing helped to ease the pain of my magazine that was wedging into my hip.

I felt like looking over to my left to see what Steve and Dennis were making of the situation, but thought better of it. I just focused on the butts waiting for my target to show its self; within seconds and not minutes, the targets suddenly appeared like a rabbit sticking its head out of its hole.

The targets seemed larger than I had first anticipated, even from one hundred metres back, I noticed one or two targets looked liked they had just come in from a good night out, as for mine, it was standing firmly to attention.

"Ready," was the next command, we pulled back the cocking handle with as much force as we could and then allowed it to spring back, the weapon was now primed. It seemed unreal that a sixteen-year-old boy was about to fire one of the most powerful weapons in the world; there was now a round of 7.62 ammunition in the chamber waiting to be fired at its respective target.

"Five well aimed single shots at your target in front, in your own time, carry on." I pulled the butt of the rifle firmly into my right shoulder and took aim; safety catch off with the thumb of my right hand, my finger was now gently squeezing the trigger trying not to snatch it when *bang!* Was the loud noise I heard from my left. Dennis had already begun. I had to compose myself once more and dismiss my thoughts from the loud banging that was circulating around the range. I was now squeezing the trigger once more, at the same time peering through the tiny pin prick of a hole in the rear sight; lined up with the fore sight, I continued to squeeze until *wow*, I felt the impact of the recoil against my shoulder, it was such a strange feeling firing my first ever round, I felt as if I had turned a corner, someone out there felt that I had enough about me to be trusted with live rounds.

After the last shot had been fired Sergeant Preece yelled, "Has anyone not fired five rounds?" There was a short pause of silence before we were told to apply our safety catch and stand up, keeping our weapons pointing down the range.

"Unload," was the next command: Safety catch, magazine off, cock the weapon three or four times, point the weapon down the range aim and fire, with the idea that there should be no more bangs.

"For inspection port arms," said Sergeant Preece, we held the rifle at a forty-five-degree angle, pointing to the sky and pulled back the cocking handle except this time, we would lock the cocking handle back so that Sergeant Preece could check into the chamber for any live rounds. Sergeant Preece walked along the detail checking each and every weapon. As he checked my rifle he tapped my shoulder. "Clear ease springs," he said, and again I would let the working parts of my rifle go forward, point the weapon down the range and fire an aimed shot and apply the safety catch.

"Wolfie," was the cry from Steve.

"What?" I said, with my ears still ringing.

"Whose target did you fire on?" he said.

"My own," I said, confused, to which he replied.

"I fired on Norris's," he said.

"You better hadn't have done," said Dennis, looking worried; if I've got more than five holes in my target then I know who they're from.

"Your rounds are probably on Wolfie's target," said Steve.

"So, I could end up with ten holes on my target then, is that what you're saying?" We just had to wait to see if we had any rounds at all if any in our targets, or in my case maybe ten.

Our targets were now being examined by the butt party for any sign of a hit, before they were being erected again; one by one Sergeant Preece got the butt party to point their pointer at where the rounds had hit, he would signal to the firing consul to let the butt party know which target he was on.

Within a short while, he reached Steve's firing position; what Sergeant Preece was looking for was a tight grouping of five rounds so that he could adjust the rifle as necessary, what he got was three left of target and three right.

"How come you have got six holes in your target, Parry?" said Sergeant Preece in a loud voice.

"It must have been Norris, Sergeant."

"Norris?" said Sergeant Preece.

"Yes Sergeant," said Dennis.

"Have you been shooting on Parry's target?" asked Sergeant Preece.

"No Sergeant," said Dennis, looking over at Steve, who was now smirking.

"I don't believe you," said Sergeant Preece. "I just hope for your sake that you have five rounds in your target."

Sergeant Preece used his tool combination to adjust Steve's weapon before going onto Dennis's firing position and then held his hand in the air to signal to the consul that he was ready for the results of Norris's effort.

"Seven!" was the cry from Sergeant Preece. "Seven, Norris!" he said again in a louder than before voice, "how the hell have you ended up with seven?!"

"Wolfendale, Sergeant," said Dennis's quick thinking brain as he looked over to me.

"Fuck off," I said looking at Dennis.

"Quiet, Wolfendale," said Sergeant Preece. "God knows how many rounds are in your target," he continued to say.

Sergeant Preece made his way over to where I was and signaled to the firing consul, three rounds was my allocation.

"Three rounds, Wolfendale, explain that one," said Sergeant Preece.

"It must have been Junior Gunner George Lynch," I said, looking to my right, "he said that my target was the one just to the right, it was only after firing my first two rounds that I realised that I was firing on George's target."

"Is that true, Lynch?" said Sergeant Preece as he turned to George. If Sergeant Preece had eyes in the back of his head he would have seen me laughing behind his back at George, it was quite obvious that I had told a porky just to get myself out of trouble.

"No Sergeant, not true," George said.

"Wolfendale, you lying bastard," said George, not finding the matter funny at all. I knew then it wouldn't be long before George would get his own back on me, something I was accustomed to. It was now time to get the result of George's effort.

"Lynch, seven rounds," said Sergeant Preece, still confused with the mathematics.

"Now who's the one lying, George," I said, looking at him with a smirk whilst at the same time, feeling slightly guilty.

"Shut your mouth, Wolfendale," said Sergeant Preece in a grouchy tone of voice, I l won't tell you again.

After all the rifles had been zeroed we were taken back to the beginning of the firing range ready for our next mission, George was still having a go at me all the way back.

"Twat Wolfie, getting me in trouble," said George, still trying to see the funny side of it.

"It was the only thing I could think of at the time," I said to George, now feeling just a little guilty.

"Listen in, get yourselves lined up on your respective targets," said Sergeant Preece. "Make sure you identify it, I don't want anyone firing on someone else's target like when you were zeroing your rifle."

Now that our rifles were zeroed it was time to see who would be the next Clint Eastwood; lined up on the firing range we were firmly told by Sergeant Preece, "You will be firing ten rounds at two five round intervals, five rounds will be fired from the prone position and then on my command, five rounds will be fired in the kneeling position, both targets will be at two hundred metres. You'll then be given your score which will be calculated electronically in the firing consul, are there any questions?" he continued. "For those of you, who remembered to take your ear defenders out of your ears, put them back in, with a magazine of ten rounds, load!"

We went through all the usual procedures before the command was heard, "Five rounds in the prone position, five rounds in the kneeling position, in your own time, carry on."

I was looking down the range with bated breath for my target to appear; it must have been at least ten seconds of concentration before the target suddenly sprung up, it felt like a life time as I continued to focus on my task in hand. I took aim, trying not to miss or fire on George's target; I believe I counted five shots before I took up the kneeling position, not as easy as it seems trying to keep your balance when being knocked off your feet by the recoil of your rifle.

Ten rounds had now been fired by all, we just stayed in the kneeling position until told to stand up and make our rifles safe; there were a few Hawkeyes among us including my mates. We waited with great keenness for the scores to be announced from the PA system.

"Number one 7 rounds… two 8 rounds… three 9 rounds… four 5 rounds… five 8 rounds, and then it was the turn of number ten, Steve's position, number ten. 10 rounds, eleven (that was Dennis) 8 rounds, twelve 10 rounds," *yes!* I was thinking, "thirteen 9 rounds…" I looked over to George who also was beaming from ear plug to ear plug, looking content with his score.

CHAPTER THIRTY-FOUR (PART TWO)
KINGSBURY RANGES
MR CLUMSY

After being brought back down to earth, the next task was to pick up all the empty cartridge cases from the range into our berets, then return them to ammunition boxes for transporting back to the barracks. With the butt party now back from their duties we were lined up in a single line for our final declaration before leaving the ranges.

"I have no live rounds or empty cartridges in my possession, Sergeant!" was the reply from each and every one of us as he walked down the line and, at the same time checking in our ammo pouches. "OK, listen in you lot; get your arses onto the four tonner now."

Unfortunately, detail one was the only detail that had not had the time to clean their rifles, with the fact that we had just come off the range; while everybody else was relaxing where possible in the back of the bouncy four tonner, detail one were hard at work cleaning their rifles; not easy, as Dennis found out.

Dennis was sitting near the back when he, and without any thought, unlocked his gas plug, not for one minute was Dennis thinking about the pressure from the spring that was behind the gas plug. With a shocked look we all just stared out of the back as we saw his gas plug catapult into oblivion and never to be seen again. The look on Dennis's face was hilarious, he looked liked a cod fish with his bottom jaw hanging on the floor. "Oh fuck" said Dennis.

"What's wrong mate" said George curiously.

"My gas plug" Dennis replied, "I have just fired it out of the back of the truck."

"Tell me you're joking" said George now looking worried.

"It just flew out" said Dennis, "into a field" I feared the worst for Dennis. "Four weeks in pokey for you Dennis," Steve said.

"Might get kicked out," said someone else.

"Anyone got a spare gas plug?" said George to the rest of the troop. "Norris has just fired his out of the back of the truck." The comment brought roars of laughter from everyone, even though we knew it was no laughing matter, the only thing to do now was to have a good sing song.

"Does anybody know a good Army song?" said a voice from the rear of the truck, Dennis needs cheering up; by chance one or two of the lads that had spent time in the cadets came forward.

"I know a gooden," said Riggers, nothing to do with a gas plug though. "It's called, *what ya gonna do when you leave the Army*, the same tune as *What ya gonna do with the Drunken Sailor*." Within minutes we were all singing along.

What ya gonna do when you leave the army, what ya gonna to do when you leave the army, what ya gonna to do when you leave the army, early in the morning.

Make my way to the nearest station, make my way to the nearest station, and make my way to the nearest station early in the morning.

What ya gonna to do when you get to the station, what ya gonna to do when you get to the station, what ya gonna do when you get to the station early in the morning.

Catch a train to civilization, catch a train to civilization, catch a train to civilization early in the morning.

What ya gonna do in civilization, what ya gonna do in civilization, what ya gonna do in civilization early in the morning.

Run like fuck to the nearest boozer, run like fuck to the nearest boozer, run like fuck to the nearest boozer early in the morning.

What ya gonna do when you get to the boozer, what ya gonna do when you get to the boozer, what ya gonna do when you get to the boozer early in the morning.

Drink to the fuckers in the British Army, drink to the fuckers in the British Army, drink to the fuckers in the British Army early in the morning.

We were now minutes away from the barracks and Dennis was now looking more worried than at any part of the journey. As we drove through the main gates we could see the Armourer making his way into the Guardroom antic-ipating our arrival.

"Everybody off!" was the order from Sergeant Preece who was looking up at us from the back of the vehicle. With the tailgate now down we made our way into the Armory to hand in our weapons. I stood behind Dennis in the queue trying to console him, and at the same time maybe thinking the worst. "Next," said the Armourer in a voice that said, *get a move on I want to get home for tea.*

"I'm afraid I've lost my gas plug, Staff Sergeant," muttered Dennis with a soft voice; we were all expecting the worst until the BQMS said in a casual manner, "No worries, I've a tray full over here." The relief on the face of Dennis was a picture as he handed his weapon over to the BQ.

"Bloody hell Dennis," I said, "people have been shot for less."

Back in the barrack room it was a quick shower and ready for tea. Tuesday morning brought more drill and PT; during our NAAFI break I went to see the TC about my hobby options.

"Wolfendale," said the TC as I entered his office, "Saddle Club."

"Sorry! Sir" I said.

"Saddle Club, you asked me to change your hobby, is that correct?!"

"Oh yes Sir, I did."

"Well, you start tonight."

"Thank you, Sir," I said with a look of appreciation written all over my face, "no more drowning for me, Sir." I saluted and marched out.

On the way back to my room I saw Sam who to was hoping to change his choice of hobby, I explained to Sam that I had changed mind and also explained that the TC was in his office if he wanted to go and see him.

"On my way now," said Sam, with his feet not touching the ground. A few minutes later Sam was exiting the TCs office with a huge smile.

"Photography," said Sam, "I start tonight."

"Good for you Sam," I said, "sounds interesting and fun."

Later on that evening I made my way out of barracks to the small stables about a five minute walk from the barracks. I found this more to my liking: saddling horses, fixing the bridle, saddle soap for cleaning the saddle, it was a new adventure that I relished. Over the next few weeks I was learning how to get my horse from a walk to a trot and from a trot into a canter. There was a lot more work to riding horses than I first thought; it was a far cry from Blackpool Beach Donkeys when I was a wee nipper.

CHAPTER THIRTY-FIVE
MILITARY PRANKS

Over the next few weeks it was more of the same things, it was a chance for George to get his own back on me for dropping him in it on the Ranges and in fact, it only took to the first weekend after live firing for George and his buddies to reap revenge.

Saturday night was everyone's chance to chill out down the NAAFI or out of barracks as long as you were back by 2300hrs. I decided to chill out down the NAAFI with Riggers and Steve. Doctor Who with John Pertwee was showing on the TV and the news at ten was revealing more misery on the events in Northern Ireland.

Police are investigating the murder of a man in County Armagh; this sort of news, as sad as it may be, would always draw our attention with the fact that we may be fighting there in the near future. It was around 2230hrs when we decided to make our way back to the block, there wasn't much activity going on apart from the duty guard walking around in their combats carrying their unmistakable pick handles. I think they were more of a deterrent as opposed to being used as a weapon; it would certainly make me think twice about giving them grief.

As we made our way into the now lit-up barrack room, we could see one or two of the lads just dozing on their beds, writing letters, chitchatting away, there was even some that were actually in their beds.

"All right Wolfie?" said George in a kind of *nice to see you mate* way.

"Yes, thanks George," I said, "been down the NAAFI with Steve and Riggers, all kicking off in Northern Ireland according to the news reports."

"Yeah, we will be there one day mate," said George.

"I will be scared; at least I think I will," I said. "At the same time, looking forward to military combat."

"Hard as nails, you," said George.

"Hard as nails," I said. "I would run a mile if I saw a spider, I fucking hate spiders, scare the living daylights out of me. Anyway, I'm off to bed now George, maybe write a letter to my parents before going to sleep."

"OK mate," said George.

I was quite taken in by George's thoughtful words; he actually sounded quite human, a side of George I hadn't seen before. As I got undressed and was now standing by my bed in just my psychedelic boxers, I could see George and his buddies had taken a kind of more, should we say an interest in my bedtime habits than normal. I was thinking *maybe it's my boxers they have taken a liking to.*

"All right lads?" I said.

"Yeah mate," was the reply from a few of the lads, I was thinking *strange,* but that was about as far as my thinking went.

I pulled back the white cotton sheets and calmly got into bed, it was only when I tried to stretch my legs out that I couldn't understand why my feet weren't able to extend any further than about half way down the bed. I was crouched up like a ball; I kicked and kicked until I could kick no more, unfortunately it was all in vain, I could hear the laughter from all around the room, George included.

They had removed my top sheet and hidden it away under my mattress, and then folded the bottom sheet over making a kind of pocket; when the job was complete it looked like a well made bed, apparently it is called a French bed. It was so frustrating, I won't repeat the industrial language I used; I think you can imagine that for yourselves. I had to make a decision to either sleep with my legs bent all night or remake my bed. I think if I'd had been drunk I would have chosen the first option, but as it was, I spent a good five minutes re-making my bed. I noticed Riggers and Steve checking their beds for any sign of sabotage; however on this occasion they were given a reprieve.

'Suitcase beds' was also something that was to become more common over the coming weeks: you would dismantle someone's bed undoing all the nuts and bolts that hold your steel framed bed together, then hide the bed and mattress behind their locker or in the washrooms, basically somewhere out of sight where they can't be found. You would then get their military suitcase that is the size of a normal suit case and fold a blanket and sheet around it. The case would then take the place of where your bed would be with a pillow placed in its normal place. Snow White would've been proud of your efforts when complete. There was many a time when you would come back having had too many sherbets that you didn't give a fig; going to sleep on a suitcase always seemed like the best option. All though Army pranks were there for a laugh, it was a case of where do you draw the line from a bit of fun to stupidity; well, we were soon to find out.

CHAPTER THIRTY-SIX
BRANDED WITH AN IRON

Blanket baths on your birthday could be a pain, I was just glad I only had one birthday each year. One night after returning back from wherever, I came into the room to find darts being thrown around by all and sundry; ducking and diving and hiding underneath your bed was the only way to avoid the darts as they flew from one end of the room to the other. On his way into the barrack room was Junior Gunner John Machin, returning from the NAAFI without a care in the world. As he entered the room and before anyone could warn him about the flying projectiles, a dart hit him full-on, in the back of the head with enough velocity to penetrate his skull. We stood still momentarily and looked on in astonishment as the dart was truly embedded in the top of his head, a loud, blood curling scream could be heard around the barracks.

"Ahhhh," was the cry from John Machin. I don't think John had a clue what had happened until Dennis and Riggers told him to keep still.

"What the hell hit me?" said John, who was now looking worried.

"There is no easy way of saying this," said Riggers. "You have a dart stuck in your head." I could hear John now whimpering with his hands trying to hide his watering eyes; who the culprit was, we may never know, all I can say is; I saw Muckers looking very sheepish on top of his bed.

John was taken down to the medical centre by Riggers and Dennis, I'm not sure if anybody saw them on the way to the medical centre but it would have made one or two eyes turn; after all, when was the last time you ever saw someone walking to A&E with a dart embedded in their head? We were all waiting with great anticipation for the return of John, Riggers and Dennis fearing the worst. There was hardly anyone that had gone to bed; we just needed to know how John was.

An hour had past when we heard the return of the three amigos. We were all staring at the two swinging doors when we heard them coming up the stairs; it sounded like more than one person but, was it two or was it three, we were asking ourselves? Had he been taken to the local hospital, was he dead, we were just seconds from finding out. First Riggers entered the room with a sad look on his face followed closely by Dennis also looking distraught.

"Where's John?" said Sam. "Is he OK?"

"I'm afraid the dart has gone deeper than first thought," said Riggers "could be touch and go."

"What?" we said, feeling scared and concerned. We were all thinking *we were in major trouble now*; we were all looking at each other for any evidence to who may have thrown the dart; seconds later the doors sprang open to reveal John and his small white stuck-on patch that was covering the shaven area of his head.

"Bastard, John," we all said at about the same time. "You had us believing that you were in hospital, so glad you're all right though." It felt like a huge weight had been lifted off our shoulders, a joke's a joke, but this was overstepping the mark. All this meant we could sleep a lot easier now and not worry too much about waking up to the consequences that we were all dreading.

There were some occasions when the weakest member of the troop would get singled out for preferential treatment for something they may have done wrong, something that would cause the rest of the troop to be punished. All for one and one for all was how it was; unfortunately this sort of cruelty was quite a common thing at times. The reason behind this behavior was to educate the soldier into not letting the rest of the troop down; camaraderie springs to mind. At times it proved to be a great deterrent, however the term 'you can lead a horse to water, but you can't make him drink it' sums up some of the troop.

Some of the lads including myself would prefer the sit down and use the chat method while, some others would take the more aggressive approach; a bass broom bath (Long handled garden broom) was thought to be the answer for the ones who were somewhat germ-infested. It certainly worked, but it's difficult to know who did it for the correct reasons and who did it just to get a kick out of it. I guess we will never know.

One of the more lesser punishments that was used as a fun prank was, whoever was singled out for the gratification of some of the lads was to be tied down to a dining room type chair. Their hands would be tied together behind the back of the chair and their legs would be tied to the legs of the chair. I remember watching from my bed not knowing what the hell was going on and making me feel very uncomfortable. After watching John getting a dart in his head and hearing about the bass broom bath, I was thinking, *what form of punishment is going to be inflicted on this young lad?*

It wasn't long before I found out. One of about six or seven guys that were surrounding the chair took an iron from his locker and plugged it into the wall socket. You could feel the nervousness bouncing off the walls. *My god, they're going to burn him,* I said to myself with my bottom jaw dropping to the floor.

"Right you bastard, we are going to brand you with the iron, understand do you?" said one of the lads angrily.

"No, please don't," was the pitiful cry that was falling on deaf ears. The iron was pushed up to within about an inch from the skin of his forearm.

"Feel the heat, can you?" said one of the lads. "The next time you feel it will be when it touches your skin."

"Please, please, don't burn me," said the guy, who was now almost in tears. I cannot believe that I was just sitting on the edge of my bed and not doing anything to stop it, maybe because I didn't really think they were going to brand him.

One of the other guys that were surrounding the chair suggested blindfolding him.

"Yeah, great idea," said someone else. This was like your worst nightmare; at least we were all spared the humiliation of seeing him crying. With the blindfold in place and the guy in the chair crying like the Niagara Falls, everything was ready.

"Are you ready?" was yelled from the guy with the iron.

"No, I beg you, please don't burn me," said the guy in the chair, but to no avail. I could see one or two of the guys that were standing around the chair starting to smile and giggle, I was thinking *what sadistic bastards,* just as I felt I need to do something about this situation, I saw the guy who was standing behind him with the iron also holding a mess tin in his hand, it was all falling into place now. Just as the guy with the iron was only a millimeter away from his skin, they shouted, "Now" and almost in the same breath took the iron away from the arm and then slammed the cold metal mess tin against the upper part of the arm. The guy in the chair squealed like a pig. The cold mess tin was to give the impression that he had been burnt and, the guy in the chair would continue shouting and screaming still believing that he had been burnt. With everybody now laughing it was time to take the blindfold off; the guy in the chair glanced over to his arm fearing the worst.

"What… What did you do?" he said, stuttering; an explanation was the least we could give. I never know to this day whether or not he ever saw the funny side of the prank, but at least he lived to see another day, and that's how it was with pranks.

Six weeks down the line and three months into our training, meant it was time to go on leave again; however, it would be for three weeks this time around and not the five days that we were allocated back in June. It's amazing how much trouble you can get into in three weeks; buying a crossbow and finding somewhere safe to fire it was proving difficult until I ran into my mate Dec. Why did Dec even dare me to fire at his dads shed?

CHAPTER THIRTY-SEVEN
A HOLE IN ONE

It was now mid August and time to receive our bounty from the TC. One hundred and thirty five pounds was what I received; with that and about twenty pounds in my Army Post Office savings account, plus a few quid already accumulated in my bank, I was feeling very wealthy and couldn't wait to go home. Three weeks at home meant three weeks before I saw any of my Army mates again so it was a case of saying, "Take care , see you in three weeks, and have a great time with your loved ones, and in your case Steve, the sheep."

"What yer mean by that, Wolfendale?" said Steve.

"Nothing at all," I said. We all shook hands as if it was to be our final goodbye, we had come so close as friends that I could feel the sense of balance changing from where I would like to be at this moment in time; even though I wanted to go home to see by family and friends, I knew deep down I would be missing my Army mates more than I could ever imagine. When I arrived home later that day I was greeted by my parents as if nothing had changed. It was like I had never been away, as if I had just come home from a day at school; visiting more of my sisters and brothers that were married and lived nearby was one of my priorities. Three weeks can be a long time to find things to do, especially after the hectic schedules we had back in Bramcote.

I met up with Dec, my best mate on several occasions and to my surprise, he explained that he was now thinking more seriously about joining up.

"Wow," I said with a feeling of jubilation, "it would be unbelievable for me if you did, to have my best mate, someone I class as another brother serving alongside me would be the best thing ever."

"Well," said Dec with glee written all over his face, "I am definitely going to make an appointment before Christmas to see about joining."

"Can't wait," I said, rubbing my hands together. The second week of my leave saw me doing some therapeutic shopping. After picking Dec up from his house we made our way into town on a beautiful Saturday morning. I wasn't sure what I wanted or needed to buy, but felt I would treat myself to something; a crossbow could be seen in the window of the gun shop calling my name.

"What do you reckon, Dec?" I said, looking into the shop window.

"Reckon what?" said Dec, wondering what I was looking at.

"The crossbow, you daft bugger," I said. "What else do you think I was looking at; I wasn't contemplating on buying the glass window."

"Crossbow," said Dec, looking bemused.

"Penny for your thoughts, Dec," I said.

"Just never saw you as a William Tell," said Dec.

"What do you think, mate?" I said.

"Go for it," said Dec in a way that suggested *it's your money, not mine.* That was it, before I knew it I was on my way back to Dec's with a crossbow in hand, oh and several hunting arrows. Back at Dec's house everything seemed quiet, in other words the house was empty. I was feeling agitated and wanted to try out my new toy.

"There's nowhere to fire it around here?" I said to Dec, in hope that he might have an intelligent answer to offer.

"Why don't you fire it at my dad's wooden shed?" said Dec. I was thinking *yeah Dec, that sounds really intelligent.*

"Are you sure your dad won't mind?"

"Nah, it will be alright, I won't tell him," said Dec in a nonchalant way.

"OK then, if you're sure," I said. Basically I just wanted to try it out. I pulled back the steel-like cable with all my might; it was hard to believe how strong you needed to be. I put the butt of the crossbow into my hip joint and just pulled until the cable was locked into place behind a small metal catch. I then placed a hunting arrow into the groove on top of the weapon.

"Loaded and ready," I said, pointing the crossbow towards the shed. With Dec at my side I took aim. I knew it wasn't going to make the sound of the SLR but I was just as scared.

With my finger now on at the ready I gently squeezed the trigger. Even the shed was feeling scared at the thought of being shot with an arrow more suited to shooting an elephant. *Twang*, the arrow flew towards the now terrified shed; a hole the size of golf ball could be seen as the arrow ripped through the front of the shed.

"Gordon Bennet!" was the shout from Dec, "my dad will go mental!"

We both walked over to the shed to inspect the damage. The arrow had gone straight through the shed and was now lying on the wooden floor smiling at us both. We could almost hear the arrow saying *told you so*; we were both astonished at the power it possessed. A little white lie now was in order: wasn't me dad, no idea what could have caused that, maybe a bird strike. At the end of the day it was just two young teenagers having some fun without thinking.

The three weeks soon went by. It was Monday 2nd of September and time to catch the train back to Nuneaton to see what the next term would bring. After arriving back it seemed like a more relaxing atmosphere as one by one and, after doing a head count we were all accounted for; it was straight to the ironing room for me making sure my kit was ready for the Tuesday morning parade. We were no longer NIGs by definition, the new intake of Junior Leaders were now arriving, the feeling of *yes, I outrank you* was what I felt even though I didn't outrank anyone. After the Tuesday morning parade we were told to make our way into the lecture room as the TC would like to address us on coming events leading up to Christmas.

Once seated, we were all told to sit to attention by Bombardier Bartlett as the TC entered the room all smartly dressed; he turned towards us and told us to sit at ease.

"I hope you all enjoyed your well earned break," he said, smiling like only the TC can. "Nice to see we have no absentees. This is the time when we tend to lose one or two of you, after being with your families and friends for three weeks it can be hard to adjust to Army life all over again. First on the agenda is, as from next Monday, which will be Monday 9th, we will all be in long sleeve order; pullovers will be the dress." Bombardier Bartlett and Sergeant Preece were standing either side of the TC taking all the information on board; having no trust in us what so ever, was quite a common thing. The TC continued his speech:

"Make sure they understand and make sure they're pullovers are immaculately ironed," as he browsed over to his left.

"Yes Sir," said Bombardier Bartlett, at the same time given us the daggers look.

"There will be several outings to various places over the next term," said the TC. "A lot of your training will be out of bounds training, starting off with an orienteering exercise in a week's time in Cannock Chase: first aid, physical training and sports will also be part of the main structure leading up to Christmas. As far as free time goes, Saturday afternoons and all day

Sunday will be at your own disposal, dependent on whether or not we have something planned for you." We all looked at each other with a *Yes, can't wait* kind of look. "Church parades will be every four weeks as normal, hobbies will be reduced to one session a week on a Wednesday night instead of the original two, there will be no more pay parades, all monies will be transferred straight into your bank accounts so make sure you spend wisely."

The lecture went on for about thirty minutes until we were dismissed by the TC to go to our welcome NAAFI break.

Who's coming out Saturday? Who's doing what on Sunday? Could be heard amongst the ranks; feeling responsible for ourselves had everybody feeling excited at the prospect of having a little me time.

In the afternoon we were taken to the Educational Block to be taught some map reading skills and, how to use a Silva Compass in preparation for the coming week, after all, they can't have us getting lost now, can they? After taking our seats in what looked like a five star education room, compared to my now forgotten school days; the lecturer dressed in his smart civilian clothes explained what orienteering was all about.

"The aim of orienteering is to navigate between control points marked on an orienteering map; as a competitive sport the challenge is to complete the course in the quickest time choosing your own route. As a recreational activity it does not matter how young, old or fit you are, you can run or walk, making progress at your own leisure." Not a chance we were going to be able to walk, however, the thought of walking did sound very appetising. Learning a new skill was very pleasing in respect that it was a pleasant change from military activities; orienteering would not be one of the skills I would have associated military training with, but now when I think about it: fitness, map reading and being able to operate and think for yourself is a big part of being a British soldier. After a quiet weekend of little activities, the only thing that was different was, that we had to iron our pullovers; they took a lot less time to iron than our shirts. It was a case of getting out the can of spray starch and spraying the cotton patches and epaulets that were on each shoulder until they were stiff and crisp; two cotton patches on each arm sleeve around the elbow area also needed to be starched and that was about it. In the coming week the TC decided that it would be a great idea to insert some fun to the orienteering exercise by offering a £4 bounty; could I really win and take the money that was on offer? Well I definitely was going to give it ago.

CHAPTER THIRTY-EIGHT

ORIENTEERING

Monday morning arrived in quick time; we paraded outside the Battery Block at our mandatory 0800hrs dressed in our smart woolly pullies. The weather was sunny with a cool breeze blowing across my face. Wearing the jumpers made us all look like we had put on a few pounds over the weekend however; I can assure you we hadn't. The main focus of the inspection was spent inspecting our jumpers.

"Too much starch, Lynch," said Bombardier Bartlett.

"Not enough starch, Norris."

"Elbow pads need more attention, Rigby."

I think almost everybody got picked up for their jumpers not being as they should; to be honest, we half expected to get grilled. After the inspection we were told to get our bodies into the block and get ready for our orienteering exercise in Cannock Chase.

"Get changed into your red PT vests and your combat jackets along with your webbing belt," commanded Bombardier Bartlett. It felt quite refreshing wearing a PT vest under our combat jacket instead of our cotton shirts that would always feel tight and itchy. A forty-five minute bus journey saw us park up in a small dirt like car park within metres of the wooded terrain.

"Off the bus and line up in three ranks," was the order from the front of the bus. The TC and Bombardier Bartlett along with Sergeant Preece were all in attendance; the only one of them that looked remotely interested in this activity was the TC, as he stood there rubbing his hands together dressed in what I would call his non-battle dress: shiny brown shoes, khaki pressed trousers and his long sleeve pullover.

We were all given our Silva Compass and map. The Silva Compass could be hung around your neck by a long cord thus making it easier to plot your course, all you needed to do was to bring the map up to your waist area and then place the Silva Compass on the map whilst, still hanging around your neck.

We were given our coordinates to which we would adjust our Silva Compass and a small card about the size of a bingo card with roughly twelve small squares on it, the idea behind the card is when you reached each point, there would be a stapler attached to a tree that you would use to punch your card. Each stapler had its own letter or number signified by small needles, so when the stapler was pressed on to your card, it would leave an indent of a number or letter. Foul play was not uncommon; you would occasionally get the odd bar-steward that would rip the stapler off and throw it away, leaving you with no way of marking your card.

"Listen in everybody," said the TC in his serious voice. "Shortly you'll be setting off at five minute intervals between each man; you'll enter the wooded area over there, pointing to the entrance, and then find yourself around the course. Each point will be clearly marked with a red and white hooped can, Wolfendale that will be black and white to you," as he looked and grinned at me like only a TC can. It brought a chuckle from the ranks however; I think everybody was just trying to be polite to the TCs so-called 'funny remark' that was now wearing thin.

"You will begin in alphabetical order, for those of you who are not sure what that means I will call out your name when it's your turn. Each one of you will hand over to me the sum of ten pence before starting, the one who finishes in the quickest time and getting all the points stamped correctly on then card,will be pronounced the winner; in return for your effort you will receive the pot of gold." I was thinking *that's about four quid up for grabs.*

"Worth giving it a go," I mumbled to myself. I could see the looks on everyone's face as we were getting nearer to the off, they all seemed to be thinking the same as me; money up for grabs, get in there. We had a choice of wearing our combat jacket over our red PT vest or take the combat jacket off. With it being an overcast day I decided to keep my jacket on; didn't fancy getting bitten by all the hidden insects.

The better half of us were told to get back onto the bus where we were given our lunch boxes while the other half of the troop alphabetically from A to M, got themselves lined up outside; white cardboard boxes the size of a shoe box were passed around the bus, a bit like pass the parcel. Riggers, Sheep and I were sitting near the back of the bus with an inquisitive look on our faces; the smell from inside the boxes was pretty odourless, so we were at a loss as to what we might find inside. I could see Steve shaking his box vigorously from side to side.

"What the hell are you doing, Steve?" I said, looking confused.

"Seeing if there is any kind of life in the box," he said.

"Well if there was, it'll be dead now," said Riggers. A quick tug of the folded down lid revealed all: cling film wrapped sandwiches, a boiled egg that was black at one end, a chocolate bar and piece of fruit. "Anybody like to swap a boiled egg for a sandwich?" could be heard from the front of the bus, my chocolate for your fruit; I think it ended up with the boiled egg brigade, the sandwich brigade and the chocolate bar brigade; food was being swapped all over the bus.

"Where's Dennis?" I said as I looked around the bus. "Dennis, where are you hiding?" I continued to shout. Just then Steve looked out of the window of the bus to see Dennis standing next to Chris Muckersie. Steve knocked hard on the glass window to grab Dennis's attention.

"Norris," shouted Steve, as Dennis made his way to the window.

"What's up?" said Dennis, looking up to the window.

"What's your surname?" said Steve with a kind of serious grin, Dennis was thinking that Parry had lost the plot but still went along with the quizzing.

"Norris," said Dennis.

"So your name begins with N, am I right?" said Steve.

"Yes," said Dennis still looking confused.

"So why are you lined up next to Muckersie?" said Steve, staring.

"We were told to line up in alphabetical order, A–M," said Dennis.

"BINGO," said Steve.

"Still not with you," said Dennis. Steve got Dennis to recite the alphabet from A to M.

"I J K L N M," said Dennis.

"Stop, I J K L and what's next?" said Steve to Dennis with his face now pushing the window out.

"Shit, it's M and then N; can't believe I could make such a cock up."

As Dennis got onto the bus he was given some abuse as he stood looking down the length of the bus, to be honest he deserved all he got.

"Yeah OK, don't milk it guys," said Dennis in a sort of *I can't believe what a dick I've been* tone of voice.

About forty five minutes had passed, we could see the first of many of the lads racing out of the wood to the finishing line from the seats of the bus, they didn't look to be too exhausted which made me feel that it wasn't going to be as tough as I first thought.

"How was it?" we all asked as the first person clambered onto the bus for their packed lunch. Without giving too much away he said, "So so, found it difficult to find a couple of the points so I just left them and made my way back." I think we were all just trying to gain the edge over the ones that had already gone first, I'm still thinking, £4 at stake here ; *not to be sniffed at*.

With most of them now back, we were called forward to the start line by the TC. "Off the bus you lot, the ones that have not yet done the course."

"That includes you Dennis," as the banter continued from one and all. I was last to go as per usual.

"OK Wolfendale: here is your compass, map and scoring card, best of luck" said the TC. I stood there facing the woods like a sprinter on the starting blocks. "Three, two, one, goooooo!" was the command in a loud voice. Once in the woods that were very dark and condensed, I made my way at some pace to the first marker which I found with relative ease; all downhill with a few small ditches to negotiate, my pace increased with each marker I managed to find. It was proving a lot less challenging than I first thought, to me it just felt like a cross country run and to my surprise, I took to the orienteering side of the task like a duck to water. I was finding it moderately easy.

It wasn't too long before I could see the light of day through the woods that were about fifty metres in front of me; all the markers were now a thing of the past; my card was looking like a pin cushion with more holes than moth bitten jumper. Exiting the woods, I could see the TC in the distance encouraging the last few of us over the finishing line.

"Wolfendale, you made it, well done!" said the TC with a stunned look on his face. "Maybe I have been underestimating you Wolfendale, get yourself on the bus."

It was now about 1500hrs and with everything packed up, the final few were ordered back onto the bus by Bombardier Bartlett and Sergeant Preece for the journey back; stepping over the empty white cardboard boxes that had contained our lunch, I made my way back to my seat.

"What was your time?" could be heard from several of the lads.

"Did you get all the markers?" was also another question that was being thrown around the bus. I was becoming more intrigued the more I heard the times and how many markers each and everybody managed to achieve. I never heard anyone claiming a time or score that had beaten the one I achieved however, I would have to wait until the TC had marked the cards back in the barracks. It was a jolly atmosphere on the way back with the so-called Military Song

Book proving to be a hit with us all; it reminded me of being at Elland Road watching my beloved Leeds United, someone starts a song and within minutes everybody knows the words. On this occasion it was a song called *A Yellow Bird*.

The prettiest girl, I ever saw, was sipping Burma, through a straw
The prettiest girl, I ever saw, was sipping Burma, through a straw

I picked her up; I laid her down, her long blonde hair, lay all around
I picked her up; I laid her down, her long blonde hair, lay all around

I pushed it in, I pulled it out, it felt so good, it made her shout
I pushed it in, I pulled it out, it felt so good it, it made her shout

The wedding was, a formal one, her father had, a white shot gun
The wedding was, a formal one, her father had a, a white shot gun

And now l have, a mother-in-law, and forty kids, to call me pa
And now I have, a mother-in-law, and forty kids to, to call me pa

A yellow bird, with a yellow bill, landed on, my window sill
I coaxed it in with a piece of bread, and stamped right on its
Its Fucking head

The following day the TC got us all together in Wingate's Block lecture room for the result of the orienteering exercise. I was feeling quite up beat with the fact that I believed I had won and, was expecting to get a £4 bounty.

"Listen in," said the TC standing there dressed in his smart pressed uniform, "before the results of the orienteering exercise, I would like to bring to your notice that there will be a need for extra duties in the cookhouse this weekend, that means anyone who gets pulled up for anything un-Army-like between now and Saturday, will be spending the whole weekend in the cookhouse." You could have heard a pin drop as we all looked at each other in disbelief. I was definitely in contention for the cookhouse reward as I had yet to do a cookhouse duty; this might just be my time.

"OK, I have the results of the orienteering exercise," said the TC as he ruffled through the sheets of paper he was holding in front of him. There was silence from the ranks as we sat impatiently waiting for the outcome.

"In third place is Junior Gunner Lester Fitzergerald."

"Well done Fitzy," we all mumbled.

"Second place goes to, Junior Gunner Parry," said the TC.

"Cheat," said George in an amusing way.

"On yer bike Lynch, not my fault you've got two left feet."

"OK, keep your noise down," said the TC, "and in first place and champion of the orienteering is…" There was a long pause and a drum roll from some of the lads as I sat there waiting in great anticipation for my name to be called out when the TC announced, "Junior Gunner Quinn, *What?* I was thinking, at the same time questioning the integrity of the TC. His arithmetic was nothing short of abysmal. I was in a state of shock, but who was I to question his ability to count in front of the troop. The last thing I wanted was a short spell in the nick.

The following day I knocked on the TCs door that was slightly ajar. "Come in," was the reply in a stern voice. I marched in, stood to attention and did the mandatory salute before blurting out my trivial but more than warranted *I have a bone to pick with you* question. I explained the situation with the utmost sincerity rolling off my tongue, which seemed to amuse the TC.

"Wolfendale," said the TC, "You believe you have won?"

"Yes Sir," I said feeling smug with myself. The TC opened his top drawer to reveal the results paper; looking up and down with his eyes no more than an inch from the ink of the paper, he finally found my name and my score.

"Wolfendale," he shouted loudly and slowly into my face, "you're correct, you did win, I apologise." An apology from the TC; *unheard of*, I was thinking.

"Well done," said the TC, "you will have to get the prize money off Junior Gunner Quinn, tell him that's an order."

"Thank you Sir," I said as I turned and made my way to find Quinn. By the end of the evening I was £4 better off and feeling good about myself after locating Quinn and explaining the TCs cock up. What happened in the next week was something that only Andy Clayton could explain; why he said what he did is beyond comprehension.

CHAPTER THIRTY-NINE
INSTANT REGRET

As one week rolled into another more was expected, our dress needed to be smarter, our drill needed to be sharper and our accommodation needed to be gleaming at all times. The first of the COs inspections that we would encounter over the coming months was due, several of what I would like to call the less menial tasks were put on the back burner (So to speak). We were told that giving up the occasional lunch break was a necessary requirement according to Sergeant Preece and Bombardier Bartlett, whose orders would have come through the chain of command.

Following our early morning parade on Thursday morning we were told to be back in the block for 1100hrs sharp, straight after NAAFI break for extra cleaning duties.

"The CO will be inspecting all of 33 Campbell Battery," said Sergeant Preece in his stern deep voice, "that includes Wingate Troop. Tomorrow morning at around 0830hrs the CO along with the RSM will inspect your rooms along with: lockers, washrooms, showers, toilets, corridors, stairs, drying room, basically the whole block." You could tell by the tone of his voice and the way he addressed us that we didn't dare cock this one up. I had never felt so much silence within the ranks, I even felt too scared to breathe at one point.

"Troop fall out," said Sergeant Preece. "Don't be late back." We had two hours to kill with not much going on in the morning so we were expected to go and see George at the barbers shop for a quick short back and sides and, to do any admin we had to do, like going down to the BQMS stores for any exchanges we might have. This is where I bumped into the smartly dressed Bombardier James; he seemed like the sort of guy who would cross the road with manners. He was part of Shrapnel troop and was there to help with their training including drill. Over the next few months we became good friends, so much that when there was no one around I was allowed to address him as Jessy.

At 1100hrs we were all in our rooms waiting for Sergeant Preece and Bombardier Bartlett to arrive to allocate us our respective room jobs.

"Wolfendale, Norris, Rigby, washrooms. Clayton and Lynch, you are on toilets, Parry and Gandy, stairs and drying room." I was thinking *favouritism, two room jobs, not fair*, as I looked across at Sam and Steve. The list of jobs went on until everybody had been detailed their respective jobs. Riggers, Dennis and I made our way to the washrooms and to be honest, I wasn't sure what more could be done to make them look like they were fit for a Queen or in our case, the CO. It wasn't long before we were presented with some red lead paint to paint around the edges of the washroom; with only two, three-inch brushes, I decided to stick to the basic cleaning whilst Riggers and Dennis tried their skills in painting by numbers.

It was now getting close to lunch time and we were just finishing off tidying up when we heard one almighty cry from Sergeant Preece. At first we gave each other a double eye take, we all looked at each other as if we had seen the ghost of Christmas past, we knew something was amiss, but were unsure what, until we heard Sergeant Preece going ballistic with one of the lads.

It was Junior Gunner Andy Clayton. We looked out the window overlooking the main road outside of the block to see what was kicking off; "Left right left right left right left, mark time," was being rattled out by Sergeant Preece, Junior Gunner Clayton was being doubled down to the Guardroom at a hundred miles a hour, it was the scariest thing I had seen since arriving at Gamecock Barracks some five months ago, his feet never even touched the freshly brushed tarmac.

Andy was being humiliated. He was almost in tears, I could see his blown out reddened cheeks that looked like they were ready to explode at any minute; seconds later he was out of sight and awaiting his fate. Rumour control was in full force; no one seemed to have any idea of what had gone on or, why Andy had been doubled down to the Guardroom. It wasn't long before Sergeant Preece arrived back at the block and paraded us outside.

"Listen in and be warned," was the cry from Sergeant Preece. "Junior Gunner Clayton is now down at the Guardroom in the hands of the Provo Sergeant, if anyone else would like to join him then please let me know, just one quick call to the Provo and I'm sure it can be arranged." We were still none the wiser what Andy had done and Sergeant Preece wasn't giving away any clues.

It wasn't until after tea that we were to find out the reason why Andy was thrown into the holiday inn for the afternoon; I didn't know whether to laugh or just mull over at what a complete idiot Andy had been. Apparently when Sergeant Preece entered the block to see how we were getting on with the room jobs, he saw Andy painting the edges of the toilet floor with red lead paint, like he was ordered to do. Sergeant Preece wasn't holding back with what he had to say.

"Clayton," he said, "you're supposed to paint the edges around the toilets not the toilet doors, get it sorted or you'll be doing it in your lunch break."

For some reason only known to Andy he flipped, he turned around and looked Sergeant Preece in the eyes and said, "If you can do any better, then do it your fucking self."

The phrase *instant regret* sprang to mind, said Andy. *Oh my god* we were all thinking, credit where credit's due, but what the hell possessed Andy to say what he did is beyond intellectual capacity. Anyone with any common sense would know that answering back to a senior rank is asking for trouble, let alone saying what Andy did. Andy became a cult hero amongst the ranks for his foolish mistake, but I am sure there must be better ways to make friends with the lads.

The following week saw us getting ready for the Junior Leaders annual regimental cross country event, not something I was looking forward to. It is an event that the TC would like to win. We had some speedy individuals in Wingate Troop that would be expected to be up with the pace makers; I would say I was among the top ten in the troop on a good day. I would prefer to treat cross country as more as a recreational sport, not a competition. It was Friday morning and the sun was showing its face once more.

"On parade now," was the order from Bombardier Bartlett, with a hop skip and a jump we were ready for action lined up outside the block. "Attennnnnntion," was the command as the TC was spotted exiting our accommodation and down the concrete steps. The TC was looking as smart as ever as he told us to stand at ease; you could almost feel it was going to be one of those; *I am going to read you the riot act* moments.

"I want each and every one of you to have an early lunch today, I would also like you to eat wisely, be careful to how much you eat," said the TC. "At 1430hrs this afternoon, as well you know, it is the regimental cross country event, I want to win it, not just win it, but win it for Wingate Troop. Bombardier Bartlett will have you lined up outside the block at 1345hrs ready in all respects: your dress will be red PT vest, blue shorts and green Army socks, let's show the rest of the regiment how strong Wingate Troop is; let's put Wingate Troop well and truly on the map."

To be honest the TCs speech made us all feel proud to be part of the troop, if that speech didn't spur us on, then nothing would. As ordered we were paraded outside the block ready for the challenge that lay ahead, and then marched down to the windbreak sports field; it was a nice gentle pace until we were in sight of the field.

"Right, listen in lads, time to impress the rest of the regiment," said Bombardier Bartlett. "Double march." For a few moments we were the talk of the town, or should I say the talk of the sports field; we must have doubled past every other troop at least once that was now awaiting our arrival until we were brought to a halt where the TC was standing. We were told to fall out and get ourselves prepared for the now ever getting nearer Charge of the Light Brigade.

"Wolfie, get over here," said Steve. I made the short distance of about two metres over to Steve and replied with, "What do you want?"

"Try and keep up with me if you can," said Steve, "that way you should finish nearer the front of the race and not nearer the back."

"Cheeky twat," I said, "two things you need to understand. First as you know, there is no way I could keep up with you even if I was on acid, and secondly, I am not going to finish near the back."

There must have been close on five to six hundred of us lined up in our respective coloured PT vests ready for two laps of the wind-break. As we were called into line, we seemed to lose all sight of where each one of us was positioned. There were red vests dotted all over the start line, which was about a hundred metres across and just as deep. You could see all of the Officers and senior ranks lining the route, they were shouting and yelling like football fans, *try not to give yourselves a nose bleed* I was thinking. We were now seconds from the starting pistol being fired. As I looked up to the start line, I could see that it was our TC that had been trusted with the gun, my main concern was, I hoped he was going to hand it back to its original owner once the race had started.

"On your marks, get ready..." *bang!* Went the gun and charge went the Cavalry. Halfway around the first circuit and running well, I was overtaken by George; I just glanced to my right for a split second and then he was gone. I must admit it didn't fill me with joy, but at the same time, I knew that

George was a strong runner. We were all being ushered along as we past the finishing line for the first time. I am just glad I saved a little bit of energy so that I could put on a show for the TC as I stepped up a gear. Second lap was now in sight as we left the roaring fans behind us, it was nice to hear the sound of silence once more as we were now entering the final mile of the race. The race was almost over for me as I could hear the unmistakeable sound of the officers and senior ranks in the distance, as I rounded the last right hand bend, I was greeted by my TC; if he had got any closer to me he would have been part of the race.

I was running alongside a smaller-than-me black lad from 2 Baker Battery.

"Wolfendale, don't you dare let that lad beat you," said the TC shouting down my ear. It was a sprint towards the line between us both; I could feel my competitive instinct kick in once more, I gave it my all and more just to cross the line before my competitor in our individual battle.

It was more than I could muster to stay on my feet after the exertions of that final sprint; I was greeted by the voice of George and Steve who now had already recovered from their efforts.

"Where did you finish?" I said to them both still trying to catch my breath.

"Seventh," said Steve.

"What about you, George?"

"Twelve."

"Well, I came fiftieth," I said, "not bad out of five or six hundred; let's hope we have done well as a troop." It wasn't long before all the competitors were back and the scores on the doors were being announced. Everybody stood around and listened to the COs speech, it was the same old speech that we keep hearing except, it just seemed to be more important in the sense that we were now being spoken to by a Lieutenant Colonel (A Crown and a Pip). A huge white board was turned around by two of the senior ranks to reveal the final standings. A big cheer went up from Wingate Troop as we saw for the first time that we were the victors. Not sure who was more excited, us, or the TC, either way it was a day to remember for us all. We were given the rest of the day off, albeit there were only two hours left before the end of the working day.

The next four weeks went past like there was no tomorrow, before we had our next five day break, which included my 17th birthday on the 14th September; a blanket bath up and down the barrack room floor getting bounced from pillar to post was cheap entertainment for the lads.

Leave came and went unnoticed; time spent with my mate Dec and precious family time to recharge my batteries were top of my things to do list. It was now early October and we were now faced with one of our longest terms before our Christmas break, about ten weeks to be precise, as opposed to the normal six or seven weeks. Up until now I had managed to stay out of trouble, which is more I can say for some of the lads in my room; however, all that was soon to change leading up to Christmas.

CHAPTER FORTY

GUILTY AS CHARGED

Tuesday 8th October and we were all arriving back at the barracks; early evening brought lots of chin-wagging from inside our now well established room. Our room was now looking like it was fit for a king: everything was gleaming, the floor was shining like a new penny and our beds lined up with regimental precision.

"How's things, Woofer?" said Steve, sitting on his bed.

"Fine, had a wonderful few days' welcome break," I said as I sat down on the end of his bed.

"Who gave you permission to sit on my bed?" said Steve in his serious but sort of joking way. More banter followed until Steve said, "Fancy a trip to Leicester at the weekend? We could go after RSM's parade." I had never ventured too far from the barracks since joining in May, but I thought, *why not*.

"How far away is it?" I asked.

"About thirty minutes," said Steve, "we could catch a taxi into Nuneaton and then catch a bus or maybe a taxi to Leicester."

"Sounds fine by me," I said, "what do you intend to do there? Not get drunk I hope?"

"Don't be stupid Wolfendale," said Steve, "what do you take me for?" I just looked at Steve, thinking, *if anyone can drown a few pints, then it's you.* I was practically tee-total compared to Steve; he could out drink a fish on a bad day. Within five minutes the news travelled around the barracks like a bad does of STDs.

"Great idea," said Riggers.

"You can count me in as well," said Sam. Before I knew it, there were enough of us to fill the green regimental bus. I feared the worst at best; what was meant to be a small outing with just one or two of us, was now turning into a stag weekend.

Saturday arrived and now with the RSMs parade over, it was a quick dash back to the block to get changed into our smart casual civilian clothes before having some lunch down at the cookhouse. A few of the lads that had originally said they wanted to go, had now decided for one reason or another that they had other plans, *fine by me* I was thinking, the fewer the better; all in all there were about ten of us including my mates: Steve, Sam, George, Riggers and Dennis, along with Slaney, Rowlands, Luckhurst and Jock Monaghan.

I must admit we looked as if we could have been going to a football match the way we were making our way to the Guardroom; we got a few stares from some of the military staff that were on duty on this fine, sunny but cold Saturday afternoon. Down at the Guardroom we gave our names and booked out; even the Guard Commander was looking confused by the mass of bodies that were going into town; *see you later,* would be going through his mind. As there were so many of us we decided taking two taxis would be a more sensible option. I believe that this was one of their busiest times of the week; they were always guaranteed a fare from the barracks. You could almost sense the merriment in their faces and the noticeable rubbing of their hands as we exited the camp.

"Where to, lads?" they would ask as they opened the doors for us.

"Leicester please," said Steve. *Wow,* the smile on the taxi drivers' face was a picture. I could see his eyebrows elevating to the top of his receding hair. The two taxis made their way to Leicester for what was to be an interesting encounter. We got the taxi drivers to drop us off near the town centre as we all agreed that this would be the best option: shops, pubs, and wouldn't you know it, a tattooist, yes a tattooist shop could be seen from where we were.

"Anybody up for a tattoo?" said Dave Slaney, like he was about to take on the town.

"Up yours," said Riggers, "no chance."

"What about you, Wolfie?" said Dave.

"Not sure," I said, "are we allowed? Don't fancy getting into trouble." No one seemed to give a damn about the consequences as some of us were still deliberating over the matter; Dave Slaney had all ready made up his mind and it seemed a little unfair to allow him to have a tattoo on his own.

"Go on then," I said, "count me in."

"Go for it Wolfie," said Dennis, who was clearly not going to have one. Malcolm Rowlands was almost falling about laughing.

"Fucking mad bastard Wolfendale," said Malcolm, holding his sides in.

"What about you then Malc?" I said. "Too scared, I bet?"

"No, just don't know whether to or not," he said. Malcolm was quite impressionable just like me; it took no more than a few seconds for Malcolm to agree to have a tattoo.

"Good man, Malc," I said, at the same time putting my arm around him and marching him towards the tattooist.

There were no more takers even though I tried my hardest to get Sam and George to participate, but to no avail. I am not sure where everybody else went to; everybody went their own separate own ways as I remember it.

"See you later," said George.

"Just ask for an amputation," joked Steve.

"Good luck," said Riggers, "even though I think you're all mad."

We made our way into the unknown; a small room that was covered with different tattoo patterns all over the walls greeted are presence. Dave made his way apprehensible into the room followed by Malcolm and then me hiding behind Malcolm.

"How can I help you?" said a man who looked to be in his thirties. He was wearing blue jeans and a short sleeve shirt exposing and marketing his artwork that covered his arms.

"We are interested in having a tattoo," said Dave as we gave him a slight but firm nudge forward as if to say, *it was your idea to come in and have a tattoo*. To my amazement the man was very hospitable towards us, after all he was in the business to make money and we were paying customers. I was quite shocked that he didn't ask for any ID to verify our age, I mean to say, I only just started to shave a few months ago and that was under duress. I looked no more than about fourteen years of age and here I was about to have a tattoo.

There is no turning back now, I said to myself, we had the cash, he had the tools; it was just a case of choosing a design among the catalogue of designs he had.

I was quite shocked at the price of some of the tattoos; I wasn't sure whether the number at the bottom of the design was the design number or the price of the tattoo. They were ranging from about £3 up to £30 and above. I chose my design carefully knowing that the tattoo was going to be with me for life. The design was a red rose with a love heart underneath the rose and a scroll that that cut the heart in two. I had the words mum and dad inscribed within the scroll; to me it was the most wonderful thing I could have done. It made me feel that my parents were with me at my time of need; they are the most precious things in my life.

I remember sitting in the chair not knowing if it was going to hurt, Malcolm and Dave sat behind me still awaiting their fate as the tattooist rolled up my shirt sleeve, and then cleansing my skin before switching on his tattoo gun; it was a buzzing sound that seem to get louder and louder as it reached my frail skin. I tried to look away, not because he had bad breath, but I didn't fancy seeing the needle penetrating my arm. I felt this kind of burning feeling as the tattooist sketched the outline on my right forearm.

"Hang on in there," said Dave as he could see the grimace on my face. From start to finish the tattoo took about thirty minutes to complete; some cream and some free advice to finish off what was to me, a masterful work of art, for the total cost of £5.

"Great tattoo Paul," said Malc, staring at the art work.

"Feeling a little sore," I said, breathing heavily. I took a seat and waited for Dave and Malcolm to have their tattoos; it took all of my mental power to prevent me from looking down at my tattoo that I was so in awe of, I just wanted to get back to the barracks and show it off to my buddies.

All in all we spent about two hours in the tattooist before leaving to find the rest of the party, we ventured into every pub we came across but without any success, they were nowhere to be found.

"Maybe they have been arrested," I said in a kind of joking way, but at the same time not ruling it out. After about an hour of trying to find them we decided to make our way back to the taxi rank in hope that we might meet up with them again. It was a lost cause, they were either in a gutter somewhere or maybe they had already gone back to camp. It was 2000hrs before we arrived back at our much-loved Gamecock Barracks. On booking back in I noticed that Steve, Pete, Dennis, Sam, George, Luckhurst and Jock Monaghan had all booked back into camp, meaning we were the last three back; making sure we had our sleeves down to cover our tattoos was now our main priority.

I think we all knew we were in serious trouble, but unfortunately, there was no turning the clock back. We made our way through the dark night to our barrack room to find the lights were shining brightly through the windows that were overlooking the road, there seemed to be lots of activity going on so we knew we were in for a prestigious welcome by the lads. We were set upon like a pack of wolves as we entered the room; a rapturous welcome made us feel like we were heroes on the battle field.

"Wolfie, you nutter, let's see your tattoo," said someone.

"Dave, Malcolm, get over here." There was no getting away from the excitement that was bouncing around the room; they all knew we were going to face the music, if not before, then on Monday morning's parade for certain.

Sunday came and went without as much as a peep from Bombardier Bartlett or Sergeant Preece so Dave, Malcolm and I knew that we were going to have to face the consequences on Monday morning. I had never known the troop so eager to see Monday morning arrive; the lads couldn't resist giving us their verdict as to what was going to happen to us in the morning. "Death row for you three tomorrow," said Steve.

"A month in the slammer at least," said George.

"Maybe kicked out," said someone else.

"Cookhouse fatigues for the next month could be on the cards," said Sam.

I tossed and turned all night until I finally fell out of bed and hit the floor with one almighty thud, the only thing that surprised me was, the fact that hardly anyone woke up. It was still pitch black in the room as I attempted to climb back into bed for a few more hours of beauty sleep. The day of execution was upon us as we were woken up by the duty guard. Dave, Malcolm and I made sure the tattoos were covered after returning from breakfast, we were all feeling nervous but thought, *what will be, will be.*

"Stand by your beds," could be heard from Bombardier Bartlett as he made his way up the stairs. I was thinking because it's long sleeve order, we might, just might get way with a short stay of execution until it all blows over; not a chance. Someone amongst the ranks must have said something: a snitch, a brown nose, an informer, either way it didn't matter; we were in trouble. Bombardier Bartlett made his way around the troop and, one by one made us roll up our sleeves. Dave and Malcolm had already been exposed and it was now my turn to be compromised.

"Roll your sleeve up, Wolfendale," said the Bombardier, breathing in my face. "What's with the white bandage?" He said, "I hope you have not got a tattoo underneath there."

"No Bombardier," I said, hoping that was the end of the matter; with a snarl and a grin Bombardier Bartlett ordered me too remove the poor excuse of a bandage from my forearm, my only concern now was that I needed to be careful not to mess up the beautiful artwork.

"What the fuck is that Wolfendale, scotch mist?" shouted Bombardier Bartlett as the tattoo exposed itself.

"No Bombardier, it's a tattoo," I said, feeling worried.

"I can see that for myself, you idiot," said Bombardier Bartlett. "Do you think I am blind? Well, do you?"

"No, Bombardier," I said, standing rigidly to attention.

I could hear the sound of sniggering and chuckling from around the room as Bombardier Bartlett laid into me. Unfortunately this got me smirking; it was like a funny joke going around when you're in church and you can't stop laughing, even though you know you shouldn't. Bombardier Bartlett looked me in the eyes and said, "Charged, BCs orders, Wolfendale." All three of us were the talk of the camp that day, unfortunately, all for the wrong reasons.

Later on that day we were summoned to the TCs office for another grilling before he announced that we were going before the BC tomorrow morning at 0930hrs. That night I spent every spare minute I had on my kit, making sure I was as immaculate as I could be for BCs orders. Tuesday morning arrived and it was best boots time. Straight after breakfast I got myself polished up for the sin that I'd committed.

"Get outside," was the command from Bombardier Bartlett. "Wolfendale, Rowlands and Slaney stay in the room until after first parade. I shall be back in about thirty minutes, I suggest you use the time to its full, anyone who gets picked up for your dress will find yourself on another charge."

Bombardier Bartlett arrived back like he said he would, bang on time. "Stand by your beds," he said, looking annoyed that three of his boys had infected his reputation. He spent a good five minutes of his precious time inspecting each one of us with a fine-tooth comb. I think he could sense what we were feeling by the way we would occasionally swallow trying to draw breath; he tried to make light of this unfortunate situation by cracking the odd funny remark, the thought of kicking a man when he is down wasn't his thing, although there were times when I had my doubts.

We were lined up facing the heavy swinging doors and marched down the stairs at pace; I am just glad he had the decency to open the doors before we crashed into them. As we exited the block we were told to mark time before we were allowed to cross the road; I am pretty sure it wasn't because he didn't want us to get taken out by a military vehicle.

"Forward," was the cry from Bombardier Bartlett in a loud voice, and within seconds we had travelled the short distance across the really busy road *NOT,* and into BHQ.

It was now the turn of the BSM to grill and inspect us. One thing I did find difficult to understand was, the higher the rank the faster my heart was beating; facing forward I could see the well painted wall with its military framed pictures hanging as straight as a die.

We could see out of the corner of our eyes the BC entering the block with his heavy frame, even though we still had to fix our now kaleidoscope eyes on the military pictures. The BC brushed past us without as much as a care in the world. I imagine that this was a regular occurrence for the BC, just another day at the office. We could see Bombardier Bartlett standing outside the BCs office before he was requested to enter; all I could hear was the stamping of his DMS boots on the polish wooden floor as he came to attention.

After all the brown nosing had taken place it was the turn of the terrible trio to face the music. Bombardier Bartlett could show no mercy, he was in the BHQ and in view of all his superiors, he was being scrutinised by everybody that held a higher rank than him. Bombardier Bartlett addressed us before we entered the BCs office.

"Wolfendale, you'll be going in first," said Bombardier Bartlett.

"Yes Bombardier," I replied sternly.

"On my order you'll turn left," said the Bombardier. "Then when I say, march forward at double quick time, turn right, and then double quick time to the BC who will be sitting behind his desk immediately in front of you. I will then get you to mark time before coming to attention. You'll then salute the BC and then talk when you're told to talk, understand?"

"Yes Bombardier," I said. Final preparation saw the BSM entering and then exiting the BCs office.

"Bombardier Bartlett, the BC is now ready," said the BSM with his pace stick tapping on the floor.

"Ready, Wolfendale?" said Bombardier Bartlett; I was feeling nervous now and accidentally said, "Yes Sir… I mean… Bombardier, sorry Bombardier."

"Attention! Left turn, double march, left right left right left right left, right turn, mark time." Before I could even draw breath I was standing before the BC.

"Junior Gunner Wolfendale, halt," was the final command.

I came to an abrupt halt and then saluted the BC with a stiff upper right arm. I felt all alone without a friend in the world as I waited for my charge to be read out.

I saw the BC look down at the charge sheet and then within seconds the BC read out the charge in a clear concise manner that had been typed up for him.

"Are you 24311682 Junior Gunner Wolfendale?"

"Yes, Sir," I said without as much as a movement of my head.

"You have been sanctioned here before me today because apparently you cannot be trusted when allowed the privilege, and believe me it is a privilege, to be allowed out of the barracks and out into the town," said the BC. "I believe that you took it upon yourself to enter the local tattooist in nearby Leicester, not only do we not allow this sort of behaviour, but it is illegal for anyone under the age of eighteen to encompass such a fate." I was now standing there concerned that I was not able to understand a word he was saying. The BC continued, "Do you have anything to say before I carry out your sentence?"

"Yes Sir," I said. "I didn't realise that I was not allowed to have a tattoo, I thought it would be alright now I am getting close to being eighteen, Sir, September next year Sir to be precise." I wish I had just kept quiet, the BC didn't find my lack of respect for military law at all amusing.

"Analytically examining the evidence and the elemental parts of your crime Junior Gunner Wolfendale, do you accept my award or would you like a trial by court martial?"I had absolutely no idea what he was saying, everything the BC had to say going right over my head; it was the toss of a coin as to which one to choose, BCs award or trial by court martial.

"I accept your award, Sir," I said; apparently, and luckily for me, that was the correct answer.

"I fine you £10 and confine you to barracks for two weeks. I do not want to see you come before me again; do you understand Junior Gunner Wolfendale?"

"Yes, Sir," I said.

That was it; it was now the turn of Bombardier Bartlett to march me out as quickly as I was marched in. I was ordered to wait outside in the small corridor until Malcolm and Dave had been charged; standing outside in the corridor made me reflect on how foolish I had been, but there was no turning the clock back, I just took it as a learning curve and promised myself not to get charged again.

Before long we were all lined up outside in the corridor getting a dressing down from the BSM and then Bombardier Bartlett. It was basically the same script as the BCs. It was now 1000hrs so I decided I would meet up with my mates in the NAAFI who would be waiting eagerly to hear the full story.

"What was the charge? What was it like? Were you bricking it? Tell us the whole story Wolfie!"

"Slow down," I said, trying to answer all their enquiries. I was certainly taking centre stage once more, they even got one of the lads to go and get me my usual cuppa and sandwich so I could tell them everything that went on. I suppose they were intrigued with the fact that one day it might be them facing the music.

As time ebbed by and the scars had healed, you'd think I'd have learnt my lesson, unfortunately I didn't think for a split second how impressionable I could be.

CHAPTER FORTY-ONE
HAVE YOU BEEN DRINKING LAD?

Towards the end of October we had a week's Battery camp to look forward to, in the UK Ministry of Defence Military training area, a small town called Sennybridge in Powys, South Wales. Although the camp is in the Brecon Beacons National Park, the training area is not and is located to the north of the National Park. The training area was acquired by the Ministry of Defence in 1939 and is a major field and firing range for the infantry and artillery. The demanding and arduous environments of the South Wales mountains, caves, rivers and lakes is with the aim of promoting the development of personal character and building team cohesion through the delivery of: mountain walking, caving, open canoeing, climbing and rope courses. The camp itself was a far cry from Gamecock Barracks; it was like going from a five-star hotel to a one-star tent.

After settling in we were ordered to parade outside our dilapidated building; let's say it could have done with a lick of paint. Sergeant Preece, Bombardier Bartlett, the TC and some of the junior ranks made up the social gathering as well as one or two civilian instructors; we were being read the riot act as per normal of what was expected of us. The itinerary for the week was one of sheer exhaustion: pot holing, abseiling, fitness training, map reading shooting etc. There didn't seem to be much spare time in our busy schedule apart from the occasional evening, when we were allowed into the nearby town. It was about halfway through the week when we had just come back from abseiling and pot holing…

"Enjoy the day?" said Dennis.

"Not sure," I said as I was getting changed into my civilian clothes, "I enjoyed the abseiling but had reservations about the pot holing; trying to crawl through small gaps in rocks that a snake wouldn't venture into isn't my idea of fun."

"Are you going out tonight, Paul?" asked Dennis. "There is a few of us that have decided to take a walk into Sennybridge."

"The last time I went out with you lot I got charged, remember?"

"Yeah, but that wasn't our fault, you chose to have a tattoo Paul, "said Dennis.

"Yeah I know, I'm not blaming anyone but it's just… I just have this funny feeling that if I venture out of the barracks tonight something serious will happen, once bitten twice shy springs to mind," I said with a worried look on my face.

"Wolfendale"

"What?" I said looking towards Parry and knowing what he was about to say.

"Don't be a party pooper, let's go out and enjoy ourselves. Pete Rigby said he will look after you if you get drunk."

"DRUNK?" I said. "I don't even drink."

"Well it's about time you started, you'll be fine."

Half an hour of being lambasted by my so-called mates meant I was now officially going into Sennybridge, for what I hoped would to be a quiet night.

It was around 1930hrs when Dennis woke me up from my Egyptian PT position.

"Wolfie, wake up mate, we are all ready to go," at the same time shaking my shoulder harder and harder until I was dragged away from my thoughts.

"What?" I said, sounding startled.

"We're off now, come on," said Dennis. Whilst still not fully awake I asked, "Off where?" as I was rubbing my eyes.

"Into Sennybridge to get pissed… sorry… I meant for a drink." It was only then when I realised what I had agreed to earlier.

"Wolfendale!" was the call from afar. "Get a move on!" I didn't need a second guess at who that was.

"Yeah, I'm on my way," I said unenthusiastically. Steve, Pete, Sam, George, Dennis and I made our way towards the Guardroom that was manned by the Guard Commander and the Marching Relief; we had to book out just like in Gamecock Barracks.

"Name?" said the Guard Commander.

"Junior Gunner Wolfendale, Bombardier," I said.

"Sign against your name," he said, at the same time looking up at the clock to put the time next to my name. By time we had all booked out which took a good five minutes; it was hit the road time. I could see all the locals in the shadows of the street lights glancing over towards us, at the same time trying to distance themselves from the presence of a group of young boys that looked like they were on a mission. They just grinned and tilted their heads towards us. There was the occasional one or two that would cross over to the other side of the road just to avoid the loud chitchat that was reverberating around the streets.

It wasn't long before the beady eyed Steve Parry set eyes on the first pub… "Aye up lads," said Steve, rubbing his hands together in the cold damp air.

"Your round first," said George to Dennis. I just took a back seat and left it to the professionals; after all, the only pint I knew was a pint of milk. We made our way through the narrow door with myself bringing up the rear; with our babyish looks we made our way to the bar not knowing whether or not we would be served. I am not sure why, but there were no questions asked by the thirty-year-old, good looking busty barmaid.

"Go and get a table, Wolfie?" said Riggers, as he, along with Steve ordered the drinks. Steve continued by saying, "Dennis, get your wallet out, your round." Reluctantly Dennis removed the cobwebs from his wallet to pay for the drinks, whilst at the same time trying not to flash the cash to all and sundry.

I had no idea what my so-called mates had decided to order for me, but I was soon to find out as they carefully brought over the drinks, it seemed like a glass of coke in a tall thin glass which would have come with my approval. Luckily for me, I had the common sense for once to take a small whiff of the coke like liquid that was presented to me.

"What the hell is it?" I said feeling confused.

"Just get it down you," said Sam in his rough Scottish accent.

"It's called a Bacardi and Coke," said Riggers in a *it will be OK* kind of voice, before long they were all joining in with their so call banter.

"Go on Wolfie, get it down you," said Parry. I was a lightweight when it came to drinking so was naturally very cautious. I lifted the glass to my lips and took my first sip followed by a gulp, then before I knew it, the glass was empty; it actually tasted rather refreshing to my surprise.

"Well done, Wolfie," said Dennis with a huge grin on his face.

As the evening moved along and 'unprompted' about five or six double Bacardi and Cokes found their way into my blood stream making me feel a little tipsy, my words were becoming slurred, Parry became Barry, Riggers became Sniggers, Dennis became Batman, oh and then there was Fireman Sam and Charlie George.

"Drink up Wolfie," someone said. I was feeling like I hadn't a care in the world; as long as my backside stayed glued to my seat I knew I would be OK, *just don't stand up* I am thinking to myself. Last orders could be heard at the sound of the bell from the landlady, this was it… it was now time to leave. To my surprise I managed to stand up on my own two feet before falling down; within seconds I was being man handled to my feet by George and Riggers… or was that Charlie and Sniggers?

"Come on Wolfie, let's get you outside, some fresh air is what you need," said George. I felt the cold night air hit my face which seemed to wake me up, one step forward and two steps back was the order of the night. One minute the lads would be behind me laughing at my staggering walk and then the next minute, I would be behind them.

It was now about 2330hrs and we could see the gates of the barracks no more than about a minute away if you were sober, about ten minutes away if you were pissed. I had to try to put on a front as I entered the Guardroom, chin up, act normal, or maybe not in my case; just try not to give anything away, try not to breathe on the Guard Commander I was saying to myself.

I was now standing in front of the Guard Commander with the rest of my so-called buddies at my side…

"Name?" shouted the Guard Commander as he was looking down at his booking-in book.

"Wolf… Wolf… er… Wolfendale, Bomb… Bomb… Bombardier," I said, slurring my words.

"Have you been drinking, lad?" asked the Bombardier loudly.

"M… Me… Me, Bombardier, No Bomb… Bomb… No, I am fine Bombardier."

"Don't you fucking lie to me you piece of shit, I can smell it on your breath, you smell like a fucking distillery." The Bombardier continued shouting by dismissing the rest of the lads and told me to wait for my troop Bombardier to arrive. It was pretty obvious that I was in serious trouble no less than a month after getting charged for having a tattoo on my arm. A quick to the point phone call from the Guard Commander saying, "I have one of your Junior Leaders with me and he is drunk as a skunk." *Drunk as a skunk*, I was thinking, *how dare he?* I may have been a little inebriated but I could just about stand up with the help of the counter. The five minute wait seemed like a life time as I was becoming more acquainted with my bowels.

"Wolfendale, I might have guessed it would be you, get yourself outside now," said Bombardier Bartlett. He was going apoplectic with rage, I am pretty sure if he could have got away with it he would have knocked me into next week.

I was doubled the short distance to the block where Wingate Troop was staying and then taken to the shower room; I had no idea what Bombardier Bartlett had in store for me until he told me to get undressed.

"A cold shower for you Wolfendale, do you understand?"

"Yes bomb."

"Fucking bomb!" said Bombardier Bartlett. "Do I look like I've got a fuse up my arse? Get in the fucking shower now!" I was left there for a few minutes while Bombardier Bartlett went to get a green army style towel. I didn't dare move from the stabbing pains of the freezing cold shower; I just waited until he returned.

"Get out of the shower now, Wolfendale," the Bombardier screamed. "Get yourself dried off, don't bother getting dressed just wrap the towel around your waist, get your clothes together and then follow me." I was marched to my bed space in no uncertain way; with the rest of the lads now tucked up in bed not daring to as much as breathe I was told to get into bed. *Bed,* I was thinking; I couldn't even see my bed let alone get in it. With a little bit of help from Bombardier Bartlett it wasn't long before I was wrapping the warm sheets around my now freezing body.

"Turn on your side, Wolfendale," said Bombardier Bartlett, still going mental. "Don't you dare lie on your back, do you understand?" He was concerned that if I was in some way sick, I might choke in my sleep. "Oh and by the way Wolfendale… you're charged." *Music to my ears* I thought before I fell asleep.

The next morning I woke to the sound of laughter from several of my so call buddies. "Wolfendale, how are you feeling?" was the question from Steve.

"Better than I deserve," I said, "just leave me alone." My head felt like I had been trampled on by Bombardier Bartlett's boot, I could hardly keep my eyes open and making my way to the washrooms was a task within itself. How I managed to get through the day without being sick I am still not sure, but got through I did; although I still take full responsibility for my stupidity, my mates will never be forgiven, having a laugh at my expense—NOT FUNNY.

The end of the week was near and although I was looking forward to getting back to Bramcote, I knew that I had this charge hanging over me when

I return. With that in mind I felt like asking Bombardier Bartlett if I could stop for another week; it wasn't going to happen.

On return to the barracks and settling in, Bombardier Bartlett came over to the block that evening to inform me that I was on BCs orders in the morning; more bulling my boots and making sure my uniform was immaculate was my priority while a lot of the lads were down the NAAFI enjoying themselves. I think I was the first one in the troop to be charged twice since joining up, not a record I was proud of but it was something I was going to have to live with; learning from my mistakes is what I needed to do. *Maybe I am hanging around with the wrong sort of people,* I was thinking to myself in a kind of joking way. The next day I was lined up as normal in the corridor of the Battery Office except this time I was on my own.

"Wolfendale," said Bombardier Bartlett in his stern voice, "I can't believe you're here again, remember the format?"

"Yes, Bombardier," I said, standing to attention and staring him in the eyes.

"Left turn, left right left right left right left, right turn, mark time, and halt" said Bombardier Bartlett. I was thinking in my mind about what the BC must have been thinking, which made me want to snigger; I just bit my lips at the thoughts that was chasing around my head.

"Wolfendale… we meet again, you obviously have not heeded a word that I said since the last time you were standing here before me no less than a month ago. There is no helping some people Wolfendale; do you understand what I am saying?"

"Yes Sir," I said, feeling guilty once more.

"Then why are standing here again?" said the BC raising the tone of his well educated voice. "I hear from your TC that you hold the record for getting from one end of the scramble net to the other."

"Yes, Sir," I said with a kind of smile on my face.

"Commendable, Junior Gunner Wolfendale," said the BC, "however this sort of record is not commendable, twice in a month doesn't make good reading, does it?"

"No, Sir," I said.

"Charged £10" March out. He never even asked me if I wanted to go for trial by court martial or accept his award. I was marched out at double pace and given the, *you've been charged* lecture by Bombardier Bartlett as he stared into my eyes.

"Don't you ever end up here again, Wolfendale, you're walking a very thin line." Shaking his head from side to side and then shouting "Get out of my sight now." I was pleased to breathe some welcomed fresh air into my lungs as I exited the Battery Block. I just looked up to the heavens and paused for a second to gather my thoughts.

CHAPTER FORTY-TWO
THOUGHT I WAS A GONNER

It was now November and we were getting all spruced up for Remembrance Day, sometimes known as Poppy day. It is a memorial day observed in the Commonwealth of Nations member states since the end of World War One to remember the members of their armed forces who have died in the line of duty. Remembrance Day is normally observed on the 11th November in most countries to recall the end of the hostilities of World War One on that date in 1918. Hostilities formally ended at the 11th hour of the 11th day of the 11th month. A few days before the Sunday parade, Bombardier Bartlett came into the barrack room with a cardboard tray hanging from his neck by a ribbon; he looked like an usherette, one of those who brought ice cream around in the cinema.

"Get your money out," he bellowed. "Remembrance Day this Sunday and no one is excused: best No. 2 dress, best boots, outside at 1000hrs sharp." Bombardier Bartlett came around us one by one and handed us our poppy. I was just about to attempt to fasten the poppy to my jumper when I was stopped in my tracks.

"Wolfendale, stop there right now," said Bombardier Bartlett, "the poppy leaf goes behind your cap badge."

"Sorry, Bombardier," I said, taking a step back. Apparently what you need to do is take away the plastic stem and then thread the hook of the cap badge through the hole in the middle of the red leaf; after a small struggle with this minor task I was ready to take a quick look in the mirror. I stood there thinking for a few seconds, *yes very smart young lad*.

Sunday's Remembrance Day parade gave me the same feeling that I felt at our passing out parade, swollen with pride, walking in the same steps of all those that had given their lives in both world wars and also the ongoing civil war in Northern Ireland.

Towards the end of November, we were once again on our way for more adventure training. This time it was Ross on Wye, a small market town in

Herefordshire; it was thought by some, and in the interest of public safety, that it would be better to keep us away from the town and put us on the water, especially after our invasion of Sennybridge.

The main emphasis was on canoeing and raft building, over the three days we were there; character building and team bonding were at the forefront of the exercises. The weather was extraordinarily warm for the time of year which made the adventure more appealing; travelling in the back of two four tonners mid November can be an harrowing experience in respect that there is no escape from the cold air that flows through the open end of the vehicle. The canvas flaps were always tied back around the metal frame-work by small tie straps.

On arrival we were herded off the vehicles like cattle and into our make-shift accommodation; white mattresses on metal frame beds was the order as we all rushed to get a bed; it was like a game of musical chairs. I'm pretty sure that there were enough beds to go around however, we were taking any chances: Riggers, Steve, Sam, Dennis, George and I were now racing at full pelt between the narrow gaps between the beds; it brought back memories of Murder Ball, the game we were subjected to in the gym. Crash bang wallop and a little *get out of my way* tactics meant we all got a bed – it was a case of dive on your bed, wrap your arms around the frame work and shout, "My bed." There would always be someone trying to grapple you off it by any means possible; if you could stay on for about a minute then you could be assured that the bed was yours.

I can still feel the pain in my fingers now as they were being wrenched from the metal frame one by one. The next stage would be to unroll your sleeping bag onto the awaiting mattress to complete a job well done. It was now early evening and we were given our curriculum for the following day by Bombardier Bartlett and Sergeant Preece; gathered around in our accommodation in a relaxed atmosphere dressed in tracksuits or smart civilian clothes we waited for the brief.

"Tomorrow the TC will be paying us a visit at around 0900hrs," said Bombardier Bartlett. "Dress for tomorrow will be battery tracksuits along with plimsoles; you'll be taken out to the River Wye in four tonners, where upon arrival you will canoe down the river in the company of the TC. It will be a whole day adventure and a pack lunch will be awaiting you at around 1300hrs depending on how fast you canoe." I could see his eyes glaring towards Sam and one or two others; I think what Bombardier Bartlett was saying with a smile on his face was, *it's going to be a kind of endurance and I look forward to seeing you struggle.*

We weren't allowed out of the makeshift barracks for the three days we were there, so a bit of entertainment in the evening was a must, a few pillow fights would do the trick, after all we were supposed to be mean, lean, fighting machines. It was a way of getting rid of unwanted energy. I must admit these sorts of nights were as unwelcome as a fart in your underpants, soldiers with energy to burn is a recipe for disaster as I was to find out later in my career.

A lovely sunny day was awaiting our canoeing trip as we were awoken by the makeshift guard. A cold shave from the washrooms wasn't ideal but it was nothing compared to what lay in store for me later on in the day. At 0930 we lined up outside in three ranks dressed as ordered: battery tracksuit and plimsoles. After a short inspection and a visible roll call we were brought up to attention.

"Squad, Squad shun," was the order from Bombardier Bartlett as the TC arrived with his unique *this how a TC walks* walk; looking very charismatic he made his way over to within feet of his merry men. It was more than we could muster to keep a straight face, that walk will haunt me forever, even Bombardier Bartlett was pinching is lips tightly together trying not to smirk. It only took about five minutes for the TC to explain the activities for the day before we were loaded onto the back of the four tonners for the short ten minute journey to the river.

"Everybody off the truck," was the command as it pulled into the public car park just next to the river. The tailgate of the vehicle came crashing down with a force that you wouldn't believe. We exited from the darkness of the truck like there was no tomorrow and into the bright sunlight that was now causing us to squint.

"Get your bodies over by the river now," shouted Bombardier Bartlett in a stern voice; glaring over to my right I could see the slow moving but quite calm river. The river was a lot wider than any river that I had ever seen before, my first thoughts were, *how the hell am I going to swim from one side to the other if for some reason or another I accidentally capsize, or one of my buddies decide it would be an amazingly good idea to turn my canoe over?*

"Listen in," said Bombardier Bartlett, "When I call your name I want you to get yourself over to the four tonne vehicle, the one with the canoes on, Wolfendale." Again, I felt he was trying to humiliate me in front of the troop.

"That's the one over there, Wolfie," said Steve pointing to the truck. Steve always had to have his say.

"Your canoe is the one with the hole in the bottom of it," I said sarcastically to Steve. Our names were called out in a kind of random order instead of alphabetical order, something I wasn't use to.

"Gandy, Wolfendale, two man canoe. Lynch, Parry, two man canoe," said Bombardier Bartlett. "Rigby, Norris, single canoes for you."

"Favoritism" shouted Ricky the Slug. 'Brown nose' 'teacher's pet' and other harmonizing words were also vibrating around the lads. To be honest it was about a fifty-fifty split as to who got what, all I knew was that I was in a two man canoe with Sam 'I don't like water' Gandy; that certainly filled me with lots of confidence. We dragged our paint scratched, worn out, red canoe from out of the back of the vehicle and made our way down to the edge of the river. They weren't too heavy to carry, just awkward to balance, a little top heavy is how I would described them. It felt like an intrusive invasion was about to take place on the beautiful meandering calm river as we assembled just inches away from the murky water.

The TC was the first to enter the water in what looked like his own personal, made to measure vessel, not a scratch to be found anywhere on his canoe; gliding gracefully with a slight tail wind meant he didn't have to introduce his oars into the river until he manoeuvered his canoe so that he was facing us.

"Bombardier Bartlett," shouted the TC from the middle of the river, "get them in the water now." We didn't have to wait for the order, it was like the Alamo; shouting and screaming we ventured into the water trying to cause as much mayhem as we could, or at least that what it seemed like. The chaos continued until the last canoe entered the water to the relief of the now slightly infuriated ducks. Lined up behind the TC we waited for the starting pistol to be fired; unfortunately the TC must have left it back at base.

"Follow me," was the order from the TC in his battle cry voice. The sun was still shining as we made our way up the river; enjoying some small-talk chitchat Sam and I made our way to the front along with Riggers. To be honest it seemed great fun, hard to believe that you can get paid for doing something that is so enjoyable, it wasn't to last.

Within about half an hour of our expedition I heard a cry from behind me, "Wolfie!" I looked over my shoulder to see Junior Gunner Barry Culf at the back of the fleet.

"What's up?" I said whilst at the same time trying not to capsize the canoe.

"Do you fancy a single canoe instead of a double canoe?"

"Why?" I asked, intrigued.

"I just fancy a change, bored on my own," he said.

"Fine by me," I said feeling ok with the reason he gave me, "Are you OK with that, Sam?"

"I suppose so," said Sam, "just be careful you don't turn the canoe over when you get out." We made our way over to the edge of the bank to a place where we could safely swap seats, as we were swapping I could hear another voice from nearby.

"Wolfendale, Gandy, I am going to report you to the TC for swapping canoes." It could only be one person, Steve the Sheep Parry. I didn't give fig about Steve until the nutter started shouting in a loud voice, "Sir! Sir! Wolfendale is swapping canoes!"

"Shut up, Parry," I said at the same time threatening to throw him in.

"What's up, Parry?" shouted the TC.

"It's Wolfendale, Sir," as he looked towards me.

"What's wrong, Wolfendale?" said the TC.

"Just saying to Junior Gunner Parry what a great TC you are, then Junior Gunner Parry said he was not sure Sir, he said he hadn't made his mind up yet."

"Is that right, Parry," said the TC.

"No, Sir," said Steve, "Wolfendale is telling fibs."

There was little or no response from the TC apart from, "Get a move on and keep up with the rest of the troop."

After safely negotiating the difficult task of swapping canoes I fastened the spray deck on and started to make some progress to catch up with the rest of the pack. Sam and Culf were already building up their speed and were closing in on the rest of the troop; daylight was forming between me and the rest of the lads that was making me feel uneasy. It was only now that I realised why Junior Gunner Culf had wanted to swap canoes; it's as if the canoe had a mind of its own, if you paddled left the bloody thing went left, if you paddled right the canoe would also go left, there was no controlling it. I was dropping further and further back from the troop and languishing even further behind with each stroke I took. It wasn't long before the situation was becoming distressing for me; like a Chinese whisper the news travelled through the pack until the news reached the TC.

I could see the TC coming to my rescue as he fought against the flow of the river, at least that's what I was thinking… not on your life, all he was interested in was giving me a rollicking.

"Wolfendale, what's your problem?" he shouted as he encroached on my space. "Get a move on and catch up with the rest of the troop." *Is he having a laugh,* I was thinking.

"The canoe won't travel in a straight line, Sir," I said nervously.

"Everyone else is managing to keep up, Wolfendale," said the TC in a now kind of angry voice. The TC insisted that I stay close to him as we made our way back to the now stationary pack; try as I might, the canoe I was in was not playing ball. I made one last attempt to power the canoe to go where I wanted it to go, but my over-exuberance caused the canoe to wobble from side to side, and then another wobble side to side, I was feeling very unbalanced now as the canoe finally tilted beyond its safety limits.

"Fuck, Fuck, Fuck!" were the last words I remember saying before the canoe capsized, throwing me into the darkness of the murky water; a conspiracy theory sprang to mind as I now faced my worst nightmare. It was a strange feeling being upside down in the water, I felt all alone for the first few seconds until my natural instincts kicked in, I tried to remember the now valuable training we had been given some five months ago, keep calm, pull the toggle on the front of the spray deck and push out. Pulling the toggle was as easy as my ABC; the spray deck detached itself from the canoe just like it was carrying out a military order. I felt quite calm and assured myself that everything was now going to plan until I went to stage two; pushing and trying to squirm my way out of the tight embrace of the canoe was proving to be a challenge and a half within itself.

Minutes later, and not seconds, I was still embedded in the clutches of the canoe. Panic was starting to set in as I continued to struggle to release myself from the vice-like grip around my waist. I was at the stage where I was giving up all hope of ever seeing the light of day ever again. I believe it was the calmness of giving up that allowed my body to relax; feeling a slight movement from my body, I felt that there was a slim chance that I was going to get out of this mess. I just seemed to allow my body to take over that was now on automatic pilot with the fact that I had no control over it; within seconds my body slithered out of the canoe, my arms and legs were now working overtime to thrust me upwards before I started taking in water.

It seemed like an eternity before I finally managed to take a gasp of fresh air as my head emerged above the water line. For some reason I still felt uneasy popping up and down in the water. I caught sight of the TC some ten metres away in his state of the art canoe.

"Wolfendale, are you OK?" he shouted in a concerned voice.

"Yes… er… yes Sir," I spluttered, at the same time trying not to swallow the contents of the river. With each minute I was in the water I felt my body getting colder and colder until I was rescued some five minutes after capsizing. The TC positioned his canoe so that I could grab the back and be towed to the edge of the far bank, whereupon I managed to climb up the grassy bank and into a local farmer's beautiful green field, a field that was full of grazing black and white cattle minding their own business; *penny for your thoughts,* I was thinking as the cows took a break from munching on the short grass to have a staring match with me.

The TC sent a couple of the lads to retrieve my now upside-down canoe along with the paddle from the water before it had time to drift away. To be honest I didn't want the damn thing back anyway, it wasn't part of my 1157 kit list as I remembered; well at least I don't think I signed for it. The canoe had absolutely no value at all to me, *let it drown* I was thinking, I don't want it back. With the canoe now safely on the bank and the cows now looking more confused than ever, I was told in no uncertain terms, that I was to stay on the grass bank along with my canoe and wait until they returned some time later-on in the afternoon; *fine by me,* I thought, although I would have liked to have completed the rest of the trip.

The TC made his way back along the slow moving river to catch up with the rest of the troop. I could see them slowly disappearing into the distance; around the small curve in the river they slowly became a figment of my imagination until there was complete silence. It was now just me, the cows and the beautiful sunshine bearing down on my saturated body. I took off my life jacket and red PT vest so that I could wring them out; in a tourniquet sort of way I strangled the life out of the vest before laying it on the warm grass and introducing it to the sunrays amongst the white fluffy clouds. I had no idea what I was going to do to pass the time away so I thought the only thing I could do was to sunbathe next to my PT vest; by this time the cows had lost interest in my unexpected visit and were more than happy to continue eating the lush green grass.

It seemed like a lifetime as I lay awaiting the return of TC and the rest of the boys; there were thoughts running through my mind that they may not return or at least until it was dark. All my fears vanished when in the distance I saw what looked liked to be international rescue; it was the TC and a couple of the lads marching over the brow of the field trying to avoid the occasional cow pat. It was time for me to get myself into gear; my red PT vest was now as dry as a bone and ready to cover my poor excuse of a body, the body that had previously frightened the cows away. I had no idea where the cows had gone; I must have fallen asleep at some point on this lazy afternoon.

"Wolfendale," shouted the TC from a distance.

"Yes Sir," I said commandingly whilst thinking, *this is going to be out of the frying pan and into the fire.* I wasn't happy being left for dead but at the same time, I knew I was going to get a mild ticking off and some undeserved ribbing from my so-called mates. No sooner had I gotten within about fifty metres of the trucks, all I could hear was my name being echoed around.

"Lazy twat, Wolfie!" shouted Muckersie. Everybody seemed to be full of laughter at my expense but to be fair, it just went over my head, even the ever so pragmatic 'Posh Peter Rigby' couldn't hold back his feelings; laughing and joking, Pete gave me a hand and pulled me up onto the back of the truck to be greeted and cheered by the rest of the troop. On the way back it didn't take long for someone to come up with appropriate song…

"Row row row your boat gently down the stream, if you see a Wolfendale don't forget to scream." We looked like a bunch of loonies as we sang the song from out of the back of the four tonne vehicle travelling through the town.

The next day we made our way back to Nuneaton for what would be our final few weeks before our well-earned Christmas break. It would be a chance to recharge our batteries, but not before I got a good wallop from Steve's suitcase as it fell of the roof rack of the train.

CHAPTER FORTY-THREE
HOME IN TIME FOR CHRISTMAS

The weather was taking a turn for the worse, which meant it was time to dig into my suitcase to find my warmer winter clothing and pack my t-shirts away. I bumped in my friend Bombardier John James for a brief moment who informed me that he would unfortunately be leaving us after the Christmas, to return back to his unit in West Germany. "West Germany" I said, "wow, I hope I get the opportunity to go there one day."

"Well, if you do, be sure to look me up" said Jessy with a firm hand shake

"Yes, that would be nice" I said, "thanks for the support you have given me over the few months I've known you." It was so nice to have a more senior figure to talk too; little did I know that in the coming year I would end up in the same battery as Jesse. It was now Friday December 20th and I was listening to 'Lonely This Christmas' by the group Mud, lying on my bed with my mini radio and ear phones. I was in my own little world waiting for lunch to arrive followed by being officially dismissed for our two week break; the end of the song was near when suddenly, my bed felt like it had been hit by an earthquake with the velocity of a ten on the Richter scale.

"Wolfendale, quick, get out of bed, we are getting attacked!" was the cry from Parry,

"What the hell is going on?" I shouted with my heart pumping out of my chest, I was so confused; my legs were feeling like jelly as they hit the floor, it took me a few seconds before I knew where I was.

"Coming to dinner?" said Steve in a now much quieter voice.

"Dinner," I said loudly, "you just scared the living daylights out of me!"

"Don't be such a mard arse," said Steve. "Come on, I am absolutely starving."

I just shook my head and at the same time thinking *it was just one of those everyday occurrences that we would be subjected to from time to time*. With everybody now on a high it was more like party time at the cookhouse, you could tell the ones that were on their way home for Christmas from the ones that would be staying.

Afternoon arrived, as we paraded outside the Battery Block I thought quietly to myself, *this will be the last time in 1974 that we will be standing here, the next time will be 1975;* how time travels so fast. It was the normal full house that addressed us; first Sergeant Preece gave us a lecture with Bombardier Bartlett occasionally getting his six pence worth. Out of the corner of my eye I could see the TC approaching, looking as smart as ever with that unforgettable tight lipped serious smirk that could only come from being a Lieutenant. We were brought up to attention in our civilian dress before the TC gave his 1974 speech…

"Well done lads on completing your training so far, seven months of intense training has seen you develop from being dependent on your families to be coming self-reliant. I have noticed a fantastic transformation in your development and attitude which is all down to hard graft from my team, consisting of the Troop Sergeant, Sergeant Preece and Bombardier Bartlett, also some of the more junior ranks for helping out with various tasks." I could see the self-righteous looks on the faces of Sergeant Preece and Bombardier Bartlett as they stood each side of the TC, standing there as stiff as a well-starched crease in your trousers. It was now our turn to receive some welcome and warranted praise; this bit I was looking forward to.

The TC moved his shifty eyes along the three ranks in a kind of slow motion fashion, occasionally pausing for a second or two on a certain individual; I am not normally the paranoid type however, I did feel that his eyes engaged with mine for more than a split second. It seemed like he was trying to be as impartial as he could as he began his speech. "First of all, I would like to thank you all for completing your basic training and various other tasks. It wasn't that long ago that you were all standing outside RHQ dressed in civilian clothes, some of you with hair touching your shoulders; standing here in front of me now, makes me feel proud to be your TC." I was waiting for the next line like, *this includes you Wolfendale*, but no, the TC was staying away from any segregation as he continued his well rehearsed speech. "It has been a long hard road for most of you, but one that you have overcome without too much difficulty. Your efforts have not gone unnoticed. After Christmas you'll be entering your final four months before joining your respective regiments; there will be no easing up on fitness and the training will be as tough as ever, will you be up for the task? Well, I believe you will. We are on the home straight Wingate Troop, keep up the good work."

The TC wished the troop a Merry Christmas and a prosperous New Year before handing the parade over to Sergeant Preece and Bombardier Bartlett. It was a strange sort of relaxed dismissal with the senior ranks still not allowing themselves to become too friendly; "Get out of my sight now before I call you back, go go go!" said Bombardier Bartlett.

We legged it into the block to retrieve our cases feeling all excited, with Bombardier Bartlett close up behind; seconds later you could almost hear the silence in the barrack room as we made our way towards the Guardroom and the main gates. The taxi drivers had already been forewarned of our departure, so it was no surprise when we exited the camp gates and saw them rubbing their hands together once again, not because it was a little nippy outside, but with the fact it was pay day for them. You could see the pound signs in their eyes, some of them with a quick motor might even get two or three journeys if they were lucky.

I shared a taxi with Dennis, Sam and Steve as we would all be catching the same train up north. Pete lived in a place called Uttoxeter and George was staying at Stu Hatton's house that meant they would be catching different trains. At the station we still had to remind ourselves that we were still members of the Junior Leaders Regiment Royal Artillery; apart from a few cake fights in the station cafeteria, we were on our best behavior. Our Army suitcases set us apart from the now overcrowded platform. The sturdy reinforced corners of the suit cases was symbolic to the Armed Forces; looking along the platform you could see Army suitcases everywhere, some in clear view and other partially hidden by the passengers waiting to board the now approaching train.

As the train pulled into the station everybody started to take a step nearer the edge of the platform, knowing that there would be limited seating. The train stopped with everybody now only inches away from boarding; the heavy doors of the train were now being flung open with some force to allow passengers off.

"Come on," I said to Sam, Dennis and Steve.

"Save us a seat," was the cry from Sam as I stepped up into the carriage. I managed to push my way through the narrow door before it became too occupied; a table with four empty seats brushed across my eyes. To someone that holds the record for getting from one end of the scramble net to the other, this was easy pickings for me; I commandeered the table and its seats in a flash.

"Over here lads," I said, shouting down the carriage whilst at the same time still trying to prevent anyone else from getting their backsides on the seats. Apart from a few small scuffles we made it quite comfortably into our seats.

"Wolfie," shouted Dennis. "Put my suitcase on the overhead netted racks, will you?"

"Pass it over," I said without realising the weight… "What the hell have you got in here, bricks?"

"No, it's just the Officers' Mess silver," said Dennis jokingly." I sat by the window next to Steve and opposite Sam as the train started its slow journey out of the station; a game of cards made the one hour journey pass quickly. About forty minutes into the journey I was given an early Christmas present from the overhead roof rack, it was Steve's suitcase, without any warning at all it managed to slither its way off the rack and onto my head. It felt like I had been poleaxed by a JCB, it brought tears of laughter from my so-called mates and lots of concern from the rest of the passengers that seemed to be in shock.

With my head now throbbing, it was time for Steve and I to disembark as the train pulled into Crewe. Steve was catching a train to North Wales whilst Sam had to change somewhere along the line for his journey to Scotland, Dennis? Well Dennis was staying on the train and making his way to Chorley near Preston; a final farewell to Dennis and Sam, and a quick goodbye to Steve, meant I was now just a small taxi fare from home. It would be difficult to describe or even hard imagine what lay in store for me over Christmas; catching a quick glimpse of a girl walking through my bedroom late at night had me thinking, *she looks fit*; beer goggles can be a strange thing at times.

CHAPTER FORTY-FOUR
A CHEST OF MAJESTIC PROPORTION

I arrived home at about 5pm that evening. It was now pitch black, but I could have found my way home blindfolded. It was a breathtaking feeling to be on my home patch again; the unmistakable sound of the air pump from the farm once again meant I was about fifty metres from my drive. With my suitcase in hand I opened the front door that was never locked to be greeted by my parents, a warm embrace from my mum and a firm handshake from my dad brought a huge smile to my cleanly shaven face. Nothing much had changed from the last time I was home but the thought of spending Christmas and New Year with my family and friends made it extra special.

After a good night's sleep and not having to worry about being woke up at six in the morning, I had myself some breakfast before making the short journey on my bike to see what Dec was up to. I needed to know whether he had thought any more about joining up. It felt like a second home to me although I would always knock on the front door out of politeness. I believe Dec had heard I was due home because he was up and waiting for me. Dec's first duty was to escort me to the back of his house and show me the shed that had now been patched-up by his father; a piece of wood nailed over the hole did the trick.

"Did your father go mental with you?" I said to Dec.

"No, he just gave me a lecture and told me not to hang around with you anymore."

"You're joking, tell me you're joking" I said. Dec couldn't hide the fact that he had made me feel that his father was going to kill me.

"You bastard, Dec," I said still in the state of shock; Dec was not the sort of person to play pranks but would always appreciate a good laugh. Maybe I was seeing a new Dec. I did see the funny side of his remark though. I always think the sign of a good man is one that can take a joke, and also laugh at himself.

"Is there any more news about joining up yet?" I asked with hope in my mind.

"Yes" replied Dec with a glowing smile, "follow me."

We went into the living room where upon Dec handed me a letter that he had received from the Army careers office, I took a seat and started to read the small note…

Dear Mr. Tomkinson, we are pleased to announce that you have been offered a place in Harrogate on April 2nd for a two day assessment.

I didn't need to read any further, I was so excited. "Tell me more," I said.

"Well, I went and took the entrance exam last month and passed it with flying colours, then two weeks ago I took my medical just like you did, the letter that you're now reading arrived just a few days ago, can't wait."

"So, are you thinking of joining the Royal Artillery?" I asked with my eyes now wide open.

"Yes, all being well," said Dec, "it would be great to follow in your footsteps." I couldn't have been any happier as I shook his hand like a real man and stared him in the eyes; not only was I proud of myself for what I had achieved so far, but I was now shaking hands with a man, my best mate, who would be walking in the same footsteps as me.

The first week of my two week break leading up to Christmas was spent Christmas shopping, visiting friends, relations, and just basically chilling out. My father and I went into the woods that were opposite our house to chop down a Christmas tree, a tree that would be left for my mother and sisters to decorate it. It wasn't the traditional pine tree that we associate Christmas with; it was a holly bush that was carefully shaped to look like a tree with beautiful red berries. I can still feel the sharp corners of the holly leaves as they made contact with my barc hands; we needed to save money where we could and this was one of the ways we did.

It was now Christmas Eve and with my brothers and a couple of my sisters down at the pub, the house was feeing quite empty. I remember watching a little TV with my parents before retiring for the night at about eleven o' clock. The layout of the bedroom that I slept in was bizarre; to get to my mum and dad's bedroom and also to get to the bathroom, meant you would have to walk through my bedroom; getting disturbed throughout the night was a regular occurrence in our house, especially my brothers when they had drunk one too many sherberts.

It must have been around midnight when I heard my sister's voice along with another unrecognisable female voice; wandering through my room trying their best not to stand on the occasional squeaky floor boards and wake me up was like walking through a well laid mine field. They made their way to the bathroom without switching the light on crashing into the walls and door frame; I would say they were slightly inebriated. I pretended not to notice they were disturbing my beauty sleep among the pitch-black room. I just turned over onto my left side, pulled the sheet around my bare-skinned body and groaned a little. Within seconds they were making their way back trying to mirror the same path without crashing into the walls this time. Instead they crashed into the end of my bed causing me to catch a quick glimpse of my sister's friend, and to be honest, on first appearance she would have been more than welcome to warm my cockles on this cold Christmas Eve; as it was, they both vanished out of the room leaving me with thoughts of what might have been.

Christmas Day was a family affair. It wasn't until just before lunch that I managed to confront my sister about the night before. "Who was that girl that you so kindly paraded through my bedroom last night?" I asked curiously.

"Carol;" my sister said "she's a friend of mine, a work colleague actually."

"Do you know if she has a boyfriend?" I asked.

"Don't think so," my sister replied.

"Could you ask her if she would like to go on a date?" My sister just looked at me with a grin on her face and continued...

"Oh yeah, you've finally realised it's not just for stirring your tea with, have you?" I just shook my head from side to side, not wanting to get involved with her sordid remark.

"Can you ask her please?" I replied.

"Yeah OK, I will be seeing her tomorrow," said my sister. With that I got on with the Christmas festivities and thought no more about it. The following day and early evening I caught up with my sister again.

"Paul," my sister shouted, "I saw Carol today."

"And..." I said, waiting for an answer.

"Carol said yes, tomorrow night if you're free. She said she will meet you at the fountain in Nantwich at seven o'clock." *1900hrs* I said to myself; I was now fully conversant in the ways of a twenty-four-hour clock so seven o'clock to me was confusing.

"Thanks sis," I said.

I was now feeling quite excited at my first real grown up date with a girl, with the fact that I now had money to spend and someone to spend it on. It was now Friday 27th December. I got dressed into my glad rags before making my way into my home town of Nantwich. I arrived about 6.45pm and stood opposite Woolworths on the other side of the road trying to keep an eye out for my mysterious date. I had been waiting no longer than about ten minutes with no sign of my date anywhere. On the fountain and sitting on a bench were three young, good looking ladies chatting away, they looked to be enjoying themselves as they casually glanced over in my direction. *It must be one of them,* I thought to myself, maybe she has brought two of her friends for a little moral support. I remember thinking *I don't care which one is Carol, they all looked like beauties,* even though they were about twenty metres away in the shadows of the street lighting.

I plucked up some Dutch courage and tiptoed across the small road to where they were sitting. I felt very uncomfortable with the situation however; it still didn't stop me making a fool out of myself. I looked all three in the face and nervously said, "Excuse me; you wouldn't happen to be called Carol would you?" Almost at the same time and in a kind of softly spoken voice they all replied, "No."

Ouch, I said to myself feeling embarrassed. "Oh, I do apologise, my mistake," I said as I turned around and at a snail's pace and made my way back to my original position; the position that was meant for losers.

I was just about ready to move off the losers square when all of a sudden, and in the distance, I saw what looked like a girl walking towards me. My first thought was *please no, surely that can't be my date.* This person looked like they were dressed for a day on the farm; *along came a heifer* sprang to mind. With her hand raised in the air and smiling at me through the gaps of her teeth, I knew this was my date. *Why didn't my sister warn me? Why didn't she switch the bedroom light on?* I said to myself.

Through politeness and not wanting to be too disrespectful, I smiled back and casually swaggered my way towards to my date. I had absolutely no idea what I was going to do with her, one half of me was saying stay well clear and the other half was saying exactly the same. I decided to be the gentleman that I was now expected to be; a gentle kiss on the cheek of her face seemed to break the ice. After a small introduction we decided to have a stroll to the local pub; I'm not sure what the definition of local means but it was a good mile and a half we walked to the Star in Acton. It was a nice cosy pub with just a few regulars: nice carpeted floor, small wooden tables and scenic type pictures hanging on the wall. We spent a few hours there getting to know each other over a pint and of course, a Bacardi and Coke; you can probably guess who had the pint. Hours later and with myself feeling a little more confident with a couple of drinks inside me, we made our way back to Nantwich; sitting on a park bench for a few minutes and taking in some of the car fumes that were being generated in our direction had me thinking about my next step. I decided to search around in my pockets for the 'what to do on my first date' manual, unfortunately I must have left it back in the barracks.

This is where I came into my own once more. I wasn't about to make a fool of myself for the second time, or was I? She was about two years older than me and certainly more experienced in the birds and the bees department; the book I was searching for never materialised so it was now down to me to use my own initiative. I looked over to my right and noticed that she seemed to be waiting for my next move; it was that kind of 'I'm bored look' that I noticed first, *do something, Paul,* I'm saying to myself, this is your time. I leaned over towards her and did the business, my lips were now firmly in place, the only problem I had now was not knowing when to stop. *What are the boundaries on your first date?* I was all fingers and thumbs as my hands made their way up her thick woolen jumper and attacked her bra, I tried to put my hands down the front of the bra but without much success.

Carol was looking very uncomfortable with my efforts as she just stared at the full moon shining in the sky; she eventually gave me a clue...

"Try pulling the bra up from the bottom Paul," she said with pain written all over her face.

"Oh, OK," I said. Within milliseconds of tugging on the reinforcements of her bra, these two what could only be described as milkers' jumped out and hit me in the face. *Wow,* I was thinking, she isn't as bad as I first thought; so shallow us men. My eyes rolled around in their sockets. Her boobs were that big that they looked like they had their own postcode, I didn't want this moment to end, but end it must. A whole five minutes of fixation made me lose my concentration.

"I think it's time to put them away now, don't you? before someone sees us," said Carol.

"Er... yes OK, I suppose so," I replied disappointedly; before I knew it they were nesting back in their hammocks until the next time, what a moment.

I walked Carol home like a good man should and then arranged another date over the festive period; I felt I could have walked the streets all night until the following morning, that's how I was feeling. I saw Carol on two more occasions before heading back to Nuneaton to tell my mates all about her. New Year had now passed and 1974 was now just another part of history. We all hoped for a great New Year and after meeting Carol I hoped this would be the start of a prosperous 1975 for me.

Thursday the 2nd January meant it was time to return to Gamecock Barracks in Nuneaton. With my suitcase packed I said farewell to my family; catching the train to the barracks was becoming what I would say, an everyday thing now. As well as missing my family I now had someone else I would miss, more than I could ever imagine.

CHAPTER FORTY-FIVE
TRADE TRAINING

Early January meant the roads in the barracks were quite slippery, not just from the ice that was cluttering the gutters, but from all the fallen autumn leaves. There would be no excuses available in any Army manual that excuses anyone from falling on their backside; 'adapt to the conditions' is what we would be expected to conform to. Falling over as well as the embarrassment could see you on BSMs sweeping the roads fatigues.

It was all the customary chin-wagging around the barrack room as everybody that had managed to return on time was busy unpacking all their Christmas goodies. We all knew there would be no let up on hygiene and discipline, so making the most of our last few hours before turning in and then the inevitable 0600hrs wakeup call was not to be missed. I sat on my bed and within seconds, the ever 'I will listen to anything you have to say' Sam came over for a chat.

"How's things Wolfie? Great Christmas I hope," said Sam in a quiet and understanding voice.

"Fine thanks, Sam," I answered, Sam was the perfect person I could possibly have wanted to have a chat with in respect to the way I was feeling; understanding someone's feelings is a wonderful talent to have and believe me when I say, Sam was that man. I explained to Sam that I had met a girl over the Christmas period, and although a soldier in the British Army, we are not immune from feelings. Sam was pleased for me as he also told me about his Christmas activities. It wasn't too long before my story was finding its way around the barrack room.

"Wolfie, if you need an educational degree on the birds and the bees, then I am your man," said the ever sympathetic Steve 'The Sheep' Parry. As far as I could make out everybody enjoyed their Christmas break; the question now that needed to be asked, was how many of us would still be here in five months' time?

I am not sure why we were all feeling the way we were, maybe the Christmas family thing, maybe it felt like here we go again, another five months, maybe I was missing mum's burnt porridge or maybe just a combination of everything, anyway, whatever it was, it was going viral. The first week saw us loose Hatton and Culf, I remember seeing Stu Hatton packing his belongings. "Can't fucking wait," he said as he was rushing around, it was just like day one but in reverse: mattress, mattress cover, pillows and blankets, they were all being marched out of the block for the last time, I could see the smile on his face, a smile that said 'they're not having me any longer'. I shook hands with Stu before he went, feeling proud that I was still part of the troop; however, that same night as I was trying to get some sleep I felt myself tossing and turning with the fact that Stu was now at home in his own bed. I thought *Wow that could be me in a few days, what do I do?* I hardly got any sleep that night; it must have been the longest night that I've ever endured since joining some eight months ago.

"Out of bed now, you lazy individuals," shouted the duty guard. My bed was being banged up and down like a fiddler's elbow before my eyes were open; it was like a nightmare from hell, a couple of weeks ago I was in heaven and now, well, just let's say it was a huge reality check

Whilst in the washrooms my mind was now made up, this was it; I had made up my mind that I was going to see the TC later on in the day about leaving. I was missing my family and girlfriend and the letters I was now receiving, it was a telling factor in my decision to leave. Perfume scented envelopes were too much for me to handle; keeping my thoughts close to my chest for the rest of the day was a difficult thing to do. I was yearning to tell someone like Sam, Riggers or Dennis, the ones that would understand; maybe I was scared that they would try to get me to change my mind, scared that they would think I was a failure, either way I was keeping it quiet. Later on that day I made my way to the TCs office feeling very nervous. "What can I do for you Junior Gunner Wolfendale?" said the TC.

"I want to hand in my notice Sir, wanting to leave, Sir," I said with a firm tone in my voice.

"Close the door and take a seat," was the reply.

I knew then by the tone of his voice that this was going to be an uncomfortable few minutes. The TC asked me to explain the reasons behind my decision. It was a one-way conversation for the next five minutes, I was talking and the TC was listening. Just when I thought I'd pulled it off, just when I thought he understood how I was feeling, he hit me with, "Can't do anything for you I'm afraid, Wolfendale." My heart sank and missed a beat for a second as I was trying to come to terms with what he had said.

It was now my turn to listen to what the TC had to say. He just smirked in a sort of 'I'm sorry' sort of way before explaining to me his reasons behind his quick-snap decision. "Unfortunately, Junior Gunner Wolfendale, because you have now been with us for more than six months your time has expired to voluntarily hand in your notice, as you so elegantly put it. Six months is the get out clause period, unless there are some out of the ordinary circumstances that will allow me the power to release you; missing your family and girlfriend doesn't come under that category. We all have loved one we miss, and surprisingly that includes me, Wolfendale." I just looked him in the eyes as I tried to gather my thoughts. I had now gotten to the stage where I felt myself pleading with the TC.

"What about Hatton and Culf Sir, they have been given permission to leave?" I said, feeling slightly angry.

"What has gone on with those two soldiers is not of your concern, Wolfendale," said the TC. "You're going nowhere; do you understand the Queen's English?" The TCs voice was now getting louder with each word he uttered to me, it was now quite obvious that this was the time to back down; this was a debate that I was not going to win.

The TC had certainly done his job, he had managed to somehow convince me that I was here to stay; on a positive note it gave me a sense of 'the Army needs men like you'. Already getting charged twice for having my tattoo and getting drunk didn't seem to have any bearings on the TCs decision. 'Let bygones be bygones'. It was now time to show some true grit and continue with my Army career. Later on that evening I decided to tell my so-called mates about my day, they had no idea that I had contemplated leaving. "Bloody hell, Wolfie," said Dennis.

"You nutter," said George. "You're the only reason why I'm still here, you can be a twat at times, but we all need a joker in the pack, you're the one that we turn to when we are feeling down in the dumps." Sympathy of plenty from my mates made me feel that the correct decision had been made.

The following week meant it was back to business as usual, it was a cold Monday morning and we were lined up outside the Battery Block; awaiting the arrival of the TC meant there was some important news to be heard. Standing next to Steve in the back rank meant that he was filling my head with all sorts of garbage.

"Maybe we are getting a pay rise," said Steve quietly, "maybe it's a rollicking because you were trying to get discharged."

"Behave," I said to Steve with a serious tone in my voice. Steve just laughed in his normal way knowing that he had penetrated my vulnerability once again. Just then the TC arrived with a clipboard in hand and told us all to relax as he had some important news to tell us.

"Listen in," said the TC. "In my hand I have a list of your names, next to your name is the trade you'll be doing prior to joining your regiments in the coming months." We were all feeling excited now, with the fact that it felt like one step closer to finishing our training as we anxiously waited for our name to be called out. With Bombardier Bartlett and Sergeant Preece at his side, the TC called out our names; apparently the judgment call was based on how well you did at the assessment centres, in my case at Harrogate some eight months ago.

I waited for my name to be called and at the same time thinking, I might get some glorified trade like a: road sweeper, washer upper, laundry etc. However, before I could get to grips with my thoughts my name was called.

"Wolfendale... Gunnery..." said the TC in a fine voice.

"Fine by me," I muttered under my breath.

"Gandy, Signals. Parry... TARA (Technical Assistant Royal Artillery)," there was an echoed "Oooo "from the ranks.

"Get you," I said as I glanced across to Steve in a confused way. "What the hell is TARA?" I whispered.

"Not too sure, but I am pretty sure it's on a more intelligent level than Gunnery," said Steve.

"Lynch... Signals" there was no surprise there. "Rigby... Gunnery" slight surprise, I could see Riggers doing something more up market. The roll called continued until I heard, "Norris... clerk." I think he was the only one to have been given that trade.

"Norris... clerk?" said Sergeant Preece, with a shocked look on his face. "You must have been the only one to have spelt your name correctly at the assessment centre." Looking back now, I couldn't in all honesty visualise Dennis and his stripped-down racing pigeon frame lumping artillery shells around. Later on that day I spoke to Riggers outside the Education Block.

"Are you OK, Riggers?" I asked whilst smiling at the same time.

"Yeah, not too bad," said Pete.

"I see we are both doing Gunnery, will be great to be together, what do you think?" I said.

"Well, I've just been talking to the TC in the Education Block," replied Pete. "He took me to one side and said '*Rigby?*' To which I replied, '*Yes Sir*' he said '*I have been thinking and pondering over the trade that I allocated to you, after careful consideration I believe that signals would be more to your liking, I would like you to join the signals course*'."

"Did you say yes?" I asked.

"Yes, I just felt the TC knew better than me. The only problem is that I will have to stay on for an extra term."

"What, until September?" I said in a shocked voice.

"Yeah, a bit gutted about that," said Riggers, "just makes leaving seem that much further away."

"I just feel grateful that I wasn't at the front of the queue when they were handing out brains," I said. "Dennis and Steve will also have to stay on an extra term as well, so at least you'll have some company."

Pete tried to reassure me as only Pete could.

"We all have hidden talents, Paul," said Pete. "To be honest, having you around keeps me going, I just hope I meet someone else like you for the last three months once you have departed;" those sorts of times and those kind words are what unites' everybody together as a unit, I just didn't know how to reply to Pete's comment without gushing, I just said,

"Thanks Pete." I knew then that Pete would be a long-term friend.

A lot of us were becoming segregated now with the fact that we were learning different trades. Although you're taught to be a soldier first and foremost, learning a trade was a welcome education. Most of the training took place in the confines of the camp but in different locations; Dennis was in the Clerical Education Wing, Sam, Pete and George were united in the Signals section while the Gunnery took place in one of the hangars. Week one of trade training had all the Gunners marching down to the hangar that housed the guns; given a short intro about the guns as we stood in the hangar dressed in combats was how it was.

"Listen in," said Sergeant Preece as he delivered his well rehearsed speech.

"The Ordnance QF 25-pounder, or more simply the 25-pounder, was the major British field gun and howitzer during World War Two. It was introduced into service just before the war started, combining high angle and direct fire, relatively high rates of fire and a reasonable lethal shell in a highly mobile piece. It remained the British Army's primary Artillery field piece well into the 1960s, with smaller numbers serving in training units.

The 25-pounder used howitzer-type variable-charged ammunition. The 25-pounder was separate-loading; the shell was loaded and rammed, then the cartridge in its brass case was loaded and the breech closed.

"In British terminology the 25-pounder was known as 'quick firing' (QC), originally because the cartridge case provided rapid loading compared with the bag charges, and was automatically released when the breech was opened. The gun was fitted with a direct-fire telescope, for use of armour-piercing shot, it also used one-man-laying in accordance with normal British practice. A crew of about six men would be required to operate the gun for maximum efficiency; four rounds a minute would be classed as normal fire unless you were having a slow day.

"The guns were made so that they could be easily towed behind an ammunition trailer, or a military truck like the four tonner we use. I've never seen one become unhitched before, so if you ever come across one in someone's garden being used as some center piece feature, then can you please return it to its rightful owner."

Stood next to Muckers we were told to gather around one of the six guns that were present. It felt like going back to basics when we were being taught how to operate the SLR, except these guns were on a far a larger scale; I was intrigued, but not excited about the prospects of being let loose on one of these guns.

After a small demonstration by Sergeant Preece it was my turn to sit in the layer's seat. In technical terms it was like sitting in the driver's seat of a car; fun in abundance I recall, I can't remember when I'd last had so much fun. I was a very competitive person and winning was in my blood. Once the gun sight was inserted into its housing it was like a competition to see who could lay the gun in the quickest time – again, in technical terms, to see who could get the gun ready to fire its first round.

There were two fixed metal spoke wheels about the size of a dinner plate that had to be turned in unison at a pace quicker than lighting, it reminded me when I would try tapping my head and rubbing my tummy at the same time, the idea behind it was to get two spirit level bubbles in the center of the spirit level at the same time; with the bubbles level, your gun was then ready to fire. I was as quick as anyone in the layer's seat, seconds and not minutes would see the gun ready for action. The afternoon continued with everybody getting to do all of the jobs that were required of a successful gun crew and within weeks, we were ready to be let loose on Lark Hill ranges for a few days to fire the guns in earnest.

Lark Hill is located in central Southern England (Salisbury Plain), and it provides a controlled safe environment for the release of land – and air-launched missile firings as well as instrumentation variation and a controlled ground impact area. With its varied terrain Lark Hill provided the sort of environment that you would expect to find in certain war zones, it reminded me of some of the old war movies I used to watch with my dad; never for one minute would I ever imagine that one day I would be chewing some of the same dirt.

It was a far cry from Kingsbury Ranges where we would be firing the SLR; with all the guns lined up about fifty metres apart and the ammunition at the rear; it was time to put our skills into practice. I was in the layer's seat and staring up the range. All I could hear from over my shoulder was, "Load," before I knew it the shell and charge were nestling in the barrel waiting to be fired. It was now my turn to lay the gun to the co-ordinates I was given, thus hopefully pointing the gun in the correct direction. We would always have a safety officer present on the range to prevent the local town from making the national news. His job would be to check the lay before being given their permission for us to fire the gun.

I wasn't sure what the impact of the gun firing would have upon me as I sat in the layer's seat fearing the worst. "FIRE!" was the noise I heard vibrating in my ear. I felt myself almost being thrown off the metal seat that my backside was occupying, smoke of plenty and cordite up my nostrils was my first experience of live firing with the 25-pounder; six young boys of seventeen years of age were now growing speedily into men.

I lost count of the number of shells we must have fired over the days we were there; however, what does stick in my mind is the burning of the cordite as it burrowed its way into nicks and cuts in your hands and fingers. It was a nice welcome return back to Bramcote: hot showers, washing machines, cookhouse food, basically I just felt comfortable to be back in my home surroundings and of course, being able venture into town on a Saturday. Venture into town you may ask; it was one of those times when Steve wished he had stayed in the barracks.

CHAPTER FORTY-SIX
STABBED IN THE BACK

More interesting news reached our ears; we were all told that bed-blocks were now a thing of the past, except on the occasional room inspection. Getting to know the men in a more enhanced capacity meant that the TC and the senior ranks would now be looking at us more closely to see who in their opinion, would be worth promoting, and to see who has the potential to lead a team of men into battle.

I wasn't expecting any stripes to be thrown in my direction so it didn't come as any surprise to me when the stripes were handed out that I wasn't getting one; the first I knew about any promotion was when I saw George with a black trimmed red stripe on his left arm.

"Wow, George," I said with my eyes wide open, "well done mate."

"Made up," said George with a huge proud smile on his face. "Slightly unexpected, but I'll enjoy wearing it with pride." I was now shaking hands with Junior L/Bombardier Lynch. George was still one of the lads, after all, how can you suddenly give up your mates just because you have been given more responsibility? With his own room, George was now even more segregated from the troop. He would be given more authority along with a couple of other now Junior L/Bombardiers that had also been promoted. Their tasks would be to alleviate some of the work from the senior ranks, however, at the same time, their head would be on the chopping block if they failed in their duties; being in charge and taking responsibility is something I've never really experienced in my sheltered life, so taking orders and not giving them was fine by me.

We were now entering February; there were just a couple of months left for me and the lads that didn't have to stay on an extra term before completing our training. Switching off though was something we had to be acutely aware of, as the TC still had a list of events for us to carry out before that day arrived.

"Listen in," said to the TC as we stood by our beds. "Tomorrow we will be finding out more about your potential. Each one of you will stand up in front of the troop and give a five minute lecture on a subject that I shall present you with shortly."

My heart sank… *bloody hell,* I was thinking, as well as other words that were crossing my mind. You could hear a pin drop as the TC continued his speech; you could just see by the look in his eyes that he was going to enjoy this moment. TC torture I would call it.

"Tomorrow you'll be able to show the senior ranks and myself your true ability to eventually be able to command your own gun. Being confident commands respect, without that ability you'll struggle to get the respect of the men that are working under you."

For the first time I felt respect being thrown my way. I felt that the TC was including me in his stern speech; it lasted for a whole three minutes until it was my turn to be told of the subject I would be expected to talk about.

"Wolfendale," said the TC, pretending he didn't know where I was.

"Yes Sir," I replied.

"Well, stand up then," he said, trying not to laugh under his breath. I stood up and made contact with his eyes from a distance of ten metres. I could see a grin that eventually was turning into a smile as he was about to announce my fate.

"A match box is what I would like you to talk about." Is it possible for your heart to sink twice in such a short time? Well, mine did. By this time the TC was laughing for Britain; he was human after all. As soon as the TC had managed to pull himself together he continued by saying, "Every time I look at you Wolfendale I have to laugh, I can't wait for tomorrow." Without trying to be flippant I replied, "I can, Sir," which for some reason not known to me caused his infectious laugh to hit me once more.

The TC left the block with all the lads having the evening to work on their respective subject; preparing a five minute speech would take a good few hours. Most of us just lay on our beds in sweet harmony trying to make sure not to disappoint the TC. With some tossing and turning throughout the night, the next day inevitably arrived. With every spare minute of the day we would try to use each minute wisely; we all had our well rehearsed speeches in our pockets so a quick read through it from time to time was imperative.

The afternoon arrived and we were all feeling nervous as we awaited our fate. We were assembled in the lecture room that was in the block. Sitting next to Parry made me feel even more nervous, it had me thinking that I should have sat next to Pete or even Sam; seconds later the unmistakable sound of the TCs shoes could be heard walking on the stairs as he got closer. "Attention," said L/Bombardier Lynch as we all sat upright in our seats.

I started to think that standing up in front of the troop has got to be the best laxative known to man. Instead of taking a front row seat, the TC decided to sit at the back in the cheap seats for a better view along with Bombardier Bartlett and Sergeant Preece, oh and some of the junior ranks just for good measure.

All seemed well until one by one we were called forward to give our lecture, from where I was sitting it seemed fine until…

"Wolfendale, you're next." Parry was giving me the elbow in my ribs.

"Go on Wolfie, get up there," he said, sniggering. Swearing is not something I do on a regular basis, but on this occasion, I felt it necessary to speak my mind.

"Fuck off," I said nervously… and I meant it.

I dragged myself through the ranks that were sitting in front of me and stood before the crowd. My eyes were working overtime; they didn't know where to look. With match box in hand I unenthusiastically started my speech.

"When I look at this match box it reminds me of my childhood. If this match box could talk it would save me the time of standing up here trying to explain its meaningless use, apart from providing my wonderful TC with some light entertainment. I was always told not to mess with matches by my parents so I would empty them into the coal fire and watch them burn. It was more fun when the dog would be warming herself by the fire to the point of almost being comatose; the sudden surge of a full box of matches going off would always make her run for her life.

"I now had a match box that, with a little thought; I could have some fun with. Finding a spider was an easy option in my ramshackle farm house, however, catching it is another thing. I would open the box just like a drawer and then with great precision place the open match box over the spider. All was left for me to do was close the box without trapping any of its eight legs and the job was a gooden.

"What came next would be quite obvious. I would place the match box on the side cupboard in the living room and take a seat. It normally wouldn't take long for one of my sisters to open the box; the scream could be heard for miles as the imprisoned spider leaped out of the box to what should be safety. Unfortunately the spider occasionally would end up embedded into the cupboard; it was a fifty-fifty chance as to whether the spider made it or not.

"I would also use the box to entice the mice from under the wooden floor-boards; the little bar-stewards would keep me awake at night. I would get a small piece of cheese from the fridge and place it in the open match box, and the match box would be placed by the side of my bed with my shoe at the ready, it was a case of *wallop*. I can't remember how many I managed to kill but I enjoyed the challenge, one thing I do remember is that the cheese made their breath smell."

I felt I had done enough to impress the TC with my lecture; he was in fits of laughter which is how he saw me, the Troop Clown. Weekend had arrived once more which meant it was time for some well earned free time. It was Saturday night and one or two of the lads were gearing up for a night on the tiles, the ones that enjoyed a pint or two. I could see Steve drowning himself in Brut, the sort of aftershave that would attract the flies and the type of birds you wouldn't give a second glance, however, we were talking about Steve here. "Wolfendale, coming down town?" yelled Steve from his bed-space.

"Not a chance," I said. "First of all I don't drink, at least not on your level."

"You're a pussy Wolfendale, get yourself ready."

"Say what you want Mr. Parry, I'm not coming," I said, "you may have a short memory, I haven't; my bank balance is ten pounds down thanks to you and one or two others."

Steve couldn't hold back with his smirk even though he knew I was right. I spent the night in the block writing a couple of letters, one to my parents and the other to Carol before getting into bed to the feel of new freshly soft sheets; sleeping for Britain was my plan for the night.

It was close to midnight when the sound of drunken soldiers was heard staggering up the stairs; this is something that I had become accustomed to over the last few months, except on this occasion I could sense all was not well. There was a kind of more serious tone in their voices and not the normal dribble drabble I was use to.

The doors swung open in their normal aggressive way as someone shouted, "Parry... he's been stabbed." The ones that were still left in bed were now sat up in astonishment at what we had heard; it took a double take before we all realised that this was no joke. One of the lads that were out with Steve that night soon explained the bare facts to the rest of the troop. We all gathered around like we were about to have a bed time story read to us.

"The night began with Steve and five of us making our way into town of Nuneaton for what we were hoping was going to be a good and cheerful night out, around about 2300hrs and a few pints later we made our way back along a narrow street whereupon we saw a crowd of about a dozen lads standing on the street corner within spitting distance. Steve said he heard one of them saying something like *'Soldiers Boys'* but keeping out of trouble was the first thing on our minds. Being let out on a Saturday night was a privilege and not a god given right."

"Then what happened?" we asked, snuggling closer together.

"Well… we started to pick up the pace a little, at the same time hoping there would be no trouble, and then before we knew, it they started chasing us; being more than a match for them with our fitness levels at a premium we had no problem getting away. Unfortunately one of the pursuers managed to get in a blow with what Steve thought was a fist on his back. It was only then that the attackers fled into the darkness of the night leaving us all to reflect on what might have been." The room was now as silent as could be as we awaited the rest of the story. "We made our way into the taxi office and took a seat on the wooden benches. I could see Steve was getting hot and sweaty and asked him if he was feeling OK.

"'My breathing feels difficult,' said Steve 'can't understand why, my back feels all sticky as well.' Steve put his hand around his back under his shirt to wipe away what he thought was sweat, we all had the shock of our lives to see the claret red blood that was now dripping off his hand and onto the floor. We were all absolutely shell-shocked and dumbstruck.

"'What the hell?' we said, "'call an ambulance and the police." Within minutes the emergency services arrived, with the police arriving just before the ambulance. While Steve was taken to the hospital we were quizzed by the police about the night's activities."

Steve was taken to the local hospital where he spent the next ten days before being discharged, and then given a week's compassionate leave. The place didn't seem the same for the week Steve was away; I was missing all of his annoying banter and his sense of humour.

We weren't quite sure when Steve would return so it was a wonderful surprise when we entered the room after a day of activities to see Steve sitting on his bed. It was great to have Steve back on board after three weeks of missing training; he explained that the knife had pierced his lung and that if the knife had penetrated any further it could have been fatal. At last there would be some good news for Steve as we all prepared for some adventure training.

CHAPTER FORTY-SEVEN
REGIMENTAL ADVENTURE TRAINING (RAT)

It was now the beginning of March and we only had about six weeks left of our training; short sleeve order was now coming into force as the days lengthened and the nights became shorter. George was now a full screw, another name for a Bombardier. He had been awarded his second stripe and was on his way to Junior Sergeant; looking at the stripes on his rolled-up sleeve made me feel like *I wish that was me.*

Steve was put on a driving course, not sure whether it was felt that after all that he had gone through it would be some sort of recuperation. 'Ours is not to reason why, ours is but to do or die' is the famous Army motto; at least it kept Steve away from some of the more hardy tasks we had to endure like RAT (Regimental Adventure Training). While Steve and a couple of other Wingate losers were out enjoying themselves with their civilian driving instructors, the rest of us were slumming it in Dolwyddelan, Snowdonia National Park for a week. We were divided into three groups to remind us of our heroes, Sherpa Tenzing, Edmund Hillary to name but two, they were the people to reach the summit of Mount Everest in 1953; "Wolfendale Tenzing Troop," said the TC as we all waited with bated breath.

"Yes Sir," I said in a sort of strange farmer's voice. I got a, *did you really say that* kind of look from the TC; to be honest I think he had more important things on his mind than to question my rudeness.

The accommodation was the worst I had experienced so far, barely habitable, grotty buildings that weren't even fit for rats; they were situated just off the main road by a huge mountain. I could sense already that this wasn't going to be a holiday; a cold fast running stream and lots of forestry made me feel like we were miles from civilisation.

We were given camp beds to erect so we didn't have to lie on the cold concrete floor among the creatures of the wild; I just kept saying to myself, *one week and we will be back in Bramcote.*

The first and for many mornings after, we would be out of our pits about

0600hrs and taken on a force march/run. This was the first time that I realised what the symptoms of asthma were; my chest was becoming tight as I ran over the tops of the Snowdonia mountings and finding it tough to breathe amongst the thin air. The runs were around about five miles long on average, but taking the terrain into account they felt more like ten miles: dressed in our red PT vest along with combat trousers DMS boots and standard Army green socks meant we were ready for action.

With myself being a more than an average runner I was right up the front with the leaders; feeling quite exhausted I was wondering how much further we had to run when out of the corner of my eye, I caught sight of the small camp at the bottom of the mountain where we were staying. Normally you would get excited when the finishing line was in sight, but not on these occasions. A fast rapid-like freezing cold stream flowed right past our accommodation, the sort of stream that you could only admire when standing on the bank next to it. Not for one minute did any of us think that we would be expected to jump in.

To me it seemed like an invasion of the stream's privacy, at the same time thinking how rude it would be not to get acquainted with the cold flowing water. "In the river now," was the order from Bombardier Bartlett as we stood in line facing our fate; like lambs to the slaughter we thundered our way into the shallow water with terror in our eyes.

"Gordon Bennett," was the cry as I hit the water. It felt like someone was sticking knives' into the bottom of my feet as the cold icy water slowly made its way through the eyelets of my boots and gradually found its way between my toes.

"Get your hands in the water and splash it over your face," said Bombardier Bartlett in a loud and aggressive tone. I could see Ricky the Slug Hill next to me clenching his teeth together and almost crying with pain. "Cheer up, Ricky," I said, feeling sorry for him with the way he was looking. I decided that I needed to find that fun element that comes with every task you undertake, it would at least take away the pain I was feeling; splashing my face with water led me to accidentally on purpose spray some over Ricky thinking it might bring him out of his coma.

"Bloody hell, Wolfie," he said, or words to that effect, "what the fuck?" Before I could grab another handful of the water Ricky Slug beat me to it, straight down the front of my PT vest it went. Standing upright, I was now feeling snatched (extremely cold), in other words my body was twitching like

I was throwing a fit; it didn't take long before everybody was having a free for all. "Whoopee," I said, "never had so much fun without laughing, takes us back to our kindergarten days." With everybody now having so much pleasure it was time for Bombardier Bartlett to put a stop to it; basically he was pissed that we were having so much enjoyment.

"Out of the pool now, sorry… I meant to say stream," said Bombardier Bartlett angrily. We were told to get ourselves back into the block and get changed into our lightweight trousers and combat jackets.

"I want you lined up outside in an hour's time, breakfast is in fifteen minutes".

After a full English and a mug of tea we were handed our packed lunch as we left the cookhouse; a white cardboard box full of surprising goodies meant that we would not be returning back to camp until later on that day, or maybe not at all. Some of us were just about to venture into our boxes when we were startled by a loud screaming voice.

"Get outside now with your backpacks on," was the command from Bombardier Bartlett. We just about had time to pack our lunch boxes away before making our way outside and lining up in three ranks. We were told that we would be going on a hike, a hike to the top of Mount Snowden. *Bloody hell*, I was thinking, we were only just getting over our pre-breakfast endurance and now they hit us with this. Climbing the highest mounting in Wales would be a challenge within itself, but one I felt ready for. Before we had chance to draw breath we were ordered to get onto the four tonne vehicle that was waiting on the road side.

"Right turn, forward march," was the command as we made our way the short fifty metres to the main road; seconds later we were all sitting on the wooden benches that were attached to the sides of the vehicle, trying to look appreciative of this holiday of a lifetime .

There wasn't much chitchat going on in the back of the vehicle, just a few lads having a smoke and one or two reading a book. I think most of us were just trying anyway we could to keep warm on this cold damp morning. The journey all in all took about half an hour before we pulled up at the foot of the imposing mountain; it's amazing how much of your lunch can be devoured in such a short time.

"Off the vehicle, hurry up and get a move on," yelled Sergeant Preece. We climbed out with our now bruised and battered bodies, trying at the same time to get ourselves orientated, I stood up and could see the terrain that we would be shortly climbing, the damp mist was laying low so seeing more than about fifty metres in front of us was as good as it got. "Three ranks now," was the cry from Bombardier Bartlett; I could see an Army Land Rover over to my left that was occupied by an SAS (Special Air Service) Sergeant also along with Sergeant Preece and the TC.

There are several routes that can be taken to climb to the summit of Snowden; the one that was chosen for us was just outside Llanberis. The path began at a cattle grid just above the Snowdon Mountain Railway Station. I could see a sign saying 'footpath to Snowden' – bit of a giveaway, really. I think the reason this route was chosen because it was one of the longest, maybe the TC wanted to make a full day of it.

With our backpacks on and in single file we started to ascend the mountain, the SAS Sergeant led the way with Bombardier Bartlett bringing up the rear. It was a lot steeper and more challenging than I expected; I seemed to be permanently bent forward as we made our way forcefully along the sometimes very narrow paths. Looking back over my shoulder gave me some idea of how far we had walked.

"Look how far we have walked," I said to Riggers, at the same time trying to take in a lung full of Snowdonia air.

"Bloody long way," said Pete, "not too far now before we reach the summit." I turned my head back and rolled my eyes in an upward manner to see how much further we still had to climb; Pete was right, and within a short space of time we had reached the top of the mountain. With everybody now present and in need of a break we found a place where we could relax and have our lunch.

"OK, let's see what Mr. Kipling has brought us," said Sam.

"Vanilla Slice, Cream Bun, may be some of his exceedingly tasty cakes." Why were we shocked when we opened the box to find exactly what we knew would be in the box, the only difference this time was there was a piece of fruit and a small carton of orange complete with straw. After our amazing lunch it was now time to start thinking of getting ourselves ready for the afternoon activities.

"Get yourselves sorted and take all your rubbish with you," said Bombardier Bartlett; I took one last look at my feet thinking, *it's all downhill from now on so please be gentle with me, no more blisters, I promise to put you in the ice cold stream when I get back.*

The journey down the face of Mount Snowdon was a much more pleasant affair; it was a case of putting the brakes on a little. However, if I knew what was to come within the next five minutes I wouldn't have ventured any further from where I was standing; in line with Riggers in front of me and Ricky the Slug Hill behind me, we made our way down the mountain like a snake would slither through the grass, but from the air, we were probably just like a bunch of wannabes.

All seemed well as we chatted away until *wham,* my feet flew from underneath my body. I was now taking the more direct and unconventional route down the mountain like an unstoppable train as I slipped on the slippery rocks. It was definitely all downhill now; I was heading for the world speed record to get to the bottom of the mountain. My boots were having no impact, even a hand brake would have struggled to stop me.

The cry from Riggers and Slug alerted the SAS Sergeant who was playing the part of follow my leader. I was heading towards a sheer drop off the edge of the mountain with no means of stopping; with my head bent forward, I could see the Sergeant turn to face me with his hands spread wide as my deathly eyes made contact with him.

"Have faith in me, you're not going to die," said the Sergeant. As I took one final look at the heavens I could see the crows circling above. Maybe this is where most people lose their lives and the crows would be the beneficiary of my death. My size 9 boots cannoned into the Sergeant's midriff with the velocity of a bullet; I still today find it hard to believe that he managed not just to hold onto me, but to stop us both from falling to certain death. Such a great man is hard to come by. I still feel if we'd have both fell over the edge of the mountain he would have found a way to hang onto me and use his body as a shield to protect me.

For me, time seemed to stop still for a few minutes, but for the Sergeant, he just brushed the incident aside as if it was an everyday occurrence.

"Bloody hell Wolfie," said George, "you alright, buddy? Thought we had lost you then, it's times like this when you realise how important camaraderie is within the Army; your so-called buddies will save your life one day." It was a great relief to reach the bottom of the mountain in one piece and, to see the four tonne vehicle waiting to take us back to camp. The next few days were much of the same thing: early morning runs, log racing with logs the size of telegraph poles, raft building and anything else that would test our stamina and leadership skills. Throughout the course we were being assessed by all the senior ranks of our qualities. I felt that I had shown enough aptitude to receive a well earned respectable mark and was looking forward to the results.

It was Friday morning, the last day we would be spending at the RAT camp when the TC and all of his merry men entered our room. After a quick inspection of the accommodation, the TC got us all gathered around in a small huddle to announce the results of the past week.

"Well done to all of you for completing what I know has been a grueling week," started the TCs speech. "I would like to thank all the staff for their participation in making this a most memorable exercise. I am hoping that you have all taken something positive from your time here. I have here in front of me the results of how we evaluated your performance."

As we all waited with bated breath the TC pulled out a piece of paper from his combat jacket. In reverse order he started to read the names out; this is the one time I didn't want my name to be called out first.

"Russell... 34pts," *Great* I was thinking, *not last*.

"Owen... 36 pts," continued the list.

"Wolfendale... 40 pts," I was gobsmacked, absolutely gutted; I had worked my socks off. I felt that I had been pre-judged just like the orienteering exercise when the TC failed to recognise my true ability. I lost total respect for the TC and the senior ranks after this showing. If I had truly done badly on the course then I would have no problem with the results, but there was no way I could agree with the mark I got; so be it, I just had to take it in my stride and get on with the last few weeks of what had been an amazing journey.

It was now time to get all our belongings together and get ourselves on the four tonner for our journey back. Most of us fell asleep within minutes, a task within itself; falling asleep on the back of a four tonne vehicle just doesn't happen. On the journey back to camp we were all felt we were now that much closer to leaving Bramcote; what we didn't realise is, we were that much closer to stepping onto the streets of Northern Ireland; a trip to the NAAFI one evening brought the message well and truly home as we were watching the news on the television. More blood being shed as the troubles between the British soldiers and the republicans was heating up.

CHAPTER FORTY-EIGHT
HARVEY ANDREWS

It was great to be back in camp and just sit on my nice warm soft bed again, to look out of windows and see that there is life outside the forest region of Snowdonia. Spring was now upon us that meant the sun was showing its face once again, the sort of day that brings back memories of my childhood, I could see the troops marching in short sleeve order with a kind of swagger in their tail; quite amazing how a drop of sunshine can change your mood. The first thing I did is pay a visit to the Battery Office to see what mail I had received if any. "Coming to see if you've got any mail?" I said to Sam.

"Yeah, wait a sec, just give me chance to lock up my locker and I will be with you," said Sam. "I'm so glad RAT is over."

"Same here Sam," I said. "Bloody hard graft that was, although I do feel a lot fitter for the excursions."

"Yeah, know what you mean, I've found muscles I didn't know existed," said Sam, looking at his biceps. We made our way into the Battery Office to see if someone had been kind enough to write us a letter.

"How can I help you?" said the Battery Clerk.

"Is there any mail for Junior Gunner Wolfendale and Junior Gunner Gandy?" I asked.

"Let me have a look," said the Battery Clerk, looking through his well organized filing system; it took less than a few seconds before he produced two letters for me and one for Sam. The smell of perfume as the Bombardier handed me my letters told a story within itself. *Carol,* I was thinking at an educated guess. The other one I was not too sure about, the hand-writing was not that of my parents or my sisters. Sam could see that his was from a family member, so no surprise there. We made our way back into the block to the greeted by the rest of the troop.

"Mail, everyone," someone said excitedly. As soon as they saw that Sam and I had got mail they were out of the swinging doors quicker than if they were going on leave.

I knew I had about five minutes to kill until the rest of the troop would be returning, so I planned to make the most of the time. I just lay on my bed and decided to open the letter that I had absolutely no idea who it was from; with the envelope now open I slid the well folded letter out. *Wow*, I said to myself as my eyes scanned the first lines of the blue note paper; it was from Dec, my home town buddy.

Dear Paul

Just a short note hoping this letter finds you well, things have been moving on at a fast pace here, I have just come back from the selection center in Harrogate, I am pleased to announce that I have been selected to join the Army. I shall be joining the Royal Artillery just like you; I need to report to the Crewe Army Careers Office at the beginning of April to sign up. I leave school in about three weeks' time and then I am finished with education, please let me know when you're home again and we can have a catch up.

Take care of yourself.

Declan.

Before I had chance to digest what I had just read, the rest of the lads were starting to return. "Riggers," I said, "Guess what?"

"What?" said Pete, wanting to know my news; I explained all the details to him about the contents of the letter.

"Brilliant," said Pete, "another gunner. When you write back to him, give him all the best from me; tell him he will love it here."

"Yes, I will, Pete," I said, still feeling excited. I never did get time to open my letter from Carol; I thought I would leave it for later on in the evening when everybody is asleep. It was early evening and I was just about to go to the cookhouse for some scran when Steve entered the block.

"Bloody hell Steve mate, how are you doing?" I said joyfully.

"Had better days," said Steve. I was just about to give Steve an embrace before he said, "Stop there Wolfendale, my back remember."

"Oh shit, sorry mate, I forgot, how is it now?" I asked.

"Better, however I've been told to stay away from any bear hugs." I just smiled; it was nice to see his sense of humour had not gone astray.

"How's your driving going?" I said.

"Passed it today, it was a week-long course," said Steve as if it was a stroll in the park.

"Well done mate," I said still trying to show my concerning side. I could be very understanding when needed and this was one of those times.

Later on that evening George, Sam, Riggers, Dennis, the walking wounded and myself decided to have a evening in the NAAFI, after everything that had gone on over the last few weeks we all felt we needed some get-together time; sitting down at one of the tables swigging alcohol down our necks brought the best and worst out of us, we were getting louder and louder with each minute that passed. We started talking about what regiment we would be joining after leaving training.

"7th Para for me," I said to George as he almost choked on the remains of his beer.

"7th Para, have you gone mad?" said George.

"Just think I could do the course, be proud to wear a red beret," I replied seriously.

"Go for it, Wolfie," said Dennis, who was always supportive with everything I did. "I think you could do the course no problem, Paul."

"Thanks Dennis," I said, with that in mind I decided there and then, why not? *Dennis, I think you could be right,* I thought to myself.

The time was getting close to 2200hrs as I looked up towards the TV screen to see News at Ten was just starting. The civil war in Northern Ireland was making the main headlines once more; in one quick movement we all glanced over to where the TV was to catch the story.

"Bomb blast kills a soldier in Belfast," said the news presenter. "A soldier whilst on patrol in the Springfield road area of West Belfast has been killed, the bomb was placed in a nearby car and was thought to be a controlled device, as the patrol passed the vehicle that was parked on the busy street the bomb was detonated killing the soldier instantly." We all just looked at each other in disbelief; the looks on our faces said it all. We were due out of training soon and in a few months' time that will probably be us patrolling the streets.

The mood on the way back to the block was something like I'd never felt before, the laughter that would normally be present after a couple of drinks was nowhere to be found. It felt as if it would be disrespectful to share a joke or two or to even raise a smile, the sort of feeling you can only envisage at a funeral; hearing about soldiers dying on the streets of Northern Ireland was like a kick up the backside for us all, we needed to grow up, and grow up fast.

With my mind focused on the atrocities I almost forgot to read my letter from my girlfriend, which seemed inconsequential now; it was a touching letter with lots of 'I Love You and Miss You' however to be honest, it just went straight over my head as there were more important things going on in my mind.

The next day we were chatting to some of the permanent staff, a couple of Bombardiers that were helping out with our training, we mentioned what we had heard the night before about a soldier losing his life in Belfast. They became very intrigued about our interest and explained that they had served two tours of Northern Ireland; the conversation went on for some time until one of the Bombardiers mentioned that he had a cassette tape of the singer Harvey Andrews that, at the time, didn't mean a lot to the majority of us.

He continued by saying, "There is a song on the cassette entitled 'Soldier' that I think you will all find fascinating, I will bring it to the block tomorrow for you all to listen to."

"OK, that would be excellent," we said, "looking forward to hearing it". The next day true to their word they brought the cassette for us to listen to; some of the lads had a cassette player so as soon as the Bombardier had left we put the cassette into the player and searched for the song.

The song that was about a soldier losing his life in Northern Ireland , it was so touching to listen to, and sung so beautifully with such a passion that the song deserved. After listening to the song I remember lying on my bed and reminiscing over the words that were now well and truly part of my feelings. I could picture the situation that Harvey Andrews described as if I was part of the song. I just stared into oblivion and enjoyed these precious moments that only come around once in a while. Harvey Andrews intended the song to transcend sectarianism, but some have wrongly interpreted it as the glorification of military heroism; played several times a day the song never lost its identity.

With our passing out parade looming ever closer we were now being handed bayonets, a sharp dagger like weapon that would be very carefully placed onto the end of your rifle. Using them for ceremonies like the one we would soon be participating in seems delightful, however used for their correct purpose by an infantry soldier made me feel that much closer to war. Put it in—twist—pull it out would be the command, making my stomach churn every time I heard those ghastly words; thrusting the sharpened bayonet into a hanging sand bag felt too real for my liking.

Drill patterns were becoming more intense now, not only were we expected to march in a straight line, but we now had rifles with fixed bayonets to contend with. After a good half hour session your arms would be feeling the strain of the weight of the weapon.

Weapon handling was considered an art within itself in the Army: saluting, trail arms, fix bayonets, slope arms all required a certain skill level, anyone found letting their rifle slip from their grasp would certainly know about it. It was now getting close for us to choose our regiments we would wish to join; I was having second thoughts about joining 7th Para but, had I left it too late to change my mind? It was now in the hands of the TC as he headed to RHQ to submit the list before a committee.

CHAPTER FORTY-NINE
CHOOSING YOUR REGIMENT

We were now entering our last four weeks of slightly toned down training; that meant we were getting more free time. It was Saturday evening and some of the lads had volunteered (a thing you should never do) to wait on at the Officers' Mess function night; a few free beers and an extra few quid in your pocket would make it worthwhile giving up your Saturday night. The only down side of this was for the ones that didn't volunteer, would end up getting woken up at an ungodly hour by the few that had drunk one too many. It must have been about 0130hrs or thereabout when I was woken by the sound of a few merry men falling up the stairs. The noise of the doors swinging open meant I was now unquestionably fully awake.

"Wolfie, I love you, you bastard," was the slurring sound I heard from Dennis as he was drunkenly trying to climb into bed, unfortunately it was the bed that I was occupying.

"Yeah, love you too Dennis, but this is my bed, there's no room at the inn."

"Yeah but, I still love you Wolfie," said Dennis with his arm now around me. I decided that this situation had gone far enough.

"Let me show you where you'll be sleeping tonight, Dennis, and it is not with me," I said whilst getting myself out of bed to escort him to the other side of the darkened room. On arrival at Dennis's bed I noticed that there was already someone lying in it. It was like something from the three bear's story; if it wasn't for me being sober I'm pretty sure we would have had a compromising situation as Dennis then tried to climb between the sheets.

"Stop there for a second Dennis," I said, "I think we have someone sleeping in your bed". It was Sheep, no… not an actual sheep, but none other than Mr Parry. God knows how, but he also had managed to find his way into the wrong bed. I spent the next five minutes trying to sort out where they both should be sleeping before I could settle down again.

"Now get yourselves some sleep" I said, "It will soon be morning;" within minutes I could hear Dennis and Steve snoring their pretty little heads off, and with that in mind, I felt it was now safe for me to get some sleep. The following morning I made my way down to the NAAFI for the morning paper; above everything else I wanted to read the sport. I lay on my bed trying not to wake up the out-for-the-count Dennis and Steve and started to read the sports section. From back to front is how I always take in the news. It wasn't long before I saw that the team I supported (Leeds United) had won; we had no chance of winning the league title like we did last year, that honour was going Derby County. I continued reading the paper when I noticed in the fixture column that Leeds was playing in Leicester on Tuesday night. It was an FA cup match against Ipswich Town; already drawn three times at Portman Road, Elland Road and Old Trafford, it was time for a fourth match between these two heavyweight teams. I decided that it was time to wake Dennis up out of his coma. "Dennis," I said, shaking his shoulder, "fancy coming to see Leeds on Tuesday? They're playing Ipswich in the FA cup."

"What the hell Wolfie, what do you want?" groaned a half drunken Dennis. I'm not sure how many times I had to repeat myself before the penny dropped, but eventually Dennis finally understood what I was asking him; with the fact that Dennis wanted to get some more sleep he agreed.

"Alright, alright," said Dennis, "now I can I go back to sleep?"

"Wow, cheers Den, yes of course you can go back to sleep," I said as he turned over for some more beauty sleep. The next couple of days felt like a lifetime until Tuesday finally arrived. I was feeling sparkling at the thought that I had the chance to see the football team I had supported all my life once more.

Tuesday evening traffic meant that we would have to leave the camp as early as possible in order not to miss the scheduled 1930hrs kick off. Dennis and I made our way to the Nuneaton train station at the double knowing we were on a tight time scale. On arrival we could hear the PA system; the train now arriving at platform three is the 1900hrs to Leicester.

"Quick Dennis," I said, "before we miss it!"

"Right behind you, Wolfie," said Dennis as we hurried to the empty open space of the platform. The train was reasonably empty so finding a seat was a simple task, well… at least compared to the task's we were given in Army training. With the doors closed and whistle blown we were now on our way to see my much-loved Leeds United.

A short taxi journey to Filbert Street home of Leicester City was the final leg of our voyage. The taxi driver dropped us off right next to the ground but unfortunately, the game had already started; we were ten minutes late to be precise. I managed to purchase a woollen Leeds scarf from one of the so-called 'sellers' located outside the ground.

"Anyone scored yet?" I asked as Dennis and I were leaving his stall at some pace.

"One nil to Ipswich," he shouted as we continued running towards the turnstiles.

In all the confusion of my mind that was now thinking about the score, I didn't realise that I was now entering the Ipswich end as I handed over my cash.

"Come on Den," I said. It was like a party atmosphere all around us; normally the best and safest policy would be to keep quiet as we stood on the terrace, but that just wasn't going to happen. Minutes later we equalised. There was no way I wasn't going to enjoy this moment; it was now a party for two as everybody else around us was drowning their sorrows. I was jumping up and down like I was on acid whilst at the same time waving my scarf to the heavens. Dennis wasn't too sure what to do. The look in his face said it all, he seemed a little petrified to say the least; I had made my existence quite clear to the thousands of Ipswich fans who for some reason, felt undeterred by my presence.

The game ebbed and flowed with Ipswich taking the lead again only for Leeds to make it 2-2. Later in the second half, Ipswich retook the lead for a third time and despite all of our pressure, it was not to be. All the huffing and puffing was to be in vain as Ipswich ran out 3-2 winners.

"Come on Dennis, let's head back," I said, feeling deflated. It must have been close to 2300hrs when we walked through the camp gates; we just wanted to get back into our beds for a good night's sleep.

Two weeks and counting, I thought as I made my way to breakfast for my usual fry up. Normally I would be one of the first to the cookhouse, but on this occasion I was close to being last. I could see George and Sam getting stuck into the final embers that were left on their plates.

"Alright," I said to them both as I sat down.

"Yeah, not too bad," said George.

"I think we are choosing our regiments today," said Sam.

"Yeah, I know, any idea what regiment you want to join?" I asked. "Rumour has it that we get three choices."

"That's right," said George, "you write your first choice down and then two alternative ones in case you don't get your first one."

"Oh, right," I replied. "I might see where some of the other lads are going before I make up my mind. West Germany sounds good, never been abroad before, I think that's where my vote will be going."

Time was getting on now. After all the chin wagging and getting excited about what regiment to join, we lost track of time. It was more of a double pace back to the block even though my stomach didn't appreciate it; we just about had time to put our eating irons away before being called outside for the morning's parade.

"Outside now!" was the command from Bombardier Bartlett. A quick inspection of our dress and then a few words were spoken about the topic of the day. Sam's intuition was about to be confirmed as the Bombardier started his speech.

"I want you back in the block after NAAFI break at 1030hrs; the TC will be joining us to discuss what regiments are available to you and what regiment you may wish to join." He wasn't telling us anything that we didn't already know, however it was still nice to hear it from the horse's mouth (so to speak).

It was off to the Armoury to sign for our SLR and then onto the parade square for about an hour of drill; passing out parade in two weeks time would be with rifles and fixed bayonets which meant there was still some work to be done before we become the finished article.

With NAAFI break now over everybody was buzzing at the thought of choosing our regiments as we made our way into the lecture room. It took a good stern, "Quiet you lot," from Bombardier Bartlett to get us to shut up. Once seated, the TC arrived. "Attention," shouted Bombardier Bartlett as we sat upright in our seats. The TC got straight to the point as if he had better things to do.

"OK listen to what I have to say, it is almost time for you to leave Junior Leaders, it's time for you to make a decision on the regiment you'll serve with. Bombardier Bartlett will put a list of the regiments that will be available to you on the notice board and then you'll need to read it carefully before making any decisions. Tomorrow morning I will be inspecting your lockers and then after the inspection, I will be asking you to tell me your choice, in the event that we cannot allocate you your first choice, I want you to choose two more regiments as backups." Everything seemed as clear as day as we were dismissed to return to our rooms for a while.

"Any thoughts anyone?" said Riggers.

"I need to check the list on the notice board," I said. I noticed that Steve was being very sheepish as he sat on his bed.

"What about you Steve, any thoughts?" I asked.

He replied in a quiet tone of voice, "It's alright for you; I've still got another term to serve." I understood what he meant, the majority of us were feeling jubilant with the fact that we would be leaving and Steve, well, he still had three more months to do; staying an extra term wasn't as bad as it seemed, you would still attend the passing out parade and then return for one last term.

L/Bombardier Lewis and L/Bombardier Hogg decided to pay us a visit. I thought they had disappeared off the face of the earth as we hadn't seen them for a few months. It was nice to see them again whilst at the same time, it was nice for them to see the results of their efforts; we were now the finished article and ready to take the next step in becoming a fully-fledged soldier.

"Great to see you again," we all said, "to what do we owe this pleasure?"

"We just thought we would come and see you and answer any questions you might have now that you're so close to leaving."

"Well, which regiment to join is proving to be a difficult decision," I said, "any thoughts?"

"It depends on where you would like to be stationed," they both said. "Some of the regiments are in West Germany and some are over here, there will be some that will be going to Northern Ireland later on in the year although you won't be able to go until you're 18."

"I'll be 18 in September," I said, "so I guess I could be sent there as early as that."

"Yes, you could," said the Bombardiers.

After a lot of thought and running my eyes up and down the list I decided that 42 Regiment ticked all the boxes for me, even though I was contemplating the 7th Para as my first choice. 42 were based in West Germany, one of the batteries was predominantly made up of people from the Cheshire area and also there was a rumour that they might be going to Northern Ireland in November, yet to be confirmed; that news was the clincher for me. Riggers became the first person to come over to me...

"Made up your mind then, have you, Paul?"

"Yeah, 42 Heavy for me that are based in Fallingbostal," I said with a colossal smile on my face, and my second choice would be 7th Para.

"What about you, Pete?"

"Still not sure, but you know what, I think I will follow in the same footsteps as you; it would be great to serve in the same regiment, I just feel that we have become really close over the last year," replied Pete.

"Wow, that would be fantastic," I said. "Let's hope we both get our first choice."

That evening, some of the lads that had not already made up their mind were still pondering over their future. Sam had chosen 4 Field regiment; they were based at Catterick, not too far from his roots in Bonny Scotland. Dennis was making his way to Gutersloh, West Germany to join 40 Field along with George. Ricky the Slug chose 50 Missile that were based at Menden West Germany and Steve was still to make up his mind. I made my way over to Steve who was putting the finishing touches to his locker.

"What's doing then, Steve?" I said. "Come on buddy, put me out of my misery, who's it going to be?"

"Where are you going?" said Steve.

"42, based in Fally," I said "that will be my first choice"

"Well, I can cross that off my list of regiments to join then."

"Cheeky bastard" I said, "Riggers has chosen joining 42 as well."

"Well then, I am definitely not joining 42, you're a bad influence."

"Bad influence!" I laughed. "It was you that got me pissed, it was you that contributed to my downfall; I didn't enjoy getting charged you know." It was a while before Steve finally decided to show a more serious side.

"42 it is then," said Steve underneath his breath.

"What did you say, Steve?" I said.

"42 it is then," he repeated.

"Why do you have to wind me up you arse? You knew all along that you were going to join 42 didn't you?"

"Just wasn't too sure," replied Steve, "wanted to see where you and Riggers were going first."

"Riggers," I shouted, "get over here; Parry is joining us in Fallingbostal." Pete was all smiles as we gathered around Steve's bed. I knew I would be first to fly out to West Germany so it would be up to me to get the feel of the place before Riggers and Steve arrived.

The following morning and after our locker inspection, the TC being true to his word stood at the end of the room with a folder in his hand; he called out our names one by one and asked for our choices of regiment. All in all, it took no longer than about fifteen minutes; choice one, choice two and choice three were now in the hands of the TC, it was a case of waiting to see if we got our first choice.

"I shall be going down to HQ now; I shall let you know later on this afternoon what regiments you have been allocated."

"Bombardier Bartlett, have them parade outside the block at 1600hrs," said the TC.

"Yes Sir," said the Bombardier.

"Attention." We all came to attention as the TC trundled his way to RHQ. It was only then that I had this strange feeling that I might be given my second choice; it was a rarity for anyone to join 7th Para so I was feeling nervous that I would be allocated my second choice. "Sir, Sir" I said as I raced after him down the road.

"What's a matter Wolfendale" he said looking shocked.

"I want to change my second choice Sir" I said trying to catch my breath, "I don't want to go to 7th Para Sir, if I don't get my first choice then please could you choose another regiment for me; not the Paras."

"Well you'll just have to wait and see then wont you" he said with a smirk on his face, "now get yourself back to the block.

The rest of the day seemed to last forever as we waited until finally, 1600hrs arrived.

"Outside, now," was the order from Junior Sergeant Lynch who had been promoted to Sergeant just a couple of days ago. George was now given more responsibility; it was his job to show his true potential and get us on parade.

Before we knew it we were halfway down the stairs, it wasn't so much that George had raised his voice, more with the fact that we couldn't wait to see if we had got our first choice. The normal position of where you would stand on parade was now a thing of the past on occasions like this; it was just a case of getting yourselves in three ranks in some sort of orderly fashion. Standing next to Dennis and Riggers we waited nervously for the TC to arrive. We didn't have to wait more than a few minutes before that moment was upon us. After being brought up to attention and then told to stand at ease, the TC wasted no time in announcing where we would be stationed over the coming months.

Instead of calling out individual names, the TC called out the name of the regiment first, and then the name of the person or persons to join that regiment.

"42 Heavy Regiment based in Fallingbostal." There was a slight pause before the TC lifted his head, stared into the ranks, and then announced the names.

"Wolfendale, Rigby, Parry." *Wow*, we just looked at each other with sheer delight; I almost missed where my other buddies were going until I heard, "40 Field Regiment based in Gutersloh… Norris and Lynch… 50 Missile Regiment based in Menden. Junior Gunner Hill… 4 Field Regiment based in Catterick. Junior Gunner Gandy…" The list went on and on until everybody had been allocated a regiment.

After being dismissed I was in state of *wow, can't believe it*. "Steve, you're the first person I met on the way here and now we will be serving in West Germany together along with Pete!" It was the first time that Steve commented without being sarcastic or making a joke about anything we did together. Most of the night was spent chatting about joining our regiments; our lockers had taken a back seat even though we knew we had a locker inspection in the morning. It was to be the last locker inspection at Gamecock Barracks before our passing out parade.

CHAPTER FIFTY

LEAVING PARTY

Thursday morning arrived, after NAAFI break I made my way to the Battery Headquarters to see if I had some mail; *one letter for Wolfendale* was written on the white board. It was a letter from my parents saying that they wouldn't be attending the passing out parade. I felt disappointed, but at the same time, I understood their reasons; passing out from recruits some ten months ago was their special moment and in their eyes nothing else was going to eclipse that.

After talking to one or two of the other lads about my parents not attending they said, "No worries buddy, my parents have decided to give it a miss as well."

"Oh, right," I said. I suppose it did make me feel considerably better in respect that I wasn't the only one whose parents weren't attending. After a quiet weekend we were all up and ready to tackle our final few days. Monday morning was completely different to any other Monday morning I've ever witnessed; it felt like we were moving house as well as putting some final touches to our drill parade.

MFO (Military Forces Overseas) boxes were being shipped into our rooms. They were small and made out of plywood, I would say they were probably about two to three foot square. We were given the address of the regiments we would be joining by Bombardier Bartlett.

"Make sure you write your name and the address in black felt tip pen on the lid of the box, as an example, you'll be called Gunner and not Junior Gunner."

'Gunner Wolfendale', *Sounds good to me,* I was thinking; no more Junior Gunner, that title was about to disappear forever. Underneath my name I had to write the address; a number was all it was, BFPO 38 (British Forces Posting Overseas). We were told to pack away unnecessary equipment like: gas masks, webbing, coveralls, rain mac; even our combats had no more use in this final week. Two boxes are what we had to cram as much stuff in them as we could. Our lockers were now looking a little bare; putting away some of my unwanted civilian clothes into the last remaining space of the boxes just about completed the clear-out.

Bombardier Bartlett came along later that evening to check that we had not accidently packed away our No.2 dress uniform by mistake. *Now why would we want to do a thing like that?* Either way, once he had inspected the contents we nailed the lid tightly to the box; a small two-pound hammer and some tacks did the trick before they were collected the following morning and put onto the four tonners.

A surprise was in store for us on Tuesday. Bombardier Bartlett and Sergeant Preece announced that Wingate Troop, under the supervision of the permanent staff, would be having a leaving party, basically at night of moderate bladderation at a club just outside Nuneaton on Thursday evening. It's great news for those who like a pint or two, me? Well, I guess it would be a chance to have a great time with my buddies; it's a well-known fact that after a few pints you find out the truth about somebody. Between Tuesday and Thursday, we found ourselves doing some general fatigues as well as continuing with our rehearsing for our passing out parade. Most of the lads were now content with just keeping their nose clean, with it being so close to leaving.

Thursday evening was on us in the blink of an eye and after a quiet day, it was time to put on our glad rags. Smart trousers and a shirt is always a military minimum requirement along with shoes not trainers. I put on my John Travolta leather jacket to the sound of, "Hoping to pull, Wolfie?" from my mate George.

"You never know what's around the corner," I said. "Pass us some of your Brut, George." *Splash it over,* I said tunefully to myself as I padded it on my angelic face. "Come on then Dennis, you ready yet?" I said.

"Ready to down a pint or two," said Dennis.

"Let's get this show on the road," I replied.

We made our way down the stairs along with Riggers, Sam and the rest of the troop, a white civilian type coach could be seen parked up by the gym.

"Do you think that's for us?" asked Sam

"Not sure, very much doubt it," said some of the lads, "too posh for us."

Within two shakes of a lamb's tail I could see the smartly dressed Bombardier Bartlett along with Sergeant Preece and other permanent staff personnel approaching from around the front of the bus. "Get yourselves on the bus, you lot," shouted Sergeant Preece.

"Bloody hell, soft seats for a change I said to Steve."Come on lads," I continued saying

I wasn't really sure why I said that because as I looked around, Steve and I were the last two, to get our arses into gear and make our way onto the coach.

On the bus to school again is what it felt like; don't half miss those school trips. We were trying our best not to become too rowdy, however, a night out on the town is difficult to disguise.

"Here we go, here we go, here we go, here we go, here we go here we gooooo!" was the tune we were blurting out.

"Keep your noise down, you motley shower," was the cry from Sergeant Preece at the front of the bus.

"Yeah, whatever," we said under our breath; taking the mick out of your superiors wasn't Army policy, we still had two more days to go before our passing out parade so we had to be careful not to cross any boundaries.

"Right, you lot," said Sergeant Preece, "the first drinks are on the house, courteous of all the senior ranks from Wingate Troop."

"Get in there!" said Ricky.

"Enjoy the moment while you can," said Bombardier Bartlett. "Remember, it's the RSM's inspection tomorrow; god help anyone that is not fit for duty."

As the bus pulled into the huge car park we were all thinking, *why have a leaving do on the night before the RSM's parade!!* Never mind. *Ours is not to reason why, ours is but to do or die* sprung to mind once more.

Once inside it was a case of commandeering a table… "Over here," yelled George.

"Table in the corner, close to the bar," he said. It was a case of the usual Dennis, Sheep, Riggers, Sam and me rattling a few chairs as we trampled our way over the plush carpet.

"Ricky, get your butt over here!" said Steve, "there's a spare seat next to Sam."

"On my way," was the snap reply. The room itself was very enchanting, almost fit for a five-star General; with everybody now settled a waitress came forth and asked for our orders, whilst at the same time reiterating that the first drink was free.

"Wolfie, double Bacardi for you," said Steve.

"On your bike," I said, "there's no way I'm getting leathered, you can get yourself legless if you want, but I'm not facing the BC again." No matter how much they pushed me it was one pint, even that had become as flat as a witch's tit by the time I had finished it. As the evening rolled on the chat was getting louder along with mountains of innuendoes. I was starting to feel slightly home sick; occasionally I would have a quiet heart to heart with Dennis and Sam. "Missing my parents, missing my girlfriend and I know for a fact come the weekend I be will missing you lot too," I said, "life can be cruel at times."

"It's not going to be that bad, Wolfie," said Sam. "I am sure we'll meet up again." Before we could babble on any further it was back into party mode; a good old military song was doing the rounds that meant not joining-in wasn't an option; with pint mugs in hands and in my case a glass of Coke, we sang to the high heavens.

Old King Cole was a merry old soul and a merry old soul was Old King Cole, he would turn out the lights in the middle of the night and call for his Gunners three, Beer, Beer, Beer said the Gunners, have another drink on me, there's none so fair you can compare to the Royal Artillery, ah rumba, rumba rumba rumba rumba rumba rum ba ba.

Before we knew it, it was time to shut up shop. "Last orders please!" could be heard from the busty barmaid. I knew there were going to be a few thick heads in the morning by the way some of the lads were staggering into the cold fresh air, but I never for one minute thought it was going to be me; a quieter affair was had on the way back to the barracks through the dark and uninhabited streets of Nuneaton. I felt like a naughty boy exploiting my curfew, I would normally be in camp for 2200hrs or face the consequences. A great night was had by all, it was now time get some beauty sleep, don't want to be worse for wear in the morning. It is possible to have a night out drinking only one pint of beer, and then waking up feeling as if you had drank the whole brewery?

CHAPTER FIFTY-ONE

MY WORST NIGHTMARE WAS ABOUT TO COME TRUE

The following morning, just one day before our training would be consigned to history; we were given the luxury of an extra hour in bed, courteous of the TC; with the guard also informed of our win fall they thought they would give us a final farewell present as they entered the room waving their pick handles.

"Out of bed now, pissheads," was the battle cry, "out of bed now you laze bastards. I think they must have had their orders to give us one of those never to be forgotten wakeup calls. They could have marched in with the Royal Artillery military band playing Rule Britannia for all we cared, we were going home tomorrow and nothing was going to dampen our mood.

As I got out of bed everything seemed fine for the first few minutes until I made my way to the washroom. With every step I took I could feel my head banging, sharp stabbing pains were causing my eyes to squint, I had to look away from the light. As I made my way to one of the vacant sinks I heard a voice saying. "How you feeling, Paul?" it was Dennis, who was trying to wake himself up with cold water.

"My head is bloody killing me, can't understand it," I said with the pain getting worse.

"It's all that Coke you drank last night," said Steve in a jovial way.

"Did someone spike my drinks last night?" I said loudly to anyone who might be listening… *no takers;* "Well if no one spiked my drinks, then why is my bloody head killing me?!" Sympathy was landing on deaf ears apart from a couple of my buddies.

"I have got some aspirin in my locker," said Dennis, "take a couple of them and that will help." On the way back to the room I bumped into Riggers, well at least that's what it felt like, I explained to Pete about how I was feeling.

"Big strong lad like you, hang in there Paul, you'll be fine by NAAFI break. I'll buy you a strong cup of coffee; that should sort you out, are you coming down to breakfast?"

"Not a chance," I said, "just going to take a couple of aspirin and lay on my bed for half an hour."

It was now 0800hrs and everybody was back in the block. My head was no better; if anything worse; there was no way that I could face the RSM and his parade. I had never been on sick parade before but my head was giving me no choice. I made my way out of the room without anyone even so much as asking where I was venturing to. I was just going to make my way to the Battery Office just a cross the road to let the Battery Clerk know of my whereabouts, when suddenly I heard. "Wolfendale, where the hell do you think you're going?" It was Bombardier Bartlett hanging around like a bad smell.

"I'm feeling unwell, Bombardier," I said, "I need to report sick."

"Sick?!" said Bombardier Bartlett, "what's wrong with you?"

"My head, I've got the worst headache I've ever had," I replied.

"Headache" said Bombardier Bartlett, "If this has got anything to do with last night you're in big trouble, understand Wolfendale?"

"Yes, Bombardier," I said, I stood there thinking *I've been charged for getting drunk, not my fault, charged for having a tattoo, my fault, nearly drowned, sabotage, and almost fell off the end of Mount Snowdon, act of nature, and now I am being accused of a hangover after supping Coca Cola all night.*

On arrival at the medical centre I was pretty certain that it would be a case of 'take some tablets for the next few days and you'll be as right as rain'; not for one minute did I think that when I walked out of Wingate Block it would be the last time that I would see my buddies. The elderly civilian nurse got her thermometer out of her well presented uniform and placed it under my tongue. "Bite down," she said, "I will be back in a moment." I just sat there mainly thinking *I need to get back to the troop pronto, RSM's parade in an hour.*

"OK, open wide," said the nurse. She took the thermometer out of my mouth, shook it up and down and then examined it. I could see by the look on her face that there was a problem.

"Oh dear, I am afraid that you won't be going anywhere today, you'll need to be admitted."

"Sorry?" I said, not quite understanding what she had just told me.

"You have a rising temperature of over 100 degrees," she continued to say. I was shocked. Missing the RSM's parade was a bonus and at the same time, nice to get one over Bombardier Bartlett, even though he should be commended for getting all of us through our training.

The nurse took me into uncharted territory; "If you would just like to get yourself upstairs and into the room on the left please." There was a single bed in the room beautifully made with hospital corners. "Get undressed and into bed, I will be with you shortly." There was a locker for my clothes and a bedside cabinet, apart from that, that was it. Once tucked up in bed by 0900hrs and feeling guilty, *not*, the nurse returned to explain my illness.

"You have Gastric flu," she said, "and until your temperature goes down, you'll be staying with us."

"What about my passing out parade tomorrow, will I be able to attend?" I replied.

"At the moment it looks unlikely" she said, "I will take your temperature every few hours and keep a close eye on any improvement."

I was now feeling gutted, what seemed like a good skive about an hour ago was now turning into living hell. I would have done anything at this moment in time just to be on the parade square tomorrow. The nurse notified Bombardier Bartlett who in due course got one of the lads to go into my locker and get my washing bag with all my accessories in.

Throughout the day my temperature was holding steady; to be honest it couldn't get much higher without me bursting into flames. I was so agitated, I wanted out. I was hoping to maybe get a visitor; however, the nurse informed me that no one would be allowed near me for the fear of catching the virus. *Unbelievable,* can't believe this is happening to me. Friday night was burger night for the troop; Friday night was orange juice and pills for me. I could almost smell the burgers seeping through the closed window.

I got my head down as day become night. Tossing and turning throughout the night meant that I had a pretty awful night sleep; missing all the banter from the lads and being on my own was driving me insane. I was just glad to see the light of day peer through the window that meant it was close to getting out of bed time. At around 0730hrs the nurse made her way up the flight of stairs.

"Morning Paul, how are you today?" I needed a get out plan even though my head was still banging, lying through my teeth I said.

"Feeling much better," with a smile on my face.

"OK then, sit up, I need to take your temperature." There wasn't anything I could do now except play the waiting game, my fate was in someone else's hand. The nurse took the thermometer out of my mouth, shook it, looked and gave me the news I didn't want to hear.

"Your temperature is still no better, Paul, there is no way you can attend your passing out parade today." I just shook my head very gingerly from side to side in disbelief. I was almost begging the nurse to show some compassion; twelve months of training and I can't pass out with my Army mates. I could see the nurse was just as devastated as me. I was heartbroken, the feeling I felt was like nothing I had felt before. My breakfast was the only thing I had to look forward to and to be honest; it was a struggle to work up an appetite.

Time was passing me by now without knowing anything that was happening in the outside world; it was only when I heard the RA military band strike up that I knew the passing out parade was imminent. My mind was awash with all sorts of things; for the next hour I went through every military move with the lads from the confines of my bed. Mid afternoon and I could sense that the camp was now feeling somewhat vacant. I was still trying to come to terms with the last twenty-four hours. I was bored to tears; feeling all alone with not a soul in the world to talk to apart from the nurse, made me anxious to want to leave. It wasn't until Sunday morning that I managed to get the nurse to show some empathy; for the first time in two days she was considering maybe letting me out of what was becoming a prison cell for me. After the regular thermometer reading the nurse was still unperturbed until I said, "What good can staying here be to me?, I can just as well go home where my parents can care for me, I would feel much better surrounded by my family."

"Well, your temperature is still very high but stable, how far do you need to travel?" she said.

"About an hour on the train from Nuneaton to Crewe, I can then get a taxi from the station to Nantwich; it is about a ten-minute journey."

I was quite surprised when she said, "Promise me that you will go straight home and then get yourself into bed, if you're still felling unwell on Monday morning then phone your local GP."

"Of course I will," I said with a serious look on my face. "Does that mean that I can go?"

"Yes, I will give you a letter explaining your symptoms for your GP if you call him out," she said. Within half an hour I was back in the now deserted Wingate Block packing the remains of my locker into my Army suitcase.

There was no one to be found anywhere, no one to say my final goodbyes to. I guess I must have been the last one from the 74 intake to leave the block. I took one last look around the room, reminiscing. I could see all of the lads in my thoughts: bulling their boots, making their bed blocks, laughing out loudly, and then, in the blink of an eye it was all gone. I turned and made my way out of the swinging doors and down the stairs for the last time. I trundled my way outside with my suitcase in hand, out onto the cleanly swept road; it was a sad moment in my life leaving Bramcote, but one I would readily do again.

The journey back home was again full of reminiscing, *when would I see my good mates again, what will become of them?* I was so busy day dreaming that I almost forgot my stop. Back home my parents were glad to see me with an embrace and a cuddle; they had been informed that I was ill by the regiment and, that I would be coming home as soon as I was able to travel. I decided it would be a good idea to take on board what the nurse had advised, although I didn't take much persuading to get myself into bed. My head was still a mess and I was starting to feel as sick as a chocolate frog in my stomach region; cups of boiling hot water were my mum's remedy that had been passed down from generation to generation.

I slept all day Sunday with the hope that the welcome rest I was receiving would see me feeling better. "If you're no better by tomorrow morning, I shall be calling the doctor," said my mum. "Here, get this mug of boiling water down you, it will do you good." The blisters in my mouth were telling me not to drink any more of the tasteless liquid, who was I to argue, my mum always knew best.

Monday morning arrived and I was still not doing star jumps, which meant that it was time to phone for the doctor.

"Get the doctor," yelled my mum to my sister, "go and use the phone at the farm, tell them it's an emergency." *An emergency,* I was thinking to myself, *does my mum know something that I don't?* I didn't feel like I was going to die.

It seemed to take about an hour for the doctor to arrive in his upper-class car. "Come in," said my mum, "he's on the couch in the living room." He was a lot scarier than the nurse I was use to; tall and somewhat old looking in his darkened suit was how I remember him. He opened his black case and got out his stethoscope in a very slow manner. A quick examination confirmed that it was definitely Gastric flu in its later stages.

The doctor addressed my mum as he was closing up his case, saying, "If he doesn't feel any better by tomorrow or Wednesday then please phone up again. Get him to take this medicine three times a day. I hope that will do the trick." It was hard and frustrating to find that throughout Tuesday there was no change in my physical condition; retching on an empty stomach and not being able to keep any form of food or liquid down was as much as I could take.

By Wednesday I was almost dead within myself. No energy, my head was worse than ever; there were times when I thought that I was never going to shake off this unfortunate virus, the medicine was having no impact at all on my condition.

"Call the doctor again;" my mum said frustratingly, "I cannot believe our Paul is still no better." A lady doctor came out to see me this time; she was a lot more caring and understanding than Doctor Death.

"Are you allergic to penicillin?" was the first question she asked me in a nice, softly spoken voice.

"Not to my knowledge," I said. "I'm pretty sure I was given penicillin when I was in hospital about two years ago."

"OK, I will try a course of penicillin, let's hope that does the trick, if not…"

"Yes, I know, call you out again," I said quickly before she had time to finish her sentence.

The doctor just chuckled and replied, "Yes, I'm afraid so."

The penicillin proved to be the tonic I needed. By the weekend I was feeling much better within myself and ready to take on the world. I needed to go and see Declan to find out about his joining date and to tell him about when I would be flying out to West Germany. With Declan now finished with school, I thought I would wait until Monday before going to see him. The weather on Monday morning wasn't feeling very charitable, rather cold to be honest; I got on my now forgotten school bike and made the short 10-minute journey to Dec's house.

"Hi there, Dec," I shouted as my bike came to a sudden stop outside his house.

"Ay up there, Paul," said Dec, "great to see you, just doing a bit of tidying the garden for my dad. Let's go inside out of the cold; you can bring me up to speed about what you've been up to."

We sat down in Dec's living room with a nice hot cuppa like two old ladies, catching up on the gossip. Dec went first and explained that everything was now in place and he was going to Bramcote on the 8th May. I was so pleased for him. I then thought it best for me to explain some of the do's and don'ts, something that I wish I had known before joining.

"One thing in particular springs to mind, Dec," I said, "never walk or trespass on the parade square. Doing so will result in a severe rollicking and possible fatigues. Let me tell you the history of the parade square as I know it. After a battle, when retreat was sounded and the unit had reassembled to call roll and count the dead, a hollow square was formed. The dead were placed within the square and no-one used the square as a thoroughfare. Today, the parade ground represents the square and hence, a unit's dead. It is deemed to be hallowed ground, soaked with the blood of our fallen, and the area is respected as such by all."

"Wow," said Dec, "I will make sure I remember that." Questions galore were thrown my way and I was only too glad to answer them. After a while it was my turn to tell Dec about what was now next for me.

"I fly out to West Germany from Luton on Saturday 3rd May, in a few weeks' time," I said. "I can't wait, first time on an aeroplane; I'll be nervous, but excited at the same time."

"Sounds exciting," said Dec, "let's hope I can join you there next year."

"Well, when you finish training just make sure you ask to join 42 Heavy Regiment, I am sure they will prioritise, just tell them you have a friend who joined 42 last year. As long as we keep in touch there shouldn't be a problem."

We spent hours over the following weeks discussing Army life until it was time for me to say my goodbyes. Over the next three weeks I was at home, my girlfriend was becoming a distance memory; saying that, I still wanted to see her as much as I could; I just felt my life was taking a turn for the better and, with so much to look forward to, it meant my mind was on other things. My parents were now getting use to my changes; the man I was now turning into is all down to them.

THE COOPER FAMILY 1954

MY SISTER, ZOE AND I 1966

MY FATHER, CHARLES WILLIAM COOPER

PATCH AND MY
BROTHER, ALAN

MUM AND DAD IN THEIR LATER YEARS

FOR INDIVIDUAL STYLING AND ATTENTION—VISIT—

FRANK STUBBS

HIGH CLASS GENTLEMENS HAIRDRESSER

20 PILLORY STREET

— SATISFACTION ASSURED —

MY LOCAL BARBER'S

RHQ JUNIOR LEADERS REGIMENT BRAMCOTE

GAMECOCK BARRACKS JUNIOR LEADERS REGIMENT

WINGATE TROOP 1974

WINGATE TROOP 1974

(above) SAMMY DOUGLAS,
GEORDIE STANTON, DINGER
BELL, DEREK CLAYTON, PAUL
WOLFENDALE, KENNY

(left) MY BROTHER, MALCOLM 1966

M107 ARTILLERY GUN

KEADY, NORTHERN IRELAND 1977

DAD 1968

DIVIS FLATS, BELFAST 1980

ALAN CARVELL, TONY ABBOTT,
PAUL WOLFENDALE, DAVE WATERMAN

FALLS ROAD, BELFAST 1980

BOMB DISPOSAL, BELFAST 1980

STARLIGHT ARMY MEDICAL VEHICLE

TYPICAL REPUBLICAN GRAFFITI, BELFAST 1980

BELFAST 1980,
FOOT PATROL

DIVIS FLATS COMPLEX

DAVE, ALAN AND I

HILDESHEIM GUARDROOM 1981

EAST GERMAN BORDER

CREW COMMANDERS COURSE 1982

MAY 1983 VISIT OF HER MAJESTY QUEEN ELIZABETH II
TO IMPHAL BARRACKS, YORK

From Lieutenant Colonel N S Nash

PMC/1

Ousefield House Officers Mess
Fulford Road
York

York Military) Ext 2266
York 59811)

May 83

Dear Bdr. Wolferdale

The visit of Her Majesty The Queen to the Mess on 16
May was the end result of months of careful planning.
In the event all who were involved in any aspect of
the visit can take great pride in what was, with
out doubt, a great success.

I really did feel that we all worked together as a
well drilled team and I was very proud to have been
the PMC and to have had you on my staff.

The enclosed photograph is with my compliments as
a memento of a day which I hope was as memorable
for you as it was for me.

Sincerely

Tark Nash

CHAPTER FIFTY-TWO
FIRST TIME ABROAD

Saturday May 3rd finally arrived; my feelings were that of when I first met Carol on that dark Saturday night back in December. Feeling excited, but at the same time being scared of the unknown; my first time on a plane and the first time I would be venturing out of my beloved country. With my bags packed and my documents all in order I waved goodbye to my family and friends.

"When will we being seeing you again, Paul?" said my mum as she gave me a hug.

"Not sure mum, it's all a mystery to me, will more than likely find out on Monday. I will write to you and dad and let you know as soon as I find out."

"Very well Paul, take care and have a safe journey."

A final shake of my dad's hand and I was off. A half hour taxi journey to Crewe station is all it took, probably one of the longest half hours I've had to endure in respect that the taxi driver was chewing my ear off about his unfortunate life. All I wanted to do is reminisce; I just wasn't in the right frame of mind to chitchat… "Crewe station," he said with relief written all over my face; changing his depressing subject to one that I was more familiar with cheered me up for the last half mile of the journey.

"Thank you," I said, "keep the change. I'm off now before I miss my train." I suppose there was an element of sarcasm in my voice that could be detected. I just turned away and made my way to the ticket office and then the platform that would see me catch the train to Luton.

The train journey took about an hour and a half with one change of train on the way; outside the station there were buses of plenty to take me to the airport.

"Anyone for the airport?" was the cry from a strange looking man.

"Yes," I said, "what's the cost?"

"Are you with the military?"

"Yes." I answered.

"No charge for military personnel, sonny," he said, "get on board, we shall be leaving in five minutes." I felt quite important for a few seconds as I took a seat at the back of the bus. The doors of the bus closed as the driver revved up his engine and made his way to the airport. It felt strange being all alone; its times like this when you need a friend, someone to talk to. The only person that I was talking to was my reflection in the glass of the window as we chugged along.

Airports were just something I had imagined in my dreams. I guess what I am saying is, my descriptive power couldn't have been any more further from the truth. What I was now looking at was nothing like the Thunderbird base I use to have as a kid. I was so glad that there were other people willing to help me find my way; I would've probably still been there now without their help and kindness.

At the check-in I showed my flight tickets and ID card (no passport needed), it was a case of don't ask too many question just do exactly what you're told. It was now time to get rid of my Army suitcase. "Could you place your suitcase on the conveyer belt please," said the well-dressed check-in lady; getting shot of my Army suitcase was pure heaven, although I did from time to time feel that I was missing something.

Once in the departure lounge I found a soft seat to sit on. I felt myself looking around to see if I could see some short back and sides, young and out of control juveniles; not a chance. Just when I needed someone of that calibre to chat to, not one could be found. I must have been in the departure lounge for about an hour before the PA system announced the call I was waiting for.

"All passengers for flight VC 1023 travelling to Hannover please make your way to gate six." The only gate I knew was a farm gate, but on looking around, there wasn't one to be found anywhere. *Follow the crowd,* my mind was telling me, *surely over two hundred passengers can't be wrong, or can they?* Either way my logic seemed to work, before I knew it, I was looking out of the departure lounge window that was bigger than my house; I could see the plane that we hopefully would be flying in. Flying wasn't going to be a problem for me; it is the fact that I would be thirty-two thousand feet up in the air and the thought of not flying that concerned me.

The plane was due to take off at 2000hrs GMT (Greenwich Mean Time) and land at 2215hrs European time. I had taken a window seat about half way along the plane as the rest of the passengers were still boarding. My feelings at this moment in time were that of pure amazement and disbelief as I heard the roar of the engines. I seem to remember the aeroplane doing some sort of three point turn before making its way to the beginning of the runway. We were stationary for about a minute before the sound of the engines kicked in again. I was being forced back into my seat as the plane picked up speed before taking off, the excitement was that of being at the pleasure beach in Blackpool and riding a new rollercoaster for the first time; *no turning back now*, I was thinking. The plane started to pick up speed down the runway and before I could even draw breath we were powering our way to West Germany. We were given some light refreshments once in the air, and then, with time passing me by quickly, we were being told by the cabin crew to fasten our seat belts and prepare for landing; looking out of the window I could see the ground that was now getting closer illuminated like the lights on a Christmas tree.

My thoughts were now well and truly on the landing, however, I was still concerned about what was I going to do when I was in the airport arrival lounge. With a slight bump we landed on West German soil and then embarked into the airport. As before, I just followed the crowd, it was time to be reunited with my suitcase once more. *Damn,* I thought as I saw my unmistakeable Army suitcase on the conveyer belt. "Come here you," I said to my suitcase, "We need to find our way out of here; I'm not sure which way to go." I felt my suitcase answer back, "Follow the crowd you idiot," … so I did.

After going through several checks, I was now in the part of the airport where I could just walk through the glass doors and into the unknown. *Where was my military transport that I was promised? What has happened to the Army that I was use to back in Nuneaton?* There, they would've never let us out of their sights let alone leave us in the confines of Hannover Airport. I was becoming a little alarmed with the fact I could see no sign or smell of any military personnel. I could see a bar across the way which made me think that would be my best option; one thing I learnt from my short but exhilarating time in the Army is, if you want to find a Squaddie (nickname for soldier) then search no further than the bar.

My instincts were correct; I made my way to the bar and stood next to, a not so baby-faced person as me.

"Excuse me," I said just as he was finishing off his pint. "Are you by any chance a soldier?"

"Yes, I am," he said without a care in the world, "Barman, ein bier bitte" (one beer please). I was still trying to get his attention away from his next pint when he replied. "What can I do you for young man?"

"I am a little lost," I said, "I have just come from Luton expecting to be met by someone from the military."

"Where are you heading?" he slurred.

"Fallingbostal 42 Regiment," I said as he started to drown another beer.

"No worries," he said, "I am waiting for the duty transport to arrive, I am stationed there, part of the tank regiment, you can get a lift with me. By the way, my name is Ken."

"Great, thank you," I replied, "my name is Paul."

After about thirty minutes and three pints later, I noticed a military figure out of the corner of my eye. "Is this the Duty Driver?" I said, looking over in the direction of where he was walking.

"It sure looks like it," said Ken, "over here!" he shouted to the soldier. "Are you the Duty Driver for Fallingbostal?"

"Yes, are you Private Proudlove?" asked the Duty Driver.

"Sure am," said Ken. "We have one more addition to the party, a gunner from 42 Regiment; will it be OK to give him a lift? It's his first time over here, straight from the Junior Leaders Regiment in Nuneaton." It was nice that they were including me in the conversation, *not*; as long as I was getting a lift to the barracks that was fine by me.

It was now close to 2300hrs. As we exited the airport I could see the unmistakable long wheel base Land Rover in the warmth of the city lights. It was parked up in the drop off and pick up zone that seemed to me as though it was on the wrong side of the road. I had never given two thoughts about the fact that they drive on the right-hand side of the road in West Germany. It was such a strange feeling sitting in the back of the Land Rover driving on the right-hand side of the road. I was trying to take in as much information as I could as we hurtled along a single carriageway and then a dual carriageway; strange as it may seem, there was just no way that I could have ever in my wildest dreams ever come close, to imagining what I was looking at out of the back of the Land Rover. I was feeling more and more apprehensive as we got within striking distance of the barracks; why did I get the feeling that I wasn't expected as I walked into the Guardroom? That explains why there was no duty transport waiting for me at the airport.

CHAPTER FIFTY-THREE
WELCOME TO 42ND REGIMENT ROYAL ARTILLERY

After travelling through the city lights of Hannover and then a stretch of the Autobahn (Motorway), it was into the rural wooded area. It reminded of back home, except for the wild boars that were roaming around on the edge of the roadside. Time was ebbing away quite quickly as I chitchatted to Ken and the driver. Before I knew, we were arriving at the barracks with my stomach still churning; with that in mind and feeling completely lost with my surroundings we pulled up outside a small red and white barrier, one that was more familiar with the one at Kingsbury's Ranges.

"OK," said the Duty Driver, "just report to the Guardroom and someone there will advise you of where you need to go."

"Cheers, thanks for the lift," I said gratefully and, at the same time shaking hands with Ken. I climbed out of the back of the Land Rover and just stared into the direction of the barracks. It looked more like an open prison as opposed to the well-designed camp back in Nuneaton. Although it was dark, I could still just about make out the outline of the accommodation blocks in the distance.

There were several lights on shining through some of the already occupied rooms, considering it was almost midnight, it was something that took me by surprise; tucked up in bed and lights out by 2200hrs is what I was use too. I made my way up the concrete stairs at the side of the Guardroom and then into a small square room that felt overcrowded, even though there were only two people occupying the room. I turned to my left to face a well-dressed Bombardier. He was sitting in a small swivel chair wearing his combat suit. He looked at me with a surprised look on his face; it seemed pretty obvious to me that I wasn't expected.

He continued to dress me up and down as if waiting for me to break the code of silence. "My name is Junior Gunner Wolfendale," I said, waiting for a response.

"Junior Gunner," said the Bombardier with a smirk on his face, "my name is Bombardier Phil Everitt, the Guard Commander." He looked over to his left to where a L/Bombardier was standing in the corner.

"We have a Junior Gunner in our midst then do we?" Said the L/Bombardier grinning. I was still slightly confused as to why they were referring to the fact that I was a Junior Leader, making me feel even more uncomfortable than I cared for. Then the penny finally dropped. "Sorry, I mean Gunner; it's just so difficult getting out of the habit of being called a Junior Gunner." I answered

"No problem," said Phil. "As I pointed out, I'm the Guard Commander and L/Bombardier Hales is the Marching Relief. He takes over my duties when I need to take a nap. I will make a couple of phone calls to try to find out more about the situation." *Why wasn't I expected? Why wasn't he informed? Maybe I should just get the next flight back to the UK.*

"OK, it seems that there has been a lack of communication (Army cock-up), you are expected," said the Bombardier. "Someone along the line has failed to inform the Guardroom but what's new."

"Well, that's a relief." I said.

"You will be joining 18 Battery," said Bombardier Everitt. "Can I see your ID card please?"

"Yes, no problem," I replied as I handed it over.

Once all my information had now been ascertained the Guard Commander sent two of the guards complete with the infamous pick axe handles to find the 18 Battery Duty Storeman; it gave us plenty of time to became more acquainted while the search for the ever elusive storeman began. I got to find out in the time they were looking for the Duty Storeman, that the Guard Commander, Bombardier Everitt, was also from 18 Battery and was keen to find out about my sporting activities, and how I would able to help 18 Battery be king of the regiment. It was a far cry from Junior Leaders. I felt so much more in my comfort zone talking about sport. It got to the point where I was doing all the talking and the Guard Commander was quite content just listening to what I had to say. Just before I put the Guard Commander to sleep, the guard returned with news.

"No sign of Limpy Lou," said the guard, "searched the block high and low; he's nowhere to be found: under his bed, in his locker, Battery Bar, I think he must have gone to Fallingbostal."

"Well, there's nothing more I can do until Gunner Lewis comes back," said the Guard Commander. "Would you like a coffee? It looks like it could be a long night."

"May as well," I replied, "however some sleep wouldn't go a miss, oh, by the way, who's Limpy Lou?"

"It's just a nickname for the storeman, he walks with a kind of wobble," said the Guard Commander, "everyone knows him by that name."

It was about 0130hrs before Gunner Lewis returned. "Lewis, get in here now," said the Guard Commander, "take Gunner Wolfendale to the Battery Block and then issue him with some bedding."

The smell of his breath was telling its own story about his whereabouts as he turned towards the door and said, "Follow me."

Gunner Lewis seemed like a funny type of guy without a care in the world; as long as he got his pay cheque at the end of each month and the beer didn't dry up, he would be content. I had now met my first two 18 Battery lads, one destined for the top, the other not. I made my way into the block and up the flight of stairs that were in front of me, trying to make as little noise as I could. I was told to wait outside the BQ stores while Gunner Lewis went to find the keys.

"Here we are," said Limpy, "found them." I'm not sure how many attempts it took him to unlock the door but eventually the correct key was found. "I will issue you with your bedding now," said Gunner Lewis, "then tomorrow you can come and get your MFO boxes that arrived last week."

"OK," I said, "thanks for that." With my bedding now firmly in hand it was now made known to me where I would be sleeping.

"This is your room," said Gunner Lewis as he quietly opened the door. There was enough light from the corridor making its way into the room to allow me to see where I would be getting my head down. It was so strange entering a room that was already occupied by two fellow soldiers. All I could see were three wooden wardrobes that were being used to partition the room. I could see that the other two beds had someone sleeping in each of them. In a matter of minutes my bed was made and I was away with the fairies.

Sunday morning sunlight brought me out of my coma; I sort of semi-sat up to get a glimpse of the two other people that I was now sharing the room with. I felt I was being intrusive as I slowly moved my head 360 degrees around the room: tapestries on the wall, lava lamps on a coffee table and a small television to watch, it even smelt nice as my eyes continued the 10p tour. I noticed that the two lads had bright flowery quilts as opposed to my Army blankets and sheets. One of them was showing more leg then I cared to see as it was hanging out of his bed, almost touching his bedside mat. I thought I would give it a few minutes to see if anyone makes a move before getting out of bed; it's times like this when I could have done with some buddies from Bramcote for a bit of moral support.

As I sat up in my bed the first sign of life was evident from across the room, the guy that had his leg dangling from his bed was now starting to sit up. I think he had to do a double take before realising that someone else was now staring towards him; rubbing his eyes and getting to grips with what he was looking at, the first words from his mouth drifted towards me.

"Oh, er, hello, my names Don, Don Bowles, sorry if I sound vague, just, er, just wasn't expecting a new person in the room, nobody informed me."

"You don't say," I said sarcastically "no one informed me."

"Typical Army communications," said Don, "anyway welcome to 18 Battery, where you from?"

"Nantwich, Cheshire, oh and by the way my name's Paul, Paul Wolfendale," I said, hoping to establish a well needed friend. I explained to Don about Limpy Lou and how I ended up in this room.

"He's harmless enough is Limpy," said Don, "means well, just got very little ambition, the stores seem to suit him."

Don made me feel so at home. He had a certain trait about him, one that I've only experienced before with my close family. I couldn't have asked for a more caring person to herald the start of my new adventure with 42 Regiment. We must have spent at least twenty minutes or so getting to know each other before dragging ourselves out of our beds. The first thing that struck me was that I was now the baby of the battery; even Don with his boyish looks was pushing twenty-one: Fair hair, slim build, about six feet tall would be how I would describe Don. He had a great sense of humour but well respected by the rest of the battery; he did mention that some of his so-called friends call him Stan; he had the looks of Stan Laurel, from the famous duo Laurel and Hardy.

Don and I made our way to the washrooms for a good morning shower. Everything to me was in comparison to how it was in the Junior Leaders; the thing that I was impressed with was the way it made me feel, it felt like you were being treated like no one had a care in the world about the way you conducted your business, you were a free man, and within reason you could do what you wanted. On the downside, it was like going from a five-star hotel, to a two-star hotel, in respect that everything seemed liked it was pre-war; complaints from me there were none, the cavalier way was something I liked.

Once back in the room and trying not to disturb the other guy who was still snoring, Don and I made our way to the cookhouse for a late breakfast. The cookhouse was only a couple of hundred metres from the block, opposite the Guardroom and with the NCOs mess above the cookhouse. Don was a gunner like me with no rank at all, so that area was out of bounds unless, one day we got promoted; L/Bombardiers and Bombardiers were the only people allowed to use it. A type of village hall welcomed me and my hungry stomach; the food was as normal, a five-star rating, never would I ever complain about Army cookhouse food.

After a good half hour breakfast it was time for Don and I to exit the cookhouse and head back to the block to be introduced to my other roommate Colin; although Colin was a good friend of Don's, the feeling I felt between us was one of 'just because you're our roommate doesn't mean that we are going to be friends'. *No problem there,* I was thinking.

"What's the dress for tomorrow, Don?" I asked curiously.

"Coveralls," said Don.

"Coveralls," I replied.

Don continued by saying, "You're not in the Junior Leaders now Paul, after first parade that is at 0800hrs we make our way down to the Gun Park." All this was going over my head. *Gun Park, Coveralls;* the only thing that did make sense was 0800hrs parade, I just thought, *wait until tomorrow and then all would be revealed*, it was just going to be another chapter in my Army career. Throughout the evening I met one or two guys that what I would call sweats, some I connected with straight away and others, well let's just say, they seem to distance themselves; making new friends wasn't going to be as easy as I first thought, I guess I struck lucky meeting Don.

CHAPTER FIFTY-FOUR
AN EVENING AT THE RED LIGHT DISTRICT

Monday morning arrived with the sound of silence; I was waiting for the normal 'Get out of bed you lazy bastards' routine, but instead, it was a case of 'at your leisure feet on the floor, no rush, enjoy the morning fresh air. There was a battery guard that came around just in case you decided to take an extra few minutes to drag yourself away from your pits; even then it was quiet and sedate. As it was approaching 0800hrs I could sense it was becoming busier around the block and in the corridors. All the pads (married personal) were arriving, with the fact that there was no special room set aside for them, they would intermingle in the block and in your rooms until it was time to get on parade. "Outside on parade," was the cry from someone with authority in their voice. This was it. I had never heard such laughter from within the ranks, and all with deeper voices than mine, everybody just seem to amble their way outside and form up wherever there was a space within the three ranks; facing forward towards the block and stood in the back rank I just waited to see what was going to happen next.

There must have been at least four Sergeants that weren't required to join the ranks; they all seemed to have their own spot on the footpath that also include some L/Bombardiers and Bombardiers; we were gunners, and we knew where our place was. I suppose we were more expendable. One of the Sergeants brought us up to attention and then just had a quick walk through the ranks to see if he could smell any alcohol on our breath, as well as a quick look at our dress. Unfortunately I was standing out like a sore thumb with the fact that my boots were shining like mirrors. Probably didn't go down to well with the rest of the troop, but there was nothing I could do about that, I was pretty sure it wasn't going to be long before they got roughed up. After the inspection it was time to be addressed.

"Listen in," said one of the Sergeants, "we have two new recruits with us today, Gunner Wolfendale and Gunner Schofield."

"NIGs," shouted someone from the ranks in a loud voice, bringing a ray of laughter from the troop.

"Walsh, shut your mouth!" said the Sergeant as he continued his talk. "I want you to make them feel welcome; I do not want to hear of anyone giving them grief. Gunner Wolfendale, you will be joining C Sub, your Gun No.1 (person in charge of the gun) is Sergeant Douglas."

"That's me, Wolfendale," said this older looking man in his advancing years; displaying thick fuzz under his nose and speaking with a very northern type accent.

"OK Sergeant," I said with respect in my voice.

"Sarge will do," said Sergeant Douglas in a kind of understanding tone. *Sarge,* I was thinking, I would have been hung drawn and quartered back in Bramcote for saying that. I understood I had a lot to learn about the so-called man's Army.

"Gunner Schofield, you will be joining A Sub," said the Sergeant, for whom I knew not of his name, well at least until someone had a question to ask.

"Sergeant Massey?"

"What is it, Walsh?" said Sergeant Massey.

"Are we allowed to beat them up?" said Gunner Walsh.

"No, not even a little bit, Walsh," replied Sergeant Massey. The whole episode was making me feel uncomfortable until Sergeant Massey ordered one of the Bombardiers to march us down to the Gun Park; a journey of a few hundred metres in the morning sun and we were there, ready for action. The Gun Park was a large concrete area the size of a football field; it housed a large building that run the length of the strip; up and over sliding doors to lock the guns safely away at close of play and that was it. Over on the left was a wash-down area complete with a ramp for the gun's maintenance.

I was amazed at the size of the M107 175mm gun that I was now look- ing at; I just took a back seat as Sergeant Douglas and his merry men took charge. The noise of all the gun subs opening their gun cages (a place where all the tools and equipment were kept) was that of a mass riot, but nothing in comparison to what was to come when the guns were fired up.

"Dinger," shouted Sergeant Douglas, "start the gun up and drive it outside onto the apron." There was a loud droning noise for a few seconds before the engine kicked in. I stepped back away from the gun not knowing what to expect next as the gun propelled forward on its huge tracks out of the hangar;

there were guns being fired up all around me, three more guns to be precise: A Sub, B Sub, C Sub and D Sub made up the four gun battery.

Once all the guns were on the apron, I just took stock of myself as I looked towards their sheer size once more. The 37ft long 5 tonne barrel stood out above anything else as it was angled towards to heavens; the width of gun was about 10ft 6in with a total weight of 27 tonnes. Basically it was enormous. As time went by I found out more about the heavy artillery gun and how it functioned; with the sound of the engines now being turned off I could once again hear myself think, at last, some kind of normality. It was now time to be introduced to Sergeant Douglas's Gun Bunnies. Actually, I was the Gun Bunny; I was no longer a NIG, I was now a Gun Bunny, the name given to a new member of the sub.

Meeting the members of C sub was interesting to say the least. Kev Rowledge, Paul Sheridan, Billy Dytor, Bombardier Nobby Naylor (cover number, the guy who would take over responsibilities if the No.1 of the gun got killed or captured in war time), L/Bombardier Dennis Heron and the gun driver John Dinger Bell.

"Kettle on," said Dennis in a stern voice to Billy, "take Wolfie with you, show him where the brew kit is." Before long I was the chief brew maker, at least until we were given a new Gun Bunny. At about ten o'clock and to my complete amazement, a van arrived; it was about the same size as an ice cream van as it drove onto the Gun Park. "Y dub van lads," yelled some of the lads. It was a case of dropping your tools and getting yourself over to the van ASAP. It was the equivalent to a NAAFI break on wheels. They sold the most amazing fleischwurst (German word for meat sausage) crusty rolls, it was like bits of meat in a cream sauce; they were cheap at half the price. I bumped into Don in the queue which was nice.

"D sub me Paul, Sergeant Massey, the guy over there." As I looked over I could see that it was the Sergeant who had taken the parade outside the block this morning. I could also see the new recruit Gunner Schofield getting familiar with his gun sub.

Lunch time came; it was time to lock up shop (so to speak) and make our way back to the block for a clean-up before setting foot in the cookhouse. I felt this would be a good opportunity to make my acquaintance with Gunner Schofield." Hi mate," I said, "you're new as well, so I hear."

"Yeah, straight from Junior Leaders," he said.

"Me too, mine name is Paul," I said.

"Mine is Steve, Steve Schofield," he said. "Most people call me Schoie, short for Schofield." Steve was a lot shorter than me, but dressed just as smart; the Junior Leaders swagger was still on show. It felt comforting to know that I wasn't the only one that was new to 18 Battery as we made our way to the cookhouse chitchatting away. Over the next few days I found out more about Steve; I found out that he had an uncle in one of the infantry regiments on the garrison who was showing Steve the ropes, and also that Steve had a fondness for kung fu. Steve was a master of the art, which made him very popular with the rest of the lads. Myself? Well, apart from my charm, I didn't fit in quite as well with the rest of the troop; in the first few days, apart from Don and the gun crew I was attached to, things weren't all hunky dory. A few of the 18 Battery lads were sending out a warning: "Wait until the rest of 18 Battery come back from Cyprus, they will show you what hard is."

"I didn't even know I was coming across as being hard." I said in a surprised voice.

"You've got too much to say for yourself" said someone else.

Most of the threatening went over my head; I wasn't the sort to be bullied. I thought… *what will be will be, I can't change the way I was brought up, hopefully in the weeks to come they would see the real me*. After the first few days and still awaiting the return of the Cyprus mob, Steve asked me if I wanted to join him and his uncle on a night out in nearby Hannover. To be honest I wasn't that keen, however, I felt it would do me good to get out of the block for the evening.

"Yeah, OK Steve," I said, "why not."

"Great," said Steve, "we need to be at the Guardroom for about seven, he's ordered a taxi." It was already five o'clock so straight after tea I got into my glad rags, put on a little smelly and touched up on what little German I had inside my head. *Ich möchte ein bier, bitte* (I would like one beer, please). Steve and I made our way down to the Guardroom and within minutes we were heading out of the garrison and onto the semi dark main roads. "Whereabouts are we heading in Hannover?" I said (not that I knew the place).

"The red light district," said Steve's uncle with a huge smile on his face. Steve and I just looked at each other in amazement as we sat in the back of the Mercedes wondering what on earth we were going there for.

"Fifty Deutsche Marks should get you laid," said Steve's uncle. I think I only had about twenty Deutsche Marks on me, so I asked.

"What can you get for twenty?"

"Mugged," said Steve's uncle. Steve and I just sniggered at each other nervously; the look in our eyes was enough to say that there was no way we were going to indulge in any sexual act. We finally pulled up into what seemed to be the city centre; street lights were burning brightly and the footways were awash with men on a mission. It was like I was witnessing things beyond descriptive power. Steve's uncle and the taxi driver exchanged a few words that I was unfamiliar with before we exited his cab and stood on the semi crowded pavement.

"Who's up for a little fun then?" said Steve's uncle, pointing the way to the area where all the action was taking place; doing a bit of window shopping was about as far as Steve and I were going to take it. There were some lovely items for sale in the huge glass windows that stretched along the street for some distance; it was a case of, up one side and down the other until you found something you liked. Steve's uncle looked more like a pro than the ones in the window, with that in mind; it didn't take him long at all before he was making his way into one of the dwellings. Before Steve and I could even ask any questions like, *how long will you be? Or, what would you like us to do while you're enjoying yourself?* Steve said to me…

"I think twenty minutes is as long as it takes, what do you think?"

"Not sure," I replied, "I'm not that experienced, I think maybe five minutes, ten tops, either way we should just about have enough time to have a quick look around." We made our way past lots of discerning men that were taking up the whole width of the pathway; suits, tracky bottoms, there was even some that looked they were in fancy dress for the occasion.

As Steve and I walked slowly past the adjoining terraced shops, we were treated to some (from a man's point of view) beautiful and unbelievably good looking ladies. They were just sitting there half naked, occasionally looking you in the eyes and nodding their head at you as if to say, *what about it young man?* There was no kind of price tag attached to each of the ladies, but by the time Steve and I reached the other side we had learnt quite a lot. We saw prospective customers knocking on the glass and asking, "How much?"

"What would you like? Would you like a Frenchie? Or do you want fucky fucky? Or maybe you would like something else?" *Quite extraordinary*, I was thinking. With the fact that Steve and I had very little collateral between us we stood well back from the windows until one of the lower class market punters decided she wanted us for breakfast. She couldn't have drawn more attention to herself if she had parachuted down and paraded herself naked on the street. *Bang Bang Bang* went her fist on the window as she looked towards us with desperation in her eyes.

"You two, come come come, I have an offer for you," she said, in her German accent. Steve and I just wanted to leg it but her aggression was getting the better of us, we made our way over to the window and at first glance, I could see why she didn't have many followers. She shouted through the double glazed window, "TWO FOR THE PRICE OF ONE."

"Good god," I said to Steve, "she wants to have us both at the same time."

Steve took one look at the lady and said, "On yer bike, we don't want anything, we are just window shopping." She was so desperate that I believe if we had gotten into a bartering match we could have knocked her down a few quid. Steve and I just turned away and never once looked back whilst at the same time continuing our window shopping.

"Steve over here," Steve and I looked across the road to see his uncle standing there looking at us with a, *cat got the cream* type of look.

"Well," I said to Steve looking at my watch, "definitely more than five minutes, you were right, nearer twenty, I must be doing something wrong; maybe I need to work on my technique;" a*n eye opener to say the least* I was thinking as we made our way back to camp. One week in and I had already been introduced to legalised prostitution. It wasn't going to be long before the lads that had gone to Cyprus were arriving back. A new Gun Bunny/ NIG in the troop needed reminding who the daddy in the troop was. Whilst sleeping in the confines of my bed one night they took their opportunity.

CHAPTER FIFTY-FIVE
FROM BAD TO WORSE

Monday morning arrived with the sun shining amongst a tempered breeze. I was now one week into finding my feet. I noticed that there seemed to be a bigger presence than normal on parade, *got it,* I said to myself. It was the welcome return of the rest of the lads that had been to Cyprus. I tried not to bring to much attention to myself by looking around; I just stood next to Don trying to hide in his shadow. We were brought up to attention with a loud cry from Sergeant Massey that was followed by a short inspection of our dress.

"Settling in, are we, Wolfendale?" said Sergeant Massey.

"Yes Sergeant, thank you."

"You don't need to call me Sergeant, Sarge will do, just try to get out of the Junior Leaders way, chill out a little, and I mean a little."

"OK Sarge," I said. It felt wrong, however at the same time, it was something I'd have to get use to. Sergeant Massey made his way back to the front of the battery and stood us all at ease before giving us a longer than normal speech. "Next week we will be going on a live firing exercise with the guns, it will be a regimental exercise starting on Monday and returning on the weekend of the 30th May, almost two weeks for those of you who can't count. Your No. 1s will bring you up to speed with what is happening once I have briefed them; anyway that's the bad news. Good news is, as soon as you get back and on the following Tuesday, we shall be having our annual Battery camp," said Sergeant Massey. "We shall be going to Amersfoort in Holland for two weeks." I felt quite excited for a split second; Germany, Holland, it was becoming quite an adventure within my first two weeks.

"We will be staying at a Dutch camp as part of a public relations exercise; it will be mainly civilian clothes with a few military items thrown-in. Details of the camp will be published on Battery Orders as well as Guard duties and fatigues." After being dismissed it was the normal get yourselves down to the Gun Park routine. It was time for me to get more acquainted with the M107 gun and its crew. I was really enjoying the days but as for the evening, I was always watching my back for anyone who fancied their chances.

It took until Thursday before one or two of the so called (I don't give a toss who you are) guys decided it was time to make their presence felt: It's amazing how brave you become when you've had a drink, it's amazing how brave you become when there are four of you, and it's amazing how brave you become when the person you're after is alone and asleep.

It was about midnight when they decided to attack me. It was hard to believe that one of the lads was my other roommate; I always did have a bad feeling about him. I just about had time to open my eyes before they attacked me.

"Don't fucking move, NIG," was the cry from one of them.

"Fucking gob shite, aren't you?" said someone else. "Think you're hard, we'll fucking show what hard is." A few punches here and there as one of them pinned me down to the bed; a razor was being bandied around with the words, "Fucking move and we will fucking slice you." They ripped the sheet cover back and pulled down my undies before shaving the area where I did manage to grow some hair, somehow, I was thinking *best not to move.* It was all over in a matter of minutes; it's what's known as an initiation ceremony, although, to me, it was bordering on bullying. I closed my eyes and thought to myself *let them have their little game, let them have their five minutes of glory.*

This sort of behaviour went on throughout the Army, I just believed they were doing what they had maybe had done to them; would it one day stop? Well certainly not it my time in the Army. There was not a chance that I would do anything like what they subjected me too; it is thankfully not in my nature. The Army is full of all sorts of individuals, it was a case of make or break time. The general air of dark depression was characterising my mood; luckily for me I was brought up to look after myself and also to show the utmost respect to my elders. I spent most of the darkened early hours of the morning awake staring at the ceiling, wishing I was somewhere else instead, like the comfort of my now distant homeland. I felt a lot more relaxed as night turned to day and isolation turned into my welcome friends.

The next day I was reading Battery Orders to see if the weekend was clear for me to do what I wanted. As I read through the small print and just scrawling down the page, I noticed the Guard duties for Saturday morning. My name was down for guard starting at 0900hrs and finishing on Sunday morning at 0900hrs. *Gutted,* I said to myself as I made my way into my room where my mate Don was putting the last touches to his dress.

"Hi Don, you OK?" I said.

"Yeah, thanks Paul," said Don, "just sorting out my civvie clothes." I took one look into Don's locker and could see at first glance he was quite a debonair person. He had an array of clothes fit for a king, ladies' man sprung to my mind.

"I'm on guard tomorrow, not happy, but ay, it was going to happen at some point," I said.

"Never mind Paul, 0900hrs start" said Don, "I was on a few weeks ago, just messes your weekend plans."

"I've got nothing planned anyway," I said. "Tonight, I will just get my combats ready for tomorrow." The following morning, I was out of bed sharpest and dressed ready for action, Don was snoring away along with our other roommate, or should I say room-not-mate when a familiar face walked through the doors wearing smart combats.

"Gunner Wolfendale," he said sternly, "why aren't you on guard?"

"I'm just leaving now, don't need to be there until 0900hrs," I said feeling confused, "it's only 0845hrs."

"0830hrs is the time you need to be there for Guard mounting (Parade of the Guard) for inspection," said Bombardier Ginge Cundliff.

"Sorry," I said, "I had no idea."

"You're on a 2.5.2," said the Bombardier.

"What?" I said, "What's a 2.5.2?"

"It's a charge sheet, you're being charged for being late for Guard duty," was his reply, I couldn't believe what I was hearing. I had been with the regiment for no more than one week and here I was facing a charge.

I had already worked out that its times like this when you just need to keep your mouth shut and don't make matters worse. The guard itself was a pain, two hours on the gate, two hours walking around the camp and then four hours off if you're lucky, and now, to top it all off, I was going to be charged, my week was rapidly going from bad to worse.

Monday afternoon meant we were going on exercise, and to add salt into my now sore wounds, there was just enough time to put me in front of the BC before setting sail with the guns. I knew I would meet with the BC at some stage, but I didn't think for one minute it would be so soon and under these circumstances. I knew the routine from Junior Leaders; I was becoming quite a dab hand at this sort of thing now. I could see that the BC was showing signs of giving me the benefit of the doubt. I think deep down he was trying not to laugh at all my excuses when I explained my side of the story, however, even against his good will, I was still found guilty, £25 march out. I just shook my head from side to side thinking, *what have I got to do to be heard?* Maybe I just needed to be more mindful when I read Battery Orders. After making my way outside I thought to myself *you know what, although I'm not looking forward to slumming it for two weeks, the break will be quite refreshing, gives me a chance to show my true colours to my gun crew, gives me chance to tell them more about myself.*

CHAPTER FIFTY-SIX
EXERCISE BEGINS

After lunch we made our way down to the Gun Park saying goodbye to my pillows for a while: Full webbing, SLR rifle along with NBC kit and skid lids (tin hats), you name it we took it; after all we wouldn't be coming back for a couple of weeks. All four 18 Battery guns were driven out of the gun sheds and onto the apron closely followed by our own personal amphibious ammunition truck (Stalwart) primarily used for transporting military shells around. It felt like the start of another war breaking out, with the APCs (Armoured Personnel Carrier) tracked vehicles known as 432s also showing their power. The BC, BK (Battery Captain), and TC all had their own personal Land Rovers with sophisticated radio equipment in them. Once all the vehicles were lined up in a regimental order we were told to line up in front of our respected gun. There were about ten of us on a good day, two lines of five. There was a short announcement: "All No. 1s to the BC," was the cry from the BSM. It was like a mothers' meeting as all the No. 1s and commanders from other vehicles gathered around the BC.

Still lined up in front of the gun we waited no more than a few minutes before for the battle cry was heard: "Mount! Get the engines started, we are moving out now," shouted the entire gun No.1s, it was difficult to know how I was feeling at this moment in time; Scared, excited, confused, I just got onto the gun and took my seat. There were removable seats, one on each side of the gun that would seat two people, the No.1 would stand up on the gun attached with a harness and then there were two singular seats as well. I believe the gun would accommodate about eight of us and then a couple would travel in the Stalwart vehicle.

As the engines roared from around the Gun Park we made our way out onto the open roads. A lot of the roads were known as tank roads, used mainly for military vehicles. I was astonished how quick the 27 tonne self-propelled M107 could go, speeds of 40 mph plus. I was told by some of my crew members to watch out for track pads flying off the tracks; I thought it was some sort of wind up until… *Wham!* One of the pads went whizzing disgustingly close to my head. They were about the size of a house brick and made of hard rubber; being struck by one of these projectiles could do some serious damage to your health.

It was about a thirty-minute journey in all before we reached our gun position. As we came off the beaten track with dust everywhere, the gun No.1 Sammy started shouting, "Get ready lads," in a *don't let me down* tone of voice. To be honest, I hadn't got too much idea what to expect, everybody on the gun seemed to be standing up and holding onto anything they could as we bounced around over the uneven dirt track. I could see someone about fifty metres in front of our gun running for his life as Dinger (our driver) sped towards him at speed. Apparently he was the person guiding the gun into its gun position; I was thinking, *slow fucking down before we run him over!* There was no mercy as Dinger increased his speed to max-out, Sammy the gun No.1 seemed to be giving Dinger his instructions by kicking him on the back of the head; the driver's head was always in close range of a size ten boot.

"Bell you jock git, fucking slow down." We were almost being catapulted off the gun; it was like a baptism of fire for me as we finally got to where the CP (Command Post) wanted us to position our vehicle.

A huge hand was flown into the air by the person guiding us to our gun position that had 'stop' written all over it, unfortunately, no one had explained to me that this is how you stop the gun, oh dear, they must have forgotten this small detail. I was thrown forward and ended up passing the driver before ending up on the hard surface of the track; sympathy of plenty, *not*, as Sammy shouted, "Wolfendale, get up you idiot before I set Dennis on you." After looking at the size of Dennis, getting up seemed the most intelligent and appropriate thing to do.

For a second it seemed like organised chaos was taking place, everybody on the gun seemed to know their place and what they had to do, it was only poor little me that had absolutely no idea what was expected.

"Wolfendale, get out of the way, stand back and learn," was the voice of Bombardier Nobby Naylor rallying his troops.

"Fine by me," I said; doing exactly as I was told seemed to be the way forward; minutes later the gun was ready for action: the barrel was elevated into the air, the camouflage net was hiding the gun, we had coms (communications), all that was left now was for the crew to do the finishing touches and we would be ready to fire; we also needed some ammunition, oh yes, and a brew.

I liked working as a team; it wasn't long before we were all sat down under the cam net waiting for Sergeant Sammy Douglas to brief his men; apart from me everybody knew their job backwards.

"Wolfendale, peg boy," said Sammy. *Doesn't sound very enterprising to me,* I was thinking, *or very challenging.* What it meant was when we came into action just like we did a few moments ago, I would have to get the bag of pegs from the driver's hatch and peg down the cam net, just like you would peg down your tent. The term 'Gun Bunny' was beginning to show its true meaning now. *Wolfie get the kettle on, Wolfie run down to the Command Post* (which could be miles away), to be honest, I couldn't have asked for a better Gun No.1. Sammy was fair to us all. It was Sammy under the cam net, but once outside the cam net, it was Sergeant Douglas.

As day became night I got chatting to Kev Rowledge (Rolo). I was asking him all sorts of questions to do with the gun. He explained the urgency of why we came into the gun position at such pace; it wasn't for the sheer thrill of it like I thought it was, but because of the rivalry between the other gun subs; in particular Sergeant Massey. It was a race to see who could report back to the Command Post first by saying 'No. 1 gun ready' or 'No. 2 gun ready'. It was all making a lot more sense now. We were quite lucky on the first night in that there was no move planned to a new location; all this meant we could get some sleep in the Stalwart vehicle. The vehicle provided some shelter with the fact that a canopy was draped over it to provide us with some welcomed warmth.

It was about 2100hrs and going dark when Sammy returned from one of many briefs he would have to attend throughout the exercise. "Listen in and gather around," he said.

"Reveille will be at 0700hrs and breakfast at 0730hrs at the cookhouse, anyone seen not wearing their full webbing and not carrying their SLR will be in serious trouble, that's the good news, the bad news is, we are going to have to provide a sentry out at the front of the gun throughout the night. We are going have to dig a trench about six feet in length and about two foot wide with a depth of about five feet."

Apart from the first stag (another name for being on duty) from 2200hrs-2300hrs that went to Bombardier Naylor, we drew straws. I ended up with 0200hrs-0300hrs (dead stag). Each one of us needed to know who we would be waking up next or you could end up doing a double shift. After the trench was dug, it was time for us all to get our sleeping bags out and try to find some space in the back of the Stalwart, we had a few torches but weren't allowed to use them just willy-nilly and, we had to be discreet. It was like a mine field, clambering over bodies in the early hours of the morning. You could always hear someone climbing up and over into the Stalwart and quietly saying, "Wolfie, come on mate, your turn for stag," a little nudge of my shoulder woke me up from the comfort of my dreams. You didn't dare go back to sleep; as one person climbed into their slav sack (nick name for sleeping bag) the other one would get out of theirs trying to be as quiet as they could, and that's how it went on throughout the night. If you were really unlucky you could end up with two stags that night.

As morning broke we made our way to the cookhouse. The roar of the No. 1 burners would always indicate you were travelling in the right direction if it was dark, on this occasion it was a case of *follow the crowd*. Some of the food was slightly rationed apart from the beans. "One sausage and one egg," said the BSM as he stood behind the tables that the food was on, then almost in the same breath he said, "help yourself to the beans," I think beans were the last thing we should have been given more of in respect that at times ,we all slept very close to together. After our '*be grateful you got fed breakfast*'it was time to make our way back to the gun and under the cam net, out of the way from all and sundry; cleaning and checking your weapon and a quick tidy up around the gun area meant we could now relax. Terms like 'crash the ash (get your cigarettes out), your turn Billy could be heard'; for those of us who smoked it was a welcome break.

"Command Post to No.1 gun," could be heard on the radio, "Gun Guides to Command Post." "Wolfendale, get your stuff together and make your way to the Command Post," said Sammy. Sammy explained what a Gun Guide's duties were that meant I had to travel with the GPO (Gun Position Officer) in the back of his Land Rover, along with his driver and three other Gun Guides, one from each gun sub. We would leave a good couple of hours before the guns would be leaving, allowing plenty of time for the GPO to make sure when the guns arrived they would be pointing in the correct direction. To be honest it was a right pain in the backside, it just felt like you were the least important person on the gun crew, a position that made me feel, 'we can afford to lose you for a couple of hours.' "We will make our own brews while you're away," continued Sammy, laughing under his breath. Once we had all confirmed our gun sub number to the GPO we headed off somewhere else, and I mean somewhere else; we just sat in the back of the Land Rover and waited until we arrived at our next location.

"OK, get out of the back, we're here," said the GPO. Each gun position took about ten minutes to complete; the guns would be positioned strategically across a huge range. I was called forward by the GPO and told that this is where he wanted my gun to be positioned; two metal poles stuck into the ground about four metres apart and painted yellow on the top were my markers. There was also a metal arrow attached to the pole at the top to show me which way the gun needed to be facing, simple really, or so I thought. We were all relaxing on a grass bank under some shade of the trees when, we must have all fallen asleep; the next thing we heard was the GPO shouting, "Gun Guides, where the fuck are you?!" The guns were literally on top of us with their engines roaring, I'm still wondering now how the hell we didn't hear them. It took us a few minutes to get our bearings again before managing to pin point our gun, and then, guide it into its correct position.

A bollocking was forthcoming and an extra stag duty was the least I deserved. No sooner had we cammed-up it was a case of, "Wolfendale, dead stag for you tonight." I suppose I had already had a couple of hour's kip. *Sounds fair,* I said to myself. After a while Sammy and the rest of the gun crew found it amusing that all the gun guides had fallen asleep, but a punishment was needed. Over the next few days it was much of the same, "Wolfendale, Gun Guide;" occasionally I was given a reprieve, just so I could see what it was like when we were told to come out of action. We were told that a move was imminent, that meant we were all ready on stand-by; a little bit of cheating went on in respect that we would have some things packed away discreetly, we would all be standing around the gun waiting for the command 'cease fire' that would come through on the radio.

There would always be a final few words from the No.1 and the cover-number Bombardier Naylor before the off. "Cease fire," was heard in a loud voice from Nobby Naylor who was wired up to the radio.

"Go, go, go!" said the crew. We all knew our job which meant it came together like clockwork; it took next to no time for Dinger to fire up the engine. Everything was thrown onto the gun it quick time: cam-net, cam-poles, webbing, rifles, brew kit, even before we were seated we were charging along at some pace bouncing around like there was no tomorrow. In the distance we could see our main rival D sub. Douggie Massey and his crew were charging towards the main track being thrown around just like us, two guns heading for one single track road meant an accident was certain; with every metre we covered, the two guns were getting ever closer to each other until the game of chicken was over. Dinger threw the gun sharply right locking the right track allowing the gun to take pride of place. We made it, we were the first gun to be lined up behind the Command Post with D Sub closely behind. It must have brought great entertainment for the command post and all of their crew watching two guns battle it out for supremacy. It was so good to stop for a few minutes to get ourselves sorted, pretty sure if we had carried on much further we would have lost an item or two. A bit of a snarl from Douggie and his crew with a few hand gestures thrown-in for good measure was a symbol of our victory. Today it was our turn to celebrate, however, tomorrow would be another day.

The live firing itself was something else, it was like learning another language; at first it would be, "Fire Mission Battery," (an order given to us by the Command Post) and we would all jump to our gun positions, next would be the order to load the gun with its shell, "H-E Mike 572 Quick Charge 3 load." The crew were like a well oiled machine as they loaded the gun. The radio instructions continued: "At My Command," which meant we weren't allowed to fire the gun without the permission of the command post, "Bearing 2526 mills, elevation 146 mills, three rounds fire for effect." After each round was fired we would still have to wait for permission to fire the next round, basically we were at the hands of the command post. Ear plugs were certainly a big part of our equipment when it came to live firing; the noise was thunderous. With myself still being a Gun Bunny I was spared the opportunity of having to stand on the gun when it was fired, my turn would come later. The recoil of the gun was so powerful it would throw you off if you weren't holding onto something. The idea of standing on the gun was so that you could reload in a short space of time; I believe the Americans stand well to the rear of the huge artillery weapon.

It was now getting close to the end of the exercise, Wednesday 28th May to be precise, tomorrow would be END-EX (End of Exercise); feeling grotty and in need of my pillow I was looking forward to returning back to the barracks along with all the rest of the lads. The 28th May to most people wouldn't mean a thing, but to me, it was one of the most important days of my life so far, my beloved Leeds United were playing in the European Cup

Final against the German champions Bayern Munich. It was the first time that they had reached the final since the club was founded in October 1919.

During the early afternoon we moved location and were settled into our new gun position by about 1800hrs, my first thought was, *I should be able to listen to the match on the radio* as no more moves were planned that evening.

"Gather around," was the command of Sergeant Sammy Douglas. His speech confirmed that there would be no move until tomorrow however; we still needed to provide sentries around the gun (stag duties) throughout the evening and throughout the night. Short straw was now swimming around my mind. I was just hoping that I would be given a stag duty that didn't coincide with the match. Sergeant Douglas was in one of his more compassionate moods meaning that he had a plan as to who would be doing which stag. "Names in a hat," said Sammy, "fairest way of doing it." Sammy would pull out a name from the hat, the first name out would be given the first stag from 1900hrs-2000hrs and so on. After the first two stags were taken care of, it was now down to stag three, 2100hrs-2200hrs. This was definitely the stag I didn't want; it would be the second half of the match. On a normal day this would've been a good stag to have, you would be guaranteed a good night sleep until about 0600hrs the next morning.

I sat eagerly next to the rest of lads who waited with bated breath, Sammy's hand entered his beret and pulled out the piece of paper, he just looked over in my direction, stared me in the eyes and then called out the name on the piece of paper: "Wolfendale, 9-10." ...My jaw dropped. I was in no position to argue with the No.1 of the gun, even though I was gutted. I just took a deep breath of air and looked towards the dirt on my boots at the same time trying to console myself. 2100hrs arrived and it was time for my stag, 0-0 was the score when I reluctantly dragged my feet to the trench; trying to concentrate on the enemy attacking us was now taking a back seat. I could hear some of the senior ranks including my gun No. 1 shouting and cheering at every pass or close call, it was doing my head in.

It was now dark, so I couldn't see a thing. Suddenly I heard a loud roar from the command post where they were all gathered, *it must have been a goal for Leeds* I was thinking. It was difficult to know what the score was from the oohs and the arhs. I was relived from my duty to find out that we had lost 2-0; apparently the cheer was for a Leeds goal only for it to be disallowed before Bayern went on to score two goals. One thing I did learn from the disappointment was that there is more to life than football, even though football was a big part of my life.

Thursday saw our return back to barracks: washing the guns down, maintenance, full tool check and getting our clothes washed was foremost of things to do; we only had a few days before we were making our way to Holland on the Monday for a two week Battery Camp. Surely I couldn't get myself into more trouble?

CHAPTER FIFTY-SEVEN
GET THEM DOWN YOU ZULU WARRIOR

The weekend was a nice refreshing change: getting hot showers, washing clothes, and getting to chill out with some music. Barry White (Walrus of Love) was music that I'd never come across before, but it was Don's taste, he had quite a few albums of the famous singer. To be honest it wasn't long before I was becoming converted to the beautiful words from his really deep voice. Monday morning arrived and yet another week had passed without me being charged for something, *a rarity,* I was thinking. Outside the block were two four tonners and a couple of Land Rovers to take us all to Holland, nothing like a bit of comfort to take us on our jollies.

"OK lads, get yourselves on the back of the vehicles," was the command from Sergeant Massey. It really did feel like we were going on holiday as we clambered on board, especially with the fact that we were all allowed to travel in civilian clothes. Denim jacket and jeans seem to be worn by the majority, a few 1960 pullovers, and yes... plenty of flares were on show.

Sitting next to my good friend Don made the long journey more enjoyable, it wasn't long before we were having a half way stop at a service station close to the Deutsche border. As we pulled in we could see the Army Land Rovers already in position.

"OK, get out and stretch your legs," said Sergeant Masscy. "Half an hour and I want you back on the vehicles. I don't want anyone buying any alcohol; and that includes you Walsh."

"What do you take me for?" said Geordie Walsh, laughing and looking shocked.

"Half an hour I said, so don't be late back," repeated Sergeant Massey.

Don and I, plus a load of other lads battled our way into the service station looking for the bogs (toilets). With that many of us wanting a pee it meant there was a queue a mile long stretching outside the door. I am not saying that the lads didn't know how to pee into a urinal however, when we left, it was safe to say it would've taken more than a mop and bucket to clean up the mess. I kept close to Don for the rest of the tour who introduced me to some German cuisine for the first time.

"What do you fancy, Paul?" said Don, looking at all the delicious food on display.

"Not sure, maybe some chips and sausage," I said. Although I spoke some German, I thought I would leave the ordering to Don.

"Zweimal pomme-frites mit Bratwurst, bitte," (two portions of chips with sausage please) said Don.

"Wow, impressed," I said, "thanks."

"No worries, you're paying for it," said Don.

"Cheers Don," I said with a smirk.

"Don't mention it Paul, that's what mates are for," he said with a huge grin on his face. I wasn't going to argue the toss with Don in respect that I was pretty sure that Don would return the complement the next time we were out together. Within minutes we were sitting down enjoying our German cuisine. "Wow Don, this sausage is to die for," I said as I started tucking into another bite.

"Can't beat a good German sausage Paul, famous for their sausages are the Germans."

"Just what I needed Don, very filling, and bloody lovely."

The half hour break flew past quickly and before we knew it we were back on the Autobahn and making our way to Holland. By the time we reached our destination most of the lads were falling asleep, it took a few speed bumps as we entered the Deutsche Army camp where we were staying to wake them up. "Ouch, what the fuck was that?" could be heard as they were being tossed about and banging their heads on the metal frame work.

"We are here," shouted someone as the vehicle came to a halt. Seconds later Sergeant Massey was calling the tune again. "Out you get, line up over by the wall." The camp was not dissimilar to the St Barbara Barracks back in Fallingbostal, only difference was that we were given less than comfortable rooms. It was more like going back to the dormitories we had in Bramcote without the luxuries: sleeping bags on mattresses, plain dull walls and no TV, food was three squares a day from the camp cookhouse and that was about it.

The first day saw us being taken to the nearby town of Amersfoort where we would be terrorising the town on cycles. The only thing about these bikes they had no brakes, or at least that what I thought; it was only when we were given the order to get cycling on this scorching hot summer's day that I realised I couldn't slow the bloody thing down. I shouted over to the peloton, "How the hell do you stop the bike? I've no brakes." There must have been at least half a dozen of us that had no idea how to slow the bike down. A voice that seemed to come from beyond the grave could be heard… "Try pedalling backwards, you stupid twat." It was Billy Dalzell ,one of three brothers, with that kind of remark ringing in my ears I really thought *yeah, pedalling backwards*, it was one of those pigs can fly moments.

"Oh, look up there," I said looking towards the sky, "Is that a porky pig I can see? Pedalling backwards, never heard anything so stupid." Something needed to be done, so I felt that maybe, just maybe, I should give this stupid idea that Billy had suggested some consideration; preventing myself from crashing into anything that got in my way seemed to be my only option.

I decided indiscreetly to give peddling backwards a go; I felt I had nothing to lose. I wasn't expecting anything to happen which proved to be my downfall; it was like doing an emergency stop as I went arse over tit onto the hard tarmac road causing minor injuries to my uncovered arms. "Alright Wolfie?" was the sympathetic cry from Brian (Betty) Davies who decided to stop and assess my injuries.

"Yeah, I'll recover," I replied, still licking my wounds. I was thinking *how nice of the rest not to stop*, they just continued on their merry way as if nothing had happened. It was a nightmare riding through the streets of Amersfoort, pedalling backwards to stop wasn't something I was getting to grips with.

The first week of our two week battery camp was spent doing much of the same thing: cycling, walking, sport activities and occasionally getting wasted in the evenings; with me still new out of training I was subjected to some things that are best left underneath my beret by the so call bullies. I will take those unforgettable atrocities to my grave. I'm still not sure what some of the bullies got out of it, maybe they will look back now and realise that what they did was unacceptable. It was getting close to returning back to West Germany and it was thought that we would have one last big bash in one of the local clubs. Whose idea it was is anybody's guess; all I remember is that it was to be a turning point in my Army career.

Most if not all of us had assembled in a huge darkened club which was packed to the rafters with people: single women, women with their husbands/partners, single men, gays and straights, black, white, I think I even saw a monk at the bar, all of God's children everyone, they just wanted a good night out… oh, and I nearly forgot, sixty plus rowdy squaddies ready to gate crash the party.

The beer was flowing quicker than the Niagara Falls; in quite a strange way and after a few Bacardi and Cokes I was also getting into the party mood. Even the bullies were becoming my friends, probably not a bad thing as there was never any place to hide; 'if you can't beat them, join them' was the motto, well at least until I was shown some respect. There was no way that I was ever going to be converted into being a bully; or a drunk, I am what I am and that's how it was going to stay.

"Wolfie, your round," said Billy.

"Fuck off," I said, "you get them in." It was only then that I realised what I had said, *must've be the drink talking,* I was thinking; it got a few laughs if nothing else, but that kind of remark probably deserved a smack in the mouth. No more was said. As the evening progressed and with everybody now a few sheets to the wind, it was time for their party trick.

"Wolfie," shouted Danny Dalzell. "Fancy doing a Zulu Warrior?" I looked Danny in the eyes, or was that three eyes? Not sure, my head was spinning.

"What? What in God's name is a Zulu Warrior?" I said, slurring my words, I was even having trouble finding my mouth with my next instalment of Bacardi and Coke. I must have been talking loudly because within seconds everybody was chanting, "Zulu Warrior, Zulu Warrior, Zulu Warrior, Wolfie is going to do a Zulu Warrior." Well, how could I refuse? How rude would it be too refuse to perform a Zulu Warrior? I still had no idea what I was letting myself in for until my mate Don explained whilst at the same time chuckling, "You have to strip all your clothes off Paul, standing on a table."

"Bloody hell," I said, "on your bike, there's no way I am showing my bits off in public, don't care how drunk I am."

"I don't think you've got too much choice, Paul," said Don, who was sounding sympathetic yet at the same time, also looking forward to tonight's entertainment.

"Go for it, Paul," said Don. Again there seemed to be nowhere to hide, I must admit it took me a while to pluck up the strength to agree to their command.

Don and Billy decided to give me a helping hand out of my seat (how kind of them) and escort me to the awaiting table that was now clear of its belongings. I still couldn't believe what I was doing as I stepped onto the table, I felt all alone as I moved my head around the club. All eyes were now on me.

I stood there thinking for a few seconds, I wonder how many people here tonight were told that tonight's entertainment would be a stripper.

"Get them down, you Zulu Warrior; Get them down, you Zulu Chief Chief Chief." I decide it was time to start. First was my shirt buttons, in slow time I unfastened them from top to bottom, just like a tease would; if I was going to do it then I was going to do it properly. I propelled my shirt a few times above my head just like a cowboy with his lasso before releasing it into the cheering crowd. God knows where the shirt ended up; I just saw it land somewhere among the lads. My six-pack was now revealed to the ever increasing noise of the lads, I am pretty sure the rest of the club would have joined in with the song if they knew the words; all that said, I did see quite a few clapping near the bar. I seemed to getting myself into a dancing type rhythm and felt quite pleased with my performance so far. The trousers were next as the volume increased; top button, and then slowly unzipping my flies with my right hand. My underpants were now on show for all to see, blue y-front undies if I remember correctly. Getting more and more nervous I just continued until, and, without tripping myself up, I managed to slip off my trousers and throw them cowboy style once again into the same direction as my shirt.

It was only now that I realised I still had my shoes and socks on; I must have looked a right prat standing there in my undies. With the humiliation I was now feeling I decided that they must go. Without even bending down I flung my shoes off into the gladiators' den. Not sure if they hit anyone, but maybe now after all these years, it's time for me to give an apology; to be honest, I think they would have been more concerned about my socks. This was it; I had nothing left to take off apart from my Y-fronts. "Get them down you Zulu Warrior," continued to rattle my car drums. What seemed like an eternity was actually only a few seconds. My hands now slid down to the waistband of my undies, I held them there for a couple of seconds wondering whether to continue. I felt I had no choice but to carry on with my shenanigans, I didn't have any time to reflect what I had just done as my pants hit my ankles, exposing my meat and two veg. There was a loud cheer from the ranks and also the locals; before I could even blink I was covered in gallons of beer, all the lads must have thought it would be a good idea to throw their drink over me whilst standing there naked on the table.

After retrieving my clothes it came as no surprise that we were ordered off the premises and told never to return. I think it's fair to say we didn't make any friends that night among the captive audience, just enemies. The next day and feeling somewhat groggy, my name was the talk of the town, everywhere I went.

"Wolfie, brilliant last night, what do you think?" said Billy and Danny.

"Not sure, just can't believe what I did," I replied, holding my head.

"One of the lads now Paul," said someone unknown to me "can't see you getting any more trouble from now on." I felt annoyed with that remark, not personally, but because it made me question, *why do you have to do something that they would class as heroic just to be part of their so called group?* It made no sense to me. My days of being bullied, picked on, humiliated, whatever you would like to call it were well and truly behind me, it was now time for someone else to go through what I endured. With the battery camp now over it was time to get our belongings together and head back to Fallingbostal to my shared room and my comfy bed. With more surprises imminent I just went with the flow, it seemed the best way to stay out of trouble. Consuming twelve bottles of Bacardi in two weeks had me asking questions about myself. Surly six would have been enough?

CHAPTER FIFTY EIGHT

MY BOYISH LOOKS PLAY HAVOC WITH MY LOVE LIFE

June and July brought lots of activity; my feet never seem to touch the ground. Considering I had never ventured far from my homeland, I had now touched base with West Germany and Holland in the first month of engaging with the regular Army, and with more adventures still to come.

The following week and only two days back into our normal working routine I was checking for any mail I might have received. A slightly different system was used compared with the system we used at Bramcote, a wooden rack with small compartments that was marked from A-Z, any mail you had would be put into the compartment with the first letter from your surname. On this day there was no mail for me, however, as I was walking back along the corridor close to the Battery Office I heard a voice shouting my name.

"Gunner Wolfendale, just the man I was looking for." *What have I done wrong now*, I was thinking, it was Sergeant Lucky; he wanted a quiet word with me.

"Fancy a trip to Denmark? Two weeks sailing around the coast, you start at Kiel just up from Hamburg."

"Nah, thank you all the same," I said. Sergeant Lucky decided it was time for a different approach as he got within inches of my face and gave me a stare that had "*you will be going sailing* "written all over it.

"I don't think you heard me correctly," said Sergeant Lucky. "Let me put it this way, you're not volunteering, it is an order, you are going to Denmark, and you will enjoy the experience of learning to sail; most people would give their right arm to go sailing for two weeks, have I made myself clear?"

"Yes Sarge," I said, "seeing as you put it like that, I would love to go Sarge, one question though, why don't you send someone else on the course if it's that good, maybe someone who actually wants to go sailing." My remark fell on deaf ears.

"I will confirm it on Battery Orders," said Sergeant Lucky, "make sure you read them, it will tell you the date you're going and other useful information you might need."

That evening, whilst in my room, I was telling Don about the sailing course.

"Go for it," said Don.

"Well yeah, I will, problem is, why me?"

"No idea mate, don't knock it, pretty sure you'll have a great time," said Don, "tell you what though, take some bottles of Bacardi with you; I believe it's very expensive over there, maybe you could make a bob or two."

"Would that be legal?" I said, "I don't want to get into trouble, I've already been charged once since arriving here about a month ago."

"It will be OK; just don't tell anybody," said Don.

"How many bottles should I take? What do yer think?" I said "half a dozen?"

"Why not, go for it," said Don.

"It sounds like a good idea that Don," I replied. "What I don't sell I can drink." Don seemed happy for me, just wished I felt the same. The next day I read Battery Orders to see my name attached to the memo that I was expecting, it was only when I got half way down the A4 sheet of paper that my breath was taken away. I would be going in two days' time, along with seven other lads from different batteries, with such short notice and time of the essence; I decided to get myself down to the NAAFI for some supplies, like Bacardi Rum. I remembered what Don had said, *six bottles* I was thinking, *if he said six, then maybe just to be on the safe side, I should up my order.* Twelve bottles is what I bought, a nice round dozen along with plenty of goodies. Later on that evening I met up with Don doing his ironing in the room. I explained to Don how I would be off in two days time and that I had bought twelve bottles instead of six.

"Bloody hell!" was his reply. "Twelve bottles, that's enough to sink the Titanic!" Don couldn't stop laughing. "Two weeks, fourteen days, by my reckoning, that's almost a bottle every day if you don't manage to sell them."

"Well done Don, not as daft as you look," I said with some sarcasm attached to my voice. I felt comfortable around Don and one or two other of the guys now, so giving them back some banter wasn't a problem anymore.

The day had arrived. With my bags packed including my twelve bottles of duty frees I made my way to the Guardroom, two Army long wheel base Land Rovers were awaiting our arrival.

"Sailing course?" said one of the drivers.

"Yes," I replied, still feeling concerned.

"Get yourself into the front Land Rover with your bags, we will be leaving shortly," said the driver. There were already three of the lads that were on the course in the back so I just clambered aboard and kept quiet. The journey took a few hours including a pit stop until we finally arrived; to be honest, I still wasn't feeling much better with what lay ahead.

"OK, over here lads," said a voice from a distance. It was an elderly gentleman, well at least compared to me, I would say about fiftyish. It turned out he was the Captain of the vessel we would be sailing in.

He explained the dangers of what could happen if we didn't do as we're told, followed by a tour of the boat before he allowed us to pick which bunk we wanted to sleep in (as if I had a choice). Luggage on board meant we were now ready to sail before it became too dark; we had about three hours of daylight left so the Captain wanted to set sail immediately. Looking at all the other lads on board made me feel so young and innocent once again. There wasn't one that was younger than twenty five years old; that again raised the question, *why was I chosen to go on this sailing course?* Meeting a new set of lads for the second time in a month wasn't my idea of fun, it was my idea of getting messed around and thoughts of my fellow mates from Bramcote were again going through my mind.

How does one describe sailing on the Baltic Sea? Let's say it was choppy and at times, bloody cold and, it felt like at any moment I would be getting my feet wet. Over the two weeks we would be mooring up each night at a different port around the coast of Denmark, places like: Svenborg, Helsingborg, and Tuborg were visited; a night sail was also included in the package deal. After the first day's sail it was time for our evening meal; compo rations made into a meal fit for the queen had us all squirming with delight. With everybody now enjoying themselves and, with the Captain's orders, I was asked to crack open my first bottle of Bacardi. "It's to sell, not to drink," I said, but unfortunately, what I had to say was of no concern to rest of the crew; I was out numbered. Before I could say another word the top was off the bottle and the clear white liquid was being shared around the crew; we were all feeling like mariners now, mariners without a uniform, *what ya gonna do with the drunken sailor* sprang to mind.

Day two was interesting to say the least. With the Captain navigating this trip on a regular basis meant that he had made a few friends on the way; we were pulling into a small marina when I saw these two wonderful looking women dressed to kill: small tight blue denim shorts and slinky well filled out yellow tops. "OK ladies," said the Captain, "come aboard." I was still trying to make sense of the situation when the Captain announced that these two beauties would be joining us, one of them would be staying with us for a few days and the other one would just be staying until we got to our next location later on in the day. As I looked towards them I was thinking *wow, another notch on my bedpost* yet at the same time thinking *they are definitely out of my league*; either way it was going to be a nice refreshing change to be looking at two stunning ladies.

That evening as expected, one of the ladies left us, it was now seven horny soldiers and one not so horny Captain, along with one oh so stunning lady; seven into one doesn't go, so it was a case of, *who do you fancy darlin'?* I do know one thing for sure, over the next few days she was with us, I certainly didn't get a look-in, that's not to say someone else didn't. One of the lads a married man at that (mum's the word) was the only person unaccounted for at breakfast, oh, apart from our female guest ; maybe she wanted the more mature man and not the choir boy-looking seventeen year old that I was. I did manage to do a little sunbathing with her on top of the boat later on that day, however, that's as far as it went.

As the weeks went on my stash of Bacardi went down, I never did get to sell any of it. I was now becoming accustomed for the taste for Bacardi and Coke; for someone who doesn't drink or at least very little, I was becoming quite a connoisseur in the art of drinking Bacardi. With the two weeks almost up the Captain treated us to a night out in the town of Helsingborg. We went to a night club that was larger than life; drinks were so expensive that it made more sense to get half cut before venturing out. It was like déjà vu; the Captain seemed to know everybody at the club. Within minutes of entering the club the Captain introduced us to his friends; gorgeous beauties again were on parade.

"Where does he find all this talent?" I said to one of the lads.

"Search me, maybe he's got something in his trousers that's more appealing than what we have," was the reply I got, not necessarily the reply I was expecting or looking for. It wasn't long before I noticed that one of the beauties that the Captain was friends with was flirting with a couple of men; I was slightly confused by this and thought *maybe I might have a chance here…* Wrong. After plucking up the courage to ask her for a dance I thought maybe I would take it to the next level.

"Who's that man over there you were talking to?" I said, getting closer and closer to her ear to drown out the noise of the disco.

"That's my husband," she shouted close up to the cheek of my face, still confused I continued…

"Well, who's the dude you were talking to at the same table?"

"Oh him, he's just someone I sleep with on a Thursday night," she said so casually, my eyes were now wide open with shock trying to take in what she has just told me. I paused for a second waiting for her to continue.

"How does that work?" I said, waiting eagerly for the next chapter.

"We swap partners on a Thursday, the girl at the bar just over there is his wife, we have been doing it for about a year now; we find it spices up our sex life."

I was stuck for words for a while, which wasn't like me, and then all of a sudden, and I don't know where it came from, I blurted out.

"Do you fancy sleeping with me tonight for a change?" I could see she was considering the proposal the way she was staring at me with her kaleidoscope eyes; for a second or two I really thought I was in until she dropped the bombshell.

"Well, maybe, nah, you look too young, I like slightly older men, you look too innocent, but thank you anyway, I do like you though and it was a close call." *Stop patronising me* I was thinking, *you have said enough.* My boyish looks were once again causing me a problem. It was times like this when I just wished I was a few years older; to be honest I did try to get her to change her mind, almost to the point of begging, but to no avail. Apart from a typical brawl that broke out later on in the club, chairs being thrown everywhere, and then two people who looked more like heavy-weight boxers just dancing around the dance floor without laying a punch on each other that I found comical to say the least; that was about it. It was now time to get back to the ship for some beauty sleep.

The trip ended with me feeling much more educated than two weeks ago. As well as learning something about sailing a boat, I learnt that Danish women are to die for, and at the same time, very liberated, you can get through twelve bottles of Bacardi in two weeks and Danish men, well let's just say, they need educating into how to fight on the dance floor. Would I ever go back? Wild horses wouldn't stop me. With news that a regimental parade was forthcoming and rumour control in full flow, I was concerned when I would be getting any more leave. It was time for me to get off my backside and dodge a few mines (so to speak) if I was to be granted leave.

CHAPTER FIFTY-NINE
FIRST CLASS AMERICANS

It was nice to be back on dry land after two weeks on the high seas. The first thing I did after unpacking was to check battery and regimental orders, at the same time, being careful not to miss out any important information like,' you're on Guard duty.' Upon close inspection I noticed that on Monday morning there would be a full muster parade at 1030hrs, straight after NAAFI break. It obviously caught my attention with the fact that 1030hrs was not the customary time you would expect to be on parade.

"What's this Monday morning muster parade for?" I said to Bill Young, the Battery Clerk, with a concerning look.

"I just type the orders," said Bill, "they don't tell me nowt."

"You must have some idea," I said, hoping for an answer. The clerk turned to me and in a quiet voice said...

"Think it's about our tour to Northern Ireland, at a guess."

"Wow," I said, "thanks, I will keep it that information under my beret."

"No need, most of the lads have all ready worked it out for themselves," said Bill as he made his way back to his office.

With no Guard duty over the weekend I just spent time with my buddies that I had become friends with: Dave Turner, Steve Schofield, Don Bowles, Paul Sheridan, Kev Rowledge to name a few; I would definitely consider them as friends, friends that I could rely on if ever needed. It was early Saturday evening when I made my way to Dave Turner's room to see if he had got any plans.

"Hi Dave," I said as I entered his room, "I've got naff all going on tonight, fancy doing something?"

"Like what?" replied Dave,

"I was thinking maybe the SKK (Soldier's Kino Korporation) cinema, see what's on."

"Yeah, why not," said Dave to my surprise, "just give me a couple of minutes and I will be ready."

"That'll be great," I said with a smile on my face. "Tell you what; I will just nip back to my room to see if Don wants' to come along." I was even more surprised when Don also agreed to venture away from his Barry White music. Saturday night is normally a relaxing night for Don, flat out in his pit, listening to his favourite music.

Apart from us wondering what was on at the SKK, the main topic of conversation was to do with the rumours of our probable tour of Northern Ireland; it would be the first time for us all so being excited was an understatement. With the SKK now insight we were all looking to see if we could see what was showing.

"The Sting," shouted Don.

"What was that you said Don?"

"The Sting," repeated Don "you need to get your ears cleaned out Paul; it stars Robert Redford Paul Newman and Robert Shaw

"Never heard of it," I said, shaking my head.

"Oh well, may as well give it a look," said Don. The film was amazing; on the way back to the barracks all we could talk about was the movie. I was feeling a lot closer now to Dave now as he was proving to be a very close friend, someone I could talk to, *another Dennis Norris, another Pete Rigby,* I was thinking

After a quiet Sunday, Monday morning's muster parade soon arrived. The anticipation of everybody could be felt throughout the ranks as we awaited the arrival of the BC. I don't think I have ever seen so many senior ranks on parade at one time, *it must be serious:* Sergeant Massey, Sergeant Douglas, Sergeant Moore, Sergeant Walsh and many more, "Attention," was the order from Sergeant Massey as the smartly dressed BC arrived from his office. Once at ease the BC started his speech.

"I know that most of you already have your suspicions about what this muster parade is about, well let me confirm your suspicions. Early in November and a date yet to be confirmed, 42nd Regiment Royal Artillery will be deployed in the Province of Northern Ireland for a four month tour, returning back in March." There was silence among the ranks as our ears were now pinned to what the BC was saying. "18 Battery will be given the task of patrolling the city centre of Londonderry." Again the silence was like something you would expect at a funeral, I just gave Dave a slight nudge with my hand as we continued to listen to the BCs speech.

"We all know that you will do a splendid job when you arrive and I feel proud to be in charge of such a magnificent battery. Northern Ireland training will commence in August in about four weeks time, during that time there will be no leave for anybody." *No leave* I was thinking, *god knows when I will get to see my family and friends again.* Apart from a few more comforting words from the BC, that was about it. The BC made his way back to the comforts of his office and left us with a mind full of 'Oh my God' moments.

Over the next couple of days the topic of conversation was all about Northern Ireland everywhere you went: Cookhouse, NAAFI, Gun Park, Battery bar, local bars, all you could hear around the camp was talk of our tour to Londonderry. We were even putting on Irish accents from time to time. It was late evening and I was lying on my bed in the now darkened room, all sorts of things were going on in my head. Writing a letter to my parents was one of them. It was only then when I decided to reply to a letter that I had received from them a few days ago that a thought suddenly struck me... *leave.* By the time I returned from Northern Ireland in March (God willing), it would have been almost eleven months since I had my last allocation of leave, eleven months since seeing my parents and loved ones. Considering I was use to having some sort of leave every six weeks or so in training, this was one of those moments I had to get off my backside and do something about it. I continued writing my letter without mentioning Northern Ireland, I thought it best to leave that subject for a while, didn't want to worry them. I know for a fact that they would be keeping up with events from the troubles from Northern Ireland on the national news.

The following day and with my mind still pre-occupied with seeing my family I decided to make a few inquiries.

"Don, have you had any leave this year?" I said, trying to find out some facts before I acted on my state of affairs.

"Yes," said Don from the comfort of his bed, "I think most of us have, April, I had three weeks back in my home town of Wolverhampton, some of the others are on leave at the moment and then there will be others that have booked leave for July, just before Northern Ireland training starts, I'm pretty sure that someone at the top would have known about the tour long before we would be told Paul."

"There was a rumour going around in Junior Leaders about this tour when we were choosing which regiments to go too, so I know what you mean" I said.

"Anyway, why do you ask?" said Don.

"Well I was thinking, I might see if I can get some leave before August" I said, "it will be almost a year before I get to see my parents and family again, I had a couple of weeks at the end of April before flying out to Germany, and that was that."

"Well, my parents are in the middle of emigrating too Australia at the moment," said Don, "so I'm going to see if it could be possible for the Army to pay for a flight for me next year."

"Will they do that?" I asked curiously.

"Not sure, if not then I won't be able to see them until I come out," said Don. "I'm only going to do three years, I signed off just before Christmas; eighteen months' notice is what I had to give."

"So when are you due out?" I asked.

"February 1977," said Don. "Three years is enough for me."

The conversation continued for about ten minutes with Don saying, "You would be better off seeing the TC," (bypass a few mines is what he was saying), "I wouldn't bother going through the chain of command, go see the TC that's my advice, see where it gets you, if you go to the Troop Sergeant he will probably just say no, and that will be the end of it."

"Cheers Don," I said, "thanks for that advice."

I was off my bed and out of the door in quick time while everything was fresh in my mind (no time like the present). Luckily for me I saw the TC in the Battery Block corridor trying to look busy, to me that meant he was waiting for something to do. *I'll give you a task Sir*, I was thinking. I made it look as if I hadn't seen him until I was just in the midst of walking past him;

"Oh, oh Sir, just the person I was looking for," I said with my 'wow nice to see you' voice.

"What can I help you with?" he replied. I explained the situation like I had explained it to Don while still occupying the corridor; to my surprise he took my request for leave seriously. "Leave it with me," he said.

"*Leave* it with me, funny that Sir, pardon the pun," I said.

"Yes, very good Wolfendale," said the TC with a welcome smile on his face, "I will see what I can do for you."

It didn't take too long for the TC to get back to me with some interesting news. "Gunner Wolfendale, just the man I've been looking for," he said as we were both heading in the direction of the Officers' Mess. "I have spoken to the BC about an hour ago; the fact that you have just come out of training, and the fact that you'll be going to into conflict at such a young age, you'll be allowed two weeks' leave starting as of this Friday." I was so thrilled with the news; however the not so good news was that I would have to pay for myself, *I can handle this,* I was thinking, my wages had just gone into the bank so on the money side of things it wouldn't be a problem.

On my return to the block I went to see Bill the Battery Clerk, he seemed to be the one who I could rely on to give me advice on the best way to get home.

"Hamburg to Harwich, Prinz Ferries is your best bet," he said in a really helpful way. "From there a train to London and then a train to Crewe."

"I cannot thank you enough, Bill," I said. Bill gave me a list of sailing times and where to purchase my tickets, also he mentioned that the Duty Driver would take me to Hamburg free of charge which would be of great help. With only three days to go I didn't have any time to inform my family so it was going to be a major shock for them to see me on the door step. The ship would be sailing at around 1330hrs so it was going to be an early start on Friday morning. Friday morning soon arrived. It was a fantastic feeling getting out of bed and getting into civvies; as I looked over to my right I could see my mate Don putting on his in coveralls.

"Lucky bugger Paul," he said with a sense of disappointment in his remark.

"Can't wait, a little nervous travelling all that way on my own, knowing my luck I'm bound to cock up something along the way," I said, still feeling mildly excited.

"Get on parade," was the cry from one of the Bombardiers that was pacing the corridor.

"See you mate," said Don with a firm hand-shake.

"You too Don," I said. In a strange way I was going to miss him just as much as I was looking forward to seeing my family. I couldn't resist one final look through the window; seeing the battery on parade while I was going on leave felt embarrassingly good.

I arrived in Hamburg in plenty of time, to be honest, everything went like clock-work. The ship was something like I could never imagine, Titanic proportion sprang to mind. I slowly scanned my eyes over the vessel to take in its enormity. As I was boarding I just sort of followed the crowd once more until I was sat in the comfy lounge type area. All in all the crossing of the North Sea took roughly 18 hours; finding somewhere to sleep proved to be a challenge within itself. Passengers without a cabin or berth (myself included) would lay their head wherever they could. I was up and down all night with not being able to sleep properly; taking in the sea breeze and occasionally looking up to the ever-glowing stars was a breathtaking experience.

A journey full of no mishaps (thank god) saw me arrive home early Saturday evening; you can imagine the look on my mother's face when she opened the door.

"Paul! Oh my god, what… what are you doing home?" she said, thinking the worst.

"Don't worry, I haven't deserted, I've been given two weeks' leave, I didn't have chance to let you know," I said trying to show some calm.

"It's our Paul," shouted my mum to whoever was at home; it was so nice to see both of my parents again. After the mandatory hugs it was time to drop the bombshell about Northern Ireland. Sat round the warm coal fire I broke the news.

"I have something to tell you I said; "I'm not in trouble or anything like that."

"What it is then?" said my mum curiously. I just took a look at my mum and continued.

"The regiment has been told we will be going to Northern Ireland in early November. You don't need to worry, as soon as I get back after this leave I will be training for the tour." There was silence for a minute as my mum raised her eyebrows to what I had said, my dad was just his normal self, he just nodded his head and said next to nothing; thinking back now, he spent more time talking to his vegetable garden than my mum and I. For the first time in my life I was actually faced with silence from my mother. Not sure what she was thinking deep down inside, all I knew from my own experiences was that she would be worried, well at least until I arrived back safely.

The conversation continued for a few minutes until I felt that I had done all that I could to put their minds at ease. The two weeks went by quickly, but unfortunately not without incident; Carol and I decided to break up, we had a small argument over next to nothing however, I'm pretty sure that the cause of the split was due to the fact that we were seeing less and less of each other. I am a true believer in the phrase absence makes the heart grow fonder, but in this case, the heart had gone AWOL (Absent without Official Leave). No worries, didn't get too upset, I had too much on my mind to be concerned with splitting up with Carol.

It would have been nice to have seen Dec before I returned back to base, however, Dec was busy with his training back in Nuneaton, exactly where I was twelve months ago. I am not very good with goodbyes so saying farewell to my family again was an effort within itself, I could feel silent tears forming in my mother's eyes as I kissed her goodbye; a firm handshake from my father signalled it was time for me to say farewell once more.

The journey back was more entertaining than when I left West Germany; after changing trains in London, and now on the way to Harwich, I became acquainted with a young American girl who was on vacation with her mother. By some strange coincidence we both accidentally ended up in a first class carriage with second class tickets (not a good idea), I ended up there because I was stupid, and with the fact that there was limited seating also didn't help, they ended up there because they were finding it difficult to understand the British Railway system; either way, we were both travelling illegally. The friendship started when the conductor of the train came around shouting, "Tickets please," in his jobs-worth voice. It was no surprise when he checked the small print on my ticket that I would soon be searching for a seat in 2nd class; he was trying to tell me what I already knew without sounding condescending.

"The last few carriages, 2nd class I'm afraid for you," he remarked. Seconds later the well presented American mother and daughter were right behind me looking for a seat, we both found it amusing to be honest.

"Where are you heading?" I said, trying to drum up a conversation.

"Germany, West Germany, we are off to Harwich to catch the ferry to Hamburg." My eyes nearly popped out of my head.

"Really," I said, "me too, I'm in the British Army, I am stationed over there."

"Maybe we can meet up on the ferry then?" She said as she gently presented her hand to me in a lady like way. "My name is Tegan by the way, Tegan Alexandra, and my daughter's name is Kim."

"That would be lovely," I said, as I smiled in the direction of her beautiful daughter with her silky blonde hair. "My name is Paul, Paul Wolfendale; look forward to meeting you later aboard the ferry."

We parted company at the train station, but only for a short while, well at least until we met up again on the ferry. The ferry was very congested so finding my American friends wasn't as straightforward as I first thought; in fact it wasn't until we set sail that I was able to find them.

"Over here, Paul," said a voice from close by. I looked over towards where the call had come from to see Tegan and her daughter Kim sitting at a table;

without wanting to shout through the crowd of people, I just smiled and made a bee line to where they were sitting.

"Would you like to join us, Paul?" said Tegan with a smile on her face.

"Love to," I said, "if you don't mind." As I took a seat opposite Tegan I only had eyes for Kim and her beautiful long blonde hair. She was stunning, everything about her made me feel that there were such things as love at first sight. Kim was only sixteen, one year younger than me.

"Whereabouts are you from?" I asked.

"California," said Kim, "3948 Palm Drive, Bonita, California is my address." It sounded so aristocratic compared to where I lived.

"What about you, Paul?"

"Nantwich," I said, "3 Manor Cottages, Edleston, Nantwich, Cheshire." There was nothing aristocratic about where I came from, although the word cottages has got a little upper-class ring about it.

I spent a good few hours chatting to Kim and her mother until Kim decided to go to her cabin for a lie down. It was a signal for me to tour the ship for a while and just have a general nose around. It was early evening before I met up with Tegan again; unfortunately there was still no sign of Kim.

"Hi Tegan," I said, "Is Kim not joining us this evening?"

"She's still asleep in our cabin," said Tegan, "why don't you pop down and wake her up?" I couldn't believe my luck.

"Well yes, if you would like me to," I said in a casual manner.

"The room number is number 302, just down the first flight of stairs," said Tegan. "Ask her if she wants to go to the disco tonight, maybe you can join us?" Kim's mum was pressing all the right buttons as far as I was concerned; maybe she wanted me to date her daughter.

"I would love to join you both," I said, "I will go and see if she's awake." Down the stairs I went until I found her room, a slight tap on the door with no answer meant it was time for plan B. I entered the unlocked door; I can still remember now how I entered the room to find her lying on the top bunk fully clothed. She looked like an Angel that had descended from heaven. Disturbing her was the last thing on my mind, I was just so happy to be standing in the room next to her.

I do believe that she must have been feeling my presence in the room as she started to stir. "Kim," I said gently nudging her shoulder, "time to wake up, your mum asked me to ask you if you would like to come to the disco tonight?" Still half asleep, Kim sat up in her bed.

"Yes, that would be nice," she said, "I shall be up shortly, I just need to have a wash and wake up first." I believe that this was the signal for me to leave the room. I made my way back to where her mum was and explained what Kim had said.

Later on that evening her mood had changed, I felt I was getting the cold shoulder from Kim; we were all sat together at the disco when Kim decided to sit next to some other older men. My thoughts were that of, she was either trying to avoid me or, she just fancied older men, either way it hurt. As the evening went on it was quite obvious to me that she was content with the situation. I decided it was time for me to say my goodbyes to her mother, almost like I was spitting my dummy out; finding somewhere to sleep was now my main priority as I made my way to the lounge area.

The next morning and only about an hour before arriving in Hamburg breakfast was being served in the dining area, I could see Kim and her mother tucking into their food, enjoying their last few moments before disembarking. I sat on my own some ten metres or so away and occasionally I would peep across despondently to where they were sitting. I was burning up inside. I really wanted to talk to Kim maybe for one last time; unfortunately due to my stubborn ways there was no way that I could ever give in. As I glanced over one more time I must have caught the eye of Tegan.

"Paul, come and join us," she said. It felt more like a cry for pity, not that they really wanted me there; however, I decided because Tegan had made the first move it would be rude of me not to join them, even though I couldn't wait. I made my way over to their table and took a seat.

"Why are you sitting by yourself, Paul?" said Tegan with a surprised look on her face.

"Without being too blunt, I just thought I would allow you to have breakfast on your own, I just felt after the disco last night that our short, but wonderful friendship was nearing its end."

"I'm not sure what you mean," said Tegan. I could see Kim who at this point had not said so much as a single word and also looking a little sheepish as I continued with what I had to say.

"I just felt there was a slight awkwardness between us last night, I felt that Kim was trying to tell me that she wanted her own space back, that she wanted me to go and haunt someone else." What I said certainly didn't fall on deaf ears.

"I'm so sorry, Paul," said Kim, feeling that she had been put on the spot.

"I was just trying to enjoy myself, I had no idea that you felt like I had abandoned you."

"No worries, I said," still feeling grouchy. "It's probably just me; I suppose I had taken a liking to you and then seeing it being all taken away in the matter of a few minutes made me feel rejected." Kim was now the one doing all the talking instead of her mum, I felt we were closer now than at any time of the journey, it was just so sad that it was coming to an end. As the ship was doing its final manoeuvre before docking, I handed over a photo of myself to Kim as we stood on the deck.

"Thank you," she said with a smile on her face.

"My address of the barracks is on the back, if at any time you would ever like to write to me then please do, it would be lovely to keep in touch."

"Mum," said Kim, "have you got a photo of me in your handbag, one that I can give to Paul?" Within seconds I was handed a beautiful photo of Kim, a close up of her face against a black background; her mum wrote her address on the back and said, "It would be nice to keep in touch Paul, we have enjoyed your company." All that said, it would have still been nice to have heard it from Kim and not her mum. It was now time to say our goodbyes and lucky for me, I did get a warm embrace from Kim and her mum before we exited the ship.

I was so gutted, at the same time I felt heaven blessed that I had met a girl to die for; it was back to the Army now for me. Life seems so unfair at times, Kim was off enjoying her vacation and I was off to Northern Ireland. How could I have possibly known, that in a couple of month's time, I would be going through this all over again on the streets of Londonderry.

CHAPTER SIXTY
NORTHERN IRELAND TRAINING

Back at the barracks all the guns had been cleaned, greased up, and put away in the hangars until after our forthcoming tour. No more Gun Park and no more exercises, it was going to be three months of preparing ourselves for what lay ahead. I was keyed up and looking forward to the training, it's one of those exhilarating moments in your Army career, one of those moments that you look forward to in a kind of strange way that makes you realise why you joined. The weather was somewhere around 30 degrees (cracking the flags) so short sleeve order was in force; rolled up combat sleeves and light-weight trousers would be the dress for the biggest part of the three-month training schedule.

We were split into several eight man sections with a Sergeant or a full Bombardier taking charge of each section, then we would be split up once more into a small four man patrol that was called a brick; two four man bricks made up the eight man section.

The first part of our training was foot patrols around the camp, well at least for the first two weeks to be precise; the two bricks would patrol at the same time, sometimes on different streets, but always within striking distance of each other. Radio communications that were normally carried by the Brick Commander were how we kept in touch with each other. My position in the brick was tail end Charlie, a position that I would take up on a regular basis. The job of the tail end Charlie was to walk backwards for about a ten second interval, then turn around and face forward again, and at the time same time, still being aware of your surroundings; walking backwards into a lamp post is the last thing you wanted. Looking professional was one thing, resembling a prat was another.

After we had managed to become skilled in how to patrol it was time to gain knowledge of how to master mobile patrols. This was a lot more fun, it was the Army's version of hot pursuit; with four men in each of two Land Rovers we would speed down the roads and then come to a sudden halt, thus blocking the road off to take up a mobile snap VCP (Vehicle Checkpoint). This sort of unexpected snap VCP would often catch any form of terrorist off their guard, as opposed to a fixed VCP that could be avoided. From my point of view the first month was so exhilarating with all that was going on that I almost forgot it would soon be my eighteenth birthday as September dawned. Training was becoming even more electrifying as I was chosen to be part of the search team, called upon to do house searches when needed; it meant that at times I would be taken from my section and be replaced by someone else from another section whilst I carried out a search: I was being trained in the use of explosives, safety fuse, detonating cord and the effects of pressure pads, trip wires, mercury tilt devices and also familiarising myself with certain equipment, some that was very similar to metal detectors.

Time was moving on quickly and our departing date was getting ever closer; however, I still had my birthday to celebrate. Unfortunately, money was in short supply and with not many of the lads having any knowledge about my birthday, I spent it just laying on my bed writing some letters and generally just having a lazy day; all it meant to me and most importantly to the Army, was that I was now old enough to go into conflict. The training was now becoming more intense as we were preparing for a two-week exercise in Sennelager which was about a two hour drive away. This is where the main bulk of Northern Ireland training would take place with highly sophisticated trained staff.

The facilities were second to none: we had two manmade small towns with housing estates. One of them was built using a mixture of corrugated iron and brick, this was known as tin city, and then more recently a more conventional fabricated type larger looking housing estate, this was more suitable for riots and car chases as opposed to tin city that was more urban with lots of hidden surprises. There were electronic explosions.' Irish music that could be heard being played in a make-believe pub with silhouettes of people in the lit-up window of the bar area, moving around on a kind of turntable; a car running on rails in the middle of the road to bear a resemblance of a moving vehicle was also something that caught my eye. How could you not be excited with all these new toys? We had to remember though that one day all this training could save your life or someone else's life that was your duty to protect, this was really serious stuff; being reminded by the well trained staff in a stern voice occasionally was necessary just to keep us on our toes . *Fine by me,* I was thinking.

On arrival and lined up on parade at the makeshift static camp, we were told of who would be in who's section. Stood next to Don and Dave Turner the list was read out: there were smiles, groans and a few *oh my giddy aunt's*.

"I've got him in my section," could be heard from within the ranks. Me, well I wasn't too concerned: Don, Dave, Steve Schofield and maybe a few others that I'd become more acquainted with would have done nicely, maybe Sergeant Douglas as the Section Commander would be nice, didn't think I was asking for much. After a few sections had been named and not too many names left to be called, my name was finally called out. "Section eight, Section Leader will be Bombardier Dodd's and L/Bombardier Naylor will be his second in command," a few more unfamiliar names were being thrown about until I heard my name called, "Gunner Wolfendale," that was it, I was in section eight. Once everybody had been allocated a section it was time to be introduced to the rest of your men.

The only ones that I was familiar with from the section was L/Bombardier Nobby Naylor, our cover number on our gun, oh, and my mate Dave Turner; I was a little disappointed to say the least that there weren't more of my mates, but having Dave in the section made me feel better. There were quite a few lads from other regiments that had volunteered to see some action, AAC (Army Air Corps'), REME (Royal Electrical Mechanical Engineers), RCT (Royal Corps' of Transport), oh yes, and a guy called Wilson, he was a gunner that resembled an officer, he walked with a stiff upper lip and talked over the rim of his glasses, his nick name was Major Wilson.

The training was unrelenting at times as we were put through our paces on a daily basis; mentally fit as well as physically fit was how we needed to be. After a few days of fitness and firing our weapons it was now the turn of our section to enter tin city. We were given a brief by the DS (directing staff) before we were allowed to enter onto the streets; sat down in the so called operational room, the DS began his brief.

"Tin city is a man made town to resemble how it will be in Northern Ireland, this is where all your training will be put to the test," said the DS. "Your patrolling will be filmed and then when you come back for your debrief I will replay the footage of how you performed."

"Bloody hell," I said to Dave, feeling anxious. Before entering we were given a flak jacket, an item that I was unfamiliar with; basically it is a bullet-proof vest that can save your life from a low velocity bullet, something like a 9mm pistol.

I was in the first brick with Bombardier Pete Dodds and my mate Dave. As we entered onto the first street through a side door it felt like we were entering into the Coliseum, live or die sprang to mind. I felt all alone at times as I patrolled the street, it was terrifying at best. "Wolfendale, don't forget to keep turning around," said Pete, reminding me of the role I had to play.

"No problem," I said at the moment I was just about to turn around.

"Dave," I said, "don't forget, about every five seconds we will alternate being tail end Charlie."

"Fine by me," said Dave, scanning all around him. I could hear the music from the make shift pub, it sounded like an Irish band were playing the Wild Rover; just when we thought we were safe, a car on the rail that we were half expecting flew down the road.

"Take cover," said Pete in a sharpened voice. We all looked for some protection to hide behind and make ourselves a smaller target.

"Wolfendale, Turner, keep an eye over there," said Pete, "thought I saw something in the top window of the shop." Before we could get our bearings, the dustbin that Dave was kneeling behind blew up, a small explosive device was placed under the bin to represent a real bomb; the dustbin lid was blown off into the air causing panic within the brick. The DS who was now walking close behind us and taking control of the situation decided that wasn't enough.

"You have a casualty," he said, looking at Dave, "this man has had his leg blown off."

"Nobby, get your men over here now, we have a casualty to deal with," said Pete hurriedly. We were now working as a section and not as a brick; one brick would be used as a cordon for protecting cover and the other brick would deal with the walking wounded. We spent about ten minutes with the incident before the DS was satisfied that our performance merited us being able to return to base.

"OK, you can return back to base now, the same way you came in," said the DS, "don't switch off until you're back behind closed doors."

After unloading our weapons it was time for the unavoidable debrief; something I wasn't looking forward to.

"Take a seat," said the DS as he switched on the TV screen, we were all still breathing quite heavily after our escapade however, I was pretty sure I would be breathing even more heavily watching a re-run of our so called mission; with cameras placed everywhere, hiding places were at a premium.

"Who's the guy behind the bin?" said the DS, freeze-framing the clip.

"Me, Sir," said Dave, putting his hand up.

"How's your hearing?" said the DS.

"Still ringing," said Dave. "Just need to get my leg back."

"No time for joking," said the DS. "Never hide behind something that can be moved, never hide behind something that a bomb can be placed into. I know at times it can be difficult to find somewhere that's safe, I understand that, however, where do you think would have been a better place to hide?"

"Around the corner away from where the bin was," said Dave, now being more serious.

"Correct," said the DS, "out of the direction from where the danger was coming from, lesson learnt?"

"Yes Sir," said Dave.

The footage continued as we sat there waiting for the next clanger we made. I could see no problem with the next clip as it rolled on, all I could see were Bombardier Dodd, Major Wilson, Dave and myself patrolling the streets in the normal way that we have been trained to do; how wrong we were.

The TV was suddenly paused once again. "What's wrong now?" I said to Dave with a surprised look on my face.

"No idea, Wolfie," said Dave, "maybe we were too close to the guys in front."

"Good call," I whispered to Dave, "can't think of anything else it could be."

"OK, can anyone tell me why I have stopped the clip at this point?" said the DS. Even the section commander was struggling to find an answer to the question as he examined the clip; there was a pause of silence for a few seconds until the DS continued.

"The guys at the back, the one on the right, identify yourself to me please." It was me.

"What the 'Eck have I done?" I said to Dave, looking confused.

"Not sure," said Dave, smiling under his breath. "I bet you a pound to a penny that you have done something wrong."

"Me Sir, it's me at the back," I said, feeling nervous.

"Take a look how he's ballooning from side to side making himself a more difficult target for a sniper to take aim, that's what we are looking for, well done, nice to see you have been listening," said the DS. I was gobsmacked to say the least, I'd never told anyone until now, but actually, that was the way I walked, never even realised I was doing it; praise from Bombardier Dodd and L/Bombardier Naylor meant I was now flavour of the day. How long could I keep this run going? Was the next question I asked myself, two days was the answer.

After a couple of days of being transferred away from my section and being attached to my search party role, it was the turn of section eight to take on what I would call a stroll through the forest. Lined up at the edge of the trees with your SLR and a magazine of twenty rounds, you would enter the woods looking for electronic pop up targets that would be hidden behind the trees and in the undergrowth.

It was the return of my favourite D Sub Sergeant Massey who would be behind me trying to give constructive criticism as I walked the path of terror, along with one of the DSs; his job was to arouse the target from its hidden place electronically with a remote control gadget.

"OK Wolfendale, with a magazine of twenty rounds, load," was the order from Sergeant Massey. To be honest he sounded quite compassionate for a pleasant refreshing change. Thinking about it now, the fact that I was the one with the loaded SLR could have definitely had something to do with it, either way it felt comforting.

"Keep a look out," was the soft voice of Sergeant Massey in my ear, and in an even louder voice, "keep your weapon pointing down the range at all times as there may be a target popping up soon." Creeping tentatively through the enclosed wooded area my first target popped up.

"One o'clock," shouted Sergeant Massey still trying to help me. I did appreciate his help, but felt I wanted to be left to my own devices; down on one knee and my rifle firmly tucked into my shoulder the target was now out of commission with a well aimed shot.

About five minutes into my mission I was feeling good, every target now was well and truly incapacitated; Sergeant Massey was now doing what I hoped he would do, taking more of a back seat, allowing me to get on with my task in hand. I was waiting eagerly for my next target to pop up as I was scanning the surrounds when suddenly, there it was; the target introduced itself into my eye line from the undergrowth with some force. I was now down on one knee with my rifle at the ready… *take aim* I said to myself… *fire*, feeling proud of my super quick reaction and waiting for some well deserved praise, my thoughts were stunned into silence. It had just occurred to me what I had done; I had shot a passive target, a target that I had been warned about; a target of a man that was holding a letter in his hand. *Holy shit*, I was thinking, *what have I done?*

"Wolfendale," was the cry I heard from over my shoulder, "you've just killed the fucking postman you idiot."

"Sorry," I said, trying to sound very apologetic.

"Cookhouse duty for you tonight, report to the cookhouse after tea," said Sergeant Massey in an angry voice. Here I am me thinking that Mr nice guy Sergeant Massey had turned over a new leaf, ouch, well that taught me a lesson not to get complacent.

After I had completed the course and unloaded my weapon I tried in vain to plead my case. "Sergeant Massey," I said with a fed-up tone to my voice.

"Yes, what is it," was the sharp reply.

"I shot one postman, just one, and at least ten terrorists, surly that doesn't warrant a cookhouse fatigue," I said, hoping he would see my side of the story. Sergeant Massey couldn't hide his amusement; trying not to laugh he turned to me in a kind of Mexican standoff and yelled,

"One postman, one fucking postman… you can't go around shooting postmen Wolfendale, if that was in Northern Ireland you would be serving life in prison for murder."

"Well if you put it like that, then yeah, I suppose you're right, good point well made Sergeant," I said sheepishly.

"Fucking right good point well made, Wolfendale," he said, "think yourself lucky I've only given you one cookhouse duty."

The training continued at some pace for the next few days, riots of plenty in the new made up village that at times were frightening; we would be confronted with hundreds of so called peace or civil right marchers (Civ Pop) that got out of control. Having well aimed bricks and any form of missile thrown at you that was meant to harm, or at worst kill, wasn't my kind of fun: Baton guns, shields, CS gas, cosh, skid lids (helmets), you name it we had it as we faced the ever increasing aggressive crowd. It was a welcoming feeling to be heading back to Fallingbostal after an enterprising two weeks; everybody learned so much in such a short time, I just hoped we could put it all into action when patrolling the streets of Northern Ireland.

Back in camp it was nice to receive some welcome mail; a birthday card and letter from my parents awaited me; although it was wonderful to hear from them I was secretly hoping there might be a letter from America, from

Kim, but it wasn't to be. Maybe she was still on vacation, maybe she had not got round yet to writing to me, or maybe she just felt that I wasn't worth writing to, anyway, no matter how disappointed I was, I still had my own life to lead.

Later on in the evening I was given a right shock as I lay on my bed listening to some music, when out of the corner of my eye I saw my buddy from The Junior Leaders Regiment, Pete Rigby, entering my room.

"Bloody hell, Pete," I said jumping off my pit, "when did you arrive?"

"About two weeks ago, Paul," said Pete, smiling for England. "I arrived early September, Parry's here as well, he's been attached to 49 Battery just up from our block."

"Wow, brilliant," I said. I felt like a kid with a new toy once again, we had so much to chat about as we spent half of the night just reminiscing about the great times we had in training.

"Must go and see Steve tomorrow," I said, "can't wait to see him again, missing his sense of humour."

"He hasn't changed at all," said Pete, "still the same, cracking jokes."

"So glad to see you again, Pete," I said repeatedly as we parted company and went to bed. The next day I managed to locate Steve in the 49 Battery bar, where else would I find one of my best mates? My life was becoming more tolerable now; having Riggers and Steve around was something I had been missing for the last three months; it was making me feel like a dog with two tails.

It was now early October and the move to Londonderry was imminent; we were being shown mug shots of known terrorists that we had to memorise and recognise if we ever come face to face with one of them. We were also shown some aerial photos of the city centre, the area where we would be stationed and our two main camps that we would be occupying: Bridge Camp, on the edge of the River Foyle by the Craigavon Bridge, and Hawkin Street, where the main 18 Battery Head Quarters was run from. These were the ones that we needed to know about first and foremost.

Ebrington Barracks where a lot of the WRACs (Women's Royal Army Corps') were based just across the bridge was also one of the barracks that we would occasionally visit. Everything was now falling into place in respect that our fitness levels were at a premium, physically and mentally, along with being highly trained in close quarter combat in how to cope with anything that was thrown in our direction. Finally we would become more familiar with all the republican paramilitary groups, there were so many to remember, but remember I did: IRA (Irish Republican Army) PIRA (Provisional Irish Republican Army) OIRA (Official Irish Republican Army) INLA (Irish National Liberation Army). And then there were the loyalist paramilitary groups, the ones that were apparently on our side. UVF (Ulster Volunteer Force), UDA (Ulster Defence Association), UFF (Ulster Freedom Fighters).

We were also graced with the company of the RUC (Royal Ulster Constabulary) and the UDR (Ulster Defence Regiment) who we would work closely with.

With now just days to go, the advance party had already set sail (so to speak). This party included the ones that would be working in the operational room, the ones that would be undertaking intelligence duties, also, one or two that would be working undercover; they would need to get a feel for the place before we arrived, then pass on all of that information to the troops when we stepped onto Irish soil. As soon as you arrived you would need to hit the ground running, without the intelligence it would make life a lot more difficult.

CHAPTER SIXTY-ONE
STEPPING FOOT ON IRISH SOIL

November 5th dawned and apart from the obvious Guy Fawkes celebrations that would be going on, it was D-Day (Delivery Day) for the regiment.

"Don, are you awake?" I said across the darkened room.

"Yeah, I am now thanks to your early morning call," replied Don, huffing and puffing.

"Big day today," I said. "I'm going to get up, can't sleep any longer; think I will go and get washed and dressed."

"What time is it?" said Don.

"Just let me switch the light on so I can see my clock," I said, before Don could say *don't you fucking dare,* the light went on.

"Bloody hell Paul, almost blinded me," said Don, rubbing his eyes, "may as well get up now I'm awake."

"By the way, it's six o'clock," I said. Don paraded his upper-class underwear off as we both made our way to the washrooms for what would be the last time for four months, then within a couple of hours we were would be formed up outside in three ranks waiting for all the senior ranks to arrive. The time arrived.

I could sense the way everybody was looking at each other what they were really thinking, *this might be the last time we set eyes on each other* was written in their faces. We were told to stand easy and relax, which is far from the normal 0800hrs parade that we were use to.

"Listen in," said Sergeant Massey, "I know some of you can't wait for the tour to start, but there are a few final things to go through before we leave in a couple of hour's time. I have here in this box your dog tags (identity tags) for you to wear; section commanders come and get your tags for your section." We all now split ranks and got ourselves into our sections; stood all gathered together our section commanders called us over to give us our dog tags.

L/Bombardier Naylor presented me with my 'you must wear at all times' dog tags. "Here you are Wolfendale," said Nobby Naylor with a nasty grin on his face. "Make sure you put them around your neck and keep them there at all times, do you know why we have them?" he continued to say in a more serious way.

"Not totally sure," I said. "Is it just in case I get killed?"

"Yes it is," said Nobby with his infinite wisdom, "and that's not going to happen is it Wolfendale?"

"No Bombardier," I said, feeling more scared of what would happen if I disobeyed his order.

"There are three discs attached to the cord," said Nobby, staring in my face. "One of them stays with your body, one of them goes on your coffin and the other one stays with the Army." *Gordon Bennet,* I was thinking, it was a scary thing to hear, however it certainly got the message across. With my ID discs now firmly around my neck it was time to be given our yellow (ROE) rules of engagement cards. It was a small card that could be fitted quite easily into your top pocket of your combat jacket. It contained all the information you needed to know about when or when not it was permissible to open fire on your enemy. Even though we were at war we weren't above the law, although even today, there are still some paramilitary groups who think in a different way.

We now had about an hour before we were leaving on Army buses so Steve (Schoie) and I decided to take a trip to the Families NAAFI for some duty free products and to say goodbye to some of the staff.

"Hi Paul, hi Steve," said Chloe who was working hard behind the till, "what time are you leaving?"

" In about half an hour," said Steve in his quiet voice.

"Listen carefully, both of you," said Chloe, "make sure you look after yourselves and return safe, do you hear me? We will be all thinking about you."

"Of course we will Chloe," we said, "you just look after the NAAFI until we get back." Chloe just smiled as only Chloe could as she waved her goodbyes to Steve and I, making our way back to the block, Steve asked whether or not I was feeling scared. "No, not really," I said, "just want to get out there and onto the streets, I'll let you know then."

"Well I won't be joining you on the streets until the 18th," said Steve, that's when I'll be eighteen and eligible to join you, guess I'll just be doing other stuff until then."

It was now only minutes from departing and I could hear the coaches arriving to take us to RAF Wildenrath for our flight. There were family members from all of the married pads arriving to say their goodbyes to their loved ones. It was nice of them to come and see us off, it felt like they were there to wish every one of us a safe return which I am sure was true as we were now gathering outside on the road. I managed to say a farewell to Riggers before checking that I had my bible with me that I was given when I enlisted some eighteen months ago. "See you when you arrive, Pete," I said.

"Take care Paul, be thinking about you buddy," said Pete with a hug that I had only felt before from my parents. "Keep your head down, mate."

"Will do Pete, I will see you in January when you come of age;" I turned and walked away to join the rest of the lads. There was one final good luck speech from the padre before we got onto the coaches that had him wishing us all a safe return; feeling proud as only one can when you're going into conflict we took to our seats. I was wondering if there had been a crystal ball present, how many of us would have taken that final step onto the bus.

The fine white coaches started up their engines and slowly moved forward allowing all of those that had come to see us off time to give us their final goodbyes. It looked like they were rejoicing among their saddened hearts and hidden tears, either way it was welcomed by one and all; I am not sure how much the wives family members and loved ones understood about the part they play in a soldier's life, well without their understanding and support, we would have no Army. We were waving and returning the compliment tenfold; even though my waving was mainly directed at Pete before we were finally out of sight and on our way.

Within an hour of the coach journey you could feel the silence creeping in as all the chit chat was now a thing of the past; everyone was now getting into their fighting mode.

"OK lads," said Sammy, "the airport is about five minutes away, get your kit together and then follow me when we get there."

"Well, this is it," I said to Steve, who was sitting next to me.

"Wish I was going straight onto the streets," said Steve, "I suppose I will just have to be patient and wait."

"Pretty sure they will find you something interesting to do when we arrive," I said, trying to gee-up his spirits.

As the coach rolled up we were told to disembark and go through the normal procedures for departing on the military aircraft, saying that, it was very much just like a normal commercial airliner, similar to the one I flew over on. Time seemed to run away with itself as we drank some refreshments in the departure lounge.

"OK lads," was the cry from Sammy Douglas who seemed to be in charge of getting us across the Irish Sea, "get all your belongings and make your way over to the departure gate." It must have been a sight for all the personnel working at the airport seeing all of us making our way across the apron to the aircraft: combat jacket, lightweight trousers and bulled Army boots, not a sight you would see every day at an airport. Once on the plane we settled down for the short two hour flight that was only minutes away. I was hoping to get a seat next to Steve again, but because of the way we boarded the aircraft, it just didn't work out that way.

"Wolfendale," was the cry I heard as I walked down the aisle of the plane, "get sat down there," said Sergeant Massey pointing to where one of the older members of the battery was sitting.

"Can I sit with Gunner Schofield, Sarge?" I asked, hoping he might say yes.

"No you puff, now get sat down there now," was his instant reply. There would be no point in arguing; one thing I have taken on board since joining 18 Battery is, don't answer back to Sergeant Massey.

I got to know a little about the guy next to me in the two hours we were in the air on our way to Aldergrove airport Northwest of Belfast. Cyril McDonald was his name and compared to me he was a veteran with years and years of experience behind him; he was an inspiration to chat to and at times it felt like he was taking me under his wing.

"You'll be fine," he said in a comforting voice, "after the first few days you'll soon get settled in."

"Thanks for that, Cyril," I said in a way that I really meant what I had said.

"Just call me Daddy Mac," he said, "that's what everybody else calls me; I'm due to leave the Army shortly after the tour."

"Wow," I said, "you're leaving and my career has just begun, well nice to have met you Daddy Mac, I will think about you when you're enjoying life away from the Army and I'm on Guard duty."

"I'm sure you will Paul," said Cyril. Just then the announcement came over the PA system to inform us to fasten our seat belts ready for landing. I was trying to peer out of the window as we got closer to the ground; not sure what I was expecting to see, it was just one of those inquisitive moments we get from time to time.

As the wheels of the aircraft touched down on Irish soil we were all now getting mentally prepared for what lay ahead. Even when we exited the aircraft we seemed to be moving at a pace that would make it difficult for a sniper to take one of us out. I am pretty sure we were being escorted in the right direction; however, it felt nerve-jangling as we made our way to the two coaches that were awaiting our arrival to take us to our base in Londonderry.

It was about 1500hrs, mid-afternoon, when we started the two hour long journey under escort to Londonderry, the weather was mild for this time of the year although it was starting to get dark in the overcast skies. With it being my first time in Northern Ireland I spent nearly all of my time peering through the window taking in the scenery and admiring the beautiful countryside that I was least expecting. Signs like Magilligan Prison caught my eye; it all seemed so peaceful as we travelled along the country roads and the occasional open major ones; *where was the war being fought* crossed my mind. It was now around 1700hrs and getting very dark. As we got within a few miles of Londonderry reality started to kick in; the familiar sound of Army Land Rovers could be heard with soldiers pointing their weapons out of the back of the vehicle. I could see the huge double tier Craigavon Bridge spanning across a river of vast magnitude.

There was a vehicle checkpoint situated in the middle of the bridge, a bridge that must have stretched the best part of a hundred and fifty metres across the River Foyle, the river that flows out to the Irish Sea. I could see the city lights shining brightly over to my right where we would soon be patrolling. It looked like a city that never slept with the traffic flow now at its busiest; the closer we got the more nervous I became as we seemed to be eating up the road faster than I felt comfortable with.

As we crossed the lower tier of the bridge I noticed more Army checkpoints at both ends of the bridge that were manned by four soldiers wearing flak jackets. It was just like the training we had endured back in West Germany, except this time, there couldn't be any mistakes; one mistake out here could cost you or one of your mates their life.

The coach finally came out of the darkened bottom tier of the bridge and turned left towards Bridge camp. The camp was only a couple of hundred metres away on the left hand side with its huge corrugated gates awaiting our arrival; the guard would have been forewarned about our arrival, so it was no surprise when the gates opened with a loud clanging noise to reveal the habitable accommodation we would be using for the next four months. We were told to wait on the coach while the section commanders disembarked for a quick debrief with the advance party that had taken up residence some ten days ago. We could see the tension and urgency as we peered through the window of the bus at the congregation of senior ranks all tightly hugged in a small circle; some smiling faces and packed suitcases from the regiment that were now going home made the four month tour feel even further away.

With the debrief now over, I could see our section commander Bombardier Dodds making his way at some pace towards the coach; stepping onto the coach, Bombardier Dodds said in a raised voice, "Eight section, off the coach now, we are on PCPs." (Pedestrian checkpoint) It got the attention of everybody else on the coach as we got our belongings. We first got issued with our flak jacket before making our way to the make shift armoury to get our SLR complete with sling that you would fasten to your wrist to prevent your rifle getting snatched. It was then on to our live rounds… yes… live rounds; this would be the first time ever, apart from controlled firing ranges, that we would be let loose into a residential surround with life rounds.

"Wolfendale, Turner, Wilson, follow me," said Ragsy (Bombardier Dodd's nickname). We made our way to the loading bay to attach a magazine of fifteen rounds to our rifle. "With a magazine of fifteen rounds, load," was the order from Ragsy. "OK, are you ready? Wolfendale, Turner, tail end Charlie," said Ragsy, "Wilson up front with me."

"Dave, I'll take the left, you take the right," I said.

"Fine by me, Paul," said Dave. Before I had time to even think about being shot at the huge gates were open and we were on the streets making our way to our first PCP.

I must admit I was feeling on edge as I was trying to keep up with the demanding pace set by the section commander. As we made our way down the Foyle Road his enthusiasm appeared to be boundless as we turned sharp left into Wapping Lane with the pace increasing with every stride. I was shocked to see how steep it was even though it was only about one hundred metres in length; walking backwards up Wapping Lane was a challenge within itself. A few more right and left turns meant we were now at the end of the 'five minute walk if you run' journey. Ferryquay Street was our destination. It was one of several checkpoints located at the foot of the city wall that isolates the city centre.

The city wall reminded me of a fortress with the fact that there were only about four or five entry and exit points; checkpoints that were guarded by the

Army. I believe that 18 Battery manned them all but one that was manned by 94 Battery. The checkpoints were like big archways, the sort you would see at the entrance to a medieval castle, just wide enough to let traffic pass with two foot ways either side. The area that we were in was predominantly loyalist which meant we were with the good guys (so to speak), but becoming complacent could cost you your life; suspecting everyone, from a child to an OAP (old age pensioner) was paramount towards our safety.

As we arrived, we were told to take some form of cover and be alert for any activity that was taking place, this allowed Ragsy to take charge of the handover from the other regiment, it took no longer than about five minutes before the checkpoint was in our hands.

"Wolfie, take over duty from the guy over there," said Ragsy.

"OK," I said making my way over to the foot of the archway.

"Looks like you're heading back home," I said, "feeling envious."

"Yes, we fly back in the morning, can't wait," he said.

"Well made up for you," I said with a touch of irony in my voice.

"Be your turn soon, four months will soon fly by, take care of yourself and keep your head down, gunner," he said.

"Thanks, I will," I replied. We were now on our own trying to remember everything that we had been taught by the Directing Staff, I felt very uncomfortable and intrusive as I was put on searching bags and belongings duty.

"Can I look into your bag please madam?" I said to the first person who approached me among the ever increasing evening shoppers. Without so much as a word or smile she allowed me to sieve through her two carrier bags like she'd had this done a hundred times; expecting to find something of any interest was like trying to find a needle in a haystack as the lady continued on her merry way into the city centre.

Time was ebbing away quickly and before we all knew it, we had been on duty for three of the six hours we were sanctioned for, can't remember how many bags I must have searched in that period but it seemed a never ending task; one that was necessary.

"Wolfie, swap over with Wilson," said Bombardier Dodds, "keep an eye out for anything suspicious."

"Will do," I said, making my way over to the other side of the footpath. I was now on Guard duty again trying hard to focus on my task in hand, occasionally bringing my rifle up to aim position and scanning around the vicinity of the checkpoint.

"What's all that barbed wire for on top of the wall?" I said to Pete, trying to make sense of it all.

"It's to stop anyone getting onto the wall and walking along it," said Pete. "If anyone was allowed on the wall it would make us an easier target."

"OK, I see," I said in agreement with his answer. It was now getting close to the end of our shift and to be honest, we never switched off for a minute. I was feeling slightly more comfortable than I was at the beginning of the shift, but still feeling on edge; a split second lapse in concentration and you would be another statistic in this endless civil war.

It was now 2300hrs and the new stag could be seen making their way up Ferryquay Street towards our location. On arrival Bombardier Dodds handed over all of his notes that we had gathered together throughout our shift to the oncoming section commander, the whole takeover took no more than five minutes before we were galloping our way back to Bridge Camp for our debrief via a different route. It was very important to vary your route from time to time so as not to form a pattern and leave yourself an open target.

Back in Bridge Camp and after a short debrief we got our belongings and were shown where we would be sleeping. Bunk beds in a small hut were to be our accommodation for the coming months; within a few minutes the cookhouse became our next port of call with it being open 24hrs a day. A late meal was set aside for the likes of our shift and any other shifts that were just coming off stag duty. Egg banjos were on offer, something I had not heard about before until now, throughout the early hours of the morning some of the patrols were coming in off the streets feeling like a hot drink and a quick bite to eat; the duty chef would leave stacks of eggs and loaves of white bread by the hot plate for them to top up their tank.

"Where does the name egg banjo come from?" I said to L/Bombardier Nobby Naylor, who was sitting opposite me.

"Bloody hell Wolfie, don't you know anything?" he said with a sarcastic grin on his face, I was tempted to say *I am not an old bugger like you,* but thought better of it if I knew what was good for me.

"Look over there where they're making them and all will be revealed," said Nobby, turning my head forcefully in that direction. We both waited with great anticipation as the first of many soldiers slapped their egg between their two slices of buttered bread. "Watch closely now," said Nobby, "watch what happens." No sooner had the first soldier bit ferociously into his egg sandwich, the yolk dripped out and onto his combat jacket like a tap that was leaking.

"For fuck's sake," said the soldier, as the yolk continued to meander its way onto the buttons of his combat jacket.

I continued to try to make sense of what was to happen next when the penny dropped, the soldier pulled out his hankie and started to wipe the yolk away from the front of his jacket at speed, his hand was moving up and down like a fiddler's elbow giving the impression that he was playing the banjo.

"Well, blown me down with a feather," I said to Nobby, still in hysterics, "you learn something new every day." It was now time for some shut eye as we were on duty again at 0700hrs on Butcher's Gate PCP just up the way from Ferryquay Street; it was six hours on and six hours off so getting to bed was a must.

The next day section eight that were all billeted together, were woken up by one of the early morning patrols, it felt like the Junior Leaders all over again without the industrial language being thrown around; 0700hrs until 1300hrs was our shift which meant we would need to relieve the section that was already manning the gate around 0645hrs. We were out of bed sharpest, ready for the Ragsy force march; arriving late at your checkpoint was not an option. Once again we were taking a slightly different route, a route that would take us up Hawkin Street, the street where we had our main HQ. It was still semi-dark so it was a pleasant relief to see the light of day dawning; my first sight of this wonderful city was upon me. The checkpoint named Butcher's Gate looked over the notorious Bogside (gateway to hell) where so many battles had been fought; we were now looking at the strong republican area, an area that had me quaking in my boots.

As I peered through the small gateway that was for pedestrians only, I could see gravity of plenty along with the infamous Rossville Flats standing out like a sore thumb. 'You Are Now Entering Free Derry' could been seen in huge black letters on the side of a building that had been painted white; a mural of petrol bomber wearing a gas mask was also a prominent feature. All of this was a fearful reminder of Bloody Sunday in January 1972, when what was meant to be a demonstration for civil rights became a real massacre; *will we ever know the full truth about the events that went on that day? Probably not,* I thought to myself.

For some reason I did feel more fretful on this checkpoint as if I was expecting trouble; the early morning rush of people going to work meant we all had to be on full alert.

"Wolfie, stop that man," I was told by Ragsy as he managed to slip through the net without being searched.

"Excuse me Sir, over here please, I need to search you," I said sternly but politely.

"Wolfie, I'll remember you," he said in his Northern Ireland accent.

"Arms up, legs apart and less of the Wolfie," I said, "only my close friends call me Wolfie and that doesn't include you." To be honest, he knew the format better than me and was ready for his every day early morning search.

"What the fuck do you hope to find," he said, shaking his head.

"Just doing my job, Sir," I said as I started to frisk him. "Just remember Sir, bad things happen if the good people like us stand around and do nothing."

"Why don't you get yourself a proper job, soldier, instead of pissing me off every morning?" I felt like telling him what I was really thinking but had to use my controlled aggression, biting my bottom lip was the theme for the day.

"OK, on your way Sir," I said as he just shook his head once more and left on his not so merry way.

Within the first hour I must have searched more men than I wish to care for without one of them so much as making me feel that I was doing a meaningful job, even the dogs that were running loose seemed to have an attitude towards the military; they say you can't teach an old dog new tricks, well these dogs were the exception to the rule.

As we continued with trying to keep the city a safe place to enter, an Army mobile unit arrived, two Land Rovers with two of our men in the back, it was Billy and Danny Dalzell with their Brick commander in the front. I was wondering what all the commotion was about until I saw a WRAC was joining us for the rest of the shift; she was a Red Cap (military police) whose role would be to search the women that we as men, were not allowed to search. It felt comforting to have a female on board and for some unknown reason, it made me feel so much closer to home. They say there is something about a woman in a uniform, well now I know why: stood there in her knee length grey skirt, white blouse, dark coloured jumper and flak jacket was bringing a smile to my face.

The six hours disappeared quickly without too much bother, although I was quite amazed at the things I was told to search: pushchairs, prams, trolleys, wheelchairs and anything else that might be used to hide a weapon or explosives. It wasn't uncommon for a weapon to be hidden under the blanket of a newly born infant that was being pushed along in a pram; in our battle against crime everybody had to be taken seriously. It was nice to see the oncoming shift thundering towards us just up the road knowing that it was our turn for a well earned rest, as for the Red Cap, she would be staying on a little longer until her duty was over; it would work out that the WRAC would be employed as and when needed on more of the notorious checkpoints. All seemed to be going well in the first week, however, that was soon to change.

CHAPTER SIXTY-TWO
SHOT IN THE FOUNTAIN

Back at Bridge Camp it was time for lunch and my first look around the place in daylight. The first thing that struck me was that the camp was built along the banks of the River Foyle that meant we would be pretty safe from that side, it provided the camp with its own protection making it difficult for a terrorist to escape without being compromised. There were a couple of red phone boxes that had a 10p or 2p slot, a call to Great Britain would cost 42p for three minutes so plenty of change was needed; to my surprise the phones weren't in great demand until there was a rumour going around that all you needed was a two pence coin to phone home. Taken aback by what I had heard I spoke to Brian Betty Davies about the rumour.

"All you need to do is phone the operator" he said "and then, tell the operator you would like to pay for a call to England, "42p" is what they would say; "If you would like to put your money in the slot now please I will connect you."

"Well how does that work?" I asked Brian, thinking his maths skills need some attention.

"You just put your 2p into the slot being careful not to let it drop into the machine and then pull it back out," replied Brian. "You will need to do it twenty one times and hey presto, she will connect you, just be careful you have a spare 2p Paul, just in case you let it drop."

I couldn't wait to try it out as I searched my trouser pockets for some change, it definitely worked, the only drawback, is that it would take you as long to put your 2p in the slot twenty one times than the three minutes you got to talk to your family; occasionally there would be some suspicion from the operator when she would ask, "Have you put 42p in, it is only registering 30p at my end?"

"Well, yes, I'm sure I have," I would say.

"Very well, I will connect you," she said reluctantly. After the three minutes it was a case of doing it all again. "Would you like to pay for another three minutes Sir?"

"Yes please," I answered… two, four, six, eight, ten, and so on. I spoke to my brother asking him to give my love to my mum and dad when he sees them; just wished they had a phone at home. Up from the phone box was a small shed that housed a couple of slot machines, and a kitchen that was run by some people call the Mojo's; they made the most amazing cheese burgers that were always welcome as a snack between stag duties. Fizzy pop and other goodies could also be purchased from the store. It provided a bit of recreation time that was needed to recharge your batteries and to stop you going crazy.

Over the next two weeks we did much the same sort of things including the Sanger VCP on the Craigavon Bridge that we passed on the way into Londonderry. Today was the day when our section would be manning the checkpoint. Even on a good day it was cold; being fully exposed to all the elements and being in the open meant that you could become an easy target for a terrorist. After searching several vehicles I noticed our BQ (Battery Quartermaster) approaching on foot working undercover trying to obtain as much information as he could on his travels, it would be quite obvious to us all that he would be was carrying a 9mm pistol; we treated him like anyone else entering the city so as not to compromise his cover.

"Bombardier," I said in a quiet voice, "I think we have one of our own approaching."

"Just treat him like you would treat anyone," he said, "try not to draw attention to the situation." He soon approached.

"Excuse me Sir; would you mind putting your arms up for me, I need to frisk you." Trying not to show his English accent and not wanting to stand out he lifted his arms up and stared me out as if to say, *you know you I am, don't you?* I could see Dave pointing his SLR towards him from the slit of the Sanger as I started to search him; I started by searching is upper body; it was at this point that I felt the gun he was carrying, to be honest, it was quite daunting for me knowing that my hand was feeling a pistol. For some reason, and I'm not sure why, I couldn't resist a little joke although he wasn't to find it funny.

"What's this, Sir?" I said, trying to keep a straight face.

"Er, it's just a cassette player," said the BQ, now feeling slightly nervous with his eyes almost leaving their eye sockets.

"Cassette player, can I take a look please Sir, Just to be on the safe side." His face was a picture; I could see his jaw drop as he was trying to think of what to say next.

"It's broken, if I get it out it might fall into bits," he said.

"Then why are you carrying it then?" I said, still pushing the boundaries.

"Just taking it to be mended," he said quick as a flash, "please don't make me take it out," he said, almost begging. I paused for a few seconds at the same time giving him my 'I'm not too sure' look, before putting him out of his misery.

"OK Sir, you have caught me on a good day, on your way." As I watched him continuing on his merry way I saw him looking over his shoulder with a scowl; knowing that, I knew I would be in for some grief when I arrived back at Bridge Camp after my shift. At the end of the day I was just doing my job, no matter which way you look at it.

Back in the barracks I saw Schoie for the first time since arriving; he was now joining us on the streets after his eighteenth birthday; unfortunately, the reunion didn't last too long as our section were now spending a week at Hawkin Street: camp guard, mobiles and stand by duties. The stand by duties would speak for themselves in respect that you would normally spend a full six hours fully dressed and ready to go at a minute's notice.

It was early evening and we were all just watching a bit of TV chatting away, waiting for something to happen, in fact we were getting so bored that we would play a game. Play School came on the TV which excited us all; we would guess which window they would be going through to tell a story, I think there were four to choose from, you would hear a huge cheer if you guessed correctly. Seconds later the call that we were all dreading could be heard:

"Standby outside now, get a move on." You could probably imagine how quick we got ourselves into gear. It was the full eight man section that went out to the incident that we were yet to find out about. "Get into the Land Rovers," was the cry from Bombardier Dodds, "hurry up; quick get in, there has been a shooting in the loyalist fountain area."

"Bloody hell," I said to Dave as we flew out of the gates trying to make sure we didn't fall out of the back; screaming up the roads like we were on a police chase had my adrenalin maxed out. I was feeling terrified to say the least. My mind was a mixture of thoughts as we made our way the short distance to the where the incident was. The Land Rovers pulled up on the Small Fountain housing estate close to where the shooting took place; with only the street lights shining it was becoming easy to get disorientated, I was at a complete loss to what was going on.

"Wolfendale, Turner; get yourselves over to the other side of the street and keep a look out for anyone that looks suspicious." Once there, I just crouched down feeling petrified that the gunman might still be at large and, that I may be next to be faced with the wrong end of his gun. The chances of the perpetrator still being around were a slim I know, but my head was telling me different.

I must have been there for the best part of fifteen minutes before I saw the body of the person who had been shot. He was being taken away on a stretcher covered in a bold stained white sheet. The blood that I saw on the sheet was making me feel sick beyond reason. All the training I had could have never prepared me for this sort of incident; squatting down on the corner of a street and feeling like a wimp had me wanting to get back to Hawkin Street pronto.

"Wolfendale, Turner, you can stand down," said Nobby, "get back into the Land Rovers; I will join you in a second." I was so relieved to be getting back into the Land Rover along with Dave.

"OK let's go," said Nobby to the driver. "Listen in, you pair in the back," said Nobby, referring to Dave and I. "A UDR (Ulster Defence Regiment) man has just been shot with several rounds to his head; waiting for him to come home to his wife and family two gunmen attacked him outside his house. They were sitting on a bench minding their own business when he walked past them, the next thing he knew, they got up and walked behind him, when he turned around, one of them put a pistol to his head... the rest is history."

"I guess he must have taken the same route home every night and formed a pattern to the route he took to get home," I said to Dave. "I suppose that all it takes, for someone out there to keep an eye on you for a few days and then they have you tagged; it would have probably just been some young kids that he had never given much thought too."

Back in Hawkin Street camp the news had escalated around the troops that a UDR man had been shot dead; apparently he was only 22 years old and had all his life ahead of him. Everybody now was put on high alert, even the ones that were on rest period, the ones who had taken our role and were now on stand-by; well, at least until we had been debriefed. It was only then that they were allowed to stand down and go back to their position of rest. I suppose our section was the main topic of conversation for the rest of the night.

"What was it like?"

"How did you feel when you were out there?"

"What actually happened?"

All these questions needed answering by the section including myself. The next day after a good night's sleep it was back to Bridge Camp but not before the BQ saw me and wanted a quiet word in my ear. "Don't you ever do that to me again Wolfendale," he snarled, "What do you think you were doing?"

"Just doing my job," I said, "didn't want to compromise your position."

"Compromise Wolfendale, you fucking scared the shit out of me," he said.

"Sorry, I wasn't thinking," I said, "It was funny at the time though, wasn't it?"

"Funny for who?" said the BQ, as he walked away feeling better now he had gotten it off his chest. Back at Bridge Camp it was more VCPs and PCPs. We had quite an extended rest period with the fact we were changing camps again; it was early afternoon before we were on stag duty again at the end of Shipquay Street. There were two checkpoints with one of them being called a soak area, the one that Dave and I would be manning. We were dropped off in a Land Rover for the reason that we couldn't patrol the streets with just two men. The area was like a small un-tarmac car park with only one way in and one way out, it was called Bank Place, right next to the city wall where trucks would be expected to be searched before entering the city itself. The name soak area derives from the trucks having to spend an hour or two there before being released, just in case they had been hijacked along the way and then terrorised into carrying a bomb in their vehicle .It wasn't uncommon for this situation to occur with a family member being used as a hostage if they refused.

The truck drivers would welcome us with open arms; the majority of truck drivers were glad we stopped them so their problem would now become ours; in other words, they would now be in the clear and safe from any repercussions that might occur. A small Sanger against the wall was where we would operate from with one soldier in the Sanger guarding the soldier outside doing the searching. It was a welcome change from searching people and vehicles on the open roads; occasionally we would be given boxes of crisps and chocolate to take back to the barracks from some of the good guys that were on our side. Six hours later we were picked up again by the mobile patrols and taken back to barracks. Within the first month I must have done all the checkpoints around the city including, the first one I ever did on Ferryquay Street, to be honest, it seemed to be the one that I would do on a regular basis.

CHAPTER SIXTY-THREE
THEY DIDN'T STAND A CHANCE

It was now early to mid December and I was back on Ferryquay Street once more. Over the last month we had all become familiar with the girl in the gift and paper shop right next to the checkpoint, Audrey was her name, without asking her, I would say she was in her middle twenties; her Northern Irish accent was always a winner with the lads. She often cheered the troops up with her flirtatious conversation.

"Hi Audrey, how are you today?" I would say as we started our morning shift.

"I'm fine, so I am, thank you for asking," she said from the doorway of the shop, "it's nice to see you again. Is there anything I can do for you?"

"Now now, Audrey," I said. "Considering that none of us have been near a woman in what seems like ages, and here you are offering your services; then yes, maybe there is something you can do for me my dear lady."

"If only," she said, "maybe one day when you're off duty."

"In other words, there is more chance of the desert freezing over," I said, sulking in an amusing way.

"All good things come to those that wait," she said.

"I go back in March, as if you didn't already know," I said. The flirting continued for a while until I said…

"Actually, there is something you can do for me, Audrey… I would like some Christmas cards and a Shillelagh (Irish Walking Stick), like the one you have in the window."

"I will sort something out for you for the end of your shift," she said, making her way back into the shop.

"Bombardier Dodds, at the end of the shift I just need to pick up a present for my mum from Audrey if that's OK?"

"Yes, but make it quick," he said, "one minute and then we're off."

As planned, the oncoming shift took over the checkpoint and then my brick formed a small cordon while I got my merchandise from Audrey.

"Here you go Paul, a pack of Christmas cards and a Shillelagh for your mum," she said smiling.

"Thanks a lot," I said after paying her, "see you around, not sure when I will be here again, shouldn't be too long."

"OK, bye for now Paul."

Back in the camp I wrote a card out and sent it to the BBC Radio Two show, Judith Chalmers' Christmas Show to be more precise. I was hoping that it would be read out on Christmas day, to show my parents how much they meant to me. The Shillelagh was for when I went home for four days between Christmas and New Year, everybody would get their RR (Rest and Recuperation) leave at sometime during the tour. It was now December 18th and the weather was becoming colder, but to me, the colder weather was an indication that it would soon be Christmas; it took more effort to slide my shivering body out of my pit than to run a four minute mile. After breakfast it was time to get myself sorted and make my way to the loading bay with the rest of the brick, whilst at the same time, chitchatting away and having some mild banter with Betty, Billy, Danny and Dave Dalzell; Mr Prankster Geordie Walsh was could also be heard cracking the jokes. Craigavon Bridge was our port of call on this cold frosty morning, it would take no more than about five minutes to reach on a normal day, but with Ragsy at the helm and striding purposefully, we were there in four, some sort of record I think.

It just seemed like any normal day up till about 1100hrs. I was outside the Sanger in the middle of the four lane carriageway doing what I do best: stopping, searching and causing as much disruption to the public as I could (at least that's what the bad guys thought). Dave was in the lookout part of the Sanger with Ragsy all wired up to his radio moving in and out of the Sanger as needed. I had just completed a search of a vehicle, and was about to do a number plate check on the next approaching vehicle when there was one almighty, deathly explosion. I could feel the quake running through my body and down my feet; it sounded more like a crack at first followed by a thud as grey smoke weaved its way into the clear blue sky.

My first thought was *what the hell was that;* I didn't think for one moment that it was a terrorist attack. Seconds later and with the traffic now being brought to a halt, radio silence had been put in force throughout the battery; absolutely no one was allowed to use their radio set until told otherwise.

I could hear the operations room trying to get in touch with the checkpoint that I was manning a couple of days ago; it was the soak area where all the HGVs got searched. It made a lot more sense now as I looked across in the direction of the city where the smoke was bellowing from. The radio silence continued for the next few minutes as the operations room continued to ascertain some form of communications with the soak area, but it was all in vain; dealing with a serious incident of vast proportion was now becoming quite evident. Starlight (military ambulance) could be heard in the distance making its way into the city at pace. Law and order still had to be maintained on the bridge as everybody was now out of their cars and trying to find out more about the situation.

"What's going on?"

"An explosion in the city," I replied, making sure not to give them too much information. It was becoming difficult trying to concentrate on my task in hand knowing that something serious had happened. I continued searching vehicles and chatting to the people who were asking questions that I couldn't and didn't want to answer, whilst at the same time trying not to vent my anger. Trying to keep law and order was my priority at this moment in time and not to inflame the situation. As I started to allow the traffic to flow again things were starting to get back to normal; being on my lonesome in the middle of the road made me feel excluded from the rest of my brick, the feeling was very much the same as that horendous evening in the fountain area some four weeks ago.

It must have been the best part of ten minutes before the unmistakeable sound of starlight could be heard once more in the distance of the city; with its blue flashing light and the noise getting ever louder, I could see the green Army ambulance thundering towards the checkpoint. As a child I was always scared of the noise from emergency vehicles; I was feeling exactly the same as it took me back to my childhood. For the remainder of the shift it was a case of wondering and thinking about the extent of the explosion some two hours ago. The checkpoint was as quiet as it could possibly be in respect that we were all shocked into silence, it was difficult to know how I was supposed to feel. *Should I feel relieved that I was nowhere near the explosion? Should I feel angry that maybe more could have been done to prevent the incident?*

I'm not sure how much longer I could have stayed on the Craigavon Bridge without losing control of my feelings; thank god it was only minutes before we could see the next shift coming to take over from us. I could see Ragsy chatting to the new section commander with total concern written on their faces just before I was relived of my duty by another Gunner.

"What's gone on?" I said, wanting to know supplementary details, "I heard and saw the explosion but that's all I know."

"As far as I know, two men dead," he said, looking disconsolate, "apparently they didn't stand a chance." I just shook my head and took a deep breath.

"Come on then, let's go," said Ragsy, wanting to get back to camp ASAP.

The short journey back in Bridge Camp was like one of those journeys you sometimes take, and when you arrive, you can't remember any part of how you actually got there. On arrival we were told the news of the explosion and what had happened, it was the sort of news that didn't go down well with the troops. The Provisional IRA had already put in their claim that it was them who had carried out the atrocity in the centre of Londonderry. Gunner McDonald and Craftsman McInnes had both been killed in the explosion, Craftsman McInnes was killed instantly and Gunner McDonald, for whom I sat by on the aircraft flying over here, died on the way to hospital. Apparently, or as rumour has it, the two soldiers were lured out of the Sanger by some young children who offered them some sweets; while the soldiers were distracted IRA volunteers lowered a bomb onto the roof of the Sanger that exploded within minutes killing Cyril and Colin.

It was a real kick up the backside for us all. It felt like day one again when we were as keen as mustard; we needed to find that resurgence once more. My ex junior leader mate Steve Parry was due to join 49 Battery this day so I was thinking, *what sort of welcome is he going to get, hardly the warm welcome he will be hoping for.* I am pretty sure that the news would have travelled back to BAOR (British Army of the Rhine) and the feeling over there would have been much of the same as we were feeling over here.

My next job and the job of many other serving lads was to phone my brother to tell my mother and father that I was still in one piece before the news was broadcasted on TV. The queue for the phone box as you can imagine was lengthy, it was a case of wait and take your turn. The next few days leading up to Christmas meant we were on full alert trying to prevent any reoccurrence of what had gone on before us; we were still in a state of mourning and trying to raise a smile was becoming difficult if not impossible. It was 0600hrs on Christmas morning and I was on mobile duties with the rest of the section. I, along with Dave was told that we would be going out with the BCs party with a tea urn that was laced with a tad of rum. It was the BCs way of trying to bring some spirit (pardon the pun) back into the troops.

"Merry Christmas," said the BC as I got into the back of the Land Rover.

"Same to you, Sir," I replied along with Dave.

"Merry Christmas, Dave" I said.

"Same to you, Paul," said Dave, and so it went on for the next few minutes until there was no one else to wish Merry Christmas too. It felt like we were giving all the troops that were on the streets an early Christmas present as we made our way around all the checkpoints. They were so appreciative of the gesture even though it was just a small token of what they all deserved; they were doing a rewarding and justifying job so everybody else in the city could sleep well and enjoy their Christmas. A Christmas dinner took place at Hawkin Street with a few extras until it was time to put Christmas behind us for another year.

A couple of days later it was time for my RR leave; saying goodbye to my mates was easy on this occasion as I couldn't wait to see my family again. It seemed so strange to be escorted into the back of a Land Rover through the city to catch my flight home; dressed in civilian clothes I made my way onto the aircraft for the short journey to Manchester Airport. I was so excited that I almost forgot to pick up my small suitcase from the conveyer belt before making my way to meet my parents. My brother-in-law Norman was there to meet me along with my father.

"Hi dad," I said, giving him the obligatory warm embrace as well as a hand shake from Norman.

"How are you, son?" asked my dad.

"Fine thanks dad, just nice to be home." I could see that he was hiding his feelings, too much of a man to react any other way; we both knew the love we had for each other was well hidden in the confinements of our hearts. It was so nice to be heading home without worrying about being blown up or shot at, although the feeling of Londonderry wasn't going away; I could still feel the sense of fear everywhere I looked, just glad I wasn't allowed to bring my SLR home with me.

Back home it was grand to see my mother, brothers and sisters again, to share some of the Christmas spirit that has been missing for so long; to my surprise my family thought it best not to quiz me over the events of Northern Ireland and just allow me to enjoy the time I had with them.

"We heard your greetings on the radio, Paul," said my mum.

"What greetings were they?" I asked feeling confused.

"The one you sent wishing your family a Merry Christmas from Londonderry," my mum replied.

"Bloody hell," I said, "I'd forgotten about that, when was it read out?"

"On Christmas Day, just as we were about to sit down for Christmas dinner," said my mum.

"Wow, never expected that for a minute, I was just hoping it would; that's made my day." Although I was only home for three full days I still managed to catch up with Dec who was home from the Junior Leaders. It was a case of telling him everything that had gone on so far; not sure how it made him feel, but he certainly had a story or two to take back to Gamecock Barracks and tell the rest of the lads.

"Won't be long now, Dec, before you join us," I said.

"Sometime in May, Paul," said Dec, "can't wait."

"Don't forget to request 42 Regiment then hopefully you'll be put into 18 Battery."

"Will do Paul" said Dec.

"Anyway, I will say my goodbyes now, Dec," I said, "I shall look forward to seeing you in May."

"OK Paul, take care of yourself; see you in May," said Dec as we shook hands and headed back to our respective duties.

It was now time to catch the afternoon flight back to Londonderry. My father came along once more to see me off which was very heart warming; just to see the look on his face as I made my way into the airport was something that would stay with me for the rest of my life, he just smiled like only my father could, shook my hand and never stopped looking at me until I turned to face the other way as I made my way through check-in. On the flight back I was hoping that there would be no more bloodshed for the rest of the tour; less than two weeks after being back, the IRA were showing their true colours once more.

CHAPTER SIXTY-FOUR
RIP MARK

No sooner had I stepped back onto Irish soil, it was straight to 18 Battery HQ, Hawkin Street to be more precise. Once there I had to officially report back for duty and then be escorted back to Bridge Camp. After settling back into my duties and looking forward to the final two months, I was told that my section were out on the streets patrolling and I would be starting checkpoint duties tonight at 0100hrs; with that in mind, I thought it best to sort myself out and get some sleep before the so call 'dead stag.' I managed to catch a few minutes with Don and Schoie which was nice as I seemed to have lost touch with them since arriving in November. The camp seemed to be back to normal now that Christmas was out of the way, the feeling of the lads was one of; *it's all downhill now* whilst at the same time remembering not to switch off.

Midnight arrived and it was time to get out of bed and get ready for our shift; a cold brisk frost lay on the ground so a little more clothing and special issued black gloves just for Northern Ireland were the order of the night. We only had to walk about a minute up the road from the camp. The checkpoint was at the lower tier of the bridge with a small Sanger on one side of the road with a sentry box on the other side; it was like the one you would see in London with one of the queen's guardsman in. I was first to occupy the metal box while Dave was outside guarding me from the other side of the road. I think it must have been the first car that came through the checkpoint I searched that brought a little nervousness to my mind; with the fact I had only just come on duty I was still not fully focused on what was to happen next.

There was little space between the car and the sentry box to manoeuvre so, when the car pulled up, it felt like I was trapped, an invasion of my privacy is how I would describe it; if I'd have wanted him to get out of his car to open his boot it would have been a struggle. There was just about enough room for his door to open.

"Can I see your licence please, Sir?" I said, expecting it to be just a routine check; without a word or prayer the rough looking gentlemen past me his photo book licence, he just stared forward as if not wanting to make any eye contact with me or show me his face. I was feeling intrusive and uncomfortable with the silence as I checked the photo on the licence so thought it better not to ask him any questions.

His left hand was out of sight down near where the hand-brake would be with his right hand just resting on the steering wheel. It took me a few seconds of thought for my brain to register that the photo I was looking at on his licence was one that resembled a photo that I'd seen in the mug shot book that we had in all of the Sanger's. I was half thinking about getting him out of the car for a boot search but for some reason unknown to me, my mind declined my first thought and told me to wave him through. "OK Sir, on your way," I said, thinking no more about it. What I was thinking was that the photo of his face was a 'report on sight' mug shot and not one of the known players (a name we would give them) that would be classified as an arrest on sight.

After my hour long shift it was my turn to have a welcome break in the warmth of the heated Sanger.

"Can I have a look at the mug shot book please?" I said to Ragsy.

"Why what's up?"

"Oh not much, I just thought I saw a report on sight man in one of the cars I was searching," I said. He past me the book and I started to open it, I didn't have to search too far to find his photo.

I was shocked when I saw the identical photo in the No 3 slot out of twelve on the arrest on site page, I thought *I could be in a spot of bother here, do I report it and get into trouble or do I just leave it and say nothing*. Not reporting it could have severe consequences in the long term, I felt I had no choice. I looked over to Bombardier Dodds and said nervously;

"I think I've made a bit of a fuck up."

"What's that then?" said Ragsy, "what fuck-up as you so elegantly put it?"

"Well, this player here on the arrest on sight list," I said, pointing to his photo, "he went through into the city about an hour ago."

"Are you certain?" said Ragsy.

"100%" I said, "it was like a double take, the photo in the book is exactly the same as the one on his licence."

"Well, it's too bloody late now, isn't it," said Ragsy. "I'd better report it right away, can't believe you let him slip through your fingers."

"Really sorry," I said remorsefully, "I just knew it was a stupid thing to do, guess I just got caught off guard."

At the end of the shift I had to explain what had happened to the operational room that were none too pleased. I got a ticking off for not arresting him, but now as I look back on the incident, maybe the choice I made of not getting him out of the car could have saved my life; I guess we will never know.

Another week passed and again at the same checkpoint there was more to talk about, a girl called Jane, apparently an IRA informer was hanging around the checkpoint wanting to chat to the soldiers. She was a young girl of about seventeen years of age that seemed to take an interest in a man in a uniform; not sure if she had ulterior motives but we needed to be on our guard just in case. To my knowledge she was a cool Irish girl just looking for a bit of fun with the squaddies and not someone who was trying to distract us from our duties. I was shocked of how easily I was influenced by the attention of a gorgeous lass and the way she spoke in her native tongue. A quick snog and cuddle at the back of the Sanger in the middle of the night made me feel like my batteries had been recharged. I know it was wrong and dangerous what I got up to that night on the Sanger, but unfortunately, I was smitten. Knowing who to trust out there on the streets was becoming difficult for me, as I was later to find out.

It wasn't long before Pete Riggers joined us; it was so nice to see him entering Bridge Camp.

"Riggers, over here" I said.

"How's it going?" said Pete. "Great to see you Paul, I've heard what's been going on, back in Fallingbostal we are kept in touch with the everyday goings on over here, we were all stunned into shock when we were told the devastating news; can't believe we have lost two men."

"Just the half of it," I said. "Anyway more to the point, how are you feeling?"

"Scared," said Pete, looking for some comfort from myself.

"Let me show you around," I said, "let me make you feel at home." It wasn't long before Pete was joining his section and getting the feel of what it is really like out there; I knew I would be seeing very little of Pete over the coming months, so all being well we would have a good catch up back in BAOR.

January 17th was now upon us and all the RR leave was now over. I was having my lunch meal when news of a shooting in the Strand area of the city just up the road from our area was filtering around the troops.

"What's happened?" said someone anxiously.

"Not sure," said someone else, "think there has been a shooting in 49 Battery." The first thing that came to my mind was Steve Parry, he was in 49 Battery; I am pretty sure everybody had a friend or two in 49 Battery so they were also just as concerned. It took about an hour for conformation to arrive to what had taken place, Mark Ashford aged 19 had been shot in the head on St James Street. Three young youths approached the checkpoint on a busy Saturday morning market, two of the men were walking side by side and then the other one was tucked behind the other two, out of sight. Mark was outside the Sanger with a lady civvie searcher volunteer (who would be unarmed). As they approached the two front runners parted towards the Sanger, which left the way free for the murderer to point his low velocity hand gun at Mark; it was over in seconds.

Mark was thrown back onto the wall and just slid down the wall onto the footpath; Mark would have died instantly without suffering. The other two youths kicked the unlocked Sanger door open and fired randomly at the two soldiers who were also taken by surprise. One of the soldiers was a friend of mine from 18 Battery that was attached to 49 Battery, Frank Sumner. Frank got shot in the arm, but in some way he was lucky that the bullet went straight through his arm and out again; as for the other soldier, I believe he had several bullets fired into his flak jacket with only one penetrating through causing severe bruising to his chest.

We were all stunned into silence with the fact that another one of 42 Regiment's men would not be returning. At the end of the day we were all easy targets for the enemy; not knowing your well despised enemy was now starting to have an impact on us all. Throughout the following week we were given the code name Mrs Brown to look out for, it was the name given to a brown Ford Cortina Mark 3 that was seen at the shooting as the getaway car according to eye witnesses. I can't remember any reported sightings, it had probably been torched somewhere. It was back onto the Craigavon Bridge for a night shift but luckily for me, it was my turn to spend the shift in Ebrington Barracks; just across the other side of the water that is known as the Waterside. This area was not patrolled by 18 Battery however occasionally we would have mobile patrols taking some of the lads who were on rest period to the camp for some social time.

Within the WRAC camp was an operational room where you would sit in the comfort of the room in front of a small TV screen along with a keyboard; this is where I would be for six hours. The task was similar to an operator's duty. The rest of my shift that were now on the bridge getting cold, would radio through the car registration number plate of any vehicle they were suspicious about. I would then type the registration number into the equipment and Hey Presto, the machine would give me all the information about that vehicle.

Stop 1, Stop 2, Stop 3, and Stop 4 were the categories that would be displayed with each number having a different meaning. It was a pleasant six hours to say the least; at times, it felt like a rest period. After the shift and back at Bridge Camp I was to find out that the lads on the bridge that night had had a lucky escape; an infantry regiment that were patrolling on a hill overlooking the Craigavon Bridge stumbled across a firing point that was in direct line and in clear site of the bridge as the crow flies. Ammunition of plenty was found on the grassy area just by some bushes; rumour has it that all the facts were adding up to a possible shooting onto the bridge that night, all it needed now was for someone to come along with a rifle and we could have been mourning another fatality.

A couple of days later I was once more on the Sanger at the lower end of the Craigavon Bridge, even I could not for one minute, imagine what was to follow over the next two months; things like this are not supposed to happen.

CHAPTER SIXTY-FIVE
A MYSTIFYING PHONE CALL

It was the evening shift from 1900hrs until 0100hrs, the checkpoint where I met Jane most recently. About half way through the shift and guarding Dave from the Sanger side of the road I noticed a small cuddly brown haired girl chatting to Dave as the night became quieter. To be honest I was more concerned with my duty and making sure that Dave was being guarded by myself until the girl came over to me and started up a conversation.

"Hi, soldier boy," she said in her native tongue, "do you have a name?"

"Yes, Paul," I said.

"Paul, nice name so it is, she said. Are you Dave's friend?"

"Yes, good friends… and you? I take it you have a name," I said, trying not to get to distracted.

"Ooooh, now that would be tellin' Mr Soldier boy, I am not tellin you so I'm not, Lydia," she said almost in the same breath, "Lydia McMullen."

"So where are you from?" I said as I looked her in the eyes.

"From the waterside, Paul," she said, "no need to worry, my daddy is in the UVF (Ulster Volunteer Force), we are the good guys."

"Good guys, bad guys, all the same to me." I said being serious.

"I understand what you mean, Paul," she said, "but you'll get no trouble from me so you won't."

As well as trying avoid what I would call a dereliction of duty, I must have spent at least half an hour chatting to Lydia, she had certainly gained my trust even though it was still difficult to establish who were the good guys and who were the bad guys; there was just something about this evening and something about this girl that that I was taking a shine too.

"Wolfendale," said my section commander, Ragsy.

"Get rid of that girl from the checkpoint now."

"Easier said than done," I said, "I can't make her move from the streets if she doesn't want to."

"Don't be so stupid," said Ragsy, now becoming more aggressive, he then looked in the direction of Lydia and said "if you don't leave the checkpoint now I will be forced to arrest you."

"Wolfendale, so that's your surname, catch you on," said Lydia. "Such a grand name, so it is, Paul."

"Well, it's the only one I've got so I'm glad it comes with your approval," I said, feeling more anxious that she was still hanging around. "Think you better go now before you get me in trouble, don't you?"

"Aye OK, I'll be on my way so I will, don't want to get you into trouble soldier boy," she said, "maybe catch you around again."

"Yeah, I would like that," I said.

"Bye for now Paul."

Once Lydia had left, I got a small lecture from Ragsy that had behave yourself written all over it, and then, I had a chat with Dave who said he met her about a week ago on this same checkpoint.

"How did you find her?" I said.

"Seems a nice girl but I would still be careful, Paul," said Dave, "you just don't know who to trust and who not to trust." It was now 0100hrs, we made our way back the whole two hundred metres into Bridge Camp; a quick egg banjo was on the agenda before retiring to my bed for some much needed shut eye. I was also conscience not to disturb a couple of the lads who were on a twelve hour break. Before I could even close my eyes the door of the room opened with some force by the duty chef.

"Anyone called Paul Wolfendale here?" he said loudly without any or no thought for anyone who might be asleep.

"Yeah that's me," I said, looking at him from the horizontal position.

"There's a girl on the phone for you, she sounds Irish."

"For me" I said, feeling confused and wanting to get some sleep.

"Yes, hurry up, she sounds like she is crying, the phone box on the camp is the one she has phoned." I got myself out of my pit and quickly put on my tracky bottoms along with my Army pullover before making my way through the semi lit camp to the phone box.

Still in shock I picked up the receiver and said, "Hello."

"Is that you, Paul?" said a voice with a soft whimper.

"Yes," I said, "Is it Lydia, Lydia McMullen?"

"Yes Paul."

"What's the problem, Lydia?" I said.

"I am worried, I think someone is trying to get into my house," said Lydia, crying, "I can hear banging outside and it sounds like they're trying to break in."

"Go and wake up your parents then." I said.

"I can't do that otherwise I will be in trouble for staying out so late, I just need someone to talk to and you were the first person that came to mind, please will you just stay and talk to me for a while Paul, just until they have gone?"

"Of course I will," I said; *to be honest what choice did I have,* I thought to myself. We must have chatted for at least an hour on the phone getting to know more about each other.

"I was talking to Jane the other night and she mentioned you," said Lydia.

"Jane, you mean the girl that I kissed on the checkpoint?" I said, sounding shocked.

"Yes, she is a friend of mine."

"Bloody hell," I said, "I thought she was one of the bad guys."

"Ah, she's OK so she is," said Lydia, "she's harmless enough so she is Paul, just don't go telling her too much."

"Not a chance," I said in an Irish accent just for a laugh.

"I would love to meet you, Paul, and have a chat to you when you're not on duty," said Lydia, who was now feeling a lot perkier. "There is a way we could meet up you know."

"What's that then?"

"Well you know Ebrington Barracks across the water?"

"Yes, "I answered.

"Well I know if you manage to get yourself over to the barracks. and there are at least five of you, I've heard that you can then book out of the barracks and go to the British Legion Pub, from there you could always sneak out and I could meet you."

"You have got to be joking, Lydia," I said, shocked at her naivety, "that sort of advice could get me into serious trouble or even killed, oh and by the way, while we are on the subject, how the hell do you know all this?"

"Don't forget, Paul, I've lived here all my life, through all the troubles, it's my business to know what goes on, you'll be safe Paul, you can be sure of that, so you will."

I felt myself being pulled into a situation that I was finding difficult to get out of, I really wanted to see Lydia on the terms that she was so elegantly describing however, deep down, my stomach was churning at the thought to what I was about to embark on.

"Very well, Lydia," I said, "I will see what I can do, I've got a twelve hour break tomorrow from 6pm until 6am the next morning, maybe, there will be a window of opportunity."

"I can phone you tomorrow then Paul, from the same phone box about 6.30," said Lydia.

"Yeah, that should be fine, Lydia," I said, "I still can't believe what the heck you're getting me to do, even though I can't wait to meet you."

"Like I said, Paul, you'll be fine with me so you will."

"Must go now, Lydia," I said, "we have been chatting for almost two hours now and I need to get some sleep."

"OK Paul," she said, "I will phone you tomorrow soldier boy, you get yourself some beauty sleep, thank you again for talking to me." With her voice now becoming more distant we hung up on each other; my head was spinning around with all sorts of things as I lay in my bed trying to get some sleep before my next duty. Did I really believe that I could honestly meet up with Lydia?

CHAPTER SIXTY-SIX
THE MEETING

Up early and my shift now finished, it was time to see if I could get some of the lads that weren't on duty to accompany me to Ebrington barracks. I was quite surprised with the fact that I was still a relatively new recruit that by asking, my influence was not falling on deaf ears. "Yeah, no problem," said a couple of the lads.

"Brilliant," I said without telling them any more about my motives. At the last count there were about four of us that were heading out to Ebrington Barracks and then onto the British Legion, I would just need one more and then I could meet up with Lydia. Duty transport was booked for 1900hrs so it was just left for me to confirm with Lydia that all being well I would be able to meet up with her. It was getting close to twenty five past six and time for me to make my way to the camp phone box before it became engaged. Luckily for me the phone box was vacant. I waited inside the cold red structure pretending to be on a call if someone suddenly came along and wanted to use it.

Right on time the phone rang. "Hello?" I said as if I didn't know who was on the other end of the line.

"Could I speak to Paul Wolfendale please?" was her reply.

"Speaking" I said.

"I knew it was you Mr Soldier boy, just wanted to make sure though before I said something that might embarrass me."

"Well, I think I should be able to meet you later," I said, "can't see there being a problem." "Catch you on, Paul," she said. "I'm so excited, what time should I be there soldier boy?"

"Somewhere around 8 ish," I said, "if I'm not there then phone the pub from a nearby phone box, Lydia listen, I must go now, someone wants to use the phone, see you later."

"On your way then, Paul, don't be late." Down at the small OP room we got into the back of the Land Rover and headed across the Craigavon Bridge to Ebrington Barracks. Once there, we made our way to the bar and had ourselves a drink; I needed to get another body with their only being four of us. It wasn't long before I found someone who was willing to join us. It was a short walk to the British Legion and once we were all seated with a pint or two, it was time for me to expose my motives to my friends.

"I have something to say," I said, trying to attract their attention.

"What's that then?" they said, swigging their beer.

"Well, I'm going to leave you for a while," I said, looking up at the clock on the wall, "Can't say too much but, I'm not going far, just going to see someone."

"See who?"

"Just someone I met on one of the checkpoints." I said.

"You mad or what?" said one of the lads.

"Just don't say anything, I'll be back shortly." I got up and made my way outside through the two swinging doors to meet up with a girl I knew little about. I was feeling so vulnerable as I made my way across the road and onto the semi busy streets, what was going through my mind was anyone's business as I continued walking at a slow pace. Within seconds and almost at the same time our eyes met.

"Paul, over here," said a voice that could only be Lydia. I made my way towards her dark shadow that was being illuminated by the street lights, a warm embrace welcomed my presence as we both couldn't believe that we had taken this next step to be with each other.

"Give me your hand, Paul?" said Lydia as she offered me hers. It was so nice to be able to hold her hand and just to feel the freedom that I hadn't felt over the last two months. I knew what I was doing was wrong, but my feeling for Lydia was overriding any fears that I had.

As we walked along the lit-up street it was only then that I realised how short Lydia was, without trying not to sound rude I said. "Didn't realise actually how tiny you were now that we are standing side by side."

"Ah, all the best things come in small packages so they do, you should know that soldier boy."

"What are you trying to insinuate, Lydia?" I said. "I hope you're not referring to me?"

"No, no of course not," she said in her funny and inelegant way.

"4ft 11in Paul and before you say something about my slightly chubbiness, I'm built for comfort and not for speed." No matter what she said in her native tongue it always amused me to the point that I was falling for her charm with every word she uttered. As we made our way to a small park where there was a bench we could sit on, I heard the noise of an Army Land Rover thundering down the roads; before we could both become invisible it went zooming past us. My first thought was of apprehension, wondering whether or not it was one of our own patrols and that I might have been compromised.

"I hope that wasn't one of our mobiles," I said to Lydia, still feeling worried.

"Yes, it was," she said, sounding undeterred.

"What, how do you know that?" I said. "How can you tell?"

"Because your Land Rovers have a yellow disc on the front of them," she said. There we go again, she knew more about my unit than me which I found unbelievable to say the least. I was now feeling more concerned than ever but knew there was nothing I could do about the situation; I would just have to wait until later on when I returned to see whether or not I had been seen.

We made our way across the grass area of the tiny park to where the wooden bench was situated; it was here that I got to know more about the girl that I was having so much fun with. We sat close to each other with our hands still warmly locked together; we were now only inches away from each other and staring into each other's eyes. We both knew what the next move was to be. As we got even closer to each other and before our lips met on this cold dark night we brushed the back of our hands on the cheeks of each other's face; the first kiss lasted no more than a few seconds before we dragged ourselves from the embrace.

"Paul Wolfendale," she said in a 'what do you think you're doing' kind of way. "I shall have to tell my Ma about a soldier that kissed me in the park."

"I'm afraid you will; hope she won't come looking for me with a gun."

"Not a chance," she said laughing at my remark. "Catch yourself on, Paul."

"So, how old are you Lydia?" I asked.

"Fifteen, fifteen years of age, I will be sixteen in July," she said, stroking my leg to try and keep me warm.

"Oh, well I'm only 18 so there is two and a half years between us."

"So there is, Paul," she said, "you know what people call me?"

"No idea." I said.

"Cuddles, because of my size, no bigger than a pint pot, that's me, I wasn't too sure what to make of her nickname, but I could have thought of worse.

"You remind me of my ex," I said, thinking *that it probably wasn't the brightest thing to say.*

"Your ex," she said. "Tell me more."

"Well I mean your long brown hair and your."

"My what?" she said.

"Erm, well my ex was quite top heavy as well."

"Paul Wolfendale, what are you trying to say?" she said. "I can feel myself blushing so I can; touch my cheeks and feel for yourself Paul."

"If I must," I said, I took both of my hands and gently touched the side of her cheeks with the tips of my fingers as she slowly closed her eyes. Lydia knew what buttons to press to get the attention she was seeking, it's as if she was telepathic and could read my mind. It was so obvious to us both that something special was going on between us. We just continued chatting to each other about anything and everything as we sat looking across the water at the beautiful lights of Londonderry.

Over an hour had passed and it was time for me to reluctantly make my way back to the barracks.

"I will walk you back, Paul," said Lydia

"It's not part of your service" I said, but if you insist and promise not to seduce me, I might let you. My mum has warned me about girls like you."

"What do you mean, Mr Wolfendale? Girls like me."

"Well it starts with a good night kiss and then…"

"And then what, Paul?" she said.

"Well now that would be telling Lydia, come here," I said, taking her by the hand. We enjoyed the short walk that seem to come to an end before it had even started; she gave me a huge hug with her loving arms before I laid a soft kiss on the cheek of her warm face. It was time now to make my way back into Ebrington barracks; the only thing that was on my mind at this moment in time was seeing Lydia again, hopefully over the next few days, somewhere in the city centre on one of my shifts.

The duty transport arrived for me and a couple of the other lads to take us back to Bridge Camp; it was my gun driver Dinger Bell sitting in the back with his rifle pointing out of the back.

"Hi Dinger," I said, trying to drum up a conversation.

"Where have you been tonight, Wolfie?" he said, "and don't lie to me." I felt my stomach drop a few inches as I knew there was something strange about the question.

"In the barracks and then on to the British Legion," I answered.

"And then?"

"And then what, I said."

"I told you not to lie," said Dinger, "I saw you with some girl walking along the road, I know it was you, we turned back to see if we could find you but you must have seen us and scarpered quickly." I was never very good at lying and although I felt the truth wouldn't do me any favours, I thought it better to own up to my escapades.

"OK," I said. "What do you want me to say, I'm sorry."

"Sorry," said Dinger, "I am taking you to see Sergeant Walsh the Troop Sergeant, he can deal with you." I had little more to say as I just sat quietly until we reached the checkpoint by the soak area where Sergeant Tommy Walsh was on duty.

"OK, Paul, get out," said Dinger in a sheepish way. Maybe he was having second thoughts; either way, I was now having to face Sergeant Walsh who was about to give me the rollicking of my life. After Sergeant Walsh had been given all the details of events, in was a case of, "stand to attention you blistering idiot, what the fuck do you think you were doing?" yelled Sergeant Walsh in a voice that the whole of Londonderry could hear. "You're on a fucking charge."He continued raging like a mad bull until there was no more to be said. "Get yourself out of my sight Wolfendale, Bell; get him back to Bridge Camp now before I do something I regret."

The next day I was the talk of the camp for all the wrong reasons as I was escorted to Hawkin Street to face my charge; there were naturally not many of the lads that were showing any sympathy, however, anyone that didn't know me before certainly knew who I was now. Standing waiting in the rest room area in my Army uniform, a call of, "Gunner Wolfendale, outside the BCs office now," could be heard from the BSM.

"Yes Sir," I said, not expecting a reservoir of good will. It was just another rollicking from the BSM just to calm my nerves down before being called to face my charge. To be honest, I was getting to the stage when I didn't give two monkeys; I just wanted to get it all over and done with.

The BSM entered the BCs office for his short but essential debrief and then within seconds came out and ordered me to attention.

"Accused quick march," said the BSM, before I knew it, there I was for the fourth time in my short Army career getting charged in his makeshift office.

"Gunner Wolfendale, we meet again," said the BC. "What on earth did you think you were doing?"

"Not sure Sir," I said, trying to find words that would fit the crime; I was literally on a hiding to nothing, standing there in front of the judge was not for the faint hearted, I was as guilty as sin, and as I said before, lying was not one of my virtues.

"I'm lost for words, Gunner Wolfendale, how you never ended up in the River Foyle with a bullet in your head I shall never know. Do you understand the implications of what you have done? Well do you?"

"Yes Sir," I said, fearing the worst.

I must have been lectured for at least five minutes before he gave his verdict, I was thinking maybe I would be posted back to West Germany and then sent to Colchester for a six month prison sentence and a dishonourable discharge at the worst end of the scale.

"Fifty pound fine and loss of all privileges, including confined to barracks," said the BC shaking his head in disbelief at the leniency of his award. Fifty quid was a lot of money on the balance of what I earn, however accepting his award seemed generous compared to what I was expecting.

It took me a few hours of rest to get my head around what I had done; keeping Lydia and I apart was like trying to keep a soldier away from a pint, it just wasn't going to happen. After a couple of days had passed and I wasn't anymore the talk of the camp, I managed to catch up with Lydia once again on one of the checkpoints. After explaining to Lydia what had gone on with my charge we thought it would be better to tone things down a little; with that in mind, she gave me her phone number and explained the times when she would be at home, it meant that one way or another we would always be in touch on a daily bases, If we couldn't see each other on a checkpoint then we would make sure we were on the phone. We would spend up to six hours at a time on the phone with each call bringing us ever closer together.

I hadn't seen Lydia for a couple of days so it was back to the camp for a catch up call. With my 2p in hand I called her number hoping she would be there to pick up at the other end; as the receiver was picked up I heard her unmistakeable voice.

"Hi Lydia," I said with a relief in my voice.

"Paul, so glad to hear from you again, I'm missing my soldier boy so much."

"I haven't got a lot of change so I might have to go through the operator and use my dodgy 2p method."

"No need, Paul," she said, "just put your receiver down at your end and I will phone you back, my Ma will think that you have called me because she won't hear me pick up the receiver."

"My god Lydia, you know all the tricks under the sun." Within seconds of hanging up the phone rang.

"Hello, can I help you?" I said.

"It's me, Lydia."

"Sorry, who is it?"

"It's Lydia, Paul. I know it's you, so stop messing."

"Don't know anyone called Paul."

"Fine then I will just hang up so I will; I must have phoned the wrong number." For a second I believed she would, so after calling my bluff I thought it would be better for me to come clean.

"Of course it's me."

"Knew you would give in," she said, "you just can't live without me can you now?" Not wanting to admit it, she was absolutely right; I was now head over heels in love with my Irish girl. It was difficult to know what was going to happen to a relationship that should never have happened and could never happen; descriptive power sprang to my mind once more into how anyone could possibly understand what was going on between us.

As the tour continued into February, things seemed to be settling down on the streets; apart from a few minor incidents there was not much to report from Londonderry. Meeting up with Lydia again on one of the checkpoints at night time almost had me in more trouble; I was standing chatting to Dave who was on the other side of the street when I saw Lydia walking thoughtfully towards me within the shadows of the street lights. I felt excited as I hadn't seen her for a couple of days, although we had spoken a couple of times on the phone.

"Hi there, cuddles," I said, "so glad to see you." I so wanted to put my arms around her once more just like we did on the waterside that night, but unfortunately I couldn't, the war that brought us together was now keeping us apart. I could see in Lydia's eyes that the feeling was mutual, a love that could never be was now bearing fruit and there wasn't a damn thing we could do about it.

"Hello there, soldier," said Lydia as she got within inches of me, "seen any good looking soldiers around on your travels?"

"You can try the Bogside," I said, "or maybe the Strand, you might find some there."

"I'm sure as not going to the Bogside, full of wee bitches that place so it is."

"Well, I'm afraid I can't help you then," I said, "Unless."

"Unless what?" said Lydia.

"Well, I'm footloose and fancy free if you would like to settle for second best?"

"Erm, I might have to then," she said sarcastically.

"Get your body over here," I said.

"If you insist," said Lydia, "Can't promise to keep my hands to myself though."

"You'd better, Lydia," I said feeling worried, "I'm in enough trouble as it is."

We had been chatting for no more than a few minutes when we heard the sound of Army Land Rovers approaching in the distance; it was the BC and his party doing their rounds. As they pulled up outside the checkpoint one of the men, Bombardier Phil Everitt ran over to me.

"What do you think you're doing with that girl?" he said. Before I could even speak Lydia was answering for me.

"Who do you think you're talking too?" she said, "I am waiting for the bus."

"Don't lie to me," he said; "get yourself of this checkpoint and make your way home."

"I'm not one of your soldiers that you can order around you know, I can stand here and wait for a bus if I want." I was gobsmacked to say the least at what she said, with the fact that I would have been hung, drawn and quartered for that kind of remark. As it was, it got me off the hook as the BC and his party departed.

"I will phone you tonight, Lydia, when I get back to camp," I said.

We were now entering the final week of our tour and the heat was being turned up again. There were riots of plenty on the bottom tier of the Craigavon Bridge, buses were being set on fire with hundreds of people thinking it would be good idea to give us a going away present; having projectiles thrown at you from such a volatile and hostile crowd was a scary experience within its self. Back in camp, everybody was now looking forward to seeing their loved ones once more, for me, well it was a case of, although I wanted to be reunited with my parents again, the love of my life was here in the land of the Provo's. I must have been the only one not wanting to return back home. That night I spent a few hours talking to Lydia again on the camp phone, she was almost in tears like the first time she spoke to me some six weeks ago, knowing that we had little or no time left together; I knew then that she was just as infatuated with me as I was with her.

"I have written you a poem, Paul; would you like me to read it out to you?"

"Yes, that would be nice."

"OK, here goes." I could almost feel her tears as she very slowly started to read her poem to me.

> *I love you and you know, I don't have to tell you so,*
> *If you love me then that's OK, there's just one thing I'd like to say,*
> *Now that we've made just a happy start, please don't let us drift apart.*

The poem summed up her feelings for me, making it even more difficult to say my goodbyes within the next week.

"Don't cry, Lydia," I said. "I'm sure we will see each other again in the coming future."

"I use to chat to a soldier before, about six months ago to be precise." She said.

"So what happened?" I said, feeling curious about what she had said.

"Well, I had feelings for him, but nothing like I have for you, Paul," she said, weeping. "I am so in love with you, I've never felt this way about anyone before." I was humbled by what she said, but still felt deep down inside I was fighting a losing battle; being able to see her again was going to require a miracle. We were pondering our thoughts for several minutes wondering if we would ever be able to solve this unsolvable problem we were faced with; all of a sudden Lydia came up with a mad idea that seemed so fanciful that you would have to be from a different planet to even contemplate what she was saying.

"Why don't you come over to see me, Paul?" she said, waiting for my answer.

"You cannot be serious, Lydia," I said, thinking *it was a joke*; "I will get bloody killed."

"Paul you won't, believe me, I will never let you come to any harm," she said in a reassuring tone.

"Lydia" I said "it would be hilarious if it wasn't so terrifying, this is a crazy idea, I could never come back here and feel safe, do you understand what I am saying Lydia? What do you think would happen if I got compromised?

I would be tarred and feather, and then probably have my knee caps shot off before the Provo's hood me and then put a bullet in the back of my head."

"Paul, don't be so dramatic," she said, "you'll be safe at my house with my Ma and my Daddy, so you will."

I was finding it hard to comprehend what she was asking me to do even though the thought of seeing her again was so appealing; coming up with an answer to our problem was causing my mind to work overtime.

"How do you know your Ma will want me staying at her house?" I said, thinking at the same time, *could this really be possible?*

"My Ma and Daddy would be fine with it, Paul, so they will, at least think about it Paul, it would be amazing." Lydia was now back to her mischievous and humorous ways, she was so energized I could hardly get a word in edgeways.

"Have a guess what I got up to today," she said in a playful voice.

"Go on Lydia, I've no idea."

"Well, just for a laugh I phoned a random number and when this lady answered the phone I said in a posh voice... *'Hello madam, this is British Telecom speaking, we are checking to see if your phone is in perfect working order, would it be possible for you to stand back from the receiver and sing?' 'Give me a second,' the lady said, she then shouted out, 'can you hear me now?' to which I replied, 'Yes, but only just, can you sing something you know.'* I was laughing my face off when she started singing 'The Green Green Grass of Home' by Tom Jones."

"Lydia, you can't do that," I said.

"Oh yes I can Paul, it is so much fun, gets me away from thinking about all the troubles."

"Well, I can't argue with that." I sniggered.

"By the way Paul, has there been a shooting in the city tonight?"

"Not to my knowledge," I said wondering what she meant.

"Oh right, no problem then."

"Lydia, what are you rambling on about?"

"Well, I heard from a source that there would be a shooting tonight, just make sure you keep your head down, Paul."

"Bloody hell, Lydia," I said, "How do you know all this?"

"Well, you know Jane "she said.

"Yes, you know too well I do."

"Well, she just mentioned something in passing."

"I wished you hadn't have mentioned it now, I should report this sort of information to intelligence, but the problem I have, if I do say something, I can guarantee I will be in more trouble once again. I feel like an undercover agent, you're telling me stuff that intelligence probably don't even know about; it would definitely be the end of my tour I can grant you that."

"Then don't say anything, Paul," said Lydia, now sounding more concerned. "Just forget what I said."

"I will have to," I said. With all that in mind I made my way back to the billet for some dreaming and personal thoughts; I had a lot to ponder over. The following night there were reports of a shooting in our area, two Land Rovers that were driving down Magazine Street by the city wall were fired upon from the top of the wall, M60 Machine gun I believe, luckily no one was hurt in the shooting, but by sheer luck rather than judgement. When I heard about the shooting I was thinking, *could this be the shooting that Lydia was talking about*, I was so relieved to hear that no one had been hurt. God knows how I would have coped if someone had been injured or even worst; the fact that I knew about the possibilities of a shooting taking place had me concerned about how I would have lived with myself. Whether or not if I had have said something would have made any difference, we shall never know. In my mind there was never any evidence linking the incident with what Lydia had said.

The next evening and with only two more days of the tour remaining I had made my decision about whether to return to Londonderry after the tour.

"Hi Lydia," I said from the infamous red phone box.

"Hi Paul," said Lydia apprehensively, "have you decided what you're doing, Paul?"

"Yes," I said, "I'm afraid."

"Please don't say another word Paul; please just leave it at that, I understand," she said, holding back her tears.

"Wait… don't interrupt, I was about to say, I'm afraid that your Ma will have to find somewhere for me to sleep. I've decided, and against my good will, to come and see you, Lydia. I love you so much and don't want to lose you to the civil war that seems to be holding all the aces. Why should we let it get in our way? I know I'll be scared, but at the same time, I know you will keep me safe."

"Oh my god Paul, are you sure? Please, please don't let me down."

"I won't Lydia; I will let you know when I get back to England about my

429

arrangements." Lydia was finding it difficult to come to grips with her good fortune and, I knew for a fact that she would not believe it until I was standing there in front of her in about a week's time. My final shift was on the checkpoint where I first started my duties some four months ago, midday to six in the evening; everybody that went through the checkpoint was getting a huge smile with it being the last one. "Afternoon Mrs Hymes," I would say, at the same time checking her bag,

"Going home today so you are, is that correct?"

"Yes," I said, "hours to go, then off home to my family."

"Well, you have a wonderful time with your family," she said, "thank you for all your support soldier, you've done a grand job so you have, your family will be proud of you." It was now getting close to the end of the shift and our turn to get a feel of what it is like when we took over from the last regiment four months ago. "Here they are," said Dave. Time to go; handing over the checkpoint was such an unbelievable feeling and that final walk to Bridge Camp for the last time. I just about remembered to say goodbye to Audrey in the paper shop before heading back. Once in the camp there was only one place I wanted to be and that was in the telephone box for my last chance to speak to Lydia for a while.

I wasted no time in making my way to the dodgy phone box to phone Lydia who I knew would be waiting in anticipation at the other end of the phone; one ring of the phone was all it took for Lydia to pick up the receiver.

"Hi, Paul," she said with her telepathic sense.

"Yes, it's me," I said, without winding her up this time. "I am missing you so much Lydia, I've finished my tour now and I'm all packed waiting for my journey back to West Germany tomorrow morning."

"Missing you too Paul, missing you so much," she said, "I just feel this may be the last time we will ever talk to each other, I just have this yearning feeling inside my stomach that this is going to be one of those pipe dreams that people have from time to time and that for some unknown reason you won't come back to see me, the thought of that is killing me, Paul."

"Lydia, please don't think like this," I said, feeling emotional. "I promised you I would come back to see you and I aim to keep that promise, I want to see you again just as much as you want to see me, I will be back Lydia."

"I so want to believe you, Paul, so I do," said Lydia with her voice now becoming more tearful with each saddened word she spoke. I was feeling helpless to do anything and to reassure her and her feelings; there was me sat in a phone box in a military camp and there was Lydia just on the other side of the water out of arms length.

"It will only be a few days, a week at most before we reunite again," I said with passion in my voice. This seemed to do the trick as I could feel Lydia's frame of mind change from that of being despondent to one of being buoyant.

"Thanks Paul," she said, "you have cheered me up no end so you have, and yes, I do believe you when you say you'll set foot on Irish soil once more." I was feeling more relaxed now that the conversation was flowing smoother than the River Foyle under the Craigavon Bridge. We had been chatting for some six hours now as the camp was almost in silence apart from the odd patrol getting their egg banjos from the cookhouse.

"Lydia, I think it may be time for me to get some shut eye. I need to be up early in the morning, got a long day ahead of me."

"Oh, do you have to, Paul," said Lydia. "Please don't hang up, just a wee bit longer, pretty please." Such a sucker I am as I agreed to just a few minutes more which turned into another three hours.

"Lydia I've got to go now," I said despairingly, "I am almost falling asleep in the phone box."

"OK, Paul," she said silently. "Go and get some beauty sleep, don't forget to phone me when you get back to England."

"Of course not," I said with my eyes barely open;"take care of yourself Lydia."

"You too, Paul," she said, slowly putting down the receiver. Those were the last words I heard Lydia say as I made my way to my bed for a couple of hours sleep.

The four month tour had been a roller coaster ride of complex emotions, one I will never forget; in some respects I was glad that it was all about to come to an end. The next morning and standing outside the billet ready for my journey back, I bumped into Don once more who had some exciting news to tell. One week between going back to West Germany and going on leave should technically have been a breeze for one and all, not for Don, even Don can't be that stupid, can he? Why did I open my mouth and tell Don he will need to get himself a tan.

CHAPTER SIXTER-SEVEN
MY EYES ARE DIM I CANNOT SEE

"Hi Don, today's the day mate," I said trying to sound bright and breezy, "bet you can't wait?"

"Damn right I can't," said Don. "I just found out the other day that authorisation has been approved for me to fly to Australia to see my good folk."

"That's brilliant Don, wow, made up for you," I said with a 'good for you' look on my face.

"Tickled pink, Paul," said Don with a Chelsea smile, "I leave the same day the regiment go on leave."

"Great news that, Don," I said. "You'll need to get yourself a tan before you go."

"Good point, Paul," said Don. The journey back to Fallingbostal was a case of catching up on some welcomed sleep, I must have slept at every opportunity I could until the white coaches rolled into St Barbara Barracks to a rapturous welcome from all family members and soldiers united. I was feeling more awake than ever now and although thoughts of Lydia were still etched on my mind I was so glad to be able to spend some time catching up with my mates without feeling like I was going to get shot.

"Schoie," I said, "coming down the NAAFI to see Chloe?"

"Why not," he said; "so glad to be back Paul, so looking forward to seeing my family again."

"Me too, Steve," I said, at the same time wanting to tell someone of my plans. Maybe I was having second thoughts, maybe I just wanted someone to advise me that what I was about to do was insane. As it was, I decided to keep my intentions secret to the point of bursting. At the NAAFI it was big hugs from Chloe as she saw us entering the store. "Paul, Steve, get over here!" she said with her arms wide open. "I have missed you both so much, so glad you got back safely."

"How could we not, Chloe," we said. "It's people like you that kept us going when we needed a boost. Walking around those streets in the early hours of the morning can be a lonely place at times."

Back at the block it was much of the same thing with everybody wanting to get back to normal; however at the same time trying to answer everyone's curiosity about the tour. We only had five days of preparation before heading back to our respective parts of the UK. England, Scotland, Wales and any other destinations where some of the lads lived; oh yes, I almost forgot, in my case Northern Ireland. Colin, my room associate, had moved rooms to my delight which meant Don and I had a new roommate. Al Green was his name, who was also from my local town of Nantwich; Al was just planning a short adventure in the Army, three years to be precise, so like Don, he would be leaving in the coming year. Al was about twenty two years of age and one of the quietist and most understanding lads I knew, he was the sort of person that suited me to the ground.

The first evening back I spent some catch up time with some of my mates that I hadn't seen for four months and then around 2200hrs decided to return to my room. I was gobsmacked to see Don sitting on the edge of his bed and no more than a few inches away from a small ultra violet lamp browning his face.

"Bloody hell Don, hasn't taken you long to get into holiday mode."

"I decided to take your advice, Paul, he said, looking at me with a pair of small like swimming goggles that were protecting his eyes. "Need to get my tan sorted before going to Australia."

"Well, it seems to be working," I said, thinking *he's gone mad* and trying not to laugh; his face was looking more like brown bread than a nice gentle tan. Out of respect, Don took his goggles off and looked me in the face, at the same time asking me what I thought of his two hour transformation.

"My god Don, what have you done?" I said trying to hide my laughter.

"What do you mean? Looks OK, doesn't it?" said Don.

"Just take a look in the mirror you nutter," I said, feeling concerned about what he was about to see.

"Bloody hell, what the fuck have I done?" said Don staring in the mirror. Don had two white circles where the goggles were sitting, the size of two well developed sliced cucumber pieces; he looked horrendous.

"Try not to get too excited, Don," I said, "no need to worry, you've got a few days to sort it out, you'll just have to be prepared for some ribbing on Monday mornings parade."

"No need to worry?" said Don with panic in his voice. "I need to sort it out and sort it out fast."

"Look, Don, I'm off for a shower now, just let me have a think about what we are going to do and then hopefully we can rectify the situation, don't do anything stupid while I'm away."

I was away for no more than fifteen minutes but unfortunately, Don hadn't listened to a word I'd said, fifteen minutes was far too long to leave a guy like Don on his own. As I entered my room once more, I saw Don exactly in the same position again sitting on the edge of his bed browning his face except this time, without the goggles.

"Don," I shouted, "what the hell are you doing? You'll damage your eyes!"

"It will be OK, Paul," said Don calmly, "just need to brown my eyes a bit." I couldn't believe what I was hearing. Maybe that's why I got on so well with Don; he was as stupid as me at times. A few minutes later the lights were turned off and silenced could be heard before we both fell asleep; silence, you may ask? Apart from waking up about mid night by Al Green entering the room and quietly getting into bed everything seemed normal. It must have been about 0500hrs when I felt my shoulder being shaken like something my mum would do to get me out of bed for school.

"Paul Paul, are you awake?" said a soft voice in my ear.

"What's the matter?" I said, still not knowing who it was.

"It's Don. I think I've gone blind Paul, I can't see." Still trying to come to my senses, I continued saying.

"Blind! Don't know what you mean, Don, "dragging my body out of my bed. "It's fucking dark, Don, I can't see either." Don didn't understand what I was implying and, at the same time I didn't understand the seriousness of his problem. All this meant that Don was now becoming frustrated with my remark.

"I know it's dark Paul, stop being a twat," he said, "I can't open my eyes is what I am trying to tell you."

"Just watch your eyes, Don, while I turn the lights on," I said tripping over Al Green's bed at the same time. It was like the blind leading the blind as I eventually found the light switch that now woke up Al with a few moans and groans.

"Sorry Al, go back to sleep, there's no problem, it's just Don, he's gone blind." Trying to keep a hold of Don was difficult as I tried to weigh up the damage, his eyes were literally knitted together, it seemed like someone had squirted glue into his eyes while he was asleep.

"OK, Don, try not to panic, but your eyes are glued together."

"Tell it as it is, Paul," said Don, "don't beat around the bush."

"Well, at least I can safely say you're not going to die, let's get you down the medical centre mate."

It was a long painful walk of what seemed like a mile before we finally reached the medical centre. I was just glad that there was no one around to see us; explaining what Don had done was something I hadn't been trained to do. On arrival and explaining to the medic about Don's eyes, the laughter could not be refrained even with the medic's professionalism; I was just glad Don couldn't see him sniggering.

"OK," said the medic, "just leave him with me, I shall be bedding him down until we manage to get his eyes to open, if you want, you can come and see him tonight however, I don't give much hope in Don seeing you."

"How long will he be in for?"

"A few days, I would imagine," said the medic, "come back tonight and I will let you know, you'll need to get some of his belongings if you can from his locker."

"Will do, see you later Don," I said, "oh, by the way I need your locker key."

"Here you are, Paul," said Don, passing me his key and explaining what stuff he wanted. Later on that evening I returned to the medical centre to see how Don was faring up.

"Ay up Don… I see your eyes are still closed, when do you think you'll be able to open your eyes again?"

"They said they should be open in the next couple of days," said Don, trying to work out where I was by the sound of my voice.

"I've brought you a wank mag (seedy magazine for the more discerning person) to read Don, just in case your eyes were open."

"Well, they're not, are they?" said Don, annoyed. "How the hell do you expect me to read it?"

"Tell you what, Don," I said. "I'll describe the colour photos as graphically as I can as long as you promise not to get to excited."

"Go for it, Paul," said Don. At the end of my half hour stay, Don was feeling more like himself as I said my goodbyes; the next couple of days saw me visit Don again before he was finally let out a day before his leave. Soon I would have to make a decision as to whether I should go back on my promise to Lydia or tell my parents that I was thinking of going back to Londonderry; either way, it wasn't going to be easy.

CHAPTER SIXTY-EIGHT
MEETING LYDIA'S PARENTS

The day arrived for us all to go on leave. Cars of plenty that looked like they were in convoy left the camp and headed for the ferry ports, duty transport was laid on for the ones that chose to fly from the local airport of Hannover. Once more the camp was being stripped of its troops apart from the skeleton staff that had not been on tour. Again I felt like a jet setter with the fact I was leaving after only five sleeps back in base camp; a two hour flight to Manchester and an expensive taxi journey on this occasion saw me walk through my front door mid afternoon. Three weeks to do what I want seemed like bliss compared to the last four months, although I did still need to drop the bombshell to my parents about my plans to return back to Northern Ireland; leaving that sort of information could wait until tomorrow, well, at least until I had had time to show my true feelings to my parents of how I was so overwhelmed to see them again.

The next day and sitting by the warm coal fire, I thought this would be my best opportunity to address my parents as they were sitting cosily watching TV.

"I met a girl whilst on duty in Northern Ireland," I said, trying to divert their attention away from the goggle box (television).

"Oh, that's nice," said my mum without too much interest.

"Yes, I'm thinking of returning back too Londonderry to see her."

"What do you mean, Paul?" said my mother, now giving me more of her devoted time.

"Well, I am thinking of travelling back in a couple of day's time to see her," I said, trying to choose my words carefully. I saw my father now glancing over towards me as he took a drag on his beloved woodbine, waiting for the next chapter of my 'please understand speech'.

"What on earth for Paul? It's dangerous over there," said my mother. "I don't want you going back over there Paul, it's not safe." I was now at a dilemma and torn between the two people in my life that meant so much to me; I was in a situation whereupon I didn't want to be a disappointment to my parents, but at the same time, I was in love with Lydia. My collective loyalties and devotion were equally divided between Lydia and my parents, at the end of the day, I felt that my choice had already been made, made some days ago back in the infamous Bridge Camp.

"I'd promised Lydia that I would come back and see her and feel that it would be wrong of me to go back on my word, mum." I was feeling really uncomfortable with what I was saying. My father was not as unrepentant as I had hoped as he said his piece.

"Can't believe that you're even considering going back over there Paul, what if you get killed?"

"So sorry dad" I said "please try and understand my dilemma, I don't want you to be angry with me."

"Come here," said my dad, giving me a hug that I wasn't use to. "If that's what you want to do, son, then that's fine by me, just make sure you take care of yourself." It was so nice to have the backing of my father and also my mother who had now accepted the fact that I had made up my mind. "Thanks mum, thank you dad," I said, feeling so much better with the situation. "I'm still at home for the next couple of days before I go, so we will have plenty of time for a good catch up." I spent the next two days tied to my mother's apron and precious time with my father chatting away in his allotment.

I made a call to Lydia the night before I left to confirm my arrangements for the next day; she was still convinced in her own mind that I wouldn't turn up.

"Please, please Paul; don't let me down," she said in a panic stricken way.

"Of course I won't let you down, Lydia," I said with tears in my eyes.

"I love you, Paul Wolfendale," she said; "I love you more than you will ever know." We only spent a few minutes on the phone as the cost to Northern Ireland was very expensive, no more of the dodgy phones like we had in Bridge Camp. I made my way to Liverpool to catch the eight-hour night ferry crossing that would arrive in Belfast early the next morning. A few hours sleep throughout the night made the journey pass quickly as I could see the lights of the ferry port.

Docked up, I made my way back onto Irish soil feeling very anxious. Soldiers patrolling the docks didn't make my return to the land of the Provo's any more welcoming, in fact I felt more anxious than ever. I was thinking to myself *not only are the Provo's my enemy, but I must make sure I don't get compromised by my own mob;* it was a case of one step at a time and see what happens.

As I made my way to the nearby railway station and onto the platform, there were soldiers of plenty; for some unknown reason, one of the soldiers decided to stop and ask me for some ID. My heart was beating ten to the dozen at this moment in time as he said, "Name please, Sir?" I wasn't prepared for this so I was caught a little bit off guard.

"Paul Wolfendale," I said, still feeling shaken by what was happening.

"Do you have any ID on you?" he said, staring me in the eyes with his gun at the ready.

"Yes," I said, searching in my wallet for my Army ID card. What on earth was I thinking about, *why would I want to compromise myself?* Which is what I was about to do. I produced my ID card and at the same time expecting to get arrested when he said, "Oh sorry, Sir, here is your ID back." I couldn't believe my luck, the only thing I thought of was that he must have thought I was some sort of undercover agent; either way I was now on the train making my way to Londonderry.

On arrival in Londonderry after the hour plus journey it was a lot more pleasant than in Belfast with the fact I didn't see any soldiers at all on the platform, even outside the station was looking deserted from a military presence as I made my way to a phone box. Maybe lady luck was shining on me once more.

I could see the Craigavon Bridge in front of me as I looked towards the phone box. I couldn't have been more than a few metres from the bridge that I used to man on the upper tier; staring at the bridge seeing the Army carrying out their duties made me feel glad that it wasn't me standing there searching cars. I made my way into the phone box to make the call that I knew Lydia would be waiting for. I was just about to phone the last digit of her number when to my surprise there was a knock on the door of the phone box, as I turned around to see who it was I was almost in shock.

"Jane," I said, feeling shocked to my ankles, "what the hell?"

"Paul," she said even more shocked than me, "what are you doing here? Catch you on, Paul."

"What do you think?" I said, shaking at the knees.

"You've come to see Lydia, haven't you?"

"Yes, yes I have," I said, trying to think *what the hell is happening, this wasn't in the script*; an IRA informer just happens to be in the exact place as me at the exact time.

"Please don't say anything Jane; you know how dangerous it is for me without you saying anything to make matters worse."

"Of course I won't," said Jane, who was now groping me in the phone box to my delight even though I knew it was wrong.

"Jane," I said, "what are you doing? I thought you were a friend of Lydia's."

"So I am," she said, "if you don't tell then I won't tell." Well, with the fact that I now feared for my life if she so much as uttered a word to anyone, I thought it better if I played ball with her, well at least for the few seconds we were in the phone box. I eventually parted company with Jane and managed to complete my phone call to Lydia.

"Hello," said the voice of the unmistakable Lydia as she picked up the receiver.

"Hi Lydia, it's me, Paul, how are you?"

"Fine," she said, still not knowing that I was in Londonderry.

"Well, are you coming to pick me up or do have to spend the night at the station?" I said, waiting for her reply.

"What do you mean?" she said with her voice now sounding confused. "Are you really in Londonderry Paul? Are you, are you really?" with her voice now getting quicker and quicker and more excitable with each word she spoke. "Oh my god Paul, please tell me you're not joking."

"I'm not joking, Lydia," I said. "I'm at the phone box at the bottom of the Craigavon Bridge; I will tell you the number of the phone that I am phoning from if you don't believe me, Lydia."

"I believe you, Paul, oh my god I do believe you Paul; I just cannot believe what you're telling me."

"Well, I'm here and waiting for you to come and get me."

"I will be with you shortly Paul. Just need to catch the bus to the station, Paul, and then I will be with you."

"OK then, I won't keep you any longer, see you soon."

"Love you, Paul," she said in a voice that I knew she meant every word she said.

"Love you too Lydia," I said at the same time, replacing the receiver.

Lydia arrived within half an hour of exiting the phone box, the feeling of meeting her again was one of perpetual bliss, a feeling that I just couldn't describe; it was just one of those moments that would stay with you for the rest of your life. A hug, an embrace, a twirl brought us together again, the never-ending civil war was not going to stop us seeing each other even though what we were doing could be described as insane. *On the bus to school again* was sloshing around my mind as we sat on the back seat of the bus as tight to each other as we could; it felt like having the freedom of the city as we continued the short ten minute journey to her house.

"This is my house, Paul," she said as we walked the final few hundred metres to where she lived. Her house was something like you would get on a normal housing estate; three bedroom semi detached was how it was.

After entering the front door, I was welcomed by her mother who seemed undeterred by my presence. "This is my mum, Paul, and this is my father."

"Nice to meet you both," I said, still feeling apprehensive about the situation.

"Peter is my name and my wife is called Freda," he said in his Irish accent. "Army lad, is that correct?"

"Yes," I said, not wanting to give too much away.

"You'll be fine with us Paul, so you will, there's no need to worry about that lad."

"That's nice to know," I said, looking in the direction of Lydia for some comfort.

"Paul, I've cooked you a Sunday lunch," said Lydia's mum. "Get yourself sat down at the dining table." Lydia never let me out of her sight for a minute as she watched every mouthful of my Sunday meal until my plate was empty.

"Can I pay you some keep?" I said to Freda after such a pleasant meal.

"Yes, of course, Paul," she said in a kind of expected way. I handed over the amount that I would normally give my parents, to her delight.

"Let me show you where you'll be sleeping, Paul," said Lydia as we made our way up the stairs. "Here we are Paul; you'll be sharing a bed with my brother, Joshua."

"Not a lot of room," I said to myself, "I suppose it will do." A three quarter bed was enough in respect that her brother was only about thirteen years old. It was Monday morning and Lydia needed to catch the bus to school which meant I was all alone with her mum at her house. Lydia and I would secretly, and, out of sight of her parents say farewell in a more of an adult manner than just a quick pick on the cheek. Occasionally her mum would have things to do like her weekly shopping so it was only in the evenings that I got an opportunity to see Lydia, and of course weekends. I felt after the first week of being under house arrest – at my own request I hasten to add – I was getting along nicely with her family, so nice that her father asked me to join him down at the local pub close to where I use to patrol on the waterside. "I'll be fine," I said, "not much of a drinker anyway, but thanks for the offer."

"Don't be silly Paul, do you good getting out for a change so it will."

"Yes," said Freda, "you will be fine with Peter." Why did I get the feeling I wasn't wanted around their daughter anymore? I didn't want to cause any undoing between us so agreeing seemed to be the only option open to me, even though it was under duress. All I wanted to do is spend as much time as I could with Lydia, I could have stayed at home in England and gone down my local boozer if I was that way inclined, but I wasn't.

"Just give me a few minutes to get washed and get changed into something more suitable," I said; this was my way of being able to see Lydia again before leaving. I made my way into my bedroom where Lydia was already waiting.

"Do you really have to go, Paul?"

"Looks like I've got no choice, Lydia," I said, "I don't really want to go."

"Yes, I know," said Lydia. "Anyway I'll be waiting for you when you get back, can you do me a favour, Paul?"

"What's that then?" I said with my mind working overtime.

"Will you bring me back a small bottle of brandy?"

"Brandy?"Well, yes, I suppose so," I said, stuttering my words.

"Don't tell my daddy, Paul, our little secret" she said, "try and hide it in your jacket somewhere if you can."

"Why do I get the feeling that I'm being set up for a nasty fall Lydia, you'll get me into a whole lot of trouble, the last thing I need now is to be thrown out onto the streets for the Provo's to tear me to pieces."

"You're so dramatic, Paul," said Lydia with a smile on her face.

"Well, just let's hope it doesn't come to that," I said seriously with a wry smile on my face.

"You ready, Paul?" said Peter from the bottom of the stairs.

"On my way now," I said. I got quick gentle reminder from Lydia of her affection for me and a swift final prompt not to forget her precious brandy before exiting into the night. It was the same bus journey again back towards the city that gave me time to find out more about Peter and his family. Unfortunately the things he was telling me were things I didn't want or needed to know; let's just say I saw enough bloodshed over the last four months so I didn't need reminding of any more atrocities that have gone on over the years. I just knew it was a bad idea to venture beyond the front door but felt there was little I could do; if I wanted to carry on seeing Lydia then I had little or no option to go along with her parent's request. Sat in the pub I was introduced to a few of his loyalist friends, but still felt extremely uncomfortable.

"Raffle tickets, anyone?" said a middle aged man as he approached the table I was sitting at.

"Yeah, go on then, I'll have a couple," I said in my unmistakeable English accent.

"20p," he said, handing me the tickets, "just write your name on the back of the ticket, here's a pen."

"Thank you," I said, not thinking any more about it until later that evening when the draw was made; unbelievably my name was pulled out. "The winner is Paul Wolfendale." Very Irish name, *not*. I should have written Seamus, Liam or something like that on the back of the ticket; how the hell did I know I was going to win the cash prize that I had to stand up in front of the whole pub to receive. With an extra four quid in my pocket it more than paid for the small bottle of brandy that I just about remembered to purchase before we left. "Great night, Paul," said Peter, putting his arm around me to stop himself falling over and then, staggering onto the bus like someone who needed his bed, "we will have to do it again sometime."

"Yeah, love to," I said sarcastically.

Back at Lydia's, Peter went straight to bed without so much as saying goodnight to anyone. Lydia and her mum were still up watching TV as I made my way into the living room.

"Hi Paul," said Lydia ecstatically, "had a good evening?"

"Great evening," I said, pointing to the inside of my leather jacket; she knew by the look on my face what I was telling her.

"Stretch your legs out, Paul, so I can sit on your lap," she said, parking her backside firmly on my vitals. I could see her mum with her astonishing peripheral vision glancing over and not looking too pleased with her daughter's advances, who may I say, was now getting more familiar with the lower region of my body.

"Lydia, will you keep still?" I said in a quiet voice with her mum just a couple of metres away and still glancing over.

"Enjoying your stay with us here, are we Paul?" said Lydia, whispering in my ear and still moving the cheeks of her buttocks in a circular motion upon my lap.

"Yes of course I am thank you Lydia" I said casually. It was getting to the point now that I didn't want her to stop, but at the same time I could still see her mum grimacing out of the corner of my eye.

"You're such a tease, Lydia," I said, staring her in her eyes. To be honest, I was having so much fun, which is more than I could say for her mum who was now finding it difficult to focus on the television.

"Think it's time you got yourself up stairs to bed now, Lydia?" said her mum.

"Awww, catch yourself on Ma," she said, "I just want to spend some time alone with Paul, please Ma."

"You know you should be in bed by now, so you should, Lydia," she said, at the same time adding more volume to her voice; a little more pleading by her mischievous daughter led to her mum agreeing for us to share no more than ten minutes together. Her Ma turned off the television and made her way to bed closing the door behind her. "Ten minutes, Lydia," she said as she made her way through the living room door. "I shall be back down if you're not up those stairs in ten minutes." With her mum now in her room it was time to get the brandy out.

"I'll get the glasses out," said Lydia, "and you get the brandy open, Paul."

"Never really drank brandy before," I said, "what about you?"

"Just a wee dram my daddy gave me once," she said. I wasn't too sure what to make of that or what Lydia's material motives, let's just say I have never seen someone get drunk so quick in such a short time; two glasses of brandy in two minutes and she was opening her personal private life to me.

"I heard my Ma and my daddy going for it last week, Paul," she said, now lying on the couch and slurring her words.

"Lydia," I said, "I do not need to know about your mum and dad," with my face almost touching hers.

"I heard my Ma say to my daddy oh Peter, Peter, you could kill a cat." I almost choked on my small share of the now empty bottle of brandy. To put things into perspective, Lydia was now becoming more and more flirtatious as she wrapped her arms around my back, pulling me down into the horizontal position.

"Turn the light off, Paul?"

"If you let go of me for a second I will, Lydia," I said stretching for the switch. "Lydia, are you sure we should be doing this?" I said as we starting undressing each other in the darkness of the room, and may I add, at some pace; ten minutes isn't a lot of time to get drunk, undressed and have some fun. I wasn't counting the seconds down but knew if her Ma was keeping her promise, she would be surveying her stop watch and be down the stairs very soon, to be honest what we were doing didn't seem right and for one reason or another her mum saved the day.

"Lydia," I said, "I can hear your mum coming down the stairs, quick, get your clothes on." Not a chance, she was now plastered without a care in the world as opposed to myself who was bricking it. I heard her mum step off the final step of the flight of stairs and then open the door about an inch to announce her presence.

"Lydia, get up stairs now," she said angrily. I was so worried that she was going to open the door a few more inches and find her daughter half undressed when I decided to call her bluff.

"Come in if you like," I said, thinking this is my only option I have to retrieve the situation, my plan worked; reverse psychology is something I didn't believe in, until now.

"No," she said, "I don't want to, now get Lydia to her bedroom right away, you have five minutes." Lydia's mum, who was now fuming, made her way back to her bedroom leaving me with the task of getting her daughter to her bedroom.

"Lydia," I said trying to wake her up out of her coma, "come on sweetheart, we are in a bit of bother; I need to get you to your bedroom before your mother lynches me." A dead weight sprang to mind as I had to drag her up the flight of stairs and into her bedroom. After opening her door I just shoved her in and left her to her own devices; closing the door was the last I saw of her until the next morning. I got myself into bed next to her brother trying not to wake him up. As I lay there for a few minutes before falling asleep I was thinking, *Sunday was supposed to be a day of rest*. I had a feeling that on this occasion it was a case of try to avoid Lydia's mum until she calmed down.

The next morning and with Lydia still sleeping off her hangover I went downstairs to face the music, I was thinking, *a few white lies wouldn't go amiss as her mum quizzed me*.

"So who was drinking alcohol last night?" she said, tidying up her house.

"Just me," I said, now sitting down on the sofa, unfortunately for me she had already done her Sherlock Holmes homework.

"So why were there two glasses on the sink top that both had the remnants of alcohol in them? And, then there was the small empty bottle of brandy in the bin. "Don't lie to me Paul; it's doing you no favours so it isn't." Again I had been rumbled.

"Sorry," I said, not wanting to get Lydia into trouble, "nothing at all of any nature went on, I love your daughter and I am not apologising for that."

"I know you do, Paul," she said, looking me in the face, "there is no doubting that, but as her Ma, I need to look out for her, the troubles over here are bad enough as it is and you seeing my daughter isn't making it any easier. We are always watching out for each other Paul, just the other night there was shooting in Belfast; do you understand what I am saying?"

"Yes I do," I said; "it's not easier for me either, is it? It was just a case of we both just needed to let off a bit of steam." That sort of remark brought a welcomed grin from her mum as I sat there with my short back and sides.

"Ay, I know Paul," she said, now showing a little more compassion. "Put the television on, Paul, I will go and make you some breakfast." It was close to lunch time before Lydia showed her drunken face. I explained that I had spoken to her mummy (a word that she would sometimes use) and that things were a lot better now than a couple of hours ago. Apart from a few evening walks when it had gone dark, I kept myself well away from the local bars.

My final day of my two week tour had arrived and with my bags packed it was all tears from Lydia as we had one final afternoon walk together; a stroll down memory lane is what we took as we sat on a park bench just like we did the first night we met on the illuminating streets of Londonderry.

"Paul, will you stay one more night?" she said, wiping away her heavenly tear drops.

"I'm not sure if your mum will like that, Lydia."

"Then let's ask her, Paul," said Lydia, squeezing my hand in hope that her mum might agree.

"OK then," I said, the only problem I had with the situation was that if not today, then certainly tomorrow this fairy tale of what had been an amazing journey must come to an end. I had my family back in England waiting for me and at the same time, I was a member of Her Majesty's forces who were expecting me back on duty early next week; delaying the obvious was just inflicting more pain on both of us, pain that we could do without. Back at the house I posed the question to her mum like Lydia had asked. Not a chance was the reply in a stern voice. "I am sorry, Paul, your time here has now come to an end; there is nothing you can do or say that will make me change my mind." She said still doing her dusting. "It was nice to have you stay with us, Paul, but to be honest, I have had enough of the entire goings on between you and my daughter to last me a lifetime. You can come back in the summer some time if you would like, but for now, well, I'm afraid it's time for you to leave." Lydia just ran to her bedroom for a few minutes, not being able to handle the news.

"OK," I said, "I understand, not a problem, it was wrong of me to ask." Just then Lydia appeared from the darkness of her room.

"I am going to see Paul off at the station," she said, staring through her tears.

"I don't want you to, Lydia," said her mum, "I'm afraid you might not come back." I could see the concern in her mum's eyes as she continued to question her daughter's mindset.

"My god," I said, "this isn't a conspiracy, this isn't something that we have talked about… of course she will be coming back."

"Lydia, please make sure you come back," said her mum, who was now almost in tears herself. I couldn't take much more of this tearful goodbye situation so decided to put an end to it and just make my way to the bus stop; I had travelled no more than a hundred metres when I heard Lydia racing towards me with floods of tears running down her face.

"Paul, Paul, I am coming with you to the railway station, I am not bothered what my Ma says, I love you so much, so I do Paul."

"I love you too, Lydia," I said with my arms wrapped around her like I was never going to let her go. We were now just ten minutes away from probably ever seeing each other ever again as the bus made its way to the train station. Not once did our hands part for the whole journey as the bus pulled into our stop next to the train station.

With my train already waiting at the platform to take me away from the girl of my dreams, we just stood there facing each other, standing all alone with not a soul to share the platform with. It's as if it was meant to be that we wouldn't be disturbed for our final last few seconds together; we hugged each other like never before as the smile ran away from my face without a word being spoken between us. We didn't need to speak, everything we needed to know was written in our eyes. We slowly let go of each other and made our way down our individual paths that seemed to be mapped out well before we met that one night at the bottom of the Craigavon Bridge. Was this to be our final goodbye? Well, in the next couple of months, things would become a lot clearer.

CHAPTER SIXTY-NINE
EASTER LEAVE BROUGHT ME TO MY SENSES

Arriving back home and still no wiser what was happening to my life, it was time for me to spend a few more days with my parents, it was the least I owed them. I felt that I needed some catch up time; unfaithfulness was a word that was running around my head, a word that that was not part of my character. In the evenings I spend time phoning Lydia from the local phone box. Reversing the phone charges from her house to Bridge Camp cost next to nothing, however, reversing charges from England to Northern Ireland would prove costly for me in more ways than one; both Lydia and I had not the slightest inclination of the implications it would bring to our relationship, but we were later to find out.

After spending the best part of an hour chatting to Lydia and over a period of several days, it was now time to make my way back to Fallingbostal to continue my Army career. Once back in the barracks my mind was still full of thoughts of Lydia, but at the same time, I knew I had to stop torturing myself and eradicate them from my mind. As I made my way into the block and entering my room I saw Don sitting on the edge of his bed listening to some Barry White music.

"Hi Don," I said, trying to clear my mind of thoughts of Lydia, "how was your time in Australia?"

"Don't ask, Paul," said Don, looking disgruntled. "Never made it, I got to the airport to find out I only needed a bloody visa to travel."

"What?" I said feeling stunned, "So sorry, Don, take it no one told you that you needed a visa then?"

"No, I had no idea I needed one," said Don, "absolutely gutted, I just went back to my sister's in Wolverhampton and spent some time with her." I felt so apologetic that I had even asked Don, however, he still managed to raise a smile as he knew that in about nine months time he would be leaving the Army for good.

Things were changing fast. I was now being sought after for babysitting duties, Sergeant Sammy Douglas and Bombardier Pete Dodds were among just a few married pads that I would be required to look after their future NCOs; it was a voluntary duty and not an order, but again, with my kind nature, I thought it rude to say no. To be honest, I had little or nothing to do on a Friday or Saturday night anyway.

Babysitting would always make me feel closer to home sat there in front of the TV Watching BFBS (British Forces Broadcasting Services) and catching up on my habitual Coronation Street. Some good nosh was always available on demand along with a record collection to die for; all in all it was a welcome break from military activities. Day by day I would be making more and more friends and becoming a more popular figure with a lot of the senior ranks; my keenness for sport was now coming to the fore, playing football with Sammy, Pete and some other unfamiliar 18 Battery faces, followed by regimental rugby with my good friend Bombardier Jessie James that I become acquainted with back in Junior Leaders. Another sport I excelled in was cricket, I was selected to play cricket for the regiment along with the Battery Clerk Bombardier Bill Young for whom I might say had a major influence on my love for the music of Neil Diamond.

I felt things had now taken a turn for the best although I knew that there would still be plenty of stumbling blocks along the way. April was now upon us and short sleeve dress was now in force. A change to our dress was the most noticeable thing; instead of wearing coveralls on parade we would wear lightweight trousers and then get changed into coveralls down at the Gun Park. What I did notice is, that when some of the higher ranking senior ranks/officers were replaced by similar ranks, they would all have different ideas of how to run the battery; this was part of the reason for the change in our dress.

I was still receiving letters from Lydia on a regular basis and occasionally up to six letters a day would be in my pigeon hole, our love for each other was still the same and nothing had changed in respect that my life was still full of heartaches, I would always try to embarrass Lydia by writing things on the back of the envelope, things like…

EGYPT (Ever Grasping your Precious Tits)
SIAM (Sexual Intercourse after Midnight)
ITALY (I Truly Adore Loving You), and then there is
IBASISAKILTOTOT (I Buy a Sigh I Send a Kiss I love The One That Opens This)

Lydia would always reciprocate my kind gesture by attempting to outdo me with the number of acronyms she would write on the back of the white envelope. It was getting close to our Easter break and the thought of having a few days off once more was filling everybody with joy. I had nothing planned as I didn't think more than a few days ahead, some might say I don't think at all, anyway, I bumped in Riggers on my travels to see if there was any mail.

"How's it going, Pete?"

"Not too bad, Paul," said Pete, "what are you doing for Easter, Paul?"

"Not sure, got nothing planned; maybe take a trip out to one of the local cities, maybe Hamburg, what about you?" I answered.

"Same as you I suppose, I tell you what though, we could have a word with Parry?"

"A word about what" I said.

"Well, Steve can drive, can't he?" said Pete. "So what about hiring a car and we can do a bit of travelling around."

"Fine by me," I said, thinking *good idea that, Pete.*

"I'll have a word with him then later, see what he says" said Pete, "pretty sure he will be up for it; I'll just tell him we are going on a pub crawl, that will do the trick,"

"Great, let me know as soon as you can," I replied, at the same time wanting to go and see if I had any post, "Just going to see if I have any mail, will catch you later Pete."

"Pretty sure there will be at least one from Lydia," said Pete as if to say *I know I am right.* I made my way to the Battery Block to find that there was a letter for me, a letter that had me wondering who it was from; it was definitely from Londonderry by the postmark, but the hand-writing was telling me otherwise. On opening the letter and reading the first line of the short message it was obvious who it was from; Lydia's mum. She had received a surmountable phone bill and was now requesting or should I say demanding, the full amount of what I would call a month's wages. I could feel the anger in her handwriting as the letter continued to spell out that I was no more welcome at her family home. "I expect payment within the next week," spoke the letter.

I was now at a loss with what I should do next, paying the bill was not an option so the chance of never seeing Lydia again was now becoming a reality. I wasn't sure what impact this was having on Lydia back home, but what I did know is, over the coming weeks, the volume of letters I use to receive was now dwindling; I tried to put the contents of the letter behind me and just concentrate on getting on with my life even though I was hurting deep down. With Easter now upon us I was looking for some fun time with my buddies. Later on that day I caught up with Riggers again.

"Have you managed to speak to Steve yet, Pete?" I said, expecting the worst.

"Yes mate, saw him earlier and he said he was up for it, he said he will sort out the car hire and then we can have a few days off together, travelling wherever we want."

"Great news Pete," I said, "could do with some cheering up," as I explained the context of the letter I received.

"Sorry to hear Paul, don't worry, we will have a great time in a few days' time."

"Thanks for that Pete, you know what, you're right, I'm just going to turn my back on Northern Ireland for a while and try to get my life back to normal; trying to erase those memories won't be easy Pete," I said passionately. I was just glad that I had Pete and Steve to help get me through this entanglement.

After early morning parade we were told that unless we were on duty we were now free until Tuesday morning at 0800hrs. With Steve being in 49 Battery we all got together the night before in the battery bar, *where else,* and arranged for Steve to pick up the hire car in the morning. The plan was to leave by lunch time if Steve was sober enough to drive, and then head out towards Holland; that was about as far as our forward thinking took us. With my small bag packed with a few essentials, I made my way to Pete's room.

"You ready, Pete?" I blasted out as I entered the room.

"Bloody hell Wolfie!" said Pete, scared the living daylights out of me, yes, ready as I'll ever be, ready to have some fun".

"OK then, let's get this show on the road," I said enthusiastically. "Let's go and see if Steve's got the car." With bags in hand we made our way over to 49 Battery to take a look at what car we would be travelling around the world in; to be honest, Pete and I weren't expecting anything out of the ordinary but even we were given a real surprise when we saw Parry loading his belongings into a 'top of the range VW Passat'. It was orange in colour which made it stand out like a sore thumb; who was I to complain, it was the best car I had ever been in, just purely because everything in it worked. It would have been nice to have driven it, but unfortunately, Steve was the only one with a full licence. That didn't seem to bother Riggers, as we were to find out.

"Right, where to?" said Steve as he started up the car.

"Holland, my good man," said Riggers who was sitting in the front; I was just sat there thinking… *what the hell are we doing? The last time I was in Holland I ended up doing a striptease in a club.* This was almost as mental as me going back to Northern Ireland; we had no plan at all apart from a quick stop off in Fallingbostal so Riggers could buy a rather large lens for his camera before navigating to Holland.

"What do we plan to do when we reach Holland?" I said, thinking that one of them might have a sensible answer.

"Get pissed," said Steve without a care in the world.

"What about sleeping?"

"Get our heads down in the car," replied Pete.

"Well, I'm commandeering the back seat," I said with a 'no questions asked' attitude. I'm not too sure why we didn't get lost along the way but within hours, we were crossing the Dutch Border and showing our ID cards to the border patrol.

"Passport," said the Border Guard as we handed over our Army ID cards; even though we knew we weren't terrorists it was always on the back of my mind that Steve would say something like, "He's got a gun in his pocket." It was a pleasant relief to be given the all clear. "On your way," was the order from the guard. We still had no idea where our next destination would be until I said to Steve the Taxi Driver, "Pull over Steve, will you."

"What for" said Steve; clearly thinking I had lost the plot.

"Just pull over, there is a lay-by on the right over there, we need to sort out what we are going to do; I don't want to end up in a brothel tonight."

"Yeah, I think we better," said Riggers looking just as concerned as me, "we need to sort something out, Wolfie's right."

"OK, Wolfendale," said Parry, "now you've got us parked up, what have you in mind?"

"Well, I don't know what either of you think, but what about catching the ferry home, back to England?" I said, trying to take control of the situation.

"Not a bad idea, Paul," said Riggers, "which port did you have in mind?"

"Well, certainly not the port Steve would be thinking about," I said jokingly.

"Just because you prefer a glass of milk," said Steve, "not my fault you're a wuss."

"Well, I'm up for it," said Riggers, "what about you Steve, a couple of days with your family do us all good?"

"Well, if I agree, what's the plan then," said Steve, "can't just drive towards the sea and hope there will be a ferry waiting."

"Let's get the man sized map out," said Riggers.

The map was as big as a dining table, so we just lay it out on the bonnet of the car trying not to look like lost tourists.

"OK," said Steve, "let's work out where we are and then we will take it from there. Go have a look at that sign over there Wolfie, see what it says."

After a short walk of about fifty metres I shouted back, "Wankum, twenty kilometres."

"What did Wolfendale say?" uttered Steve.

"Sounded like wanker," said Riggers.

"Who the fuck does he think he is calling us wankers? Tosser!" shouted Steve.

"You idiot Parry," I yelled, "The name on the sign says Wankum."

To be honest, we all found it pretty amusing once we had established I wasn't calling anyone a wanker. We located the town on our non-tourist map and then decided that if we carried on the same route we would pass through Belgium and then into France, once in France we could make our way to Calais and catch the Calais to Dover Ferry. The idea seemed crazy, another one of my crazy ideas, but at least this time I wasn't the only crazy one, I had my crazy mates Riggers and Parry with me. "How are we for fuel?" I said to Steve, still trying to take control of the situation.

"Almost empty," said Steve, "there's a garage just ahead, think we better pull in and fill up."

"Hope they take Deutsche Marks," said Riggers.

"Bloody hell, never gave it a thought," I said, looking over to Steve.

"Don't look at me Wolfendale," said Steve, "I was put in charge of hiring the car."

"Yeah, that includes the fuel, it's not going to run on fresh air," I said. "Just let's hope they take Deutsche Marks." We didn't think it would do us any favours to fill up before asking so with that in mind, we got Posh Riggers to ask; stood behind Pete, Steve and I were somewhat sniggering at the accent Pete was trying to put on. "Do you take-er Deutsche-er marks or you no take-er Deutsche-er Marks bitte?"

"I speak perfect English," said the cashier in a way that said *why didn't you ask before making a fool of yourself?* Pete just looked at Steve and I who were now heaving with laughter.

"Well done Riggers," I said, trying to pick myself up off the floor.

"Fuck off," said Pete, at the same time chuckling to himself.

"No, we do not take Deutsche Marks," was the reply we received; our heads hit chin strap proportion as we tried to think of a way out of this mess.

"Is there any way we can get some fuel?" said Pete to the cashier with an English twang to his voice.

"Yes" said the cashier, "if you cross the border back into West Germany there is a small town called Wankum."

We were all thinking *everything is fucking Wankum*, we have only been travelling a few hours and already everything is looking Wankum. With no other option available we made our way back through the border and then after refuelling continued on our way; a strange look from the border patrol summed up our day so far.

The journey to France was enduring to say the least which meant once on the ferry, it was a case of a few hours sleep for the short trip across the English Channel. It was early morning when we disembarked in Dover; listening to the sound of the seagulls flying over the white cliffs and that good English fresh air along with the smell of fish and chips brought us out of drowsiness. We were now looking like we had just come of a mackerel trawler and smelling just as bad. We made our way to Uttoxeter to drop Pete off first. Pete's dad was working in the front garden as Steve was tear-arsing the car up the drive without any thought for Pete's dad.

"Get off my drive now, you hooligans," said Pete's dad furiously as the car came to an abrupt halt; it was only when he realised that his son was sitting in the front that he calmed down. "I thought you were German tourists," he said; unfortunately we had forgotten that we were displaying West German number plates.

"See you in three days time on Monday, Pete."

"OK," said Pete, "take care lads, have a nice journey."

"You nutter Steve" I said as we reversed off Pete's drive.

"What!"

"Scaring the living daylights out of Pete's dad," I said. Steve just laughed and even I was finding it funny now thinking back on it.

I was next to be dropped off, probably not a bad thing in respect that Steve was the driver. It was only about an hour to my house, but then Steve had the best part of a two hour journey to Penmaenmawr in North Wales. A quick goodbye to Steve and that was it until his return on Monday. I was hoping to see Dec, but unfortunately, he wasn't due home until the following weekend, however, I knew it would only be a matter of weeks before I saw him again. It was a nice pleasant surprise for my family to see me so soon again even though I had hardly enough time to put my feet underneath the table. Monday arrived in quick time and it was time to make our way back to West Germany to see what the Army had in store; Riggers driving with no driving licence concerned me a tad, but what of it, we just needed to get back, I just closed my eyes and waited for the loud noise you only get from two cars colliding. Three hours late getting back meant we got an extra Guard duty but the memories of the Easter break will last forever.

Now back in camp the main thing I was looking forward to was meeting up with my mate Dec and taking him under my wing; hard to believe that we met when we were about nine years of age and grew up together like brothers, only for us now to be joined at the hip once more as soldiers in the British Army. I was hoping that the arrival of Dec would help me stay out of trouble. No more getting charged for me, I promised myself that I would try and behave; surely my luck must change at sometime, easier said than done as the Christmas spirit was flowing.

CHAPTER SEVENTY
WELCOME DEC GOODBYE DON

Arriving back brought more up evil, as I was to find out that there had been a few changes in where people were sleeping. This was due to people leaving or getting posted to other regiments meaning that some two men rooms became vacant. My good mate Don had moved into a two man room with Geordie Walsh which meant there was just Al Green and myself in a three man room, well at least until they decide to transfer someone else into our room, little did they know that it was tailor made for my mate Dec when he arrived; when one door closes another one opens.

Between April and May I was put on my basic guns course allowing me to get a slight pay rise and a more understanding of the M107 self propelled gun; not sure if anyone fails the three week course, I was just relieved that I passed it. Early May arrived quickly and it was time for me to go and meet Dec off the Army bus up near the cinema, luckily the weather was kind on this Sunday afternoon so the half mile walk meant I didn't get soaked.

I waited feeling excited at his arrival that was now forthcoming; I could see the bus approaching as I was reminiscing about the good times we use to have growing up together. I got my first glimpse of Dec as the bus came to a sudden halt; waving my arms furiously I could see Dec making his way to the exit door dressed in his denim jeans.

"So how's it going then, Dec?" I said, giving him a tap on the back.

"Well, flying for the first time was interesting to say the least, then landing in West Germany without being able to speak a word of German cemented the fact that I would need to learn the lingo."

"I know exactly how you feel Dec, it was the same for me some twelve months ago, at least I can show you the ropes, unlike when I arrived. I knew no one at all apart from Steve Schofield who was in 2 Baker Battery. I have so much to tell you, Dec." Before I could blink we were at the 18 Battery Block and then onto the Guardroom to get booked in. It was easy going for Dec as I knew the format backwards, the only thing I needed to do was to convince the 18 Battery Guard Commander that I had been told that he would be staying in the same room as me, *lying like a drain*.

"Who said he would be in the same room as you, Wolfendale?" said the Guard Commander.

"Sergeant Massey, Bombardier," I said. "I spoke to him on Friday before he went home and he said it would OK for Dec to be put in my room."

"OK then," he said "go and find Limpy Lou and get Gunner Tomkinson's bedding." I explained to Dec on the way to the BQMS stores about Limpy and his nickname whilst at the same time asking Dec if he had been subjected to any nicknames "Tommo," replied Dec.

"Well, that will do for me," I said. "Wolfie or Woofer I get called." After settling in I gave Dec the ten Deutsche Mark tour before turning in and getting some sleep before Monday morning's parade.

Over the next few months and with Dec attached to Sergeant Douglas's C Sub, we were in each other's pocket like a set of twins, I was seeing less and less of Riggers and Steve now with Riggers working in the Signal Department and Steve in 49 Battery, however, we were all getting new sets of friends. Summer leave arrived and Dec and I caught the Hamburg to Harwich ferry, an eighteen hour journey that meant another stay over on the ship. In a strange way soldiers always seemed to have money to burn, especially on pay day, so why is it we didn't have money to pay for a cabin; finding a comfy sofa was as far as it went, this not planning ahead thing was certainly becoming a stumbling block in my itinerary.

I was hoping for a relaxing just Dec and I sail; not a chance. Yet again I managed to get with a bird of the non-feathered type, cutting to the chase, I'm pretty sure she fancied Dec more than me, however, it was me that ended up in her bed; regrets of plenty came to mind as I ended up having to see the doctor on return to the barracks, and so here endeth the lesson. Early August arrived and a regimental parade was the talk of the camp, just like when we were told about our tour to Northern Ireland, we knew something was brewing.

It was to be a sad day in 42 Regiment's history. We were given the unwelcomed news that the regiment would be disbanding in early February, the time my good buddy Don would be leaving the Army for good. 18 Battery would be joining 5 Heavy Regiment in Hildesheim which meant we would not need to be retrained. 5 Heavy had the same guns as 42 Regiment; all twelve guns would be amalgamating with 5 Heavy to make a twenty four gun regiment, four batteries with six guns in each battery. My good mate Steve from 49 Battery would be joining 40 Field Regiment where Dennis and George Lynch were.

It was hard to know how to feel as more disruption was inevitable, I can understand the saying now, 'Join the Army and see the world'. At least Dec and Pete would be joining us, as for Steve, well he would be going to another regiment and keeping in touch with him would become difficult. Leading up to Christmas I was still receiving the occasional letter from Lydia and, oh yes, I finally received a letter with the post mark San Diego on the stamp, it was from Kim, she was inviting me over to Beverly Hills, saying that she had passed her driving test and that she would take great pleasure in showing me around the sights. I was so tempted to go, to this day I wished I had, I just felt that the time wasn't ready to cross the pond, as well as what it would have cost; my parents and my close friends were now playing an even bigger part in my Army career.

Christmas arrived and yet again the phrase 'A leopard never changes its spots' sprang to mind; although I felt I was a becoming the ideal soldier that the Army was looking for, I just couldn't stay out of trouble. It was Christmas Eve and I was enjoying the company of Dec and Don in the 18 Battery bar along with my other so called mates when the BONCO (Battery Orderly Non-Commissioned Officer) came in dressed in his combats. His job was to keep law and order, wake people up in the morning for parade, albeit there would be no one to wake up on Christmas morning. Stood at the bar, the BONCO, who was my gun driver Dinger Bell, was having a drink or two. I'm not sure if it was allowed when on duty however, it was Christmas Eve and could be overlooked with some discretion. I was pretty sure that I had no axe to grind with Dinger although I felt we were always butting heads with each over.

After a short while a few unsolicited words were exchanged. My mate Don wasn't helping the situation by saying, "Why don't you smack him, Paul?" Thumping someone was the last thing on my mind until Don kept pushing the issue. Out of the blue Dinger got wind of what Don was saying and then turned to me to say, "Anytime Wolfendale, I'll fucking have you." Not sure where it came from to be honest, I was gobsmacked; although I am a quiet person most of the time I just snapped and took up the challenge as Dinger continued his rant. "Come on then Wolfendale, outside now." Followed by half of the battery, we made our way in an aggressive manner out of the bar and into the corridor that led to the exit door which also included the Guard Commander Roger Glanfield.

We got as far as the exit door before the fist fighting took place, I remember Dinger landing the first punch on my nose but then, I just let fly putting Dinger on the floor before the Guard Commander decided that, although he was enjoying the fight, enough was enough and pulled me off. "Bell, follow me down to the Guardroom," said the Guard Commander aggressively. "Wolfendale, get your arse back into the bar and out of the way." It wasn't long before the ROS arrived.

"Wolfendale, get yourself outside now," said Sergeant Harkin the ROS. "Wolfendale, what did you think you were playing at lad, you just can't stay out of trouble can you? How many times have you been charged since arriving?"

"Twice, Sergeant," I said fearing the worst.

"And now look," said Sergeant Harkin, sounding pissed off. "You're in trouble again, aren't you?"

"Yes Sergeant."

"Well, I've spoken to some of the lads that were in the bar and you can thank them that you're not being locked up for the night. L/Bombardier Bell is locked up in a cell until the morning. Be warned Wolfendale, you can't go around fighting with the BONCO or anyone else that is on duty, now get out of my sight."

With time now ebbing by, I made my way back to the block as it was now close to Christmas Day. The following morning Dec and I were invited to Sergeant Pete Dodd's married quarters for Christmas dinner; Pete was my section commander in Londonderry and had more recently been promoted to Sergeant. Being invited to married quarters was a thing that went on a lot in the Army, all living-in soldiers were invited to spend the day with the married families; the wonderful turkey dinner washed down with a glass of wine and great hospitality made it a memorable occasion to cherish.

With Christmas soon over, it was time to see what next year would bring. January was much about getting ready for our disbandment parade; the block was looking like the painters and decorators had moved in, with all rooms and basically anything that stood still getting a lick of paint. A lot of the lads were having to move into different rooms while their rooms were being painted which meant I ended up in a two man room for the first time with my mate Don; it was quite fitting with the fact that Don was the guy

458

who made me most welcome when I arrived some twenty months ago, and now here I was reunited with him again just before he leaves.

"Who's the photograph of, Don?" I said. "The one on your bedside table, I've never seen it before."

"No, my sister gave it to me when I was on leave, it's of my little sister Jess, she's fifteen years old and I haven't seen her for almost two years now."

"Good looking girl, she is," I said, being polite, even though she was.

"Why don't you write to her Paul? She would like that."

"Write to her" I said feeling humbled that he thought I was an alright guy.

"Yes, she would like that" said Don without any qualms.

"OK," I said, *why not?* With the fact that Lydia was out of arms' reach along with my American girl, it would be nice to receive a letter or two from Don's sister. Don gave me her address and the same night laid on my bed, I started to write to yet another girl that I thought was just going to be a type of pen friend. *Wrong again, Wolfendale.* Before I knew it we were sending cassettes to each other.

The cassettes were so welcome, every day I would make my way down to the Battery Office in hope that there would be a small package for me. It was probably about the third time that I received a cassette from Jess in which I realised from her comforting words that this was turning out to be something more than just a casual relationship on paper. After inserting the cassette and listening to her voice she was becoming more intimate by saying, "Paul, I hope that one day you'll be able to come over and see me, I love you so much, and when you do come over it won't just be puppy love we make." Falling in love with yet another girl from overseas was again playing with my mind; sometimes I would play the cassette over and over again just to hear her beautiful voice and her meaningful words.

February soon arrived and not only was the battery getting ready for our farewell parade, but for me, it was a case of saying goodbye to a true gent and great friend in Don Bowles. Don was doing his rounds, saying goodbye to all his friends after handing all of his Army clothing back to the BQMS stores; I was hanging around in the drying room when Don popped his head around the corner of the door.

"There you are," said Don, full of jubilation. "Glad I found you Paul, I wanted to say my goodbyes to you last with you being such a great friend of mine."

"Well, Don," I said with a tear forming in my eye, "I feel proud and privileged to have had you as a friend, wish you were staying though, without trying to sound gay, I'm going to miss you Don."

"Just promise me you'll keep in touch," said Don, giving me a man hug.

"An M107 driven by Dinger couldn't stop me, Don."

"Keep in touch with Jess, Paul, I know she loves you," said Don. We looked at each other with mutual admiration and a smile that was hiding our pain; 'unfortunately' there was no cure for the way we were feeling. Don turned and made his way down the stairs and out of the block for the last time leaving me on my own for a few minutes to ponder over the great times we had together. I can't remember Sergeant Boucher back in the Army Careers Office saying anything about all the heartbreak that comes with being a soldier. Carol, Kim, Lydia, my mates at Junior Leaders and now Don; it felt like a living bereavement I was enduring.

Losing Don made me a better person in respect that I had a better understanding of how other soldiers would feel when this sort of thing happened to them. I was always a caring person, but now felt I had a degree in the subject. Having a heart to heart with some of the lads was becoming a speciality of mine.

With Don now back with his family in Australia it was time for the regiment to make their way to Hildesheim in dribs and drabs; a new start and new mates was what I was thinking. Hildesheim was proving to be a hit with all the guys; it took no more than a few weeks for us all to settle-in, luckily for me I managed to accommodate a two man room with Dec, well at least for the time being.

I was almost out of my teens and still just as easily influenced. I was just hoping that the next few months or so would see me settling down a bit more, would buying a motorbike be the answer?

CHAPTER SEVENTY-ONE
YELLOW PERIL

It was early spring. Dec and I were just chatting away in our room when some dude in a smart suit was doing the rounds.

"Hi there," said the man standing by our open door.

"Can I help you?" I said, wondering what he was doing.

"Yes," he said, "can I come in and have a chat?"

"Well, you're halfway in already," said Dec, "you may as well come the whole way now you've come this far."

"Can I sit on the bed?" he said politely.

"Yes, make yourself at home," I said, "What is it you're selling?"

"Well, first off my name is Bernard, Bernard Farrell. How do you fancy owning a motorbike? I have some photos if you would like to see them."

"A motorbike," I said, "never ever crossed my mind."

"Well now is your chance to own one."

"Bloody hell Dec, what do you think?" I said. "I can't even ride one."

"Me neither," said Dec. "Can't be any different than riding a bike." The guy on the bed must have been laughing under his breath whilst at the same time thinking, *what a couple of mugs*; I bet he was already seeing Deutsche Marks in front of his eyes. We sat down and browsed through the catalogue of motorbikes on offer; Dec had the luxury of passing his driving test back in Junior Leaders just like my mate Steve, but me, well, I didn't even have a fishing licence. Before we could pose that important point to him, he said, "Oh by the way, you only need a provisional driving licence and not a full licence, you can ride up to a 250cc on your provisional without passing a test." Well that was it, he was about to make the sale of the century, not one, but two motorbikes, the thought of owning my own motorbike was too much to resist.

"What do you think, Dec?" I said hoping for a positive answer.

"Can't see why not," answered Dec, voicing his opinion. "I think we should go for it, we can ride home to England on them in the summer."

"OK," I said to Bernard, "we would both like to buy one."

"Fantastic," said Bernard, "is there any one in particular that takes your fancy?" We both looked through his brochure and after a short deliberation; we decided to buy the Honda 250cc T with Dec choosing a dark red one and myself a bright yellow one.

"I will get all the paper work sorted right away and the bikes should be ready for you to pick up in about two weeks' time," said Bernard, who looked like he was about to book his family holiday at our expense. Soon after he had left, Dec and I mulled over what we had just ventured into, only one of us could drive and that was on four wheels; now here we were about to be the owner of a 250cc motorbike, stupidity once again sprang to mind. Two weeks had passed and we got confirmation that the machines were waiting for us in a shop in Hamburg, a city of mass proportions. Bernard came to pick us up in his Merc and drove us the two hour journey to the shop where our bikes were being held.

On arrival we entered the shop to catch our first glimpse of the two bikes that were awaiting their owners. We could see the polythene wrapped around the seats and that smell of newness that you only get from a new brand new bike. Looking at the gleaming bike made me just want to get on the bike and ride it; little did I realise that my eagerness was going to be my down fall. The bikes were wheeled out of the shop and onto the edge of the quiet residential street (It wouldn't be quiet for long) with the polythene still covering the seats. It seemed like kids' stuff until I kick-started the engine.

"Just have a little ride around the block to get use to its power," said Bernard like we knew what we were doing, "and then when you both feel comfortable you can follow me to the Autobahn where you can navigate your way back to Hildesheim. "We went at a slow pace with Dec taking the lead and myself close up behind, the first couple of left turns were negotiated with consummate ease as I was just following the same line as Dec. It was on the third left turn that I came a cropper as I lost the concept of which control made me stop and which one didn't; I believe I accelerated at the same time trying to brake, thus gravitating my bike into a nearby wall. After dusting myself down with just a few minor lacerations it was time to examine my new toy: front head light smashed, dent in the lower regions of the fuel tank, bent gear lever, oh, and one consolation, the polythene that was on the seat was still intact. I managed to get the bike started again and decided to push it along the final straight to the shop.

"What the hell has happened?" said Bernard.

"Don't ask," I said, looking worse for wear. "Let's just say there's more to riding a Motorbike than I first thought." It wasn't going to deter me from giving it another go; one more lap of the estate did the trick.

"You OK, Paul?" said Dec, looking worried.

"Yes, just let's get going before I change my mind," I replied. Riding through the streets of Hamburg was daunting to say the least, the journey through the busy streets seem to last a life time as we tried to keep pace with Bernard; I can't remember how many red lights we ran to keep Bernard in our sights, but it was more than I could count on my fingers. We finally said goodbye to Bernard as he pointed towards an Autobahn sign that we needed to get us back to camp; even now I'm still not sure how I ever managed to get back without inflicting more damage to my pride and joy.

I managed to get my bike fixed up over the next week apart from the dent in the tank; all Dec and I were concerned with now was our leave in late March. Before all that we were told of a regimental parade that was pending; the last two regimental parades brought contrasting news, the first news was to inform us of our tour to Londonderry Northern Ireland, the second, news about the disbandment of 42 Regiment. *What's next?* I thought. Well, I was finding it hard to believe what I was hearing as we stood in three ranks on the regimental parade square; another tour to Northern Ireland in September was on the cards. This was not normal, a two year gap is what normally happens, however, with the fact that we had joined another regiment the time gap was unavoidable; County Armagh, bandit country is where 18 Battery would be deployed and details would follow in due course.

We had leave to look forward to first and then we would start thinking about Northern Ireland after we get back. There were three of us with motorbikes now: Dec, a guy called Phil Card who was also from Nantwich and me. Phil was a lot more experienced on a motorbike or at least that's what he had us believe. He gave us the 'how to keep safe' speech that lasted all of thirty seconds. Did we listen? Not on your Nelly. We made our way out of the camp gates and onto the nearby Autobahn with Phil taking the reins. Dec and I were now oozing with confidence as we were getting to grips with the Autobahn and its ride as fast as you like speed limits; it was only when we came to a traffic jam that it all went wrong.

Phil had already warned us not to undertake on the inside if there was slow moving traffic, he explained that we would be better going through the middle of the stationary vehicles. Unfortunately, Dec had by some means managed to get to the front with myself close up behind, a gap seem to open up on the hard shoulder side that didn't require a second invitation. Dec decided to weave his way alongside a huge articulated truck with me close up behind. It took less than a couple of seconds for the inevitable to happen, the truck driver decided to move further over into the hard shoulder not sensing that we were in his blind spot.

I could see Dec panicking as the truck was practically in his shadow, a second later Dec hit the hard surface; there was little I could do to avoid him as I crashed into him pushing us both down the grass bank. A few tumbles could be seen as we finally came to an abrupt halt with our bikes resting on top of our battered bodies. I looked over towards Dec and to my amazement, he just started laughing his head off.

"What the hell are you laughing at?" I said, thinking he'd lost the plot.

"No idea," said Dec. "I think it's because you crashed into me, causing us both to crash." I could see where he was coming from as it wasn't long before I joined in with his laughter. We managed to get ourselves sorted and back on our way without too much damage to our bikes. This time we decided that Phil could take the lead once more. Twice now I had crashed my bike, they do say things come in threes, well in my case they came in fours: I crashed it once more while enjoying my leave causing more damage to my bike. On the way back to West Germany after Dec and I had just filled up with fuel, we both got caught out with how sharp the bend was exiting the petrol station. Dec managed to escape by banking over as far as he dared, but me, well I went arse over tit once more onto the grass at the same time bending my gear lever.

Crashing my bike was becoming an everyday occurrence now. I just straightened my gear lever and made my way back onto the Autobahn to catch up with Dec who had no idea I had crashed , until I caught up with him later. Well, at least I had more sense than Dec when he used the naked flame of his lighter to see how much fuel was in his tank.

An adventure and a half was had by Dec and I, one I shall never forget, however it was now time to get back to business with Northern Ireland looming in a few months' time. Training was much the same as it was for Londonderry except we were to carry out more rural type exercises. Lucky for me, Dec and I were put in the same section with the section commander being Sergeant Douglas, our gun No.1; other names were Geordie Stanton,

Les Sheared and a REME guy attached to us just like in Londonderry; a better section I could not have wished for. During weekend time off, Dec and I would venture out a lot more on our bikes, mainly just to get us away from the barracks. What would be the chance of Dec and I meeting two girls on separate nights in a night club and then find out they were sisters, surely not? Well, I was definitely dealt the hand of fate.

CHAPTER SEVENTY-TWO
WATER SLIDE SPEED RECORD

Another week passed and yet another Monday morning parade brought some interesting news, we were informed that we would be flying around in helicopters in preparation for what lay ahead. The AAC, with their sky blue berets who were stationed on the same camp as us (Tofeck Barracks), were going to be taking us up in their helicopters and then dropping us off in various locations to simulate the rural areas of County Armagh. It was the first time for most of the lads and an experience I wouldn't forget in a hurry; the smell of the aviation fuel and the sounds of the rotor blades whizzing above your head as you entered through a huge side door emphasised the danger when boarding.

Once in the air it was an amazing experience flying over the local villages that surrounded Hildesheim. "OK lads, get yourselves ready for landing," was the barking voice of Sergeant Sammy Douglas. The doors of the helicopter were already open so banking over to the left didn't do my nerves any favours, all I could see was the wooded grass area through the open doors as the helicopter banked even further over.

The helicopter hovered about three or four metres from the ground and then it was our turn to jump out in an orderly fashion without trying to land on your mate, a short run into the wooded area was next before the helicopter took off; landing on terra firma would delay the helicopter from making a quick escape in the event of an ambush occurring; hovering just above the ground was the way it was done for a quick getaway. Weekend arrived and apart from going to Hildesheim on Friday evening to do my laundry, I had a leisurely night watching BFBS television from the luxury of my bed, unlike Dec. Dec was getting out a little more now that he had his two-wheeled transport. It must have been close to midnight when I heard his motorbike on the car park at the back of the block, within minutes Dec was in the room.

"Good night Dec?" I said with some sort of interest.

"Yeah, went to the Sound Club in Bad Salzdetfurth, about fifteen kilometres away."

"I wouldn't mind getting out myself." I said.

"Well, I'm going back there tomorrow night, why don't you join me?"

"Not sure if it's my sort of scene," I said, now having second thoughts.

"It will do you good," said Dec. "Remember Paul, there is no such luxury in negative thoughts."

"Seeing as you put it like that then," I said, "why not" I'm still not sure what he meant.

"I have just started dating a German girl by the name of Angela (An-gay-la); she speaks quite good English, which helps."

"I've had enough of girls for a while," I said, "not that I'm changing my allegiance, it's just that I seem to fall in love too easily and then get hurt." The following night Dec and I made our way to the Sound Club which was bursting to the seams with locals and a small amount of squaddies that managed to scrape themselves from the battery bar. I felt a little uncomfortable sitting on my own at times as Dec was strutting his wiry frame on the dance floor to a song called 'Yes Sir I can Boogie'. As the evening went on and again sitting on my own, a young, good looking, dark haired girl decided to make her presence felt. *Is it possible to accidentally brush yourself against another person when there's ample space to get past?* A ten out of ten smile and a glare with *'come to bed eyes'* gave it away as she returned to the dance floor and, still looking in my direction. I never gave much attention as to what her intentions were so just continued enjoying my own company until I felt I was ready to leave. The night was still young, well, at least by some people's standards, but for me, it was late enough. I decided to make my way back to camp leaving Dec to enjoy the company of his good looking lady.

The next morning and in the washrooms I confronted Dec about the mysterious girl, after describing her to Dec he said. "Now I know who you mean, Angela's sister."

"What" I said, feeling shocked.

"Yes, her name is Marlene."

"Wow, do you know if she is going out with anyone?" I said. "If not, could you put a word in for me?"

"I'm going to her house tomorrow night, so I will mention you to her if you like."

"Cheers," I said, "that would be great if you could."

I had almost forgotten about the whole episode until a couple of days later when Dec mentioned that he had spoken to Marlene and, that she would love to go out with me. She met me at the Sound Club the following Friday evening, in fact she brought me a chain with the letter P on it to hang around my neck (probably from her ex). I was thinking *here I go again*, another girl in my life and one that I could do without. The following weekend it was back to the Sound Club to meet up with Marlene once more; whilst there, I bumped into Riggers and a couple of his new mates.

"Riggers, come over here for a minute."

"OK there, Paul," said Riggers, "dare I ask why you're here?"

"Got a date with a German girl that doesn't seem to be here yet," I said, feeling let down.

"What's her name?"

"Marlene," I said, whilst at the same time catching a glimpse of her in the dark distant room. "Here she is now, over there," I said excitedly "the one with the dark hair."

"I would stay clear of her, Paul," said Riggers. "I have seen her here a few times and I know for a fact that she is going out with a guy called Smudge from Q Battery, I was even thinking of asking her out until I found out she was going out with one of the lads from the camp." I was quite shocked at what Riggers had said, although at the same time, felt undeterred.

"You'll have a job to keep her, Paul," said Riggers, swigging his pint, "you would be better off finding someone else."

"Well, thanks for the advice, Riggers," I said. "I'll just see what happens, where is her so called 'boyfriend' then?"

"He's on leave until next week, answered Pete, don't think he will be to best pleased when he comes back."

"Cross that bridge when I get to it" I said." I spent the evening with Marlene and at the same time quizzed her about Smudge.

"Don't need to worry about him," she said, "we were going out with each other but not anymore." Not sure why she said that because a few days later he was back on the scene. News was now travelling around that I was now seeing Marlene and that I had a yellow motorbike, so it was no surprise when I left the sound club late that night to find someone had cut the leads to the spark plugs with the intentions of immobilising my pride and joy. It almost worked, I just connected the leads back on to the plugs again; mind you, I did get a few electric shocks on my way back to camp as my bike became live, that's about as far as it went until I managed to get it fixed.

Later on that day in the camp cookhouse I confronted Smudge and his mates who blatantly denied that they had any knowledge of the incident. Proving it would difficult, so I decided that rather than get myself into trouble I would just leave it and hoped it would all be forgotten about in a few days' time, unfortunately not. A couple of days later I was at Marlene's house along with Dec when a car drove up outside. Before I could even blink, Marlene was at the window. "It's Smudge," she said smiling, "I am going to see him."

"Stay where you are," I said. "I'll go and see him; I have some unfinished business with him." I made my way to his now stationary car that he was driving along with a couple of his mates.

"What do you want?" I said politely.

"You'll fucking know if I get out of this car," he said angrily.

"Well then why don't you get yourself out of the fucking car?"

"Do you want me to then, do you?" he said furiously with his mate sat next to him.

"Your choice" I said. There was no reply, just the look of a loser was enough for me to feel he was finally getting the message; a quick wheel spin was heard as he sped away with his tail between his legs. It was so refreshing that he didn't get out of the car; getting charged again for fighting was something I could do without.

Over the next few weeks Dec and I were getting our feet under the table, finding out more about their family; seven daughters and five sons made up their huge family, almost as big as my family. Marlene was the third youngest and Angela the fourth in the household, again like my family most of them were now married and living elsewhere. Dec and I decided that we would have one final weekend with the girls before we went to Northern Ireland; it was a water park outside Hildesheim that would be our destination.

The weather was boiling and the park was full to the rafters making the queues for the water slides extensive. In for a penny in for a pound was my motto as I made my way up the stairs doing my best to look breathtaking in my flower power trunks; trying to impress my girlfriend was also at the forefront of my mind.

I was not averse to heights, but looking down from the top of the slide had me having second thoughts about taking the quickest route to reach the bottom. Fastened to the railings I noticed a sign that was written in German and English, it read 'WAIT UNTIL THE SLIDE IS CLEAR BEFORE YOU ENTER THE SHOOT'. *No problem with that,* I said to myself.

All this seemed straightforward as I was now getting closer and closer to my turn. I stood behind some young German lads that were looking all keyed up and raring too go; one thing that did spring to mind was the loudness of the boys with their deep voices, a far cry from my voice at their age.

The speed they went down the slide was one that I was determined to match as I gave a short, but noticeable wave to Marlene, who by now was getting a stiff neck; standing first in line and waiting for the person in front of me to exit the slide I made my way forward. With an Olympic type push I flew the first ten metres without touching the slide thinking I was going to slide down at a speed that was second to none. I was shocked to say the least as I came to an abrupt halt and found myself paddling my arms furiously to try to impress my girlfriend. I must have held the slowest record for getting from top to bottom, I looked up to see the queue had increased tenfold as they waited for me to finish my run.

"Well done Paul," said Marlene and Angela along with Dec clapping his hands as I exited the pool.

"Can't understand it," I said, feeling embarrassed, "did you see my Olympic push off?"

"Yes," said Dec still laughing his nuts off, "and then you stopped, what happened?"

"No idea," I answered, feeling like a complete idiot, and not for the first time I hasten to add.

"It was a good effort, Paul," said Angela feeling sorry for me.

"Well I'm going to give it another go and try to beat my last time," I said with aggression in my voice.

"Shouldn't be too difficult," said Dec giving me no hope at all. I made my way back up to the top of the slide with more determination than ever, at the same time trying to evaluate where I went wrong. Suddenly, I noticed that all of the younger generation that were standing in the queue had a technique to their style: before they threw themselves into the shoot they would put their trunks into the crack of their bum so quickly you hardly noticed it, and the ones that were wearing shorts would slide them down a little so their bottom would be on the slide and not the material. I wasn't sure at this moment in time what impact it would have, but felt it was worth giving it a go if I wanted to impress.

A one off elderly gentleman with a sort of penalty spot on top of his head had managed by some means to get in front of me in the queue; normally this wouldn't have any bearing on the situation with the lethargic speed I would be travelling at, but all would be revealed in the next thirty seconds or so.

Next in line I could just about see the penalty spot disappearing around some of the bob-sleigh like bends and seemingly well out of my range; ignoring the warning sign I discreetly give myself a so-called wedgie and, just like before, threw myself into the mouth of the slide.

"Fucking hell," I blurted out, I was now totally out of control without any brakes, the first couple of bends saw me almost flying out of the slide as I shot up the sides picking up momentum with every second, it wasn't until I saw the elderly gentle in my sights that I really knew I was in trouble. I tried in vain to get the gentleman's attention by shouting what little German I knew. "Fooking hell, I no brakes have." I could see the look on his face quite clearly now as he looked over his right shoulder to get a glimpse of what he was about to endure.

The man with the penalty spot was now trying to pick up some speed of his own; fearing for his life he frantically started pushing himself forward with his arms and legs. There was only one thing for it, I put both of my arms onto the side of the slide and used them as brakes. I could feel my skin being ripped off as I was reeling-in the elderly man closer and closer, within seconds I hit the man with such strength that he was now at my beck and call. We were both now travelling towards to end of the slide without any way of slowing down; we shot around bend eight and then projected about ten metres forward into the swimming pool before disappearing under the water.

It seemed like forever until I emerged to a rapturous applause from the onlookers; they had never seen so much fun at the water park. It wasn't until a few seconds later that I caught sight of the elderly gentleman on the surface of the water coughing up the contents of the pool; getting his breath back he looked at me and gave me a right volley in his native voice. I made my way over to Dec and the girls and explained that I thought it was time we left with the fact I was going to be kicked out of the park anyway. "Good call," said Dec, still laughing his head off; we were out of the park within five minutes and on our way back to the girls' house.

After spending the evening with our respective girlfriends it was time to make our way back to the barracks; it was nice to get a warm send off from their parents who, 'just like the whole world', knew about the conflict in Northern Ireland. "Take care Paul take care Tommo," they said as we made our way out of the door. Two big hugs from our love ones meant it was now time for us to start our motorbikes up and be on our way; it felt like our own personal farewell that was appreciated by both Dec and I.

With Northern Ireland now upon us it was going to be four months or so before we would ever be able to see them again. We had been together for about six weeks, but our relationship would now be tested, four months away from each other can be a long time; would we still be together when we came back from our tour of duty? Only time would tell. It was now September and I was saying goodbye to my teenage years as I celebrated my twentieth birthday just before our tour of Northern Ireland. We were all hoping that it would be a tour without any casualties, a tour that would see everyone arriving back safely; however, we didn't take into account that we were in more danger from one of our own men as he was unloading his LMG (Light Machine Gun).

CHAPTER SEVENTY-THREE
KEADY, COUNTY ARMAGH

The build up to the eagerly awaited tour on Wednesday the 28th September, was pretty much the same as the first tour so for me, mainly because I knew what to expect. I wasn't looking forward to four months away from my home comforts. As for Dec and some of the other lads, it was their first time so naturally for them they were feeling a little excited, for want of a better word. Reminiscing about my unforgettable tour of Londonderry to Dec as we sat together on the flight over to Aldergrove was the main topic of conversation, along with trying to answer all of his inquisitive questions.

After a smooth landing it was quite a trek to the main city of Armagh before we were transported to Keady, the place that would be our main location for the next four months. Keady is a small rural town with limited streets; let's just say if you fancied a night out, then Keady wasn't the place for merrymaking. The camp was a tiny affair that was occupied by a small section of RUC personnel; one of our duties that we would be expected to carry out was to work in unison alongside the RUC when required. Three sections occupied the camp which to be honest, was plenty with the size of the camp. Guard duties were required with one Sanger overlooking a rural hill, and then a couple of men on the galvanized gates adjacent to the loading bay. About five to ten miles away was 18 Batteries main location in a derelict place called Middletown; right on the border of the Republic, making it an easy option for the Provo's to escape.

The tour started off sedately; instead of the PCPs like we had in Londonderry, we were now doing neatly planned foot patrols everywhere apart from the occasional mobile patrols. We were issued heavy type parka coats to protect us from the elements that we were subject to in the rural outback's; climbing over stiles and walking across fields made me feel like I was back at home on the farm. It was now the 3rd October just five days into our tour that saw our section united with a new face. He was a guy call Gavin, Gavin Hamilton from Barrow-in-Furness. Gavin had just celebrated his 18th birthday and finished his NIRTT (Northern Ireland Reinforcement Tactics and Training) which was done in Ballykindly; Gavin had to learn in two weeks what we had to learn in three months.

"How are you doing?" I said to Gavin, trying to make him feel welcome as I showed him where he would be sleeping.

"Fine thanks, a little nervous." He said

"Only to be expected, I've already done one tour in Londonderry mate so I am pretty sure I know how you're feeling." I knew how important it would to make him feel welcome however, I had no idea that throughout the tour we would forge such a fantastic relationship and he would become one of my best buddies, we just seemed to click.

"My Name is Paul, Paul Wolfendale; my buddies call me Woofer or Wolfie so take your pick."

"Woofer, yeah I like that," said Gavin, "most of my mates call me Hammo."

"Sounds good to me, that, Hammo; I will introduce you to the rest of the section." Hammo came across as being a very studious person; with his quick wit and sense of humour he was proving to be a hit with the rest of the section, not to mention his blonde hair and the fact that he was one of the smallest guys in our section. It was so refreshing to have someone who shared the same sort of feelings as me; he was kind hearted and someone who you could turn to if you ever had a problem. Hammo: Tommo, Geordie Stanton, Sammy Douglas and Dinger Bell meant we had a well-knit section, a section to be proud of.

In some strange way it was like de-ja-vu for me, I remember only too well that just a couple of weeks into my tour of Londonderry our section were called out to an incident where a UDR man had been shot dead; well this time it only took ten days for the same thing to happen. It seemed like a welcome present from the Provo's to warn us of their never-ending resilience against the British. They were cowards, how could anyone shoot a poor, innocent girl in cold blood and be called a hero by their counterparts. Well, that's what we were up against. It was the evening of Saturday 8th October and we had just come in from a foot patrol in Keady, a lot of shouting could be heard from the operational room. "Section two; get yourselves ready to move out now."

"Bloody hell," I said to Tommo, "wonder what's up."

"No idea," said Tommo as we were now heading at full pelt towards the loading bay,

"Hammo, get over here now" I said "something's going off, but not sure what." We were all now on edge even though I had been through this sort of thing before.

"OK two section, get yourselves into the back of the Land Rovers now," said Sammy with some urgency in his voice. "Dinger, (Brick Commander) take the rear vehicle with Geordie Stanton and Les Sheared. Woofer, Tommo, Hammo in the first Land Rover with me." Everything was at a frantic pace as the main gates crashed open; sat in the back with our rifles at the ready, Sammy explained what little he knew. "There has been a shooting on Doogary Road near Tynan, a section from Middletown has been sent out to the incident and we are providing back up, when we get there we will be forming a cordon under my instruction, at the moment that's all I've been told."

Apart from Sammy, I was the next most experienced man in the Land Rover so I was trying my best to keep a cool head which I knew was needed in the circumstances; leaving the camp gates with a sudden burst of speed had us hanging on for dear life. It only took about five or six minutes to reach our location before jumping out of the back of the now almost stationary Land Rovers. "Wolfendale, Hamilton, get yourselves squat down by the hedge," said Sammy, listening in on his radio. "Tommo, you come with me." There were all sorts of bits of information being spouted around as Hammo and I just continued to do what we were there for, keeping an eye open for any sign of trouble; within minutes of getting settled down on the damp and cold grass we heard a commotion going on in the growing dark of the night.

"Found the weapon," could be heard from one of the lads in a loud and excitable voice... "An Armalite rifle," continued the shouting. Finding a weapon was like finding a needle in a haystack so you could imagine the excitement from the lads. After a good hour of freezing to death it was time to head back to camp for a debrief and to find out more about the incident as opposed to listening to rumour control; "Get yourselves sorted and then straight into the briefing room," said Sammy, who was now somewhat calmer.

Once in the briefing room and after receiving praise for our efforts, we were gathered together like we were going to be given a press conference; with a few of the senior ranks now in position we were ready to listen to what had happened.

"Tonight, and through no fault of anyone, three young men claiming to be part of the IRA committed an outrageous and brutal killing. The killing was nothing short of what the IRA is renowned for, but even by their standards a killing that can only be described as appalling. The three young men drove casually along the rural country road and then with an Armalite rifle in hand, made their way to the front door of their targeted house. They were searching for a young part-time UDR Greenfinch by the name of Margaret Hearst. (Greenfinch is a name given to a female member of the UDR). Private Hearst was off duty. At the time she would have naturally been unarmed due to Army policies. On opening the door the three men barged their way in, terrorising her more elderly parents and her two brothers before being told under duress that Private Hearst lived in the caravan at the side of the house, along with her three year old daughter.

That was it, they knew where she was so one of the young lads made his way out of the house and headed towards the caravan while the other two waited for the few seconds it would've taken to murder the poor young girl, a vast number of rounds were fired even though one well aimed shot would have been enough to kill her instantly. Her three year old daughter was thought to have been sleeping with her Kermit the Frog cuddly toy, which after examination was found to have had a stray bullet gone through it, was there any intention meant? I guess we will probably never know the answer to that. In the follow up search to the shooting, an Armalite rifle was found in the hedge row by Gunner Robbo Robinson, some few hundred metres from the scene. With that evidence, the chances of the perpetrators still being in the North are slim; it is likely they have fled back over the border and into their safe haven in the Republic."

Private Hearst was the first Greenfinch to be killed while off duty, and although a flare was set off from the dwelling to alert the Army of the monstrosity, it was to be in vain.

Back in the barracks and after a good night's sleep it was time to get a brief before going out on patrol. We already knew what the main part of the brief would be about, last night's atrocities, so it was a case of enlightening us to any other overnight developments.

"Get sat down," was the order from TSM Hardy (Troop Sergeant Major) as we entered the operational room. "Your task for today is to gather as much information as you can about last night's shooting. The chances are that all the locals will be too scared to approach you so I don't want you make it too obvious, just stop the occasional person on the street and, in a friendly manner, make a note of their name and where they are going, if they do decide to tell you something related to last night's shooting then make sure you write it all down. More news has reached us overnight about who might have been involved in the killing of Margaret Hearst." We just sat there patiently waiting for a name to be thrown in our direction when the name of a well known terrorist hit our ears.

"One of the young men is called Dessie O'Hare," said the TSM, "he is the most wanted man in Northern Ireland at this moment in time. He's nicknamed the Border Fox around these parts for reasons you can work out for yourself." We were given a more up to date photo of his boyish looks even though he was twenty one years of age, this guy wouldn't think twice of pulling the trigger if you were on the wrong end of his gun; staying out of his way was the main concern of most of us, catching him would make you a hero.

"OK," said Sergeant Sammy Douglas, "make your way over to the loading bay now." Luckily for us with it being an urban patrol we didn't need to take the LMG that weighed a tonne, on some of the more rural patrols taking the LMG was a must in case we were ambushed, having the LMG and plenty of ammunition would allow us time for reinforcements to arrive.

Once out in the small town and the weather being kind on this occasion, it was a case of just doing what we were told; there was hardly anyone to chat to apart from one or two going to Church.

"Hammo," I said, "there's a woman coming towards you, see if she wants to chat."

"I thought we were told not to stop them."

"I know what was said, but what was said and what we do are two different things. Just sort of accidently get in her way and then start up a conversation, it will work believe me, I've done it myself a few times in Londonderry."

"OK," said Hammo, "I'll give it ago." It worked a treat as Hammo almost knocked her off her feet; I could hear Hammo across the street apologising to the middle aged lady whilst at the same time trying to drum up a conversation, we all took covering positions while Hammo continued chewing the woman's ear off before they finally parted company.

"How did it go, Hammo?" I asked.

"Tell you about it when we get back, Woofer," was his reply, feeling self-satisfied with himself. The whole two hour patrol saw us chat to no more than a handful of locals, some that were just passing through the town. I was finding it very difficult to take on board how quiet the town of Keady really was, in some respect it made it more dangerous with the fact that you could easily switch off and become a more vulnerable target. We were now only about fifty metres from the camp gates and the men in the Sanger would be radioing the guard on the gate to forewarn them of our arrival; with the gates now open it was straight to the unloading bay to unload our rifles before making our way to the operational room for our debrief. Once seated, it was time to divulge any information we had ascertained on our patrol.

"Anyone got any information of any kind?" said the TSM.

"I have a few notes," Hammo replied.

"Let's hear them then," said the TSM.

"I spoke to a woman and after chatting away, I eventually got on to the subject about the events of last night hoping that she would have something to say, she wouldn't give me her name however, she gave me some interesting information. She said Dessie O'Hare is well known around these parts and it was him that was behind the shooting last night, rumour has it that he and his accomplices fled over the border and into Monaghan where they just casually went on a night out at a club." The TSM was handed the note paper that Hammo had for the TSM to pass on to intelligence.

"Well done, Gunner Hamilton," said the TSM at the same time getting praise from Sammy.

"Did well, Hammo," said Sammy, "good man, Wolfendale."

"Yes Sarge," I said.

"Take a leaf out of Hamilton's book and you won't go far wrong," said Sammy with a grin on his face. Not to let the cat out of the bag that it was my idea to stop the lady, I just looked over to where Hammo and Tommo were to see them putting their finger up in front of their mouths as if to say, don't you dare say anything. It was now lunch time. After lunch, we were on rest period for a good six hours before being on Guard duty around the camp. With the camp being so small and isolated there wasn't much to do apart from sleep; being cooped up in our accommodation that had no windows wasn't my idea of fun.

"Fancy having a stroll and get some fresh air?" I said to Hammo and Tommo who were just lying on their beds.

"Why the hell not!" they said.

Dressed in casual clothes it was nice to roam the camp and have a catch up. Just being able to look up at the blue sky was a refreshing moment within itself, not having to worry too much about getting shot. We decided to sit down on the loading/unloading bay for a while and chat away, unknown to us all that in a few weeks time the loading/unloading bay would be part of an investigation that could have cost someone their life.

"What was it like in Londonderry?" said Hammo, drumming up a conversation.

"It was more intense," I said, "I met an Irish girl while I was there."

"Tell me more."

"Ah, it was one of them moments that I shall never forget mate," I said, looking up to the skies as if to say *where are you Lydia?* "I really loved her you know, I really did," I said, feeling sad and lost without her by my side. I explained to Hammo all about our affair that had him totally mesmerised.

"Wow, Paul," he said. "That's some story, must have took some nerve going back to see her."

"Yeah, it did buddy," I said, still thinking about her. "I haven't heard from her for a while, I just hope one day she will try to get in touch with me again."

"Do you have a photo of her?"

"Reluctantly, no," I said. "Giving me a photo wasn't her sort of thing; she said that if she gave me a photo of herself it would bring bad luck, maybe bring an end to our relationship."

It was now early November and just about two months into our tour. RR leave was now in full swing and I was due mine the first week in December. In respect to Londonderry where there was always something going on, it had been a very sedate tour so far but things were soon about to change. Sat in our room and just passing some time away playing a game of cards, the sound of a machine gun could be heard which seemed to be coming from inside the camp gates. Tommo and myself along with the rest of the section rushed out of our rooms and into the court area of the camp fearing the worst. There was all sorts of pandemonium going on without us knowing what had taken place, we just stood and stared at the loading/unloading bay where all the commotion seem to be coming from.

"What the hell do you think has happened?" said Tommo feeling confused.

"God knows," said Hammo, at the same time looking at me for some answers.

"I have no idea," I said. Lots of obscenities could be heard from some of the lads, they looked as though they were as terrified as I was feeling; minutes later and still standing in the court yard it was now quite obvious what had happened. One of the lads from one section had been unloading the LMG when he accidentally fired the weapon, in Army terms it is called an ND (Negligent Discharge). Several rounds had been fired causing panic within the section, narrowly missing some of the men that were standing nearby. It was pure luck that they escaped being injured or even killed by the out of control machine gun; the mood around the camp for the rest of the day was one of sorrow, sorry for the guy who was responsible for the accidental ND.

Kicking a man whilst he is down wasn't how it worked in the Army so we could only feel remorse for the guy who was now serving twenty eight days in the makeshift Army prison in Armagh camp. Looking back some eighteen months ago I was thinking *'how the hell did I get away without being incarcerated for my crime of seeing Lydia on the streets that one night in Londonderry?'*

At the same time all this was happening news was reaching us that another one of the lads had unfortunately lost his mind and was having a break down while on Sanger duty in Armagh camp. The stress that we were under at times was now having its toll on some of the lads. It took a cool Bombardier to keep him talking whilst another one of the lads (I believe it was my good mate Steve Schofield) managed to lay a glove on him before disarming him and making the situation safe; it was a strange sort of week with the fact we seemed to be more of at threat from our own guys than the Provo's.

We were now over two and a half months into the tour and it was time for my RR leave. It was a nice welcomed break to catch up on some precious family time and to be able to walk freely around my home town of Nantwich. Although you felt relaxed with your home comforts I still found myself scanning the buildings for any form of danger, even the slightest sound of a car backfiring would have you on edge; it would take months even years as opposed to days before your head would become fully cleansed of the events of Northern Ireland.

My father was now looking more aged than the last time I saw him, which for me was a major concern, he was now using a walking stick to get around and his sight was becoming impaired; using the furniture to navigate around the house was now how it was. His health had deteriorated in such a short time that I felt the end might not be too far away. To lose my father now would be catastrophic as I was only twenty years of age and would be hoping to spend many more wonderful years with him and my mother. I tried to put my father's health behind me as I returned to Keady to finish of my tour. On return I met up with Riggers for the first time since leaving West Germany in September.

"For what do we owe the pleasure of your company, Pete?" I said, feeling great to see him again.

"Just standing in while some of the lads are on RR, it makes a nice change to get out onto the streets instead of sitting in the operational room listening in on the radio."

"Well, not a lot going on here in Keady," I said, " but yes, I understand, I would rather be where any action could be and not stuck in the OPs room." Christmas came and went with a ceasefire announced by the Provo's. *How nice of them*, it meant nothing at all to us; we still had to be just as vigilant although a few drinks when we were not on duty were allowed over the festive period. We were now entering January and had two weeks left when the Provo's decided to give us a farewell present again, just like in Londonderry. *How very kind of them*. My mates and I were all asleep in the comforts of our beds when the lights in our room suddenly went on with someone shouting at the top of their voice.

"Out of bed now, the camp is under fire!" I could see now how changing parades back in Junior Leaders some two and a half years ago were an important part of our training; out of bed and fully dressed with the rest of the lads in less than two minutes meant we were ready for action.

In a strange sort of way it felt like we were going into the unknown as we exited the huge corrugated gates. "Hammo, Wolfendale, follow me, "was the cry from Sammy as we charged up the steep road to where the shooting had come from. "Dinger, Tommo, Geordie, keep an eye out behind you just in case the gunmen are still around," Sammy continued to say. Within seconds the firing point was located just off the road and on the grass bank, there was a massive amount of empty cartridge cases lying in the grass next to where the machine gun would have been positioned; as Hammo and I stood there in the darkness of the night, we could see the line of sight that the gunmen had as we looked down on our camp that was now feeling empty.

We spent a good hour searching the area for any more evidence that we could find, but as normal, whoever was responsible would've been well gone over the border; it was difficult to know whether or not it was just a wakeup call from the Provo's to show us that they were still an active force or they were out to kill someone; I am pretty sure that if someone had have been killed, they would've claimed the rights to the incident as if it was premeditated.

It was now Sunday 15th January and we were getting ready for our departure, and just like in Londonderry, the excitement was growing around the troops; we were saying goodbye to Dessie O'Hare and his associates, well, at least until the next time I might be setting foot on Irish soil. For some unknown reason I was really glad the tour was over, even though I enjoyed fighting alongside my best buddy Tommo and my new best mate Hammo, also, not forgetting Dinger and Geordie Stanton for whom I couldn't understand a word he was muttering in his Geordie accent. On the flight back I was wondering what 1978 would bring. Well, even I was taken by surprise at what the battery had in store for me when I returned from my annual leave at the beginning of February.

CHAPTER SEVENTY-FOUR
DEATH OF MY FATHER

It was the middle of February and everything was getting back to normal, long sleeve order was still in place and the camp was feeling more like a camp should feel with the fact everybody got back safely from Northern Ireland; mail was at a premium now as all my three sweethearts Lydia, Kim and Jess had unfortunately lost touch, mainly due to another tour of Ireland. After arriving back on the Sunday I thought it best to read Battery Orders as I didn't want to get caught out again and find that I should be on Guard duty tomorrow. As I was reading down the sheet I did notice that I was being transferred to the Officers' Mess for the short term. *Why?* I asked myself, *was it a punishment? Had I done something wrong?* Working in the Officers' Mess was normally regarded as a position for someone who was surplus to requirement (not wanted) *so why was I assigned there?* There was little I could do until Monday morning when Sergeant Douglas would be present and then I could be brought up to speed with the issue.

Sunday gave Tommo and me the first opportunity to get on our motorcycles and make the half hour journey to see our girlfriends. It felt like a huge rapturous welcome for us both as we arrived outside their house, the unmistakable sound of the engines had them both looking out of the window and then it was hug for Tommo and no hug for me. I was quite taken aback by what seemed to be the cold shoulder treatment. Tommo and I made our way into the downstairs bedroom with the two girls and another one of their sisters Maria; at this moment in time I wasn't sure whether or not Marlene was still wanted to share a relationship with me.

After a little gentle persuasion by her sister everything was back on track. I could see that Dec and Angela's relationship had a strong bond about it, well, as for mine, although I felt I loved her, I always felt that I would need to put in some serious work to make it work; with hindsight I probably should have seen the signs and called it a day, but my heart would not allow it. After spending the day at their house it was time to head back to camp ready for Monday morning's parade. It was nice to see the battery amalgamated together again outside the Battery Block ready for a brisk march down to the gun hangars.

Once down at the hangars it was a case of a formal parade for the BC with all the senior ranks and officers present. It was a longer than normal parade with the fact that we were being told the agenda for the coming year, plenty of exercises with the M107s was going to play a huge part in the months to come. With the parade over I made my way over to Sergeant Douglas to find out about my sudden attachment to the Officers' Mess. "Sarge," I said, "can I have a quick word about why I've been volunteered to work in the Officers' mess?"

"Says who," said Sammy grunting, "first I've heard about it, who told you that?"

"Battery Orders, I read them yesterday and it says I start today."

"So what are you doing here then?" he said chuckling.

"Well, I thought I would speak to you first to see what you can do," I said.

"Just wait a minute," said Sammy. "I'll try to get it sorted." A few minutes later Sammy returned to inform me that it was only going to be for a month and that they needed to replace one of the lads that were working there for some unknown reason. "Better get yourself changed into your barrack-room trousers and No. 2 dress shirt along with your pullover," said Sammy sternly. "I want you back on my gun, Wolfendale, so I will make sure you're there no longer than a month."

"OK," I said thinking, *well… Sammy knows best.*

After getting changed I made my way down to the Officers' Mess without a clue to what my role would be and feeling lost in my new environment. "Gunner Paul Wolfendale arriving for duty," I said to the Bombardier in charge of the mess, still feeling confused.

"Oh right, we have been expecting you," he said with a huge smile on his face. "I will introduce to the rest of the crew, just follow me, oh, and by the way, my name is Bombardier Rick Parry."

"I have absolutely no idea what to do," I said, hoping for some advice.

"Don't worry Paul," said Bombardier Parry. "I will explain all."

"Can't wait," I said sarcastically as he explained my duties. He gave me a tour of the mess whilst at the same time explaining what my duties were: basically waiting on the officers at set meal times, cleaning silver, making brews and essentially just doing what I was told. The mess itself was something I would compare to a hotel, not that I had ever been in one, just the ones that I had seen on TV; it was luxury at its best. Guard duties were now a thing of the past which suited me down to the ground; with the fact that the officers held regular functions it meant occasionally I would be expected to work some weekends on a rota basic and also some evenings.

After a couple of weeks away from the battery I was actually enjoying working in the mess, there was a more relaxed type of atmosphere, no offence to Sergeant Massey, but not getting a bollocking on a daily basic was quite refreshing. I'm not sure why other soldiers didn't see it this way, most of the friends that I had spoken to had the attitude of *'why should I waiter-on so called Ruperts'* (name for officers). Well, I didn't see it like that, and to be honest, I saw the officers in a different light, I felt that they respected my position as a waiter and didn't take anything for granted; still keeping a safe distance from being impertinent to my superiors felt that I could chat to them in a less formal manner and still feel I was on safe ground, 'don't bite the hand off that feeds you' is a famous saying that sprang to mind.

A sort of normal day in the mess would see me arriving via the side door (tradesman's entrance) and not the main entrance at about 0800hrs unless I was on the early breakfast shift; from then it would be helping out the early shift and then preparing for a 1000hrs mini type of NAAFI break: coffee, tea and toast would be the norm, occasionally we would have to prepare for a special lunch in a separate room for one or two of the officers, apart from that, it was a case of setting the huge shiny oak tables for lunch. The mess naturally had its own cooking facilities with some of the top chefs you could have hoped for. The food was to die for. At home it would be called stew; in the Officers' Mess it is called Beef Bourguignon. At lunch the food would be served from the hot plate, but dinner in the evening would be served in entree dishes on the table. We would bring them their main choice of meat/fish etc on a warm plate and then they could help themselves to the veg and potatoes. A three course meal washed down with wine and then retiring to the Ante Room for coffee and a good gossip of the day's activities was how it was.

There would always be someone on duty until at least 2100hrs for any emergency, like I need some more coffee (joking of course), I felt as long as they treated and talked to me with respect, I would have had no problem staying on a little longer. Easter break was now upon us, which meant we had a long weekend unless on duty.

"Paul," said Bombardier Parry, although I usually addressed him as Rick, "I have just made out the rota for the Easter break, I've put you in on Easter Monday, there is not a lot going on, but one or two of the officers will still need feeding."

"Yeah, fine by me," I said, "what time do you want me in?"

"Around nine o'clock will be fine," said Rick, "apart from that, the rest of the weekend is yours to do what you want with."

"Cheers for that," I said. Three days of rest for me, with that in mind, there was only one place that I wanted to be, with my girlfriend. Normally if you were planning to stay somewhere other than the camp you needed to let the Battery Clerk know in case of an emergency; knowing where everybody is at short notice is important even though I thought I knew different. Why would it be a problem if I didn't inform anyone? Well, I was about to find out. The weather was kind over the Easter break with soaring temperatures that made my stay at Marlene's feel like I was on holiday in somewhere like Spain; riding around on my motorbike getting to see some of the sights around West Germany and visiting some of Marlene's relatives was how I spent the first two days.

On the second night of my three day stay, Marlene decided to pay me a visit as I slept in the downstairs bedroom.

"Paul, are you awake?" she said softly.

"Yes," I said, feeling aroused to see her in her baby doll outfit.

"Move over so I can get into bed with you."

"What about your mum?" I said feeling worried.

"She is asleep," was her reply as she endeavoured to pull back the quilt; before I could blink we were snuggled up together and then the inevitable happened, yes, you guessed it, we both fell asleep. It must have been the early hours of the morning when with me being a light sleeper, I heard the bedroom door open. I didn't need a second guess as to who it was, her mum, she was doing the rounds like the tooth fairy. I pretended to be asleep like I was hiding from her presence as she came closer. I felt the bed rock as her mum grunted in her rough voice, "Marlene, auf stein," (get up now) or words to that effect; all sorts of words in her mum's native tongue were being thrown around until her daughter got up and was marched back to her bedroom; leaving me feeling a little guilty I just continued facing the wall at the same time shaking like a bag of jingles, With the room now in silence I just closed my eyes and went back to sleep.

The next morning sat at the breakfast table and for some unknown reason I didn't understand a word of German any more, no matter what her mother said I just said, "Nicht verstehn."(Don't understand) I suppose her anger was written all over her face, but what the hell, I just decided time would be the healer and left it at that. It was now getting towards lunch time as I said to Marlene, "It's back to work for me tomorrow."

"Can I come with you?" she said, more in hope that I might say yes.

"Well, I am not sure," I said, "maybe if I phone the Officers' Mess someone there will let me know, can't see why it should be a problem. Tell you what, let's walk down to the bottom of the road to the phone box and I'll call them."

"OK," she said, "just need to get my coat." Minutes later we were in the phone box searching in my pocket for a Deutsche Mark to make the call. After a few short rings the voice of one of the soldiers answered the call.

"Hello, Officers' Mess, Ian speaking," he said politely.

"Hi, it's Paul," I replied, "Who's in charge today Ian?"

"Tony, Tony Doherty," said Ian, but before I had chance to say *can I speak to him for a moment,* he said he had some news for me.

"The Orderly Officer needs to speak to you, Paul, urgently; you need to come into camp today."

"Why what have I done?" I said, feeling uncomfortable with what Ian had said.

"I can't tell you, Paul," said Ian, "all I know is that he needs to see you right away."

Still feeling confused and even more curious that maybe I have done something wrong I replied. "Well if you don't tell me then I am not coming in until tomorrow."

"Look Paul, you've done nothing wrong as far as I know, you just need to come in to see the Orderly Officer." Unfortunately, I got to the point where I was pushing the issue so much that he felt he had no choice but to tell me.

"It's your father, Paul."

"What about him?" I said, now feeling worried.

"He has died," said Ian, waiting for my reply; I just went numb for a few seconds as I dropped the receiver. Marlene knew then that there was something wrong; she could see the tears in my eyes sliding down my face.

"What's wrong, Paul?" she said, looking worried.

"It's my father, he is dead," I said still in a state of shock. Marlene consoled me by wrapping her warm and welcome arms around me. "He's dead," I said again, "dead, I have lost my father." We made our way back up the stairs to Marlene's house that sat on the hill; Marlene explained to her parents the devastating news that was now eating me up. Marlene's mum was as caring as only a mother could be, she comforted me with her kind words and the mandatory cup of tea.

"I must go now," I said, still crying.

"Take care, Paul," said Marlene and her mum as I made my way outside and onto my motorbike; to be honest, it wasn't the best idea riding the bike in my condition, but what choice did I have? Back in camp feeling my world had come to an end I made my way to the Officers' Mess to meet up with the Orderly Officer. Everybody that was working in the mess had already received first-hand knowledge of my father's death so it was a case of sympathy all round, I had never known so much silence in the mess as I set eyes on the Orderly Officer awaiting my arrival.

"Paul," he said, "Take a seat, I am sorry that you had to find out about your father's death in the way you did, it wasn't meant to happen like that, we have been trying to locate you for a couple of days now. Your father passed away on Good Friday from a heart attack whilst asleep in his bed. I am so sorry for your loss, Paul, but please remember, we are all here to help you through your traumatic time; with the fact that your father has already passed away, your leave will be classed as compassionate B as opposed to compassionate A. What that means is if your father was on his death bed, it would be compassionate A and a more urgent arrangement would be put into place. The first flight we can get you on is tomorrow morning, we have organised a flight for you from RAF Wildenrath at 0600hrs, duty transport will be ready to take you to the base at 0430hrs and will pick you up from your room, you have been allocated two weeks' leave before you need to return, do you have anything you would like to ask?"

"No," I said silently. "I just need to get back home to be with my family." I returned to my room and packed my suitcase ready for my early start which included my No. 2 dress uniform; everybody I spoke to and everybody I passed in the corridor of the block showered me with kind words that meant so much to me at this moment in time. I didn't realise how many friends I had, even the ones that I was not that close to were offering me their condolences.

It seemed like an eternity as I waited up all night for the duty driver to arrive to take me to the RAF base, a two hour flight to London and then the customary train journey to Crewe before a final taxi journey the final five miles. I arrived home early afternoon, I was ready for the tears to start all over again as trundled my way up the garden path. I opened the front door that was never locked to see my mum still carrying out her household duties.

"Hi mum," I said softly as she looked me in the eyes; seeing angel type tears running down her pale cheeks for the first time started me off as she explained to me the circumstances surrounding my father's death. I must have hugged my mother for a good five minutes before we let go of the tightened embrace. This is the first time I had ever been faced with a death in the family apart from when I was about ten years of age when my grandma died; luckily for me my older brothers and sisters were taking charge of the situation which gave me time to grieve. Over the next few days leading up to the funeral, I met distant family that I had never met or heard of before; it felt like I was reliving my father's life with everybody knowing something about my father's past, I could have sat all day by the coal fire and listened to their stories, but there just wasn't enough time.

The day of the funeral arrived; it was my good and very close school friend Graham Tresidder and his father who conducted the service. The hearse arrived about an hour before the funeral was due to take place so that we could have the coffin underneath the window in the living room with the lid open. I didn't want this moment to end. As I held his cold hand that was warm to me I just stared into his closed eyes, he looked so peaceful dressed in a red dressing robe. "Wake up dad," were the last words I uttered as I gave him one final kiss on his forehead before paying my last respects; saying goodbye to the most hard working and wonderful family man you could have ever wish to meet had me crying.

With tears rolling down my face it was now time to fasten the lid down for the final time. I was trying to show little or no emotion as the lid was fastened into place by the very caring undertakers.

With the sun showing its face it was time to take the short ten minute journey to the church. On arrival five of my brothers and I made our way over to the hearse to carry the coffin into the church under the guidance of Graham and his father; memories of my passing out parade in Nuneaton came flooding back as I could see a vision of my father standing next to my mother, feeling proud of me and what I had achieved. Dressed in my Army uniform once again is the way my father would have wanted it.

After an overwhelming service, it was time for my brothers and me to lower the coffin into the sacred ground and, for the last time, lay my father to rest. I hung around for a short while not wanting to leave my father alone a second longer than I needed to before making my way back home for the close family members and friends to reminisce over my father's life. Reminiscing wasn't enough for me so later on in the afternoon and on my own, I made my way back to my father's grave for a personal catch up. I just sat down on the ground and admired all the wonderful flowers that were now covering his grave. I must have spent some half an hour chatting away until I felt I had developed a relationship with him once again; out of sight, but certainly not out of mind were the last words I uttered as I turned and unenthusiastically made my way back home to be with my mother.

My paperwork arrived in the post the next day with all the information about when I was to return to camp. I needed to make my way to Woolwich in London, home of the Royal Artillery. I was to spend a night there before my flight from Heathrow the next day; saying farewell to my mother in the absence of my father was one of the hardest things I have ever had to do, I just felt that the parting of my father made me grow up into the man my father would have wanted me to be. The next couple of days before arriving back in West Germany were the longest of my life, I just needed to get back to my friends and get things back to normal; little did I realise that later on in the year I would be arranging my own wedding, yes my own wedding.

CHAPTER SEVENTY-FIVE
TWIN PREGNANCIES

When I arrived back, I was to find out I was no longer employed by the Officers' Mess, my No. 1 Sergeant Douglas was true to his word and made sure I would be humping shells around in the coming months. I was put on to the advance gun course that was to start in two weeks' time. It was nice to get back onto the guns again and also to see Hammo whom I had become good friends with. He was attached to our gun along with Geordie Stanton making it a gun sub to be reckoned with; we must have had one of best gun subs in the regiment.

Two weeks had passed and I made my way to the gun hangars for my advance gun course. The hangars were fitted with lecture rooms the size of a normal type class room. The course was a lot harder than I first thought it was going to be, but at the same time, enjoyable; letting my No. 1 Sammy Douglas down was not going to happen as I thrived to be the best I could. I guess it was that competitiveness I was blessed with kicking in once more. I was up against some stiff competition from all of the other batteries, including some lance jacks and an ex-full Bombardier who had been busted to gunner. After two intense weeks of theoretical and practical tests, it was now time not only to see if I had passed, but hopefully to have done well on the course.

As we sat at our desks and in front of the training staff I just hoped that I had done well. Memories of RAT came flooding back when I was sure I had done enough to be in the top five, only to find out I finished third from bottom. "Listen in;" said Bombardier Walker in a commanding way, "I am pleased to say that you have all passed the course although some of you have just scraped through. I am not going to read out all of your names, I am just going to read out the top five." I waited with bated breath to see if I had made the top five as Bombardier Walker called out the names. The first three places were taken by L/Bombardiers which made me believe that I would need to check the list on the notice board to see where I came; it was only then that

Bombardier Walker looked over in my direction and said, "Second place goes to Gunner Wolfendale, well done on your effort."

I was so pleased that my efforts had been recognised which was also echoed by Sergeant Douglass when we met up again later on that day. "Wolfendale, well done, son," he said, "I want you to be my layer on the next exercise; you can share the laying duties with Dinger."

"No problem," I said feeling proud. We were now into April and Tommo had some interesting news to tell me as I entered the room.

"Paul," said Tommo. "How are things with you and Marlene?"

"Fine," I said, "are you going up to their house tonight?"

"Yes, after work," said Tommo.

"Me too, "I said.

"I have something to tell you first," said Tommo anxiously; with there just being Tommo and I in the room it seem the correct time to tell me what was on his mind.

"Go on then, Dec," I said, wondering what was so secretive.

"Well, Angela's pregnant."

"What?" I said. "Tell me you're joking."

"No, I'm not," he said, "found out last week; Angela went down to the doctors to get it confirmed."

"How far gone is she?" I said, feeling shocked, "didn't know you had it in you."

"Two months," said Dec, what do you mean I didn't think you had it in you? We're hoping to get married next month, in May."

"Bloody hell," I said. I was finding hard to take it all on board: my best mate getting married and also becoming a dad.

"Have you thought it through?" I said, trying to make sense of it all.

"Yes," said Dec. "I am going to tell Angela's mum tonight about her being pregnant and about the wedding."

"She doesn't know yet?" I said, sounding astonished.

"No, we will tell her together tonight," said Dec. "Just hope she doesn't go mental."

"Best of luck with that one, mate," I said with a smile on my face, "tell you what, I will come up a little later, let the air clear a bit first. God help me if I get Marlene pregnant, my feet wouldn't touch the ground I'm standing on." (Famous last words) Later on that evening I made my way to Bad Salzdetfurth on my 250cc to see Marlene and find out more about how her parents had taken the news. The first person to open the door was her mum who couldn't wait to preach me the riot act. Although she spoke no English, I got the gist at what she was saying before I could put one foot through the door. (Literally translated) she said with aggression in her throat…

"Have you heard?"

"Heard what?" I said, acting dumb.

"Angela is pregnant, my god she is only eighteen and she plans to get married next month in May."

"Wow," I said frowning, "I had no idea." I was now expecting a lecture on my behaviour like, "don't you dare get Marlene pregnant" when to my surprise, her attitude changed, she was all smiles as if to say 'what will be, will be'. I was now allowed into the house to see Dec and Angela to congratulate them and at the same time looking for Marlene; it was an evening of celebrations for the soon to be Tomkinson family. News around the camp travels fast and it wasn't long before the cries of, "Tommo has become a man and he's going to be a daddy," were flittering around.

The next few months went by quickly with plenty of exercises in the hot summer heat that made it so much more special when the exercise was over. Dec had now moved out of the barracks and was allocated a married quarter in the nearby village of Sarstedt. Dec and I were still very close as friends even though I saw less of him. However, it wasn't going to be too long before all that would change. It was early August and I was about to go on my annual leave; not seeing Marlene for three weeks was something I wasn't looking forward to, however, I needed to see how my mother was coping without dad by her side. I decided that maybe, just maybe, Marlene's mother would allow me to take her daughter back to England on the back of my motorbike (classy) for the three weeks, but first I needed to ask Marlene. It was a few days before I was due to go on leave when I popped the question; sat in her bedroom, I said, "how do you fancy a trip to England with me?"

"What?" she said in a shocked voice.

"Yes, to England," I said, "on the back of my bike." She must have asked me about fifty inquisitive type questions before she finally said she would love too.

"I need to ask my mum first," said Marlene, now feeling excited.

"Well, let's go and ask her," I said. "No time like the present." We made our way down the stairs and into the living room to where her mum was watching TV. Although Marlene's mum was a kind person, she certainly wasn't the sort of person you would want to mess with.

"Mum," said Marlene, "I have something to ask you."

"Ask me what?" said her mother looking at me for some answers.

"Can I go with Paul to England for three weeks?" said Marlene, who didn't even give her mum a chance to answer before explaining all about the so called holiday; with that in mind, what choice did her mother have? She knew I would look after her daughter and that she would be in safe hands even though she was only sixteen.

"Yes, OK," said her mum, "as long as you look after her, promise me that, Paul."

"Yes I will, she will be safe with me," I said as I continued to reassure her. That was it, all the talking was over and we were given the green light.

The next two days were spent getting all our belongings together for our long tiring endurance; I had no idea how much luggage one could carry on the back of a motorbike, but I was about to find out. As I attached the two suitcases to the back of the bike fastened down with elasticated straps, we were looking like we were moving house. Back in England and with the bike over-balancing a couple of times it was time to introduce Marlene to my mother and the rest of the family, well at least the ones that were still living at home. It was so strange for me having to be an interpreter in respect that Marlene was the first person in our house to speak a language that didn't resemble farm-yard English.

My mother wasn't keen on us sleeping in the same bed together which I understood, just like it was in West Germany; not sleeping together wasn't a problem with me although Marlene felt different about the sleeping arrangements.

As one week rolled into another it was quite obvious to my sisters, but not to me, that Marlene seemed to be piling on the pounds, but not through over eating; 'women's intuition', they call it. My sister said, "Paul, can I have a word with you for a minute?"

"Yes," I said, "what's the matter?"

"Is Marlene pregnant?" she said, as if to say *tell me the truth*.

"What?" I said feeling shaken at the remark.

"You must have noticed the swelling, ah Paul," said my sister as if I was stupid.

"Not really," was my honest reply, "why, do you think she is?"

"Well I'm no doctor but I think we need to get her checked out," said my sister with concern written all over her face.

"I will speak to her and see what she says," I said, feeling worried. After a short but difficult chat, and with me doing all the translating, Marlene confirmed that she had not had a period for a few months. I was gobsmacked to say the least, I wasn't ready for this; I was just hoping that the test would prove negative, not because I didn't want to eventually have children with her, but because her mum would kill me. An appointment was made for the following day for Marlene to have the test. My sister kindly went with her to comfort her; within the hour they were back home to inform me that the test was positive and she was five months gone.

"Five months!" I blurted out trying to hold myself upright. "Your mum will go mental with me. I'm a dead man."

"I will speak to her," said Marlene as calmly as you like. My family seemed unperturbed by the news, thinking, *well… you're twenty now and responsible for your own doings,* even though it was a shock to my mother. It was now time to head back to West Germany with even more weight to carry; the closer we got to Marlene's house then the more nervous I became. On arrival we both tried to keep calm until the right moment arrived to tell her mother, but unfortunately, the swelling that was now obvious attracted attention from Marlene's mum. I was downstairs in the room where I sometimes slept when her mother came bursting in. "Ist meine tochter schwanger?" (Is my daughter pregnant?) She raved in a loud voice.

"Yes," I said, squirming, with my head bowed looking at my worn out shoes.

"Mein Guter," (she was shocked) she said and then continued by saying in her native tongue, "so what are you going to do about it?"

"Get married," I said, thinking, *have I said the right thing?* Feeling all alone I was just hoping that Marlene could be by my side to take some of the flak I was being bombarded with. Lucky for me and right on cue Marlene appeared to give me some welcome support.

"Mum, stop having a go at Paul," she said. "We know what we're doing, we are going to get married," she said to her mum with some authority. The situation was a carbon copy of what Dec and Angela had gone through some months ago, it was just the fact that her daughter was only sixteen years of age and I was feeling the full wrath of her mother. I managed to ascertain a date to get married at the local register office in Crewe for October 9th; a small gathering of my family attended the wedding that cost me no more than seventy pounds including the rings and then a small reception back at mine.

I was now a married man without a married quarter. Getting a married quarter was very much like trying to get a council house, it worked on a point system and I hadn't earned enough points to be allocated one yet. I was now living at the mother-in-law's, which meant I had to commute every day, unfortunately for me, I managed to pick up a speeding ticket from the armed police on my way into camp.

November arrived and Tommo became a daddy, a little baby girl was born on the 1st of the month. "Congratulations, Dec," I said, "so pleased for you Dec, have you thought of a name yet?"

"Yes," said Dec, looking proud. "Caroline is the name we have chosen."

"Really nice name," I said, giving him a hug.

"When is your baby due?"

"January," I said, "round about the 9th, can't wait."

"What's the betting it's a girl?"

"You never know," I said. "I hope so; I would like a little girl."

CHAPTER SEVENTY-SIX
"A BELT" I SAID, FEELING CONFUSED

Back in camp and reading Battery Orders I noticed that I had been put on a basic driving course. I couldn't believe it, I was so excited at the thought of being able to drive; it was to be a two week course starting on the Monday. The first week was all classroom work and then, providing you passed a small written and practical exam you would be allowed onto the roads for a week's intensive driving. Although I had absolutely no idea about the running of an engine, I still felt I was a reasonably quick learner and felt I would have no problem. *Ouch, how wrong can one be?* Monday morning arrived and I made my way down to the MT (Motor Transport) bay along with two more potential drivers from 18 Battery. I was so pleased to see one of the 18 Battery Bombardiers running the course along with some other ones from different batteries. "Hi there Ken," I said with a look of glee on my face.

"Bombardier Bailey to you, Gunner Wolfendale, do you understand?"

"Yes, Bombardier," I said feeling betrayed; I thought he was a friend. I soon found out that friendship goes out of the window at times like this, he was running the driving course and he wasn't going let me forget it. It was pretty much all about how the engine functions that I found uninteresting. For the life of me I literally had no interest in what was under the bonnet of an Army Land Rover, but at the same time, I knew if I didn't get through the first week I wouldn't be allowed to drive. Each and every day we were learning all about the components of the engine and how everything worked, to me all I could see was a chunk of metal every time I looked into the bonnet; for some unknown reason not known to me my brain just couldn't find any form of connection with the engine.

Throughout the week I could feel I was struggling with the knowledge I needed to know for the test we would be doing on Friday, whilst at the same time, I still felt I would pass with consummate ease.

It was Friday and time for our exam. "Take your seat," said Bombardier Bailey. "This is it, in front of you is your test paper, you've got one hour to complete as many of the questions as you can, does everybody understand?" There was a pause of silence from us all that meant we were ready and understood what was said. The hour for me went by quicker than I would have wished, I must have answered at least half of the questions, but whether that would be enough I would have to wait and find out.

"OK, papers down," said Bombardier Kenneth Bailey, "leave your papers on the desk in front of you and get yourselves down to the NAAFI, I want you all back in the classroom at 1100hrs sharp." To be honest, I was just glad to get the exam over and done with; a couple of meaty bread rolls washed down with a cuppa was enough for me to re-energise my batteries before returning back to the MT bay classroom for the eagerly awaited results. "Take your seats," said Bombardier Bailey with his ever serious look. "It will be easier to tell you who have failed, not the ones that have passed. There are only three of you who have not reached the required mark." At this moment in time I felt quite relieved knowing that the chances of me being one of the failures was slim; I was stunned to hear my name called out along with two others as Bombardier Bailey continued talking. "Wolfendale, Wood, and Westall, you will be given another chance in one hour's time to answer the questions you got wrong, the rest of you are dismissed until Monday morning when the driving will start."

An hour later and with the classroom feeling empty, we were read the riot act. To be fair the DS was very lenient in respect that they wanted us all to pass however, after the other two lads had been told they had passed, I unfortunately, was told that I had failed once again. I was mortified. "Wolfendale," said Bombardier Bailey, feeling pissed that one of the 18 Battery lads couldn't pass the course, "I cannot believe that you have failed again."

"Sorry," I said, looking sheepish and gutted that I wasn't going to be able to do my driving next week.

"I'm going to give you one last chance after lunch even though you don't deserve it. Get out of my sight now before I change my mind; I will see you back here at 1400hrs sharp." Although I was classed as a married pad (Married Personnel) I was allowed to eat in the cookhouse because I was on a military course; meeting up with some of my mates and telling them the truth wasn't something I was looking forward to.

"How's the course going?" said Hammo.

"Great," I said lying through my teeth, "get our results this afternoon then if all goes well I will be doing the driving part of the course on Monday."

"You'll pass no problem," said Hammo, not knowing I had already failed the first part of the course twice. Back at the MT bay I heard the familiar voice of Bombardier Bailey shouting me over to the corridor area of the classroom. "Stand there," he said, still looking cheesed with me. Bombardier Bailey decided it was time for a change of tactic, he decided to use a few props to help me pass as he could see I was still struggling to answer a simple question. He pointed to his military belt with all his might. "For god's sake what am I pointing at? This thing that is holding my trousers up," he said, shaking his head from side to side.

"A belt," I said, feeling thick and slightly panicky.

"And what is that over there?" he said, pointing at the fan.

"A fan," I said, still not totally understanding where this was going.

"OK," he said in a quiet and slow voice, "put the two words together and what do you have?"

"A fan belt," I said, still feeling confused.

"Bingo," he said, scratching his head and looking exhausted. "Now get out of my sight, you've passed." It was another one of those wow moments for me, I was still not sure why the answer was a fan belt, but I didn't give two figs, I had passed and was ready to take to the road on Monday morning.

With my experience of driving tractors and also my motorbike, I took to the driving like a duck to water; half tonne short wheel base Land Rovers, with three of us going out at any one time was how it was. We would drive out to Hannover and then to the local town of Hildesheim. About every hour or so we would swap around taking our turn in the driving seat; there were no dual controls in the vehicles so it was a case of get your own back time on Bombardier Bailey if you were that way inclined. To be honest the instructors had nerves of steel, there was no way I would have wanted to be sitting on their side of the vehicle. There were times when I felt for their lives as I was driving through narrow roads and almost taking a few extra wing mirrors back to camp.

After four days of intense driving it was time for us all to put our skills into practise as Friday morning arrived. We were all feeling nervous as we were chitchatting away on our way to the MT bay. "OK, get yourselves into the classroom," said Bombardier Bailey and his staff, "there are three military examiners that have been appointed to be with us today to conduct your driving test. The test will last about thirty minutes and will be conducted first on the apron around some cones then, on the streets of Hildesheim."

We were told when we would be doing our practical test and lucky for me, mine was going to be early afternoon which meant I could relax and have the morning off.

I decided to get myself down to the Gun Park and join up again with my gun crew to see if they needed any work doing. The last thing I wanted to happen was be caught skiving by some senior rank and be asked what I was up to; finding me something meaningless to do like sweeping the parade square is what I would have ended up doing.

My test time arrived and I was introduced to my examiner, who, I believe was the rank of a Sergeant Major. After a short brief it was straight onto the Gun Park to spiral through the strategically placed cones then on to the emergency stop. "OK, Paul," he said with a smile to put me at ease, "we are now going to make our way out of the barracks, I will give you clear instructions of where to go, if you don't understand, then please ask."

"OK," I said, feeling a little more settled now. As we exited the camp gates I just tried my best to focus on the task in hand and not to see if I knew who was manning the gate. With the sun shining in my eyes I continued the test route into the heart of the town; it wasn't long before I came across a situation that Bombardier Bailey had explained about during the training. His exact words were, "If there are two vehicles already in the middle of a traffic lighted crossroads that are both turning left then don't enter into the middle, if your lights suddenly turn to red you might not have enough time to complete the turn, thus causing vehicles from the opposite direction to be grid-locked."; it worked a treat as I did exactly what I was taught. *More brownie points for me,* I was thinking.

The rest of the test seemed to go to plan without any trouble. We were now close to the end of the test and turning into the camp that had me saying to myself, *a few more metres and it will all be over.* We stopped on the Gun Park where the test had begun. "Turn your engine off please," said the examiner, looking at his driving report. There must have been at least a minute of silence before the examiner decided to put me out of my ridiculously nervous state. "I'm pleased to say that you have passed your driving test," he said, looking me in the eyes. "In fact, it's one of the best drives I have had for a long time."

"Thank you," I said, feeling on top of the world and relieved that it was all over. After the examiner had exited the Land Rover I was told to take it back to the battery MT; it felt so unreal driving the vehicle on my own across the Gun Park and then into the hangar. "Wolfendale" was the cry from some of my buddies, "Did you pass?"

"Yes, with flying colours." I answered.

"You need to get a motor now," they said. To be honest with a baby on the way it sounded a good idea, once I could afford it; *time to get rid of my 250cc* was going through my mind. Moving into December meant I was getting even closer to being a daddy and wondering what 1979 would bring for me and my buddies. My Army career seemed to be progressing in the right direction even though I felt I still had some growing up to do. Does cutting your sleeves of your shirt sound like I was growing up, or was I still just a little kid inside a man's body?

CHAPTER SEVENTY-SEVEN
GETTING SHIRTY

After spending Christmas with my mother-in-law and her family it was back to the grindstone. I was still pondering about getting a car as the freezing cold weather was telling me to get rid of my bike; riding through the slush of the melted snow would always make my neatly ironed trousers look shambolic, or at least that was the word that Sergeant Massey used when he inspected the troop; understanding my dilemma was not his concern, I was a soldier that needed to think on his feet even though at times I was told I was not paid to think, just paid to do as I was told (work that one out if you can).

After a normal day's work it was time to get myself wrapped up for the journey back to Bad Salzdetfurth. On arrival I was greeted by my mother-in law who explained that Marlene had gone into labour and that she had been taken to BMH (British Military Hospital) Hannover. "Bloody hell," I said, trying not to panic. "I need to get there as quick as I can."

"She has all she needs," said her mum, "she just needs you now to be by her side." I was on my bike and on my way before I could blink; a good hour away saw me arrive about 1830hrs looking as if I had been dragged through a bush backwards. It wasn't too long before I set eyes on my wife as she lay on the hospital bed panting, no sooner had I reached the side of her bed she was given me grief. I was told by the sister that giving me grief was part and parcel of the labour stages so not to take anything personal. "OK, can't wait for her to give birth," I said sarcastically.

It was now past midnight just about eight hours into my shift when my mind was thinking, *how much longer can my wife be in labour?* I was almost on the brink of falling asleep when from down the corridor, the sister arrived. "We have come to take your wife down to the labour ward now," she said, "it shouldn't be too long."

"OK," I said. Looking towards my wife I continued saying; "Won't be long now love, anyway I don't know if my hand can take any more of your squeez-ing." I stayed by her side as she was wheeled down the corridor and into the delivery room; it took no more than half an hour before I became a daddy for the first time; a beautiful girl weighing in at 7lbs 14oz who would be named Melanie was making me feel swollen with pride. Later on that morning I still had to go back to work, I promised my wife I would see her later on that evening. "Dec," I said, "Marlene has given birth, a beautiful little girl."

"I knew it," said Dec. "Just knew you would have a little girl just like Angela and I."

"I'm so thrilled," I said, "You know what the ironic thing about it is though?"

"No, what?" said Dec.

"Your Caroline was born on the first of the eleventh and our little girl was born on the eleventh of the first, hard to believe," I said, shaking my head. I couldn't wait to get back to the hospital later that evening as any father would; within a few days Marlene was back home being a mother to our child, all that was needed now was for me to get an Army quarter; a short visit to the families office to show them the birth certificate meant that I had enough points to be allocated a married quarter. "Next week, Wednesday," said the family's officer, "we have a married quarter that has come vacant in Sarstedt."

"Wow," I said, feeling eager to move in, "my wife will be pleased in respect that her sister and my best mate live there too."

"Well, that will be nice for both of them," he said. "No.5 Brieger weg, ground floor" he continued to say; I couldn't wait to tell Marlene and also Dec.

A few months down the line and now fully settled in my new home, oh yes, and a few exercises later I was put on an NCOs Cardre Course, someone somewhere must have thought that it was about time I was given the opportunity to prove myself, to see if I was worth promoting.

The course itself ran from Monday through to Friday which meant I had to sleep in camp. The standard required to pass was like the standard that would be expected back in Junior Leaders some four years ago, however, I was a lot wiser now and had learned to side step a few mines; like cutting the sleeves of my shirt so it would fold more neatly into a small square no more than about 9in in length and about an inch in depth, then folded around some cardboard for stiffness. It was something that was common on these sort of courses, just don't get caught defacing Army clothing or for the high jump you would be.

My locker layout was at a standard to be proud of as Sergeant Major Mick Thorpe did his rounds with the rest of the DS. With the luck that would normally embrace me, or should I say lack of, I was half expecting the Sergeant Major to sniff out my flea-bitten shirt that would have severe consequences if compromised. As it was, it was my lucky day; I got nothing but praise for my efforts. "Well done, Gunner Wolfendale," he said.

"Thank you Sir," I said, feeling full of admiration for his kind words. The five days went by almost unnoticed with a pass-out parade and the end of the course. With most if not all showing their NCO qualities and passing with merit, it was time to head home; however, little did I know that the commencing week the same shirt that I had defaced would come back to haunt me.

One of my so called mates Hector Heath paid me a visit once the course had finished. "Ay Wolfie, can I have a word a minute," said Hector excitedly, "can I borrow some of your locker layout?"

"Why?" I said inquisitively.

"I'm on the NCOs Cardre course next week," he said, begging me to lend him some of my hard work.

"Can't see why not," I said, "what are you after?"

"Anything to make my life easier," said Hector.

"Got some stuff here you can borrow," I said, handing over part of my locker layout. "There is a shirt here that I've dismembered, make sure you don't get caught with it, if you do get caught, then no matter what, don't mention my name."

"Cheers Wolfie, you're a mate," said Hector, feeling smug with himself.

"Don't mention it," I said, "just make sure you bring my stuff back after the course." After a relaxing weekend with my family it was time to get back to normality; although a promotion was still just a pipe dream it was a step closer to getting my first stripe, even my buddies Tommo and Hammo were saying things like, "Shouldn't be long mate, just got to keep your nose clean."

It must have been about half way through the week when I was told that Sergeant Major Thorpe wanted to see me on my lunch break; this had me wondering as to whether, was it good news, or was it bad news? It wasn't long before I found out.

As I entered the block and close to the Sergeant Major's office I just made sure my uniform was looking of the highest quality, didn't want him to think that I had lowered my standards in just a few days; a nervy gentle tap on his door and I was ready for my fate. "Come in," was the reply from the Sergeant Major. "Gunner Wolfendale, just the man I want to see," as his eyes made contact with mine.

"Sir," I said.

"I was inspecting the NCOs Cardre course this morning, and guess what I discovered in Gunner Heath's locker!" At this moment in time my legs were feeling like jelly.

"No idea, Sir," I said, lying through my teeth.

"This flea-bitten shirt," he said, producing the goods, "Gunner Heath has told me that he borrowed it from you. I have a good mind to make you do the course again, do you understand?"

"Yes, Sir," I said. All I could think about now was, *wait till I get hold of you, Hector.*

"I recommended you for this course," said the Sergeant Major, feeling let down. "Using your initiative is one thing, taking the piss is another; get out of my sight now before I put you on a charge."

I felt so betrayed by Hector, and thinking, *any promotion that I may have been forthcoming would now have to wait a little longer.* It wasn't long before I caught up with Hector down at the NAAFI. "Hector, get over here now," I said angrily. "Why the fuck did you tell Sergeant Major Thorpe about the shirt I lent you?"

"I'm so sorry, Paul," said Hector apologetically. "I just froze for a minute when he catapulted the shirt out of the locker with his pace stick, I just didn't know what to say, I was just caught off guard."

"Well, the one thing you shouldn't have said is, that Gunner Wolfendale lent you the shirt should you?" I said, shaking my head. "I got a right ticking off, bang goes my promotion for a while, luckily for you I've calmed down a bit now, I am still fuming, just don't ask me for any more favours again."

"Like I said Paul, I'm sorry, it was just the first thing that sprang to mind when he asked me whether or not it was my shirt," was Hector's reply.

Now feeling sorry for him I said, "Don't worry Hector," feeling like I had gotten my point across, "just let's leave it at that."

Going into the summer I was once again being shifted from pillar to post. Although there were lots of different jobs open to you within regiment I didn't envisage doing them all, I was quite happy on the guns. Without any warning and completely out of the blue, I found myself being volunteered to be attached to the 18 Battery MT wing; something I really didn't want to do, but as it was, I had no choice in the matter. I had been nominated to be the BKs driver (Captain Snowden). In charge of the MT wing was stoned face Sergeant Frank Smith along with a more light-hearted guy called Bombardier Dave Waterman, Dave was a lot easier to get on with although you wouldn't want to cross the path of either of them.

I was allocated my own Land Rover to fit it out any way I wanted, well at least with the BKs approval. I wasn't told how long I would be on the MT, but if I had my way, it wouldn't be long. It was just one of those jobs that I had little or no interest in; Sergeant Smith, the MT Sergeant and I, just didn't see eye to eye.

Each day I was there made me feel that much further away from my mates; I was trying to find the fun element in my job that seemed to have disappeared since leaving the guns. Anything you did was never good enough; I don't think I can ever remember one time that Sergeant Frank Smith smiled or threw any praise in my direction; I'm not saying is approach was wrong, but for me, he took his job far too serious for my liking. I just needed to get back on the guns and get my life back.

CHAPTER SEVENTY-EIGHT
CHERRY BRANDY AND WHISKY

It was a few weeks into my new job when we were told that we would be going on exercise and I needed to make sure that my vehicle was up and running for the BK. " Wolfendale, the BK will be coming down to inspect the vehicle later on today," said Sergeant Smith.

"No problem," I said, trying not to crack a smile. I suppose the one thing I did like about my new job was that you would be left to your own devices to get on with the task in hand. I developed the long wheel base Land Rover into a kind small camper van, there was a small cabinet for all sorts of goodies and also plenty of sleeping space for the BK and I; compared to the guns, it was luxury even though we had the ever-impressive Stalwart vehicle to sleep in if it didn't break down. Later on that afternoon the BK arrived right on cue. "Gunner Wolfendale," he said, looking over the rim of his glasses.

"Yes Sir," I said, at the same time saluting the Queen's commission.

"I believe you're going to be my driver for the foreseeable future," said the BK, looking me up and down with his wandering eyes, "is this the chariot?"He smirked.

"Yes Sir," I said, trying to snigger at his wit. The BK took a leisurely walk around the vehicle believing he knew what he was looking for before getting into the passenger seat.

"Not bad, Wolfendale," he said, looking at the frame work that held up the canvas roof. The BKs inspection brought a smile from Sergeant Smith in respect that it was a feather in the cap for the MT department. "Exercise next week, Gunner Wolfendale," said the BK. "I will require you to meet me at the Officers' Mess to load up my bits and pieces."

"Bits and pieces Sir?" I said curiously.

"Yes," he said, "my belongings: webbing, holdall, sleeping bag and some personal items that you do not need to know about."

"OK, Sir," I said. The following week was spent putting the finishing touches to my long wheel base Land Rover: jerry cans full of water, all the essential tools including the jack in case of a puncture, steel tow rope that would sit inside of the spare wheel, a spade and pick for digging a trench or two, and last but not least, the camouflage net complete with poles. On the more domestic side of things, a small gas stove complete with the brew kit was a must, my life wouldn't be worth anything if I had forgot to load the more important items: biscuits, squash, bread, plus an Officers' Mess type ceramic plate were also part of our own interpretation of an 1157. With everything now packed I made my way to the Officers' Mess as ordered to find the BK. It was quite strange seeing all the officers running around like they were on a mission in their combats and webbing slung over their shoulder. I was so use to seeing them in their khaki trousers and neatly pressed shirts; pace sticks and multicoloured stable belts were now a thing of the past, well at least for the next couple of weeks.

I didn't have to wait long before BK arrived looking as if he would rather be somewhere else than roughing it on exercise. "Morning Sir," I said in an energetic way and with the mandatory salute.

"Everything OK?" said the BK, putting his webbing and holdall in the back of the Land Rover.

"Yes Sir," I said, giving him a helping hand.

"OK, let's get going," he said. We made our way onto the parade square where I lined up my vehicle next to the BCs. With this being my first time as a driver on exercise I wasn't sure what was expected of me apart from the obvious chauffeur duties; it was a case of learning the ropes as I went along. All the guns and APCs were regimentally lined up just like they were going into battle; I couldn't resist walking over to my old gun sub and have a chat to bring some well needed laughter to my person.

"Wolfendale, you don't belong here anymore," said the crew with huge laughter, "get yourself back with the Ruperts you turn coat." This is what I was missing. I had broad shoulders and was always open to sarcasm. I had only been with my Gun Bunny buddies for five minutes and already I was feeling so much better. "Wolfendale," was the cry from afar, it was the BK wondering where I was.

"On my way, Sir," I said, feeling like I was already in trouble.

"Go on Paul you naughty boy," said the lads in a kind of gay sort of voice. "You're wanted somewhere else, go and lick some cherry blossom Paul, see you later darling."

"Yes, I can probably guarantee that knowing you lot," I replied, smiling. After a mild ticking off from the BK it was now time to leave. We were actually one of the first to leave along with the BC, in some ways it did feel relaxing and certainly a lot quieter on the roads; map reading was the BKs responsibility and just doing as I was told was mine. It was nice to see the other side of what goes on in respect that it gives you an overall representation of how much is involved in organising an exercise of this magnitude.

Most of the time I would be driving around without being informed about how the battle was being won, however, what the BK was impressed with was my knowledge of the German language; it was probably a good job as we were about to cross a unmarked level railway crossing. "What are you stopping for?" said the BK abruptly.

"The crossing, Sir," I said.

"What's the problem?" was his reply.

"It says trains pass at regular intervals and you must phone the train master for clearance before crossing."

"Bloody hell," said the BK, feeling relieved at what I had noticed on the sign. "I think it would be you better if you phoned, you sound like you know more about the German language than me."

"OK, Sir," I said. I think this was one of these moments when the BK realised that there was probably more to me than just being the BKs driver. The exercise was going well from my point of view; however, as per normal when I do something right there was always something bad waiting just around the corner. For some unknown reason and off the beaten track, the BK had us driving on the Autobahn and, considering we were on exercise, this was not the norm. We had only been travelling a short while when I felt my vehicle starting to slide from side to side, I was becoming a little concerned about what was causing the problem on this hot sunny day. "Wolfendale," shouted the BK as he was trying to study his map, "keep the vehicle straight."

"It's not me, Sir," I said, gripping the steering wheel tight.

"Well, you're the one driving," he said stupidly. I tried in vain to steer a straight line but the vehicle continued to become uncontrollable.

"Wolfendale, for the last time keep the vehicle in a straight line." Within seconds I was driving in lane one, then lane two and then finally the hard shoulder, drastic action was now a must; slowing the vehicle down I managed to pull the vehicle over to a controlled stop to the disgust of the BK.

"What's the problem this time?" said the BK.

"Not sure, Sir," I said, scratching my head. "I will get out and see what's wrong. It's a puncture Sir, front wheel."

"Can you fix it?" was his reply.

"I think so Sir," I said. "I will need to get the Bottle Jack out of the back and then take the spare wheel off the bonnet."

"Let me know when you're finished" said the BK, helping himself to some refreshments. Parked on the hard shoulder I began to put my training into practise. "How's it going, Wolfendale?" said the BK from the comfort of his seat.

"Nearly done, Sir," I replied, trying to be polite, "just need to tighten up the last of the wheel nuts and then I am finished." *That's it,* I said to myself as I tightened the last wheel nut, all I needed to do now was to drive off the Bottle Jack like I was taught and then we would be back on the road. As I got back into the driver's seat the BK was full of praise.

"Come on then let's get going, we need to make up some time."

"Yes, Sir," I said. Within seconds we were picking up speed in lane one when I had this horrible thought. "Oh no," I said with the colour running out of my face.

"What's up now, Wolfendale?" said the BK, looking towards me.

"I forgot to pick the Bottle Jack up, Sir," I said, "I have left it on the hard shoulder."

"You idiot Wolfendale, what are we going to do now?"

"We will have to turn around at the next exit, Sir" I said.

"I was wondering why we were getting flashed and beeped at," said the BK. "There is an exit in five kilometres, we will turn around there." The whole escapade took about half an hour before we caught sight of the Bottle Jack. "Lucky for you, Wolfendale, it hasn't caused an accident," said the BK. To be honest, I was more afraid what Sergeant Smith would say like paying for a new jack than whether or not it had caused an accident.

Later on that evening and now back onto the so called range roads, there was still plenty of driving to do. For some reason I don't ever remember reading anything in the driver's training manual about what to do if you feel fatigued. I was feeling bedraggled and in need of a rest. Driving in the dark was playing tricks with my mind; every few hundred metres or so I kept seeing a bush jumping out in front of me, the fact of the matter was, I was actually driving off the road and into the bush. "Wolfendale," was the cry once more from the BK. "Keep a straight line." I knew for certain that this time it wasn't a puncture, it was me not being able to keep my eyes open through lack of sleep, how I managed to keep the vehicle on the road for the next few miles I will never know; it was such a relief when the BK announced that we were stopping and meeting up with the BC.

I managed to get about an hour's sleep before the BC and his party arrived. "Wake up Wolfendale," said the BK, "the BC is here." Rubbing my eyes, I tried to look as if I was full of energy and having a fabulous time. "Care for a small tickle?" said the BK to the BC.

"Wouldn't say no," said the BC not knowing what he was letting himself in for. The BK opened the passenger door and then leant over to where the hand-brake was located. There were two small hip flasks full of some sort of liquid that I knew nothing about; with mugs in hand the BK poured the contents of one flask and then the other flask into the two mugs. "What is it?" said the BC curiously.

"Just take a sip," said the BK "should warm up your cockles, cherry brandy and whisky wouldn't be without it." I could see the BCs eyes light up like a fruit machine as the liquid slid down his throat and into the chest region.

"Wow," he said, trying to catch his breath, "I can feel it burning inside."

"Would you like some more?" said the BK.

"Not at the moment, maybe another day, back in the mess." The BK informed me that we would be getting some well-earned sleep until about 0700hrs, sleep that was definitely overdue. "Would you like a taste, Wolfendale?" said the BK.

"Don't mind if I do, Sir," I said, "maybe just a small one for medicinal purposes." It was to die for, I'm not a whisky drinker, but the two together complemented each other splendidly, I had been converted. Whisky and cherry brandy had become my signature drink.

Days later it was nice to see the exercise coming to an end; apart from one more puncture and the gear lever snapping off everything went to plan. It was a case of dropping the BK off back at the mess and then sorting my vehicle out for the next time, if there was to be a next time.

Now I was on the MT my roles had changed, I was being put on Duty Driver more often than not, although occasionally I would cop for a Guard duty. Doing a Duty Driver meant I was still having to sleep in the Guardroom but my duties were very much the same as a taxi driver, sometimes you would have a couple of hours' rest without much happening and then there were the times when you would never seem to stop. Each vehicle would have its own work ticket folder that would hold all the information about the vehicle's whereabouts, keeping a record of the mileage and getting authorisation of each journey by a senior rank was essential; even the Army runs on a budget.

Occasionally, and in the middle of the night, you could be called upon to travel to an Army base that could be absolutely miles away to collect an urgent package; it would normally be something like a part for the M107 that was needed by the REME to get the gun back on the road. Those sort of journeys could be a right endurance especially if you got back to barracks just before first parade; no remorse would be shown by Sergeant Smith and his understudies, getting the vehicle washed down and then straight back to work was how it was.

Summer was now over and we were back into long sleeve order. My 22nd birthday had passed unnoticed and my mate Hammo was now in the piggery; the gun sub that was so well knitted was now being fragmented and a new era beckoned. After another normal type day on the MT, I thought I would check Battery Orders before making my way home to unite with my family once more; hoping I wasn't down for any duties I noticed a section that had me scratching my head. *Grape picking, what the hell is grape picking?* I mumbled to myself, "Priggers," I said to my mate Pete Prigmore, "what the hell is all this about?"

"Not a clue," said Pete, looking just as stunned as me. We both read down the sheet and to our interpretation, it read that volunteers were needed for two weeks for an adventure in the Mosel helping to harvest the grapes from the vineyards. "Sounds like a bit of a skive to me," I said to Pete, "at least it will get me out of the MT for a couple of weeks, although I will miss my wife and little girl."

"Well, I've got no ties," said Priggers. "Think I'll put my name down."

"Me too," I said "Just need to speak to her indoors tonight." We carried on reading down to find out that it was paid work which added more gloss to the reason why we wanted to go. The next day I was in the Battery Office giving my name to Bombardier Young along with Pete and Pete's best mate Dave Hewer, to be totally honest, there were very few married pads that had volunteered; it was mainly the single lads who were looking for a two week alcoholic holiday that was paid for by the lovely West Germans.

CHAPTER SEVENTY-NINE
FEELING TIPSY IN THE VINEYARD

It was now the middle of October and I was saying goodbye to my family for two weeks. Four tonne vehicles could be seen outside the Battery Block (travelling in style) accompanied by Sergeant Vickery who I assumed, must have been volunteered to take charge of what seemed like a chartered party. The idea of what I would estimate to be around 300 soldiers descending on the famous wine town of Bernkastel was to establish as good PR (Public Relation) between the British Forces and the West Germans. We were all for keeping the peace where possible; after all, we needed to respect the fact that we were in their country. Five hours in the back of a four tonne vehicle was enough to drive anyone insane as we trundled towards the nearby border of Luxembourg, especially when you needed a pee. I always wondered what the small square holes in the floor of the four tonne vehicle were used for, although I was later to find out.

After a tiring journey we arrived early evening at our destination which meant it was pitch black by now. "OK, off the trucks," said Sergeant Ron Vickery in a quiet but authoritive voice, "just stay where you are until I tell you where you're going." We just stood there chatting away to each other until Sergeant Vickery could sort out where we would all be going.

"OK, gather around," said Sergeant Vickery "Listen to your names being called out and then stay with that group until I tell you where you'll be going." Within minutes and getting colder, Sergeant Vickery started to announce who would be with who and our locations; there were some small groups of about two or three and some groups of four or five.

"Wolfendale, Hewer and Prigmore, you'll be going to Mulheim to stay with the Fischer family," said Sergeant Vickery.

"Ah, Wolfie," said Priggers, "going to have a great time, bring it on." His remark brought a chuckle and a laugh from Dave Hewer who seemed just as pleased that we were one step nearer to the local nightlife. Once everybody knew where they were going we were loaded back onto the four tonne vehicle and, strategically dropped off at our locations. Ten minutes down the road had us shaking hands with the family where we would be staying.

"Glad to meet you," said this stern, well-dressed bearded man in his German accent. "My name is Matthew, and yours?"

"My name is Paul," I said, "this is Dave and the smaller guy is Pete."

"Excellent," he said with a huge smile. "I will show you where you'll be sleeping and then I will show you where my family and I live, have you eaten?"

"No," we all said, thinking *thanks for asking.*

"No problem, my mother has prepared an evening meal for you." We were absolutely starving, hearing Matthew saying there was food on the horizon was music to our ears, we couldn't have been more grateful that we were going to be fed. We were escorted across the main road that ran through the town to a small hotel.

"OK, this is where you'll be staying," said Matthew. "The hotel is closed at the moment, well at least for the next month; the owner has allowed me to use it for you to stay in."

"Is there anyone else staying here?" said Pete.

"No," replied Matthew, "you have the hotel to yourself."

"Bring it on," said Dave, chuckling like an Australian with flu.

Matthew continued, saying, "I will be back in about half an hour to show you where we live and in the mean time, it will give you a chance to get unpacked; your room is just up the stairs on the right."

We made our way up the carpeted stairs and onto the first floor. There were about ten rooms however; there was only one bedroom that was not locked, the one that had been set aside for us. In fact, after checking out the building we found that ours was the only room in the hotel that was unlocked: the bar, reception area and basically the whole of the hotel was out of bounds. Maybe our reputation had arrived here a long time before us.

After settling in, Matthew returned. "Hello," was the cry from the bottom of the stairs, "are you ready?"

"Yes," we all said in unison, "be with you right away."

"Can't wait for tea," said Pete, "bloody starving." We quickly made our way downstairs to where Matthew was waiting with a key.

"Make sure you lock up the hotel when you leave," he said as he handed me the key. "OK then, follow me, my mother has been busy making your evening meal." It was only a short walk just across the road and into the farm before we entered the huge three storey house. "This way," said Matthew. The dining room reminded me of the Officers' Mess with its enormity; a large wooden oak table beautifully decked with delicious hot food was far more than we were expecting as we sat down to eat.

Seconds later Matthew's mother arrived with a few rules of her own; she was a lovely lady who happened to remind me of my mother at times. "I want to see a clean table," she said in a commanding voice, "and if you need more food then please ask."

More food, we were thinking; there was enough food to feed an Army; "Wow, so much food!" I said to Dave and Pete, who were now getting stuck-in. Every five minutes or so Matthew's mother would pop in like a well trained waiter to make sure we were enjoying our German cuisine.

"Everything OK?" she would say. "Oh and by the way, my name is Maria."

"All OK, Maria," we said, munching away. Just then we noticed a black Labrador entering the room.

"Zenta," she said, "don't you start looking for food, whatever you do, please do not feed her, she has her own food."

"Not a chance," we said, but as the evening passed by our stomachs were feeling swollen, there was still food left on the table, food that we needed to shift.

"Here, Zenta," said Pete quietly, "here girl, come on girl." Not sure if Pete's English was having any impact on the dog, but the dog didn't need asking twice when she saw food being thrown under the table.

"Keep an eye out for Maria," I said to Dave as I helped Pete to clear the table. Before we knew it, the table was looking drained of the feast that we were presented with.

"She's on her way back," said Dave hurriedly.

"Zenta, get from underneath the table now," said Pete, giving her a swift helping hand with his foot.

"Wow, nice to see you have an appetite," said Maria, who was now in the room. "Would you like some more?"

"No, no," we all said, at the same time blowing out our cheeks. "We couldn't eat another thing." We looked over to where Zenta was who was now looking very coy lying on her full replenished belly trying not to give any clues away; a few unnoticed licks of her lips that had us worried meant we were now in the clear, well at least for another day. It was now late evening and time to make our way back to the deserted hotel.

"One last thing," said Maria, "breakfast will be at 7:30 in the morning and then everybody will be leaving around 8:30."

"Thank you," we said as we waved one last farewell to Zenta. "See you in the morning Zenta." Back in the hotel it was a case of getting a good night's sleep, although Pete and Dave were in two minds whether or not to hit the town and sample the German beer.

"Don't even go there," I said, trying to be the responsible one. Luckily it didn't fall on deaf ears as they both agreed to give it a miss; well, at least until tomorrow.

Without an alarm clock I was up sharp and dandy which is more than I could say for Pete and Dave; a short reminder by shaking their beds was all I needed to do to get them to vacate their pits and get ready for the day that lay ahead.

"Woof woof," said Pete to Dave. "Here boy," they continued to say, and they weren't referring to my nickname; they couldn't wait to feed Zenta again. My only concern now was how big Zenta would be by the end of the two weeks.

"Morning, get yourselves sat down" said Maria as we entered the dining room." There was food of plenty that included: bread and bread rolls, jam, sliced meats and also some boiled eggs on demand. It was definitely VIP treatment once more as we tucked into the well decorated table.

"Don't know where to start," said Pete, looking around the table.

"Crusty bread rolls for me," I said. "Think I will try the meat."

"I'm going to order a couple of boiled eggs," said Dave, clicking his fingers in the direction of Maria.

"Don't need to click your fingers, young man," said Maria, looking cross. "What would you like?"

"Two boiled eggs please," said Dave with an apology written all over his face.

It wasn't long before we were left all alone again with Maria now in the kitchen. "Zenta," we said, who was now becoming familiar with the English language, "Over here girl." Zenta didn't need to be asked twice as she took up her position under the table. Within five minutes the table was looking empty again and Zenta was feeling satisfied as she once again could been seen licking her lips. Marching on a full stomach was something that had been instilled into us soldiers for decades which meant we were now ready to take on the world.

It was 0800hrs military time; we were now standing in the small farm yard when we saw Matthew approaching in his fine attire: britches, thick woollen socks with leather boots and a jumper to die for. As for Pete, Dave and I, we were looking like a soldier should look when off duty: jeans and t-shirt and our Army boots instead of the habitual trainers that you would normally associate with a squaddie.

"Morning, men," said Matthew, "are you feeling ready for your first day?"

"No," said Dave.

"What?" said Matthew "What's wrong?"

"Dave is just having a joke," I said to Matthew. "English humour, and yes, we are all ready."

"Ah, I see," said Matthew. "I will remember in future." Just then a civilian type Land Rover appeared to take us to the steep mountainous vineyards. "OK, get on board," said Matthew, "it will take us about fifteen minutes before we get there. How was breakfast? I hope my mother looked after you."

"Yes," we all said, "Really nice food." The fifteen minutes took no time at all before the Land Rover came to a sudden stop. As we got out, we just stared at the abnormity of the so called mountain whilst at the same time thinking, *how the hell are we going to climb this monstrosity?* We were given a short lecture on what our duties entailed. "These are called Hods," said Matthew, pointing to these big cone shaped containers. "You put your arms through the leather straps and the Hod will then rest comfortably on your back."

"Looks bloody dangerous," said Pete, taking a step back. The Hod was about four to five foot in length stemming from your shoulders all the way down to your backside. It was wide at the top and then it became narrower at the bottom; with our Hods now attached to our backs we just paraded around like ballerinas wondering what the hell we would look like in a mirror. "OK," said Matthew checking that the Hods were in their correct position, "follow me up the mountain." It was a bit of a slog; however, we weren't going to show any weakness to Matthew and his workforce.

It took us about five to ten minutes to reach the top of the mountain before we got our first glimpse of the ladies picking the succulent grapes from their vines. "Just rest your Hod on the ground facing upright," said Matthew. "When the small buckets are full, your task will be to empty the contents into your Hod, when the Hod is full to the rim, you then sit yourself down on the ground and attach the Hod to your back. You'll need to be very careful when you stand up because of the weight of the Hod and the strain it can put you on your back."

Matthew stayed with us for our first attempt to see how we fared. It took no more than a few minutes to fill the Hod with the buckets that were already full from the early shift. "Pete, give us a hand," I said, trying to prise myself up from the ground. "Harder than I first thought."

"Just lean forward," said Pete, holding my Hod, "one, two, three… now."

"Wow," I said, feeling relieved, "Feels better now I am standing upright."

"Looking good, Wolfie," said Dave, laughing his head off.

"Wait until it's your turn Dave" I said, "then you'll realise how heavy they are." Dave took the same stance as me as he connected with his Hod, "Bloody hell" said Dave looking as if his legs were about to give way.

"I told you so Dave," it's like trying to walk with an Elephant on your back". We all waited for each other to be ready before descending the mountain with the sunlight shining through the majestic valley; with an angled back and trying to keep our balance we started taking tiny steps down the mountain.

At the bottom of the mountain and lying in wait was a tractor with two huge round tank-like containers fastened to a flat bed trailer. Our job was simple; well, at least that what it seemed. We had to step onto the trailer and project the Hod forward over our shoulder and then empty the grapes into the containers. I had a slight chuckle to myself as I launched my grapes into the container; it reminded me of the blackened coal man filling up our coal bunker when I was a wee nipper. Up and down the vineyard all day was how it was. One thing we did notice was that if you got caught short then there was nowhere to pee; the ladies had to discreetly and sometimes not so discreetly drop their panties and go for it. Finding a dry patch to sit down with your Hod was proving a task within itself.

At around 1200hrs we would have our lunch brought to us by Matthew or one of his co-workers: Salad sandwiches, freshly cooked meats, cake, German biscuits or just some sort of light snack washed down with a soft drink and, if we were lucky, occasionally a cold beer; within half an hour we were ready to take on the mountain again. In the evening and around 1700hrs it was time to head back to the hotel. Pete and Dave were ready to venture into the nearby town, while me, well; I was content just to read a book in the room.

After the first week Pete and Dave were getting a little short on cash so thought it would be a good idea to ask for an advance on their wages. "Yes, of course," said Matthew, reaching to his back pocket for his wallet. "I will give you what you have earned so far and then, I will give you one final payment at the end of next week, is that OK?"

"Yes, thank you," said Pete and Dave. Matthew handed over several Deutsche Marks that brought smiles of plenty from Pete and Dave. 'Beer, beer, beer said the gunners' sprang to mind as they got themselves ready for another night on the tiles.

"Fancy joining us?" said Pete.

"Nah, not for me," I said. "I'm here to make a profit and not to spend all of my earnings."

"Sucker," said Dave. "Enjoy your book." Working through the weekend wasn't an option, halfway through the next week Pete and Dave were again feeling the strain of continuous drinking; they were flat broke.

"Wolfie," they said, "we need a favour."

"What?" I said curiously.

"Well," they both said with a puppy dog like look on their faces, "we were wondering if you would mind asking Matthew for an advance on your wages."

"Now why would I want to do that?" I said, knowing what they were up to.

"Oh come on, Woofer," they said, "don't make us beg."

"Aye, OK then," I said, shaking my head. I was being embraced by both of them to the point where I couldn't breathe. "Get off me, you nutters," I continued to say as I became their next best friend, well at least for the next few days. The end of the week was now upon us and as a treat, Matthew decided to bring a bottle of Mosel schnapps along for our lunch as this would be our final day on the vineyards (huge mistake). One by one Pete, Dave and I made our way down to the bottom of the mountain in the scorching heat. "Here we are, lads," said Matthew with a smile on his face, "get some of this down you."

"What the hell is that?" I said to Dave, looking confused.

"Looks like some sort of schnapps," said Dave, rubbing his hands with glee. "Come on Pete, let's get stuck in." Matthew was now set upon by Dave and Pete who, if they had been any closer, would have been in danger of Matthew having to buy them a meal. Matthew opened the screw top lid and started to pour the white liquid into the small snap glasses that we were all holding.

"It is called Tresda," said Matthew, "a product of the Mosel. Please take a drink."

With our glasses now charged it was a case of down the hatch. I'm afraid I was a little slow on the uptake so before I could even think of knocking mine back Dave and Pete were searching for a refill. "Get it down you," said Pete, getting a top up.

"Just need a second to compose myself," I said, trying to avoid the inevitable. One, two, three and it was lining my stomach; it was disgusting, I could feel my throat burning whilst at the same time trying to regain my voice. I think I managed one more and that was my lot; as for Dave and Pete, I lost count. After the so called 'happy half hour' it was time to make our way up the mountain for our final shift, but for some unknown reason and with every step I took, my head was giving out drunken signals. I was starting to feel a little dizzy as I struggled to fill my Hod with the freshly picked grapes. With my Hod now firmly on my back, I gingerly made my way down the mountain.

Everything was looking good apart from the fact that I could see two tractors instead of one waiting at the bottom of the mountain. Unfortunately, one of them was real and the other one was a figment of my imagination. *Which one do I choose?* I said to myself as I was now only feet away. Within seconds it was quite obvious that I had made the wrong choice as I cart wheeled off the small wall and onto the road scattering grapes everywhere.

"What are you doing?!" shouted Matthew, who was standing by the real tractor, "get the grapes picked up quickly."

"Thanks for asking if I am all right," I said angrily.

"Well, are you OK?" said Matthew, now sounding just a tad concerned.

"I will live," I said, "just a broken leg."

"Your leg is broken?" replied Matthew.

"Of course it isn't," I said, shaking my head, "but it could have been."

With the help of Matthew we managed to collect all the grapes up and put them where they belong, on the real tractor and not where I wanted to put them. After an exhilarating afternoon, all good things must come to an end; it was now time to say our goodbyes to the hard working ladies on the mountains, ladies who we had become acquainted with. In a strange sort of way I was sad to be leaving the Mosel and all of its majestic beauty, but I had a family to get back to; giving my wife and child a big hug each morning was something that had been missing for the last two weeks.

There were a few loose ends to tie up before we made our way back to Hildesheim the following day, like receiving our final pay packet from Matthew. Our wages were handed to us after breakfast on the day we were leaving.

"Here you go, lads," said Matthew, handing over our wages. "On behalf of my family , I would like to thank you for all of your help. It has long been a tradition for the British soldiers to come to the Mosel and help harvest the crops and, at the same time it is a tradition for my family to give you two bottles of the finest Mosel white wine for you to drink at your leisure."

"Wow, thank you so much," said Pete, Dave and I. "We had a lovely time."

"Well, take care of yourselves and maybe I will see you next year," said Matthew, shaking our hands.

"You never know," we said, thinking, *why not?* We made our way back to the hotel to gather our belongings and then open our pay packets. Unfortunately, Dave and Pete owed me the remains of their wages, which meant they had next to nothing to show for their efforts apart from a few hangovers. Me, well, I was rolling in the clover, which is the reason I volunteered in the first place. On the way back to Hildesheim in the dark of the night the temptation of opening the bottles of wine was too much for some of the lads who had also been given gifts in the form of alcohol. I was just being my normal self sat by the tailgate of the truck when the wine swigging lads decided that it was time for a toilet break; not a conventional one I hasten to add. "I need a leak," said Jock Eddie Burns politely.

"Well, we are at least an hour away from a service station," said Pete.

"I won't last that long," said Eddie, now feeling worried.

"You will just have to stick it through one of the holes in the floor of the truck," said Pete. I was now thinking, *this could be one of the most stupid ideas of all time.* Minutes later it happened; with his body lying on the floor and his dick in place, I could see the car that was travelling behind us getting the full blast. I could see his window wipers coming into play as the ordeal seemed to last forever. Unfortunately some of the other lads also felt this was a great idea to relieve themselves; before long there were cars of plenty getting showered.

Continuing on our merry way, we finally pulled into the service station only to be followed by one of the unfortunate victims; a row of huge proportion broke out with Sergeant Vickery having to take the brunt of the anger which was felt by this German guy. We knew at this stage that we were in for a rollicking when we finally returned to camp hours later.

After arriving back at camp the next day we were given a stern lecture on our behaviour. To be honest, no one was giving any names away as to who was responsible for the unfortunate incident; pinpointing the blame on one individual was not going to happen. "All for one and one for all" we all said.

It was now November and with not too much going on in respect of exercises with our M107s, Hammo had now volunteered to take full charge of the piggery after his short time there, and my time on the MT reached an end as I was back on the guns again, not before time I hasten to add. I knew where my place was, and under the command of a new No. 1 Bombardier Stretch, I was back in my comfort zone with a lot of new faces, Paul Drabarek, Paul Hanson, and Kenny just to name a few. Christmas came and went unnoticed with a sprinkling of snow, the only thing of any importance was we were told that that there was to be a COs parade after our Christmas break. We weren't too concerned about the announcement as it would be quite normal to be addressed by the CO to inform the regiment of what lay ahead for 1980. However, what he had to say would come as a shock to us all, as rumour control was non-existent.

CHAPTER EIGHTY

FEARING THE WORST FOR BOMBARDIER STRETCH

"On parade now," was the cry from Sergeant Massey on this cold 1st January Monday morning. We were put in open order so that Sergeant Massey and his men could walk up and down the three ranks and inspect our dress before the COs parade. All this took no more than a few minutes before we were marched down to the Gun Park to join the rest of the regiment.

Once there we lined up in a relaxed manner chitchatting away waiting for the CO to arrive and to find out what 1980 would bring. "Attention," was the command from the RSM as the CO appeared from around the corner of the gun shed. A few neat salutes from one and all before we were told to stand at ease and then stand easy (basically, relax, but don't fall asleep). There was complete silence as the CO dropped the bombshell.

"I have been informed and, at short notice, that the regiment will once again be called upon to perform another tour of Northern Ireland." You could have heard a pin drop; we were all in shock looking at each other with raised eyebrows as the CO continued his speech.

"The tour will begin early May and finish in September; it will be in the heart of Belfast."

I just looked over to Tommo who was standing next to me and said, "Bloody hell, Belfast, wow, it's only four months away."

"Sure to be eventful," said Tommo, looking just as shocked as me. "This will be our first time away from our wives for such a long period."

"Yes," I said, "four months with RR in between." The CO continued by saying that Northern Ireland training was to start at the beginning of February. "Your senior NCOs from your respective batteries will enlighten you more over the next few weeks once we have had time to reflect on the up comings." Before training began we had a small exercise of a week to attend to; an exercise that would allow us to get use to our new No.1. Taking over from Sammy was a challenge within itself; was he up for the task? We were soon to find out.

It only took me a couple of days to establish that Bombardier Stretch was going to be a hit with the crew. As well as taking control of the men, he was always looking for advice from the more experienced ones like Dinger and me along with the cover-number Bombardier Naylor. Still getting to grips with being the Gun No.1, Bombardier Stretch was finding life comfortable; just like Sammy, he was a very determined man and just as competitive.

"Fire mission battery," was heard from the command post which meant we needed to get the gun ready for firing in quick time; being the first gun to report back to the Command Post that we were ready to fire was always the priority.

"No. 5 gun ready," reported Bombardier Stretch back to the Command Post before anyone else did. "Well done lads," he said, feeling proud of his men, "first to report ready." Within minutes all the guns were firing their 147lb shells across the range with accurate precision; although we never did get to see the target area with it being some twenty miles away we were always given feedback from the Command Post. We were given several fire missions over the next hour which didn't give us a lot of time to draw breath. Within the excitement and, for some unknown reason, we fired a round off with the order of 'at my command' still in force; 'at my command' meant that you must get permission from the command post before firing a round. If the command was not in force then you could fire when ready.

"Cease firing," could be heard over the tannoy. To give cease firing in the middle of a fire mission means that there is something not quite right, something somewhere has gone wrong. It had become quite obvious that No. 5 gun had dropped a clanger and fired a round when not ordered to do so. We all just looked at each other and then at Graham who was now wanting the ground to open up.

"Will the No.1 of E Sub," (another name for our gun), "report to the Command Post," said a voice over the radio. With Graham now searching for his webbing and SLR, he left Bombardier Naylor in charge while he made his way under the cam-net for a short walk to the awaiting CPO (Command Post Officer).

All we could do now is wait for Graham to return with what we were hoping would be no more than a slap on the wrist. However, when he returned we were to find out that this sort of incident may have to be taken further. It would need to be reported to the SMIG (Sergeant Major in charge of Guns) and then the CO. For the next few days leading up to the end of the exercise, we were all very concerned for Graham as we returned back to base camp. The regiment got together at the end of the exercise in a wooded but open area for the CO to address us on the regiment's performance.

Feeling grotty and uninterested in respect that we just wanted to get back to barracks and have a overdue shower, we were brought up to attention and then told to stand easy. Most of the jargon that was spoken by the CO went over our heads until the CO caught our attention by saying, "The exercise hasn't gone unscathed. Unfortunately, there was an incident involving the No.1 of one of the guns in 18 Battery." We all raised our eyebrows at the same time, especially with the fact that we knew who the CO was referring to.

"Could Bombardier Stretch please step forward please," said the CO with all the rest of the senior ranks around him. I could see Graham looking worried and embarrassed as he marched swiftly towards the CO.

"Hope he doesn't get demoted," I said to Tommo.

"Not sure what will happen," said Tommo, feeling shocked. Bombardier Stretch was no more than a metre from the CO when he came to a halt and saluted his fate.

"Bombardier Stretch," said the CO, lowering his chin, "it has been quite an exercise for you, hasn't it?"

"Yes Sir," said Bombardier Stretch, breathing heavily.

"I have been informed of your, let's say, out of character error, a fucking cock up in military terms, do you agree?" said the CO.

"Sir," said Graham, not knowing whether to snigger at the remark or just keep a straight face.

"Well, you're certainly not the first and will certainly not be the last to make a cock up; however, your conduct is noted. Let's say this is a warning to you, do you understand?"

"Yes Sir."

"After conferring with your BC and TSM we have reached a decision. I'm afraid that after due care and consideration we have decided that the NCOs mess is not the place for you. 'Congratulations', you're being promoted to the Sergeants' mess. You'll be expected there tonight to buy the first round."

We were all thinking, *he must have made a pact with the devil* as the CO handed over the already-prepared three stripes to sew onto his pullover, along with a firm hand shake.

Everyone standing in the ranks just cheered at the unexpected news. Just when we all thought he was going to be demoted, he ended up being promoted to Sergeant. "Well done Sergeant Stretch," we all said as he returned to the gun; it was one of those unexpected moments that only come around once in a while. Back in camp some hours later, it was time to say goodbye to the guns, well at least until October. A quick rush down to the wash-down and a lick of paint, followed by a few tins of grease meant the guns were technically out of action until we returned from Northern Ireland.

It was now time to once again be moved around from pillar to post, with the fact that the NCOs were being allocated their sections and the men they would be working with. This sort of news was always a tense moment hoping that you were in a section with someone you knew; however there would be even better news in store for me towards the end of the tour.

CHAPTER EIGHTY-ONE
NONSTOP GOODBYES

With everything now stored away, it was Northern Ireland training once more. I was expecting to be in a section that was not dissimilar to the gun sub I was attached to, but for some unknown reason, that didn't materialise; the section leader was Bombardier Dave Waterman and the section 2IC was L/Bombardier John Philip, more commonly known as JP.

These were men I had worked with in the past on the MT; Dave was second in command on the MT section whilst JP was Sergeant Major Dick Moore's driver; however, I was still surprised that I wasn't in the same section as Sergeant Stretch. Bombardier Waterman, Alan Carvell ex Q Battery and once a full screw (Bombardier) busted down to a gunner, along with Frankie Abbott and I made up our four man brick; JP, a guy called Manby and Eddie Burns who I got to know when we were down the Mosel were part of the other brick, although occasionally we would mix and match a bit.

The training was the same as ever for me, in other words, I was now becoming a veteran in the heart of combat in Northern Ireland with it being my third tour in five years; the only difference on this tour would be that we were expected to have a round in the chamber of our SLR when we would be patrolling the streets. It was quite a scary thing having your rifle cocked and at the ready; firing your weapon accidentally was now an easy thing to do, it was so imperative to have the safety catch applied at all times. Very often I could feel myself playing with the little blighter as it was positioned next to my thumb; occasionally taking it from the safety position and applying it to the ready position was something I needed to control. It was like one of those fidgety moments you get from time to time when you feel nervous. A quick squeeze on the trigger at this point and that was it; a round of 7.62mm ammunition would be fired.

During the three months of training, which included the mandatory two weeks in Sennelager, we all had our personal lives to lead. This saw Tommo and I get rid of our motorbikes; we were now well and truly family men which meant there was no place for two wheel transport. Tommo sold his to Hammo and I sold mine to Geordie Roberts also from 18 Battery. No transport meant I would now need to get myself sorted and purchase a car that would be more suited for my family.

"What do you plan on doing now that you have no motorbike?" I said to Tommo.

"Not sure, might look at getting me a car."

"Same here," I said.

Within a couple of weeks I had my first car parked outside my flat in Sarstedt: a yellow Fiat 127 hatchback, a small vehicle with just enough room for a small family. I bought it from one of my Army mates for a small fee although it felt like a king's ransom to me. As for Tommo, well he decided to wait until after our tour of Belfast. It was now getting close to the end of March and we were just tidying up loose ends to our training, lots more riot type training was the main focus that told us more of what we could expect. 18 Battery were going to be located in North Howard Street Mill, just off the Falls Road in the heart of West Belfast where riots were a common thing.

Londonderry and Keady saw me being part of the search section and Belfast was to be no different; I'm not sure why, but once again I was part of search team whilst at the same time I was also trained on the FRG (Federal Riot Gun), commonly known as a baton gun. We were given stern guidelines about how to fire the baton gun if needed, and for me, it was a good job, as I was to find out half way through the tour. The ammunition for the FRG for those who are non-military personnel would be best described as a piece of moulded hard plastic as opposed to the earlier model that was like a women's play thing; this more updated model was about one and a half inches wide and about six to eight inches in length. The end of the projectile was flat, which meant it could cause severely damage your ego if you happened to be in its line of fire.

With the hot summer weather now upon us it was time to say our farewells. The early morning sunlight shone through the curtains of my bedroom which sounded the call to get out of bed. Saying goodbye to my wife who now lay next to me filled me with sadness knowing that tomorrow morning I would be waking up alone surrounded by emptiness. My little girl, who was now 15 months old, stood up in her cot that was in our room as if to say, goodbye daddy, take care of yourself, mummy and I will be fine.

A cooked breakfast and then it was time to say my tearful goodbyes. I was thinking to myself, *all of the other married personnel would be doing the same thing so I wasn't the only one feeling gloomy.* Suddenly, there was an uninspected knock on the door. On opening the door, and to my surprise, it was Tommo and his family.

"Come in, mate," I said, trying to hide my sadness and my watery eyes.

"Thought we could leave together," said Tommo with his daughter Caroline in his arms and his wife Angela holding his hand.

"Yes, great idea," I said. "I am just about ready, I just need to get my suitcase and webbing and then that's it." It was combats and kisses time for the two sisters and our children. I'm one of those people that are no good with goodbyes, when I saw the gentle tears rolling down the faces of Marlene and Angela I found it difficult to control my feelings. My eyes could not contain the water that was gathering anymore; putting on a brave face was as much as I could muster as I said, "Behave yourselves you daft buggers; we will be back before you know it." Tommo and I made our way to the main road to catch the duty transport that was due any minute. We could see a lot of German people minding their own business yet at the same time, probably wondering what we were up to; after all, we did look like we were on a mission.

With the transport now upon us we got ourselves into the long wheel base Land Rover for the ten minute journey into camp. It looked like a war zone as we entered the camp; there were soldiers everywhere in respect that most of them were coming out from their last visit to the NAAFI. There was one last farewell I needed to do and that was to my mate, Hammo, who would not be joining us. Hammo was due to leave the Army in two weeks' time after completing his three years that he signed up for. Normally I would be looking for him in one of the battery bars, but on this occasion, I knew where to find him, The Piggery. I made my way to the back of the block to where the where the Piggery was located. I didn't have to look far to find him as there he was in front of me sitting down having a fag.

"Hammo," I shouted, "Get yourself over here, that's an order."

"Hey there, Woofer," was his reply, "how you doing man?"

"Come to say my goodbyes, mate," I said, feeling sad. "Can't believe here I am, about to go to Belfast and you, well in two weeks time you'll be at home enjoying life with your family."

"Looking forward to it," said Hammo nodding his head. "However, going to miss the Army and in particular you, Woofer." I could tell Hammo was getting more emotional with each kind word he said, and to be perfectly honest, so was I.

"Listen mate," I said, "just keep in touch, it wasn't so long ago that I was saying goodbye to Don, another great mate. I never thought I would have to go through this again. Unfortunately, and for some unknown reason I've lost all contact with Don. I know how easy it is to lose track of your mates so promise me you'll keep in touch."

"I will search high and low for you if we ever lose touch mate, you can count on that," said Hammo, wrapping his arms around me like he didn't want me to go.

"Thanks for that, Gav," I said, using his first name, "it means a lot to me."

Within seconds we were talking like squaddies would normally talk trying not to be softies. "Get back to your pigs, Hammo, I don't know who smells worst, you or the pigs," I said, turning away and heading back to the block.

"Go and lick some arses Wolfendale, you never know, one day you might get promoted."

"Not a chance," I said, "but I can live in hope." Deep down we were both hurting, but that's what the Army does for you.

With the entire farewells now out of the way it was time to concentrate on the task ahead as we were rushed onto the awaiting coaches; a drive to RAF Gutersloh and then onto a Hercules aircraft for our final journey to Aldergrove airport.

CHAPTER EIGHTY-TWO
WELCOME TO THE DIVIS

The two hour journey in a RAF Hercules plane and sat next to Robbo Robinson had us believing we really were going to war, no such luxury as cabin crew bringing us an aperitif; we just placed our backsides in canvas seats down the middle of the plane facing outwards for the two hour journey. On landing in Northern Ireland we only had a short escorted journey of about fifteen miles in the back of a four tonner to the notorious West Belfast, before arriving at North Howard Street Mill. You could almost sense the tension on the streets from the locals as we thundered our way along the Falls Road and then through the main galvanised gates that were being manned by some smiling faces, faces that were saying, "we're about to be relieved of our duties and heading back home."

The camp itself was like the name suggests, a large old factory type like building with a court yard similar to a small car park that housed the Saracens we would be needing, along with about four Land Rovers; *welcome to a guaranteed explosive four months* was what was going through my mind as we all made our way into the building. The accommodation was the best that I had come across so far in respect of my other two tours in Londonderry and Keady. The rooms were similar to the ones in Junior Leaders and pretty much sound proof. There was a stand-by room that had a TV and also a small cinema, lucky for us one of the lads had been trained as a projectionist; table tennis and a small gym along with a sauna was available to complete the tour.

It was nice to have these home comforts, although, as I lay on my bed for the first time scanning the room with my eyes, I just knew I was going to find it tough not waking up next to my wife and the happy smiling face of my child "two section, get yourselves to the OPs (operational) room now for a brief, "was the cry from Sergeant Massey.

"Great," I said to Alan Carvell, "just Like Londonderry again, straight out on patrol."

"Come on," said Alan, chuckling under his breath, "stop your moaning, let's go and show the locals what we're about." I suppose he was right, that was the sort of remark that I needed to get me motivated; I jumped off my bed and put on my stripped down webbing. I was ready for action along with the section commander Bombardier Dave Waterman and Frankie Abbott.

It was a longer brief than normal with it being the first one. We were all given a map of the area we would be patrolling that, included the infamous Falls Road just outside the gates along with the Shankill and Springfield roads; the way the brief came across made us feel like, *keep your head down and we hope to see you back in an hour and a half. Hope?* I was thinking; that certainly filled me with confidence.

Outside at the loading bay it was time to do what we had never done before, and that was to prime our SLR, "With a magazine of twenty rounds load," said Dave sternly. With our magazines now firmly fixed to the rifle, the next order was, "READY." It felt very imaginary as we all cocked our weapons putting a round into the chamber of the rifle; my first thought was *don't mess with the safety catch Wolfendale,* with my now itchy fingers.

"OK, let's go." Even though I had experience in patrolling, I actually feared for my life not knowing exactly what to expect as the gates closed behind us, leaving us vulnerable to the enemy. Within a short walk we were on the Falls Road amongst the Irish population who just seemed to be minding their own business as if to say, "It's just another day in the life of this endless civil war." Where possible we tried not to upset the neighbourhood, but occasionally we would stop the odd person or two and take down their details on a small note pad that we were issued with; name, address and their reason for being on the Falls Road was pretty much how it was. Finding out as much as you could about them was imperative if we were to enforce law and order.

Towards the other end of the falls which we referred to as the 'corridor of uncertainty' we came across the Grosvenor Road, which was adjacent to Springfield Road. The Grosvenor Road was the home of the famous RVH (Royal Victoria Hospital) that would have seen more casualties than any other hospital around; a stroll up the Springfield Road and then onto the Shankill was the route we took before making our way back to the barracks.

With so much activity on the streets, the hour and a half flew past unnoticed; one thing for sure though that did stick out more than anything else, was the Divis flats. We got a glimpse of the enormity of the flats when we left the barracks, but were treated to a more panoramic view on our return back to camp. They were located on the Lower Falls just off the Shankill. The

Divis flats were built in the late 1960s because of the deprivation around the area, thinking it might help the situation; unfortunately, because of the so called 'troubles' it became a haven for the IRA and then was correctly named 'Fort Divis'.

Spanning over 15 acres, 850 flats were linked by walkways to create a kind of community, but unfortunately, the walkways became an easy getaway for the perpetrators who occupied the flats. Standing tall and towering about 200ft tall was the Divis Tower itself; it was built on the edge of the complex. The 20-floor structure became an ironic part of West Belfast. I could see the Army OP on top of the tower which was an essential part of trying to keep the peace; although the OP was dubbed a spy post by the locals (no difference in my book), it served its purpose and that's what counted.

In the height of the troubles, the only way for the Army to get to the OP was by helicopter, until we were to find a safer way of using the lift. We would radio through to the men in the OP that the next shift were about to arrive for duty, and on that note, one of the men from the OP would take control of the lift by using an override system so the lift could not be stopped until it reached the ground floor; three days at a time was the norm we would stay in the OP, which was kitted out to provide us all the facilities that we needed.

Back in North Howard Street it was time for a quick debrief and to mull over our first escapade on the streets. "How did you find it?" I said to Alan.

"Enjoyed it," he said, "but I'm sure it will get a lot more intense over the next few weeks, I'll let you know then." It was now time for us to unpack and get some food inside us before our next patrol the following day, although I must admit I was looking forward to my first close up of the Divis, whenever that might be.

The following day and up at 0700hrs we made our way to breakfast and then to the OPs room to be briefed on our patrol. Once sat down we were told of our task; showing us photos of certain members of paramilitary groups and then informing us that we would be entering the Divis Complex. "Wow," I said to Alan and Frankie, "didn't think it would come so soon."

The operational officer continued his brief by saying, "Your task will be to stop and search as many people as you can, on and around the Divis area, we want as much information as we can get about the people living there."

"OK, get yourselves down to the loading bay," said Dave; all pumped up and ready to go Dave took a final few notes down that included checking his map. The yard was busy with patrols coming in and out at regular intervals, including mobiles. "Line up," said Dave, "with a magazine of twenty rounds load." There was a slight pause before again Dave said, "Ready."

The noise of us all cocking our weapons would always have an impact on the lads that were standing around. "Don't shoot," could be heard in a joking way. It was a surprising left turn this time out of the camp gates, which almost caught us off guard as I was about to turn right.

"Wolfendale, we're going left not right," said Dave.

"Sorry," I said, feeling like a numpty. With the early morning heat of the sun beating down on us we made our way across the waste land which was about the size of a football pitch. Being caught out in the open meant we had to be as vigilant as ever as we weaved our way across the derelict ground before reaching a residential and more built up area.

We patrolled for about thirty five minutes before we reached the Divis complex; half of the section made their way up the cold bloodshed concrete stairs with its overpowering smells around the eight block complex. Dave, Alan, Frankie and I made our way around in the other direction. Once on the walkway that was no more than a couple of metres wide, we walked along in single file about twenty metres apart. The doors of the flats resembled the colours of a rainbow: blue, orange, yellow, red, green, purple, you name a colour and I can guarantee there would be a door painted that colour. Each door also had its own small window at the side.

We were in the complex for about forty five minutes and during that time we managed to ascertain a barrel full of information, under duress I hasten to add, for the OPs room to rifle through; snarls and unwelcome language along with spitting and threats like you're dead when the IRA get hold of you was all part of what we expected.

As we left the Divis complex I took one last look up at the Divis Tower thinking *it won't be long before I'm up there with my section*; I seemed to be mesmerised by the eye watering sheer size of it until I was brought out of my trance. "Wolfendale, stop staring at the tower and concentrate on patrolling," said Dave with a Divis snarl.

"Sorry," I said as I got back to my task in hand for the final fifteen minutes of the patrol.

North Howard Street Mill Belfast
Incident of events from 07-18 August 1980

07 1425hrs – Hoax bomb Mackkies Factory
07 2330hrs – Riot outside Pound Loney
07 1715hrs – 2 busses blocking Sorrella/Grosvenor Rd
08 1750hrs – 2 busses blocking RVH (Royal Victoria Hospital) entrance
08 1907hrs – Hijacked vehicle abandoned set alight Ross estate/Falls rd
08 1925hr – 3 x HV (High Velocity) shots fired at patrol Ross estate
from area 93-95 Falls Rd
3 x HV shots fired from Lesson St at patrol in Falls Rd
08 2127hrs – 8-12 HV shots fired at RUC (Royal Ulster Constabulary)
mobile along Falls Rd
08 2148hrs – 3 x HV shots fired from area Cyprus St/Leeson St at patrol
on Falls Rd
08 2344hrs – 3 x HV shots at RUC Springfield Rd, FP (Firing Point)
thought to be Colligan St
09 0027hrs – 2 x LV (Low Velocity) shots fired at SF (Security Forces)
area of Clonard St
09 0056hrs – Hijacked vehicle set on fire Falls/Springfield Rd junction
09 0423hrs – Shots-Explosion Springfield Rd RUC station from
Colligan St
09 0623hrs – Blast bomb Colligan St/Springfield Rd
09 1233hrs – Nail bomb junction Cupar St/ Lawnbrooke
09 1411hrs – Shots at SF patrol Falls Rd from area Clonard St/ Falls Rd
junction
09 1417hrs – Shots at SF patrol from junction Clonard St/ Falls Rd
09 1700hrs – Hijacked Oil tanker left outside RUC Springfield Rd.
09 1800hrs – Explosive device thrown at RUC Land Rover Falls Rd/
Linden St junction
09 2100hrs – Nail bomb thrown at vehicle in Falls Rd from Dunlewy St
or lower Clonard St
10 0014hrs – 2 x LV shots at RUC Hasting St sangar
10 1104hrs – Find Linden St 2 x Nail bombs
10 1610hrs – Van set alight on Falls Rd between Leeson St and Spinner St
12 1500hrs – During the PSF march attempts to erect barricades
13 1340hrs – Heavy stoning junction Leeson st/Falls Rd

13 1820hrs – Hijacked truck set on fire across Falls Rd outside Walshes Bar
15 0745hrs – Hijacked van Spinner Rd
15 1540hrs – Hijacked van blocked junction Sevastopol/Falls
15 1900hrs – Hijacked vehicle set alight junction Springfield Rd/Falls
16 1918hrs – Suspect device Dunville Park, hoax
18 1918hrs – 1 x LV shot fired at mobile patrol junction Kashmir Rd/ Clonard gardens

After the first two weeks had gone by without too much difficulty it was time for our section to be on OPs. One half of the section would be going to the Divis Tower and the other half to an OP on the Springfield road. I was in the half that was going up the Divis Tower and to be honest, I was looking forward to it. We arrived at pace in the pig (Armoured Vehicle) that subsequently backed up as close as it could to the entrance to the flats. "Out now," was the cry from Dave, "go go go." The armoured plated doors flew open forcefully to allow us to exit the vehicle; as we entered the tower we were met by one of the men from the OP that was guarding the lift.

"OK, get yourselves into the lift and I will take you to the top two floors," he said hurriedly. Shortly after, we felt the lift come to a halt only to be were greeted by yet another guy as the sliding door opened. "Bloody hell, Tommo," I said with a huge smile on my face, "how's it going?"

"All right Woof," he said, looking as surprised as me.

"What's it like?" I said, needing to get my skates on.

"Interesting," was the reply from Tommo. "Glad to be heading back to camp though, will be nice to be back in North Howard Street for some recreation and comfort." Tommo was now heading back to camp and I was looking forward to three days in the OP; climbing through a small hatch in the roof saw us enter the OP.

The OP was a lot more spacious than it looked from the ground. It came with its own kitchen area and sleeping space that was more comfortable than I expected, there were some comfy chairs to sit on, then across the other side of the room was the lookout, you could see for miles. We had a piece of equipment called Noddy in respect that it was the same shape as Noddy's hat, a small eye piece at one end and then it coned out at the other end; looking through the sight was an experience within itself, it was that powerful that you could see a fly on someone's bedroom wall in the flats. I just couldn't believe how much it magnified things.

It was on the second night of the three day stay when Alan shouted me over to the lookout in an animated voice, "Paul, get over here now, hurry up."

"What's up?" I said from the comfort of my bed.

"Just get over here now?" he said looking through the sight of Noddy.

"What's so interesting?" I said as I lay down beside him.

"Have a look at the window that hasn't got the curtains closed," said Alan, allowing me to have a nifty look. It took me a few seconds before I realised what Alan was looking at; there were a man and women in the clutches of ecstasy, really going for it, It was like our own personal peep show as Frankie also got in on the act; feeling intrusive we decided that enough was enough and left it at that, however, at the same time, why would you not close the curtains? We made a note of where the flat was and thought we would pay the flat a visit the next time we were on foot patrols; purely out of curiosity of cause. In the mean time we decided to check out with the OPs room about who lived in the flat; we couldn't have been more shocked when the reply was "Mr and Mrs Darcy live there, however her husband is serving time in the Maze Prison in Long Kesh"

"Wow and Ouch" we all said at the same time.

Throughout the night as the city became silent we continued to scan the streets for any kind of trouble. There were times when I felt a chill running through my veins as I stared down the Falls Road; it was like a ghost town, hearing the sound of nothing, but at the same time visualising the bleeding and the dying as the terrorists tried with all their might to break communities apart. Before I knew it the ever so peaceful sun was trying to send out a message to the smiling locals that were going about their business and their respective places of work.

An interesting first time on the Divis flats opened my eyes to the bird's eye view we got of Belfast. "OK, get your gear together," said Dave as our three day tour was at an end. The takeover from the other shift went smoothly and before we knew, we were once again back in North Howard Street Mill. A quick but thorough debrief took place, then it was on stand-by duties for the next week. Standby duties meant that we would be first on call if there was any sign of trouble around the area, however, little did we know that in a couple of day's time we would be called upon to an incident on the Falls Road.

CHAPTER EIGHTY-THREE
TAKE COVER FOR YOUR LIVES

It was now three weeks into the tour and everybody was getting into the swing of things. Although there had been no major incidents to report you could still feel the high profile hard action stance we were undertaking. Switching off and lowering your guard was something we had been trained for, and the consequences that would materialise if we ever assumed normality was taking place; soldiers on the street were a kind of reassurance to the majority of people, but unfortunately, there was always that small fraction of people that wanted to destroy the freedom of the ground they cherished.

It was early evening and the stand-by section, including myself, were watching some TV in the stand-by room. There seemed to be lots of activity going on in the room where we were resting.

"Alan," I said "fancy a NATO standard brew?"

"Cheers Woofer, yeah would love one, especially if you're making it" said Alan

"Don't go too far, just in case we get called out," said Bombardier Dave Waterman, looking over towards me.

"Just going to the tea urn over there," I said, prising myself out of my seat.

"You may as well get me one," said Dave.

"Me too," said Frankie Abbott, more in hope.

"Yeah, don't mind me," I said. "Do I look like a fucking tea boy? In fact, don't even answer that."

"Good man Wolfie," they all said.

"Do you want sugar?" I said, shouting across to Dave.

"Yes, one," said Dave. "I thought you would have known that by now tea boy, sorry, I meant Gunner Wolfendale." I felt like telling them to get off their arses and get their own tea when all of a sudden, a huge explosion could be heard that sounded like it was from the Falls Road area.

"Standby, get outside now," was being shouted by the ever pre-occupied

Sergeant Major Thorpe; well, you can imagine where the tea went. Let's say it was fucking hot.

"Wolfie, Alan, Frankie, get outside now," said Dave, "JP, get your men to the loading bay now."

We hadn't got a clue what we were about to be confronted with, but deep down inside, we I knew it was something serious. We were kicking our heels for a few seconds before intelligence came running out of the building shouting. "Lower Falls, a bomb has gone off, not sure on casualties, get going now."

"Get into the pig now," said Dave, trying to keep his composure at the same time shouting his orders. The RCT (Royal Corps' of Transport) well trained driver was already in first gear as we attempted to close the heavy armoured doors; trying not to fall out of the vehicle was now my main concern as the huge galvanised gates came crashing open. We raced onto the Falls Road like there was no tomorrow. It took less than a few minutes before our vehicle came to a screeching halt bringing trepidation to our thoughts.

"Get ready," said Dave, trying to give us a sit-rep (situation report) on what he could see. "When you get out, just stay close to the pig and use it as a shield until we know for sure what is going on. Out now, Wolfendale, Carvell, around the front; Abbott, follow me around the back."

I made my way to the front of the pig in quick time, taking up a crouched position with my SLR at the ready pointing towards where the bomb had gone off.

I must admit I was feeling nervous but at the same time also saying to myself that, *fear is a place we sometimes have to pass through*. Amongst the screaming and shouting from the terrified locals I could just about hear myself shouting at Alan, "Alan, just keep right by my side, don't let me out of your sight."

"Right up your arse," said Alan.

"Fuck off, you fucking Brits," shouted the mob of youths that were now forming across the other side of the road. "We know it was you that planted the bomb," they continued to shout in their native tongue. I was now feeling concerned with the situation as I looked at the pub that had been blown up, the pub that was ironically next to the Sinn Fein shop. I could hear Sirens that sounded miles away given our circumstances; help was needed and needed fast.

In the distance I caught a glimpse of the other pig approaching with the other half of the section; it would be too late. Seconds later a vast number of the youths ran into their terrace houses opposite us, on the other side of the road. They came out holding petrol bombs in their hands that had already been lit. "Take cover," said Dave, fearing for our lives. I was now in a state of panic as my adrenalin was kicking in; my main concern was trying to keep calm as the first petrol bomb was thrown with great accuracy towards the pig. It exploded with force, sending white hot flames metres into the air engulfing the armoured vehicle, "You OK Alan?" I said hurriedly.

"Yeah, fine," was his reply. Before we could draw breath we were hit with another and then another; my lightweight trousers were caught by the flames as we were nearing the point at which we may have to open fire. Unfortunately we had a code of conduct to adhere to called 'Rules of Engagement' and unless petrol bombing had persisted in your area for a good part of the day, or someone's life who it was your duty to protect was in grave danger, then opening fire with a live round was definitely a no go; being charged for a provoked murder wasn't something I fancied.

The second pig arrived within moments of the attack, which seemed to have the impact that we were looking for; the petrol bombers retreated back into their safe houses and out of sight while we were left to clear up the mess that they had caused.

The pub was still standing (just) which told us that it was probably a small IED (Improvised Explosive Device) that was set off. This sort of thing would be classed as a distraction to test the skills of the so called Bastard Brits and to give the Provo's an open window of chance to bring in a few weapons.

"You alright?" shouted Eddie as he was exiting the pig along with the rest of the section.

"A bit late to the party springs to mind."

"Come again?" said Eddic, looking confused.

"Well, let's just say the party's over," I said, feeling glad that the good guys had arrived. Bombardier Watermen filled JP in on what had gone on who, at the same time was looking as if he and his brick had let us down; arriving when they did went a long way to bringing an end to the petrol bombing. If we were the brick at the rear, then I'm pretty sure we would have been feeling the same way. There was still a job to do in trying to keep the peace and find out what had gone on; the last thing we needed now was for the situation to become a full scale riot. With more troops now on the ground, normality was restored.

It was time to head back to the camp for a well earned rest after spending more than a couple of hours on the Falls Road. We still had to be alert and ready to go at a moment's notice until the next morning when we would be relieved from stand-by duty and put on rest period for six hours.

For the next few days it was much the same, stand-by and rest periods, until Bombardier Waterman came into the room and said that we were to carry out a dawn raid tomorrow morning that meant we would be relieved from stand-by duty. "Get in there," I said to Alan and Frankie.

"What are we searching?" said Alan to Dave.

"It's a car garage just off the Springfield Road," said Dave. "Patrols will be providing a walking type cordon around the area close to where we will be searching. Reveille will be 0430hrs and we will be leaving at 0500hrs in the pig, make sure you get a good night's sleep."

Considering this was my third time on the search brick in the three tours so far, I was well up for putting my new developed skills into action.

The next morning we were up and ready whilst trying not to disturb the rest of the section that were still sleeping. We made our way to the OP room for a brief on the reason behind the search.

"Take a seat," said a DS. "We have information that the garage that you'll be searching just off the Springfield Road has been used by the IRA either for a shooting or for meetings, your task is to turn the place over and see what you can find. Chances are there will be nothing significant there, however, if you manage to find anything then tell your commander and we will bring in SOCO" (Scene of Crimes Officer)

Well, the search went well amidst the morning twilight although nothing of any importance was found; it was only when I heard the cry from Alan that the search became interesting.

"Wolfie, take a look at that treasure up there," said Alan

"What treasure up where, what am I looking at?" I said, looking towards the roof top of the garage where Alan was pointing.

"Up there, fastened to the chimney "said Alan.

"Bloody hell," I said with my jaw dropping. It was the familiar orange, white and green vertical striped Republican Flag that was a typical feature of the Falls Road. "We're going to have to rip it down Alan." I said.

"Damn right" said Alan.

"Dave," I said "fancy a souvenir?"

"What are you on about?" he replied, looking bewildered by my comment. I explained to Dave what Alan and I had seen and that we would like to climb up on the roof and get it. "Make it quick then," said Dave to my surprise, "you need to get going now before I change my mind."

"Will do," I said. "Alan, come on, let's go." I made my way carefully up the roof like a cat-burglar with Alan close behind. "OK Alan," I said, "stop there and I will pass the flag down to you when I have unfastened it from the chimney."

"OK," said Alan, keeping his head down from any unexpected onlooker on their way to work. As I reached the apex of the roof there was only one thing on my mind, that was to capture the flag. On first inspection I noticed the flag was fastened to a piece of wood that was fastened to the chimney by a thick piece of lead. Not to be perturbed by the state of affairs I started swinging the pole back and forwards as hard as I could until it was at the point of being released from its entrapment. It was now only one jolt away from being mine. I had absolutely no idea that there was a device attached to the bottom of the wooden pole that escaped my attention. "It's free," I said to Alan, feeling relieved.

"Well done, Wolfie," said Alan. Just as I was about to reel the flag in, a small package made to look like a bomb went tumbling down the roof heading towards Alan.

"Alan," I cried out loud. "Watch out, there's a fucking package heading towards you at speed." I could see the fear in Alan's face as he moved his body to one side to let the package pass. The package catapulted off the roof and onto the garage floor.

"Bloody hell, Wolfie, you idiot," he said, "didn't you see it?"

"Yes of course I did, that's why I continued to rip the flag down," I said sarcastically.

"Let's get out of here now," said Alan, before we get fucking blown up. The flag was now firmly in our grasp and would be heading back to North Howard Street. On the debrief we thought it better not to mention the bit about the package that turned out to be nothing but a scare mongering device, it was there to deter anyone with any bollocks not to step an inch closer. They didn't take into account that someone (like me) with not too much intelligence would not even think to check it out before bulldozing it down.

CHAPTER EIGHTY-FOUR
ORANGE DAY MARCHES

It was mid June some six weeks into our tour. RR leave was now starting which meant the sections were becoming more fragmented. We were heading onto the streets again but this time, we were joined by Eddie Burns from our other brick, a guy that I had become friends with during Northern Ireland training and now on the streets. Eddie was always up for a laugh which was always welcome at times when we were feeling down in the dumps; however, at the same time he took his job seriously when called upon. He reminded me of Hammo, maybe that's what I liked about him.

His deep Scottish accent was something that had me saying 'what?' As we made our way onto the Lower Falls, Eddie said something that I found difficult to understand. "What did you say, Eddie?" I said, looking puzzled.

"Am no repeating masel pal," said Eddie.

"Don't need to call me Paul, Wolfie will do," I said.

"I seed Pal, not Paul, ye numpty." I rest my case, trying to understand Eddie to me was like trying to understand why we were here in the first place.

We continued our patrol which was now driven by Sergeant Douggie Massey in the absence of Dave. "Wolfendale, stop that person coming towards you and take his details?" said Douggie. "Don't you fucking shoot him though," he obviously remembered my altercation when I shot a passive target during training some years ago.

"Will do," I said, trying to ignore his sense of humour.

"Eddie, cover Wolfendale?"

"OK pal."

"Sergeant Massey to you," snarled Douggie.

"Sorry, Sarge," said Eddie sheepishly as he took up a defensive position. A quick minute of the gentleman's time and I had all the information I needed.

"OK, let's head back now," said Douggie, looking at his watch, "Wolfendale, at the front with me."

"Right away Sergeant Massey," I said in a kind of creeping way to get more brownie points.

"Brune nose," said Eddie, "teacher's pit."

"I think you mean brown nose Eddie, and teacher's pet," I said, still trying to get to terms with the Scottish accent.

It felt like a promotion being allowed to patrol up front rather being tail end Charlie. After unloading our weapons, I said to Eddie, "I think I will go have a sauna."

"Mate join yeah there pal," he eagerly said.

"It wasn't an invitation to get more acquainted Eddie, make sure you keep to your side of the sauna and we will get on just fine." After a welcomed sauna I made my way to the gym area where Pete Riggers and his brother Steve were. Steve had joined the regiment more recently and was part of the PT staff. I challenged him to a game of table tennis which he immediately took up; I hadn't had so much fun in ages, Steve was a really skilful player, a player that would give you a good game. After several games and almost out on our chin straps we decided to call it a day.

"Thanks for the game, Paul," said Steve, "it was nice to have someone to play against that can hit the ball back more than once."

"Same here," I said, now needing a shower.

With a few minor incidents over the next few weeks, we were all still in great shape however, the 12th of July Orange Marches were now up on us. We were fully prepared for everything that was going to be thrown at us, but until you're faced with an adversary, you just don't know how you're going to react. The Orange Marches are held annually by members of the Orange Order in Ulster and Scotland and occasionally England to mark William of Orange's victory over James II at the battle of the Boyne in 1690. The parades have faced opposition from Catholics, Irish and Scottish Nationalists which meant we would need to be on full alert not just on the 12th, but throughout the days leading up to the 12th and thereafter.

Intelligence was keeping us informed of any hostile situations that were imminent as the day was unfolding. There were very limited foot patrols going on around the area as we were all ready in our riot gear for any possible sudden surge of action. It wasn't long before we got the call from the OPs room to get outside in the yard under the command of Sergeant Douggie Massey and coupled with Lieutenant Mills, an ex junior leader. "Wolfendale, Burns, baton gunners," said Sergeant Massey.

"OK, Sarge," I said.

"OK pal," said Eddie. How he got away with saying that I will never know.

There must have been about four of us with baton guns including Alan Carvell, the rest were given shields along with the snatch squad being allocated wooden batons; with our riot helmets on we made our way into the awaiting pigs that had been drafted in to ferry us to the Shankill Road.

"OK, listen in," said Lieutenant Mills, "a crowd of a few hundred people have gathered on the Shankill Road and are starting to cause a disturbance among opposition forces. Let's get out there lads, let's show them no mercy."

You could feel the adrenalin running through our veins as we exited the camp in unison. I believe that deep down there were one or two that were feeling a little nervous, me included, as to what to expect. It took less than about five minutes to get to our designated location before the familiar voice of Sergeant Massey was heard shouting his orders. "Out now, keep close to the pigs until we have established exactly how we are going to deal with the rioters." Our pig lined up in the centre of the road facing the marauding crowd, who were now getting more and more agitated with our presence now firmly on show.

The noise was deafening. "Baton gunners…Load your guns and get lined up behind the shields," shouted Lieutenant Mills, "snatch squad, stay close to the baton gunners with your batons ready." Shouting orders was the only way of communicating with each other above the ever increasing crowd. With everybody now formed up in a straight line from one side of the road to the other, about a hundred metres from the crowd, we waited with bated breath; it was a case of, *who is going to make the first move first?* Our task was to keep peace and order where possible and not to antagonise those perpetrators who, according to them, were fighting for what they would call a justifiable cause.

With the crowd now becoming more and more restless and shuffling themselves inch by inch closer, it was a case of, when would be the right time for us to show our hand; knowing the range of our baton guns was something that the experienced crowd were good at.

It was becoming difficult to keep our calmness with our adrenalin now on an all time high. Closer and closer they inched their way towards us until the advancing crowd were on our doorstep and in the pupils of our eyes. There was a small section of the crowd wearing black balaclavas, a symbol of what they stood for. Standing next to Sergeant Massey and close to the pig, the first unappreciated missile was chucked in our direction hitting the helmet of one of the lads.

"Keep a tight line," said Sergeant Massey now fearing the worst; a shard of metal came flying through the air hitting him on his loose-fitting helmet. It took less than a few seconds for the crowd to follow like lemmings as the missiles were now raining down on us in clusters: Bricks, batteries, metal objects of all shape and sizes were now flying through the air.

I could see out of the corner of my eye that Sergeant Massey was getting more and more agitated with the amount of strikes he was receiving causing his helmet to be dislodged and, at the same time becoming slightly disoriented.

Having been trained to give precise and clear orders, it should have been straightforward for someone of authority to give the order to the baton gunners to open fire; however, when confronted by a crowd of this magnitude, I think the calmness went out of the window. This caused Sergeant Massey to take matters into his own hands. With a rather uncomplicated order Sergeant Massey yelled at the top of his voice. "For fuck's sake, some fucker let off a baton round." Not the sort of order I was use to; I didn't need to be asked twice. Peering through a small gap in the riot shields I took aim at a designated target and without any remorse, pulled the trigger causing a young-looking youth to fall to the ground. Normally this would be when the snatch squad would be called upon to charge forward and drag the youth back behind the shields, and then into the pig, unfortunately amongst the confusion, the order for the snatch squad never materialised.

The firing of my baton round meaningful as it might sound, did the trick; the crowd were now retreating which was our main objective. Within the hour everything was just about back to normal; after having their bit of fun it was now time for the rioters to return to their safe houses, well, at least until another day.

Back in camp and looking forward to time off, I was called to the OPs room along with Sergeant Massey. "You'll need you to fill in some forms," said one of the intelligence staff. "Just in case of any comebacks, we need to have all the details of the shooting."

"Bloody bureaucracy gone mad," said Sergeant Massey. "Come on then Paul, let's get it done and then we can get some rest." It took at least an hour filling in the paperwork so it could be put away on file: *Who gave the order? What distance did you fire your weapon from? Did you identify your target? Did you aim at the torso? What was the target wearing?* I felt like I was on trial myself.

A few days later and with RR now in full swing, we were graced by the arrival of Sir Harry Secombe, an ex-Gunner. The Welsh singer and comedian allowed us the pleasure of his company although I believe he was just as excited as we were. Sir Harry came into our sleeping quarters and spent a good twenty minutes or so chatting to us all. "Excuse me," I said, "would you mind giving me your autograph?"

"My pleasure," he said in a tone that said 'you deserve it soldier.' I took my map of West Belfast out of my pocket which he duly signed whilst at the same time sharing a joke; listening to his trademark high pitched laughter and blowing raspberries always made everybody smile. The day was soon to be over; it was time to get back to business as the riots still continued in small moderation across the area. Before then, I had my RR to look forward to; choosing one of the last RR dates was something that I always did.

CHAPTER EIGHTY-FIVE
GOOD NEWS TRAVELS FAST

"Have a good RR, Wolfie," said Alan, feeling slightly jealous. "Say hello to Hildesheim for me."

"Will do, matey," I said as I was leaving the camp in my civvie clothes. I was certainly ready for my four days off and couldn't wait to see my wife and little girl again; in a strange way it felt like I was deserting my mum, brothers and sisters, but now I had a wife and child to share my love with. The weather was kind as the plane landed at the nearby Hannover Airport; it was nice to be greeted by the duty transport that was waiting to take me straight to my married quarter in Sarstedt.

A warm embrace from my wife and child greeted me at the front door but, it was soon time for Melanie to have a sleep; say no more, a few months away from your wife meant there was plenty of catching up to do. Over the next few days I hardly ventured out of the block of flats, although I did pay a visit to the camp to catch up on any gossip.

"Hi Paul," said Taff, one of my buddies from when I use to work in the Officers' Mess.

"Hi Taff, how's it going?" I said, standing proudly with my family.

"I suppose you have heard about Tony?"

"What about Tony?"

"Oh, I thought you knew," he said sounding surprised at my remark. "He shot himself not long after you went to Belfast."

"What the fuck?" I said, raising my eyebrows.

"He was on Guard duty with live ammunition because of the threat of terrorism, and with the fact that most of the regiment were away in Northern Ireland we were on high alert; apparently he just went to his room and shot himself, he was found later on that day by the guard."

I couldn't believe what I was hearing. "Bloody hell," I said, looking towards my wife who also knew Tony. "I have just spent almost three months in the heart of Belfast with thankfully no loss of life, and now, I come back to the safe haven of Hildesheim to find one of my close friends has shot himself; it made no sense at all."

"Sorry, Paul," said Taff, "I thought you would have been told."

"Well, maybe there were reasons why we weren't," I replied. "Maybe that sort of news wouldn't go down too well, there's enough death on the streets as it is, to be told that sort of news wouldn't be doing anyone any favours." For the next couple of days all I could think about was Tony. I had to get him out of my mind and fast, it was now time to face my final six weeks across the water. I didn't feel too down in the dumps returning to Belfast, as I knew the six weeks would go past quickly.

Back in Belfast, not only had my mood changed, but the weather was also feeling grumpy. Lots of surface rain meant the lads on foot patrol were getting a right soaking; the more I thought about it, the more it brought a slight snigger to my face. It was straight into action as soon as I got back.

"Wolfie, welcome back," said Alan smiling, "we are on stand-by duty in half an hour."

"Brill, glad to be back," I said sarcastically, "Let's go and get out there." Sat in the stand-by room, I was chatting away to anyone who wanted to know about my RR leave when we were told to get ourselves ready for action.

"There has been some trouble near the Springfield Road," said Bombardier Dave Waterman. "Wolfendale, I want you to take the radio when we get out there."

Wow, I was thinking. "No problem," I said. I was effectively taking charge of the four man brick even though Dave was working alongside me; doing a job that, by rank, I wasn't qualified for was something that had a bearing on my decision to leave the Army in the coming years.

It was a wonderful and proud feeling to be walking the streets being semi in charge and responsible for the lads in the brick. Once on the Springfield we could see up ahead in the distance where the trouble was, compared to what we were use to, it looked more like a domestic was taking place. There were roughly about ten to fifteen young youths just causing a disturbance over next to nothing, however, we still needed to keep the calm; a heart to heart with one or two of them seem to do the trick as eventually they saw common sense and continued on their way.

Dave asked me to radio the OPs room and explain that the situation was under control, and to send out the pig to take us back to North Howard Street; being on stand-by meant we needed to get back pronto. Minutes later the pig arrived along with Sergeant Major Mick Thorpe in the back. Occasionally some of the intelligence staff would get themselves onto streets to get a better picture of what we were up against and also to get them out of the OPs room for a welcomed break.

Sat next to the Sergeant Major in the pig and just chitchatting away to the lads, the Sergeant Major suddenly hit me with, "How's it going then?"

"Yes, fine," I said in a 'thanks for asking' type of way.

"Have you ever thought about being promoted?" he said in a serious voice.

"Yes, all the time," I said. "To be honest, I am very surprised I haven't been promoted already."

"Really, why's that then?" said Sergeant Major Thorpe, looking shocked at my frankness.

"I just feel I have kept my nose clean and not been in too much trouble apart from the occasional misdemeanour."

"Well, make sure you keep your nose clean a little longer, well at least until we get back in six weeks' time; if you do, then I can assure you there will be something in the pipeline," he said, nodding his head.

"Thank you," I said, not knowing what more I could say. I could see Alan and Frankie looking over towards me with smiles that were saying 'well done mate'. Back in the barracks I couldn't wait to tell Tommo my news, who was as pleased as punch for me even though nothing was yet confirmed; the feeling of being a Lance Jack had me stepping up to the mark if I hadn't already. The final six weeks went by without too much difficulty; well, at least with 18 Battery. However, the regiment saw its first casualty in the way of a gunner from K Battery that had been shot in the shoulder.

Brummie Roelake was shot on the top of the New Lodge tower. It was about half the size and not too dissimilar to the Divis Tower. The tower itself was not too far from the Divis in an area that joined up with our boundaries close to the Lower Falls. An opportunist gunman thought he would try his luck as he lay in wait for that crucial moment; more luck than judgement saved Brummie Roelake from certain death, a better well aimed shot and we could have been looking at a fatality rather than casualty.

It was now the 13th September the day before my twenty third birthday and time to get our bags packed before saying goodbye to an eventful tour. "Gunner Wolfendale, can I have a word with you for a minute" said Sergeant Major Thorpe.

"Yes Sir."

"When we get back to BAOR and after our annual leave, you'll be working down the Guardroom as a Regimental Policeman. You will be promoted to Local L/Bombardier initially, which means you will be given a stripe for the purpose of the job, and then shortly afterwards you will be made acting L/Bombardier."

"Thank you, Sir," I said with a huge smile on my face. I really couldn't wait; five years with 18 Battery and I finally get promoted. I tried to keep the news under my belt, well at least until I came back from leave, not a chance. As soon as our feet were firmly on West German soil the cat was out of the bag. Within days of arriving back in Hildesheim it was time to go on leave. I decided along with my family to drive over to England to see my mother, brothers and sisters for a couple of weeks. Everybody at home seemed well; at least the ones that were still living at home; Zoe and Mary were the only ones left. The ones that came to see my passing out parade some six years ago, how ironic was that? I did the expected tour of all my other brothers and sisters over the following days before heading back to barracks. Joining the RP staff was something I was looking forward too, however, due to my ignorance of let's say, misinterpreting an order from the Provo Sergeant, I managed, and all on my own, to make life really uncomfortable for dozens of officers.

CHAPTER EIGHTY-SIX

TWO FOUR DOUBLE SHUFFLE
KNIVE FORK SPOON

It was Monday morning and I was saying goodbye to my wife and little girl before heading into camp. The inclement weather was now showing its true colours and long sleeve order was now in force. I wasn't too sure where I should be or what I should be doing so thought it best to read today's Battery Orders. There was nothing of any interest that affected me even though I was expecting some sort of news; as I read down the sheet the only thing that caught my eye was battery parade at 0745hrs outside the block. It was such a welcomed change to feel that camaraderie amongst the troops as we chatted away in our woolly pullies; pullovers and lightweight trousers.

"Attention," said Sergeant Massey, bringing us all up to attention and then putting us in open order ready for inspection. It was quite a gentle first inspection back, but no one was getting off lightly. "Burns sort your beret out," said Sergeant Massey, "and don't call me pal."

"No, Sarge," said Eddie smirking

"Turner, report to the Battery Office after the parade is finished, Bombardier Young will be expecting you, you're today's Battery Runner," (dogsbody) said Sergeant Massey.

"Yes Sarge," said Dave as we were all chuckling behind his back.

"Keep your noise down otherwise you'll cop for a Guard duty," was the voice of God once more. The inspection continued until he stopped in front of me; staring me in the face I was expecting the usual: Guard duty, cook-house fatigues, or even working on RSM's fatigues. Luckily for me it was neither. "Wolfendale, make sure you read Battery Orders tonight," he said quietly, "don't forget."

After a no more than any other normal day, it was time for my over reacting mind to be put out of its misery. I made way into the Battery Block along with Tommo to squint over Battery Orders before heading home. After the first couple of paragraphs I saw my name standing out like a sore thumb: *'as from tomorrow Gunner Wolfendale will be promoted to acting Lance Bombardier'.*

"Wow," I said to Tommo, "thought it was just going to be local initially."

"Well done, Paul," said Tommo, "well deserved mate."

"Thanks Dec," I said, feeling overjoyed. I continued reading down the orders to find I was joining the RP staff at 0830hrs in the morning: Dress would be barrack room trousers along with pullover, bulled boots and No.2 dress hat; I just about had time to get my stripe from the BQ before they closed up for the night and then get home to sew it onto my pullover before tomorrow morning. Being promoted meant a small pay rise, which was always welcome, and also access to the NCOs mess. Once my stripe was visible on my Army uniform I knew then that trying to keep a balance of maintaining my friends was going to be difficult; well, at least the ones that were still gunners. Their turn would eventually come; your true friends would understand that with promotion comes, responsibility.

The following morning I made my way into camp wondering how many people would notice my bird shit (Army jargon for my stripe) on my right upper arm. The feeling was one of jubilation; I felt that my days of having a joke were over, but at the same time, I needed to be careful not to lose my identity. Being a joker was probably part of the reason why I got promoted in respect that I had earned the admiration of most of the lads; I had become a popular figure now, but how long would it last?

I was feeling slightly nervous yet at the same time looking forward to my new position as I entered the busy Guardroom.

"Can I help you?" said Sergeant Brewster, the Provo Sergeant (Sergeant in charge of discipline).

"L/Bombardier Wolfendale from 18 Battery, Sarge," I said. "I have been told I am joining the RP staff."

Looking through his paperwork he said, "Yes, here we are, L/Bombardier Wolfendale, get yourself around the back where you'll find a rest room with the rest of the RP staff there."

"OK Sarge," I said with no questions asked.

Once in the small rest room it was nice to be greeted by the second in command Bombardier Catrell and the rest of the staff. The majority of them were all Lance Jacks like me; a couple of the lads were also here for the first time, which helped with the fact I wasn't the only one being christened. After having a short but informative chat with them, I was to find out that they had just also just been promoted to local L/Bombardier, with the hope that it would become more permanent in about a month's time. The rest room itself was kitted out with all the essentials: a dart board, pack of playing cards and a fridge that had me looking forward to my break periods. Just behind the rest room down a small corridor were the prison cells and a court yard for the prisoners to exercise when they were allowed.

It was about 0815hrs when Sergeant Brewster came into the rest room to read the riot act to us new additions. It wasn't like a normal brief, it was more like a stern lecture that said, *'if you do not abide by my rules you be sharing a cell with one of the prisoners'*. On a good day his mood was just about tolerable; on a bad day, just stay out of his way was the message I was getting. The Provo Sergeant was under authority from the RSM, so he too had his superiors to answer to. Between them they would be responsible for the maintenance of good order and military discipline, with the criminal offences being passed to the specialists of the RMPs (Royal Military Police), more commonly known as Red Caps, the colour of their hats.

After the so-called riot act was read out, it was time to be issued with a brassard or in more simple terms, an armband.

"Get these put on your arm," said the Provo, handing them over to us.

"Wow, I feel important," I said to Mick, one of the new lads.

"IMPORTANT! IMPORTANT!" shouted the Provo, overhearing my remark and staring me in the eyes. "It's not a fucking holiday camp, get it on now and make sure the RP letters are visible." Well, that put me in my place, it was one of those 'yours is not to reason why yours is but to do or die' moments; at least underneath I felt important.

The first morning was finding my feet. At the front of the Guardroom and on a white board was a list of all the prisoners: their number, rank, name, when their sentence started and when it was finishing; anything from a few days to a maximum of twenty eight days was how it read. This was important information that we all needed to digest.

Lunch time arrived and I was told that I would be taking the prisoners to the cookhouse along with a guy called Pete, one of the more senior RPs. "Wolfendale," said Sergeant Brewster, "go and get the prisoners ready for lunch, L/Bombardier White will be waiting for you in the back."

"OK Sergeant," I said. There would be no more 'Sarge' in the Guardroom. I made my way into the back to where the cells were for my first encounter with the prisoners.

"OK Paul," said Pete who was waiting for me, "I will run you through the basic procedures, the rest I'm pretty sure you'll pick up as you go along."

"Fine by me, Pete," I said, watching with anticipation. The prison cell doors were open which actually surprised me, but apparently, they had all just come back from doing regimental fatigues and were now getting ready for lunch. "Stand by your cell door!" said Pete stridently, within seconds they all emerged at the edge of the cell door as if there was an imaginary line marked out, a line they were not allowed to cross. I couldn't believe that a L/Bombardier could warrant so much respect. We walked along and passed the cells as if we were inspecting trouble. Not a sound could be heard from the eagerly awaiting SUS (Soldiers under Sentence) as they stood there with their eating irons firmly behind their backs. "Outside now," said Pete at the top of his voice; like a well drilled troop, the prisoners were outside lined up awaiting Pete and I.

We could have waited an hour before making our way outside if we had wished and I could have guaranteed the prisoners would have still been there waiting. That's how it was, the prisoners had next to no rights, albeit we would be in serious trouble ourselves if we over stepped the mark. With Pete and I now standing alongside the prisoners it was time to escort them to lunch. Lined up in their coveralls and without their berets, it was time to bring them up to attention. "ATTENTION!" was the loud cry from Pete. "By the front, double march," They were off down the road at a pace I was unfamiliar with. I was thinking, *I hope I'm not expected to keep up with them* when all of a sudden, I heard Pete shout an order that I was familiar with from my training days, "MARK TIME!" The prisoners came to a sudden halt and were now marching on the spot. This procedure was in force all the way to the cookhouse; Pete and I covered about three hundred metres and the prisoners three thousand.

At the cookhouse we led the prisoners to the front of the queue (one luxury they did get), and with their lunch in hand they were then taken to a more secluded area of the dining room. Pete and I sat next to the men, making sure they didn't become too excited at the freedom we were providing for them; within reason, Pete said that a little natter was acceptable, but not to convey that sort of information back to Sergeant Brewster. After their lunch and with the odd sausage hidden away in their pockets, it was time to march them back to their luxury hotel. Having now got full stomachs we weren't allowed to double them back, it was a more dignified stroll and then a little more pace as the Guardroom came into sight.

Throughout the next few days I was finding my feet and getting to know the prisoners by all sorts of different names, at the same time keeping my distance, in other words not becoming too familiar. I still had a job to do so the attachment of friendliness was only seen when warranted. One of the prisoners I found myself bonding with was a Gunner Lomas, a guy from my own battery; he was full of humour and knew how to get the better of Sergeant Brewster and his merry men. Deep down inside I think his attitude was *'you can throw anything you want in my direction, but you can't take away my individuality'*. We seemed to have an understanding of each other, although there were times when he almost overstepped the mark to the point of being insolent.

It was a cold frosty morning and I had just arrived for duty. The night's guard were getting ready to return back to their batteries as we would now be taking over the Guardroom. One of the first jobs was to escort the Orderly Officer around the cells to inspect the prisoners; this was a daily routine, a routine that was paramount to the daily running of an efficient Guardroom. On duty this day was Lieutenant Ross, the Orderly Officer from last night's guard. "Excuse me, Sir," I said. "Are you ready to inspect the prisoners, Sir?"

"Yes," said Lieutenant Ross, "ready when you are." We made our way to the cells where the prisoners were adding the finishing touches to their well laid out kit that was on their beds. "Stand by your beds!" I shouted down the corridor; with the cell doors open the inspection began. They all knew the routine by now, so as soon as the Orderly Officer and I positioned ourselves by the cell door, all that could be heard from the first prisoner was, "24245678 Gunner Croft Sir," at the top of his voice and with speediness attached to it. This sort of action became a competition between the prisoners to see who could reel off their number, rank and name the quickest.

The Orderly Officer strutted his way into the cell to do his mandatory inspection of the cell that included the soldiers' 1157 kit issue; looking forward and staring into oblivion without so much as drawing breath, the prisoner would just stand there until the short but toughened inspection was over. As the Orderly Officer and I made our way along the corridor, the announcement of each of the prisoners could clearly be heard getting faster and faster. It was getting to the point where it was becoming impossible to say your number, rank and name without cocking it up. *How wrong could one be*; stood next to Gunner Lomas by his cell Lieutenant Ross is now staring him straight in the face waiting for Gunner Lomas to recite his lines.

"Twofer doubled knife foon Sir." I looked towards the Orderly Officer at exactly the same time he looked at me, wondering what the hell had just happened. Lieutenant Ross, looking now displeased, replied politely, "What did you say, Gunner Lomas?"

"I said my number, rank and name Sir."

"I know what you thought you said," replied Lieutenant Ross, feeling he had missed a trick, "all I heard was something like double knife and spoon." At this point, as serious as the remark was, I had to bite down hard on my lip to stop myself from laughing.

"I must have said it too fast Sir, maybe that's what you thought you heard, Sir," said Gunner Lomas, knowing he had committed a sin.

"Well, I hope you're not trying to be flippant," said Lieutenant Ross, not looking too happy.

"Flip what Sir?"

"Never mind, Gunner Lomas," said Lieutenant Ross, looking at me and saying, "don't even go there, I've got better things to concern myself about than the literacy skills of Gunner Lomas." All in all the inspection went to plan with no major issues of any concern.

After the inspection and with the Orderly Officer now on his way back to the Officers' Mess, I decided to have a one to one with Gunner Lomas.

"Gunner Lomas" I said wanting to get to the bottom of the matter "get over here now, get over here and explain to me in the Queens English what on earth you said."

"Don't know what you mean Bombardier Wolfendale," (easier than saying Lance Bombardier) was his reply with a wry smile on his face.

"Listen carefully, and listen well, you may have pulled the wool over the Orderly Officer's eyes, but please give me some credit. I know what you said wasn't your number and to be honest, I was finding it difficult not to laugh; owing me an explanation is the least I deserve."

"OK then, Bombardier," he said, "I was just trying to confuse the Orderly Officer and at the same time seeing how much he really was listening to what I said."

"So what did you say?" I said, searching for an intelligent answer.

"Two four double shuffle knife fork spoon Bombardier."

"What?" I said, rolling in laughter, knowing that he had managed to get away with it. "To be fair, it was brilliant, just don't try it again, well certainly not on my watch; I don't fancy joining you in one of the cells."

The rest of the last few months went well with me now being a well established RP, although there was one last incident to add to my résumé before I headed back to the battery and back onto the guns. It was time to have some fun; catching the officers of the regiment unawares and annoying Sergeant Brewster at the same time adds up to a double whammy.

It was early February and I was on the front gate when Sergeant Brewster came over to have a word with me. "The new CO is due in within the next hour Bombardier, make sure you salute him and check his ID, he will be driving a cream coloured Reliant Scimitar." He didn't know I was colour blind or that he had forgotten to inform me that I must let him know as soon as the CO arrived; being dumb was a quality that I possessed.

It wasn't too long before I caught sight of the car approaching the gates. Dressed in smart civilian clothes the CO handed over his military ID card on asking. "Thank you Sir," I said, handing it back to him and trying to be professional.

"Could you direct me to the Officers' Mess please, Bombardier?" he said politely.

"Yes Sir," I said. After giving the CO directions and the mandatory have a nice day salute, it was time to get on with my duty; I wasn't sure how long it would take, but I knew a bollocking was expected forthwith. About five minutes had passed when there was one almighty cry from the Guardroom.

"WOLFENDALE!" said the red faced Sergeant Brewster, "you fucking idiot, why didn't you inform me that the CO had arrived?"

"You didn't tell me to Sergeant," I said, trying to look dumb, "all you said was; just make sure you check his ID."

"Didn't tell me to, do I have to spell everything out?" bellowed the Provo, at the same time raising his eyes to the heavens. "The adjutant has just been on the phone going ballistic; everybody has been caught off guard, which could have meant that there were going to be a few officers right for the high jump." I was a little concerned that my joke had gotten so many people into trouble, but at the same time, it was nice to see my one stripe could get the better of Sergeant Brewster and a number of officers. I never did get any type of reprimand; after being charged four times since joining the Army it was nice feeling to be not guilty for a change. Just act dumb and you can get away with murder.

1981 was quite a mundane year for me without too much happening. After the events of Belfast and my promotion, it was hard to see what could match that as far as excitement was concerned; it wasn't long before I was to find out when my wife hit me with news I wasn't expecting

CHAPTER EIGHTY-SEVEN
BORDER PATROL

It was now the end of February and I was on my way home in my Fiat 127 with Tommo. We were just generally chatting away about all or nothing when Tommo said, "Did you read on Battery Orders about volunteers wanted for border patrol, on the East German border?"

"Yes," I said, "sounds interesting, how long was it for?"

"Four days," said Tommo. "Think it starts on a Monday and then return on Thursday."

"I might put my name forward" I said, "what about you?"

"Yes, wouldn't mind," said Tommo "should be interesting if nothing else."

"It will get us out of camp for a few days," I said, "away from the missus, I'll just tell her that it's like sex, compulsory, she'll never know any different."

"Yeah, me too," said Tommo, smiling like a naughty child.

"That's it then," I said, "When I get home I'll tell her the good news, tell her to pick the bones out of that one darling."

"Here we are," I said to Tommo as we pulled up outside the flats. "See you in the morning."

"Yeah, OK," Tommo said.

"Hi darling," I said entering the flat, "how's my little girl?" I was just trying to find the right moment to tell her the news when she hit me with, "Which one?"

"Sorry?" I said not quite understanding her reply, "What do you mean which one?"

"I'm pregnant," she said, giving me the look of 'don't worry it's yours'.

"Good God," I said, feeling like I'd just been hit with a hammer, "how far gone are you?"

"I'm due in September," she said, "the first week."

I was absolutely bouncing off the ceiling at the news as I gave my wife a hug. My news now seemed immaterial although I still needed to inform her; waiting until we were lying in bed together gave me the perfect opportunity to tell her my news. "Yes, of course I don't mind," she said, as if to say, *do I have any choice in the matter?*

The next morning it was congratulations from Tommo as we made our way to camp and then to the Battery Office to put our names down for border patrol. Down at the Gun Park it was a case of, "Ah, Wolfie has had his leg over again for the second time in two years," from the comedians in 18 Battery "Congrats Paul," was said from Billy and Danny Dalzell and my No.1 Sergeant Stretch. "Nice to have you back on board again Paul, or should I say L/Bombardier Wolfendale," said Graham.

"Sounds good by me" I said.

"Dinger, take the gun out of the hangar," said Graham, "take the rest of the lads with you and get ready for track bashing." (Replacing the track)

"Should I go and help them?" I said.

"No, I need a word with you," said Graham; we went into the gun cage (office) where all the gun equipment was. "Pull the cage door shut," said Graham. "I have spoken to the Troop Sergeant Major and have informed him that I would like you as my cover-number."

"I don't know what to say," I said, feeling proud.

"Well, it isn't an option," said Graham, "you're now officially my cover-number."

"Brilliant," I said, "just one thing though."

"Go on," said Graham.

"I have volunteered to do border patrol next week along with Tommo," I said, feeling like I'd already let him down.

"Well, no worries," said Graham, "you weren't to know, from now on though, no more volunteering for anything without consulting me first."

"Yeah, sure," I said.

"Congratulations once more," said Graham, "let's go and do same track bashing." My first week of being cover-number went down well and it was now time for Tommo and I to get our gear ready for border patrol; with our bags packed we climbed onto the back of the four tonner for the two hour journey, our dress was lightweight trousers and combat jacket, the sort of dress that would scare the enemy. On arrival we were greeted by a couple of military attached personnel that escorted us to a sports centre: camp beds on a wooden floor along with sleeping bags were how it was going to be for the next three nights.

"Listen in," said one of the staff, "my name is Tom Jones, no, not the guy from Wales before you ask. I am a civilian attached to the military. You don't need to call me Sir, Sergeant, Bombardier or any other military term you call each other, Tom will do fine. This is where you'll be staying for the next three nights," (already worked that one out), "there is a kitchen where you can cook your compo rations in the morning and at night; lunch will be at your expense at the local shops unless you bring your lunch with you. You'll also be able to buy some of the local produce like eggs, bacon, milk, German sausage or anything else that takes your fancy."

"Wow," I said to Tommo, "sounds good!"

"Looking forward to it," said Tommo.

It was a quite a casual and untainted speech compared to the one we would be subjected to by the infamous Sergeant Massey. "I want you up and ready for about 0930hrs, ready to leave in Army style Land Rovers," said Tom, "although discipline is at an all time low, please still remember you're still soldiers of the British Army." To be honest, with only about ten of us present it was quite easy to keep law and order. "Are there any questions before I vacate and leave you to enjoy the town's cuisine (beer)?"

"How far is the nearest boozer?" said one of the lads.

"Just walk into Walkenreid and down the main street, there you'll come across quite a few," said Tom, now exiting the hall. Tommo and I decided it would be a good idea to replenish our now grumbling stomachs. It was a case of finding a Schnellimbiss (fast food take away); a ten minute walk and there it was right in front of us.

"Bloody starving," said Tommo as the aroma from the food that was cooking reached our nasal passages.

"Me too," I said, "my stomach thinks my throat's been cut, I'm going to try a couple of Frikadellen mit Sauerkraut und Pomme frites" (Small type burgers and pickled cabbage with chips.) "What about you?"

"Think I'll have a Currywurst mit Pomme frites, maybe even two," said Tommo. It was so nice to fill our bellies once more; a quick look around the town for about an hour and then it was back to the sports hall to get some sleep. The next morning we were up and ready for our first look at the East German border after a small compo ration breakfast.

"OK lads," said Tom in a casual voice, "there are two Land Rovers outside waiting to take you to a part of the border, it will take about twenty minutes to get to our first stop and then there will be several more along the way, I will brief you more when we get there."

"Come on then, Tommo," I said, "let's go and try to antagonise the East Germans."

"Yeah, but not too much," said Tommo. The weather was being kind with the sun shining through white fluffy clouds; all this meant was that we should be able to see as far as the eye can see.

"Got your camera Tommo, we should get some good shots today." (Pardon the pun)

"All ready," said Tommo; "got a film of 24 exposures." Without realising how far we had travelled the Land Rovers came to a halt in a wooded area.

"OK lads, we are here," said Tom, "get yourselves out and I will give you a small, more detailed history of the border."

"Can't wait," I said to Tommo, although to be fair, I was looking forward to being educated on how it all came about. Gathered around the Land Rovers Tom began his first of many speeches.

"From 1949 up till now, the NATO-aligned West Germany and the socialist East Germany was divided by the Inner German border. Not including the similar but physically separate Berlin Wall, the border was 1,393 kilometres long and ran from the Baltic Sea to Czechoslovakia. On the eastern side, it was completed as one of the world's most heavily fortified frontiers, defined by a continuous line of metal fences and walls, barbed wire, alarms, anti-vehicle ditches, watchtowers, automatic booby traps and minefields. It was patrolled by 50,000 armed GDR (German Democratic Republic) guards who faced tens of thousands of West German, British and US guards and soldiers. After 1961, the Berlin Wall physically separated West Berlin from East Berlin as well as from East Germany. The situation ended when East Germany was dissolved and its five states joined the ten states of the FRG (Federal Republic of Germany) with the reunified city-state of Berlin.The Berlin Wall was a barrier constructed by the GDR beginning in 1961. The purpose was to completely cut (by land) West Berlin from surrounding East Germany and East Berlin."

"Wow," I said to Tommo, "found that really interesting."

"Same here," said Tommo, "Tom is certainly an encyclopaedia of facts and knowledge."

"OK, follow me," said Tom, "then you can get your first glance of the border." We made our way through some wooded area along a dirt track, then out into the open to get our first look at history; I was taken aback by what I saw; words could not express how I was feeling as I stared across the open ground in front of me. A huge mesh type fence just close to where we were standing welcomed us along with signs that read "Achtung Nach 50m Grenze" (Attention 50 Metres to Border). The fence stretched as far as the eye could see over a grassy hillside and then out of sight: A mine field followed by a man-made ditch, a dirt track road running adjacent to the fence and then finally, the lookout towers that were spread strategically apart standing tall into the sky line.

"Follow me," said Tom as we were walking a little closer to the border fence. Suddenly Tom said, "STOP!" Tommo and I were thinking, *what's the matter,* as we came to a halt at the edge of the road. "Why do you think I've stopped you?" said Tom, searching for some sort of intelligent answer that was not forthcoming.

"Have a look what is standing next to you," said Tom.

"Can't see anything," I said to Tommo, who was the only thing standing next to me.

"Me neither," said Tommo. Within seconds Tom pointed out what we should have been looking at; there were was some white posts about 4ft in height and about fifty metres apart.

"These posts represent the border," said Tom, "the ground in front of you leading up to the fence is known as an Exclusion Zone. In other words, if you step over the boundary of the white posts you're officially stepping into East Germany. The idea behind it is so that if you just by chance wander over into the Exclusion Zone then you will get a stern reminder from the East German Guards that you're now in the GDR."

"Bloody hell Tommo," I said, at the same time trying to give him a little nudge into the Exclusion Zone.

"You idiot," said Tommo, looking shocked.

We were given some binoculars and told to look at the guard towers, basically to show the East German guards that we were on a mission. It became a barrel of laughs to be honest as I set my sights on the tower, all we could see was the guards looking at us through their binoculars; waving frantically at the guards must have had them wondering if we had escaped from somewhere. "If you would like to take some photos and upset the East German guards even more, then now's the time before we leave," said Tom. No sooner said than done, we were all clicking away like Chinese tourists.

We got back into the Land Rovers and made our way to another section of the border that was a good hour away. "OK lads, out you get," said Tom, "you know the score now, so get the binoculars and cameras at the ready." As we were looking and snapping our camera Tom gave us another interesting piece of information. "Last year in September two families escaped over the border by building a hot air balloon."

"Wow," I said, sounding interested, "and what happened, Tom?"

"Well, a young boy and friend of the family tried to drive a bulldozer through the fence; he was shot dead by machine gun fire. The news of his death angered both families and they decided that enough was enough, they needed to find a way of getting over the border to better their lives; how to manufacture such a daring attempt was another thing. One of the men came up with a unique and clever plan to build a hot air balloon. The first attempt that was in July failed, the balloon dropped agonisingly on the wrong side of the fence amongst the midnight sky, they were no more than a few hundred metres away from freedom when the balloon hit the ground. The attempt alerted all the authorities, who would continue searching until the perpetrators or escapees were brought to justice."

"And what happened next?" we all said as we were gripped by the story.

"Well, they knew that eventually they would be found so the only option left; was to try to purchase enough material to build another balloon without bringing any suspicion to themselves. Two months later they launched their second attempt and under East German search lights they managed to land just over the border onto West German soil. Many have tried and many have died or been recaptured, all they wanted was a better lifestyle, although some do it for political reasons."

It was a week of stories from Tom; 'pull up a sand bag and I'll tell you a story' was how it was. Thursday arrived and it was time to return to camp in the four tonne vehicle. Apart from Friday it was a weekend off to catch up on some prime family time, just what the doctor ordered. You would think that I had learned my lesson about never volunteering for anything; especially after giving Graham my word, but unfortunately, that fell on deaf ears.

CHAPTER EIGHTY-EIGHT
CONFRONTING THE ENEMY

The calendar turned several pages and before I knew it summer was upon us. My wife's pregnancy was now there for all to see and exercises with the guns were now in full flow. Late July brought my first exercise as cover number for E Sub, under the command of Sergeant Graham Stretch; with a new BC now in place everybody wanted to put on a good show. The exercise was one of the largest so far. We were to travel to a place called Grafenwoehr in Eastern Bavaria, not too far from the Czechoslovakia border (more borders). It would be my second time venturing to the U.S Army base and one that I was not looking forward to; three weeks away from civilisation and my family was now taking its toll.

All the guns and track laying vehicles along with stalwarts (six wheeled amphibian vehicle) and APCs were driven down to Hildesheim railway station, which was no more than ten minutes away; with me now being the cover number more responsibility was thrown my way.

"L/Bombardier Wolfendale," said Sergeant Stretch.

"Yes," I said loudly amidst the droning of the guns.

"Guide L/Bombardier Bell on the train."

"OK," I said; using first names with so many officers and senior ranks around was something we had to be careful about if you knew what was good for you. "OK Dinger," I said, making sure there was no one of any importance close by (like the cook), "let's get the show on the road." The train and its flat bed carriages were as long as the eye could see; trying to guide Dinger on was like trying to thread a piece of cotton through the eye of a needle. I guided the gun onto the first flat bed with precision accuracy. The track of the gun was hanging over about two inches from the edge of the carriage on both sides; to be honest, and I know we had had our differences; I wouldn't have wanted to see the gun fall off the carriage with Dinger at the wheel. I must have guided Dinger almost the full length of the train before I could breathe more comfortably again.

"OK Dinger," I said, "let's leave the gun in the hands of experts to fasten down."

"Fine by me," said Dinger, climbing out of the hatch.

It must have taken a couple of hours to load all the vehicles, in the meantime, all of the troops were finding themselves a seat in the carriages at the front of the train; with everybody crammed into small carriage compartments the train gave a chug and we were finally on our way. The journey would take the best part of a day to complete in respect that we had zero priority on the railway lines; every time there was a express train due we would pull into a side-in and wait for up to an hour at a time, some of the lads would get some sleep on the luggage racks while others would sleep on the floor. The only problem with sleeping on the luggage rack was that one certain person (who shall not be named) decided to pee himself; a nice warm shower was had by the guy sleeping on the seat underneath, not what the doctor ordered.

After spending a full day dressed in combats it was nice to arrive at Grafenwoehr (never thought I would hear myself saying that) on a scorching hot day. All in all it must have taken us a couple of hours to get all the vehicles off the flat bed trailers before we made our way to base camp. I pretty much knew what to expect when we arrived at the village hall type huts, they were as barren as the Sahara desert; a camp bed and sleeping bags was how it would be for the next three weeks. The first few days were spent dry firing (pretending to fire real rounds). We would set the guns up like we were at war and just go bang! Unfortunately, the new BC that was still a little wet behind the ears decided that it would be a great idea to get us as close to the Czechoslovakia border as possible, a position that we would take up only if war broke out; with the barrel of the gun elevated into the air pointing towards their border, all hell broke out.

Within minutes of us going Bang, Bang, Bang, we were ordered to get the hell out of there. The Czechoslovakia authorities had got wind of our fool hardy tactics and were ready to start World War Three, I am not sure what was said on at the other end of the chain of command; all I knew was that someone was for the high jump. As the days went on we were getting to know the Americans soldiers a little better, better being the operative word. "Trade you my beret for your shirt, trade you my pullover for your trousers, I've got a nice set of mess tins to swap," and so it went on. Fair trade not robbery was how it should have been, so why was it I always felt I'd been robbed. Even now thinking back, I still can't work out what the fascination was, all I can say is that we were a few items missing from our 1157 kit check, including someone swapping his gasmask.

After the first two weeks, we were looking like we had been let loose in a flour mill; the dust that was kicked up every time we ventured out was beyond comprehension. The dust at times was that bad that we were issued face masks to stop us all from choking to death; lucky for us there was a launderette on the camp that we could use. An afternoon off meant a short trip down to the launderette, which would cost a couple of American dollars. The American cinema was interesting to say the least, popcorn with salt and, I've never heard so much noise from the Americans; a mere flash of a boob on the cinema screen was enough for them to shout and scream without a care in the world for anyone else, spoiling our enjoyment? Well, I guess it did.

The last week of exercise saw us come second in the regiment best gun competition for the second time; last time we were here we came second with Sammy Douglas and his merry men, maybe we weren't destined to win the best gun competition. For me this would be my last time in the dust bowl of Grafenwoehr. The guns were loaded back onto the train for one last final journey back to Hildesheim.

Back in camp it was déjà vu time once more. Upon reading Battery Orders I found myself volunteering for yet another adventure in a long line of voluntary tasks; I knew I shouldn't, I just couldn't resist.

"Hi darling," I said as I walked through the door of my house. "It's so nice to be back after three weeks."

"My god, you're filthy!" was her reply.

"Wish I could say the same about you, darling," I said, more in hope.

"Get your clothes off and I'll get them washed."

"Don't you mean get our clothes off, it's been three weeks," I chuckled. Before I knew it we were in the bedroom with my combats somewhere on the floor collecting more dust. "By the way, darling," I said with now a huge smile on my face, "I have just volunteered to fly with the AAC tomorrow."

"What, you're going away again?" she said angrily.

"No," I said, fearing she was going to give me a volley. "It's only for a day, they need to practise their skils, dropping troops off and then picking them up again, it's in preparation for when they go to Northern Ireland next month."

"What time can I expect you home?"

"Not sure, it's a full day, I need to be in camp for six in the morning, then, well it will depend on when they think they have mastered what their aim was."

"Fine," she said, shaking her head, "just don't wake me up when you get out of bed."

The next morning I was up ready for action. Once in camp I made my way to where the AAC were based at the other end of our camp. With my L/Bombardier status now there for everybody to see, it meant I was in charge of a section of men that had also volunteered, and you know what? This volunteering lark was not as bad as some people thought. I had a fantastic time flying around in helicopters all day. We even had our lunch brought to us by helicopter and, at night time, I got to sit close to the pilot to see all the all dials and instruments that were impressively lit up; this sort of thing would have cost a small fortune had I not been in the military, so why not do it for free; getting all the money back that I'd lost thorough getting charged over the years had me smiling.

September saw a new addition to my family; my second child, a gorgeous little girl called Tatiana was born, albeit with complications, in BMH Hannover.

Towards the end of 1981 the BC decided that he wanted all cover numbers to be Bombardiers and not L/Bombardiers. *Wow* I was thinking to myself, maybe more promotion was coming my way. Sergeant Stretch decided to have a formal chat with the ever elusive BC upon hearing the news. "L/Bombardier Wolfendale is doing a superb job as my cover number," said Graham. "I would certainly have no hesitation in recommending him to be promoted to the rank of Bombardier, Sir."

"Well, I am sure you're correct," said the BC, resting his chin on his hand and looking at Graham. "Looking at my records, I've noticed that he hasn't done his Crew Commander course yet. Don't get me wrong, I am sure he will make a No.1 one day and believe me when I say it, his time will come. I think I will get him on the next Crew Commanders course early next year and then see how he performs." There wasn't much Graham could say without sounding like, *I know better than you*; undermining the BC authority wasn't something the BC would take lightly. "OK Sir," said Graham reluctantly.

"In the meantime I am going to put a full Bombardier onto your gun sub to take over as your cover number. Bombardier Booth is his name, from the QM stores."

This was a major pivotal point in my career; being demoted just because I needed to do my Crew Commanders course was a kick below the belt. I had to bite the bullet, under duress I hasten to add, and just get on with carrying out my duties to the best of my capability; trying to drum up some interest on the next exercise was proving to be a bridge too far as I found myself becoming very frustrated and, you could say, resentful.

CHAPTER EIGHTY-NINE
CREW COMMANDERS COURSE

Other highlights from 1981 saw Graham and I competing and finishing the charity Bielefeld Marathon. I was probably as fit as I would ever be at the ripe old age of twenty four: rugby, football, cricket and now tug of war and boxing were also sports I was participating in; being able to fight with Dinger and Billy Dalzell under boxing rules was a far better way of getting rid of aggression, and also not getting in to trouble. Marching relief instead of Guard duties was also a welcomed change, especially on those dark, cold, winter nights; sitting inside the warmth of the Guardroom as opposed to standing guard on the front gate at 0300hrs was far more appealing.

With another cold snowy Christmas out of the way including the odd duty it was back to work early January. In the corridor I bumped into Pete Prigmore. "Hi Pete," I said, "How's it hanging?"

"It's hanging like it should be hanging," he said, sniggering.

"What you sniggering at?" I said

"Battery Orders, take a long look about half way down." Searching with my amazing selective vision, I got wind of what he was referring to. There it was in black and white for us all to see: Crew Commanders course with a lot of familiar 18 Battery names written for us all to see, including Pete's and mine, Karl Baron Rimicans, Bernie Tittle my roommate, and last but not least, old man Paul Hansen from the same gun crew. I was thinking *this could be fun with so many familiar faces;* however, I didn't take into account the names of DS who would be running the course. Sergeant Judy Garland, Sergeant McPherson, Sergeant John Callard along with Sergeant Major Bernie Evans. John was from one of the other batteries and a complete meat head (with respect) when upset. I had worked with John on the RP staff for a short while and he was certainly someone not to mess with; joking apart, they were all there to beast us and to get us into shape. Being at my fittest now was going to be put to the test.

"Up for it, are you Pete?" I said, pushing my chest out to impress.

"To be perfectly honest I'm surprised I'm on it, not something I was expecting," answered Pete.

"Well, let's say I was expecting it, maybe not so soon, but I need it so I can get my second stripe and get back to being Graham's cover-number." Over the next few weeks leading up to February Monday 15th it was a case of getting my 1157 to the highest standard I could, even though I knew deep down the standard we produced would never be good enough. Orders stated that we would need to report to one of the blocks set aside for the course at 1400hrs on the Sunday, we needed to be lined up inside the block for a quick brief and to put our stuff in our lockers; don't underestimate the power of rank.

I said goodbye to my wife with all my worldly goods in hand and told her I would see her later on that day, to celebrate Valentine's Day. "OK," she said, "don't be too late."

"As soon as I've unpacked I will be back, not going to be hanging around longer than I need to." There must have been a good thirty to forty of us on the course as we gathered in the block like a mothers meeting was about to take place; six or more smartly dressed senior ranks standing staring at us with intent flowing through their veins was enough evidence for us all to take them seriously.

"Listen in, and listen in carefully," said Sergeant Major Evans, "you're now the cream of the regiment, well at least for the next few weeks, and if just one of you! I repeat, just one of you steps out of line, you will be in serious trouble. You're now on show for the regiment to see. They will be laughing at you, they will be mocking you, there will be times when you will feel like retaliating, but believe me, your feet won't touch the ground if you so much as take one step out of line; play the game and you'll get your rewards, if you don't, then all of you will suffer. Tomorrow morning at 0830hrs you will be mine! Until then, you're in the hands of the rest of the DS."

These sorts of remarks had me almost quaking in my boots. I was just about to ask at what time can we to go back to our loved ones before arriving back tomorrow when we were hit with, "In a minute, you'll run up the stairs like there is no tomorrow and get yourselves sorted before we meet again in the morning, the course starts as of now!" I couldn't believe it. I felt that my heart had been ripped out and trampled on, there was no more going home for me; phoning my wife later if time allowed explaining the situation was also something I needed to do. Once upstairs I couldn't believe what my eyes were telling me: there were bits of metal frames strewn all over the floor, frames that belonged to a bed, there were lots of shouting and barracking from the DS, who seemed pissed at the fact they had to come in on their precious Sunday day off. Nuts, bolts and a bit of hard graft meant our beds were now ready for a mattress that we were yet to obtain.

The lockers were next, grey metal lockers that looked that they had no earthly place in the 1980s. They looked like something from the '60s; scrubbing with wire wool until your fingers could take no more was how it was. We were up most of the night preparing our locker layout to a standard that would never be good enough; polishing the floor to a shine fit to eat off was also expected. "Reveille will be at 0530hrs," said Sergeant Garland. "I want to see you all standing by your beds dressed in PT kit." Lucky for us that was the last final word we heard before turning in. All in all we must have had no more than two or three hours welcomed sleep before we were woken up by the overnight guard.

"Get out of bed, now!" was the cry from the guards, who were under strict instructions to give us as much grief as they could, albeit their rank didn't allow them to give orders. I suppose it was a case of, let them have their five minutes of glory, at the end of the day they all knew that when the course was over, payback time could be a bitch. Lined up outside the block freezing our nuts off at 0530hrs meant the course had now started in earnest; one of the lads was called forward to take charge of doubling us down to the gym. It was all part of leadership; anytime we needed to be marched or doubled anywhere one of us would be given the responsibility of getting us there. At the gym it was no different; after we had all been beasted for ten minutes it was now the turn of us all individually to show our leadership skills by taking the class.

At 0630hrs it was time to return to the block and get ready for breakfast; it was a case of a quick shower and then getting dressed into our pullovers and lightweight trousers ready to be doubled down to the cookhouse by one of the lads on the course. Part of the course requires the DS to push us to the limits of our capabilities however, not even having enough time to swallow down a Big Mac and chips brought me to boiling point. For some unknown reason I always seemed to be the last in line, either by name or by my height; either way it got a little frustrating when the first guy in line had finished his breakfast and I was just starting mine. "Get outside now in three ranks," was the cry from Sergeant Garland, "outside now!"

"What the fuck?" I countered, looking towards Sergeant Garland "I have only just sat down."

"Don't you dare fucking answer back Wolfendale, everybody outside now."

Unfortunately, my outburst had us all exiting the cookhouse at lightning speed and having to run around the running the athletic track a couple of times before being allowed back in the block; given an individual rollicking and made to do extra cleaning duties was my punishment. After a frantic fifteen minutes or so the cry from the corridor area was, "Stand by your beds now."

I was stood next to Pete as he was a good friend, but that was to soon change as Sergeant Garland and Sergeant McPherson entered the room like they were on a mission while Sergeant Callard stood guard on the door looking like a bouncer in a military uniform. The room stood silent even though it was squeaky bum time. "Wolfendale, Walker and Llewellyn, get your belongings and make your way to room one," they said. Basically they were separating us all, putting us with guys from other batteries to see how diverse we were; half an hour later we were all allocated rooms and ready for the fun to begin.

The first day was a complete nightmare as you can imagine, we were on our haunches by the time it had gone dark. As I sat on my bed all I could hear was ringing in my ears from all the unnecessary shouting, screaming and bellowing. With so much pressure put upon us we found it difficult and infuriating that there wasn't enough time in a twenty-four hour clock to complete all of the tasks; getting to bed at two, maybe three in the morning once again meant we were deprived of our precious sleep.

Tuesday morning was much the same as Monday, 0530hrs we were up and out of bed, 0600hrs PT at the gym and then 0700hrs at the cookhouse fast food chain for breakfast. At 0745hrs it was standing by our beds time for our first major room and locker inspection. Stood next to the window, I turned to my left and grinned at George Walker. "This is it, George."

"Bricking it," said George, giggling though his teeth.

"What about you Carl?" I said, still trying to calm my nerves.

"Nervous," he said in a quiet, soft spoken voice.

"George," I said, now being serious, "promise me that whatever you do, *don't* laugh when the contents of my locker gets slat out of the window."

"No mate, no worries there, make sure you do the same too," was his reply. Keeping a straight face would be like trying to sneeze with your eyes open, it wasn't going to happen.

"Stand by your beds!" was the recognisable voice of Sergeant Garland. Our room was the first on the tour so we were ready and standing bolt upright for the DS to enter. "Name!" said Sergeant Garland, staring me in the eyes (as if he didn't know my name).

"L/Bombardier Wolfendale, Sergeant!" I yelled in his face.

"Called them creases, Wolfendale?" he said, looking at my well ironed trousers, "they're about as razor-sharp as your brain, do you understand? Well do you?"

"Yes Sergeant Garland!" I could see George biting his bottom lip trying not to show any signs of emotion with my extraordinary peripheral vision now working overtime.

"Walker, stop sniggering!" was the warning he got from Sergeant McPherson as Sergeant Garland started questioning my locker.

"Open the window Wolfendale, now!"

"Which window would you like me to open?" I said, when I knew there was only one window, *why the hell did I ask such a stupid question?* I guess it was just my nature once again.

"Which, which, which window" "Which fucking window did you say? I'll show you which fucking window if you don't hurry up and open it." I was pretty sure I knew what he meant; my best boots would be going through a glass pane if I didn't open it immediately. How George and Carl were keeping a straight face was beyond comprehension; I'm not sure how much of my locker layout was on the main road or whether it would still be there when the inspection was finished, all I knew was that my locker was looking deprived of its contents.

Next in line was the turn of George so I thought, *what's the point of smashing a perfectly good pane of glass? Leave the window open,* I said to myself. Unfortunately, trying to keep a straight face was nothing more than insanity. My sniggering turned into chuckling and then my chuckling turned into laughter as the contents of George's locker ended up with mine, on the main road. I felt we could have made a fortune from the crowd that gathered down below; I would have certainly paid top dollar to see this show. My laughter became too much for the DS and rightly so, I was heading the same way as my locker layout; lucky for me I was allowed to use the stairs. I spent the next hour of the inspection running around the infamous athletic track in front of the block before being allowed to gather up my belongings along with the rest of the course.

"Bastard, George," I said as we met up again"

"I've never laughed so much in my life" said George holding his sides.

"To be honest George, thinking about it now, it was funny, but at the time fucking scary, I'm already knackered and it's only 0900hrs."

After the first few days of the sixteen day course we were given a stern warning that lights would have to be out by 2200hrs, we were literally falling asleep early evening when the RSM was giving us the occasional lecture; matchsticks would have struggled to keep our eyes open, you could see the RSM directing his voice towards you, but not one ounce of information was getting through to our sleepy brains.

With one or two of the lads doing their homework before the course commenced, rumour was, that we would be made to cross the nearby fast flowing, rat invested river; not something we were looking forward to, however, the day had arrived and today was our turn.

The block was now looking fit for a king and our locker layouts were taking me back to how they were in Junior Leaders. Marching with rifles and getting ready for the passing out parade in about ten days was also high on the agenda. "Outside now," was the battle cry from the DS. This was it, we were going to drown. I believe the rats would have struggled to stay alive in the murky water, so what chance did we have of surviving in their excrement? Lined up outside in three ranks and dressed in DMS boots along with lightweight-trousers and red PT vest meant we were apprehensively ready for action. We were doubled down to the gym where we were split into six sections; each section had to carry the dreaded log that was the size of a telegraph pole in width and about half its length.

It looked like the PT instructors were out in force as they gathered around; I'd never seen so many as a group. It felt like it we were going to be humiliated for the second time in a few days. "Logs at the ready," said the PT staff in their smartly dressed vest and lightweight trousers. "On my command and when I say, you will pick up the log." There was a slight pause before we heard those words ringing in our ears. "Pick up the log" said the PTI. With a bend of the back the log was firmly in place (so to speak), on our shoulders, "Forward march."

"Bloody hell George," I said, "the log's almost as big as what is in your trousers."

"Well I guess you've heard the rumour about us black men then, Paul."

"Yes George, but I try not to think about it too much, doesn't do anything for my reputation." Within about ten minutes and our shoulders feeling sore we finally made it to the river on this quiet and pleasant day in February.

"Put down the log," was the welcomed order from the PT staff. Our moment had arrived. "OK, shortly, and on my command I want you to get lined up at the edge of the river; I then want to see the last man across the other side."

"For fuck's sake, George," I said, feeling concerned for my life.

"Just go for it Paul, I can't even swim," said George.

"You nutter, how the hell do you expect to survive?" I said, fearing for his life. I could see my 18 Battery buddies Pete, Bernie, old man Hansen and Baron to my left looking like I was feeling, terrified.

"Get lined up by the edge of the river," was the order; we were now seconds from being turned into amphibious specimens. I think most of us were about to deliver a specimen, and I don't mean of the liquid kind. "Ready, steady... Go." For some unknown reason and I haven't got a clue why, I decided that this was one of those moments in my life that I didn't want to be first in the queue; after watching everybody else jump in apart from George, myself and about another three of the lads, one of the PT staff turned to us and said, "Bloody idiots that lot, the rivers full of shit, I'm going to use the footbridge." Probably for the first time in a long time I had made the correct decision.

"Follow me, lads, if you like," said the PTI grinning like a Cheshire Cat, we just roared with laughter as we stopped on the middle of the footbridge to admire the rest of the lads throwing obscenities in our direction whilst at the same time, swallowing the rat infested water. All didn't seem fair so we decided that a helping hand wouldn't go amiss. Clapping our hands seemed the correct thing to do adding just a little more fuel to the fire. Unfortunately, the whole escapade did have its casualties. Throughout the next few days we lost about three of the men, they were diagnosed with pleurisy from the dirty water; being admitted to hospital meant the end of the course for them. Up until now there were about five men fewer on the course for one reason or another. The course was now entering the last week and everything was all looking good for the final passing out parade at the end of the week, everybody that had made it this far were now feeling proud and just needed one final last push to get them over the line. The last four days were going to be the hardest so far; we would be participating in a three day exercise that would be gruelling beyond limits.

It was Tuesday evening and we were all lined up in the corridor of the block with more equipment than you would find in a Garden Shed: full webbing with complete backpack, pick and shovel in case we found a nice beach to build a sand castle, compo rations and a small burner, sleeping bag and poncho. Believe me, it was going to be tough: thunder flares, SLR with blank rounds, compass, maps of plenty to complete the setup. Late that night we were driven out to a place unknown to us all in a four tonner. The back canvas was pulled down to add more reality to the exercise; the DS didn't want to make it easy for us, keeping us in the dark about our location was paramount to our task. I would say we were taken about an hour up the road in pitch black darkness until we reached our destination; we were dropped off at varied locations along the way in groups of four, our group being comprised of George, Carl, myself and we also had the pleasure of Pete Prigmore who had joined us.

"OK, out of the vehicle now!" said Sergeant Garland with anger written all over his face. "Here's your grid reference, I want you at the next location by 0800hrs tomorrow morning; that gives you nine hours, plenty of time."

Why did we believe him? Nine hours in the dark, twenty miles over mountainous terrain, there wasn't a hope in hell's chance of us getting there unless we caught a taxi; we did our best but were still a few miles short of our checkpoint after a punishing walk. It wasn't long before we were compromised. A patrolling Land Rover that was searching the area caught a glimpse of us as we tried to hide away in a ditch without much success; we basically gave up as the ever beaded eyed Sergeant Garland lay into us.

"Where the fuck have you been hiding?" he said with anger in his voice, "you should have been at your location some two hours ago."

"We have not stopped walking all night," was my angry reply.

"Then you should have run then shouldn't you, all the rest have managed to make it," he said (not true) throwing another grid reference in our direction: "Wolfendale, you can take charge of the next stage as you seem to have a lot to say for yourself, make sure you're not late, now get a move on."

We had no time to rest at all, it was a case of get yourselves dusted down and on your way. It would be another fifteen miles or so we had to walk and a meagre amount of five hours to get there. How we made it I will never know, but made it we did. As we reached the location I said to Pete, "thank god for that, never thought we would get here, I'm absolutely dead on my feet."

"Same here," said Pete, "I have got blisters on blisters." We were just about to rejoice with the fact that we had made it when out of the blue, and unexpectedly, we got fired upon. Sergeant Garland and his crew had a little surprise waiting for us.

"Hit the ground now," I said to my men. That actually was the easy bit, however, getting back up was a nightmare. "George, Pete cover fire, Carl follow me." Once Carl and I had hit the ground we did the cover fire as Pete and George made inroads towards the enemy; it must have taken about three or four skirmishes along the ground before the task was announced as complete.

"Well done lads," said the gushing Sergeant Garland, "you did well; now get yourselves a brew and a bite to eat." Half an hour was all we had to conjure up some welcomed food before setting sail once more.

Another fifteen mile hike took us into the early evening. I was trying to calculate how many miles we must have walked; I came up with a figure close to fifty miles. It was enough to bring any man to his knees, which is where I could see myself if I had to carry on any further. On arrival and not knowing what to expect, we had to demonstrate our first aid skills that we had been taught on the course. This was bliss compared to what we had done over the last twenty four hours.

"OK lads, I know it's been a gruelling twenty four hours, but believe me, it will get a lot worse than it is now," said Sergeant McPherson. "After tea you can get your head down for a few hours until we come to get you out of your sleeping bags." *Brill* I was thinking; *fucking hurray for humanity*; not one for normally swearing, but the exercise was definitely having its toll on me.

Wondering what was for tea having consumed all my compo rations it was soon made clear to what we would be eating. Just when I was getting to like Sergeant McPherson a dead chicken was thrown our way. "Here, get this down yer, that's your tea for tonight."

"You know what," I said, not giving a shit, "I think I will pass on this one." I was too drained to even think about mutilating the poor feathered chicken.

"Wolfendale, shut your mouth, you will have your share of the chicken," he said, "even if it's only the beak, none of you will be getting any sleep until the chicken has been cooked and then eaten, do you understand?"

"Gin clear, Sergeant McPherson," I said, giving up on life. George and Pete started ripping the chicken apart as Carl and I made a makeshift spit to roast it on. I could tell that Pete was as pissed as me as he started singing a song to the chicken, "Chick, chick, chick, chick, chicken, play a little song for me".

"What the fuck are you singing, Pete?" I said.

"Not a fucking clue," he replied, "my head's gone; I need to get some sleep."

"You've lost it mate, big time."

"Yep, think you're right Wolfie." All this stupid singing and crazy talking was now having us in fits of laughter; the chicken was finally cooked and devoured in rapid quick time before we were told to get our heads down.

"We will be back sometime in the early hours so make the most of the time you have to get some sleep," said Sergeant McPherson, making his way to the waiting Land Rover.

Seconds later, someone, if not all of us, decided that across the road on a nice grass bank would be a better location for us to sleep. Where we currently were was full of all sorts of flies and bugs; never for a minute did we think that it would cause a major melt down with Sergeant Garland and his merry men. It wasn't until about 0400hrs that one of us heard a familiar voice.

"Where are you, yer bastards? I know yer here somewhere."

"George," I said, shaking his shoulder.

"What is it?"

"I think we are in deep shit, I can hear them looking for us." George woke up Carl and Pete as I called across the road. "Over here."

"Over fucking where?" was the cry.

"Across the other side of the road," I said feeling worried.

"I told you to stay where you were, do you not understand the Queen's English?" I thought better of being flippant as they seemed totally pissed off. "We have been searching for you for thirty fucking minutes, wasting our fucking time aren't you?"

"Sorry Sergeant," we all said together.

"Get yourselves sorted; you have a long walk ahead of you." It was now about 0430hrs and we were running a little behind time. Getting a move on was a priority as we had about ten miles in front of us to cover. Carl was next to take charge of us so called men as we made our way to the next checkpoint; a pretty straightforward route meant we made up some time. We were stopped a few hundred metres from where we were supposed to be by the DS. "OK lads, this is an area that has just been contaminated, there was a gas attack yesterday, so on my mark I want you to get into full NBC suit complete with gas mask."

My heart sank for a minute until we were given the order, "GAS, GAS,

GAS!" We had less than a couple of minutes to get into our suits. "OK, now make your way to the checkpoint where you'll have to make and eat breakfast with your gas mask still on."

It was a right old chore, lifting your gas mask up a fraction, taking one bite of your food then blowing out again before chewing; breakfast should have taken about fifteen minutes, but on this occasion you could double that time. It was a pleasant relief to be told stand down, our suits and gas masks were off in double quick time. It was still early morning on day two so we knew that we would have at least two more hikes to do.

"Wolfendale, take charge of the next stage," said the DS, "it's about a twenty mile trek so I expect to see you about 1500hrs this afternoon, oh, and by the way, all of the BCs will be joining us today at some time to see how their lads our getting on."

"Great," I said, "hope I don't meet 18 Batteries BC on my task." The hike went remarkably well in respect that we managed to get there with time to spare.

"Right lads," said the DS, who were already waiting for us, "your next task will be to build a bridge out of some items that have been accidently left in the forest: there are planks of wood, some barrels, rope, tyres and basically anything you can use from the forest. You'll have about thirty minutes to construct the bridge and then walk across it without falling off, one other thing, 18 Batteries BC has decided to pay us a visit; he wants to see how his lads are faring up. What battery are you from Wolfendale?"

"18 Battery Sergeant, as if you didn't know," I said, feeling a little panicky.

"God help you," he said, trying not to laugh.

"Right then," I said, "let's put on a good show lads; let's go." We sprang into action with the BC standing there observing our every move. Within minutes and after a consultation, the bridge was taking shape; It took no more than about twenty minutes to construct and, to my delight, we all managed to get across the other side without so much as a creak from the bridge.

"Well done L/Bombardier Wolfendale," said the BC, "bloody good effort, great leadership skills."

"Thank you Sir," I said, feeling as though I'd done enough to impress. I was just hoping now that he may have realised that he could have promoted me earlier; completing the task successfully was also a feather in the cap for the DS, after all, if they were looking for more promotion then this was their ideal opportunity to put down a marker.

After a more reasonable night's sleep we were entering the last full day of activities before finishing the course tomorrow. We were given our mandatory grid reference with George now in charge and told to make our way to the next rendezvous. Unfortunately there would be a slight twist to the task. "You will find a Land Rover trailer about half way on your travels, if you don't get lost," said the DS, "from there you'll have to push it the final five miles to a make shift base camp."

"Stone me," I said wittering away. "Have you seen the size of our quartet; we're not exactly heavy weights, can we borrow Sergeant Callard for a few hours?"

"Yeah, I tell you what, why don't you go and ask him, I'm sure he will have an answer for you. Improvise and adapt, Wolfendale," was the reply I got. "Now get on your way, don't let us catch you en route." The first part of the long hike went well until we reached the trailer; it was like trying to push a brick wall over. With one of us on each corner we eventually got the damn thing rolling up and down the dirt track. It must have been about a mile of huffing and puffing and effing and jeffing before we heard an Army Land Rover approaching. "Quick, let's take cover," said George, the team leader.

"Yeah, nice one George," I said. "What the fuck are we going to do with the trailer? It won't hide itself now, will it?"

"Good point well made, Wolfie," said George.

"I know, let's hide under the trailer and maybe they will just drive past and think that we haven't got this far yet." Somehow I think we all knew that it wasn't going to work. Unfortunately, we were running out of time so didn't have time to come up with a plan B. We tried to play dead as the Land Rover stopped alongside the trailer. To be entirely honest they were just playing games, they knew all along where we were hiding.

"You idiots get from underneath the trailer now," said the familiar voice of Sergeant Garland; it was all he could do not to laugh at our pathetic attempt not to be compromised.

With a well rehearsed shuffle we were all finally standing upright next to each other, feeling like we looked. "Walker, it's your task, what have you got to say for yourself?" said Sergeant Garland trying to hide his amusement.

"Sorry Sergeant," he said, "it just all happened so quickly."

"Quickly Walker; if you had been quick then maybe you wouldn't have been caught; would you? You've got another four miles to go so you better get a move on, remember, improvise and adapt." Just then George had a plan swilling around inside his head.

"Improvise and adapt, you said?" *Where's this going,* I was thinking.

"Yes," said Sergeant Garland, waiting patiently for his brain to kick into gear.

"Well, why don't we attach the trailer to your Land Rover and then you can take us the final four miles?" We just looked at George in disbelief at what he had said, but then, and to our surprise, Sergeant Garland agreed.

"You're the only group so far to ask for help, so yes, let's get going before I change my mind."

"Well done George," we all said, giving him a pat on the back. We just couldn't believe our luck as we headed back to base camp, oh yes, we were definitely first back.

It was nice to get back early in respect that we managed to get some food down us at a pace more suited to gentlemen, and also, a chance to sort our kit out before the final hike that lay ahead. It must have been around 1900hrs when Pete was put in charge of the final task. We were to make our way through thick forestry areas and keep a keen lookout for the enemy who would be searching for us. If we made it to our rendezvous then that would be it, we could get our heads down until morning, but that just wasn't going to happen.

It must have been around about midnight and feeling quite upbeat that we were still on the beaten track; with only a short distance to travel we were feeling pleased with our progress until all hell broke loose. It was a first degree ambush; Pete and I were set upon while Carl and George managed to escape. We were pounced on like a lion had just attacked its prey; getting up off the ground with my heavy pack was just not going to happen.

"Wolfendale, Prigmore, glad to see you again," said Sergeant Garland.

"Get spread eagled at the side of the Land Rover," said Sergeant Callard in the deepest voice I had ever heard. Pete was taken away somewhere else to be beaten up while I was spread eagled to make me feel uncomfortable for the next hour or so; kicking my legs further apart and a few kidney punches was as far as it went.

"Number, rank and name!" was shouted at me constantly in the hope that I would crack and say something; I had been trained to say nothing apart from, "I cannot answer that question." As soon as you say something else away from those well rehearsed words you'll find yourself opening up to the enemy. To be honest I was doing such a good job that Sergeant Callard decided to try the softly, softly approach, calling me his buddy. "Would you like a biscuit? You seem like a nice lad, your mate has already told us lots of information, I just need to hear it from you."

I believe that Pete and I would have still been there now if it wasn't for the Troop Sergeant Major saying, "OK, let's leave it there." We were given a new map as ours was with George and Carl and told to make our way to the next checkpoint, and then when we get there we would be able to get some sleep. *Yeah right,* I was thinking. With night now becoming day we were closing in on our final destination; all we needed to do now was to rendezvous with the rest of the course. "Bloody hell, Pete," I said. "Looks like we are last back;" we couldn't believe what we were looking at; everybody was back at base camp standing around in their combats. "Get your arses over here now," said Sergeant Garland and his men; we never even had time to even draw breath when we were lined up facing a hill that had no right to be that steep.

"On your marks, go!" was the battle cry. My legs couldn't take any more of this abuse. "Come on, Pete," I said, dragging him up to the top.

"Not going to break me, the bastards aren't," said Pete, giving it his all. We basically fell down the hill on the way back; at the bottom it was a case of *stand on your feet.* God help anyone who dared to sit down, we were getting beaten with sticks every time we looked to be flagging. The only thing keeping me going now was the sight of the waiting four tonne vehicles that were there to take us all back to our barracks; apart from a couple of the lads that didn't manage to complete the exercise, we were all now just a day away from our well deserved passing out parade. All we needed to do was to make sure we looked as smart as we could for the parade, at the same time, still remembering that the course wasn't over until that final march off the parade square. The total of the lads that had now not managed to pass the course for one reason or another had risen to eight; their chance would come again in the near future. After the passing out parade that close friends and families attended, it was back to our room and then to the Education Block for a final debrief. At the debrief I was to find out I got a well earned C grade with B being the highest grade that anyone got; I believe three of the lads got a B grade and about ten of us got a C grade with the rest achieving D or below.

Getting a C grade in military terms meant that a promotion should be achieved within six months or less, depending on vacancies within the battery or regiment. *Happy with that,* I said to myself, *should get my cover-number job back and hopefully one day become No. 1 of my own gun.* After a few months, my patience was wearing thin as there seemed to be no inkling of any promotion coming my way, something had to be done.

CHAPTER NINETY

TIME TO TRY NEW PASTURES GREEN

With my Crew Commanders course now firmly behind me I was back onto the guns; it was a case of *watch this space* over the next few months to see where my career was going. I had been with 18 Battery almost seven years, done three tours of Northern Ireland, worked in the Officers' Mess, BKs driver, RP staff and volunteered for practically everything that was on offer, played every sport for the battery and regiment; it's fair to say I was getting as much out of the Army as they were getting out of me. I did another four months on the guns before I decided my career was going nowhere. Promises, promises, promises from the BC was doing me no favours at all; how long do you just sit on your arse before doing something about it, I was on the case straight away. I noticed an opening for a L/Bombardier to join the staff in the Officers' Mess; it was to take on bar accounting duties. Feeling that down in the dumps meant I didn't need a second invite as I put my name forward once more. Down at the Gun Park I called Graham over. "What's wrong, Paul?" he said.

"I've put in a request to join the Officers' Mess as a bar accountant, I just can't get my head around why I haven't been put forward for a promotion yet," I said, feeling I was letting Graham down.

"Don't worry mate. You know what, I perfectly understand, it has got me beat as well, you need to do what you think is best for you, maybe you'll come back to us later on in the year."

"Well, I certainly won't rule it out; it would be nice to be your cover number again one day."

We chatted for a while and then later on that day I found out that my position had been confirmed. As from Monday I would be taking on a new task; mathematics was always a subject I excelled in at school, so bar accounting wasn't going to be a problem. I spent about three months in the mess learning my trade until once again, and after reading Battery Orders, a posting to Herford was on the cards; 4 Armoured Div HQ and Signals Regiment was the outfit.

It would be an internal posting, which meant I would still be on the books of 18 Battery and any chance of being promoted was now truly put to bed; there was just no way on this planet that I would be promoted. Being allowed only a handful of Bombardiers in the battery meant I would be surplus to requirement in the BCs eyes. The posting was to be quick, in fact that quick I barely had time to tell my wife that I would be leaving next week and that she was to follow later on when an Army Quarter became available. Luckily for me, though, my wife and I had become friends with a REME guy that was attached to the Army Air Corps'; he and his wife said they would be delighted for us to stay with them until something could be sorted out.

After all my goodbyes it was time for me to regrettably leave the battery I had become so fond of. The lads from the Officers' Mess threw a small party for me as well as throwing me into the pool at the back of the mess. How kind of them; where would we be without friends? A short journey of about an hour saw me arrive at the mess. "L/Bombardier Wolfendale arriving for duty, Sir," I said to the Sergeant Major in charge.

"Ah yes, take a seat," he said politely. "I've been expecting you, when there's no one around you can call me George, George Clarke. I suppose you have been brought up to speed as to why the posting was urgent."

"Not a clue," I said, feeling confused.

"Well, this mustn't go any further," said George, "the guy whose place you're taking has been screwing a married man's wife, hence the urgency."

"Bloody hell," I replied, "welcome to the mess"

"Well, that's the end of it as far as I am concerned." George introduced me to the rest of the lads. "This is Corporal Black."

"Duncan is fine," he said in his broad Scottish accent.

"You will be working alongside Duncan when you go on exercise; you'll be looking after Major General Riley and about another six high ranking officers," said George.

"Sounds good by me," I said, thinking *General*.

"In the meantime you'll be working shifts, taking charge of matters when I'm not around," said George. I was taken around the mess to be introduced to Bombardier Mick Bounds and then Sergeant Barry Mason; there was so much rank compared to the Officers' Mess in Hildesheim, but thanks to George, I was made to feel right at home.

Later on that evening I managed to find out where my Army Air Corps' friend lived and settle down there for a few days until my wife arrived along with my children. Even Duncan was being hospitable, inviting me round to his house for tea and to meet his lovely wife.

After a few days had passed, I was starting to become a popular figure among the staff and the officers. My wife had now arrived, kids and all, to my delight; the missing piece of the jigsaw was now in place. It was only about a week or so before I was handed the keys to my luxury apartment (married quarter) that was just up the road from the Officers' Mess. With the fact that I would need to be on call at a moment's notice it felt that a more local dwelling would be more practical; working in the Officers' Mess does come with its perks, which I was later to find out as my time in the mess developed.

CHAPTER NINETY-ONE
MY FIRST EXPERIENCE WITH THE ADC

I was now getting my feet firmly under the table and things were running like a well oiled engine. I got to see Major General Riley for the first time at one of the many functions that took place; sitting at the top table with a couple of Brigadiers and a full colonel meant the CO was no more centre stage, his place was about three to four places to the left of the General. Throughout the day there was also an opportunity for some of the more senior officers, normally Lieutenant Colonel and above, to have what would we would call a special lunch.

A small but beautifully decorated, oblong shaped room would be where they would hold their gathering. It would keep them separated from the normal lunch that would be going on at the same time; this type of function would allow me to show off my attention to detail qualities that I took great satisfaction in. I was always the one when available that was totally trusted to organise the function, along with some of the other waiters that I felt wouldn't let me down. The lunch would always take pole position over the also-rans, at the same time we had to be careful not to forget that an officer is an officer. Normally in the kitchen area there would be a separate chef or cook working on the special lunch; precision timing was paramount along with flexibility that I had in abundance. I can't ever remember one of the functions ever going wrong.

With Christmas now out of the way, which included the staff Christmas party, it was time to return to business. Early January brought my first exercise, albeit just a week; I got to see firsthand how everything functioned.

"Paul," said Duncan, "I will show you the ropes so that one day, if I ever decide to leave for some reason, you can take over the reins."

"I can't see that ever happening," I said, "anyway my BC seems to have some sort of problem about promoting me" (I explained the reasons).

"That's not right," said Duncan, feeling as disgusted as I was. "Well if you ever take over from me then they will have to promote you, this position requires a full screw to be in charge. There is so much responsibility that goes with the job that you need the rank to issue authority."

"Well," I said, "I'll tell you for nothing, getting blood out of a stone would be easier than the BC having to find a reason to give me my second stripe."

"There's a lot of Army brass (high ranking officers) around these parts, Paul," said Duncan, "a lot higher than your BC."

"Time will tell," I said,"

Out in the fields it was a case of finding a panoramic view for the General's tent to have his meals from; the tent was large enough for seven to eight people to use and of course, the mandatory bar. We were totally self-sufficient in respect that the General had his own chef a Corporal that worked alongside Duncan and I. "I can see now why I would need to be a full screw," I said, "technically I would need to have at least, if not more authority than the chef if needed."

"Yeah, but it should never come to that," said Duncan. "Ay up Paul, here comes the ADC (Aide-De-Camp) Captain Murray. He's the General's personal helper, he's in charge of everything of, let's say, of slightly lesser importance, like organising his personal diary on a day to day basis."

"I take it we come under the diary category," I said, looking towards the ever advancing pace of Captain Murray.

"Oh yes," said Duncan, "even when he's wrong he's right, if you get my drift."

"Morning Sir," we said from beneath the cam-net of our four tonne vehicle.

"Morning," said the ADC, still pacing around. "Everything all set up for the General?"

"Yes Sir," said Duncan.

"Can you show me where the General will be eating?" he said hurriedly as if he had a train to catch.

"This way Sir," said Duncan; I followed along to get some experience of what to expect if I was to ever be left alone.

"Here we are Sir," said Duncan with me by his side.

"Open the flaps of the tent can you?" said the ADC looking at me as if to say, *you're the lowest rank on parade, you do it.*

"Yes Sir," I said, "there you go Sir, is that OK?"

"Not sure if I like the view," he replied. I just looked at Duncan in disbelief when he said, "I think we should move it about ten degrees to the left, the General will get a better view of the hill." I almost fell about laughing but felt I would leave that until the ADC had parted from our company.

"I will catch up with you later," he said. "You can expect the General at about 1300hrs unless you hear any different." Wow, were we glad to get rid of him, at least for a short while. With the tent now moved, Duncan showed me how to set the two six-by-three tables: white crepe paper for table clothes and the normal place mats, cutlery, wine glasses, cheese board and a selection of soft and alcoholic drinks on demand. *Oh yes,* I'm saying to myself; not got a problem with it, however, it was interesting to say the least to see how the other side of the Army functions even though we are all on the same side. OK, maybe a little over the top for my liking, but I had a job to do, and that's how I saw it.

I learned so much in my first week, including being able to sample the goods at night time before turning in; a couple of whisky and cherry brandies along with some cheese and crackers was what the doctor ordered. 1 x General, 2 x Brigadiers, 2 x Colonels including the Chief Of Staff and 1 x Lieutenant Colonel, the CO, oh yes, and occasionally the ADC might be asked to sit in, but he always seemed preoccupied with taking care of other meaningful matters, like making sure the tent was facing the correct angle.

With the exercise now over it was a case of getting sorted for the next one which would be a few months away. Back in camp it was nice seeing all the civilian staff that worked in the mess, it made me feel there was more to life than playing soldiers. I was really enjoying my new position and things seemed to be moving along nicely; would it be too much to ask for it to continue in the same vogue, yes it was, a call from the Regimental Clerk was to bring more misery to my Army career, news that I was never to get over.

CHAPTER NINETY-TWO

I JUST KNEW IT WOULD BE DEVASTATING NEWS

Although my duties were in the Officers' Mess, we still had to prove our fitness. Personally, fitness is still very important to me; passing my BFT (Battle Fitness Test) became second nature. I believe I was given about ten minutes to complete the one and a half mile run; eight minutes thirty was my time as I ran on my own alongside the PTI who was just doing it for fun. After a quick shower and feeling good about my time, it was back to work. As I entered the mess I was asked by George to step into his office.

"Paul, can I have a word with you please?" said George. "I have put you down for duty this Sunday 6th, I wouldn't normally do it, especially to the married personnel, but I'm afraid we are a little understaffed this weekend."

"No problem," I said. "What time's the shift?"

"Well if you can get in for about two-ish, do the late shift, that would be great," said George. "Oh and by the way, next week there are a couple of special lunches for the CO and Colonel Gerardo."

"Absolutely fine, George," I said. "Better get myself back to work now, the mess won't run by itself."

I spent most of the rest of the day sorting out the silver room as I had been put in charge of the mess silver; *wow*, I said to myself, so many beautiful pieces to admire, pieces that had been bought or more importantly, awarded to the mess for different reasons. Either way they would be a credit to have on any dining table.

Sunday arrived and saying goodbye to my family just for a short while was not going to be an issue. I arrived bang on time as I normally would to take over the shift from one of the more senior waiters, Signalman Russell. Russell had become a good friend of mine over the last month, not sure what direction his Army career was heading. I found him quite an articulate person, although at times, he probably needed to grow up a little; he was still a young nineteen year old lad with a lot to learn.

It was just a quiet day, a day that I wasn't use to. I must have spent most of the afternoon chatting away to the duty chef and the civilian waitress. "I think it's about time we get ready for dinner, it's already 6.30." I said to Christine the waitress (don't think she worked on a 24 hour clock)."

"OK," she said, "I'll start preparing the cheese board and coffee." As the officers that were living in the mess started to arrive, I heard the phone ring in Sergeant Major Clarke's office.

"Be with you in a minute," I said to the Christine, "just need to get this call, it might be important."

"Hello, Officers' Mess, L/Bombardier Wolfendale speaking," I said after picking up the receiver.

"It's the Regimental clerk here," he said in a clear and precise voice. "Is that L/Bombardier Paul Wolfendale?" confirming my status one more.

"Yes, speaking," I said, now deep in thought.

"Oh hi Paul, I have just received a call from the Orderly Officer, he needs to see you immediately; he said he will be in his office in RHQ."

"What it's about?" I said, feeling anxious.

"Not sure Paul, just passing on the message."

"OK, thank you." I answered.

After replacing the receiver I just stood still for a couple of minutes, pondering my thoughts. I was pretty sure I'd done nothing wrong, like nicked a piece of silver or something along those lines, and then it hit me: the last time I needed to speak to the Orderly Officer was the time my father died. I was thinking to myself, "Please God no, I couldn't cope with anything happening to my mum." I was absolutely beside myself with worry as I made my way out of the mess and heading towards RHQ. It must have been the longest five minutes of my life as I finally arrived at RHQ with my head in my lap.

With a gentle tap on his door I was told to enter. "Come on in, Paul," he said in a delicate manner, adding more worry to my thoughts. *Paul,* I was thinking, I understood quite clearly that he knew me, but to address me as Paul was very unusual. "Take a seat, Paul," he said. I must admit that he was very well educated in the way he explained what he needed to say. "Before I start, Paul, not all is lost, however, we have just received information that your mother has had a major stroke; she has been admitted to your local hospital. I believe it to be Leighton Hospital, is that correct Paul?"

"Yes," I said with tears now slowly sliding down my face.

"Here, Paul," he said, passing me some tissue. "I'm so sorry Paul, let's hope and pray that she recovers from her ordeal. At the moment, we are in the process of getting you a flight to England ASAP, Paul."

"Thank you," I said, trying to hide my tears with my hands.

"It's OK to cry, Paul, I would be doing the same thing if it was me," said the Orderly Officer trying to comfort me. "Carrying on with what I was trying to say, Paul, we are classing your mother's stroke as category A compassionate leave, which means you'll be on the first flight leaving West Germany to the UK no matter where it's from. Just bear with me a minute and I will make a call to the Regimental Clerk to see where we are up to." The call was no more than a couple of minutes before he then explained to me what was going to happen.

"OK Paul, I now have all the details. There is a flight from Hannover Airport at 0700hrs in the morning, it flies to Heathrow Airport and then, there will be a connecting flight to Manchester. Once in Manchester we will have a staff car waiting to take you to Leighton Hospital."

"Thank you," I said, "what about my wife?"

"Well unfortunately, she will have to make her own way if you want her there with you."

"Yes, of course I do."

"We will sort all that out Paul, you don't need to worry about that." I made my way back home with the Duty Driver giving me a lift. I explained all to my wife before trying to get some sleep for my early start.

It was about 0400hrs when the Duty Driver arrived to take me to the airport. I was travelling light with just a small suitcase for my essentials; a quick hug from my wife and I was off. The flight was a normal scheduled flight that would take about two hours before reaching Heathrow; luckily the flight was on time which meant that I should arrive in London about 0900hrs all being well. We must have been about ten minutes away from landing when there was an announcement over the PA system. "Could Paul Wolfendale please press the light button above your head, one of the cabin crew needs to speak to you."

With the light now on and arousing public interest, I was approached by one of the cabin crew. "Hi Paul," she said. "We have been told about your mother, we are so sorry to hear of the news. When we land and start to taxi, I would like you to leave your seat and make your way forward to the exit door, I will be there waiting for you. As soon as we have come to a standstill I will open the door, there will be a bus to take you to the other end of the airport where an aircraft will be waiting on the runway for you to board; we will do our best to get your luggage off the aircraft so that you have it with you."

It felt so strange, I was so use to being at the back of the queue than being at the front; getting preferential treatment was making me feel important, I would have give it up instantly for my mum to recover from her stroke. The flight to Manchester was only about thirty to forty minutes, and once again, just like the first flight, I was told to make my way forward to the exit door before we came to a standstill. I was now being whisked through customs without showing any documentation at all and, luckily for me by time I got to the arrival lounge my luggage was waiting for me to collect. Looking around I could see a smartly dressed military man looking as lost as me; it felt like the time when I was arriving in Hannover some eight years ago when I hadn't got a clue what to do. I made my way over to the man and to my relief he was the driver I was expecting. "L/Bombardier Wolfendale is it?" he said.

"Yes, just call me Paul,"

"OK Paul, if you would like to follow me there is a car waiting for you outside." It took about forty minutes to get to the hospital. I was thinking *three cheers for the Army*, what they did was to be applauded. Giving me a chance to see my mother once more if the worst was to happen was something I will never forget. Large parts of my family were at her bedside to meet me, there wasn't a dry eye to be found. I just looked over to my mum and gave her a kiss on the cheek; she was in a coma, but looking peaceful as she lay there. There was absolutely no way that I was leaving her bedside. I spent the next two nights with one of my sisters chatting away to her in the hope that she would come out her long sleep.

"Mum, mum," I would say, "come on mum, it's time to put the kettle on, Alan and Robin will be home soon, you need to get their tea cooked." That's how it was, on both nights my sister and I would try finding something that she would respond to.

Wednesday arrived and I had news that my wife would be joining me at the hospital later on in the afternoon; a bit of loving and caring was certainly needed at these troubled times. It was around about half five and with most of the family gathered around her bedside, including my wife, that my mum finally gave up on her life. Her final breath could be gently heard. I do believe that once she had seen everybody for one last time, she decided that all her children were now in safe hands, she must have felt that there was no more she could do.

What a woman she was, sixteen children and each and every one of them loved so much. She was now on her way to see dad, a place I knew that would be her final resting ground. "Bye mum," we all said, "enjoy your time with dad, we know it's what you wanted, enjoy your well earned rest." There was little more we could do; one by one we entered the room to pay our last respect as her angelic face said it all. This has got to be the most traumatic time in my life so far, here I am worrying about my pathetic promotion when there are lots more important things going on in the world. I was angry, I was bitter, over the next few days I just wasn't myself; turning to cigarettes again, even though just for a short while, is something that I regret.

The funeral took place about a week later. It was exactly the same as my father's some five years earlier, coffin under the window with an open lid and then on to her place of rest where mum would be re-united with dad her loving husband once more. I found it unsustainably hard coping with the grief; not returning back to West Germany unfortunately wasn't an option, there was little more I could do. I was determined to push on as one must in times of darkness. I knew deep down it would have been what my mum and dad would have wanted.

Back in the Officers' Mess everybody couldn't have been more supportive if they tried, I was so grateful; it helped me continue in what would be my last eighteen months. I needed something to take my mind off things, so found myself putting my name forward for the Verden Marathon that would take place in November of that year. However, before that I would be returning back to the UK in May for a mess steward's course and, at the same time, to meet someone very special.

CHAPTER NINETY-THREE
A VIP COMES TO TOWN

It was now early May and I was packing once more for an eighteen day mess stewards' course that would be in Aldershot, home of the Parachute Regiment and the ACC (Army Catering Corps'). I seemed to be doing more flying than an RAF pilot; with my two children Melanie and Tatiana now growing up to an age I was unfamiliar with, I was finding it difficult to keep track of time.

On arrival at Aldershot, I was in a determined mood trying to put the last three months behind me. It was my first time in Aldershot so seeing lots of the infamous red berets warned me to stay away from their manor, although to be honest, I had little or no intention of venturing too far from the boundaries of the barracks anyway.

There must have been about thirty or forty of us on the course which included two WRACs. They would always attract attention by the sheer fact that they were female and, the males outnumbered them by about fifteen to one; luckily for them they had their own room, well away from ours.

The first morning saw us get introduced to James Ginders, an ex military man. I would say James was in his mid forties and a very pleasant man. He explained the course in its entirety and how we could get our City and Guilds qualifications, 'passing being obligatory'. "Throughout the next two weeks you'll be trained to the highest standard that can be achieved from each and every one of you: bar accounting, silver service, hotel management, hygiene and all sorts of food poisonings, you'll also learn about all the food accompaniments and, you will be expected to know all military ranks of all forces."

"So much to learn," I said to Josh, who was someone I was becoming acquainted with after the first night.

Josh was already a full Corporal, the highest ranking person on the course as I remember it. We were only into day two when shortly after breakfast it was quite obvious that the two girls were going to be trouble;

they must have thought that the course was going to be a walk in the park, and that Army discipline was now becoming non-existent. How wrong they were; ten minutes late with the course already in full flow, they graced us with their presence.

"Sorry we are late," they both said sheepishly, "we overslept and have just got out of bed."

"Oh yeah," said Josh, "and who got out of bed after you?"

"Keep your noise down," said the instructor as we were creased up with laughter. "Wait outside, girls, I will be with you in a minute, the rest of you start learning the military ranks until I get back." I'm not sure what went on, but all we know is, that they were given a warning and were being threatened to be RTU (Returned to Unit). In a way I was glad that the instructors were taking no prisoners; passing the course and passing it well was my main aim and I didn't want to be disturbed by any people who were not interested, in my mind they may as well have not bothered turning up.

That same night I was hard at work trying to get educated with the military ranks, something that was important to me in my new role back in Herford. I knew all the ranks from 2nd Lieutenant to General and how to recognise them by the amount of pips, crowns and cross-swords; however, the RAF and RN (Royal Navy) took a lot more studying, but with a great deal of perseverance I eventually managed to retain the information.

Towards the end of the first week we were all gathered together in the class room for some interesting and surprising news. What James had omitted to tell us was that basically, he was like the Queen's right hand man; if there were any royal functions going on around the country then he would be called upon to organise and perform the event to the best of his ability. "OK, listen to what I have to say," said James, grabbing our undivided attention. "Next Tuesday, Her Majesty Queen Elizabeth II will be attending a military function at Imphal Barracks in York. I have been asked to provide an adequate amount of staff needed to make it an occasion to remember. I shall be in total charge of the function which will start mid morning with drinks and then lead on to lunch. There will be masses of dignitaries on show which means I will be using a select number of you on the main lunch, the rest of you will have some sort of part to play, but may not have the pleasure of seeing or meeting Queen Elizabeth herself."

"Bloody hell, Josh," I said quietly, "it would be a great honour, what do you think?"

"Once in a life time experience," said Josh, still trying to take in the information that we had been told.

"Over the weekend I shall be keeping a close eye on you leading up to Monday morning when we shall be leaving. I need to see who has got what it takes and who is flagging." I knew it wasn't going to be too difficult for me to impress as I was giving it my all; if there was a weakness in my armoury, it was carrying out silver service, getting to grips with a slippery fork and spoon between my fingers wasn't natural for me. Unfortunately for me, the lunch would require a steady hand, and yes, you've guessed it, the event was to be all silver service.

Over the weekend we were all wondering who would be chosen. One thing I was pretty sure of was, the WRACs wouldn't be on the short list, or would they? After a top of the range coach journey that had us travelling past the beautiful and very scenic Ascot Race Course, we arrived at the barracks. You could feel the vibrancy around the camp with everybody cleaning and polishing anything that stood still long enough for them to lay a duster on.

We were escorted to our rooms which, to be honest, had quality written all over them. "I will meet you all at the Officers' Mess at two o'clock where the function will be held. In the mean time, get yourselves some lunch and get settled in." After a wonderful lunch and gathering around the kitchen area of the mess, we were giving the news of who had made it onto the short list and who hadn't. About fifteen names were called out, but not mine; I really thought there had been a mistake, even the WRACs were included. That made no sense at all to me. "Gutted for you," said Josh, whose name had been called out.

"No hard feelings here mate," I said with a vote of approval, "looks like I will be on queening duties."

"Nice to hear you can still see the funny side of it, Paul."

"I always was the troop joker, Josh, no problem with it at all." With a brush in hand I was now just one of the also-rans until suddenly...

"L/Bombardier Wolfendale; there has been a change in plan," said James, "you're no longer chief brusher upper, you have been promoted to cleaning windows."

"Great," I said, thinking *when is my torture ever going to end?*

"No, I'm only messing," said James. "As from now you'll be serving on the Queens Lunch, the two WRACs are not needed, the staff from the establishment are primarily females which means the balance of female and males needs to be more equal." I was so delighted and to be completely honest, felt I deserved my place on the team.

Later on that afternoon and gathered just inside the front gates, two huge articulated trucks entered the camp. What was in the trucks was anyone's business, but we were soon to find out. It was full of wooden crates waiting to be opened. "Right lads," said James, "take the crates off both trucks and line them up in the room next to the kitchen, don't anyone even so much as try and open them. I have an inventory and need to tick everything off the list, talk about a king's ransom; it would take you a whole twenty two years of service to pay for what's in these crates."

With the crates now unloaded I could see what James meant: gold band plates, crystal glasses, china cups, silver cutlery and silver pieces. I had never seen so much wealth in one room. With the crates now unpacked it was the job of everybody to check, polish, and clean every item that would be going onto the tables later that evening; cleaning and polishing silver was the task I was given which, luckily for me, was right up my street. A couple of hours later all the items were sitting proudly on the side tables ready for us all to start dressing the tables after tea, or should I say dinner.

With dinner now out of the way it was all hands on deck under the supervision of James. We were all given certain tasks to complete until the tables were looking fit for a Queen. The table layout was two legs and a top table for Her Majesty and the ones that were lucky enough to sit close to her. "OK, lads," said James, "the tables look fantastic, you have done a great job. Tomorrow morning around 0930hrs, we will put the finishing touches to the tables before the Queen arrives around 1130hrs. I will give you all a briefing as to what station you have been allocated and how many people you'll be serving. There will also be some tasks for you in the kitchen area; again, I will inform you of your duties." James then left us to our own devices, basically to get ourselves a good night's sleep.

"Big day tomorrow Josh" I said trying to drum up some chat.

"Yeah, can't wait, bound to be a little nervous though." Said Josh

"Be nice if we are both working on the same station," I said. "Maybe we can ask James, unless he has already decided." There wasn't much going on in the barracks so an early night was had by all; not sure about the WRACs, they had their own accommodation away from ours.

It was now the morning of the 18th May and we were all eager to see what lay ahead; lined up and ready for our brief, we awaited the arrival of James which was imminent. "Here he is," said Josh.

"OK men," said James, "this is how the day is going to unfold." First of all we were given our stations, and by chance, not only were Josh and I were working together, but we were also given the task of making all the Melba toast for the starter, which was paté. "Wow, making toast for the Queen, Josh."

"That will be something to tell our grandchildren later on in life, Paul," said Josh, in an "Excuse me, who am I" kind of way. It was all hands to the grindstone now as the time quickly ebbed away; thirty minutes was the time we were given and not a minute more to get into our best bib and tucker (smart waiters' dress) before returning to be inspected.

Our first task was to carry trays of drinks to the now ever growing crowd that were congregating in the mess, and then, you could almost feel the mood change by the way that people were reacting when news arrived to announce the arrival of Her Majesty Queen Elizabeth II. For some reason, I could feel my tray starting to shake like a jelly in a bowl. Stood still and close to the main entrance, I got my first glimpse of the Queen as she entered the room, beautifully dressed in her three-quarter-length mauve-looking coat with matching hat. As she entered the room I would have liked to say she was looking at me as if to say, "Hi Paul," but unfortunately for me, she was just getting on with her royal duties.

I past within whiskers of Her Majesty with my tray of drinks as she continued chatting away; so nice to be involved in this memorable day that had only just begun. We were now ready for lunch as everybody was told to take their seats with a loud but polite announcement from Mr James Ginders.

"OK, get yourself lined up," he said to us all. Josh and I had an inside station close to the top table, however looking towards Her Majesty was definitely a no go. The first course was easy as the plated paté was sitting there on the table, it was just a case of, on the order of James, we would have to march into the room in single file, and then stand completely still. We would be expected to wait until we got the nod from James, who was standing centrally in the room for us all to see. Once the nod was given we would collect the plates from the diner, and again, take one step back looking at the same time for the infamous nod; leaving in military fashion and swaggering with pride was how James wanted it.

The main course was delivered exactly the same way, except this is where our silver service skill came into force. I was just glad to get this part of the lunch over with without spilling anything; one thing I did notice though, was that there was no way anyone was going to stop Her Majesty putting on her lipstick between each course. The rest of the day went by without so much as a step out of place; after clearing up and putting everything back into its crates we still had to time to see Her Majesty leave in her chauffeur driven vehicle.

The following day it was back to Aldershot to sort out the Paras (not). Didn't fancy eating my food through a straw, just a little swotting up on what I had learned so far was the format for the evening and then to bed; there was still a lot of work to get through before the course was at an end.

The first day back saw some changes. The two WRACs were once more in trouble as again they failed to turn up on time; unfortunately, this was to be their last chance. They were told to pack their belongings and were sent back to their units. We were now being used all over the camp to waiter on in all the messes, the more we did the better we became.

We had some written exams to do now that the course was nearing its conclusion and then on the final day, we would see who had passed and who had failed. "What do you reckon Josh, how do you think you have done?"

"Well I certainly gave it my all, just like you," he replied. "I will be disappointed if I don't get at least a B grade."

"Me too," I said. "I think 66 to 75 marks is a C grade, 76 to 85 is a B, over that then it's an A grade."

"Well, we will find out tomorrow when the results are announced." The next day we assembled in the classroom with our bags already packed for the journey home.

"Get sat down," said James. "Congratulations to you all, apart from the two WRACs, you have all passed the course, some of you just, and one or two of you really outstanding. Unfortunately, not one of you has managed to achieve an A grade."

"Gutted," I said to Josh, "thought I might, just have to see what I get." The list of names were read out starting with the lowest score first, we were now into the eighties and Josh and I had still not had our scores read out.

"Oh well, we've done alright Paul," said Josh, feeling satisfied; Eighty two, eighty three, eighty four, and then, "Eighty five, L/Bombardier Wolfendale." My head sank for a few seconds as I was trying to digest the news. *So close to an A grade,* I was thinking. I was so busy in my own thoughts that I almost forgot about Josh and his score. "Eighty five and a half Corporal Loomes."

"Bloody hell, Josh," I said, "that's harsh, half a mark off an A grade."

"Same could be said about you, one mark away."

"Yes I know," was my reply, "and I know where I went wrong, I was 3p out on my bar accounting figures; I forgot to bring onto stock a solitary match box that meant I was 3p down, well at least on paper, for that I dropped one mark."

"You know what, Paul," said Josh, "we have both done brilliant, thanks a lot for gracing me with your company Paul, at least we can go back to our units with our heads held high." As far as the City and Guilds were concerned, I got distinction in both parts.

The next day I was back home in Herford, Brahms Street to be precise, after informing the Sergeant Major on how well I had done, it was back to work as normal. The only thing that felt different now was that I was feeling more self assured about my duties. After a couple of weeks my results had reached the BCs office and I was informed that he wished to see me. "Come in, Bombardier Wolfendale," he said, although I think it was just a slip of the tongue. "I would like to congratulate you on the effort you put in on the mess stewards course you attended."

"Thank you, Sir," I said not wanting this special moment to end.

"Your report speaks volumes, you came second on the course and were only one mark away from an A grade. The report continues saying that you're a competent individual and that no task is too much for you to handle, you should be proud of yourself, young man."

"Thank you again, Sir," I said, masquerading my feelings. Even though I'd passed the course I was shocked to hear that Duncan was to leave. Would that mean I would be taking over his duties? After all, I'm still only a L/ Bombardier.

CHAPTER NINETY-FOUR
DUNCAN HITS ME WITH A BOMBSHELL

It was now the end of May. After discussing it with my wife and my Sergeant Major, I felt it was time to sign off, with no sign of my career elevating to the level that I had hoped for. I felt that I had given my all without getting any rewards, even though I felt my job was rewarding enough. Normally, you have to give eighteen months. Even now I was still pushing it to be discharged by September 1984. I had my reasons as to why I left it a little late, it was just a case of side stepping a few mines; again, working with senior offices' as its perks.

"Paul, can I have a word with you please," said George, "just step into my office and close the door behind you. How do you feel about taking over the role of being in charge of the General from Duncan, Corporal Black?"

"Come again?" I said, pondering my thoughts.

"Duncan has been asked to return to his unit in two weeks' time and we need someone to take over his role."

"In charge of the General" I said, feeling honoured.

"Yes, that's correct," said George.

"I'm only a L/Bombardier, don't I need to be a full Bombardier to carry out those duties?"

"Technically yes" said George," but first we need to fill the gap that has now been left and then, well, I will certainly be looking into getting you your second stripe."

"I suppose signing off isn't going to help my cause, is it?" I said. "I came down here with no aspirations at all, I pretty much knew that getting promoted was not going to be forthcoming, I would rather have a mindset of, *I am not going to get promoted,* than have my ambitions squashed all the time, that's part of the reasoning behind my decision to sign off; talking about promotion is best left alone."

"Sorry you feel that way, Paul," said George, "sounds like you've had a rough deal." I was so sorry to see Duncan leave, great guys are never easy to find and in Duncan, I'd found a true friend.

My first major exercise went well, and getting to know the high ranking officers almost on first name terms was a delight; just don't step over the mark and life would be made easy for my understudy and I. The officers would always call me Bombardier, something they would have been use to with Duncan; in fact, I am pretty sure they didn't even notice how many stripes were on my combat jacket, as long as I was keeping them fed and watered they were happy. I was all set up ready for lunch when the cry, "Bombardier," could be heard above the noise of the roaring No. 1 burners that were heating up some water for a brew and washing up.

"Yes Sir," I said, recognising it to be the voice of one of the two Brigadiers.

"Ah, good morning Bombardier, is there any possibility of finding someone who has a toilet set up around here?"

"Well, there's one in the building over there Sir, it's supposed to be for the General," I said smiling.

"Do you think the General would mind if I placed my one star arse on his two star toilet Bombardier?"

I was in fits of laughter before I could say, "Go for it Sir, I promise not to tell, as a matter of fact I could do with going myself whilst on the subject."

"Mum's the word," said the Brigadier, and that's how it was with the Magnificent Seven. I had started to realise that if needed, I could get away with murder; all I needed to do was quote the General's name and I would have more power than the RSM. It was nice just to do a small, one week exercise to get me into the swing of things; I suppose it was like being a gun No.1 without the loud bangs, map reading and the responsibility of making sure my crew were kept happy. The end of my first exercise brought thanks and praise from my Sergeant Major as the feedback slid its way down the chain of command. I must have done about three more exercises over the summer period with each one landing me with more and more praise.

Towards the end of November, I took part in my second charity marathon based in Verden along with my PTI buddy and one of the waiters, Private Tony Heeps from bonny Scotland. Tony was a great guy of about no more than 5ft 8in tall and a little on the overweight size. He struggled to pass his BFT so why the hell would he want to be entered into a marathon of 26 miles 385 yards? Credit to him though, after all it was for charity. I thought I would find it easier in respect that I had already completed one last year, but no, it was just as gruelling. Getting closer towards the finishing line I gave one last concerted effort to impress the crowd that were cheering and toe tapping to the sound of the military band; women, men and children of all sizes and colour made the effort worthwhile as I crossed the line. I could see that the PTI was back and dressed in his tracksuit ready for the off, what I didn't expect is to see Tony next to him.

"What the hell," I said, not trying to sound disrespectful, "how the hell did you get back before me?"

"Looks can be deceiving," said Tony.

"Deceiving," I said in a shocked voice. I was just about to give him all the praise I could muster from my shattered body when he hit me with…

"I got a lift back in the ambulance after about ten miles, couldn't go on any longer." Although I wanted to give him some of the credit I felt he deserved, I just couldn't.

"You twat," I said, which got raptures of applause from all that heard my remark. "I really thought that you had beaten me to the finishing line."

"Not a chance," said Tony. I was still full of praise for the effort Tony had put in; a true Scotsman with a heart of steel is Tony.

"Come on," I said, "time we got home, I need a long soak in a bath of hot water to soothe my limbs."

Christmas had now come and gone. I would have normally gone home to see my mother, but instead, I had my own family to enjoy Christmas with. 1984 was going to be my last year in the Army unless there was to be an unexpected twist in the tale.

CHAPTER NINETY-FIVE
KARMA IS A BITCH, ISN'T IT?

There was a quite a large scale exercise brewing early March, an exercise that would probably be my last one; it was an exercise full of incidents from start to finish. With my four tonne vehicle loaded and ready there was a last minute change of plan. "L/Bombardier," said the ADC as I was busy in the mess.

"Yes Sir," I said.

"Is everything in place for the exercise?"

"Yes Sir, no worries on that account," I answered "everything is packed on the four tonner ready for its departure in about two hours' time Sir."

"Which dinner plates have you put onto the truck?" said the ADC, pinching some food from the kitchen area.

"Blue band as normal, Sir," I said, looking bemused.

"Well I think we should take the gold band, I want it to be an exercise to remember," said the ADC.

"Is this a suggestion or an order, Sir?" I said, waiting for an answer.

"It's an order Bombardier."

"With all due respect Sir, that's not going to happen, if you take the gold band I can guarantee you, it will be an exercise to remember," I chuckled still thinking, h*e's not being serious.*

"What are you sniggering at?" he said. "It's not a joke."

"Sir," I said, "what do you think will happen if the plates get broken or someone stole them? They're not meant for exercises, Sir."

"Don't care," he said firmly. "I'm in charge, and if I say I want them, then that means I want them, understand?" I was finding his abruptness hard to believe; not being his biggest fan was certainly having an impact on how I was now feeling.

"Yes Sir," I said with an attitude in my voice, "I know one person who won't be very happy, Sergeant Major Clarke."

"He'll be fine with it," said the ADC in a blasé way. The conversation ended with me having to inform the Sergeant Major of the ADC's stupidity, a situation that I had no control over; explaining the matter to George had him up in arms, he was livid to say the least. "He's not taking any gold band plates on exercise," said George, storming out of the office, "wait here until I get back Paul, while I go and sort this matter out."

"OK."

Ten minutes later the Sergeant Major returned red faced and breathing fire from his nostrils. It seemed like it was time for me to put my tin hat on as he entered his office. "Get the gold band onto the truck," said George, throwing a fit. "If any of those plates get broken they can bloody well pay for them, it will be going on their mess bill that's for sure." *Isn't hindsight a marvellous thing and karma a bitch?*

With the truck already loaded I had no choice but to put the plates on the back of the truck; they were placed in a wooden cabinet that was fastened to the side of the vehicle by a strong adjustable webbing strap. There seemed to be no major issues as this is how the blue band plates would normally be transported; however, this was not going to be one of those normal days.

On arrival at our beautiful disused type of farm buildings I was trying to fathom out the best possible position to erect the General's living quarters. *Got it,* I said to myself, it was perfect; looking over the tops of the buildings you could take in the majestic view of a forestry mountain. "OK," I said to Sean, the truck driver, "here is where we will set up for today."

"OK Paul," he said.

"Steve, we're here," I said, "let's get unloaded; start undoing the webbing straps from the cabinet."

"Will do," said Steve, carrying out an order. All was going well until out of the corner of my eye, I caught sight of Captain Murray approaching at pace, a pace that told me he was on a mission.

"Bombardier Wolfendale, a word please," he muttered. "I have just been looking around the area and I think I have found the most idyllic spot."

"I have already found one, Sir," I said, expecting the worst, "we are just about to unload the truck."

"No, no, no," he said, talking to me like I was a child. It was so frustrating; he was a Captain a few years younger than me trying to tell me how to do my job.

"Excuse me Sir, with all due respect, I know my job backwards," I said, wanting to give him a volley of my thoughts, "it's fine here Sir, there is nothing at all wrong with this location." Sean the driver and Steve the brew boy just stood there observing from afar, waiting for the next blow to be heard. The tension was becoming heated, well at least from my corner. I could have taken the argument to another level, but there was little or no chance of me being allowed to be correct.

"No, I've made my decision Bombardier; get your driver to follow me." I was so infuriated that I had to let off some steam whilst at the same time thinking there is no reasoning with an idiot.

"Fucking hell," I said, looking away from the ADC. "Get in the truck Sean, let him have his own fucking way, Steve, mind out off the way while I back up the truck, Do Not, stand too close to the ADC, his arrogance might be contagious." My outrage could have gotten me into serious trouble if the ADC had have wanted to take the matter further; keeping a safe distance from me knowing that he was getting what he wanted was satisfaction enough for the ADC; he may have won the battle, but the war between us would continue.

With all that was going on and with the fact that I wasn't thinking straight, I started to reverse the vehicle slowly. I had completely forgotten that Steve had undone the webbing straps and that the tailgate was down, oh yes, and there was a small ramp. It doesn't take a genius to work out was about to happen next. There was one almighty crash that brought a cheer from all troops that were settling in. I can still see the opened mouth look of Captain Murray counting the cost of his next mess bill. There wasn't a gold band plate left unbroken. I'm not sure if there were any procedures in place for this sort of avoidable monstrosity, all I know is that it took a lot of men to clean up the mess that had been left by an act of stupidity.

"So, blue band plates it is then, Sir," I said sarcastically. I'm afraid that was the last I saw of the ADC for a while, I think he was still licking his wounds; speaking to George was still something I had to do as I headed towards the nearest phone box. Sergeant Major Clarke didn't know whether to laugh or cry when I got through to him, I just heard him whimpering at the other end of the phone. The only good thing that came from this expensive ordeal was that the ADC took more of a backseat role when it came to making decisions that involved me and my men. Without trying to be rude to him, I was just hoping that he had realised that by letting me do my job and him do his, everything would run like clockwork.

CHAPTER NINETY-SIX
PRAISE FROM THE CO

The following day, the General and his men were expecting breakfast, however the General's chef was not due out until later that afternoon, which meant the only place I could go to get there breakfast was from the soldiers' cookhouse that was some two hundred metres away from where the General would be dining; unfortunately, getting past all the red tape that the RSM was enforcing, especially on the first day of exercise, was no mean feat.

I was there to welcome the General with a nice glass of fresh orange and a brew. Cereal with fresh cold milk was also something I could provide. "A nice, hot, cooked breakfast would be welcome Bombardier," said the General, dressed in his battle dress and donning cross swords on his epaulets for everybody to see.

"I will get onto it right away Sir, should be no more than about ten minutes."

"Splendid," he replied.

"Steve, could you make sure that the General and anyone else that are supposed to be here are looked after?" I said, having total trust in Steve. "Keep an eye on my webbing Steve, there is no way I can carry that with me when I have the General's breakfast to deal with. I will take my SLR with me just in case I get mugged." I got a few strange looks from people that didn't know me as I squirmed my way to the front of the queue with my Royal Artillery cap badge on show, not something you do unless you're tired of living.

"What can I do for you, Bombardier?" said one of the chefs. "I have come to get breakfast for the General," I said. I could see the sheer presence of the General's name sounding alarm bells throughout the kitchen.

"Breakfast for the General!" someone said loudly.

"Leave it to me," said the Sergeant in charge. It was like organised chaos, they all seemed to have a nick name: "Jed fry the eggs, Leon cook the bacon, Aangers on the Bangers, Dean heat the beans;"within minutes, a full English breakfast on a warm plate that had a cover over it was presented to me.

"Hurry along, Bombardier," said the Sergeant, wanting to take as much credit as he could if all went well.

I made my way out of the cookhouse and across the open court yard only to be attacked by the camouflaged RSM waiting in hope for someone to step out of line; he must have thought it was his birthday when he saw me with my Artillery cap badge bringing food out of the kitchen. "Stop there now!" he yelled with sadistic pleasure written all over his face.

"What the fuck are you doing Bombardier, no one, and I mean no one is allowed to take food out of the cookhouse, I made that quite clear yesterday, did you not listen to a word I said, well did you?" I played along for a few seconds, finding it quite amusing at his outrage.

"Yes Sir, every word of what you said was Gin clear, Sir."

"And you still disobey my orders, take that food back now to the cookhouse and you can have an extra duty when you return to Herford next week." If only he had asked the right questions at the beginning of our conversation then the General's breakfast would not be going cold.

"What should I tell the General, Sir?" *Now that was a brilliant question,* I said to myself

"About what?" said the RSM; still trying to work out what the fuck I was going on about.

"Should I tell him that I wasn't allowed to bring him his breakfast, if he wanted to be fed he would need to eat in the soldiers' mess?" The penny finally dropped. The RSM didn't know whether to give me a rollicking for leading him down the garden path or just to let matters go as a misunderstanding. He chose the latter. I had only just realised the power I now possessed, without taking any liberties I was in a comfortable position; it worked out that if the General was happy then so was everybody else.

Later on that week and with the General's chef now on board, I was informed by the CO that there would be a PR (Public Relations) exercise. British officers from far and wide would host West German and a few other NATO officers of all different nationalities for lunch. Military Precision timing was going to be the key to getting it right. I was sent some reinforcements from the Officers' Mess in Herford to cope with the sheer volume that would be attending, somewhere around a hundred bodies or more were expected. I could tell the CO was anxious by the way he kept coming up to me on the day in question.

"Everything in place, Bombardier?" he spoke quietly.

"Yes Sir," I said, "one hundred and twenty places have been set, chef is cooking as we speak, nothing to worry about."

"OK, well done, they should all be arriving in about thirty minutes' time," said the CO looking nervous.

"OK Sir," I said, "you really don't need to keep checking, I have it all under control." The way I spoke to the CO was a way I wouldn't even dream about some years ago, however, it was all polite and again, with the backing of the General's name, I was on safe ground. It felt more like a friendship rather than a, 'I'm far more superior to you Bombardier, so that means you will address me with that in mind'.

Twenty minutes later the CO was doing his rounds once more, parading up and down the beautiful derelict farm building. He approached me with concern written all over his face.

"Bombardier, we have a problem," he said, trying to get his words out, "I'm afraid that the General's party is running late."

"I think we can handle that, Sir," I said, not seeing that as a problem.

"Let me make it clear," said the CO, "lunch is going to have to be split in to two settings, there are about fifty of us including some of the other nationalities that will be eating soon and then, well, there will be the General's party about thirty minutes later. I am so sorry about this, I really can't apologise enough."

"Just leave it to me, Sir," I said, trying not to worry the CO any more than he already was. "I will sort it sir, I will go and speak to the chef now. I wasn't given this post for my good looks Sir; I was given it because someone somewhere, felt that I've got what it takes to think on my own two feet."

The whole lunch went like clockwork thanks to the chef and my very capable staff. "OK lads; let's start cleaning up operations and then we can have a nice cold beer." That did the trick. Later on that day and just before we were about to move out to our next location, there was one final thing the CO needed to say.

"Bombardier Wolfendale, I cannot thank you enough for a most splendid lunch."

"It was down to team work, Sir, I have some high-quality men working under me," I said.

"That being said, it was a wonderful effort from you to show such diversity; I won't forget to pass on your efforts to your Sergeant Major." It was so pleasant to hear such praise from a high ranking officer like the CO.

The next morning I was up early making my way down to the local shops to buy fresh produce: bread rolls, eggs, cheese, orange juice and some fresh meats. Walking down the main road at 0600hrs in the morning sunlight and carrying my SLR brought lots of concern from the locals. I mean to say, when was the last time you were driving down the road and saw a soldier carrying a rifle over his shoulder?

The exercise was almost over, but there was still one last get together for Major General Riley and his men. During the General's reign, he made quite a few friends on his travels and I was finding it hard to believe where we ended up for our final night. It was a superb, huge, out of this world dwelling that I felt I had no right to enter. Inside there was a swimming pool and gym that I was allowed to use; technically I had next to nothing to do, the evening meal and breakfast were out of my hands as they were provided by the owners.

I decided that a little German cuisine would be in order so a bratwurst and chips from the local Schnellimbiss would see me right for my evening meal, and then, in the morning, some bread rolls and cereal.

The next morning we were all packed up and ready to take to the road. Heading back to Herford was always a wonderful feeling, especially when you know the exercise had been a success; I think just getting out of your battle dress and in to the more comfortable barrack room trousers and No. 2 dress shoes had a bearing on it. What the next few months leading up to leaving the Army had in store was anyone's business; even I was taken by surprise at what the Sergeant Major had to tell me.

CHAPTER NINETY-SEVEN
THE END IS NEAR

I was now entering my final five months, unless there was to be a sudden change in fortune; all the praise I was receiving still seemed to be falling on deaf ears. After a couple of weeks had passed I could hear George asking, "Anybody seen L/Bombardier Wolfendale?"

"In the kitchen," said Steve.

"Ah, there you are," said George, "just the man."

"I'm just making sure that everything is in place for the special lunch for the CO." I replied.

"Don't worry about that at the moment," said George. "I've got more important news for you than that."

"What's that then?" I said monotonously.

"I have just been chatting to the CO," said George, "he couldn't praise you enough for your effort on exercise."

"That's good of him." I said.

"Well, he said he is going to get you your second stripe, he is going to try and push it forward after speaking to the BC of your battery," said George. "Great news Paul, what do you think?"

"What do I think? I'll tell you what I think" I said in a kind of measured way, I will believe it when the stripe is on my shirt. You haven't met my BC have you; if you had, then you would know that he has no intention of promoting me, stubborn as a mule springs to mind, he wouldn't recognise a leader if the RSM was standing in front of him ."

"We are talking CO here Paul, Lieutenant Colonel Status, if he can't get you your second stripe then I don't know who can." I had heard it all before so I didn't want to get my hopes up, to be honest; although I was doing a good job, I was now looking forward to leaving, I needed to be thinking about what I was going to be doing with my life when the day came for me to say my goodbyes.

Another month had gone by and I was still L/Bombardier Wolfendale;

even George was finding it hard to understand why I hadn't been promoted. I still hadn't made up my mind about what I was going to do when I left the Army until I got chatting to the wines rep, a German guy by the name of Conrad that I got to know back in Hildesheim.

"What's doing with you, Paul?" he said.

"I will be leaving soon," I said, "long story, but I've got about two more months left, then it will be back to the UK."

"What job have you got lined up?" said Conrad.

"Not given it too much thought," I said, not realising he had something up his sleeve.

"What about working alongside me?"

"Selling wine?" I said, trying to process what he had said.

"Yes, Ian and I that run the business are thinking of expanding, Ian will be operating down the south and I will be working more to the north. We are looking for someone else to join us, you would be working with me, You would be working on the British side of things and I would be working the German side of things." I was actually taken aback by Conrad offering me a job selling wine; at last I felt that someone was seeing the potential I could offer given the chance.

Within the next week I had made up my mind after speaking to my wife, I spoke to Conrad and told him that I would love to join the company if his offer still stood. "Yes, of course it does Paul, glad to have you on board." I was now being able to make concrete plans. I knew where my life was heading and it was certainly the end of my Army days; just when I thought this was the end of all the uncertainty there was still yet another twist in the tale.

With less than six weeks to go I was working on a special lunch once more. It was for COS (Chief Of Staff), a full bird colonel and a wonderful chap at that. While chitchatting away over a glass of wine or two and totally enjoying themselves, I saw the colonel trying to gain my attention.

"Bombardier," he whispered in my ear, "I believe you'll be leaving us soon."

"Yes Sir," I said, "about another two weeks here and then, a four week pre-release course."

"The Sergeant Major has told me the story behind your decision," he said, "I have a lot of clout Bombardier you know, and believe me… when I say I can sort this mess out, I can pull a few strings to reverse your decision to leave and I will definitely get you promoted."

"I appreciate everything you say, Sir," I said, "but I am afraid it's too late for that, I've given my word to a wine company that I shall be working for them here in West Germany."

"Loyalty, another great quality you have," said the Chief Of Staff. "I will be here if you decide to change your mind Bombardier, I would like you to remember that, otherwise I will wish you all the best of British in your new career."

"Thank you Sir, that means a lot." It felt like I was deserting a sinking ship, the way his kind remarks came across, although I am pretty sure they would have already had somebody else lined up to take over the helm.

I have never been very good with goodbyes, but this was one of those once in a lifetime experiences that I wasn't going to get away with; with my wife in attendance the whole of the mess staff and a couple of off duty officers shut up shop to enjoy an afternoon of controlled bladderation. 'All good things must come to an end' is a famous quote I would use and, after saying all my emotional cheerio's to each and every one of my friends individually, it was time to leave the mess.

As I left through the front doors of the mess I just turned around and reminisced at the last almost two years of my Army career; ups and downs maybe, but it was a wonderful experience that on reflection, I will never forget. Now sat here on the balcony of my holiday apartment in Rhodes, looking over a beautiful swimming pool, and with the sun beating down on me, I was thinking *gosh, where has all that time gone?* It is now June26th 2018 almost one year after receiving my well earned Army pension. 1974 – 1984 is a period of my life that felt I needed to share with the rest of society.

WHERE ARE THEY NOW?

Keeping in touch with so many of what I would call love ones and friends would have been an impossible task had it not been for technology; in the first few years of leaving it was barely a handful.

Mary: My wonderful sister who came to see my pass out parade, sadly passed away in May 2008 age 53 due to a car accident, whilst sitting in the backseat with her husband who survived the ordeal, they were struck from behind by a truck. RIP Mary, you are sadly missed.

Duncan and George: I would like to think are living life to the full; unfortunately I've not been able to locate their whereabouts since leaving the Army.

Dave Turner: One of my early friends I met when joining 18 Battery in 1975; Dave and I have managed to re-unite through social media although I did bump into Dave when he was working in Ellesmere Port at the local hospital. Dave is now semi retired and keeps in touch.

Declan Tomkinson (Tommo): Served twenty-two years and lives minutes away from me in Nantwich. Dec, after several jobs, as now settled down with two grown up daughters and drives trains for a living.

Gavin Hamilton (Hammo): served three years and although we lost touch, Hammo searched high and low to frequent our friendship; going through the Yellow Pages and several books at that, in his local library, eventually he managed to get hold of me. Hammo has now set up home in Egypt working in construction with his beautiful Egyptian wife. Occasionally, my new wife of 25 years and I will get on a plane and go and visit him.

Don Bowles (Stan): I've searched the universe for Don without any success of finding him or his sister Jess. I hope that one day and, god forbid he is still with us, that we will rekindle the relationship and bond we shared some forty years ago. He was last seen emigrating too Australia.

Steve Schofield (Schoie): Unfortunately it was through a social media site that I found out from his lovely wife Maria that Steve was taken away from us on the 3rd November 2009 after a short illness, so sadly missed by all who knew him. RIP Steve.

Pete Prigmore (Priggers): Another Gunner and true friend of mine also passed away due to ill health (cancer) on the 10th of December 1999 at an early age. RIP Pete.

Bernie Tittle: Bernie was one of my old roommates and it wasn't until more recently that he heard me on Dee 106.3 early one morning doing a radio interview. After making contact with the radio show he managed to regale our friendship. Within two weeks we met up once more at Bernie's house in Helsby, Cheshire, only for me to discover that he had been suffering from cancer for many years; looking at Bernie I would say he looked healthier than me. Again and unfortunately just when it seemed like he over the worst, Bernie made the decision that he had had enough of his chemo treatment, a decision that would see him lose his battle, a decision that would see him lose his life. Bernie decided he wanted to go out with a bang (so to speak); we had one of the biggest gatherings of Army personnel since our time on battle fields. Sadly Bernie was taken away from us weeks later. RIP Bernie.

My Junior Leaders buddies: Steve Parry, Dennis Norris, George Lynch, Ricky Hill, Pete Rigby, Andy Clayton, Sam Gandy and many more are all in good health and doing well for themselves, last year we had a reunion at my house and hope to do it again soon.

Douggie Massey: Douggie is now enjoying his retirement and spends a lot of time visiting Berlin with his wife Elaine.

John Bell (Dinger): John, although not as old as Douggie, has also hung his boots up, due to a major road accident in Egypt that almost cost him his life. John now finds it difficult to walk without the use of a walking stick.

Lydia (not her real name): Well let's just say that about fourteen years after our short but wonderful relationship I received an unexpected letter from her. She had written her phone number on the bottom of the letter with hope that we could rekindle those precious moments we shared. We spoke for a while bringing all the feelings we shared for each other flooding back; I'm married now and so is she. We did plan on meeting up one day, but that day still hasn't materialised. I'm still in contact with Lydia, although we did lose touch with each other for many a year.

Rodger Glanfield: unfortunately Rodger passed away some years ago through illness. RIP Rodger.

Sergeant Frank Smith: My MT Sergeant has also more recently been laid to rest RIP Frank.

As for the rest of the lads including the ones I've mentioned in this book, we regale our friendship with an 18 Battery reunion every two years in the month of September in my local town of Crewe. We are all getting a little long in the tooth for a good ruck, so catching up with them and having a good chin wag is what it's all about, and naturally a few beers or two. As for me… well, my wine connoisseur days lasted about six months before I eventually moved back the UK with my family.

I have had several different meaningless jobs just to pay the bills before trying my luck back in Hildesheim Germany, working in a sugar beet factory. Four months later I was heading home once more with my family as things were just not working for me; needing a career type job, I went in search and wouldn't stop until I found one. After several visits to the job centre I finally saw a job that I felt would suit my personality, a Driving Instructor was what was advertised. After twelve months of training I passed the course to become a fully qualified driving instructor. On my marriage front, well, soon after arriving back in England my marriage came to an end, thirteen years of marriage and the rest is history.

I have since remarried and have been married now for twenty-five years with two more beautiful children; Melanie age 39, Tatiana age 36, from my first marriage, and now Emily age 24, and Joshua age 21, from my marriage to Julia. I also have three grand children so far; Christopher age 21, William age, 14, and Benjamin age, 10.

***

Whilst the characters and events in this story are based on actual characters and events, certain areas and very minimalist areas have been added to fill in certain gaps in my loss of memory after such a long time, speaking to the characters in this story have helped me to pinpoint the full truth of events.

Lightning Source UK Ltd.
Milton Keynes UK
UKHW011345160419
341109UK00001B/38/P